Guangxi and ASEAN Bronze Culture Conference Proceedings

广西与东盟青铜文化学术研讨会论文集

广西壮族自治区博物馆
广西文物考古研究所
广东省博物馆
云南省博物馆
海南省博物馆
贵州省博物馆
编

科学出版社
北京

内 容 简 介

青铜文化是人类进入文明时代的重要标志，本书主要介绍了2011年在广西与东盟青铜文化学术研讨会上，来自中国湖北、四川、重庆、云南、贵州、海南、广东、广西等省、市、自治区以及越南、老挝两国专家、学者提供的青铜文化、铜鼓文化、青铜器科技保护等方面的学术研究成果；探讨了青铜文化在这一区域的产生与发展的历程，显示了青铜器的分布、类型、铸造工艺、装饰、属族、交流等诸多的青铜文化内容以及青铜文化遗产的保护和传承，尤其是对在本区域内占有很大比重的铜鼓文化研究，涉及中国广西、云南和越南、老挝等地的铜鼓来源、分类、纹饰、功用、属族、保护、传承等各个方面。

图书在版编目（CIP）数据

广西与东盟青铜文化学术研讨会论文集 / 广西壮族自治区博物馆等编. —北京：科学出版社，2012.12

ISBN 978-7-03-036064-9

Ⅰ.①广… Ⅱ.①广… Ⅲ.①青铜时代文化－中国－国际学术会议－文集 Ⅳ.①K871.34-53

中国版本图书馆CIP数据核字（2012）第277108号

责任编辑：李 茜 / 责任校对：包志虹

责任印制：赵德静 / 装帧设计：北京美光设计制版有限公司

科 学 出 版 社 出版

北京东黄城根北街16号

邮政编码：100717

http://www.sciencep.com

文物出版社印刷厂 印刷

科学出版社发行 各地新华书店经销

*

2012年12月第 一 版 开本：889×1192 1/16

2012年12月第一次印刷 印张：25 1/2

字数：731 000

定价：450.00元

（如有印装质量问题，我社负责调换）

广西与东盟青铜文化学术研讨会论文集

Guangxi and ASEAN Bronze Culture Conference Proceedings

编委会

广西与东盟青铜文化学术研讨会剪影

2011年10月19日，广西与东盟青铜文化学术研讨会在南宁举行

广西壮族自治区文物局常务副局长谢日万（中）出席大会并讲话

广西壮族自治区博物馆吴伟峰馆长（右五）致欢迎辞

云南省博物馆长马文斗（右三）代表广西、广东、贵州、海南、云南等省、自治区参与承办的博物馆致辞

广西与东盟青铜文化学术研讨会会场

广西与东盟青铜文化学术研讨会会场一角

黄启善（广西壮族自治区博物馆原馆长、学术委员会主任）主持学术研讨会

吴伟峰（广西壮族自治区博物馆馆长、研究员）作总结报告

广西与东盟青铜文化学术研讨会现场讨论气氛热烈，台下代表与台上报告者进行交流。图为广西民族大学万辅彬副校长（站立者）与报告者交流

出席大会的部分专家作学术报告剪影

莫鹏（广东省博物馆副馆长、研究员）

陈洪波（广西师范大学副教授）

武国贤（越南国家博物馆副馆长、研究员）

玛莱湾·考本玛（老挝国家博物馆副馆长）

涂高潮（海南省博物馆研究员）

韦丹芳（广西民族大学副教授）

吴世丰（越南国家博物馆研究员）

小林公治（日本九州国立博物馆研究员）

郑生（越南考古研究院研究员）

李飞（贵州省考古研究所副所长、副研究员）

周志清（成都文物考古研究所副研究员）

阮文好（越南考古研究院研究员）

程能钟（越南考古研究院研究员）

樊海涛（云南省博物馆副研究员）

2011年10月19日上午，全体与会代表列席由文化部、国家文物局、广西壮族自治区人民政府联合主办的在广西南宁召开的“2011中国—东盟文化产业论坛，博物馆运营管理与博物馆文化产品创意开发”的大会。图为国家文物局局长单霁翔（发言者）作主旨报告

研讨会代表在广西壮族自治区博物馆和桂林、柳州等地参观与学术交流剪影

2011年10月20日下午，会议代表在广西壮族自治区博物馆参观学习

2011年10月20日下午，会议代表在广西壮族自治区博物馆参观学习

2011年10月23日下午，会议代表在柳州博物馆参观学习

2011年10月23日下午，会议代表在柳州博物馆参观学习

广西与东盟青铜

Representatives of Academi

越南国家博物馆副馆长武国贤先生在柳州参观胡志明旧居后留言

老挝国家博物馆副馆长玛莱湾·考本玛在柳州参观胡志明旧居后留言

化学术研讨会会议代表合影　2011. 10. 19　中国·广西·南宁

ference on Guangxi and ASEAN Bronze Culture

永恒商务摄影

目 录

Contents

Part 1
Research on Bronze Drum Culture

Part 2
Research on Bronze Culture

Part 3
Research on Technological Conservation for Bronze Wares

Part 4
Research on other Topics

广西与东盟青铜文化学术研讨会欢迎辞

吴伟峰
广西壮族自治区博物馆馆长

各位领导、各位专家、各位来宾、女士们、先生们：

大家下午好！

在广西与东盟青铜文化学术研讨会开幕之际，我谨代表广西壮族自治区博物馆和大会组委会，向来自越南、老挝、日本以及区内外的领导、嘉宾和专家们表示热烈的欢迎。同时，还要感谢与我馆共同承办这次盛会的广东、云南、海南、贵州等省博物馆，对你们鼎力支持表示衷心的感谢。

中国与东盟是好朋友、好邻居、好伙伴。近年来，双方的文化与经济交流不断取得新的进展。今天，我们欢聚在一起，展示和交流各自在青铜文化领域里的研究、保护、传承等方面的最新成果。这对于保护和传承青铜文化遗产将具有十分重要意义。中国与东盟青铜文化的交流已具悠久的历史，如广泛散布于这一区域的铜鼓文化，至今仍在传承和发展。去年，自治区人民政府决定在南宁兴建广西铜鼓博物馆，这一举措，标示着铜鼓文化的研究、保护、传承将推向更新的一层楼。铜鼓文化、青铜文化是多样文化中的一员。由此，我相信通过这次学术研讨会会加深对青铜文化遗产的研究与保护、传承与发展，从而促进中国与东盟之间的文化交流，推动中国与东盟文化事业的繁荣与发展。我们衷心地希望各位专家、学者以及各界同仁们一如既往地热情参与和鼎力支持青铜文化研究，共同把青铜文化研究推向新的高潮。

最后，预祝2011年“广西与东盟青铜文化学术研讨会”圆满成功！

The Greeting Speech in the Academic and Cultural Conference on Guangxi and ASEAN Bronze Culture

Wu Weifeng
The Curator of Museum of Guangxi Zhuang Autonomous Region

Honorific leaders, experts, guests, ladies and gentlemen,

Good afternoon!

At the beginning moment of the Academic and Cultural Conference on Guangxi and ASEAN Bronze Cultures, representing the Museum of Guangxi Zhuang Autonomous Region and the organizing committee of the conference, I would like to show the warmest welcome to all the guests and experts from Vietnam, Laos, Japan and our country. Meanwhile, many thanks to provincial museums from Guangdong, Yunnan, Hainan, Guizhou etc. which hold the great meeting together with us. We are so grateful for your presence and support.

China and ASEAN are best friends, friendly neighbors and intimate partners. In recent years, the cultural and economic communication between China and ASEAN have developed progressively. Today, getting together cheerfully, we show and exchange the newest achievements being made on bronze cultures about research, protection and conservation. This is significant for the protection and conservation of bronze cultural heritage. The mutual communication between China and ASEAN Bronze Cultures has a long history. For instance, the bronze cultures which were in popular in this area is still inheriting and developing. Last year, the government of Guangxi Zhuang Autonomous Region made a decision to build Guangxi Bronze Museum in Nanning, which indicates that the research, protection and conservation for bronze cultures will advance further. Bronze drum culture and bronze culture are components of various cultures in this area. Therefore, I think that this conference will promote the further research, protection, conservation and development of bronze cultural heritages, improving the cultural communication between China and ASEAN, driving the development of China and ASEAN cultures. We truly hope that everyone here will take part in and support the bronze culture research, bringing the research to a new phase.

At last, best wishes *2011 the first Academic and Cultural Conference on Guangxi and ASEAN Bronze Culture* to be successful!

广西与东盟青铜文化学术研讨会致辞

马文斗
云南省博物馆馆长

尊敬的各位领导、各位专家、各位来宾：

下午好！

在金风送爽的10月，我们欢聚在美丽的南宁，共同举办“广西与东盟青铜文化学术研讨会”，这不仅是一次学术的盛会，也是一次友谊的盛会。作为承办单位之一，我谨代表云南省博物馆向参与本次研讨会的各位领导、各位专家、各位来宾表示热烈的欢迎与诚挚的感谢。

青铜时代是以使用青铜器作为标志的人类文化发展的一个历史阶段。世界各地进入这一时代的时间早晚不一，大约从前4000年一直到公元初年左右。青铜铸造技术的发明，在人类文明的发展史上，具有划时代的作用。它代表着人类生产力水平的大跨度提升，标志着人类进入了一个崭新的文明时期。中国南方青铜文化、东南亚青铜文化在亚洲乃至世界青铜文化中，占据着重要的一席之地。例如云南的“滇文化”、贵州的“夜郎文化”、广西的“句町文化”、泰国的“班清文化”、越南的“东山文化”等，都在亚洲青铜文化史上留下了独具特色而又浓墨重彩的一笔。

在国内外专家和同仁们的努力下，我们对中国南方青铜文化、东南亚青铜文化的研究和认识已经有了一定的基础，但我们也要清醒地认识到目前仍存在许多的缺项和不足。随着时代的发展、研究模式的转变以及认识水平的不断提高，中国南方青铜文化、东南亚青铜文化之间的客观存在的种种联系逐渐被人们所重视。闭门无法造车，敝帚也无须自珍，只有通过不断的交流与合作，未来的研究道路才会越走越宽广，我们的交流与合作也会向着更深的层次、更广泛的领域不断拓展。

相邻的地理范围、相似的文化风俗，让我们血脉相连，倍感亲切。今天，借助于中国与东盟这个文化交流与合作的平台，我们对中国南方青铜文化、东南亚青铜文化展开了多方位、多层次的研讨，这是一次具有重要意义的合作，也必将是一次成功的尝试。

作为承办单位之一，也作为参会的一员，我谨代表云南省博物馆及所有参会代表对广西壮族自治区博物馆为本次会议付出的辛勤劳动表示衷心的感谢。最后，预祝“广西与东盟青铜文化研讨会”取得圆满成功！也恭祝在座的各位身体健康，阖家幸福！

谢谢大家！

The Greeting Speech in the Academic and Cultural Conference on Guangxi and ASEAN Bronze Culture

Ma Wendou
The Curator of Yunnan Provincial Musuem

Honorific leaders, experts and honored guests,

Good afternoon!

In the merry October, getting together in beautiful Nanning city, we hold the Academic and Cultural Conference on Guangxi and ASEAN Bronze Cultures which are not only for academy but also for our friendship. As one of organizers, I represent the Yunnan Provincial Museum giving our warm welcome and faithful thanks to attending officials, experts and guests today.

Bronze Age is a historic period of human civilization development characterized by using bronze artifacts. The time entering Bronze Age in various areas in the world are different. It approximately ranged from 4000B.C. to about Chirst. The invention of bronze casting technique had played an epochal role in history of human civilization. It represented the high rise of human productive level and marked the entry of human race into a new era. The bronze cultures in South China and Southeast Asia have constructed an important part in the bronze cultures in Asia and even in the world. Such as Dian Culture in Yunnan Province, Yelang Culture in Guizhou Province, Gouding Culture in Guangxi Province, Ban Chiang Culture in Thailand and Dong Son Culture in Vietnam, each of them is unique and brilliant in the history of Asian bronze cultures.

Based on the hard working of experts and scholars from China and abroad, researches on bronze cultures of South China and Southeast Asia have achieved some accomplishments. However, we are aware of there being lots of problems and blankness. With the time moving, research pattern changing and knowledge increasing, we emphasize increasingly various associations between bronze cultures of south China and those of Southeast Asia. There is no doubt that we cannot make progress without communicating each other. Therefore, only constant communication and cooperation with other countries will make more research achievements. And the communication and cooperation will also promote a higher level and become more comprehensive.

The neighboring location and similar cultures and customs make south China and Southeast Asia related tightly, being intimate with each other. Today, with the assistance of cultural bridges between China and ASEAN, we hold the Academic and Cultural Conference on Guangxi and ASEAN Bronze Culture to make multi-directional and multi-level researches on bronze cultures in south China and Southeast Asia. The conference will be a significant cooperation and a successful attempt.

Representing Yunnan Provincial Museum and all the representatives, I would like to express our gratitude to the Museum of Guangxi Zhuang Autonomous Region for their hard working. At last, I wish the Academic and Cultural Conference on Guangxi and ASEAN Bronze Culture be successful! And best wishes for everyone!

Thank you!

广西与东盟青铜文化学术研讨会致辞

谢日万
广西壮族自治区文物局常务副局长

尊敬的各位专家、女士们、先生们：

大家好！

广西与东盟青铜文化学术研讨会隆重开幕，我代表广西壮族自治区文物局表示热烈的祝贺，并向与会的专家学者、朋友们表示诚挚的欢迎。

我区以铜鼓为代表的青铜文化曾经兴盛发达，青铜文化遗产丰富。这些珍贵的文化遗产成为文物、博物馆界广泛开展学术研究和交流合作的重要资源。回顾以往，我区文物、博物馆界历年举办的各类学术研究活动中，青铜文化、铜鼓文化占了很大比重，不仅培养造就了一批又一批造诣深厚的专家，而且研究成果丰富，学术影响较大，受到社会各界的好评，有力地促进了文化遗产保护和博物馆事业的发展。广西铜鼓博物馆等大型博物馆的建设，与铜鼓文化研究的成果和影响密切相关。借此机会，向长期坚持青铜文化研究的专家学者表示由衷的敬意。

本次研讨会是近年来我区举办的又一个规模较大的学术研讨会。与会专家学者围绕主题，交流学习研究成果，探讨热点难点问题，对推动深入开展青铜文化研究有重要的意义。特别是，本次学术会议被列为2011中国—东盟文化产业论坛的活动内容，从另一个角度启发我们，不但要重视青铜文化本身的研究，还要重视青铜文化遗产保护利用的研究，发挥青铜文化遗产在发展文化产业、服务社会的作用。相信本次会议一定会取得新成效，达成共识，将青铜文化研究推向新阶段。

欢迎各位专家学者为我区文物、博物馆工作多提出宝贵意见和建议。

祝大家在桂期间身体健康，研究考察顺利。

最后，预祝本次学术研讨会取得圆满成功！

The Greeting Speech in the Academic and Cultural Conference on Guangxi and ASEAN Bronze Culture

Xie Riwan
The Deputy Director of the Relic Bureaus of Guangxi Zhuang Autonomous Region

Honorific experts, ladies and gentlemen,

Hello, everyone!

The Academic and Cultural Conference on Guangxi and ASEAN Bronze Culture has been held ceremoniously. Representing the Relic Bureau of Guangxi Zhuang Autonomous Region, I congratulate the conference and give our truly welcome to the attending experts, scholars and friends.

Bronze cultures in Guangxi represented by bronze drums had been very prosperous and abundant bronze cultural heritage has been preserved. The precious cultural heritage has been the significant resources for academic research, communication and cooperation of cultural relics and museology academia. Reviewing those years, we can conclude that researches about bronze cultures and bronze drum cultures have been main part in the various academic research activities. Not only many experts have grown up, but also a number of research accomplishments have been achieved, great academic influence having been made. Furthermore, these academic research activities are praised highly by the public and have promoted the development of cultural heritage conservation and museums. Large museums, such as Guangxi Bronze Museum, are closely related to the achievement and influence of bronze cultural researches. Here, I want to give my truly respects to the experts and scholars who have devoted themselves to bronze culture researches for long time.

The conference is one of large academic conferences held in Guangxi Province in recent years. Focusing on the themes, the attending experts and scholars communicate achievements and discuss the important and difficult issues, which is of great significance to promote the bronze cultural researches. In particular, this conference has been listed in the activities of *2011 China—ASEAN Cultural Industry Forum*, which remind us to realize that we must not only emphasize the researches on bronze cultures themselves, but we must strengthen the researches on conservation and utilization of bronze cultural heritage, making bronze cultural heritage to play an important role developing cultural industry and serving the society. I believe that this conference must achieve new progresses and make agreements, driving the research on bronze cultures to a new period.

Welcome experts and scholars to bring advices for Guangxi cultural relics and museums.

Wish everyone to have a good time in Guangxi and have a favoring investigation!

At last, congratulate this conference to be successful!

广西与东盟青铜文化学术研讨会会议纪要

黄启善
广西壮族自治区博物馆研究员

2011年10月18～23日，“广西与东盟青铜文化学术研讨会”在广西南宁召开，这次会议是由广西壮族自治区文化厅主办，广西壮族自治区博物馆、广西文物考古研究所、广东省博物馆、云南省博物馆、海南省博物馆、贵州省博物馆六家单位联合承办。广西壮族自治区文物局常务副局长谢日万、广西壮族自治区博物馆馆长吴伟峰、云南省博物馆馆长马文斗、海南省博物馆馆长丘刚、贵州省博物馆党总支书记张兰冰、广东省博物馆副馆长莫鹏、广西文物考古研究所所长林强等领导出席了会议，来自日本、越南、老挝以及北京、湖北、四川、重庆、云南、贵州、海南、广东、广西等省、自治区专家、学者等近百人出席会议。会议开幕式上。吴伟峰馆长致欢迎辞，马文斗馆长代表承办单位讲话。广西壮族自治区文物局常务副局长谢日万代表文化厅讲话。广西壮族自治区博物馆韦江副馆长主持开幕式。黄启善、韦江、林强分别主持大会学术交流。会议代表还参加了由文化部、国家文物局、广西壮族自治区人民政府联合主办的“2011中国—东盟文化产业论坛（会议主题：博物馆运营管理与博物馆文化产品创意开发）”开幕式，听取了国家文物局长单霁翔在该论坛开幕式上所作的主旨发言。与会代表还参观考察了广西壮族自治区博物馆、广西民族博物馆、柳州市博物馆、越南胡志明主席在柳州的旧居遗址以及位于兴安县的秦代“灵渠”古运河。

这次会议共收到46篇论文，内容涉及铜鼓文化、青铜文化、青铜器科学技术保护以及其他与青铜文化有关的论文。有16位专家、学者在大会上作了学术交流。经专家评审决定将37篇论文汇集出版。

一

铜鼓文化研究

铜鼓是中国南方与东盟地区最有代表性的青铜文化，在本次会议论文中，有不少文章涉及铜鼓文化的研究，对铜鼓来源、分类、纹饰、功用、族属等方面的问题进行讨论，从而更加深入地了解铜鼓在青铜文化中所占据的重要位置，尤其是对早期铜鼓的认识讨论比较热烈。比如：

樊海涛在《万家坝铜鼓与石寨山铜鼓的比较研究——从社会组织结构方式再论铜鼓的起源问题》一文中认为：铜鼓的起源历来备受学术界的关注，有“一元说”和“多元说”之争。他认为“铜鼓是特定地区、特定民族在特定历史时期的特殊产物。并非所有地区、所有民族均有可能成为铜鼓的发明者”。由此可见，铜鼓的起源问题仍然是学术界最关注的课题。因此，他在文章中再度提出了“铜鼓起源问题的再思考”。他通过对万家坝和石寨山墓葬、铜鼓等方面资料的对比研究，认为万家坝古墓群比石寨山古墓群早，而且石寨山古墓群比万家坝古墓群更成熟、更复杂、更高级。铜鼓在社会组织结构中的地位，万家坝要高于石寨山，其职能则从神圣不可侵犯而逐渐走向世俗化，最终变成滇国贵族夸富逞强的工具。从历史的角度看，石寨山古墓群所体现的社会组织结构代表着万家坝聚落未来的发展方向，但由于“濮人”东迁，万家坝衰落了，它所承载的“铜鼓文化”被石寨山吸纳并发扬光大。如果我们承认物质世界的永恒的发展规律是一个从低级到高级、从简单到复杂的运动变化过程，那么我们就应该认识到万家坝铜鼓在铜鼓产生、发展的过程中确实排列在石寨山铜鼓的“前列”，更何况还有其他诸多的考古学证据和科技考古数据的验证。

范舟在《云南早期铜鼓起源新探》一文中认为：云南早期铜鼓与北方游牧文化之间可能存在着一定的历史关系，由于古代气候的变迁，造成北方的草原游牧民族较大规模的南迁，游牧文化对于云南早期铜鼓的形成起到了重要的推动作用。他从云南的早期铜鼓、先秦时期中原和云南的地理气候、先秦时期云南游牧族群的“昆明”和“叟”及其发展历史背景、西南地区的岩画与游牧族群、铜鼓的原型——南方铜釜与斯基泰铜釜的结合、太阳崇拜与梵天等六方面内容进行探讨和论证。他认为在云南的青铜时代，出现了两个较大的游牧族群，一个是与操突厥—蒙古语的乌孙人有关的“昆明”人，一个是与操印欧语的斯基泰人有关的“叟”人。乌孙人故地在斯基泰人以东，更为接近三江的源头，因此南迁到云南的“昆明”人数多，为大种；“叟”人数少，为小种。“塞”人在云南的出现，同全球气候骤变之后斯基泰人的四处扩张有关。更进一步，他们当中的一些族群可能还沿江而下，到达更为遥远的南方，这就是我们在广西左江流域和四川金沙江流域岩画中可以看到的众多的骑者形象。对于云南早期铜鼓，从气候、生态、历史文化等方面考虑，一方面强调它所处的南方稻作文化的背景，另一方面也不能无视在它诞生之初北方游牧文化所起到的重要作用，游牧文化在云南青铜时代的独特地位从诸多方面看都是十分重要的。但除了众多抽象的文化现象之外，现在还没有太多的实物证据证明云南早期铜鼓和游牧文化之间的直接关系，这就需要人们作更多研究和探讨。同时，通过这种方式来探讨云南早期铜鼓的产生与发展，也是研究铜鼓文化不可多得的新途径。

李晓帆在《早期铜鼓与巫觋》一文中认为：铜鼓是巫觋的神物和法器，在巫术较为盛行的古滇社会，巫觋是身份地位最为显赫的人群，他（她）们占据着氏族部落中的绝大多数财富，是人们权威的精神领袖，同时也是某一特定文化（巫觋文化）的传承者。云南发现的早期铜鼓与巫觋文化有很大关系，巫觋文化的影响渗透到人们生活、生产的各个领域，社会意识形态的方方面面。早期铜鼓所展现出的文化特色正是古滇时期巫觋文化特色。

阮文好在《越南出土的万家坝类型铜鼓》一文中认为：越南发现的16面万家坝型铜鼓，可分为五个不同式别，其年代大致从前4世纪至1世纪，并认为越南发现的万家坝型铜鼓与东山铜鼓是平行的，但和东山铜鼓没有根源关系。

郑生在《中国广西和越南北部发现的黑格尔Ⅰ型铜鼓的比较研究》一文中认为：中国广西西林、贵县、桂平、田东等地出土的石寨山型铜鼓与越南北部玉缕、黄下、沱江、古螺、庙门等地出土的黑格尔Ⅰ型铜鼓，器形、纹饰相似。表明中越两国以铜鼓为媒介的文化交流在两汉时期已存在了。

玛莱湾·考本玛（Phetmalayvanh Keobounma）介绍了在老挝湄公河流域发现的1面迄今为老挝看到的最大铜鼓。认为这是1面黑格尔Ⅰ型铜鼓，与越南东山铜鼓文化有很大的联系。

程能钟、阮光绵在《越南高平省博物馆铜鼓》一文中，介绍了高平省博物馆收藏的15面铜鼓，按照黑格尔的分类，把15面铜鼓分为黑格尔Ⅰ、Ⅳ型和Ⅰ-Ⅳ过渡型，并对每类铜鼓的年代、族属等问题进行了探讨，认为高平省南光1号鼓鼓面图案的设计与中国广西西林发现的第283号铜鼓非常接近，鼓庞3铜鼓和中国广西258号麻江型铜鼓十分类似。同时他还认为，在高平省的黑格尔Ⅳ和Ⅰ-Ⅳ型铜鼓与中国广西麻江型铜鼓组中的某一类铜鼓有着一定的联系。这个有趣的课题值得进一步深入研究。

李文、张伟在《石寨山型铜鼓纹饰的民族学阐释》一文中认为：石寨山型铜鼓的纹饰研究必须结合民俗学来研究，只有运用民族学理论和方法才能比较好地诠释铜鼓纹饰的文化艺术内涵。他们通过对铜鼓的船纹、太阳纹、翔鹭纹、舞人纹、雷纹、锯齿纹、同心圆纹等纹饰的民族学阐释，认为石寨山型铜鼓及其纹饰在祭礼中充当联结天人的中介，同时也被赋予了沟通至高无上神灵的功能。可以看出这一时期云南三湖区域的滇文化已经拥有自己的文化、宗教和礼制，祭祀已经成为国家组织和政治实体最为重要的社会活动。同时，信仰统一的本身也暗含着三湖区域古代滇人政治演化的轨迹。到了后期，由于等级制度的建立与强化，以写实为主的铜鼓纹饰，逐渐被抽象为几何型图案。铜鼓的纹饰不再是社会统一和虔诚宗教的视觉代言，反而演变成了纯粹的装饰，这时铜鼓的功能从此由联系神灵与世人之间的媒介转换为区分社会等级的象征。

黄秋艳在《百色古代铜鼓文化述论》一文中，详细介绍百色地区发现的万家坝、石寨山、冷水冲型等11面铜鼓。并探讨其年代和来源，指出了百色地区的铜鼓有可能来自滇池地区，然后很快就往东南、北、南三个方向传播。由此而提出百色是滇池地区铜鼓文化向东南地区传播的接收站和中转站，甚至认为“若田东右江出水铜鼓为石寨山型向冷水冲型发展的过渡者或冷水冲型最早鼓之说成立，则百色地区还是继后的广西铜鼓文化中冷水冲型鼓的诞生地，居地先民的革新开创了广西灿烂铜鼓文化的先河，历史功绩不可湮没”。

吴伟峰、潘汁在《广西铜鼓陈列的构思》一文中认为：铜鼓是广西民族文化的标志和象征，铜鼓在其漫长的历史发展过程中，与当地各民族的社会、经济、文化生活紧密地联系在一起，形成独特的铜鼓文化。以铜鼓元素为主题的广西铜鼓陈列展览，将全面展示铜鼓文化，诠释广西民族文化的卓越成就，对弘扬中华民族文化带来重大而深远的意义。

二

青铜文化研究

本次会议共收到涉及青铜文化的论文20余篇。内容丰富，类别繁多，对先秦及两汉时期青铜器进行了深入的研究，从而探讨青铜文化的产生与发展的历史进程，尤其是广西与东盟青铜文化的探讨，主题明确，内容丰富，显示了区域性青铜文化研究的深入与发展。更反映了区域性青铜文化研究的独特性。比如：

黄启善在《广西羊角纽铜编钟的研究》一文中认为：羊角纽铜编钟是中国南方和越南北部地区古代青铜文化中一种最具有特色的打击乐器之一，大约流行于战国至两汉时期，它与这地区的古代铜鼓文化有着千丝万缕的联系，是古代西瓯骆越青铜文化的重要组成部分。文中分析了羊角纽铜编钟演奏时采用的悬挂方式，并非绳悬法或勾挂法，而是架挂法。因此，过去运用绳悬法或勾挂法等方式测试其音频乐律等结果是不准确的，是值得怀疑的。

蓝日勇在《广西古代社会进入青铜时代的时间问题》一文中认为：广西古代社会进入青铜时代的时间当为春秋晚期，而不是过去所说的商代。他认为：大量的事实证明，广西青铜文化是在中原青铜文化影响下发生的，由于自身缺乏原创动力，从而导致广西青铜文化发展缓慢的局面。

郑超雄在《广西先秦青铜兵器反映的瓯骆方国武装实力》一文中认为：广西出土的先秦时期青铜器中，以青铜兵器最多，青铜兵器的大量出现，表明先秦时期瓯骆方国社会已有王权政治和军事武装力量。

陈小波在《广西汉代铜马研究》一文中认为：广西发现的铜马数量虽少，但意义重大。西汉铜马的发现，结束了广西无马的历史。马匹初传广西时，马的役用类型有挽用型和骑乘型两种。其中以挽用型马为主，骑乘型的马为辅，但西汉时期的马大多为挽乘兼备的马，是广西畜马史上挽乘兼用的混杂期。马的来源，主要来自我国西北的养马区。所见的铜马，有的挽拉墓主专用的华丽马车，有的背上跨坐着护卫墓主的骑士，有的是墓主生前相马用的铜马式。有铜车马陪葬的墓主，多为北方南下的军政要员，蔑视并破坏铜鼓的墓主，基本都不是南方少数民族的人。出土的这些铜马，是反映墓主身份、地位、职业和财富的重要实物史料。

蒋廷瑜在《镂孔圈足铜壶研究》一文中认为：镂孔圈足铜壶，可能是由陶匏壶发展变化而来的，它们都是西汉南越国时期铜器。这种铜壶都出在南越国时期中下级官吏的墓葬中，代表了所有者的一定身份地位。

覃芳、李珍、黎福金在《广西荔浦县双江镇永吉村墓葬出土青铜器》一文中，介绍了广西荔浦县双江镇永吉村大塘屯发现一批青铜器、陶器和石器，其年代大约在春秋晚期或战国早期，对研究岭南地区青铜文化有着重要意义。

何安益在《广西左右江流域早期青铜文化遗存的认识与研究》一文中认为：广西左右江流域所见的早期青铜文化特征总体上是承袭岭南文化大传统，依然流行夹砂陶和石器，但区域特色也明显，与广东同时期的文化遗存相比，既有共性，也有差异。共性方面，该时期两地均有自己的典型断代器物组合，出现凹刃石凿、石范、石戈、骨牙璋等；差异方面主要是二者的典型断代器物陶器不同，广西主要为夹砂圈足壶、簋、双耳小圈足罐等，而广东主要为尊、凹底器、带流器等一类标准器物，纹饰装饰也存在明显不同，这种差异主要是小区域环境中史前文化发展不同形成，广西当受到本地新石器时代末期文化的影响产生。但不管是广东或广西，在早期青铜文化阶段，岭南的两大区域均出现符合自身小环境发展的典型器物群，当然左右江流域早期青铜文化遗存中，诸多文化特征与广东接近，而与云南存在较大差异，或许暗示该区域的早期青铜文化是受广东影响产生，但最后殊途同归，促使社会复杂化，促进社会文明的进步。

涂高潮在《中国南方青铜工具的发现及研究——再论海南青铜文化及其相关问题》一文中认为：海南昌江等地出土的“青铜环形器”，实为青铜圆锯，这一成果将海南青铜文化的研究提高到一个新的层次，这不仅是对该类器物名称的“拨乱反正”，更重要的是还原其本来面目，使海南青铜生产工具的种类更丰富。类似的青铜器在云南、广西两地也有发现，表明了中国南方滇、桂、琼等地区青铜文化的发展脉络、承继关系、文化传播、民族交融存在着千丝万缕的联系。

李勃在《海南古代青铜器的来源——“舶来品”说质疑》一文中，对海南岛发现的青铜环形器、铜釜、铜鼓、铜铃、铜钟、铜锣、铜斧等战国至汉代的青铜器进行了分析研究，并引用大量文献史料进行佐证，从而认为“海南岛所发现的古代青铜器当多属本岛产品”。

院文清、冯少龙在《湖北随州出土西周噩国青铜器研究》一文中，通过对湖北随州新发现的鼎、簋、甗、尊、卣、爵、觯、彝、罍、盉、斝、盘等一批噩国青铜器的研究，认为这批器物造型及纹饰都是西周青铜器，尤其是扉棱兽首面纹尊、兽首面纹提梁卣、噩侯方彝造型典雅，纹饰精美，是西周青铜器中难得一见的精品。大量重要的噩侯青铜器在湖北随州安居出土，解决了历史学、考古学关于“噩国”历史上的千年悬案。

周志清、李晓帆在《中国南方青铜器上羽人船纹图刍议》一文中认为：青铜器上的羽人船纹图是南中国和东南亚地区青铜文化中特有的装饰，其流行地区为云南中部、广西南部和越南北部古代越人传统的居住区，是当地居民适应其生存环境一种独特的仪式诉求，体现了人与自然的融合，同时也反映出南中国地区由于相近的地理或环境，人群的交流与互动频繁，古代族群之间可能有着共同的族群认同或族群记忆，羽人船纹图或许是他们共同信仰传统的体现。

刘文在《柳州博物馆馆藏几件青铜器的研究》一文中，介绍了柳州市博物馆收藏的铜剑、匕首、编钟、角形器、钺等青铜文物，认为广西青铜文化传播路线可能是从桂北传入中部然后到达南部，其中不乏在中原青铜文化传播的影响下而产生的南方百越青铜文化。

覃国宁在《广西百越青铜文化的探讨》一文中，介绍了广西一百多种百越青铜器，探讨了百越青铜文化的发展历程，从而深刻地揭示了广西百越青铜器在艺术、工艺、造型、纹饰等所蕴含的民族文化特色。文中认为广西百越青铜文化不仅深受中原地区青铜文化和滇、楚文化的影响，并通过民族与文化互动融合，创造了百越民族优秀的青铜文化艺术。

何英德在《广西铜器珍品简论》一文中认为：广西青铜器中不乏珍品，尤其是铜鼓，数量居世界之首，堪称世界一流。通过对这些比较珍贵的青铜文物研究，以事实说明广西并非南蛮之地，精湛的铜器制作技术在我国科技史上也占有一席之地。

陈桂芬在《汉代青铜博山炉的审美内涵》一文中认为：西汉时期上层社会中流行熏香。因此，汉代青铜博山炉如“井喷”一样骤然掀起。人们把博山炉与香的作用，视为一种怡情逸性的高雅享受，不少名人还为博山炉与香的意境赋诗题铭，描述了博山炉的美丽与超凡以及博山炉与香熏的形与神、情与境，从而彰显了博山炉丰富的审美内涵。

闫玲君在《羽纹铜凤灯与图像巫术符号》一文中认为：羽纹铜凤灯的艺术造型构成了一种图像巫术符号，其目的是为了达到避邪之意。以其随葬，是替墓主镇妖辟邪，祝吉化凶，以保墓主在冥府平安生活。羽纹铜凤灯的艺术造型所蕴含的巫术思想，对于研究西汉美术史、宗教思想史均有重要的价值。

三

青铜科技保护研究

莫永昇、莫鹏在《广东博罗横岭山先秦墓地出土西周铜鼎的修复研究》一文中认为：由于泥土的砸压和化学物质的腐蚀，铜鼎等青铜器出土时腐蚀氧化和破损严重，不利于日后的陈列、研究和保管，更不利于青铜文化的弘扬。为保护修复好青铜鼎，在科学检测分析的基础上，通过缓蚀处理、浸透加固、封护、黏接、修补复原等技术手段，最终完成青铜鼎修复任务。

韩玉燕在《略论青铜文物的保护与利用——以柳州博物馆的实践为例》一文中认为：金属文物的腐蚀是一个不可抗拒的自然现象，如何减缓文物被腐蚀的进程是关键。因此，加强环境监控、清理锈蚀等，并在保存或展览时采取有效保护措施，使其延年益寿。

李欣妍在《浅论三十年来我国学者对古代铜鼓铸造工艺之研究和试验》一文中认为：古代铜鼓铸造工艺的研究，时至今日已经走过了三十年的历程。但研究仍有不足，认为泥模合范法铸造铜鼓，我国实验至今仍未成功。而利用泥模合范法铸造铜鼓的痕迹也未找到，也没发现古代铸造铜鼓的泥范，而在今天的越南却得到保存？这是什么原因？其次，我们是否可以怀疑古代中国根本就没有使用泥模合范法铸造铜鼓。可是如果没有使用该法，那么又会使用什么方法呢？是韦启初、韦启叁兄弟采用的翻砂法吗？还是在中国冶金史上占据绝对地位的陶范法呢？若能回答这个问题，那么我们研究铜鼓铸造工艺中存在的许多谜团都能迎刃而解了，因此这应是我们今后研究的重点方向。

四

其 他

肖君在《青铜记忆刻录瓯骆文化印记》一文中认为：古老的青铜器承载着许多不为人知的文化印记，尤其是瓯骆青铜文化，年代久远，内涵丰富，积淀深厚，更需要人们去梳理，诠释、解读其丰富的文化内涵。

周学斌在《从出土的青铜器试看梧州汉代的社会面貌》一文中认为：梧州是一座历史悠久的南方古城，古称苍梧、广信。考古发现表明，早在旧石器时代中晚期就有人类在这里繁衍生息。夏为荆南境，商周为百越地，秦统一岭南后在当地设桂林、南海、象三郡，梧州隶属桂林郡。至今这里已发现铜鼓、鼎、盘、壶、釜、镜等大量的青铜器，尤其是錾刻青铜花纹工艺，更显示了本区域青铜文化的发现状况。

陈虞添在《广西先秦古国研究综述》一文中，介绍了广西先秦古国研究成果，从总的来看，在取得研究成果的同时也存在不足。由于文献和考古资料等原因，广西先秦古国的研究还不够深入。在理论方法层面上，史学方面主要是用文献考证、酋邦理论、军事民主制和奴隶社会等方面的分析。考古学方面主要还是运用类型学分析方法对出土器物的分析研究，还有些学者利用民族学的方法和考古学方法的综合研究。目前较少见有学者运用聚落考古、文化因素分析、数据分析研究的等研究方法和研究手段。

吴春明在《从东山文化的多元因素看“瓯骆国”的形成》一文中认为：东山文化既有红河下游土著文化的延续，又表现为百越诸王国社会文化的直接交流与融合，并从东山文化的多元文化因素说起、红河下游土著文化传统的延续、东山文化与华南百越文化的共性、中原华夏与汉文化透过岭南地区对东山文化的影响、东山文化与东南亚半岛同期古文化的不同程度共性或交流、从“雄王”之“文郎国”到安阳王之“瓯骆国”的考古推测、东山文化——瓯骆国的史迹等多方面内容进行论述，认为瓯骆国的东山文化正是在华南百越王国、中原周汉帝国间南征北伐、激流涌荡的社会文化背景下融合形成的。

广西与东盟青铜文化的交流已具悠久的历史，尤其是铜鼓是这一区域独具特色的青铜文化。通过这次学术交流，获益匪浅，不少专家代表呼吁，类似这种学术交流会，应多开多交流，使青铜文化成为中国与东盟国际间交流的一个平台，通过文化交流达到经济、贸易等方面交流的繁荣与兴旺，从而促进国际间的和平与友谊。

A Summary of the Academic and Cultural Conference on Guangxi and ASEAN Bronze Culture

Huang Qishan
Guangxi Zhuang Zu Autonomous Region Museum carator Professor

The International Academic Conference on Guangxi and ASEAN Bronze Culture had been held in Nanning on October 18th～23rd, 2011. Guangxi Cultural Department has sponsored this conference. And six departments, including of the Museum of Guangxi Zhuang Autonomous Region, Guangxi Relics and Archaeology Institution, Guangdong Provincial Museum, Yunnan Provincial Museum, Hainan Provincial Museum and Guizhou Provincial Museum, had carried out the affairs. Mr. Xie Riwan (administrative deputy director general of Guangxi Cultural Heritage Management Bureau), Mr. Wu Weifeng (the curator of Guangxi Museum), Mr. Ma Wendou (the curator of Yunnan Provincial Museum), Mr. Qiu Gang (the curator of Hainan Provincial Museum), Mrs. Zhang Lanbing (the CCP branch chief of Guizhou Provincial Museum), Mr. Mo Peng (the vice curator of Guangdong Provincial Museum), Mr. Lin Qiang (the director of Guangxi Relics and Archaeology Institution), and other representatives from Japan, Vietnam, Laos and some Chinese provinces such as Beijing, Hubei, Sichuan, Chongqing, Yunnan, Guizhou, Hainan, Guangdong and Guangxi, total of near one hundred, had attended this meeting.

On the opening ceremony, Mr. Wu Weifeng addressed salutatory, and Mr. Ma Wendou representing service departments and Mr. Xie Riwan representing Guangxi Cultural Department made speeches. Mr. Huang Qishan, Wei Jiang and Lin Qiang respectively moderated the academic convention.

The representatives of the conference also presented the opening ceremony of 2011 Strategic Interaction Dialogue of China-ASEAN Cultural Industry (the Topic: the museum's management and the creative design and development of the museum's cultural products) which was sponsored by Ministry of Culture, State Administration of Cultural Heritage and the Government of Guangxi Zhuang Autonomous Region. They listened to the speech made by Shan Jixiang, the minister of State Administration of Cultural Heritage. The representatives visited the Museum of Guangxi Zhuang Autonomous Region, the Nationalities Museum of Guangxi, and Liuzhou Museum. They also visited the former-residence site of Hu Zhiming (the ex-President of Vietnam) in Liuzhou and Ling Qu Canal of Qin Dynasty on Xingan County.

The conference has accepted 46 papers which involve bronze drum culture, bronze culture, the scientific conservation technology of bronze wares and other topics. 16 experts and scholars gave reports on the conference. *The Volume of Theses of the Academic Conference on Guangxi and ASEAN Bronze Culture* which include 37 papers being selected by experts will be published by Science Press.

Part 1
Research on Bronze Drum Culture

Bronze drum is the best model among bronze culture in south China and ASEAN area. A lot of theses discuss bronze drum culture, involving the source, classification, decoration, function and ownership. So we can better understand the importance of bronze drum in the bronze culture. The bronze drum in the early period is an especial focus.

Mr. Fan Haitao in his paper *A Comparison between Wanjiaba-style Bronze Drums and Shizhaishan-style Bronze Drums—Once Discussion about the Source of Bronze Drums from the structure of the Social Organization* expresses that there are two controversial perspectives about the source of bronze drum. Some scholars think it has only one origin and others consider that it has several origins. This issue always attracts a lot of attention in the academic circle. He considers that bronze drum is the particular product made by individual nationality in individual area in special historical time. Not all the nationalities in all areas are able to produce bronze drums. So, we can infer that the source of bronze drum is still the most attention-getting topic in academic circle. He puts up an idea that " rethinking on the source of bronze drum" in his thesis. By comparing the tombs and bronze drums of Wanjiaba with those of Shizhaishan, he draws a conclusion that the ancient tombs of Wanjiaba are earlier than those of Shizhaishan, and what's more, the latter are more mature, more complex, more advanced than the former. The status of bronze drum in social organization is higher in Wanjiaba. It was sacred at first, then it came into temporal, and in the end it was used by the aristocrats of Dian Chiefdom to boast wealthy. From the perspective of history, the social organization presented by Wanjiaba ancient tombs pointed out the prospect of the Wanjiaba settlements. However, resulted from the downfall of Wanjiaba which was caused by the eastward emigration of Pu nationality（濮人）, its bronze drum culture was later accepted and developed by Shizhanshan. If we are fully convinced that the substantial world is developing from junior to senior, from simple to complex, we will draw the conclusion that Wanjiaba bronze drum is ahead of Shizhaishan bronze drum in the history of bronze drum, the rather that there are a great deal of archaeological evidence and the data of technological archaeology.

In *A New Perspective on the Source of Early Types of Bronze Drums in Yunnan*, Mr. Fanzhou considers that the early types of bronze drum in Yunnan may deeply connect with the north nomad. Because of the changes of climate in ancient times, the north nomadic ethnic groups moved into the south area. Nomadic cultures had played an important role in the formation of early types of bronze drums in Yunnan. He discusses this theme from following six aspects: the early types of bronze drums in Yunnan; the geographic climate in Central Plains and Yunnan in Pre-Qin period; the Kunming and Saka in Yunnan during Pre-Qin period and their historical background; the cliff paintings and the nomadic ethnic groups in southwest area; the original type-the combination of the south bronze pot and the Scythian bronze pot; the worship of the sun and Brahma, etc.. He considers that there were two big nomadic ethnic groups in Yunnan in Bronze Age. One was the Kunming, relating with Wusun（乌孙） nomadic group speaking Turkic—Mongolian language. The other was Saka, relating with Scythians speaking Indo-European languages. The hometown of Wusun nomadic group was in east of where Scythians inhabited and was much closer to headwaters of 3 big rivers: the Changjiang River. So amongst the people which emigrated to Yunnan, Kunming took up the greater proportion and Saka took the smaller proportion. The appearance of Sairen nomadic group in Yunnan was connected with the abroad expansion of Scythians after the emergent changes of the world climate. What is more, some of the Sairen nomadic group had possibly gone down the river to the farther south area. And these people are the riders whose we have found on the cliff paintings in the Valley of Zuojiang River in Guangxi and the valley of Jinshajiang River in Sichuan. As for the early types of bronze drums in Yunnan, we should not only emphasize the background of the southern rice culture, but also we cannot ignore the importance of northern nomadic culture at its beginning period. Northern nomadic cultures play very important roles in Bronze Age of Yunnan from many aspects. However, in addition to a number of abstract cultural phenomenon, there are no many practical evidences to prove the direct relationship between early types of bronze drums in Yunnan and nomadic culture. This field still needs more researches and discussions. Meanwhile, studying the appearance and development of the early types of bronze drum in Yunnan in this way is a new method to research the bronze drum culture.

Ms. Li Xiaofan in her work *Wizards and Early Bronze Drums* suggests that the bronze drum is sacred artifact and wizard implement. In the ancient Dian socioty where wiftcraft is wildly prevailing, wizards took the most eminent position and control the overwhelming mojority of properties. They were both the authoritative spiritual leader and the inheritor of some one particular culture (wizard culture). The early bronze drumes excavated in Yunnan display a great deal of relationships with wizard culture. The wizard culture involves into every inpect of people's life, work and even social ideology. The culture characteristics of early bronze drums are equally refect the wizard culture of the ancient Dian period.

Mr. Nguyen Van Hao expresses in his paper *Wanjiaba-style Bronze Drums Excavated in Vietnam* that 16 Wanjiaba-style bronze drums which are discovered in Vietnam can be classified into five types covering from 4th century B.C. to 1st century A.D. and that Wanjiaba-style bronze drums in Vietnam are in the same period with Dongson bronze drums but there are no relationship between them.

Mr. Trinh Sinh proposes in *A Comparison of Heger Type I Bronze Drums Found in North Vietnam and Guangxi China* that the Shizhaishan-style bronze drums being found in Xilin, Gui County, Guiping and Tiandong of Guangxi are similar to Heger type I bronze drums being found in Ngoc Lu, Hoang Ha, Song Da, Co Loa and Mieu Mon in the northern Vietnam on shape and decoration. This proves that the cultural interaction through bronze drums between China and Vietnam had existed in Han Dynasty.

Ms. Phetmalayvanh Keobounma introduces the biggest bronze drum that has ever been found in the valley of Mekong River in Laos. She considers that it belongs to Heger Type I and has affiliation with Dongson bronze drum culture in Vietnam.

In *The Bronze Drums of the Cao Bang Provincial Museum, Vietnam,* Mr. Trinh Nang Chung and Nguyen Quang Mien introduce 15 bronze drums being collected in Cao Bang Provincial Museum and classify them into Heger Type I, Type IV and transitioning Type I-IV according to Heger classification and researches every types' age and ownership. They think that patterns on the face of the Nam Quang No.1 bronze drum in Gao Bang Province are similar to No.283 drum being discovered in Xilin County, Guangxi, China. And Coc Pang No. 3 bronze drum is quite similar to No. 258 Majiang type drum in Guangxi, China. They also consider that Heger Type IV and Type I-IV bronze drums in Gao Bang are somehow related with certain kind of bronze drum of Majiang type in Guangxi, China. This interesting topic needs to be profoundly studied.

Mr. Li Wen and Zhang Wei express in the paper *Ethnological Explanation for Decorations of Shizhaishan-style Bronze Drums* that the decorations of Shizhaishan-style bronze drums must be researched through folklore, for only by using ethnology theory and method can the cultural implications of decorations of the drums be properly explained and understood. By explaining the drums' decorations such as boats, suns, flying birds, dancing people, thunder patterns, saw teeth patterns and homocentric circles from the perspective of ethnology, They draw a conclusion that Shizhaishan-style bronze drums and their decorations are used as the media to the god during the sacrificial rites, and meanwhile they are given the function to communicate with the sacred god. From this we can know that during this period the Dian Culture in three lakes areas of Yunnan had already possessed its own civilization, religion and ritual system, and that the sacrifice had become the most significant social activity for the state or polity. In the meantime, the unification of their beliefs indicates the trace of political changes of ancient Dian people in three lakes areas. Later the drum decorations which describe the real life have gradually been replaced by abstract geometric motifs because the hierarchy system has been built and intensified. The drum decorations are no longer the visual representation of the society unification and the loyal religion, but have simply become decorations. Accordingly, the function of bronze drum being a medium between the humane to the god has transferred into the representative of social ranks.

In her paper *A Review on the Ancient Bronze Drum Culture in Baise Area,* Ms. Huang Qiuyan introduces 11 bronze drums such as Wanjiaba-style drums, Shizhaishan-style drums and Lengshuichong-style drums being discovered in Baise and studies their ages and sources. She points out that the bronze drums of Baise have probably been diffused from Dian Lake and then was spread to southeast, north and south directions. She therefore puts up an idea that Baise area is the receiver and transfer of the bronze drum culture of Dian Lake area to southeast area. She advances further that if it is true that bronze drums being discovered in Youjiang River are the transition of Shizhaishan type to Lengshuichong type or the earliest one of Lengshuichong type, then Baise area is also the birthplace of the Lengshuichong type of Bronze Drum, which initiates the subsequent Guangxi Bronze Drum Culture.

Mr. Wu Weifeng and Pan Zhi express in the paper *The Conception on Bronze Drum's Exhibition in Guangxi* that the bronze drum symbolizes Guangxi natural cultures. The unique bronze drum culture formed in the long history is tightly connected with socioty, economy and cultural life of local nationalities. The exhibition of Guangxi bronze drums will comprehensively display the bromze drum culture and the great success of Guangxi natural culture. It is profoundly significant of promoting and developping Chinese natural culture.

Part 2
Research on Bronze Culture

More than 20 theses relating to bronze culture are published on this conference. These theses which contain abundant contents and many fields make a profound research on the bronze wares of Pre-Qin period and Han Dynasty. And these theses with the noticeable theme and abundant evidence discuss on the advent and development of the bronze culture, especially the bronze culture of Guangxi and ASEAN. All of these things prove that the research on the regional bronze culture is significant and unique.

Mr. Huang Qishan suggests in his paper *A Study of Bronze Chime Bells with Horn-shaped Knobs in Guangxi* that bronze chime bells with horn-shaped knob is the one of the most peculiar percussion instruments in ancient bronze culture of south China and north Vietnam. They are very popular from Warring States Period to Han Dynasty and somehow have close relationship with the ancient bronze drum culture in south China and north Vietnam. And they played an important part in bronze culture of ancient Xiou and Luoyue. In his thesis he analyzes the way of the bronze chime bell being played, and considers that the bells should be placed on a shelf to play instead of hanging by a rope or hook. Thus there is an argument to the result of audio frequency test to use hanging or hooking in the past.

In his article *Discussion about the Time of Guangxi Entering Bronze Age,* Mr. Lan Riyong considers that it was in late Spring and Autumn Period when Guangxi ancient society entered the Bronze Age, not Shang Dynasty which people used to think. A great many evidence proves that bronze culture in Guangxi came into birth under the influence of bronze culture of Central Plains. Because it lacks creative dynamics, the process of its development is very slow.

Mr. Zheng Chaoxiong expresses his idea in his paper *Ou-Luo Ancient Country's Armed Force reflecting from Unearthed Bronze Weapons on Guangxi in Pre-Qin Dynasty* that bronze weapons take up a greater proportion in unearthed bronze wares of the Pre-Qin period in Guangxi. This indicates that in Pre-Qin period the Ou-Luo state already possessed the kingdom polity and armed force.

In the article *A Study on Bronze Horses of Han Dynasty in Guangxi,* Mr. Chen Xiaobo considers that bronze horses discovered in Guangxi is less but significant. The discovery of bronze horse of Western Han put an end to the era when it is considered there was no bronze horse in Guangxi. When horses are first spread into Guangxi, they belonged to two kinds: the draft horse and the ride horse. The former was more important. But most of them were combined with draft and saddle functions together in West Han Dynasty. These horses are mainly from northwest China. Amongst the bronze horses seen in Guangxi, some are drawing the tomb owner's luxurious carriage, some are with the riders who safeguard the tomb owner while some are the tomb owner's horse models. The tomb owners who are buried with horses and carriages are usually the important members of army and government emigrating from north. The tomb owners who disregarded and destroyed bronze drums are not the members of minority ethnics of south China. These excavated bronze horses are the important evidence to indicate the tomb owner's identity, social status, profession and wealth, etc.

Mr. Jiang Tingyu points out in his paper *A Study on Bronze Pots with openwork and round foot* that bronze pots with openwork patterns and circular legs have probably developed from gourd-shaped pottery pot and all of them are the bronze wares of Nanyue in Western Han. This sort of bronze pots were all found in junior officials' tombs of Nanyue kingdom and represented the owners' status.

In their thesis *Bronze Wares Excavated in Tombs of Yongji Village, Shuangjiang Town on Lipu County in Guangxi,* Ms. Qin Fang and Mr. Li Zhen, Li Fujin introduce the bronze wares, pottery and stone wares which are unearthed in Datang Tun, Yongji Village, Shuangjiang Town, Lipu County, Guangxi whose age are possibly in late Spring and Autumn Period and early Warring States Period. This discovery has significant meanings to the study of bronze culture in Lingnan Area.

Mr. He Anyi considers in *A Review on the Early Bronze Relics in Basins of Zuo Jiang and You Jiang in Guangxi* that the early bronze culture found in the valleys of Zuojiang and Youjiang Rivers mainly follows the general tradition of Lingnan culture. Sand pottery and stoneware were popular, but it had its own local features. There are similarities and dissimilarities between the relics of Guangdong and them of Guangxi. As for similarities, they both possess their own typical ware complex judging age, such as stone chisel with recessed edge, stone mould, stone dagger and bone or tooth *Zhang*（璋）in both places. As regards dissimilarities, the typical ware complex judging age in Guangxi are circular-footed pot with grit, Gui（簋）, pot with double handles and small circular foot, while in Guangdong they are Zun（尊）, ware with recessed foot, ware with spout. The decorations of the wares in these two places are also distinct. The differences between these two places result from the difference of prehistoric local cultures. The culture in Guangxi wais influenced by local cultures in late Neolithic Age. In early Bronze Age there are typical ware complex which accord with their own environments. A lot of culture features of the early bronze culture in the valleys of Zuojiang and Youjiang Rivers are similar to Guangdong and rather different from Yunnan. This suggests that the early bronze culture of this area was affected more by Guangdong. However, in the end they reached the same goal by different routes. They promoted the society more complex and reached civilization.

Mr. Tu Gaochao points out in his thesis *Discovery and Research on Bronze Implements of South China—Rethinking about Bronze Culture in Hainan and other Questions* that the bronze ware originally named "the bronze ring" which is unearthed in some places such as Hainan Changjiang is actually a bronze circular saw. This research promotes the study of Hainan bronze culture to a new level. Denominating the bronze circular saw not only accurately identifies the name of this sort of bronze ware, but also returns such wares to its original appearance. These discoveries make the types of bronze tools more affluent and abundant. The similar bronze tools are found in Yunnan and Guangxi. It suggests that the developing route, the succeeding, the cultural diffusion and the national amalgamation of the bronze cultures are closely connected. in south China.

In his thesis *The Source of Ancient Bronze Wares in Hainan, An Argument to the "Foreign import" Theory*, Mr. Li Bo analyses the bronze wares being discovered in Hainan from Warring States Period to Han Dynasty such as bronze ring, bronze pot, bronze drum, bronze bell, bronze gong and bronze axe. Citing massive written documents, he considers that most of the ancient bronze wares discovered in Hainan are original products.

In *A Research on E State (in the western Zhou Dynasty, 11th century-771B. C.) Bronze Wares Unearthed in Suizhou, Hubei,* Mr. Yuan Wenqing and Feng Shaolong make a research on the bronze wares of E State which are unearthed in Suizhou, Hubei such as Ding, Gui, Zun, You, Jue, Zhi, Yi, Lei, He, Jia, plate etc. and consider that the shape and decoration of these bronze wares prove that they all belong to Western Zhou Dynasty. Some are rare relics of Western Zhou Dynasty, such as Zun with animal-mask and arris design, loop-handled You with animal-mask design, square Yi of Marquis E. The fact that numerous significant bronze wares which belong to Marquis E are excavated in Anju, Suizhou, Hubei have solved the mystery of E State in history and archaeology.

Mr. Zhou Zhiqing and Ms. Li Xiaofan consider in *Brief Research on Boat Patterns with Feathermen on Bronze Wares of South China* that the boat motifs with feathermen are the unique decorations among the bronze cultures in south China and southeast Asia, which were popular in Middle Yunnan, south Guangxi and north Vietnam where ancient Yue Nationality inhabited. It was a special ritual adapting to the environment and embodied the assimilation of man and environment. It also indicates that because of the particular geography and environment in Southern China there was frequent exchange and interaction with neighborhood regions. There was probably common recognition and memory of ethnic identity between these ancient groups. The boats maybe express their common tradition of belief.

Mr. Liu Wen introduces some bronze wares being collected in Liuzhou Museum such as bronze sword, dagger, bronze chime bells, horn-shaped bronze wares and bronze Yue-poleaxe in his thesis *A Research on Bronze Wares Collected in Liuzhou Museum.* He thinks that the bronze culture of Guangxi has probably first spread from the north Guangxi, then to the middle and at last to the south. There are also the bronze cultures of Baiyue which is affected by bronze culture of Central Plains.

Ms. Qin Guoning introduces more than 100 sorts of bronze wares of Baiyue in Guangxi in her thesis *Discussion on Baiyue Bronze Culture in Guangxi.* She talks about the progress of bronze culture of Baiyue and reveals the ethnic characteristis of Guangxi bronze culture in art, craft, shaping and ornamentation. She considers that the brilliant bronze culture of Baiyue not only has been affected by bronze cultures of Central Plains and Dian, Chu cultures but also has interacted with other ethnic cultures.

Mr. He Yingde points out in *A Brief Review of Precious Bronze Wares in Guangxi* that the Guangxi bronze drums could play the most important role in the world for its quantity and quality. Through studying the precious cultural relics, Mr. He points out that Guangxi was not a barbarous place and its bronze tecnology are important components in the scientific history of our country.

Ms. Chen Guifen thinks in *The Beauty inside Bronze Bo Shan Stove in Han Dynasty* that because incensing was very popular in the upper class in Western Han the bronze Bo Shan stove suddenly came into fashion. People took use of Bo Shan stove and incense to get the graceful spiritual enjoyment. Many celebrities had written poems for Bo Shan stove and incense to describe the beauty and elegance of it, to praise the appearance and enriched spirit of Bo Shan stove and incense that enable people comfortable and relaxed.

Ms. Yan Lingjun considers in *Phoenix-shaped Bronze Lamps and Symbols of Magic Images* that the phoenix-shaped bronze lamp is a kind of image witchcraft symbol, whose function is to exorcise evil spirits. The phoenix-shaped bronze lamp is buried with the tomb owner to exorcise evil spirits to safeguard the tomb owner in the other world. The witchcraft implied in the artistic shape of the phoenix-shaped bronze lamp is very valuable to research on arts history of Western Han and ideology history of religion.

Part 3
Research on Technological Conservation for Bronze Wares

In their paper *Restoration for Bronze in Pre-Qin Period Tripods Unearthed from Henglingshan Cemetery on Boluo, Guangdong,* Mr. Mo Yongsheng and Mo Peng think that because of soil crushing and chemical corrosion, the bronze Ding damaged from serious oxidation and pressure when bronze wares were unearthed, which are difficult for next exhibition, research and storage. Based on scientific tests and analysis, the staff eventually restored the bronze Ding by technical means of corrosion processing, soaking reinforcement, sealing protection, bonding, patching, etc.

Ms. Han Yuyan considers in *A Brief Discussion on Conservation and Development for Bronze Relics—A Case about the Practice of Liuzhou Museum* that metal wares' corrosion is an inescapable natural process, so it is the key that how to slow down the process. Therefore we should pay more attention to control the environment, clear the eroding remains and adopt effective protective measures for storage and display.

Ms. Li Xinyan argues in *A Brief Review on Chinese Scholars' Researches and Experiments for Bronze Drum Casting Process in the Last 30 Years* that the research on ancient manufacturing craft of bronze drum is still not enough even having been being continued for 30 years. He doubtfully argues that not even the aborted test of producing bronze drum by assembling mud moulds method, but less archaeological evidence of producing bronze drum by such method has found including the mud moulds would result to a fact that the ancient Chinese may not apply assembling mud mould method in production of bronze drums. However, that method is still used in Vietnam nowadays. Does any reason can explain the differences between those in China and in Vietnam? There are further questions: What method is applied to produce bronze drum in ancient China? Would it be foundry method applied by brothers Wei Qichu and Wei Qisan, or the pottery pattern method which took a major position in the history of Chinese metallurgy? It should be the key point in further research to answer those puzzles on ancient manufacturing craft of bronze drum.

Part 4
Research on other Topics

Mr. Xiao Jun thinks in *Bronze Wares have Recorded Ou-Luo Culture* that the ancient bronze wares have recorded a number of unknown cultural impressions. In particular Ou-Luo bronze cultures which have long history and abundant contents need to be sorted out, explained and understood.

In *The Society of Wuzhou in Han Dynasty Revealed by Unearthed Bronze Wares,* Mr. Zhou Xuebin considers that Wuzhou is an ancient southern city with long history. It used to be called Cangwu and Guangxin. Archaeological discoveries indicate that as long ago as the middle and late Paleolithic Age ancient men have inhabited here. In Xia Period Wuzhou was the southern area of Jing Zhou, and it was ruled by Baiyue in Shang and Zhou periods. Qin Dynasty had built up 3 county, Guilin, Nanhai, Xiang after Lingnan Area had been unified. And Wuzhou belonged to Guilin County. So far, numerous bronze wares have been discovered here such as bronze drums, bronze Dings, bronze plates, bronze bottles, bronze pots and bronze mirrors. What's more the technique of engraving decoration in bronze wares shows the development of local bronze culture.

Mr. Chen Yutian introduces the achievement of studying pre-Qin ancient countries in Guangxi in *A Review of Research on Guangxi Pre-Qin States.* Generally speaking, it has achieved a lot and also has some questions. The research on pre-Qin countries is not profound enough because of less written documents and archaeology data. As for theory and method, historical researches mainly use written documents, chiefdom theory, military democracy and slave society. Archaeologists mainly study unearthed wares in the method of typology. Other scholars combine ethnological method with archaeological method. And few people have taken use of settlement archaeology, culture factors analysis and data analysis etc.

Mr. Wu Chunming in *Perspective of the Formation of Ou-Luo State from multi-factors of Dongson Culture* considers that Dongson culture has not only followed native culture in the lower Red River, but also has interacted and integrated with cultures of Baiyue countries. He discusses from the following aspects: multiple culture factors of Dongson; the continuation of native culture of the lower Red River; the similarity of Dongson culture with Baiyue culture of south China; the influence of Central Plains culture and Han culture towards Dongson culture through South of the Five Ridges; varying degree similarities and communication of Dongson culture and simultaneous culture of Southeast Asian Peninsula; the archaeological hypothesis of Wenlang Kingdom of King Xiong developing to Ou-Luo Kingdom of King Anyang; Dongson culture—history and remains of Ou-Luo Kingdom. He comes to the conclusion that Dongson culture of Ou-Luo Kingdom has been formed with the social context of the wars between Baiyue Kingdoms in south China and Zhou, Han Kingdom of Central Plains.

The mutual communication of bronze cultures between Guangxi and ASEAN had a very long history, especially bronze drums, which are the unique and distinguished local bronze cultures. Benefiting a lot from this conference, many experts propose that this kind of conference should be held frequently, making the bronze cultures to be a communicating media between China and ASEAN. Consequently cultural communication will bring the flourish of economic and trade which can promote the international peace and friendship.

第一部分

铜鼓文化研究

Part 1

Research on Bronze Drum Culture

万家坝铜鼓与石寨山铜鼓的比较研究

——从社会组织结构方式再论铜鼓的起源问题

A Comparison between Wanjiaba-style Bronze Drums and Shizhaishan-style Bronze Drums
—Once Discussion about the Source of Bronze Drums from the structure of the Social Organization

樊海涛 / 云南省博物馆 馆员

[摘要]

楚雄万家坝、晋宁石寨山两地是出土古代铜鼓的最重要的地区，其时代清晰、伴出器物丰富，对研究铜鼓的起源具有重要参考价值。从楚雄万家坝、晋宁石寨山青铜时代墓葬分布方式以及两地出土铜鼓的功能与地位比较研究看，万家坝仍然是铜鼓的重要起源地，它的社会组织结构方式吻合铜鼓诞生所需的基本条件。铜鼓起源的“多元说”，只是一种假说。

[关键词]

楚雄万家坝　晋宁石寨山　铜鼓比较　社会结构　鼓的起源

Abstract

The bronze drum that being excavated form Chuxiong Wanjiaba site and Jinning Shizhaishan site have important position in the world. there are many similarities and dissimilarities about Social organization in Chuxiong Wanjiaba site and Jinning Shizhaishan site among the grave way, the function of bronze drum, the position of bronze drum and so an. The social organization of Chuxiong Wanjiaba site is more antiquited than Jinning Shizhaishan site's, it has provided fundamental condition for bronze drum comes into being. Bronze drum only has an origin.

Key words

Chuxiong Wanjiaba; Jinning Shizhaishan; Comparation between bronze drums; Society stucture; Source of bronze drums

一

铜鼓起源问题的再思考

哪一类型铜鼓最早？迄今仍无标准答案。我国学者一般认为万家坝型铜鼓是最早的铜鼓，而越南学者大多认为黑格尔Ⅰ型铜鼓（即东山铜鼓）是最早的。中国学者与越南学者均认为铜鼓起源于自己国家。这两种观点中，不乏一些非学术性的因素，双方长期以来聚讼不休。因为东山铜鼓缺少可靠的考古学依据，而楚雄万家坝古墓葬群经科学发掘，伴出器物丰富，可信度较高，万家坝铜鼓出土后，铜鼓起源于滇中偏西地区的观点，逐渐在我国学术界占据了主流。部分越南学者也开始承认东山铜鼓原始形态的问题还有待解决。从20世纪90年代起，一些学者对万家坝古墓群、滇青铜文化的年代问题进行了新的探讨，提出了全新的看法，他们认为万家坝墓葬的年代处在西汉时期，万家坝型铜鼓与石寨山型铜鼓时代相近①。保守一点的提法是“滇式铜鼓的出现当是在万家坝Ⅰ型铜鼓出现不久受其影响而生产。滇式铜鼓自产生后便与万家坝铜鼓并行发展……”②激进者则认为“万家坝型铜鼓不可能早到春秋战国，更不可能是石寨山型铜鼓的起源或前身，两者应是同时并存的两型铜鼓。”③事涉铜鼓起源等重大问题，我们有必要对此进行细致的考察。

对万家坝墓群的年代问题，笔者认为万家坝的碳-14测年数据虽有早晚之差，但其科学性、客观性应可以肯定。与其认为被检测对象可能受铜锈污染，而使数据偏高的猜测，不如相信中国社科院考古研究所等科研单位实验室发布数据的严谨性，而且其测年数据并非单一，其中年代最晚也在战国早中期。唯数据论只是一叶障目，但完全无视科技考古的成果也不够客观科学。云南高原地区的碳-14测年数据确与其他地区略有不同，这可能是高原地域差异引起的，但在目前尚无更科学的论证前，不应轻易判定万家坝的碳-14测年数据完全不准确。万家坝无论早晚期墓葬均未出现铁器，因此其墓葬下限应可确定在西汉中期以前。从碳-14测年数据、发掘报告以及近年来科技考古的成果综合分析，谨慎判断，其上限至少不晚于春秋晚期④。

万家坝古墓群共出土铜鼓5面，均经科学发掘而出，层位清晰，伴出物丰富，是目前已知的最古老的铜鼓之一，可以将其视为探究铜鼓起源的重要坐标与参照物。其他地区所出土的万家坝型铜鼓，无论从科学研究价值还是可靠程度，目前尚无法与万家坝铜鼓可相比者。万家坝铜鼓是研究铜鼓起源最重要的材料之一，这一点无可置疑。

晋宁石寨山古墓群是滇青铜文化的核心区。该地出土的金质“滇王之印”证明石寨山古墓群是滇国王侯贵族的墓葬，其重要性不言而喻。该墓群共出土铜鼓17面，同样也是经科学

① 徐学书:《关于滇文化和滇西青铜文化年代的再探讨》，《考古》1999年第5期；徐学书:《关于岷江上游石棺葬文化同滇文化、滇西青铜文化相互关系的探讨》，《铜鼓和青铜文化研究——中国南方及东南亚地区古代铜鼓和青铜文化第四次国际学术讨论会论文集》，贵州人民出版社，2001年，131～144页；李龙章:《楚雄万家坝墓群及万家坝铜鼓的年代探讨》，《文物》2003年第12期。

② 徐学书:《关于岷江上游石棺葬文化同滇文化、滇西青铜文化相互关系的探讨》，《铜鼓和青铜文化研究——中国南方及东南亚地区古代铜鼓和青铜文化第四次国际学术讨论会论文集》，贵州人民出版社，2001年，131～144页。

③ 李龙章:《楚雄万家坝墓群及万家坝铜鼓的年代探讨》，《文物》2003年第12期。

④ 李晓岑、韩汝玢、孙淑云:《云南楚雄万家坝出土铜、锡器的分析及有关问题》，《文物》2008年第9期。

发掘出土，层位清晰，伴出物丰富，年代准确[①]，是研究石寨山型铜鼓的最可靠的材料。

本文不想深究哪一类型铜鼓最早或者是哪一号出土铜鼓的墓葬时代最早的问题，而拟从社会组织结构方式的角度出发，对铜鼓产生的必要条件作一些简单比较探讨。在解决铜鼓诞生的“必然性”后，铜鼓的起源问题应可得到更清晰的解答。一孔之间，谨此就教于海内外诸方家。

二

万家坝铜鼓与石寨山铜鼓之比较

铜鼓是特定地区、特定民族在特定历史时期的特殊产物。并非所有地区、所有民族均有可能成为铜鼓的发明者，只有在原始的氏族部落后期，文明萌生阶段，社会生产力发展到一定程度，阶级分化明显的情况下，当铜鼓成为社会发展的客观需要时，铜鼓才能出现。促使铜鼓诞生的最大动力，我们认为主要是原始宗教祭祀活动与战争的需求。铜鼓在原始宗教祭祀活动中可用来盛物，既是飨祭通神的礼器，又是歌舞活动的伴奏乐器，在紧急状态可以敲击集众，战争时候还可以指挥军阵活动。

下面我们试将万家坝与石寨山两地的墓葬分布方式以及两地出土铜鼓的功能、地位进行简单的对比和分析。

（一）墓葬分布方式比较

万家坝古墓群1975年进行发掘时，共发现79座古墓，皆为竖穴土坑墓，有的墓有棺椁，其中大墓13座，多数位于发掘区的中部，小墓则分布在大墓的两侧：西北一侧墓葬分布密集，且有相互叠压、打破的现象，东南一侧分布较为稀疏[②]。发掘报告认为“万家坝墓地是奴隶社会方兴时期的写照”，但目前看来，整个云南青铜时代是否已经进入奴隶社会都还存在很多争议，即使是最发达的滇国，学者们研究认为它更大程度上是一个具有复杂酋邦特征的早期国家，或称“方国”，还不能说已经进入了奴隶社会[③]。万家坝聚落比滇国社会组织更原始和古老，不应轻易将万家坝墓地归入“奴隶社会方兴时期”。我们认为，万家坝古墓群属于原始氏族部落时期的公共墓地，墓葬分布体现了明显的阶级分化。这种大小墓分布在一起，以大墓为中心、中小墓围绕周围的墓葬分布形式反映出原始氏族部落社会族葬制的特征。

因为万家坝第26号墓出土的“凸沿玉镯”与西汉时期滇池、抚仙湖区域青铜文化墓葬中所出无异，所以万家坝古墓群的年代甚至可能从春秋晚一直延续到了西汉初。但我们必须注意，不能以万家坝古墓群的年代下限来判断万家坝鼓的年代下限。万家坝最

① 许多学者对江川李家山古墓群的年代问题有不同意见，如米歇尔·皮拉·左里，参见《滇文化的年代问题》，《考古》1990年第1期。为避免混乱，本文对李家山出土的石寨山型铜鼓不予讨论。笔者认为，李家山M21等早期墓葬年代还是应依照发掘报告分析的战国末——汉武帝以前，如果一定要参考碳–14测定的数据，最多也只能推到战国晚期为宜。参见云南省博物馆：《云南江川李家山古墓群发掘报告》，《考古学报》1975年第2期。

② 云南省文物工作队：《楚雄万家坝古墓群发掘报告》，《考古学报》1983年第3期。

③ 谢崇安：《壮侗语族先民青铜文化艺术研究》，民族出版社，2007年，148页。

发达的时期当在春秋晚至战国初，已发掘的79座墓中，铜鼓仅出现在M1、M23两墓，最晚不过战国早期（M23），其后未见。万家坝79座墓中仅出土5面铜鼓，第1号墓出土1面，第23号墓出土4面。最新研究成果发现，第1号墓时代早于第23号墓①。这说明随着时间的推移，社会财富越来越集中到氏族部落的酋长手中。万家坝聚落的发展趋势属于早期发达、中后期逐渐衰落的情况，这可能与其原居民“濮人”的东迁有关。战国时期，一部分万家坝居民可能陆续迁徙到今昆明官渡地区。昆明羊甫头墓地前期一部分文化因素就是沿袭万家坝而来，填塞膏泥、边桩、垫木、腰坑是两地大墓的共同特征②。

石寨山古墓群自1955年起，已先后历经5次发掘，共发现86座墓，大中小型墓均有，以前认为石寨山大墓多而小墓少的认识，在1995年第5次发掘中得到了修正。石寨山同样也是竖穴土坑墓，因为当地石多土少，所以在埋葬时候经常因地制宜，选取岩石下凹的地方略加修整作为墓穴，不能因此称为“石缝间葬”。据第5次发掘过程中所揭示的最新的墓葬分布情况，大墓间相邻很近，小墓分布大墓旁，“早期墓葬主要是小型墓”，其年代可暂定在战国中期以前③。其中第76号小墓后经发掘领队蒋志龙先生考证，年代可推至春秋中期以前④。

综合石寨山5次发掘的情况，我们发现石寨山古墓群的墓葬分布形式与万家坝有相似之处，即大墓居中，小墓分布大墓四周。但万家坝的墓葬分布显示出更加古老的文化色彩，大中型墓数量仅占全部墓葬16.45%，与小墓数量悬殊甚大，大墓与小墓的关系犹如“众星拱月”。万家坝古墓群已经存在明显的阶级分化情况，出土铜鼓的M1、M23的主人应该就是当时的氏族部落酋长等级人物。

石寨山古墓群早期无大墓，西汉初期开始有大墓，同时小墓相对大墓数量迅速减少。西汉以前几无大墓，小墓分布无规律。西汉以后，石寨山古墓群分布逐渐呈现一些规律性，以第2次发掘的20座墓为核心，大墓周围零星分布中小墓葬。大墓有叠压、打破小墓的情况，而小墓从不叠压、打破大墓。石寨山古墓群的发展趋势是早期相对原始落后，中后期突然发达起来。早期的小墓应该是氏族部落时期的聚族而葬，但到了西汉初期，石寨山的性质发生巨大改变，它变成了滇王及其贵族的墓地，大墓数量激增。石寨山第9号墓的断肢葬甚至可能是被杀殉的仆从墓，显示出滇国残酷的阶级斗争的血痕。这与滇国及滇王的势力在西汉时期的迅速增长有密切关系。

石寨山86座墓出土17面铜鼓，分别出土于10座墓中，在数量和普及程度上都比万家坝多得多。早期小墓无铜鼓，西汉初期以后，大中型墓中才出现铜鼓，数量多寡不一，少者1面，最多者3面。石寨山的墓葬分布形式所体现的社会组织结构显然比万家坝更晚、更高级、更成熟，但1座墓中出土铜鼓数量却比万家坝23号墓少，其他随葬品的种类、数量则远远超过了万家坝。石寨山古墓群所体现出的社会组织结构的发展过程是早期原始落后，中后期才逐渐兴旺发达起来。如果单纯地将万家坝、石寨山两地铜鼓出现的时间比较，万家坝铜鼓最迟在战国就出现，比石寨山西汉初才出现要早得多，石寨山铜鼓是万家坝衰落之后才出现，两者之间平行关系并不明显。

① 李晓岑、韩汝玢、孙淑云：《云南楚雄万家坝出土铜、锡器的分析及有关问题》，《文物》，2008年第9期。

② 云南省文物考古研究所、昆明市博物馆、官渡区博物馆：《昆明羊甫头墓地》，科学出版社，2005年，863页。

③ 云南省文物考古研究所、昆明市文物管理委员会、晋宁县文物管理所：《云南晋宁石寨山第五次抢救性发掘简报》，《文物》1998年第6期。

④ 蒋志龙：《滇国探秘——石寨山文化的新发现》，云南教育出版社，2002年，182页。

就社会发展成熟度而言，万家坝铜鼓所生存的文化土壤比石寨山铜鼓要原始得多，万家坝在社会组织结构层面上更可能成为铜鼓的诞生地，石寨山体现出的相对成熟的社会组织结构所能容纳的只是一种成熟的“铜鼓文化”，它不会是铜鼓起源地。

（二）铜鼓的功能、地位比较

万家坝出土的5面铜鼓，时间上有早晚之分。发掘报告根据碳-14数据，将出土5面铜鼓的M1、M23断为同一时期，但最新科技考古的研究成果认为，M1时间上要早于M24。万家坝发掘简报所得出的结论也与此相同，应予重视①。我们从发掘报告可知，M1仅出土1面铜鼓（M1:12），位于墓葬腰坑中，鼓上无烟熏痕迹，鼓内壁无纹饰（图一）；M23出土4面铜鼓，位于墓葬棺木底部垫木下，两两相对，鼓上有烟熏痕迹，内壁有云纹、网纹、四足爬虫纹等阳纹纹饰，最多者达7组。M1所出的铜鼓经成分检测为红铜器，M23的4面铜鼓中，2面为红铜器，即M23:158、M23:160，其余2面为青铜器，即M23:159、M23:161②（图二）。从M1到M23，社会发展的成熟度、随葬品的丰富度、铜鼓纹饰的华美度，铜鼓的铸造水平均呈现出逐渐上升的趋势，这与社会发展的基本规律吻合。所以我们同意M1时间比M23更早的论断。而且M1出土了铜釜而M23未见，说明M1的主人是氏族部落的公推首领，掌握着食物分配与原始宗教祭祀的权力。M23出土了大量的兵器，尤其是铜矛，竟多达350余件，可见它的主人还是氏族部落的军事首领，掌握着神权与军权。虽然M23出土的4面铜鼓上满布烟熏痕迹，但我们不能据此说它一定是炊具，它更可能是在祭祀时候以“燔祭”的形式祭祀神明而形成的。

万家坝聚落的形成与发展初期，铜鼓逐渐从食器中分离出来，成为氏族部落的乐器、祭器，还可用来指挥军队战斗。这一时间段虽无考古学的证据，但它应该在M1之前，M1出土的铜鼓不一定是M1的墓主人所铸。M23出土的4面铜鼓合金成分不同，有红铜鼓、青铜鼓，它们也不是同时铸造的，有的铜鼓，例如红铜鼓（M23:158、M23:160）可能就是部落早期传承下来后被M23所独占。M1（春秋晚期）出土的那面铜鼓是原始氏族部落公鼓逐步私有化的开端，到了M23时期（战国早期），铜鼓已经变

图一　万家坝出土铜鼓（M1：12）

图二　万家坝出土铜鼓（M23：161）

① 云南省博物馆文物工作队、四川大学历史系考古专业七四级学员：《云南省楚雄县万家坝古墓群发掘简报》，《考古》1978年第10期。

② 参见李昆声，黄德荣：《再论万家坝型铜鼓》附表二，《考古学报》2007年第2期；李晓岑、韩汝玢、孙淑云：《云南楚雄万家坝出土铜、锡器的分析及有关问题》，《文物》2008年第9期。

成了典型的部落王鼓，全部集中在部落首领手中，甚至死后都要全部带入地下。M23还出土了1件铜鼓形铜凿（楚万M23:209），其顶部是一小铜鼓，鼓面朝上，鼓足下方延伸出细长的凿身。这件铜凿构思巧妙，具有很强的实用性与装饰性，也是我们迄今发现的较早的以铜鼓作为装饰附件的铜器，标志着铜鼓世俗化的滥觞。

到了石寨山时期，铜鼓的功能随着社会发展的复杂化也越来越多样。它至少有以下几个功能：①乐器。②祭祀礼器。③指挥军阵。④权力象征。⑤财富象征[①]。此外，铜鼓还大量应用在生活实用和艺术装饰等方面。2001年，昆明官渡区羊甫头墓地出土的1件漆木跪坐女巫最为典型，她头顶1小铜鼓，跪坐在1大铜鼓上，铜鼓是她服饰的一部分，又是她的座椅，在宗教祭祀活动时还是她的法器。铜鼓既具有神圣的一面，又有强烈的世俗化倾向。

万家坝部落酋长集神权、军政大权为一身，而石寨山滇国贵族神权与军权已经分离，男性贵族主持军政事务，女性贵族管理耕织，巫师掌握宗教祭祀，社会分工逐渐明晰。万家坝铜鼓是原始氏族部落唯一的通神礼器，石寨山铜鼓则仅是滇国宗教祭祀中重要的祭祀法器或崇拜对象之一，除铜鼓之外，柱、杖等也具有祭祀礼器的作用。与万家坝相比，石寨山铜鼓的乐器功能甚至可能还有一些下降，万家坝M23出土的4四面铜鼓经测音，具有演奏乐曲的可能，石寨山铜鼓在1座墓葬中出土的数量组合比万家坝少，单独演奏乐曲的可能性也因此减少，但石寨山西汉时期墓葬出土文物表明当时已经出现了多种乐器配合演奏的“乐肆”。

有的学者将铜鼓与中原的铜鼎比较，认为铜鼓是滇国统治阶级权力的象征。但他们也同时指出“铜鼓虽是这些君长权力的象征，但还没有像铜鼎那样发展到国家象征的地步……也就是说铜鼓还未成为明确和维持社会等级秩序的角色。”[②]这一认识是准确的。铜鼓在滇国确有象征权力、地位的作用，但不是说它一定标志着王权或其他某种地位。石寨山铜鼓最重要的功能是象征着财富与地位，而财富象征又在两者中占据了更重要的位置。石寨山出土的17面铜鼓（图三、图四）。多出于墓的前端或后端，其中11件内贮满海贝，其他正置的铜鼓鼓面上大多放置1铜俑。可见它们与万家坝原始氏族部落时期的铜鼓在功能、地位上区别已经很大，它们被用来贮藏海贝，或者成为持伞铜俑的座椅。铜鼓也不再被某一墓葬所独有，17面铜鼓分别出土于9座墓葬当中，而且同一时期内的不同墓葬都拥有铜鼓，例如西汉早期墓葬M14、M15、M16、M17，这4座墓时代接近，位置相邻，均出铜鼓。万家坝铜鼓仅被部落首领所拥有，而石寨山铜鼓已经变成了滇国王侯贵族的私有物品，不再神圣不可侵犯。

石寨山第6号墓是滇王墓，但该墓中并未出土铜鼓，说铜鼓是滇国权力的象征，未免与考古发现的事实相悖。在阶级社会中，社会财富往往集中在统治阶级手中，铜鼓作为社会财富的重要组成部分之一，当然也只能出土在滇国王侯贵族墓葬中。战国、西汉时期，滇国仅是一个处于早期国家阶段的“复杂的酋邦社会”，我们没有必要以真正意义上的国家的标准来评定。石寨山铜鼓确实具有财富与地位的象征作用，这是社会发展所必然赋予

① 万辅彬：《铜鼎与铜鼓的社会文化功能比较——兼议技术传播发展中的文化多样性》，《广西民族研究》2003年第1期。

② 万辅彬：《铜鼎与铜鼓的社会文化功能比较——兼议技术传播发展中的文化多样性》，《广西民族研究》2003年第1期。

图三　石寨山出土铜鼓（M14：1）

图四　石寨山出土铜鼓（M10：3）

它的历史使命，但它所能象征的程度，不能离开滇国这个尚处于早期国家发展阶段的社会形态来认识。

从万家坝到石寨山，我们发现这样的一种趋势，即随着时间的推移，铜鼓的功能越来越多样化、世俗化，但铜鼓的社会地位却越降越低。在万家坝，它早期是神圣不可侵犯的礼器、神器，是部落公鼓，后逐渐演变成部落王鼓，一直是部落首领地位、权力的标志，具有唯一性、不可替代性；在滇国，它变成了众多王侯贵族夸富逞强的炫耀工具，变成了精美的装饰附件，它的财富与地位的象征功能也逐渐被滇国独有的贮贝器所取代。

万家坝铜鼓是部落神器，石寨山铜鼓是铜鼓走向世俗化的典型。两者分别代表了铜鼓文化发展的不同阶段。它们是相承关系而非平行关系。当然，它们的相承不是指前者消亡而后者继起，而是指后者是前者发展的更高级阶段。就时间而言，万家坝型铜鼓的下限，已经到了战国晚期，甚或更晚，它与石寨山型铜鼓的确存在一些共时性，但两者起点不同，不能说成是“平行关系”。

铜鼓的社会功能演变，离不开它所根植的经济基础以及它所存在的社会组织结构。它的社会功能越复杂，它所对应的社会组织结构也就越成熟，换言之，复杂的社会组织结构中具有复杂的社会功能的铜鼓不会是刚刚“诞生”的，它只能从简单到复杂、从低级到高级逐步成熟发展起来，就像新生婴儿的成长过程。石寨山型以及与它类似的铜鼓都不是最早的铜鼓。

以上比较可参见表一。

通过比较我们可知，在社会组织结构方式上，石寨山古墓群比万家坝古墓群更成熟、更复杂、更高级。铜鼓在社会组织结构中的地位万家坝要高于石寨山，其职能则从神圣不可侵犯而逐渐走向世俗化，最终变成滇国贵族夸富逞强的工具。从历史的角度看，石寨山古墓群所体现的社会组织结构代表着万家坝聚落未来的发展方向，但由于“濮人”东迁，万家坝衰落了，它所承载的“铜鼓文化”被石寨山吸纳并发扬光大。如果我们承认物质世界的永恒的发展规律是一个从低级到高级、从简单到复杂的运动变化过程，那么我们就应该认识到万家坝铜鼓在铜鼓产生、发展的过程中确实排列在石寨山铜鼓的“前列”，更何况还有其他诸多的考古学证据和科技考古数据的验证。

表一　万家坝古墓群与石寨山古墓群出土铜鼓及相关情况比较表

	万家坝古墓群	石寨山古墓群
时代	春秋至战国末	战国中期至西汉
社会发展程度	原始部落社会	复杂酋邦社会
已发掘墓葬数量	79座	86座
墓葬分布形式	竖穴土坑墓，大墓为中心，中小墓围绕周围	竖穴土坑墓，大墓间相邻很近，小墓分布大墓旁，大墓有叠压、打破小墓的情况
大中小墓葬数量	大中墓13座，小墓66座，晚期无大墓	大中墓21座，小墓65座，早期无大墓
墓葬显示的发展趋势	早期发达，中后期逐渐衰落	早期相对落后，中后期突然兴盛起来
墓葬性质	族葬墓	贵族墓取代了原始的平民墓，有殉葬墓
出土铜鼓墓葬数量、铜鼓数量	2座墓，共5面铜鼓	10座墓，共17面铜鼓
铜鼓的合金成分	红铜鼓、青铜鼓均有	青铜鼓，尚未发现红铜鼓
一座墓出土最多铜鼓数量	4面	3面
铜鼓的拥有者	不同时期唯一的部落领袖	同一时期不同的贵族
出土铜鼓墓葬的其他主要伴出物	铜釜、铜锄、铜斧、铜矛、铜镞等	铜贮贝器、铜扣饰、铜兵器、铜弩机、铜镞、铜柄铁剑、铁矛、铜马具、铜臂甲、铜镜、铜钱、小铜俑、铜牛头、铜鹿头、金臂甲、金饰片、玛瑙珠、玛瑙扣、绿松石珠、玉器等
与铜鼓伴出的乐器	羊角纽钟	铜葫芦笙
铜鼓的演奏方式	四面铜鼓配合使用	与其他乐器如錞于、葫芦笙等配合使用
铜鼓的主要功能	部落王鼓，祭祀用具，乐器	贵族专用，祭祀用具，乐器，财富、权利象征
最高领袖的职能	集神权、军政大权为一身	神权与军权已经分离，男性贵族主持军政事务，女性贵族管理耕织，巫师掌握宗教祭祀
铜鼓的社会地位与功能演变趋势	地位崇高，功能少，开始有世俗化倾向	地位逐渐降低，功能多样，世俗化严重

三

余　论

在世界范围内，铜鼓与墓葬文化关系之密切，与本土文化融合之深入以及考古发掘伴出物之丰富，未有如云南者。从古老的氏族部落社会到早期国家，铜鼓都扮演着重要的社会角色。所以我们选取了最典型的万家坝、石寨山两地进行比较。这种比较对于众多出土铜鼓的墓葬、地区而言，确是不完全的，但由于两地的重要地位，这种比较又具有一定的典型性。我们比较的目的在于揭示铜鼓起源所必须具备的“文化土壤”，即一种特殊的文化背景下的特定的社会组织结构。离开了这种“文化土壤”，铜鼓不可能诞生。

许多学者常讨论研究铜鼓起源的“一元说”与“多元说”，这实际上是一个伪命题。在目前铜鼓出现的大致时间、发展脉络已经基本清楚的情况下，还要人为地去寻找不同的

“祖型”、不同的民族、不同的起源，这种看似细致科学的研究实际上忽略了一个文化的基本特性——传播性。正如一些学者所言“古代东南亚与中国南方，地理毗邻，气候环境相似，但又分为不同的地域，从新石器时代始，就有经济文化联系，通过民族迁徙，贸易往来，到青铜时代各地区之间交流更加频繁，铜鼓文化相互传播和影响日益密切是必然的”[①]。所以我们对铜鼓起源的“一元说”、“多元说”应有科学的认识。用个不恰当的比喻，我们很难想象，在电视机发明后的几十或几百年内，世界各地都独立地发明了电视机。

铜鼓最早出现的具体时间，因为考古工作不断有新发现的缘故，目前还不能完全确定，但就现知的材料看，春秋时期铜鼓已诞生应无可疑。从整个亚洲的宏观视角来观察，此时，东南亚地区业已先后进入青铜时代，但由于东南亚的青铜文化遗址中常伴存铁器，青铜器与铁器同时并用，故有些学者将之统称为“早期金属时代”，而不划出一个单独的青铜时代。目前大陆地区的泰国、越南有众多遗址发现，可供研究，而印度尼西亚、菲律宾等海岛地区出土遗物较少，所以我们在探讨铜鼓的起源时，也只能将目光聚集在泰国、越南和中国南方三地。泰国班清遗址、依诺他遗址的断代目前尚有争议，班清遗址出土的1面铜鼓小而精美，不会是早期的形态。东山文化的前期发掘因不是在考古学家的主持下进行，时代、地层存在很多问题，经多次新发掘后，目前对东山文化的年代一般认为与滇国相近，即战国至东汉左右。东山文化后期，铜器种类开始增多，才出现铜鼓[②]。东山铜鼓与石寨山铜鼓实际是同一类型的不同发展形式。我们通过前文的比较研究可知，东山铜鼓也不会是最古老的铜鼓。

万家坝型铜鼓目前全世界已经发现了62面，其中中国发现51面，越南发现8面，泰国发现3面。中国是发现万家坝型铜鼓最多的国家，云南是中国发现万家坝型铜鼓最多的省份，而云南中部偏西地区又是云南出土万家坝型铜鼓最集中的地区[③]。万家坝是目前经考古发掘出土铜鼓并且伴出物丰富的早期墓葬群，近年来铜鼓铅同位素研究成果已经证明万家坝鼓的原料可能采自禄丰、牟定及附近地区[④]。从社会组织结构的角度来看，处于原始氏族部落后期的万家坝聚落具备了生产铜鼓的能力与客观需要，它是目前最具说服力的铜鼓的发源地。从造型、纹样的演变分析，万家坝出土的5面铜鼓还不是最古老的形态，一些学者在型式划分上也未将万家坝出土的5面铜鼓归入最早的第Ⅰ式[⑤]，但它始终是判断铜鼓起源的最重要的坐标与参照物。

铜鼓自滇中偏西地区诞生后，呈放射状向周边地区传播，它遇到最适合的土壤时，就迅速生长壮大起来，与当地文化结合，发展出新的型式，如石寨山文化、东山文化等所见者，而当它未遇到适合生长的土壤时，则一直保持了原始稚拙的形态，昌宁天生桥铜鼓就是这种情况，它的形制古朴，鼓面上还有4组立体雕塑，时代可能已经晚至战国末或西汉初。“自西向东”只是铜鼓传播的主轴线，其他还有北传、东传、南传的各种途径[⑥]，只是在目前考古资料还不是很完整的情况下，具体的传播路线还无法作清楚的揭示，相信随着越来越多的地区不断发现万家坝型铜鼓，我们将对其传播、发展做更全面、更深入的认识。

① 梁志明：《东南亚的青铜时代文化与古代铜鼓综述》，《南洋问题研究》2007年第4期。

② 刘美崧：《雒越铜鼓与东山文化——驳“越南北部是铜鼓的故乡”说》，《中南民族学院学报》（哲学社会科学版）1996年第6期。

③ 李昆声：《论万家坝型铜鼓》，《考古》1990年第5期；李昆声、黄德荣：《再论万家坝型铜鼓》，《考古学报》2007年第2期。

④ 李晓岑：《中国铅同位素考古》，云南科技出版社，2000年，18～32页。越南阮文好先生为本书提供新资料，越南万家坝型铜鼓有16面。

⑤ 李昆声：《论万家坝型铜鼓》，《考古》1990年第5期。

⑥ 木基元：《云南型铜鼓传播路线新探》，《云南民族大学学报》（哲学社会科学版）1990年第4期。

云南早期铜鼓起源新探

A New Perspective on the Source of Early Types of Bronze Drums in Yunnan

范　舟 / 云南省博物馆 副研究员

[摘要]

铜鼓，作为亚洲东南部青铜文化最具代表性的器物之一，诞生年代久远，存在时间绵长，分布地域广袤，留存数量众多。自奥地利学者黑格尔以后，对铜鼓的系统研究已进行了多年，但目前在不少问题上仍存有较大的争议和未解之处。本文谨就云南早期铜鼓与北方游牧文化之间可能存在的历史关系作一些探讨。由于古代气候的变迁，造成北方的草原游牧民族较大规模的南迁，游牧文化对于云南早期铜鼓的形成起到了重要的推动作用。

[关键词]

万家坝型　石寨山型　铜鼓　游牧文化

Abstract

The bronze drum is a remarkable representative of ancient Southeast Asia culture. For recent years, many researches have been done about it. This thesis is on account of climate change to infer that from later bronze age to early Iron age，the nomadic ethic group from Eurasian steppe moved south into Yunnan. The early types of bonze drum in Yunnan may deeply associate with the nomad: the Saka and the Kunming. The influence of nomadic culture reflected from many aspects: Bronze ware, Petroglyph, and the myth etc.

Key words

Wanjiaba type; Shizhaishan type; Bronze drum; Nomadic culture

一

云南的早期铜鼓

云南早期铜鼓是指万家坝和石寨山型两种铜鼓。

万家坝型铜鼓出土于楚雄万家坝，被很多学者认为是最原始的铜鼓，按铜鼓分类学，不同的学者将其定名为A型铜鼓（汪宁生）、Ⅰa式铜鼓（李伟卿）、先黑格尔Ⅰ式铜鼓（今村启尔）。他们所指都是同一类型的铜鼓，本文均以万家坝型铜鼓称之。石寨山型铜鼓以晋宁石寨山滇文化墓葬出土的一批装饰华丽的铜鼓为代表，黑格尔将此铜鼓列为第Ⅰ式，本文以石寨山型铜鼓称之。

对于早期铜鼓的研究，文献不足是一个重要制约因素，这使得我们对于它们的确切纪年无从认定。万家坝墓群有5个碳-14测定数据，年代约在前7世纪到前3世纪左右[①]。石寨山墓群的年代，根据皮拉佐里的意见，大约是前250年至50年之间[②]，这一观点是比较接近实际的结论。

学界近年来对万家坝型铜鼓和石寨山型铜鼓的年代研究表明，时代上前者略早，二者基本是前后衔接的，从长期历史进程的整体来看，可以认为是同一时代的产物。从分布来看，以往认为万家坝型铜鼓主要分布于云南中西部。随着考古和文物收集的新发现，它的分布范围也扩大了，延伸至广西以及四川、越南和泰国北部，万家坝和石寨山两类铜鼓的分布范围是基本一致的[③]。二者在地域上同属一个地区，时间上可以相互衔接，基本的型制也一脉相承，可以认为是同一种器物的两个发展阶段，这方面已有很多研究成果，不再赘述。

云南早期铜鼓的族属，目前主流的观点认为其创制者是南方族群，“可以合称为濮僚或濮越族群，即现代壮傣语的先民。”[④]也有学者提出万家坝型铜鼓是“昆明人”创制，石寨山型为古越人创制的观点[⑤]，前者是主流观点，但后者却为探讨云南早期铜鼓的起源提供了新的思路和线索。早在新石器时代，云南就形成了多元文化并存的状态，这已被众多考古成果所证实。文化的多样性，表明各种文化不是孤立发展的，而是处于不断的交流之中。青铜时代云南存在的众多文化中，源自北方草原地区的游牧文化占有重要地位。来自北方欧亚草原地带（Eurasian steppe）的游牧族群沿三江地区南下，对云南早期的历史发展产生过重要而深远的影响。这种影响也反映在早期铜鼓上，云南早期铜鼓与游牧文化的关系，值得作深入的研究。

① 李伟卿:《铜鼓及其纹饰》，云南科技出版社，2000年，35页。

② 米歇尔·皮拉左里:《滇文化的年代问题》，《考古》1990年第1期。

③ 李昆声、黄德荣:《考古学报》2007年第2期。

④ 李伟卿:《铜鼓及其纹饰》，云南科技出版社，2000年，55页。

⑤ 张增祺:《“万家坝型”铜鼓与“石寨山型”铜鼓的关系》，《铜鼓和青铜文化的新探索》，广西民族出版社，1993年，23页。

二

先秦时期中原和云南的地理气候

从自然地理的角度看，云南早期铜鼓集中的云南中西部正是亚洲东南部几条大江大河流域集中交汇之处，长江、珠江、红河、澜沧江—湄公河、怒江—萨尔温江在这里汇集，尔后分头流向不同的方向。这些江河是古代文化交流最重要的通道之一，云南中部于是成为沟通北方草原地区、中国内地与北部湾和中南半岛的十字路口。特别是云南以西均为高山密林，没有大的江河通向西部印度方向，云南以西很少发现铜鼓，同江河通道的缺乏有很大关系。

气候历来是影响文化历史的重要因素。根据气候史的研究成果，夏商时期（前3000～前1000年），中国东部的气候比现代温暖，亚热带的北界达到山东兖州、河南安阳一带，商代遗址中出土了獐、竹鼠等亚热带动物和犀牛、亚洲象等热带动物骨骼，其中“圣水牛目前在中国已绝迹，现生种仅见于东南亚低地森林中。”[①]“周朝的气候，虽然最初温暖，但不久就恶化了。《竹书纪年》上记载周孝王时，长江一个大支流汉水，有两次结冰，发生于前903和前897年。《竹书纪年》还提到结冰之后，紧接着就是大旱，这就表示前第10世纪时期的寒冷。《诗经》也可证实这点。”“周朝早期的寒冷情况没有延长多久，大约只一两个世纪，到了春秋时期又和暖了。《左传》往往提到，山东鲁国过冬，冰房得不到冰。在前698、前590和前545年时尤其如此。此外，像竹子、梅树这样的亚热带植物，在《左传》和《诗经》中，常常提到。”[②]这是中原的情况。东南亚地区的气候史研究提示了同样的气候巨变：距今1万年前，东南亚地区海平面比现在的海平面低出40～60米之多，而前5000～前4000年，海平面高度却又比当前高出2.5～5.8米[③]。云南缺乏历次气候变化的文献记录，可以推断类似的剧烈气候变化在云南也是同步的。

另外一个与气候人文有关的关于游牧区和农耕区分界问题涉及充满争议的“15英寸等雨线”。“15英寸等雨线”是指从我国东北至西南的一条年均降水定型线，它的中段与长城大致符合，其西南则使青海与西藏和中国中东部分隔。等雨线的东南，平均每年至少15英寸的雨量是常态，符合拉铁摩尔（Owen Lattimore）所说的“中原农业茂盛，人口繁殖”。等雨线的西北，“几千英里内人类全然不事农桑”，他们与牲口来往于干燥的地区，让牛羊自觅水草[④]。这条线可以看作亚洲东部草原游牧地带同农耕地带的分界地带。云南中西部尽管所处纬度较低，但海拔高带来的低温对农业也有重要影响，除河谷坝区之外大量的山地不能农耕而只宜放牧，

① 施雅风：《中国历史气候变化》，山东科学技术出版社，1996年，283页。

② 竺可桢：《中国近五千年来气候变迁的初步研究》，《考古学报》1972年第1期。

③ Charles Higham. *Early cultures of mainland southeast Asia*. River Books Ltd, Bangkok，2002:8.

④ 黄仁宇：《中国大历史》，生活·读书·新知三联书店，1997年，22～24页。

因此也处于分界带上。有关这条分界线有关的其他领域的研究，童恩正从考古学的角度提出了“边地半月形文化传播带”，基本与这条分界线重合；费孝通20世纪80年代从人类学和民族学的角度提出西南地区的“藏彝走廊”，大概就是这条分界线的南段。可以认为，不同领域的学者对这条分界目前都达成了较为一致的认识：不论是15英寸降水线或是“边地半月形文化传播带”或是“藏彝走廊”，都是从不同角度描述的同一条界线，它不仅是中国农业区和游牧区的分野，同时也把游牧文化同农耕文化区别开。围绕这条分界线中国历史上游牧族群同农耕族群展开过多次纷争与战争，而和平时期两种文化的交流则从未中断过。与人们通常认为的一成不变的自然生态景观不同，历史上这条分界始终处于不断地变化当中，甚至在某些历史时期，它随气候的变化产生相当剧烈的变化。随着全球气温的变化所引发的游牧农耕交界带南北向移动，在古代云南，农耕族群和游牧族群之间的边界也相应地同样运动。

三

先秦时期云南的游牧族群
——“昆明”和“叟”及其历史背景

有关青铜时代云南的游牧族群，常常被认为出自氐羌。但氐和羌只是中原文献对黄河上游地区各部落的统称，往往氐、羌连用，表示同一类人群。这些部落各有自称，显然不是“氐”或“羌”。“羌”字最为古老，商代甲骨文卜辞中就已出现。“羌”从羊从人，《说文解字》释“羌”：“西方牧羊人也。”羌人的活动范围一直都在变化，商代的羌方大约在今陕西东部、晋南一带；春秋战国则指称陇西、青海一带的异族；秦汉时远至河西四郡的部落也被称为“羌”。先秦时期的羌人并不是纯粹的游牧族群，而是长期居住在河湟地区以农耕为主的古老华夏族群的一支。他们在主营农耕的同时兼营以羊为代表的畜牧，他们与周人有深厚的渊源。章炳麟《检论·序种姓》说“姜者，羌也。”有学者认为“‘羌’字金文作，从羊从女，实为羌字之变体。故《诗》所谓‘姜嫄’，实即‘羌嫄’”[①]可见羌是周人的始祖之一。很早以前羌人就与西南地区有密切关联，先秦时的羌人可能就是北迁的三苗族群和黄河流域中上游文化结合的产物。《后汉书·西羌传》“西羌之本，出自三苗。”武王伐商，羌人是周人盟军之一：《尚书·周书·牧誓》“及庸，蜀、羌、髳、微、卢、彭、濮人。”孔颖达《尚书正义》“此八国皆西南夷也”，论及羌人的起源，不应只考虑他们作为从北方南下到西南地区的可能性；结合文献

① 何光岳:《氐羌源流史》，江西教育出版社，2000年，192页。

和商代和西周前段普遍的温暖气候条件，我们倒是可以考虑相反的情况：即先秦时期的羌人是南方的三苗族群北迁到河湟地区。另外，说藏语的各民族在古代和羌人有紧密的联系：《新唐书·吐蕃传》“吐蕃本西羌属，盖有百五十种，散处河、湟、江、岷间”；《一统志》“西蕃即吐蕃也，其先本羌属”。由此可以理解汉藏语系诸民族的联系有着深远的历史文化基础；从局部的地方史的角度，同样也可以解释唐代吐蕃和南诏的密切联系并非空中楼阁。

先秦时期云南地区真正的南迁游牧族群，应该是来自草原地区的以骑马为标志的斯基泰族群和突厥——蒙古族群，这在文献中有明确的记载:《华阳国志·南中志》载“夷人大种曰昆，小种曰叟”。

塞人在《后汉书·南蛮西南夷列传》也有记载，被称为“塞夷”：“建武二十三年，其王贤栗遣兵乘箄船，南下江、汉，击附塞夷鹿茤，鹿茤人弱，为所擒获。”《华阳国志》中的叟人，张增祺先生认为即是“塞”人：“《华阳国志·南中志》中的叟人，《后汉书·西南夷列传》中的塞夷，都是指南迁的塞人而言。”[①]“塞”人，在西方典籍及铭文中多称为Saka（译为塞迦或萨迦）；希腊人称之为Scythians 即斯基泰（又译西徐亚、塞西安或斯奇提亚）。塞人在中国古代文献中所指就游牧的斯基泰族群。斯基泰人是纯粹的游牧民，他们占据着欧亚草原广大地区，支系众多，是一个包含了许多部落或部族的游牧民族的总称，语言主要是印欧语。大约在前8～前7世纪，专门从事畜牧的斯基泰部落变得异常活跃，他们的社会化程度大大发展，出现了社会阶层，物质产品和精神文化快速增长，物质成就中最突出的是马具和武器的完善，兵器也多样化。同时铁器开始出现[②]。这种变化直接的表现是斯基泰人离开故地，对周边地区进行大规模侵扰。具体原因可能源于气候的巨变：大范围的降温（可能还伴随着干旱）对塞人的游牧生活产生了巨大影响，迫使他们不得不另寻佳境。

在西方，“根据希腊历史学家提供的证据，并得到亚述王国编年史的补充，在前750至前700年间，来自突厥斯坦和西西伯利亚的斯基泰人从辛梅里安人手里夺走了南俄罗斯草原。”[③]这起事件其实只是冰山一角，塞人的这次西侵包括了对南高加索、小亚细来、亚美尼亚、亚述帝国等古老文明大举入侵，其后果已经超出了政治史的范畴。塞人的入侵造成了中东政治动荡的多米诺骨牌效应，这一重大变局，因牵涉过远，此处不再详述。这次西侵对斯基泰文化自身同样产生很大的影响。一些学者认为，正是同亚述的接触，使得斯基泰产生了以动物纹样为特征的斯基泰艺术风格；也正是同西亚地区的密切接触，他们完成了从铜器时代向铁器时代的过渡。

在东方的中国，塞人的活动同样引起了严重的后果。西周末年因受犬戎侵扰，西周被迫放弃关中而东迁，宣告西周的结束，时间在前770年。犬戎的东侵和斯基泰

① 张增祺：《滇国与滇文化》，云南美术出版社，1997年，287页。

② Vladimir A. Bashilov and Leonid T. Yablonsky. *Kurgans, Ritual Sites, and Settlements Eurasian Bronze and Iron Age*. British Archaeological Reports，2000:10.

③ 格鲁塞:《草原帝国》，商务印书馆，1999年，25页。

人的活动时间上是高度吻合的，犬戎可能是以狼为图腾的一个草原游牧部落。欧洲汉学家普实克（Jaroslav Prusek）认为，“欧亚草原东部‘蛮族’移徙及入侵中国，与草原西部Cimmerian和scythian（塞人）的大迁徙有关，而两者都肇因于约前1000年欧亚草原上一个新经济社会形态的产生；这新经济社会形态便是立基于畜养大量驯养动物——特别是马——的游牧。这种新经济浪潮造成新的资源领域瓜分，产生一些向邻近地区扩土的游牧武士，也因此让整个欧亚草原风起云涌，一端发生变动很快地波及另一端。”[①]东周开始以后气温快速回暖却打乱了游牧民族的迁徙步伐，南方族群迅速返身北上，春秋战国时期以吴、越、楚南方诸国为代表的稻作文化的北移也反映出当时气候变化的剧烈程度，也正是这一阶段出现了少有的文化交流和碰撞局面，对我国历史产生了深远的影响。

在中国的北方草原地区，稍晚于上述两者的另一起重大事件，是匈奴迅速崛起，这个进程至两汉发展到了顶峰。匈奴的文化和斯基泰文化有极大的相似性但时代稍晚，可以认为是受到斯基泰文化东迁的强烈影响，成熟的匈奴文化从广义上说也属于“斯基泰—西伯利亚文化圈”的一部分。

云南地区游牧族群出现的时间现在还无明确的结论，较新的研究表明，“欧亚草原地带以马、牛、羊为主要畜牧的游牧，一般认为最早出现在前1000年左右。”[②]如果这种观点成立的话，游牧族群到达云南的时间上限应该晚于前1000年，时代大约相当晚期青铜时代至早期铁器时代。他们依仗以驯马和铁器为代表的先进生产技术，可能在很短的一段时间内就从北方草原沿横断山脉进入云南乃至西南地区，这和前7世纪左右亚欧大陆各临近草原区域的文明古国是一样的情形。综上所述，前8～前7世纪以斯基泰人为核心的游牧族群的扩张是全方位和大规模的，受此影响这一时期欧亚大陆与草原地区相邻地区的历史表现出鲜见的同步性和相似性，地处东亚草原地带最南端的云南不能置身事外不受影响。历史文献中“叟”人的出现就说明了斯基泰人的一部南迁到了云南。时间大约在公元前8世纪或稍晚，这和万家坝墓群的时代上限基本是一致的，这些塞人与当地濮越族群融合后创造了兼收并蓄、异彩纷呈的滇青铜文化。

“昆明”是先秦时期分布在云南西部广大地区的另一游牧族群，其源头可能来自乌孙。许慎《说文解字》释“昆”：“从日，从比。”像两人并立于日下，与广西左江流域岩画的形象极其类似。叶玉森说：“卜辞昆为国名，疑即昆夷。”[③]“昆明”一词应是“昆弥”一词的音转。我国史书中，昆弥是乌孙的王号。《汉书·乌孙传》说：“昆弥及太子左右大将都尉皆遣使……”，可知昆弥是“王”的意思。《史记·大宛列传》记载：“闻乌孙王好（号）昆莫”，昆弥、昆莫为一词，系乌孙语。“在古突厥语和现代维吾尔和哈萨克语中，‘太阳’被称为‘KUN’，其汉字译音即作‘昆’。在吐火罗语（不论甲种吐火罗语还是乙种吐火罗语）中，‘太阳’同样

① 王明珂：《游牧者的抉择：面对汉帝国的北亚游牧部落》，广西师范大学出版社，2008年，69页。

② 王明珂：《游牧者的抉择：面对汉帝国的北亚游牧部落》，广西师范大学出版社，2008年，67页。

③《古文字诂林》，第六册，上海教育出版社，2004年，436页。

为‘KUN’，这在列维的《吐火罗语考》中也有明确结论。又据8世纪突厥文碑铭，有‘biη’词汇，意思为‘一千’。‘biη’亦可书写为‘bing’，而在古突厥语中，‘b’和‘m’是互通的，‘bing’亦即‘ming’……而“孟”、“莫”、“弥”，很明显，都是“ming”的同音异写。由以上分析，我们认为，‘昆莫’、‘昆弥’，即乌孙语‘Kun ming’的音译，其语意，直译之为‘一千个太阳’，意译则为‘像天一样广大’”[①]。古代云南的“昆明”，可能就是乌孙之“昆弥”，表示部族首领或者是主持祭日仪式的巫师，同时“昆”也代表太阳。新疆地区乌孙人墓葬研究表明乌孙人兼有印欧语族群和突厥—蒙古语族群的特征。从人种上看既有明显的印欧人种的体质特征，深目高鼻，同时也有一部分人表现出蒙古人种的体质特征[②]。关于乌孙人的语言，现在很难定论，但它明显受匈奴文化影响很深。《乌孙研究》一书引羽田亨《西域文化史》的研究认为是突厥语[③]。考古发掘的乌孙墓葬也明显有别于斯基泰墓葬[④]。乌孙徙居伊犁河流域后，有相当数量的塞人逐渐融合到了乌孙族群之中，《汉书·西域传》载：“故乌孙民有塞种、大月氏种云”。鉴于草原地区频繁的交流，这种现象可以理解，但这句话的核心在于表明乌孙既非塞种，也非大月氏种，应该是突厥—蒙古语族群，与匈奴同。乌孙语很可能是突厥—蒙古语。乌孙的文化特征据《汉书·乌孙传》称：“不田作种树，随畜逐水草，与匈奴同俗。”这与《史记》中所记录的云南古代“昆明”人的生活也是一致的。“与匈奴同俗”表明乌孙人不仅是情感上接近匈奴人，还意味着社会经济、政治制度方面的类同。因此乌孙人和匈奴关系更为密切，文化上也相对周边的说印欧语的塞人落后。

乌孙“原来活动在河西走廊西部；汉初，西迁伊犁河流域”[⑤]。乌孙西迁的原因是迫于匈奴大规模西侵的压力，几致国灭，时间约在前3世纪：《史记·匈奴传》说：“其明年（前176年，汉文帝前元四年）（匈奴冒顿）单于遗汉书曰：……‘（匈奴）定楼兰、乌孙、呼揭及其旁二十六国，皆以为匈奴，诸引弓之民，并为一家。’”这次河西地区的动荡引发了大规模民族迁徙，其中一部分乌孙及邻近的部族沿“藏彝走廊”向南逃亡到云南，这一时间正处于万家坝墓群的末期和石寨山墓群的早期。他们的南迁使得先期到达滇西地区的塞人不得不再次东迁至滇池区域，这也是万家坝型铜鼓和石寨山型铜鼓风格产生显著转变的原因。

通过以上分析可以得出下述结论：在云南的青铜时代，出现了两个较大游牧族群，一个是与操突厥—蒙古语的乌孙人有关的“昆明”人，一个是与说印欧语的斯基泰人有关的“叟”人。乌孙人故地在斯基泰人以东，更为接近三江的源头，因此南迁到云南的“昆明”人数多，为大种；“叟”人数少，为小种。“塞”人在云南的出现，同全球气候骤变之后斯基泰人的四处扩张有关。更进一步，他们当中的一些族群可能还沿江而下，到达更为遥远的南方，这就是我们在左江流域和金沙江流域岩画中可以看到的众多的骑者形象。滇文化木椁墓同他们有密切关系，这种葬式

① 王明哲、王炳华：《乌孙研究》，新疆人民出版社，1983年，76、77页。

② 王明哲、王炳华：《乌孙研究》，新疆人民出版社，1983年，43页。

③ 王明哲、王炳华：《乌孙研究》，新疆人民出版社，1983年，42页。

④ 王明哲、王炳华：《乌孙研究》，新疆人民出版社，1983年，199页。

⑤ 王明哲，王炳华：《乌孙研究》，新疆人民出版社，1983年，1页。

也是斯基泰文化的特点。而“昆明”人南下的时间可能要迟至战国晚期至西汉初，他们同云南中西部祥云、中甸的石棺墓关系密切，这种石棺墓也见于川西地区，蒙古东部和外贝加尔的“石板墓”文化，同处于“边地半月形文化传播带”范围内，应与匈奴同属一种文化体系。万家坝型铜鼓的出现时间和斯基泰人南下的时间基本相符，石寨山型铜鼓出现的时间与“昆明”人南下的时间比较接近。

在铜鼓的起源传说中，有大量的记载称铜鼓是两位来自中原的军事首领马援和诸葛亮所创。尽管现在已经明确铜鼓远在汉代以前就已出现，同马援诸葛亮并没有关系，但不能忽视这些传说的价值，在它们的文本背后有着真实的历史底蕴。民间传说，作为历史记忆的载体，其影响力和持续性并不亚于文字记录，它们是普通人的历史记忆，和历史文献具有同样的价值。无论是“孔明（诸葛）”还是“马援”，都是古代的北方军事首领符号，他们隐喻着来自北方的大规模军事活动。这种历史记忆即便是经过若干年在铜鼓上都明确表现：广西壮族自治区博物馆藏263号鼓，在各种图案中有“孔明将君”的反文和横书，可见历史记忆的持久[①]。

四

西南地区的岩画与游牧族群

游牧文化在西南地区的岩画中也可窥其对青铜器影响之一斑。一般认为广西左江流域崖壁画为著名的战国至秦汉时期骆越人文化遗址，岩画中出现大量的铜鼓图案，共绘有铜鼓254面[②]。众多图像中大量展现了古人崇拜太阳的场面。尽管它们的画法多采用抽象化的简练方式，但是这也使我们更容易从为数不多的细节中辨识出古代铜鼓文化的核心内容。宁明花山这组岩画中最为显要的人物是骑马者的形象。这些骑者的共同之处在于：①体型明显比周围众人高大，甚至有的比周围陪衬人物高出一倍之多；②大多腰部挎刀，其中几个形象中为明显的环首刀，根据刀身长度判断，应为铁制；③基本为正面像，和周围大量的侧身像明显有别，应是仪式的主祭者。花山岩画的骑者形象并不是孤例，还见于长江流域四川珙县岩画[③]和珠江、红河流域云南文山壮族苗族自治州等地[④]。岩画所描绘的人物基本类似。许多学者认为这些骑马人像是表现骑兵，源自战国时期赵武灵王胡服骑射。如果是这样的话，那么这些岩画的上限就不早于战国[⑤]。与广西地理上最接近的是战国时期的楚国，但岩画上却没有楚文化的元素，这是难以解释的。因此，这些人像的源流除考虑来自中原以外，也可能是来自云南中西部南下的游牧族群。其实在我国北方的阴山和贺兰山岩画中也发现类似主祭者的形象，只是未见骑乘，他们都被描绘成双手上、下

① 黄燕熙：《铜鼓非物质文化研究》，《声震神州——文山铜鼓暨民族历史文化国际学术研讨会论文集》，引蒋廷瑜：《铜鼓艺术研究》，云南人民出版社，2005年，197页。

② 陈远璋：《左江岩画铜鼓图像的初步探讨》，《中国铜鼓研究会第二次学术讨论会论文集》，文物出版社，1986年，198页。

③ 盖山林：《中国岩画学》，书目文献出版社，1995年，69页。

④ 曾跃明、王林斌：《平远镇大山村岩画》，《云南文物》2001年第1期。

⑤ 林晓：《40年来国内学者对左江流域崖壁画的研究概述》，《广西师范大学学报》2000年第1期。

体蹲踞的蛙形舞姿，这可能是与祷祝有关的宗教仪式。在我国西南地区发现的岩画中，云南沧源岩画、四川珙县岩画也同样发现类似的人物形象，同样的造型在滇青铜器中也大量出现，滇青铜戈往往就铸有类似蛙形人纹的图案，壮族地区也有类似舞蹈保存[①]。更有甚者，在著名的新疆呼图壁县康家石门子岩画中也可以看到类似的人物形象，这些形象和西北彩陶文化中的蛙纹在姿态上是一致的。这种祷祝姿态广泛分布于欧亚大陆各地，可能是同蛙崇拜有关的一种古代仪式演变而来。我们不能认定这种现象是人类思维发展的一种必然选择，难道它不可能是某种古老文化传播的结果？我们不能忽视新疆康家石门子岩画和西南岩画在衣着（如果说肯定有衣着的话）和头饰上惊人的相似之处，尽管它们在地理上相隔遥远，但其中的联系是无法回避的。据研究，康家石门子岩画“是公元前3世纪以前塞人的作品。”[②]另外，江川李家山出土两件骑士猎鹿扣饰，“骑士头部有包头，其上有两块片状饰物。”[③]这种略向两侧外撇的片状饰物从正面看同康家石门子岩画和左江流域岩画中的人物头饰是完全一致的，可以认为是同一类型发饰，是新疆和广西岩画形象的中间形态。

同见于花山岩画和珙县岩画的环首铁刀的起源现在还无定论，一般认为是来自中原[④]。但是大量的考古资料可以说明欧亚草原游牧族群使用铁器的时间要比中原地区为早，“大约前8世纪至前6世纪，即当中原春秋时期，新疆地区铁器应用已较普遍，而这一地区铁器的最早出现，远在前1000年以前。”[⑤]从考古材料来看，迄今为止，我国最早的成熟铁器出土于新疆、甘肃灵台和陕西等西部地区[⑥]。如果花山岩画中的环首刀为铁制的话，从时代上看，它比之于西汉时中原广泛流行的环首刀更早，其原型就是草原地区著名的环首青铜刀。

综合前述有关游牧文化的观点和中原的历史情况，西南地区这一时期岩画上为数众多的骑者应为游牧族群的形象。在云南祥云大波那铜棺墓发现的六畜模型，其中唯独马背上骑有一人，应是这些古代族群在云南中部游牧生活的青铜写照。

五

铜鼓的原型——南方铜釜与斯基泰铜釜的结合

铜鼓的原型是什么？这个问题在学术已有很长时间的争论。现在大多数学者承认：“铜鼓是铜釜演变而来的，万家坝铜鼓与铜釜共出，酷似铜釜，是最原始的铜鼓。”[⑦]但是铜鼓单纯是来源于铜釜的结论还有讨论的余地：早期铜釜与铜鼓常常共存于云南青铜文化墓葬中，因此有的学者主张“铜鼓起源于炊具陶器，但不以双耳鼓陶罐为然，而主张是鼓形陶釜。这种鼓形陶釜在新石器时代便已出现，应该是

① 罗坤馨:《铜鼓与壮族“蚂（蚜）节”考》，《铜鼓和青铜文化的新探索》，广西民族出版社，1993年，147页。

② 盖山林:《中国岩画学》，书目文献出版社，1995年，59页。

③ 玉溪地区行政公署:《云南李家山青铜器》，云南人民出版社，1995年，图版说明25页。

④ 林晓:《40年来国内学者对左江流域崖壁画的研究概述》，《广西师范大学学报》2000年第1期。

⑤ 唐际根:《中国冶铁术的起源起源问题》，《考古》1993年第6期。

⑥ 华觉明:《中国古代金属技术》，大象出版社，1999年，304页。

⑦ 蒋廷瑜:《古代铜鼓通论》，紫禁城出版社，1999年，32页。

原始铜鼓和铜釜的祖先。”[①]这种鼓形陶釜在湄公河流域的新石器时代遗址中也有发现，如泰国Mun Valley的Ban Sanuan，时代大约为前2300～前1500年[②]在湄公河下游的青铜时代墓葬如Ban Lum Khao遗址中也出现了这种陶釜，型制与万家坝墓出土铜釜几乎完全一致。与之伴出的还有陶纺轮、陶牛模型等器物，与祥云出土同类青铜器造型也几无差别，其时代约为前1400～前500年[③]。可见铜鼓的造型的确借鉴了鼓形陶釜这种贯穿东南亚新石器文化和青铜文化的代表性器物。但是鼓形陶釜仅仅是日常生活用品，与墓主的社会阶层、等级、身份无关。而铜鼓是象征权威的重器，只有“邑君”、“头人”才能拥有，鼓式陶釜显然不具备这样的社会功能。因此，只能说源于东南亚本地文化的鼓形陶釜是铜鼓的原型之一，但铜鼓应该还有其他原型。

甲骨文中的“鼓”字作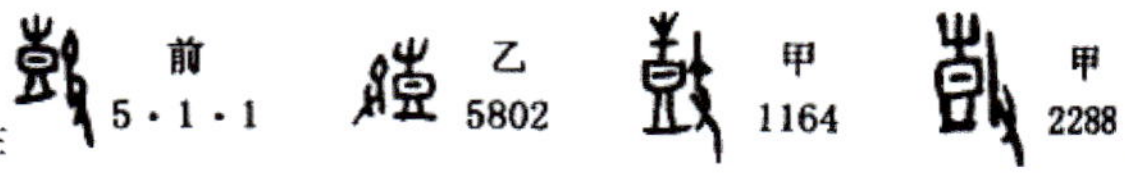

，甲骨文中鼓的形象与西南地区的铜鼓非常接近，击鼓方式与滇文化器物所见图案也是一致的；“鼓”字中的器物（有人认为是豆，并不准确，豆不能用于敲击）其形状与现存商代中原铜鼓及后世广为流传的建鼓大相径庭反而很接近南方的铜鼓，但在商代铜鼓还没有出现。甲骨文“鼓”字的原型应在北方地区，很可能就是斯基泰青铜釜的早期形态。

斯基泰青铜釜，我国学者一般称为青铜鍑，直立双耳，筒形或球形腹，底部接一喇叭形圈足，广泛分布于青铜时代欧亚草原地区。除了作炊具外，还可作盛食器和祭祀礼器。这种器物分布很广，1951年北高加索地区发现的单突耳青铜鍑[④]与陕西凤翔雍城采集青铜鍑型制基本相同，同是欧亚草原文化的产物，年代约为春秋早期[⑤]，可见斯基泰文化影响之广泛。根据希罗多德的《历史》，青铜鍑是斯基泰人祭祀仪式的重要器物，所有的祭品，都放到青铜鍑中煮熟再进行奉祭[⑥]。我国先秦时期匈奴人杀马请龙的宗教盛典，献祭的马被杀死以后就放到青铜鍑烹煮，可见游牧文化的青铜鍑在宗教活动中具有神圣的地位，西方文化中的圣杯（GRAIL）也可能和它有关。西汉时期滇池区域也有祭马的习俗。《汉书·郊祀志》记载：“或言益州有金马碧鸡之神，可醮祭而致，于是遣谏大夫王褒使持节而求之。”晋宁石寨山出土诅盟场面贮贝器上就有祭马的形象，易学钟先生认为即是马祭[⑦]。铜鼓中心的太阳纹在斯基泰青铜鍑上也有出现，在哈萨克斯坦出土了有太阳纹的青铜鍑[⑧]，在昆明羊甫头出土的大陶瓮，和斯基泰铜鍑在形制上非常接近，二者的关系有待进一步的研究。

希罗多德还记录了一件有趣的事件：在埃克撒姆派欧斯地区有一个巨大的青铜鍑，它的来源是这样的：一位斯基泰国王想知道它部族的人数，于是他命令每一个斯基泰人把一个箭头给他，并威胁说不这样做将被处以死刑；结果便有极多的箭头送到他这里，他决定用它们制造一个纪念物留传后世，于是他用这些箭头制造了这件青铜大鍑[⑨]。这个典故尽管看似偶然，但它涉及上古一个重要的文化关系：箭镞与

① 蒋廷瑜：《古代铜鼓通论》，紫禁城出版社，1999年，32页。

② Charles Higham. *Early cultures of mainland southeast Asia*·River Books Ltd, Bangkok. 2002:93.

③ Charles Higham. *Early cultures of mainland southeast Asia*·River Books Ltd, Bangkok. 2002:146.

④ 郭物：《鍑中乾坤：青铜鍑与草原文明》，上海社会科学院出版社，2003年，9页。

⑤ 郭物：《鍑中乾坤：青铜鍑与草原文明》，上海社会科学院出版社，2003年，10页。

⑥ 郭物：《鍑中乾坤：青铜鍑与草原文明》，上海社会科学院出版社，2003年，110页。

⑦ 易学钟：《晋宁石寨山12号墓贮贝器上人物雕像考释》，《考古学报》1987年第4期。

⑧ Jeannine Davis-KimBall, Vladimir A. Bashilov, Leonid T. Yablonsky. *Nomads of the Eurasian Steppes in the Early Iron Age*. Zinat press Berkeley,CA. 1995:213.

⑨ 郭物：《鍑中乾坤：青铜鍑与草原文明》，上海社会科学院出版社，2003年，112页。

部族之间的密切关系，即潘光旦说，“‘族’，也许是最初的氏族，或后来的氏族的某种综合，当初便不止是一个社会组织的单位，而也是一个军事组织的单位……这样一个血亲的而兼军事性的单位就叫做‘族’”。“原始的氏族不止是一个血亲单位、生产单位与文教单位，而也必然是一个军事单位了。就它的所以为前三种单位的性质说，我们称它为‘氏’，就它所以为最后一种单位的性质说，我们称它为‘族’，合起来，称它为‘氏族’；分说是不完全的，合说才完全”①。甲骨文“族”字从（㫃）从矢，丁山引《唐书·突厥传》中突厥十个部落以箭为称号的典故解释“族”字本意：“族字从矢，当然又与部落称箭的涵谊相同，有是四旗十箭的故事印证，我认为族制的来源，不仅是自家族演来，还是氏族社会军旅组织的遗迹。”②“族”最初是氏族间共同结成的军事组织，这种以箭代“族”的传统在欧亚草原游牧地区更为久远和典型。万家坝型铜鼓鼓面几乎全都铸有太阳纹，一些鼓在太阳纹之中还有箭矢的符号，如弥渡青石湾鼓、广南者偏鼓③，表明铜鼓与早期军事组织的密切关联。弥渡青石湾鼓太阳纹芒间有箭矢符号一个，可能是一“族”的象征。而广南者偏鼓芒间有五个箭矢符号，也许象征着五“族”的联合体。这些箭矢符号表明，这种铜鼓还保留着北方地区以箭示“族”的传统，掌握铜鼓的人就是族内的军事首领与族长，这与希罗多德历史中的记载是十分吻合的。随着铜鼓的演进，这种文化传统逐渐消失，原有的以军事活动为核心的箭矢符号已不能适应多元化的文化环境的需要，因此铜鼓上的箭矢纹也很快消失，铜鼓的核心纹饰变成以翔鹭纹、船纹等更为和谐的纹饰为主。通过对云南铜鼓原型的探讨，可以得出这样的结论：云南的早期铜鼓可能均与斯基泰人有关，万家坝型是斯基泰文化初入云南向南方本文化过渡的中间形态，石寨山型铜鼓的时期，才出现真正融合了南北文化的成熟铜鼓形制。

① 潘光旦：《潘光旦文集》，北京大学出版社，2002年，13卷，294～296页。

② 《古文字诂林》，第六册，上海教育出版社，2004年，481页。

③ 李昆声、黄德荣：《再论万家坝型铜鼓》，《考古学报》2007年第2期。

④ 利普斯：《事物的起源》，四川民族出版社，1982年，356页。

六

太阳崇拜与梵天

西南几处岩画的核心都是太阳纹，云南早期铜鼓鼓面的中心都铸有太阳纹，与太阳崇拜有关的仪式是铜鼓社会功能核心。太阳崇拜是在世界各大文明地区普遍存在的文化现象。“太阳神可以是一个神、一个英雄、可能以仅是一个人，或者是一根燃烧的柱子。太阳的光芒是太阳神射向地球的箭……”④太阳和箭的关系在神话传说中十分密切。比较神话学家坎贝尔（Joseph Campbell）认为，把太阳的光线比喻为箭可以上溯到狩猎时代，在几乎所有狩猎民族的神话中，太阳都是伟大的猎手，他们的狩猎武器就是箭。巴比伦的太阳神马杜克（Marduk）手中所持的主要武器就是弓和箭；古希腊太阳神阿波罗放出的光芒被认为是杀敌的金箭，因此阿波罗同时也是射神与战神[1]；云南沧源岩画中有一持弓箭者站立于太阳内的图像，也是太阳神和射手关系的反映。因此，太阳纹也有战争的隐喻。铜鼓以太阳纹为标志，暗示着铜鼓的社会功能最初与战争有关，是一种战鼓。在有关铜鼓的民间传说中，铜鼓的神威也大多同战争有关[2]，这也可以说明铜鼓应该起源战鼓。在晋宁石寨山12号墓出土贮贝器上有演奏铜鼓的场面，值得注意的是一面铜鼓和一枚巴人的虎纽錞于并置，表明它们的社会功能是一样的。先秦至汉代流行以鼓和錞于的组合为军乐。《周礼·地官·鼓人》："以金錞和鼓"。郑玄注："錞，錞于也"。《淮南子·兵略训》："两军相当，鼓錞相望"。

在我国南方地区和东南亚，太阳崇拜和梵天及创世神话有密切的关联。广西壮族地区普遍流行是有关布洛陀传说，但却少有直接的有关太阳崇拜的传说，这与铜鼓上以太阳纹为核心的崇日观念略有矛盾。布洛陀应是音译，其意义有不同的解释。有学者认为，根据壮语的发音，"布"（pau5）是指地位崇高的祖公；"洛陀"二字解释为：洛（成lwk8，即孩子），"陀"（念tok8，即单独、独自），"洛陀"（lwk8 tok8，即孤儿）。神话传说中的布洛陀可以解释为早期居住在山间弄（原字为峙）场，后来居住在岭坡谷地间的无所不晓、无所不能的会施法术的骆越人的祖公[3]。但是，布洛陀的传说非壮族所独有，越南北部地区、老挝和泰国也有类似神话传说，缅甸克伦族称为蒲貌陶，也是神话中的祖先[4]。可知布洛陀传说存在于广大的地理区域内，起源可能相当古老。因此，我们可以考虑可能布洛陀是外来语而非原创词汇的可能性，可以从透过其他文化来寻找"布洛陀"的原意。吐火罗人被认为是最初的印欧人，古吐火罗语中保留了大量的古印欧语，在吐火罗语乙种方言中，创造世界的梵天称为"Brahma"，其音与"布洛"音相近，而神字作"nakte"，可以视为"陀"字的音转。在缅甸的缅族（Bamars）语中，表示神灵的词"nat"与古印欧语中的"nakte"也十分相近。吐火罗语中专有"brahma-nakte"一词，意为梵天[5]。梵天，梵文也作为"Brahama"。在古印度婆罗门教中，创造世界的梵天就是太阳和祖先："太阳，大梵也。""大梵，绯红色，四出，为大父。"[6]梵天既是太阳神，同时也是创世者。由此我们是否可以设想，布洛陀是由印欧语的"梵天"而来？它也许就是隐在历史传说中的太阳神和创世者。

中国古代创世神话中最著名的是盘古神话。据何新研究，"盘古神话在华夏的出现地，确如（梁）任（日方）所指出的，是在'吴楚'、'南海、桂林'一带华南地区，其时间不会早于东汉末季。"[7]他认为盘古就是印度婆罗门教中的创世神梵天。并引申出它们与古代希腊创世神活中的"Pan"（潘）神也是同一起源的可能性，论述颇详。他认为这些创世神话的源头就欧亚草原西部："约在前14～前13世纪，来自西亚和中亚一带的雅利安人进入南亚次大陆，而《吠陀》等婆罗门经典正

① 户晓辉：《岩画与生殖巫术》，新疆美术摄影出版社，1993年，106页。

② 蒋廷瑜：《古代铜鼓通论》，紫禁城出版社，1999年，11页。

③ 覃乃昌：《布洛陀文化体系述论》，《广西民族研究》2003年第3期。

④ 蒋廷瑜：《古代铜鼓通论》，紫禁城出版社，1999年，9页。

⑤ Douglas Q. Adams. *A dictionary of Tocharian B*. Rodopi B.V. 1999.

⑥ 徐梵澄译：《五十奥义书》，中国社会科学出版社，1995年，148、169页。

⑦ 何新：《诸神的起源》，光明日报出版社，1996年，237页。

是这些雅利安人的圣书。因此在（巴比伦创世史诗中）创造宇宙的Ban神与Braham（梵）神之间，很可能存在一种演变关系。”[①]但是，梵天信仰未必是从印度传入：印度婆罗门教从未在中国流行过，而中国佛教的神祇中，梵天并不太重要，当今的印度教，专门供奉梵天的寺庙也极少。反之在东南亚，特别是在泰国，梵天的影响力却相当大，信众极多。这种信仰可能源自比佛教和印度教更为古老的宗教。梵天形象为四面，华人常称为“四面佛”，其实应是“四面神”，其原型就是太阳，梵文中说他“四出”，是指其光芒照向四方，这和上古时期出现在欧亚草原地区的四芒太阳纹是一个意思，古拙的万家坝铜鼓中心的太阳纹最初也有四芒的形象出现，而后才发展成多芒的造型，这种演化并不是偶然。梵天的信仰如果是从北方传入，那么其传播者就可能是塞人，他们是欧亚草原地区古老文化的直接继承者。

梵天和飞鸟关系密切，缅甸神话传说：“梵界住着一群梵天，因为他们命数将尽，纷纷离开梵界，化身来到世界上。但是他们仍然具有梵天的本质，所以遍身泛着祥光，终日欢乐自得。他们不吃不喝，就像飞禽那样在高空翱翔、嬉戏。”[②]这里梵天直接表现为“遍身泛着祥光”的太阳形象，同时他们像飞禽一样翱翔，飞禽即是梵天的化身，是神界和人间的中介物。在古代印度教，梵天的坐骑就是孔雀或天鹅。成都金沙遗址的著名太阳神鸟金饰，上有复杂的镂空图案，分内外两层，内层为周围等距分布有十二条旋转的齿状光芒；外层图案围绕着内层图案，由四只相同的朝逆时针飞行的鸟组成，这和石寨山型铜鼓所开创的飞鸟纹环绕于中心太阳纹的构形是同样的意匠，是符号化的骑在神鸟上的梵天形象。

① 何新:《诸神的起源》，光明日报出版社，1996年，248页。

② 张玉安:《东方神话传说》（第六卷），北京大学出版社，1999年，124页。

七

结　语

全球气候系统的非线性特征，自洛伦兹（Edward Lorenz）的开创性研究以后已得到越来越多的认可，它使我们注意到复杂系统的非线性变化。特别是大范围的降温现象，往往是在很短的时间内完成的，而并非总是缓慢长期的过程。人类社会对于自然环境高度敏感的依赖程度，使得气候的骤变很容易就引发大范围的文化变迁，对于游牧文化来说，这种变迁往往就表现为远距离的迁徙和战争，这在中外历史上屡见不鲜。但是，历史上跨区域的文化交流，我们不能看做是单向的——仅仅由西向东或由北向南。伴随着一次次较大的气候变迁和技术革新，青铜时代东南亚地区的南方稻作文化和北方草原游牧文化的领地不停地在做着钟摆式的运动，因此我们在注意到游牧文化南迁的同时，也不能忽视南方农耕文化北移的力度和规模，比如古代羌人北迁的问题就值得深思。

对于古代民族，尤其是古代游牧民族的迁徙到变动的能力常常被人低估。亚欧草原地带与我国的古代交流历史非常悠久，这一点已被人们逐渐认识。“远在原始社会时期，新疆和内地的居民已经有了密切的联系。”[①]草原文化是东西文化的重要中介，但是它与东南亚和中国南方的文化影响现在还研究不多，但已有考古证据表明这种交流的存在。“在罗布泊的古墓中，发现过海菊贝制成的饰珠，这种美丽的贝壳只出产在我国东南沿海地区。”[②]从上述斯基泰文化与滇文化的比较，我们可以认识到游牧文化的巨大影响力不仅仅限于现代的草原地区，在特定的历史时期，它的影响甚至有可能到达闻所未闻的遥远南方，尔后随着农耕文明的扩张他们如同融化的冰川渐渐淹没于南方文化的洪流之中。

关于云南早期铜鼓，从气候、生态、历史文化等各方面考虑，一方面我们应强调它所处的南方稻作文化的背景，另一方面我们不能无视在它诞生之初北方游牧文化所起到的重要作用，游牧文化在云南青铜时代的独特地位从诸多方面看都是十分重要的。但除了众多抽象的文化现象之外，现在还没有太多的实物证据证明云南早期铜鼓和游牧文化之间的直接关系，比如它们同斯基泰青铜鍑之间的实物关联。这种矛盾也提示我们如何看待文化的连续性的问题：文化如果是一个持续不断的连续体（continuum），那么我们应该从哪些方面来认定某种文化特质，是物质传统还是核心的文化习惯和思维方式？文化传播主义往往纠结于传播的技术细节和物质层面[③]，但物质表象背后的意识形态才是文化的核心构成。

① 新疆社会科学院考古研究所:《新疆考古三十年》，新疆人民出版社，1983年，186页。

② 户晓辉:《岩画与生殖巫术》，新疆美术摄影出版社，1993年，213页。

③ 庄锡昌、孙志民:《文化人类学的理论构架》，浙江人民出版社，1988年，24、25页。

百色古代铜鼓文化述论

A Review on the Ancient Bronze Drum Culture in Baise Area

黄秋艳 / 广西田东县博物馆 馆员

[摘要]

本文汇集百色市三十多年来所发现的铜鼓资料，并据之研究百色古代铜鼓文化的特征，论述其在广西铜鼓文化中的地位问题。

[关键词]

百色　广西铜鼓文化　接收站　中转站　新型铜鼓诞生地

Abstract

Since 1972, there has been 12 ancient Bronze Drums were excavated in Baise area, they respectively belong to Wanjiaba type, Shizhaishan type and Lengshuichong type. Through analysis, we know that both the Bronze Drums of Wanjiaba type and the Shizhaishan type in this area are the results of the eastward spread of neighbouringYunnan Province ancient Bronze Drums, they proved that Baise area was the earliest receiver of Bronze Drum Culture in Guangxi. It didn't simply receive, but also made some creation with the wisdom of the local people and it turned into a kind of new product with local style. After the Shizhaishan type of Bronze Drums developed in this area, they spread through the You River waterway along the Drainage Area of Yu River, to make Baise a transfer station of this type of Bronze Drum Culture. The Bronze Drums that discovered in You River are the transition of Lengshuichong type or the earliest one of Lengshuichong type, so Baise area is also the birthplace of the Lengshuichong type of Bronze Drum, which belongs to the subsequent Guangxi Bronze Drum Culture.

Key words

Baise; Guangxi bronze drum culture; Receiving station; Transfer station; Birth place of new bronze drum

从那坡县感驮岩遗址所出土的铸造铜器石范和青铜残块判断，于商代末期，百色地区已出现早期青铜文明。发展至春秋时期进入青铜时代以后，以几十年来在田东、田阳、西林、百色、隆林等县出土及出水的先秦至汉代青铜器观之，呈现出纷繁复杂、多姿多彩的青铜文化面貌。其中，铜鼓是这个地区的一种特色和代表性器物，它们不仅表现出多样性和与周边文化的密切关系，还表现出广西铜鼓文化的渊源价值等。本文即就有关方面展开论述。

一

百色地区古代铜鼓的发现与特征

埋存于百色地区的古代铜鼓，历史上有出土并载入方志等文献的极少，现知仅有民国三十七年《靖西县志》记下“民国十一年，铜鼓一面，于县之南区出土，体圆，高一尺九公分，面径宽二尺九公分。束腰，两耳。鼓面边缘四蛙环立，各面文纹精妙，似古文字形，完全铜质。其声硿硿[①]”可惜实物已不可见，其年代无从查考。而经考古发现和零星出土且有实物留存的汉代以前铜鼓则始于20世纪70年代，至今计有七次记录。

1972年修公路时，在西林县普驮屯发现1座古墓，墓中以铜鼓为葬具，揭开了百色地区考古发现铜鼓的序幕。此墓共发现4面铜鼓，出土时大小互相套叠成棺。按出土顺序，分别编号为280、281、282、283号鼓[②]。

280号鼓，用作套棺时将之从胸腰相接处截断。身高52、面径77.5、足径90厘米。鼓面13晕，中心太阳纹16芒，芒间填斜线，第2、3、4晕为勾连点线纹，第6晕素，第7晕饰20只翔鹭、勾连雷纹，第8～13晕为勾连点纹、锯齿纹夹勾连圆圈纹。胸上部与腰下部同饰点纹、锯齿纹夹勾连圆圈纹，胸中部饰6组船纹，每船载8～11人，位于船台前者戴羽冠，其余均项髻。其中立者上身裸露，腰系物；坐者全裸，划船。船间有鸬鹚或鱼。腰部用圆点纹、锯齿纹夹羽状纹带纵向分隔成12格，每格又被勾连圆圈纹带分成上下两层，上层饰鹿2或3只，下层饰羽人舞蹈纹每格2人。腰下部饰圆点纹、锯齿纹夹勾连圆圈纹（图一）。

281号鼓，身高49、面径72、足径83.3厘米。鼓面纹饰锈蚀，只见中心太阳纹14芒，芒间填斜线角形纹。鼓身纹饰亦锈蚀不清，胸部隐见船纹，腰部有翔鹭和羽人舞蹈纹，在胸的上下部和腰的分格内饰锯齿纹、同心圆纹或锯齿纹、羽状纹组成的纹带（图二）。

282号鼓，身高41、面径52、足径56厘米。鼓面以二弦分晕，共9晕，中心太阳纹8芒，芒间填翎眼纹。第2晕饰变体雷纹，第3、4晕与第7、8晕是栉纹与勾连雷纹纹带，第5晕为珠襦残片覆盖，纹饰不知，第6晕为翔鹭纹。

283号鼓，仅存上半部，腰以下被锯掉。面径57厘米。鼓面以二弦分晕，共8

① 凌树东：《广西靖西县出土铜鼓资料》，《中国古代铜鼓研究通讯》第七期。

② 广西壮族自治区文物工作队：《广西西林县普驮铜鼓墓葬》，《文物》1978年第9期。

图一 西林280号铜鼓

图二 西林281号铜鼓

晕，中心太阳纹8芒，芒间填复线角形纹。第2晕饰变体雷纹，第3、4晕与第6、7、8晕是栉纹与勾连圆圈纹组成的纹带，第5晕为主晕，饰翔鹭6只。

1977年6月田东县祥周乡甘莲村锅盖岭发掘1座古墓，所出的14件铜器中有1面鼓。此鼓面径23厘米，腰以下部分已失，存高28.3厘米。鼓面太阳纹8芒，芒间饰斜线纹；太阳纹外设计3晕，主晕纹饰为4只翔鹭，另两晕内饰锯齿纹和圆圈纹。胸部突出，饰勾连回纹和弦纹①。

1977年9月百色县（现为百色市右江区）龙川公社平乐大队出土1面铜鼓。鼓身高28.5、面径41厘米。鼓面分7晕，中心太阳纹10芒，第2、3晕纹饰模糊，第4晕素面，第5～7晕为锯齿纹夹同心圆纹纹带。鼓胸及鼓腰下部纹饰相同，皆是锯齿纹夹同心圆纹纹带。腰部上部以羽状纹带纵向分隔成8格，其中4格内饰牛纹，其余空白。

1983年田东县祥周镇康元村塘槐屯出土1面变形羽人纹铜鼓。鼓身高50、足径65、面径63厘米。鼓面为20晕圈，边缘突出，四蛙呈逆时针方向排列，中心饰12芒太阳纹，主晕纹饰为变形羽人纹，其余为定胜纹、同心圆圈纹、栉纹等。鼓胸外凸，鼓腰内收，鼓足外撇。腰间有两对扁耳，足部饰蕉叶纹。

1990年9月隆林县扁牙乡共和村出土1面铜鼓，鼓身高30、面径44.4厘米。鼓面二弦分晕，中心饰锐角太阳纹8芒，主晕为4只翔鹭纹，其他晕饰锯齿纹或带切线的圆点圆圈纹。腰部由锯齿纹分隔成6格，每格内饰一伫立公牛纹，牛躯体硕壮，弧大弯角，眼瞪神厉，具象生动②。

1993年3月田东县祥周镇联福村联福小学门口拔取铁柱时发现2面铜鼓，随伴出土有铜罍、铜棺钉等。因联福小学位于南哈坡上，故将两鼓称为南哈坡A、B鼓③。

南哈坡A鼓，身高32、面径50、胸径60.5、足径66厘米。鼓面仅于中心装饰太阳纹，太阳纹隆起,周围散射出不规则的16芒。腰部由正倒“V”字纹带分成空格,格内无纹。近足处有一周三叉纹和一周雷纹。

南哈坡B鼓，身高38、面径48、胸径60.5、足径66厘米。鼓面中心太阳纹隆起,有短小杂乱的22芒，芒外布有杂乱的晕圈，外围饰以绳索纹。腰部由纵向的曲折纹带分成6个空白格。近足处有一周勾连雷纹，雷纹带两侧是绳索纹（图三）。

① 广西壮族自治区文物工作队:《广西田东发现战国墓葬》，《考古》1979年第6期。

② 陈应生:《隆林县首次出土石寨山型铜鼓》，《中国古代铜鼓研究通讯》第十五期。

③ 陈其复、黄振良:《田东县出土两面万家坝型铜鼓》，《中国古代铜鼓研究通讯》第九期。

图三　南哈波B铜鼓

图四　大岭坡铜鼓

图五　平马铜鼓鼓面

图六　平马铜鼓鼓身

1994年6月13日田东县林逢乡和同村大沙屯农民黄善贵、李南儒在大岭坡种地发现1面铜鼓。第二天在出土铜鼓的地方又挖出铜甬钟1枚。铜鼓身高29、面径34、胸径40、足径50厘米。鼓面中心太阳纹隆起，带11芒，其余部位光素。胸腰间两对小扁耳。腰上半部用绳索纹夹对角三角纹纵分成格，格间无纹。下半部3晕，分别饰“V”字纹、绳索纹、回纹[①]（图四）。

2007年5月，田东县平马镇中山街居民黄友兴在右江捞沙时出水1面鼓。鼓已残，面、身分离，身大部分缺失。鼓面保存较好，径43.5厘米。将鼓面与鼓身残片拼接，知鼓高约35厘米。鼓面中心太阳纹8芒，芒间饰斜线三角纹，主晕为6只翔鹭和类羽人组合纹，其他为勾连雷纹和栉纹。鼓胸饰类羽人组合纹、勾连雷纹和栉纹。其中类羽人组合纹为主纹，纹带宽大（图五、图六）。

① 陈其复、黄振良：《广西田东县再次出土万家坝型铜鼓》，《中国古代铜鼓研究通讯》第十期。

二

百色地区古代铜鼓的分类与年代

铜鼓是中华民族古代文化宝库中的一朵瑰丽的奇葩，资料非常丰富。我国学者对铜鼓的研究，虽然比外国学者晚了半个世纪，但凭借丰富的资料优势，对铜鼓的起源、类型、分布、年代、族属、纹饰、用途、合金成分、铸造工艺以及使用习俗等方面进行了一系列的探讨，硕果累累，令人惊叹。在铜鼓的分类上，《中国古代铜鼓》一书作了八大类型的权威归纳，成为铜鼓类型研究的标准。百色地区出土的古代铜鼓的类型，除了2007年右江出水的1面之外，皆早有学者按八大类型标准作了区分，即南哈坡A、B鼓和大岭坡鼓为万家坝型，普驮四鼓与锅盖岭鼓、龙川鼓、扁牙鼓属石寨山型。这一分类是正确的。于此，笔者仅谈右江出水鼓的归类。该鼓出水时已面身分离，而且碎成数块，有较多的缺失。所幸将碎块拼合，尚能大致窥见其面貌。从鼓型上看仍有较多的石寨山型晚期鼓风貌，鼓面太阳纹突起，主晕除了翔鹭之外，另加别样纹饰，与邻近的云南文山壮族苗族自治州（以下简称“文山州”）石寨山型晚期鼓的装饰做法相似。不同的是，文山州石寨山型晚期鼓鼓面的另一主纹是4头瘤牛，如孟梅1、2号鼓是例①。右江出水鼓则饰类羽人组合纹，而且胸部也有这种纹带，为前所未见之特例。而羽人纹是冷水冲型鼓的特征装饰，据而判断此鼓是石寨山型鼓向冷水冲型鼓过渡的转型者，或言是冷水冲型的最早型鼓。

关于万家坝型鼓的年代，我国铜鼓研究的权威学者所采用的意见是上限在春秋早期或更早，下限到战国末期。李昆声、黄德荣两先生将万家坝型鼓详细分为4式，Ⅰ式最原始，胴部最大径在中部以下，通体光素无纹，个别仅饰太阳纹，腰部未被分格，有的足内无折边。Ⅱ式鼓面一般饰太阳纹和芒，胴部最大径在中部以下，腰部出现分格，格间无纹，但腰与足内壁饰几何纹和爬虫纹。足内一般有折边，鼓身带烟熏痕迹。年代属春秋中期。Ⅲ式鼓面通常有太阳纹和若干芒，胴部最大径在中部以上，腰部分成数格，格间无纹饰，腰内壁无纹。足内一般有折边，鼓身无烟熏痕迹。年代为春秋晚期至战国早期。Ⅳ式鼓面除了太阳纹及芒之外，已出现晕纹，但无主晕纹。胴部最大径在中部以上，腰部往往采用上下分格形式，上格格间或饰纹或无纹饰，下格由若干晕构成，年代属战国中晚期②。

用以上标准来考量百色所出的3面万家坝型鼓，它们并不是同一时期的铸品，有早晚之别。南哈坡A鼓太阳纹周围散射出不规则的16芒，腰部用纹带分成空格,格内无纹，符合Ⅱ式鼓的标准，年代约为春秋中期。南哈坡B鼓太阳光芒短小杂乱尚未定型，与A鼓有联系之处，但芒外晕圈，表现了Ⅳ式鼓的特征，而晕圈杂乱，又体现原始之状。因此它应是介于Ⅱ式鼓与Ⅳ式鼓之间的地方发展形式鼓，年代当在春秋晚期。与这两面鼓同出的还有1件铜罍、1件铜钵、7枚铜鏊钉和3件玉管。其中保存相当完整的铜罍，可作铜鼓年代判断的参考。该铜罍圆体，小喇叭形口，溜肩，圈足，肩部为一对相背向的兽耳，颈下饰勾连雷纹，肩饰两纹带，腹饰三角形夔纹，具有西周圆体铜罍的作风。与之相似的铜罍，在广西宾阳、陆川、荔浦亦有发现，它们的年代是西周晚期或春秋初期③。大岭坡鼓，腰上半部用绳索纹夹对角三角纹纵

① 文山壮族苗族自治州文化局：《文山铜鼓》，云南人民出版社，2004年，81、82页。

② 李昆声、黄德荣：《试论万家坝型铜鼓》，《考古》1990年第5期。

③ 广西壮族自治区博物馆：《广西近年来出土的先秦青铜器》，《考古》1984年第9期。

分成格，下半部由3晕组成，显示了Ⅳ式鼓腰部的装饰特征。但此鼓鼓面太阳纹和芒外光素无晕圈，表明还是这式鼓的早期作品，年代应为战国早期。伴出的铜甬钟，合瓦体修长，于部内凹较甚，铣尖锐，枚长有景，钲间、篆间、舞部、于部饰精细的云雷纹，隧部饰夔龙纹，表现了春秋晚期铜钟的特点，这就佐证了大岭坡鼓年代不会太晚。又此鼓形体较高，胸部较圆突，与南哈坡鼓有区别，应体现早晚关系。

属石寨山型的田东锅盖岭铜鼓，其所出的墓葬年代，发掘简报断为战国晚期[①]。后来有学者将墓葬出土的铜器与云南滇池地区的同类器作比较，认为锅盖岭两座墓的"文化面貌兼有云南青铜文化和两广越族青铜文化的因素，其年代起码处在西汉中期"[②]。对这面铜鼓，《中国古代铜鼓》一书将之作为最早的石寨山型中期鼓举例，而中期鼓存在的时限是战国晚期至西汉中期[③]。因此，两家之说皆有道理，只是在时间上取早取晚的问题。依笔者之见，判断地域文化墓葬的年代，应多考虑地方特有的文化现象，锅盖岭墓葬出土的铜器中，有一种叉形器是云南青铜文化中所不见的器物，在广西现知的考古材料中也仅宾阳韦坡村战国墓曾有出土，后来的广西汉墓中再没有出现这种造型特殊的器物。所以，将锅盖岭铜鼓定为战国晚期比较合理。龙川鼓和扁牙鼓，它们腰部纵格中装饰牛纹，表明它们是石寨山型中期鼓，此型鼓流行的时间从战国晚期到西汉中期，这两面鼓装饰比锅盖岭鼓精美，发展的特征表露，牛纹写实性很强，说明它们属于中期鼓的较早者，时代可定在战国末期或西汉初年。西林280、282、283号鼓，《中国古代铜鼓》一书划分归属两型。280号鼓是石寨山型晚期鼓，该书定本型晚期鼓的流行时间上限始于西汉初年，此鼓的年代应在这一时限内。另外的两面鼓为冷水冲型早期鼓,这型早期鼓最早出土于汉文帝前元五年（前175）以后至汉武帝元狩五年（前118）的墓葬中[④]。此年限在岭南汉代考古分期中属于西汉前期后段。据此而论, 将两鼓年代断为西汉早期还是可取的。右江出水铜鼓,为石寨山型向冷水冲型的过渡者或冷水冲型最早鼓,其年代当在西汉早期前段为宜。

① 广西壮族自治区文物工作队:《广西田东发现战国墓葬》，《考古》1979年第6期。

② 李龙章:《广西右江流域战国秦汉墓研究》，《考古学报》2004年第3期。

③ 中国古代铜鼓研究会:《中国古代铜鼓》，文物出版社，1988年。

④ 广西壮族自治区文物工作队:《广西西林普驮墓葬》，《文物》1978年第9期。

三

百色古代铜鼓在广西铜鼓文化中的地位

关于铜鼓起源于哪个国家和什么地区的问题，经过一百年来国际学术界的争论，直至今日，中国云南省因有几十年来考古不断发现的最原始的万家坝型铜鼓作为科学支持从而奠定了古代铜鼓起源地的地位。在云南，最先制造和使用铜鼓的地区是滇中—滇池地区，铜鼓产生后，很快就往东南、北、南三个方向传播。其中东南传播路线上最近的接受铜鼓文化地区是今文山壮族苗族自治州，有力的证据是在全世界（国外仅越南）现知的40面万家坝型铜鼓中，有6面是在文山州出土。文山州出土的万家坝型铜鼓中年代最早的为春秋早期，最晚的为战国晚期，与整个万家坝型铜鼓的年代框架一致。因此有学者甚而提出："云南文山州极有可能是世界铜鼓起源地之一。"[①]文山州不仅出土6面万家坝型铜鼓，而且还出土6面石寨山型铜鼓，表现了早期铜鼓延续出土的特点。

百色地区的原百色县（今右江区）及那坡、田林、西林与文山州接壤，文山州广南县境内发源于九龙山南麓的西洋江，由西南东流出县境入广西后，汇于驮娘江注入右江，这条在郦道元《水经注》中称为文象水的河流，在古代既是交通要道，也是早期铜鼓继续向东传播的线路。百色田东南哈坡A鼓造型上与文山广南沙果村1号鼓相近，在鼓面太阳芒的安排及做法上两者也有相似之处,这就透露了这段传播历史的存在。同时也说明，百色是广西地区最早的铜鼓文化接收站。田东县所出的3面万家坝型铜鼓，各有自己的特点，在年代有早晚继承关系，它们让世人看到的，一是这里又形成了一个万家坝型铜鼓分布主要地区，二是这一地区的万家坝型铜鼓，不是原样简单接受，而是有所创造，融入当地民族的智慧，成为具有地方风格的新产品。

通过对云南早期铜鼓的矿料来源的铅同位素分析，得出的结论之一，是石寨山型铜鼓与万家坝型铜鼓的铅同位素分布场绝大多数互相重叠，其平均值在误差范围内一致，两型铜鼓所用矿料来源相同或相近，证明石寨山型铜鼓为万家坝型铜鼓直接继承者[②]。从实物上看，云南晋宁石寨山古墓出土的铜鼓，在形制、大小、装饰纹样上与楚雄万家坝所出的早期铜鼓确有许多的形似。考古资料又显示，这一新型鼓是万家坝型铜鼓向东传播时，首先在滇池地区的晋宁、江川、呈贡等地出现的。后来由于战争造成动乱环境，迫使上述地方铸造使用石寨山型铜鼓的民族向东、向南或东南迁徙，便由此带来了铜鼓文化向外传播。其中向东的有"南盘江流经贵州和广西交界地区，与北盘江汇合后流入广西，称红水河即古时的牂牁江"一路[③]。百色地区出土的石寨山型铜鼓资料，证实了这条传播路线的存在。田东锅盖岭鼓、隆林扁牙鼓和百色龙川鼓都属于石寨山型中期铜鼓，其中出土扁牙鼓的隆林县，正处于南盘江上游，与云南省毗邻，又与贵州省交界，恰在石寨山型铜鼓播迁的红水河线路上，如此即可以说，来自云南的石寨山型铜鼓是从隆林传入百色地区的。我们将百色地区四县出土的石寨山型铜鼓综而观之，可以发现，百色地区接受石寨山型铜鼓文化传入后，曾一度将之发展、壮大，使这一地区成为古代广西铸造、使用石寨山型铜鼓的主要地区。若进一步将区内贵港、贺州两市出土的石寨山型铜鼓纳入研究视野，则这一地区同时还是这类铜鼓文化的中转站，通过右江水路，当地的铜鼓文化得以继续向东播迁。再是，若田东右江出水铜鼓为石寨山型向冷水冲型发展的过渡者或冷水冲型最早鼓之说成立，则百色地区还是继后的广西铜鼓文化中冷水冲型鼓的诞生地，居地先民的革新开创了广西灿烂铜鼓文化的先河，历史功绩不可湮没。

① 李昆声：《云南文山在世界铜鼓起源研究中的地位》，《文山铜鼓暨民族历史文化国际学术研讨会论文集》油印本，文山州人民政府，云南大学，2004年。

② 李晓岑：《中国铅同位素考古》，云南科技出版社，2000年。

③ 雷从云：《关于铜鼓起源的认识》，《古代铜鼓学术讨论会论文集》，文物出版社，1982年，55页。

石寨山型铜鼓纹饰的民族学阐释

Ethnological Explanation for
Decorations of Shizhaishan-style Bronze Drums

李 文 张 伟 / 南宁孔庙博物馆 副研究员

［摘要］

本文在大量收集整理石寨山型铜鼓纹饰的基础上，结合其他考古材料和民族志资料试对石寨山型铜鼓的纹饰做一全面的研究，提出一些初步的看法。同时本文仅就云南三湖区域的石寨山型铜鼓的纹饰展开研究，因为文化有其特定的地域性、民族性、相对性，因此在特定的范围内进行研究更能深刻地把握铜鼓纹饰背后所蕴藏的丰富文化内涵。

［关键词］

石寨山型铜鼓 纹饰 释意

Abstract

In recent years, there are lots of researches about the decorations of Shizhaishan-Type bronze drums, but most in specialized study for a kind of decorations,there are few comprehensive research achievement.On the basis of previous studies, I analysed a large number of decorations of Shizhaishan-Type bronze drums, studied the special ones as a whole and traced their origins and implications.At the same time, because of culture has its particular regional, national character and relativity,so this paper only do a research on three lake areas of Yunnan.

Key words

Shizhaishan-type bronze drums; Patterns and decoration; Explanation

一

石寨山型铜鼓分布与分式

（一）发现与分布

石寨山型铜鼓就目前掌握的资料而言，发现最早的是云南的开化鼓和广南鼓。开化鼓出土的时间大约为19世纪末期，广南鼓出土的时间为1919年。迄今为止，根据不完全统计，中国境内的石寨山型铜鼓共发现70面①。如果按照发现的情况来看，主要分为三类，第一类是传世品；第二类为单鼓出土的非科学发掘品；第三类则是科学发掘品（图一）。

1. 传世品

传世品主要指祖上流传下来的，来源不明的铜鼓。这类鼓情况十分复杂，多数系各地博物馆从不同渠道征集而来，少数为保存在一些现代民族村寨中的铜鼓。云南、四川、上海、广东等地的各级文物部门分别保存过这类铜鼓。其中云南4面，它们是开化鼓、富宁县孟梅Ⅰ号鼓、孟梅Ⅱ号鼓、甲式ⅠA鼓。上海2面，T4753号鼓、24339号鼓。广东1面，3-796号鼓。河南1面，罗山鼓②。

2. 单鼓出土的非科学发掘品

此类鼓出土时大多无伴出土物，以单鼓形式出土，未见墓坑痕迹，基本在基建过程中发现。云南、贵州、四川、广西等省、自治区均发现过，共计18面。

3. 科学发掘品

经正式考古发掘的石寨山型铜鼓，以云南为最多，其中又主要来自晋宁石寨山③、江川李家山④、呈贡天子庙⑤、昆明羊甫头⑥等墓地之中，在云南三湖区域（滇池、抚仙湖、星云湖）青铜时代墓葬中发现的石寨山型铜鼓共34面，占石寨山型铜鼓科学发掘品中的大多数。截至2007年石寨山型铜鼓的科学发掘品共计44面，全部出自墓葬之中。

4. 主要分布范围

此处主要以科学发掘品为主，因为此类铜鼓伴出的器物比较多，年代准确，较能正确反映出石寨山型铜鼓的分布。从目前石寨山型铜鼓科学发掘品的出土地点来看，绝大部分出自“滇文化”⑦墓葬之中。其中又以晋宁石寨山、江川李家山、呈贡天子庙为主，由此可以看出石寨山型铜鼓的核心分布区集中于云南三湖（滇池、抚仙湖、星云湖）附近（图二）（这里仅指科学发掘品，因为相对于传世品，科学发掘品在年代断代上更具有研究价值）。而滇文化的中心分布区大致在滇池东岸的南

① 李昆生、黄德荣:《中国与东南亚的古代铜鼓》，云南美术出版社，2008年，75页。

② 李昆生、黄德荣:《中国与东南亚的古代铜鼓》，云南美术出版社，2008年，79页。

③ 云南省博物馆:《云南晋宁石寨山古遗址及墓葬》，《考古学报》1956年第1期。

④ 云南省博物馆:《云南江川李家山古墓群发掘报告》，《考古学报》1975年第2期。

⑤ 昆明市文物管理委员会:《呈贡天子庙滇墓》，《考古学报》1985年第4期。

⑥ 云南省文物考古研究所等:《昆明羊甫头墓地》，科学出版社，2005年。

⑦ 此处的“滇文化”指的是广义的滇文化，即考古学上命名的石寨山文化。参见蒋志龙:《再论石寨山文化》，《文物》1998年第6期。

	云南	广西	贵州	上海	广东	河南	四川	浙江
传世品	4			2	1	1		
单鼓出土非科学发掘品	12	3	1				2	
科学发掘品	34	8	1					1

图一　中国石寨山型铜鼓数量分布①

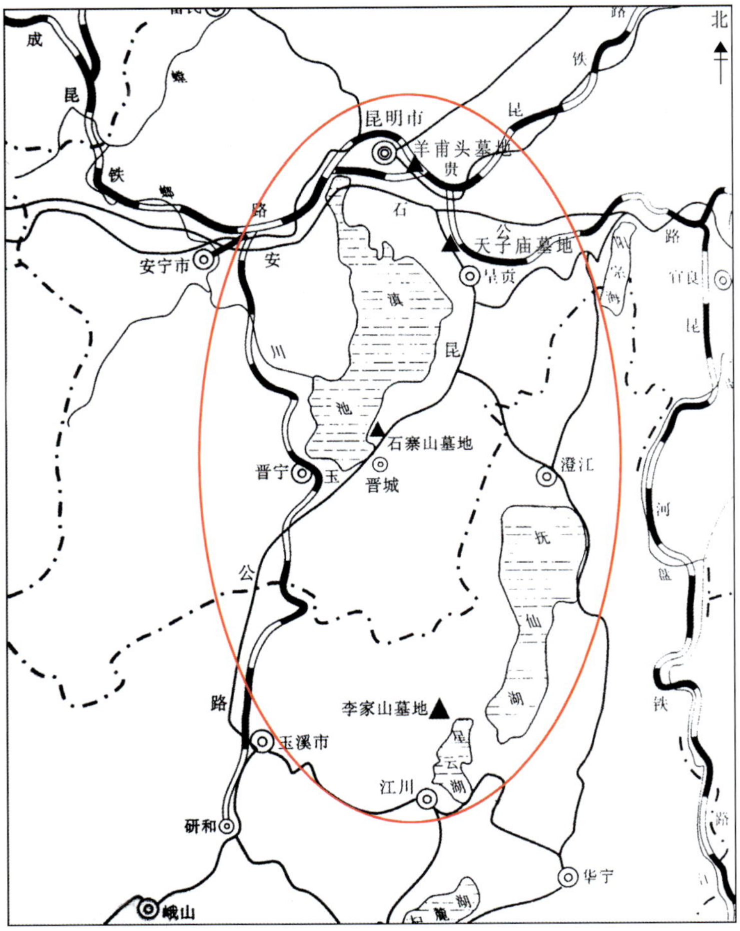

图二　云南三湖区域石寨山型铜鼓主要出土墓葬分布图

北相距约60千米的范围以内，地处滇池周围的昆明坝子和玉溪三湖地区的江川坝子，具体而言就是滇池、抚仙湖和星云湖之间的狭长地带②。所以可以看出石寨山型铜鼓的核心分布区与滇文化的中心分布区是相重合的，同时在其周边又有外延区，其范围北达四川会理，东北到贵州赫章可乐，东南至广西西林和贵县罗泊湾，西部范围不详。

① 数据采自《中国与东南亚的古代铜鼓》。

② 蒋志龙：《滇国探秘——石寨山文化的新发现》，云南教育出版社，2002年，23页。

（二）年代问题

在晋宁石寨山第一次和第二次发掘时发现的17面铜鼓，多出自墓葬分期的Ⅰ、Ⅱ类型墓葬中，即早期墓，Ⅰ类墓地的年代属于西汉早期，Ⅱ、Ⅲ类型墓葬虽然同属西汉中期，但是Ⅱ类墓葬中仅出文帝半两钱，而Ⅲ类墓葬出武帝五铢钱及滇王金印，年代仍有早晚之分。同时在Ⅲ、Ⅳ类型（晚期墓）墓中均没有发现铜鼓[①]。在江川李家山第一次发掘过程中，在23座Ⅰ类墓中（M17、M23、M24）共发现8面铜鼓，而Ⅰ类墓葬的年代为战国中期至西汉初年[②]。同时根据晋宁石寨山和江川李家山出土的石寨山型铜鼓的碳-14测定的年代数据和与其伴生的出土器物，大致可得出石寨山型铜鼓的年代为战国中期至西汉晚期[③]。

综上所述，我们可以在时间和空间上对石寨山型铜鼓加以界定，即在战国中期至西汉晚期，以云南三湖区域为其核心分布区。

① 云南省博物馆:《云南晋宁石寨山古墓群发掘报告》，文物出版社，1959年。

② 云南省博物馆:《云南江川李家山古墓群发掘报告》，《考古学报》1975年第2期。

③ 蒋志龙:《滇国探秘——石寨山文化的新发现》，云南教育出版社，2002年，305页。

二

石寨山型铜鼓纹饰

石寨山型铜鼓的纹饰为所有八个类型铜鼓中纹饰最为精美的，可以说是铜鼓纹饰发展过程中的全盛期。其花纹以刻范铸花为主，但是在云南三湖区域已有多种不同的表现手法，如阳纹的范铸线描方法，阴阳纹结合的装饰作风，阴纹的细线针刻法。早期特别强调组合排列的韵律感，鼓面除去太阳纹不计，又可分为三区。中区主晕饰翔鹭纹，内外两区则为两晕锯齿纹夹一晕圈圆纹，呈对称布局。鼓身胴部为横排晕圈，主晕有船纹。腰部用直段饰带分格，格内分别饰有峰牛、舞人等纹饰。鼓足一般光素无纹。四耳稍大，饰有绳辫纹。晚期的纹饰较之前的写实性图案，已经表现为几何型纹样，不如早期的画面表现得那么生动入微了。

（一）写实性纹饰

写实性纹饰是相对于抽象性纹样而言的，是通过创造性的视觉形象，去反映自然物象或社会生活的装饰性纹饰。它和抽象性纹饰相同的是均统一于铜鼓的整体布局，而写实性纹饰的画法更接近于绘画。由于选材和画法的差异，写实性纹饰蕴含着深层次的母题含义，往往和特定的民族历史、风俗礼仪有重要关联。

1. 翔鹭纹

装饰于胴部或鼓面上的同心晕圈之中翔鹭纹是石寨山型铜鼓纹饰中最富动态的图

图三　连体式

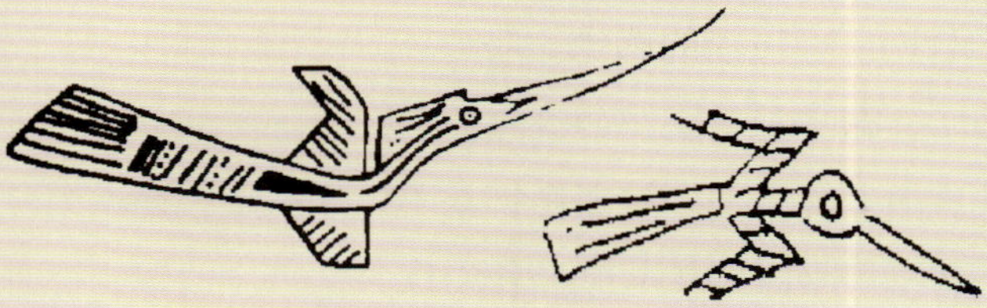

图四　分解式

图五　石寨山出土的铜鼓船纹拓片（石寨山M14：1）

1　　2

图六　广西的两面石寨山型铜鼓船纹

1. 广西西林出土的280号铜鼓船图　2. 广西罗泊湾铜鼓船纹

案，一般为逆时针绕成一圈，数量以四只为主。在四只为主的翔鹭纹图案中，其排列方式均以散点排列为主。而在翔鹭纹数量较多的图案中，则变成了首尾相连的排列方式，甚至出现交错的密集排列方式。与此同时，除了同一元素的简单重复排列，还有与其他纹饰相结合的复合排列方式，如翔鹭纹和舞人纹相复合的排列方式。同时翔鹭的结构也有两种不同的表现，一种是连体式（图三），另一种为分解式（图四）。

2. 船纹

船纹是铜鼓的装饰性母题之一。位于鼓腰和胴部，一般由四至六条船纹组成。船纹铜鼓的种类很多，具有十分强烈的写实风格，是三湖区域的古代先民多种多样水上生活的写照。

早期的船纹，船形简单，不分首尾，没有装饰。船底部长而平，两头上翘，船中坐裸体羽人三到四人，船的一边有时候端立一鸟。有的船还在外部装有一块停鸟板。中期的船纹其特点为，一般于胴体饰有四条船，船体细长，成弧线型，给人一种轻巧而灵活的感觉。船首饰有鸟首纹，船上一般坐三至四个裸体羽人，双手执桨，作奋力划行状。铜 鼓船纹中此类占较多（图五）。晚期的船纹一般饰于胴部，以六条船纹居多，船首尾饰鸟首，船身大而长，首尾翘起，每船九到十一人不等。船上的人物活动基本相同，大多数人物均戴羽冠或羽饰，裸身（图六）。

3. 舞人纹

舞人纹一般位于鼓腰或胴部，也有少数位于鼓面。舞人纹多为立式，个别也有坐式。半裸者着裙状物，全裸着露其阳具。发式为椎髻，其上一般戴有羽冠或羽饰。“滇人”[①]是一个能歌善舞的民族，在石寨山其他的青铜饰物上也有体现。舞人纹所表现的舞蹈大致分为两类，一类为徒手舞，另一类为执物舞（图七）。徒手舞没有任何道具，徒手舞蹈，其特点是强调拇指与另外四指相分离，而以四肢的伸屈运动为主，动作刚健有力，节奏感十分鲜明，很有特色。执物舞则为舞蹈者手执兵器，一般为斧、矛、盾牌等，是一种模拟战斗动作的舞蹈。在当时的艰苦环境下，这种乐舞应与原始信仰有密切联系。

4. 牛纹

牛纹一般施于铜鼓腰部，巨角隆脊，形象十分生动。牛纹的线条一般以封闭式线描为主，牛角为正视，而牛身则为侧视，四足。轮廓内填满几何形纹饰。因其背脊处隆起如峰状，故称其为峰牛，它是东南亚国家古时较为常见的一种牛。滇文化中的青铜饰物，以牛为母题者，数量和种类很多。

（二）几何形纹饰

对于写实性的纹饰，学者均给予较多的关注，而对于几何形纹饰却少有系统的研究。石寨山型铜鼓的几何纹饰包括同心圆纹、锯齿纹、点纹、弦纹等。石寨山型铜鼓的几何形纹饰主要是继承前式的风格，同时又有扬弃、有所创新和发展。下面就将石寨山型铜鼓纹饰中较有代表性的几种几何形纹饰作一分析。

1. 太阳纹

石寨山型铜鼓鼓面的太阳纹的特点为体与芒合为一体，同时在芒间饰有纹饰。下面就从体、芒与芒间纹饰三个方面对石寨山型铜鼓的太阳纹进行分析。石寨山型铜鼓太阳纹的体一般略高于鼓面，呈凸起状。文献中称“鼓脐隆起如球”[②]，体的变化较小，其直径长度一般长于芒。其次在光芒的数量上，以12芒较为多见，10芒和8芒次之，芒数太多或太少以及奇数者罕见[③]。从中我们可以看出芒数多以偶数出现，这也体现出芒数从无序逐渐走向规范化。同时，芒的长度一般与体的大小相关，体大则芒相对较短。若体小则芒一般较长。最后，芒间的纹饰这是光体进入繁荣期的主要标志。芒与体连成一体后，使得芒与芒之间形成了三角形空白，而芒间纹饰的作用就是填补这一空间。芒间纹饰又分为两种类型，一类是简单的芒间纹饰，一般

① 此处主要指生活在云南三湖区域的古代先民，后文中的“滇人”均同此。

② 杨慎:《滇载记》(卷一)，11页。

③ 李伟卿:《铜鼓及其纹饰》，云南科技出版社，2000年，85页。

图七　徒手舞与执物舞

由一种纹饰构成，如斜线纹、人字纹、叶脉纹等（图八）。另一类是复合的芒间纹饰，一般由两种不同的纹饰组合而成。

2. 锯齿纹

锯齿纹的基本单元是一个三角形，多见为等腰三角形，一般位于鼓面、胴部、腰部，足部较少见。锯齿纹的排列方式只有一种，但有的会在两齿之间均有空隙处填上小点，使图案显得十分饱满的同时又可以起到互相映衬的作用。我们认为锯齿纹是太阳光芒线图案化的体现。

3. 同心圆纹

同心圆纹就其形式而言，可以从形象和排列两个方面加以分析。从形象上看，可以分为实心和空心两种类型。与此同时，同心圆纹还有多种变体，如点圆纹、圆涡纹、圆圈纹等。其次在排列方式上，有紧密排列方式、散点排列方式和复合式排列方式，所谓复合式排列就是在两个同心圆纹之间用斜线纹连接，呈“S”形结构。

4. 雷纹

雷纹在石寨山型铜鼓上的出现也较多，形象饱满。无论是方形雷纹、矩形雷纹还是斜形雷纹都是不留空隙的，因而也就排除了和其他纹饰相复合的可能性。同时它的变化形式也较为复杂，无论是单向雷纹、并头雷纹还是勾连雷纹，均有多种不同的形式。在排列方式上以重复排列为主。

三

纹饰的阐释

铜鼓是区域性的文化现象。作为一种文化载体，铜鼓的数量多，分布范围广，延续时间长，类型和纹饰复杂，内涵丰富。使用者又包含了若干不同民族，各地的铜鼓文化内涵也不尽相同，因此分析时不能过于简单化。将铜鼓看作建立于地缘关系之上的区域性文化也许更为合适。具体到石寨山型铜鼓，应联系当时云南三湖区域内的具体自然地理环境加以分析，只有这样才能够得出较为可靠的研究结论。

（一）太阳纹与礼日神

石寨山型铜鼓的太阳纹占据着铜鼓鼓面的中心位置，而且一直处于中心位置，始终不变，所以其含义不容小视。古代先民对太阳的崇祀与他们生活的自然环境是相适应的，是古代先民自然崇拜的一种表现。在当时的条件下，他们即使对最为直观的自然现象也无法解释，他们认为太阳决定着人类的生老病死，于是乎“万物悉为妖怪，日月亦为妖怪”[①]。同时，由攫取性的生产过渡到生产性的生产，是早期人类社会的一次最伟大的变革，这种社会变革必然会反映到原始信仰当中。农业形成之后，由于各种自然现象对农业的生产影响很大，因而逐渐产生自然崇拜。

农业是滇人最主要的生产部门，《史记·西南夷列传》载：“西南夷君长以什数，夜郎最大；其西靡莫之属以什数，滇最大；……此皆魋结，耕地，有邑聚。”这是滇人属于定居农业民族的最早记载。新中国成立以来，滇池地区出土了许多青铜时代的农业生产工具。这些农业生产工具，主要从墓葬中出土，绝大多数是青铜制造。计有用于起土的铜镬五十六件，铜臿一件；用于中耕薅锄以及其他用途的铜锄三十六件；用于收获庄稼的铜镰三十四件；用于砍伐树木、开辟耕地的铜釜两佰八十七件[②]。显而易见，只有在农业民族中才会出现以农具随葬的风气。农业生产在滇人的生产资料中占据着重要位置。

云南三湖区域主要的作物为水稻，这里的新石器时代遗址中就有稻壳痕迹和稻谷遗存的发现[③]。1975年5月，在昆明黑林铺大团山滇文化墓葬（M3）出土的陶盘上发现明显的稻壳痕迹[④]。同时文献记载，西汉晚期，文齐任益州太守，曾兴修水利，开造稻田两千余顷[⑤]，发展了农业生产。因而，三湖区域的稻作农业，距今已有三四千年的历史了[⑥]。由此可见，战国至西汉时期三湖区域正处于稻作农业阶段。所以，在这样一个农业社会中对阳光的渴求就必然成为日常生活中一个重要的主题。

云南三湖区域的滇人虽然已经步入了农业社会，但在原始信仰产生之初，人们的认识和思维方式十分简单，与此相伴的则是严酷的生产环境以及落后的生产方式，那时的滇人最关心的就是农业生产问题。为了农耕和渔猎，他们更需要知道大自然所赋予这块土地的季节、风雨和冷暖。在这场与大自然的抗争过程中，最为粗陋的经济形态和古老类型的思维方式相适应”[⑦]。大量的考古发现及其出土文物也证明，我国古代很多民族或部落之中均广泛存在着日神崇拜。

1. 考古学证据

我国新石器遗址发现的太阳崇拜遗存至少已有七八千年的历史，在长江和黄河

① 薛尔曼著、郑绍文译：《神的由来》，上海文艺出版社，1990年，62页。

② 王大道：《滇池区域的青铜文化》，《云南省博物馆学术论文集》，1989年。

③ 黄展岳、赵学谦：《云南滇池东岸新石器时代遗址调查》，《考古》1959年第4期。

④ 云南省博物馆于1975年在昆明黑林铺大团山清理土坑墓3座，资料现存云南省博物馆。

⑤《后汉书·南蛮西南夷列传》：“及王莽政乱……以广汉文齐为太守，造起陂池，开通灌溉，垦田两千余顷”。又据《华阳国志·先贤仕女总赞》：“文齐字子奇梓幢人也。孝平帝时以城门校尉为犍为属国，迁益州太守，开造良田，民咸赖之”。

⑥ 汪宁生：《远古时期云南的稻作栽培》，《思想战线》1977年第1期。

⑦〔苏〕叶·莫·梅列金斯基著、魏庆征译：《神话的诗学》，商务印书馆，1990年，217页。

流域新石器时代的遗址当中均有发现大量的古代先民太阳崇拜的遗存。在郑州大河村仰韶文化晚期遗存中发现了绘在陶片上的太阳或光晕图案（图九），在河姆渡遗址发现的象牙器上也有太阳的图案（图一〇），明显带有太阳崇拜的意识。

图八　石寨山型铜鼓太阳纹拓片

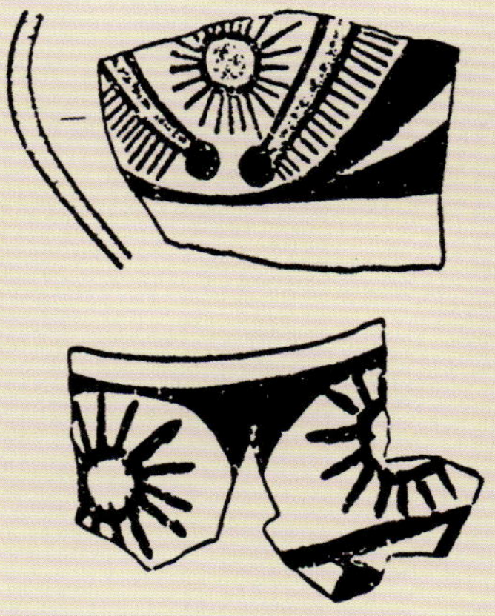

图九　彩绘太阳纹陶片（仰韶文化，郑州大河村出土）

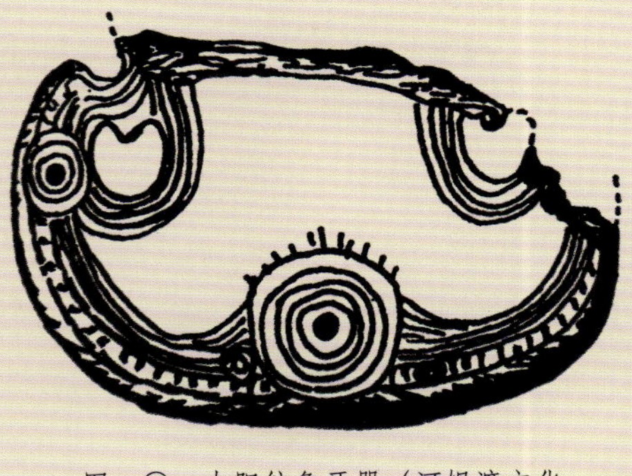

图一〇　太阳纹象牙器（河姆渡文化，浙江余姚河姆渡出土）

与此同时，还有几何化的太阳形象的表现，这一类图案多为八角形。我们认为它应是太阳图案的变形，反映的也是日神崇拜。如1960～1961年在上海发现的崧泽文化，有一例是环绕陶豆足一周的八角形图案，这似乎也是抽象和图案化的太阳纹。1963年江苏邳县大墩子大汶口文化44号墓地出土的陶盆上，在环绕陶盆颈部一周共有7个八角形图案。1971年山东邹县野店大汶口文化墓葬出土的1件陶盆上，与其他纹饰组合的4个八角星图案（图一一）。1974年在内蒙古自治区敖汉旗南台地小河沿文化遗存中出土的彩陶器座上，与其他纹饰组合的4个八角星图案（图一二）。1978年江苏海安青墩17号墓出土的2件陶纺轮上亦有类似图案（图一三）。江西靖安樊成堆文化墓葬中发现的1件陶纺轮上也刻有八角星图案。1987年安徽含山凌家滩4号墓出土的1件玉版上，刻有圆形图案，其中心也是八角星纹饰（图一四）。由此可以看出在我国境内，太阳崇拜在古代是十分普遍的一个现象。

从以上我们可以看出，这些带有日神崇拜意识的遗存大多出自新石器时代的遗迹当中。而日神崇拜观念，一般认为其产生的时代也是农业诞生的时代即新石器时代，所以太阳崇拜意识与农业生产是密切相关的。

同时，关于日神崇拜常见到的图像还有人的形象，而且人格化了的日神不仅具有人形，还具有人性。而将自然崇拜的事物人格化，也是早期原始信仰的一种表现形式。在我国的内蒙古阴山、广西宁明花山（图一五）、云南沧源等地均普遍存在有关日神崇拜的岩崖画。在黑龙江岩画的三个人体头上的太阳和三颗星星，表现得

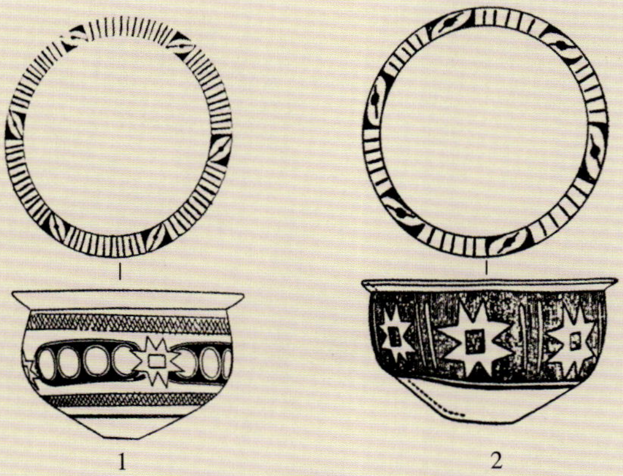

图一一　八角形图案彩陶盆（大汶口文化）
1. 山东邹县野店出土　2. 江苏邳县大墩子出土

图一二　八角形图案彩陶支座（小河沿文化，内蒙古敖汉旗南台地出土）

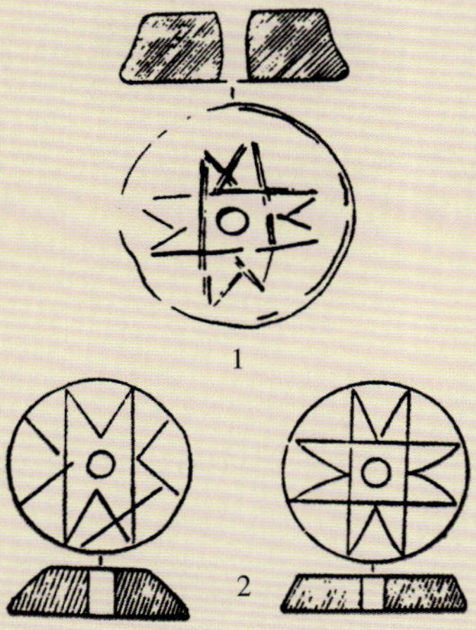

图一三　刻八角形图案陶纺轮
1. 樊城堆文化，江西靖安樊城堆出土　2. 青墩类型，江苏海安青墩出土

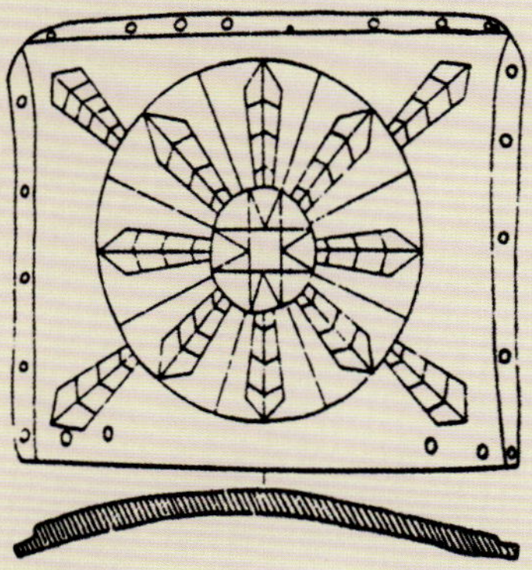

图一四　八向刻划图案玉牌饰（凌家滩文化，安徽含山凌家滩出土）

极具图案化，含有很多的示意性。用圆圈表现太阳，用“×”标示光芒，用15根放射状的线条模拟太阳的光华（图一六）。

美国加州岩画太阳的造型手法也一致强烈地反映出古代先民的日神崇拜意识（图一七）。美拉尼西亚岩画中的太阳人面，更是明确地反映出绘画者日神崇拜的意识，这些人面和太阳图案相融的图形，双目圆睁，光芒四射，在画面上十分突出（图一八）。这都表明了日神崇拜的广泛性。除此之外，锯齿纹在美洲岩画中是常见的纹饰，我们认为铜鼓上的锯齿纹应是太阳光芒线图案化的体现。相似的纹饰发现于世界不同地区的原始文化遗存中，说明这种图纹已经规范化，虽然个别有变体。但它们所表现的仍无疑应是与农业有着千丝万缕联系的太阳①。

2. 民族学材料

从全球的范围讲，几乎每一个民族、每一个地区都存在过或存在着日神崇拜及

① 张道一：《工艺美术论集》，山西人民美术出版社，1986年，12页。

图一五　广西宁明花山岩画

图一六　黑龙江岩画中的太阳图案

图一七　美国加州岩画中的太阳图案

图一八　美拉尼西亚岩画中的太阳人面

其神化传说内容，从时间上而言，日神信仰在原始时代及上古社会中较为常见，而近代某些原始土著部落中仍然存在着这一信仰。因为作为一种原始信仰，日神崇拜具有普遍意义，它在原始文化研究中占据着显要的地位。人类学家爱德华· 泰勒曾说过，凡是太阳照耀的地方，均有日神崇拜的存在，尽管有些人对这一说法并不认可，但是不容否认日神崇拜是自然崇拜的一个主要内容。在各大洲，无论是从一些土著民族还是从古代宗教的起源方面，我们都会实时感受到日神的存在。

在美洲，印第安人通过被埋在地下的种子长出来以至于开花结果这一现象感受到了大地创造生命之力，他们把“太阳视为活的精灵”[①]。越是追溯各民族文化的历史源头，我们就更容易感受到神话与历史在拉近，太阳崇拜和太阳神话就是原始时代的主要信仰和神话。对于太阳这一每天有规律运行的天体，古代先民认为它是活物，“白天它时刻监视着人们的言行，夜晚它还能透知其梦境。可以想象古代先民是多么的崇拜这个充满了光和热的火球。”[②]纳切斯人是印第安众多部落中的一支，他们有着完整的太阳教体系。居于北美的纳切斯人视伟大的日神为宇宙的统治者，他们的酋长被视为太阳王，死后葬于金字塔中。纳切斯人的太阳教有着严格的仪式，每天早晨当太阳升出地平线时，酋长们便面对日神示敬，他们要举手过头，并随着太阳运行而不断地改变方向。正如泰勒所言，纳切斯人的太阳教有着所谓完整

① 〔英〕爱德华·泰勒著、连树声译：《原始文化》，广西师范大学出版社，2005年，219页。

② 高福进：《太阳崇拜与太阳神话·一种原始文化的世界性透视》，上海人民出版社，2002年，8页。

的“太阳圣秩制度”[①]。

同样在我国，日神的信仰也是广泛存在的，云南永宁纳西族认为，天上以太阳为大，只有太阳的存在，才有万物的生长；大理白族认为太阳能驱除云雾，促使庄稼生长成熟，只有祭祀太阳神才能保佑谷物丰收；阿昌族认为，有了太阳与月亮，万物才会生长，人才有吃有穿，所以对日月供奉最勤[②]；彝族在古代所发明的十月太阳历，完全是根据地球环绕太阳运行的周期制定的，它的精密度要比古埃及历和古玛雅历高得多；西藏东南部的珞巴族也崇拜太阳，在举行仪式时要挑选一头大而强壮的牛宰杀，用来向太阳献祭；在博嘎尔一部落，人们在门外搭建有“打洛脚”篷架，其上方中央绘着太阳图像，经常献祭，以此祈求太阳女神赐予庄稼丰收[③]；鄂伦春族每逢正月初一早晨，族人们便聚集在部落中心热闹处，伏地向东跪拜太阳。小声或默祈，感谢太阳神给人们带来光明与幸福，并祈祷新一年的平安与丰收[④]。对于日神崇拜，在中国的很多民族中是一种很普遍的现象。

（二）翔鹭纹与鸟使者

古代先民把太阳和鸟视为有着极其亲密关系的伙伴。他们相信太阳和鸟是同栖其处，在古文献中也有关于太阳鸟的记载，《山海经·海外东经》云：“汤谷上有扶桑，十日所浴……九日居下枝，一日居上枝。”又据《山海经·大荒东经》云：“汤谷上有扶木，一日方至，一日方出，皆戴于乌。”说的是就十个太阳，居住在汤谷。它们轮流值班，每天有一太阳居上枝，高悬于空，给大地带来光明。可是每天太阳怎么上下哪？靠的就是飞鸟。太阳凭借飞鸟飞翔的神力，鸟离扶桑，日出。鸟归扶桑，日落。《尚书·尧典》载“日中星鸟”；王充《论衡》里也有“日中有三足鸟”，这些均是有关太阳鸟的典型记载。除了文献之外，太阳和鸟相伴的遗存在黄河流域、长江流域及华南各地的大量新石器遗址均有发现，体现了鸟作为太阳使者的悠久历史。

1. 考古学的证据

在我国新石器时代的考古遗存中就曾发现大量的鸟与太阳相结合的形象，20世纪70年代确定的河姆渡文化中就出现过，一例是刻在骨匕柄部上的双头鸟图案，鸟身中部还刻有太阳纹纹饰（图一九），另一例是双鸟朝阳或双头鸟朝阳象牙雕刻（图二〇）。而在良渚文化中，在一玉璧上有鸟纹和太阳纹，另一玉璧上刻有两只鸟逆时针绕玉璧作飞翔状，两只鸟之间夹有两只羽毛。安徽含山凌家滩出土的鸟兽合一玉雕也有太阳与鸟结合的图案（图二一）。2001年在四川成都金沙出土的四鸟绕日金饰（图二二），与河姆渡文化的双鸟朝阳象牙雕有异曲同工之妙。这些太阳和鸟结合的图案，形象地反映了原始农业产生以后，先民们对知时鸟和照耀万物生长的太阳的崇拜，同时也标示了太阳与鸟的密切关联。

① 〔英〕爱德华·泰勒著、连树声译：《原始文化》，广西师范大学出版社，2005年，728页。

② 何星亮：《中国自然神与自然崇拜》，上海三联书店，1992年，135、136页。

③ 刘芳贤等：《珞巴族的原始宗教》，《中国少数民族宗教初编》，云南人民出版社，1985年。

④ 关小云、王宏刚：《鄂伦春族萨满教调查》，辽宁人民出版社，1998年，81页。

图一九　双头鸟图案骨匕柄（浙江余姚河姆渡出土）

图二〇　双鸟朝阳象牙雕刻（浙江余姚河姆渡出土）

图二一　鸟兽合一玉雕（凌家滩文化，安徽含山凌家滩出土）

图二二　四鸟绕日金饰，四川金沙遗址出土

2. 民族学材料

对于鸟的崇拜在民族志中也有较多的记录，在埃及太阳鸟的代表是鹰，在中国太阳鸟则以凤凰为主，印第安人的太阳鸟则为秃隼。尽管名字不同，但是它们均是太阳鸟的变体，代表了不同时期不同地区太阳神的化身。究其原因，上文已述，鸟类尤其是候鸟随季节飞行是古代先民视其为太阳神鸟的一个重要因素。每当夏季来临，太阳把鸟类带往北方，冬季来临又会回到南方。而古代先民不可能科学地解释这一常识，自然会认为是日神导致了这种季节性迁移，而鸟类便被看做是太阳的使者，驮着太阳做周期性的运行。

综上所述，古代先民将鸟和太阳结合在一起，并将鸟看作太阳的使者并非是古人的凭空臆测，而是他们长期直接观察的结果。由于太阳对农业生产的影响很大，与人们的生产、生活发生直接的联系，因而促使人们去观察太阳、崇拜太阳，而在此过程当中又将与太阳关系密切的鸟纳入到这一信仰体系之中，并将其视为沟通天地的使者。

（三）船纹、同心圆纹与祭水神

石寨山型铜鼓上船纹的出现也就不足为怪，它与滨水而居的滇人有密切关联。从晋宁到江川有滇池、抚仙湖、星云湖等，因此船纹的出现并非是偶然，它和铜鼓上的同心圆纹均象征着古代先民们对于水的敬畏和崇祀。当时虽然农业是社会生产的主要部门，但渔猎也是一个不可缺少的生产资料的重要来源。因此，古代先民对于水神的崇祀也很重视，而铜鼓上的船纹所表现的正是人们对水神的祭祀场景。

1. 船纹与祭水神

首先，就船本身而言，这些舟船大多头尾相翘，身材颀长，首尾饰羽或作鸟首状。云南、广西、越南等地的许多铜鼓船纹中船首船尾大多画一圆圈以似鸟眼，在太平洋诸岛土著民族的舟船上，往往也有这种头尾相翘、饰羽、画鸟眼的装饰，其与祭祀活动密切相关。滇人擅长用舟，善于捕捞水中螺蛤贝壳及鱼虾龟鳖，这是他们的生产生活与水息息相关的另一个方面。然而，正是由于他们接近水，又自然地畏惧为水所害。无论是在江河湖的水上舟行，还是潜没入水的捕鱼采贝，其危险性都是时时存在和令人畏惧的。为了保障生命安全，祈求航行顺利，滇人自然将祭祀水神视为一种可行的办法。因此，铜鼓船纹中滇人祭祀的对象应有水神的一席之地。

从目前已发现的考古材料中，也有表现此类祭祀水神的遗存。如在日本北海道富勾贝洞窟的岩画中就有表现渔夫舞蹈的场景，有的双臂上举，弓步跳跃；有的全身摇摆，或仰或卧；舞蹈的周围有圈养的牲畜和小船，似乎在取悦水神和庆祝渔猎的丰收，而牲畜则作为牺牲献给水神，与石寨山型铜鼓上出现的牛纹和其他动物图案不谋而合。位于珠海的大坪石岩画也有类似图案，画面长5米，宽3.3～4.3米。画面中心的上部刻有两条船，下方刻有19个人和动物的图案，造型简略，人物的动作多为蹬踏起舞和奔跑①。

① 李洪甫：《太平洋岩画》，上海文化出版社，1997年，77页。

2. 同心圆纹与水神崇拜

在铜鼓的胸部和腰部有大量的同心圆纹，关于同心圆纹的研究前人较少给予关注，但是我认为同心圆纹也是古代滇人自然崇拜的一个重要表现。上文已述，石寨山型铜鼓分布范围主要位于滇池、抚仙湖、星云湖周围。当时滇人对于水的重视程度是不言而喻的，因为水是生命之源，直到今天仍是这样。因此，对于水神的崇拜也是自然而然的事情。以同心圆纹来表现对于水神的崇拜在世界其他地方的古代遗存中常有发现。同时，发现同心圆纹和旋涡纹的地方也大多位于沿河和沿海地区，如在黑龙江的乌苏里江崖畔、福建漳州、连云港的将军崖、台湾万山以及美拉尼西亚的恩威罗扑尔德、夏威夷群岛等地的岩画中旋涡纹都是主题纹饰（图二三）。大量的同心圆纹显示着滇人对水的依存意念，和对水神的敬畏和崇祀，而这也是自然崇拜的一种表现。

铜鼓纹饰和岩画一样均是当时社会生活的真实反映，如铜鼓上大量的水波纹和旋涡纹显示出当时云南三湖区域滇人的日常生活与他们傍水而生的自然环境是分不开的，到了后期的同心圆纹则应是图案化了的旋涡纹。

（四）舞人纹、动物纹与祭祀仪式

在石寨山型铜鼓的船纹上经常可以看到船员，每船都有三至九人或更多不等的

图二三　美拉尼西亚的恩威罗扑尔德岩画

船员。这些船员在大多数船纹中的装饰都非同常人，他们或头饰羽毛、羽冠，或身披羽衣、衣着羽尾等，这里通称“羽人”。除羽人外，云南晋宁石寨山出土铜鼓的船纹中，船员有的身披兽衣、髻饰双角，衣领中插牦牛尾，手持斧、钺等武器，并且作舞蹈状。这些奇异的装饰和动作都有其特殊的含义和目的。

我们认为铜鼓上的舞人纹和动物纹是表现向日神和水神祈求农业丰产和渔船平安的祭祀活动的一部分。铜鼓上的舞人通常上身赤裸。在船纹图案中，羽人与船、鸟、鱼及各类祭具密切相连而占据重要的地位。我们认为这些船员，包括饰羽的羽人、不饰羽的船员、舞祭的羽人和划船的羽人等，都应是祭祀活动的参与者。

1. 舞人纹与巫术仪式

随着三湖区域农业的产生和发展，此时巫术也随之而出，主要用于祈求日出。古代先民已经认识到太阳对于农作物生长以及人类生活有直接的意义，只是对于有时太阳久不复出或热力不足没有科学的认识。于是采用巫术手段达到目的，这是祈祷日出的朴素的巫术行为发生的最初原因。这些舞人戴羽冠或羽饰，统称其为“羽人”，他们应是部落中原始巫术仪式的巫师或主祭人。

在一些铜鼓船纹上，可见到羽人祭祀过程中手持斧钺砍杀或擒拿人牲的场面，如广西西林鼓、云南广南鼓等。此外，云南晋宁石寨山等处出土的贮贝器等青铜器纹饰及雕塑中繁多的原始宗教祭祀活动场面，也从一个侧面反映了古代滇人祭祀活动的存在。因为作为饰有羽人船纹的铜鼓与这批青铜器都是同时出土的，它们之间仅是因为图案展示的内容不同而可以让后人了解当时原始信仰祭祀对象及仪式是多种多样的。祭祀活动主要包括：一是祭祀日神，二是祭祀水神。

祭祀日神的情况在我国的内蒙古阴山、广西宁明花山等地的岩画均有反映，有多幅一人或多人高举双手以祈求日出的内容，如果仅仅从巫术的角度出发而言，它是早期人类祈求日神的一种仪式。滇人祭祀水神是有其特定的社会基础及环境原因的。铜鼓舞人纹展示的祭祀活动，是古代滇人在农业耕作、渔猎捕捞、航行安全等方面备受威胁，没有保障的环境条件下发出的无声呻吟。

首先，滇人主要种植的作物——水稻需要大量用水，没有了水田地会干裂，人畜会焦渴而亡，此时祈雨巫师便是极其重要的人物。巫师为完成其职责而采用的方法虽然不总是相同，但通常是基于顺势或模仿的巫术原则。

其次，众所周知滇人生活的三湖区域多靠近湖泊，是一个典型的近水民族，滇人的渔猎捕捞业，在其社会经济中也占有重要的位置，《史记》、《汉书》等对他们采食螺蛤鱼鳖等活动都有生动的记载，因此保证航行的安全就成为重要内容，当然也少不了巫师的参与。

2. 动物纹与祭祀牺牲

铜鼓船纹除了表现上述主体内容之外，在许多船纹的周围或上下，工匠们还往往费神刻上几只目光炯炯、长嘴高脚的水鸟，尖嘴长身、鳍鳃发达的大鱼以及一些默默站立的牛、鹿等动物。这些动物我们认为也与滇人的水上祭祀活动有关。这些动物形象不是纯粹的装饰，而是服务于祭祀活动的。

船纹四周乃至船头舟尾站立的水鸟，应该是将其当做沟通天地人神的使者，这点在上文中已做了分析。至于鱼类和牛、鹿等，它们似乎象征着献祭给日神和水神的牺牲。广南鼓腰部出现的椎牛图像真实地再现了羽人杀牛献祭的情景。晚近壮侗等民族椎牛祭祀的活动仍司空见惯，史称“椎牛酌酒欢相嘘，春秋赛社南铜鼓。”[①]因此，铜鼓中牛及椎牛图像的出现，与滇人的原始祭祀活动有密切的联系。

在民族志材料中也可找到献祭牺牲给日神和水神的证据。印度的婆罗门在清晨奉献贡品是为了给太阳催生，人们相信如果不这样奉献，它肯定不会升起的。古代墨西哥人相信太阳乃是一切活动的源泉，于是把太阳称为“伊帕尔尼莫华尼”，即“人们赖它生存”的意思。但如果他赋予世界生命，那他也需要从世界获得生命。由于心脏是生命的基础和象征，于是人和动物血淋淋的心脏便奉献给太阳以保持其活力，使他得以维持横越天空的行进[②]。我国古时藏族人在祭献日神时，以牛、羊、犬、驴等动物的血进行祭祀，即所谓的“大红祭”[③]。

（五）象征符号系统

1. 符号体系

石寨山型铜鼓上各种纹样的组合并非是杂乱无章的，它是一个严密的具有象征意义的符号系统，与当时的经济生产、原始信仰有着密切的联系。生存是人类的最基本需要。要生存便一定要从事劳动生产，而以农业为主的古代先民是靠天吃饭的，没有能力抗御水旱天灾，安全感只能靠想象力去求得。但人的想象并不是凭空产生的，而是按照人本身的方式，去解释一切生命的根源。并由之而产生了一系列的象征符号和操作系统，即原始信仰、祭祀礼仪、交感巫术等。用人自己的方式去对自然现象作出解释，并加以人格化。实际上对日神和水神的崇祀均是自然崇拜的一种表现。而石寨山型铜鼓纹饰上所体现的就是

① 《柳州县志》，卷10。

② 〔英〕J·G·弗雷泽著，徐育新、汪培基、张泽石译：《金枝》，新世界出版社，2006年，80页。

③ 周锡银、望潮：《藏族原始宗教》，四川人民出版社，1999年，300～321页。

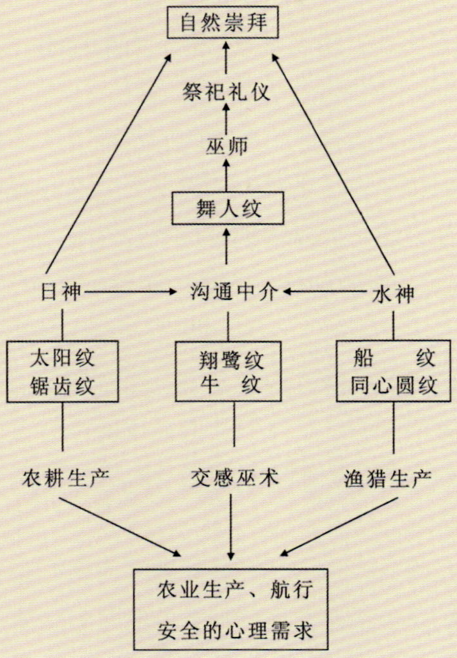

图二四 石寨山型铜鼓纹饰的象征符号体系

日神崇拜和水神崇拜为核心的，二元一体的自然崇拜系统（图二四）。

2. 符号背后的意义

任何一种信仰产生之后，都会滋生若干文化元素，由这些文化元素又构成一个文化系统。石寨山型铜鼓纹饰的文化系统又可分为信仰系统、政治系统。

（1）信仰系统

信仰系统属于自然崇拜的心理层面，包括自然神和自然精灵信仰。自然神和自然精灵观念是自然崇拜文化中两个最基本的文化元素，其他文化元素均是在这两个基础上衍生出来的。每一个自然神都有属于自己本身的神性和神职。云南三湖区域的古代滇人所崇拜的日神，人们不仅仅祈求它赐予阳光，而且把它视为丰产之神。自然神的本质是善的，但是如果不遵守禁忌或者不尊重神灵也会带来灾难，所以就产生了对于日神的祭祀。同样对于自然精灵的信仰也是一样，由于自然精灵的本质是恶的，于是人们也会对其进行信仰和祭祀以求得平安幸福，具体表现在滇人身上就是祈求渔猎作业时保证航行的安全。归结到一点，古代滇人的信仰日神和水神与稻作农业的丰产和操舟捕鱼是密切联系的。

（2）政治系统

“沟通手段的独占是中国古代阶级社会的一个主要现象，促成阶级社会中沟通手段独占的是政治因素，即人与人之间关系的变化。”[①]天地之间的沟通必须以特定的人物和工具为中介，具体到云南三湖区域的滇人就是依靠巫师和铜鼓。统治者只要掌

① 张光直：《中国古代史在世界上的重要性》，《考古学专题六讲》，文物出版社，1992年，13页。

握了这两者以及附属于它们的巫术、纹饰等物事，就占有了与上天沟通的本领，也就取得了政治的权威。石寨山型铜鼓及其纹饰正是这种天人之间沟通的一种工具。

从考古方面的资料来看，石寨山型铜鼓主要出土在晋宁石寨山、江川李家山、呈贡天子庙等少数滇文化墓葬之中，而且又集中出土于大型的贵族墓葬之中，而云南三湖区域的其他小型墓葬均未发现石寨山型铜鼓。可见石寨山型铜鼓是集中于一部分人的手中，而这一部分人以晋宁石寨山和江川李家山墓群的大型墓墓主为代表，这也为彰显政治权威提供了证据。当时的政治、宗教环境要求王朝统治者创造出一个统一的宗教和礼仪的信仰体系，以平衡和接纳各部落和地区相异的礼仪和信仰，从而成为神权社会的领袖，正是在此背景下石寨山型铜鼓及其纹饰应运而生。因此，在石寨山型铜鼓表面纹饰所流露的信仰系统和社会系统下隐藏着深刻的政治权威。

四

结　语

当一定数量的神圣事物确定了它们相互之间的并列关系或从属关系，并以此形成了某种统一体，形成了某个不被其他任何同类体系所包含的体系的时候，这些信仰的总体及其相应的仪式便构成了一种宗教①。而凝聚着神性的石寨山型铜鼓在云南三湖区域就曾扮演着至关重要的角色，它们被塑造成与最高集合神沟通的必不可少的媒介。石寨山型铜鼓及其纹饰在祭礼中充当联结天人的中介，同时也被赋予了沟通至高无上神灵的功能。可以看出这一时期云南三湖区域的滇文化已经拥有自己的文化、宗教和礼制，祭祀已经成为国家组织和政治实体最为重要的社会活动。同时，信仰统一的本身也暗含着三湖区域古代滇人政治演化的轨迹。到了后期，由于等级制度的建立与强化，以写实为主的铜鼓纹饰，逐渐被抽象为几何型图案。铜鼓的纹饰不再是社会统一和虔诚宗教的视觉代言，反而演变成了纯粹的装饰，这时铜鼓的功能从此由联系神灵与世人之间的媒介转换为区分社会等级的象征。从发现石寨山型铜鼓的墓葬大多为贵族大墓，也可以看出这时的铜鼓已不具有宗教信仰意识，而是渗入了彰显权利和显示富贵的心理动机，已经沦为区分社会高低贵贱的重要标志性器物。

在漫漫历史长河之中，有文字记载的历史极为短暂，尤其在西南边疆地区，文献的记录更少。我们只能从文物遗存中去感受历史的影子，它们对于今天的大众来讲，似乎很难理解，但是它们却是古代先民原始信仰和风俗文化的缩影。对于石寨山型铜鼓纹饰的研究我们还要深入探索，这种探索的最根本目的还是在于揭示古代滇人的信仰体系及其政治系统，从而加深对于石寨山型铜鼓纹饰的认识和理解。

①〔法〕爱弥儿·涂尔干著，渠东、汲喆译:《宗教生活的基本形式》，上海人民出版社，1999年，47页。

铜鼓“太阳纹”身份探源

An Study on the Identity
of the Sun Pattern on Bronze Drum

李 攀 / 广西壮族自治区博物馆 馆员

[摘要]

本文从视觉文化、图像学的角度，查阅历代铜鼓实物和相关研究文献资料，探究铜鼓最重要的纹饰——“太阳纹”的来源和身份。结合铜鼓的起源，联系当时的自然环境、社会生活、精神追求等因素，认为“太阳纹”实为火纹并展开论证。

[关键词]

铜鼓 太阳纹 火纹

Abstract

This paper explores the source and identity of sun pattern, which is the most important decoration of bronze drum from the point of visual culture and iconology, the author refers to the real object from the history and some related documents. Combining the origin of bronze drum and contacting the natural environment, social life, spiritual pursuits, the author believes that “sun pattern” is actually the fire pattern and discusses this viewpoint in the paper.

Key words

Bronze drums; Sun pattern; Fire pattern

“铜鼓与蛮歌，南人祈赛多。”[1]一千多年前的五代时期，孙光宪就用优美的诗篇记录了铜鼓在我国南方地区社会生活中扮演的重要角色。铜鼓造型优美，数量众多，流传地域广阔，延续至今经久不衰，它见证了世代的生产、娱乐、战争和权力。

如此重要的器物，必定有它独特的发展历程和精神内涵。“太阳纹”是铜鼓上最重要的装饰纹样，居于铜鼓的中心位置，略有突出。这种纹饰承载着岁月痕迹和集体意识，长久以来对于它的研究认为是先民对于太阳形象的再现，笔者认为这种“太阳纹”的身份应为火纹。

① 郑超雄:《壮族审美意识探源》，广西人民出版社，1991年，77页。

② 蒋廷瑜:《铜鼓史话》，文物出版社，1982年，57页。

一

从铜鼓的起源看“太阳纹”

铜鼓是内部中空、一面开口的形制，与木鼓两端蒙皮的样子相去甚远。从形态、材料上来看，铜鼓起源于仿制革鼓的说法不能信服。

《游梁杂记》记载“诸葛鼓，乃铜铸者，其形圆，上宽而中束，下则敞口，大约若今渣斗之倒置也。《戎州记》中描述铜鼓为“状似覆盆”[2]。1975年云南楚雄万家坝古墓葬出土的铜鼓，是目前公认的铜鼓的原始形态。它是由铜釜改制而成的，出土时是倒着放置的，和铜釜的放置方法相同。而且，这件铜鼓鼓面上还留有明显的烟熏痕迹，更加肯定了铜鼓起源于炊煮器的说法，这也符合艺术起源于劳动、来源于生活的规律。

云南楚雄万家坝出土的铜鼓还处于炊煮器、乐器分工不明确，混合使用的阶段。这件铜鼓上没有纹饰，只有烟熏的痕迹，这就是铜鼓上“太阳纹”的母体。先民将铜釜架置于灶火之上使用，燃烧的火焰会在釜底留下痕迹。这种灶火灼烧的痕迹在干净的釜底呈现的就是中心辐射的形状。并且，旺盛的火焰遇到铜釜底部也呈现出辐射状的变形。先民看到这种自然现象，惊奇又欣喜，于是在后来的铜鼓上人为装饰上这种火焰的形象。

铜鼓纹饰经历从无到有，最早出现的纹饰就是“太阳纹”，可见其与铜鼓有最亲密、最直接的关系，这正是炊煮与火相伴的真实写照。笔者认为，铜鼓上装饰的“太阳纹”不论从装饰的位置，还是纹样的形态都是对灶火火光及其痕迹的模仿。

二

“太阳纹”是有意味的形式

人类对火的认识从惊慌恐惧到采集火种，到钻木取火，再到刀耕火种，经历了上百万年历程。恩格斯曾说过：“摩擦生火第一次使人支配了一种自然力，从而最终把人同动物分开。”

火在人类生存中具有重要意义，文献资料中有许多有关火的记载。《书经》和《周易》认为“火能化育万物”。《孟子・许行掌》记载“舜使益掌火，益烈山泽而焚之，禽兽逃匿。”《管子・立政》“修火宪，敬山泽”、“山泽不敬于火，草木不得殖成，国之贫也。”《尚书・大传》中所说，“水火者，百姓之所饮食也。”

对于火的崇拜遍布中西，彝族、蒙古族、景颇族都有与火有关的节庆活动，希腊、埃及、印度都有与火相关的故事传说。先民的生活存留有着火的意识，传达出美好的生活意愿。

早期的铜鼓延续着铜釜的使用功能，配之以火，发挥功效。铜鼓上装饰的“太阳纹”是对火的记录，也寄托着使用者的理想愿望。铜鼓上火的形态是炊煮的灶火，灶火不仅能给人带来温暖，更重要的是能够满足生存需求。灶火火焰的大小关乎食品的味道，火焰的多少关乎食品的数量，与味觉感官、温饱水平息息相关。所以，先民希望灶火旺盛，饮食充沛，祈求富足兴旺的生活。

后世的铜鼓歌唱词中有：

大鼓响一声，万村得太平，不受水旱灾，不受虎狼侵。

大鼓响二声，五谷得丰登，一穗三百粒，十粒有半斤。

……[①]

云南的彝语支的祭词中有：

火神藏家中，人畜得安宁……[②]

验证了铜鼓与饮食、生存的关联，蕴含丰收的意味。

铜鼓鼓面在中心位置装饰火的形象，寓意着“民以食为天”的生存法则。火纹直接寄托着这种丰衣足食的理想，后来的铜鼓上有过蛙饰、云雷纹、翔鹭纹、羽人纹、划船纹、佛道纹饰的更迭变换，但火纹始终在每一面鼓的中心位置出现，再次印证火和饮食的重要性。铜鼓火纹沿袭至今一直凝结着劳动人民对富足生活的向往。

① 潘世雄：《铜鼓入土原因论》，《广西民族研究》1985年第2期。

② 张劲松：《论中华巫摊艺术中的火符号》，《东南文化》1993年第4期。

图一　云南弥渡三岔路出土的铜鼓

三

“太阳纹”形象的追溯

“太阳纹”实为火的形象还可以从与火有关的原始图像中找到端倪。

象形的“火”纹样在大汶口文化时期的器物上就有表现。出土的陶尊上刻画有形图形，学者认为这是古老的“炅”字。字体的下方就是用尖角的形状寓意火的样子。铜鼓上的“太阳纹”形象表达与其类似。

解释铜鼓的“太阳纹”形象，象形文字为我们提供了最好的物证。甲古文中的“火”字为三尖形状，写作、、等形式。这与铜鼓早期出现的“太阳纹”形象类似，可以认为“太阳纹”就是火之形象的图像表达。

云南弥渡三岔路铜鼓是较早出现“太阳纹”的铜鼓（图一），这个“太阳纹”中心光体是实心圆形，周围有六道光芒。这是值得注意的现象，在一个圆上等量划分为四份、八份都是容易的，而技艺尚不发达的先民却要将圆形均分为六份，就有一定的技术含量。是先民要挑战技术难度吗？完全没有这种必要。那么将圆均分六份的思想又是从哪里来的呢？还是象形文字给出最佳答案。

象形文字的“火”是模仿竖直燃烧的火焰，分为三个尖角。铜鼓上的“太阳纹”是模仿火焰遇到釜底后发散的形态，用两个“火”字，六个尖角的形态表示发散状态的火焰就是强调火与釜的接触。于是，六道芒的“太阳纹”最早出现在铜鼓上。

四

“太阳纹”解释的不妥

长久以来，铜鼓上的火纹之所以被人们认为是“太阳纹”，究其原因既有火纹与“太阳纹”的亲缘关系，也有人们的误读成分。

火与太阳都能发光发热，同属于能量体，带来光明与温暖。很多地方都有火崇拜、太阳崇拜，并且相互关联。华夏族的始祖炎帝就既是火神，又是太阳神。《淮南子·天文训》也存有“积阳之热气生火，火气之精者为日”的说法。可以说，火与太阳在先民的精神世界里有含混的、亲近的关系，但是早期铜鼓上的“太阳纹”作为太阳纹解释有其欠妥之处。

首先，从铜鼓的起源来看，太阳与炊煮之事并无直接关联，而火是与釜之搭配起效的。再就是，如果铜鼓上的纹饰作太阳纹解释，就是太阳崇拜的体现。先民对事物的崇拜表现为膜拜和供奉，铜鼓将太阳放置于中心位置供乐者敲击，用于取悦于人，毫无敬畏之感，显然不是对神灵图腾的崇敬之举，更显失礼和亵玩。还有，如果铜鼓上的纹饰是太阳纹，那必然有代表天界、沟通天际的作用，先民在铜鼓上敲打，发出或激昂或沉重或轰鸣的声音，演奏铜鼓的时候还配以歌曲、舞蹈，这种不安与躁动的表现就有打扰天界的嫌疑，惹怒了太阳、天界会遭受不详的报应。况且，自然界的一些巨大声响，比如电闪雷鸣、风雨交加并不是人们的渴望，而空气的运动可以使炊火更加旺盛，在炊火上敲打运动蕴含祈求温饱兴旺的意愿。

综上所述，通过探寻铜鼓的起源、分析“太阳纹”的形象，可以说明铜鼓上的“太阳纹”实为火纹。这种火纹寓意着先民求强富足兴旺的美好愿望，承载了先民的审美理想与精神追求。

早期铜鼓与巫觋

Wizards and Early Bronze Drums

李晓帆 / 昆明市博物馆 副研究员

[摘要]

铜鼓因被赋予神力而受人们所尊崇，成为巫觋手中专用的法器，被其使用和占有。另一方面铜鼓在被巫觋使用过程中历经改造、创新并得到衍生。在此过程中，铜鼓或铜鼓形器物也为我们记录和展现了巫觋在宗教祭祀巫术礼仪中承担的角色，享有的权力及地位。本文试图发现并揭示铜鼓与巫觋之间的这种密不可分的联系和影响。

[关键词]

铜鼓 巫觋 法器 衍生

Abstract

The bronze drums considered sacred are wizards special instruments. In ancient, wizards are usually tribal chief, so bronze drums are regarded as power and divine. The possessions and using bronze drums symbolize the wizards have power to control the tribal possession of wealth and status.

The bronze drums have function to communication with the god. With increasing these functions, the wizards also gradually decorate many specific designs, such as the sun, bird, all kinds of activities design, frog on the bronze drums.

The early bronze drums derive a lot of bronze artifacts forms.

These artifacts can be divided into two types: one kind is directly modified or counterfeit bronze drums. Another kind is absorbing the drum's shape as modeling elements.

Two types are used limited, such as special devices on sacrifice activities, or special implements for dead wizard.

Bronze drums are the most distinctive artifacts in ancient Dian bronze culture. In this period, the influence of wizard culture through to the people's life, the product and social ideology. Early bronze culture characteristic of showing is the wizard culture.

Key words

Bronze drum; Wizards; Religious instrument; Derivation

关于铜鼓起源、族属、年代、分布、类型等方面的研究，诸多学者多年潜心研究，大体给我们建立起一个对铜鼓认识的基本框架。按照中国古代铜鼓研究会提出的“八分法”，分布在我国西南部、南部及东南亚地区的越南、老挝、缅甸、泰国等地的铜鼓可以分为或对照为万家坝型、石寨山型、冷水冲型、遵义型、麻江型、北流型、灵山型、西盟型八个类型。本文所探讨的早期铜鼓界定为春秋战国至西汉晚期的万家坝型和石寨山型，这一时期既是铜鼓的起源期，也是铜鼓发展史上的第一个鼎盛时期。

一

铜鼓是巫觋的神物和法器

中国古代文献中对铜鼓最早的文字记载见春秋时期典籍《世本》。《世本》曰：“巫咸作铜鼓”，“巫咸，古神巫也”。在最早的记载中就显示出铜鼓与巫的关系，这对我们研究铜鼓的用途和功能提供了最初的依据。对于铜鼓的用途和功能，中外学者都有很多相关论著，总结如下：用以演奏的乐器，赛神或娱神工具，用以传信的工具以及作为地位和权利象征[①]。笔者则认为在“国之大事，在祀与戎”的古滇社会，铜鼓是由某些扮演特定角色的人创造、使用、占有的，这些人被称为巫觋。《说文》曰“觋，能斋肃事神明也。在男曰觋，在女曰巫。”合称“巫觋”。巫觋是原始部族中被认为能沟通天与地、人与神的使者。她（他）们被赋予超自然的能量，能施巫，与神灵沟通。为逃避或解除神灵的惩罚和祸害，释放心中崇拜敬畏的心理，取悦神灵，获得福佑，巫觋创造许多繁杂的祭祀礼仪巫术活动仪式，包括占卜、祈祷、祭祀、歌舞等。在进行祭祀礼仪巫术活动时，巫觋需要借助一些神物通达神灵。铜鼓就是被巫觋创造、使用，并不断改造的进行祭祀礼仪巫术活动的神物和专用法器。

在远古的氏族社会和部落联盟时期，军权神权往往集巫觋于一身，巫觋通常也是部落头人或联邦酋长，所以铜鼓也被视为礼仪重器和神物，对铜鼓的拥有和使用象征着对氏族部落统治权力的掌控、地位财富的占有。如果失掉铜鼓，意味着统治地位的丧失，而缴获对方的铜鼓，则作为胜利的象征。这些含义在后来仍有遗留。如《隋书·地理志》：“有鼓者，号为都老，群情推服。”唐代刘恂的《岭表录异》中有：“南蛮酋首之家皆有此鼓。”

铜鼓被巫觋当作法器使用，是因为巫觋认识到铜鼓具有通神的功能。通过对铜鼓鼓面部位的锤击或拍打，铜鼓能发出浑厚庄重悠远的声音，鼓音穿透力极强，能穿越重重障碍传递到很远的地方。所以在祭祀礼仪巫术活动开始之初，巫觋会借助

① 云南省博物馆：《云南晋宁石寨山古墓群发掘报告》，文物出版社，1959年。以下例举的材料出处同此，引自该报告。

铜鼓发出的悠扬鼓音，通告神灵，祭祀仪式即将开始。晋宁石寨山1号墓出土的祭祀场面鼓形贮贝器（M1：57）[①]，盖顶圆雕52个人物，形态各异，中央为1柱，柱身上缠绕2巨蛇，柱两侧各立1大铜鼓。巫觋通过柱两侧硕大铜鼓将祭祀活动通达神灵。在铜鼓被赋予神性的同时，铜鼓被首先作为神灵的象征，崇拜祭祀的对象出现在祭祀场景中，如晋宁石寨山20号墓出土的杀人祭铜鼓贮贝器（M20：1），三重叠垒成的铜鼓柱状物就是古滇先民的祭祀对象。

巫觋为增强铜鼓通神的能力，还逐渐地在铜鼓上装饰了许多特定的纹饰和图案，增强铜鼓作为法器的那种庄重而神秘的色彩。这种现象在万家坝型铜鼓上只表现为鼓面太阳纹的装饰。而在石寨山型铜鼓上这种装饰则极为丰富多彩，有太阳纹、鸟纹的装饰，各类祭祀礼仪巫术活动场景的表现，甚至鼓面还铸造有立体青蛙。这些特有纹饰图案圆雕造型的出现并非只是为器物装饰的美观，更深层次的原因是和铜鼓被作为巫觋通神的法器有关，装饰各种纹饰和图案都是为强化铜鼓的通神能力，体现祭祀法器的神秘、庄重、神圣。就以下几种铜鼓上常见纹饰或图案为例，来解读当时巫觋意识层面上的认识和考虑。

太阳纹：是铜鼓鼓面上最早出现的纹饰。太阳是世间万物生长的根本，对太阳的顶礼膜拜是不分地区、不分民族早已达成的共识。在全世界范围内我们都可以看到，原始信仰中很早就有对太阳、太阳神的崇拜和祭祀，而且这种崇拜一直保留在人们的意识形态中。这与为什么铜鼓鼓面中心一直保持太阳纹装饰不无关系。铜鼓鼓面上的太阳纹，一方面体现出人们对于太阳的崇拜和敬仰，另一方面，铜鼓的使用者——巫觋试图通过铜鼓告知太阳神灵，所有的祭祀礼仪巫术活动是以对太阳的崇拜为中心和根本的，并试图获得太阳神灵的许可而进行的。由于以上的原因，太阳纹虽因时代不同、地域不同，在形式上光体和芒有所差别，但它被作为铜鼓鼓面中心唯一纹饰一直无法取代，影响到后来的铜鼓直至现在。

鸟纹：鸟因能展翅高飞，接近太阳，到达人所不及的天空被认为具有沟通神灵的作用，被视为神物。在滇文化青铜器物之上，鸟的形象常被使用，如鸡、鹰、雉、鹈鹕、孔雀、鸳鸯、鹦鹉、翔鹭、水鸟、大雁等，这些形象的使用不仅仅为装饰目的，而是器物的使用者希望借鸟通神的灵性增强自身的神力。如滇文化显示出来的巫觋形象多为头戴各式羽冠，或背插羽翎，或手持羽翎。巫觋所使用铜臂甲、铜头盔、漆箭箙等器物上也装饰有孔雀、雉等形象。巫觋使用的漆质仪仗器的曲柄上，也装饰有鸟眼纹饰，整个器物形状为鸟首[②]。

铜鼓鼓面太阳纹外装饰的翔鹭纹最早出现在石寨山类型早期的铜鼓之上。这种纹饰的启用应该是受到中原及楚文化的影响。《诗经》中有翔鹭和鼓的相关记载；考古发掘的楚墓发现有翔鹭装饰的鼓架。除了翔鹭作为神物之外，它们还被认为是一种很有秩序的典范，它们列队飞行，小不逾大[③]。在铜鼓鼓面上的围绕太阳纹的逆

① 云南省博物馆：《云南晋宁石寨山古墓群发掘报告》，文物出版社，1959年。以下例举的材料出处同此，引自该报告。

② 云南省文物考古研究所等：《昆明羊甫头墓地》，科学出版社，2005年。以下例举的材料出处同此，引自该报告。

③ 王大道：《云南铜鼓》，云南教育出版社，1986年。

时针盘旋翔鹭常见的有4只，多达10余只。

铜鼓胸部、胴部（腰部）多装饰有各类船纹场景，其中船首和船纹也常装饰有鸟形图案。这种装饰于铜鼓船首之鸟是“鹢鸟”。《淮南子·本经训》高诱注：“鹢，大鸟也，画其像于船头”。以鹢鸟饰舟，目的在于“厌水神”、“惧江神”，以确保行船安全。“鹢首”一词在汉代甚至成为船舟之代称[①]。鹢鸟就是一种像鹭鸶的水鸟，能高飞。笔者推测铜鼓鼓面所绘的翔鹭也是鹢鸟。这些以鹢首装饰的船舟是巫觋用作祭龙神祈雨、祭河神保平安、祭亡灵或节日庆典娱神竞赛的专用舟船[②]。

各类活动场面图案：作为巫觋的专用法器，铜鼓的胸部、胴部（腰部）作为载体，记录保存有巫觋的形象或巫觋主持的各类祭祀礼仪巫术活动场景的图案。如晋宁石寨山13号墓出土的1件铜鼓（M13：3）胴部（腰部）刻划的巫觋形象，巫觋头饰复杂，戴兜鍪，顶端置三旄牛尾，两侧饰羽翎，身着甲片缀成的铜铠，双手持弓。更为常见的是出现在铜鼓胸部或胴部（腰部）巫觋主持各类祭祀礼仪巫术活动场景的图案，此类图案通常表现的是盛装装扮的巫觋，或头戴羽冠，或身披带尾兽皮，手持羽翎或兵器，进行祭祀仪式、娱神活动的场面。其中巫觋装扮成羽人在舟船上进行的祭祀娱神活动最为常见。《楚辞集注》载“昔楚南郢之邑，沅、湘之间，其俗信鬼而好祀。其祀必使巫觋作乐，歌舞以娱神。”娱神活动是巫觋祭祀仪式中的重要组成部分。通过铜鼓为载体记录下来可辨识的祭祀娱神活动有很多，多以乐舞或竞技的形式表现出来。从内容上我们看到的有祭神乐舞、祭祖乐舞、祈神活动等。就乐舞而言，根据舞者所持物品和装扮的不同，学者将其分做羽舞、旄舞、人舞、干舞、葫芦笙舞、翔鹭舞、圆圈舞、巫舞、刑牛舞等[③]。以竞技形式出现的娱神活动多见龙舟竞渡。

立蛙装饰：石寨山型铜鼓已出现立体青蛙。如晋宁石寨山M10：3铜鼓鼓面边沿立有四只青蛙，有的学者也称其为蟾蜍。因蛙能知天时，蛙鸣便有霖雨，故青蛙被视为通达雷神的神物。铜鼓用作祭祀礼仪巫术等活动，鼓面上立蛙，与祈雨、求雨、祈求风调雨顺有关。立蛙装饰更多地被冷水冲型铜鼓继承和发展，到西盟型铜鼓上还有出现两三只青蛙垒蹲装饰，其涵义是祈求蛙多雨大。

二

铜鼓形器物的衍生和使用

在石寨山型铜鼓盛行的同时，衍生出许多铜鼓形器物。这些衍生出来的铜鼓形器物可分为两种类型：一类是直接改造或仿造成形铜鼓而产生的器物。此类器物仅见铜鼓形贮贝器、叠鼓形贮贝器。另一类则汲取铜鼓形状作为器物造型的元素，或

① 李昆声、黄德荣：《中国与东南亚的古代铜鼓》，云南美术出版社，2009年。

② 李晓帆：《古滇巫觋初探》，《中华历史文化探源——云南抚仙湖与世界文明学术研讨会论文集》，云南人民出版社，2012年。

③ 李昆声：《云南青铜时代的音乐、舞蹈和杂技》，《云南省博物馆建馆五十周年论文集》，云南教育出版社，2001年。

图一　漆木女巫形象（羊甫头M113：381）

独立成形，如用金、银、玛瑙、绿松石制成的装饰品等鼓形器；或保持铜鼓基本形态将其融入某一器物造型中，使铜鼓形成器物的一部分，如铜杖头，基本上杖头底座都为铜鼓。有的器物銎口设计成铜鼓状，有的底部为铜鼓座，有的顶部或器盖为铜鼓形，有的将铜鼓的形状设计为器足。

通过对衍生器物器形、工艺、装饰、功能及出土情况的分析，笔者认为，两种衍生铜鼓形器物的使用是有所限制的，常人不能随意使用，它们的使用是局限在一定的人群范围内，即巫觋和具有巫觋身份的人才能使用。大量出现如此多带有铜鼓元素的器物，究其原因，是与当时巫术之风盛行、巫觋身份地位较高有很大关系。巫觋掌控着世俗社会中的财富和权利，也是人们精神世界的领袖。他（她）们不仅仅用占有财富的多寡来显示自己的实力，同时他（她）们也需要用一些独特元素、特殊物品以及其中的特定内涵来彰显自己特殊身份与地位。被赋予神力的铜鼓所展现出的神圣和庄重，是甄别巫觋地位身份最好的符号和元素。因此铜鼓形衍生器物是巫觋和具有巫觋身份的人的专属器。这一推断在考古发掘出土器物中可以得到证实，如用金、银、玉、玛瑙、绿松石制成的铜鼓形饰件多为墓主人衣物上的装饰，此类墓葬均是滇文化中的大型墓葬。在滇文化出土器物中我们还可以看到，巫觋的形象出现时，多有铜鼓相伴。昆明羊甫头113号墓（M113：381）出土的漆木女巫，女巫跪坐1铜鼓之上，头顶1小鼓（图一），而呈贡天子庙出土的巫师鼎上巫觋足下端铸成铜鼓形①。

衍生的铜鼓形器物或是巫觋的专用法器，或是特意为巫觋和具有巫觋身份的人特制的器物，普通人不得随意使用。以象征着权力和地位的巫觋专用法器——杖为例，云南祥云大波那铜棺墓中出土的铜杖被论定为权杖②。滇文化出土的杖均出土自

① 昆明市文物管理委员会：《呈贡天子庙滇墓》，《考古》1985年第4期。

② 梁晓强：《云南祥云战国木椁铜棺墓墓主族属与身份》，《三星堆与南方丝绸之路青铜文化研讨会论文集》，文物出版社，2007年。

图二　李家山出土铜贮贝器上的纺织场景

随葬器物丰富的大墓中，杖首多为铜质，也偶见木质杖首，如昆明羊甫头113号墓中见漆木杖首。杖首多作动物、人物圆雕造型，其下多作铜鼓形圆銎，下装木柄。

另外带有铜鼓形造型元素的器物，还有剑、矛、戈、凿、钺、啄、壶、狼牙棒等，铜鼓形元素的运用或见器物的銎部、口部、器盖等，这些器物上往往有精美、细致、奢华的装饰图案或人物、动物圆雕造型。从制作工艺和用途上分析，此类器物已经不具备原本器物的实用功能，应为巫觋祭祀等活动所使用的专用礼器，或为逝去巫觋特制的陪葬器物。

在滇文化中可看到铜鼓有被人踞坐的用途，从而有的学者认为铜鼓被人们当做凳子使用，其使用功能显示出世俗化趋势。然而仔细观察和分析，这种现象的出现有以下两种情况：一是身为巫觋或巫觋身份的人踞坐于铜鼓之上。如李家山M69：139铜贮贝器纺织场景①（图二），器物表面中部为一鎏金女性踞坐于铜鼓之上，周围女性或纺线织布，或持伞，或侍奉。踞坐在铜鼓上的女性地位显赫，为格外突出其身份，将其表面鎏金。推测该女子是执掌纺织、农作生产祭祀权力的巫觋。在古滇祭祀仪式中，女巫较男觋更为常见，这一点我们可以从出土的滇文化器物上得到证实。许多祭祀仪式，如祭农、祭鼓、祭柱等仪式，主持者、主祭者往往为女巫②。这些女巫除祭祀之外，还负责监督纺线织布等手工劳作，掌控氏族部落衣食供给的权力。另外在铜杖上，也可以看到巫觋踞坐铜鼓的现象。有的巫觋面目狰狞，圆目龇牙，甚至装有獠牙，很容易识别，有的则是尊容华贵的女巫形象。二是有持伞铜俑踞坐在铜鼓上的现象，这些持伞俑有男俑和女俑，男俑为男主人持伞，女俑为女主人持伞。而端坐在伞下的主人也被多数学者认为是巫觋，这种伞的

① 云南省文物考古研究所：《江川李家山第二次发掘报告》，文物出版社，2007年。以下例举的材料出处同此，引自该报告。

② 李晓帆：《古滇巫觋初探》，《中华历史文化探源——云南抚仙湖与世界文明学术研讨会论文集》，云南人民出版社，2012年。

使用功能一直受到学者的关注，这种伞被认为有两个功能：一为招魂，二有其实用功能，即遮阴，但使用者的身份地位都很高。从持伞男女俑的衣着、头饰和配剑上看，有的学者认为持伞的铜俑形象就是墓主人本人的形象[①]。而笔者则推测这些俑平时作为巫觋的贴身随从照顾巫觋的饮食起居，在巫觋进行祭祀仪式巫术活动时作为巫觋的助手。这里我们暂不讨论以上推断的对错，但很明显的是这些都与巫觋有关，除此之外，常人是不得踞坐铜鼓之上的。另外在铜鼓形贮贝器或桶形贮贝器上还见铜牛站立鼓上的圆雕造型，如李家山M47：23，这里的牛是供奉给巫觋的，牛在滇文化中是财富的象征。

铜鼓形贮贝器是滇文化墓葬中极具文化特色的器物，是铜鼓形衍生器中最奢华、最有分量的器物。铜鼓形贮贝器器形大，设计考量，制作精湛，工艺复杂，器物的纹饰和各类圆雕表现出宏大的场景、叙述出完整的故事，展现的人物形态各异，精雕细琢，无一雷同。每件器物都是独一无二的精品。这类器物仅见晋宁石寨山和江川李家山大型墓中，目前共出土10余件，有单鼓形、叠鼓形两种。单鼓形整体形状与铜鼓相差无几，有的在铜鼓底部铸有器足。叠鼓形贮贝器有两种叠垒方式，一种鼓一大一小，小鼓底置大鼓面上。另一种两鼓大小相差无几，底底相对。其墓主人的身份多被发掘者确定为巫师（即巫觋）。笔者认为出土的铜鼓形贮贝器是为身为巫觋的墓主人特制的随葬器物。如江川李家山69号墓出土的播种祭祀场面鼓形铜贮贝器（M69：157），整个器物为铜鼓形，鼓面铸成器盖。盖上铸立体圆雕人物35个，马2匹，盖中央有1圆孔，穿孔立1圆柱，柱顶为圆盘状，柱身装饰云雷纹、虎皮纹、兽皮纹，柱底为铜鼓形。中心人物是1乘舆的女性，发作银锭髻，穿长衣，双手垂膝。该女性通体鎏金，身后有持伞侍者，舆为四人肩抬。舆前、后、左、右，有扛长柄铲者、持点种棒者、背种袋者、头顶薪者、持圆盒者、抱罐者、捧物者、持葫芦者、提竹篮者、持布者、跪拜者、行礼者等，这些人是携带着播种祭祀仪式所需的物品前来参与祭祀仪式的。坐于舆内的女性，就是祭祀仪式的主祭女巫。器物盖上雕铸的场景应是女巫生前主持祭祀仪式活动的真实写照。也有的铜鼓形贮贝器是通过铜鼓鼓面中心或胸部、胴部（腰部）平面图案来记录和纪念巫觋生前参与或主持的活动及仪式，常见的多为祭农的各种仪式或舞蹈，如播种图、报祭图、上仓图等。在笔者看来，将这些重要的场景记录保存在被视为神物的特制铜鼓上，是古滇先民的有意识的行为，也是对作为巫觋身份的墓主人最持久的纪念和敬仰。铜鼓形贮贝器在石寨山型铜鼓时期极度盛行，也向我们表明当时巫觋在社会中极高的社会地位和社会影响。

① 黄德荣：《持伞俑考》，《中华历史文化探源——云南抚仙湖与世界文明学术研讨会论文集》，云南人民出版社，2012年。

三

结 语

早期铜鼓起源于春秋战国，兴盛在西汉时期，是极具地方特色和民族特色的器物，在古滇青铜文化中占据着极其重要的地位。对铜鼓的研究，一直以来都是从事青铜文化研究的重要课题。我们在对铜鼓本身进行研究的同时，也不妨另辟蹊径，从铜鼓背后的创造者、使用者、拥有者身上找到彼此之间的联系和相互的影响，从而来解释一些我们尚未找到答案的问题。

早期铜鼓的创造、使用和发展历经上千年，这与古滇青铜文化出现、发展、步入鼎盛的时期是相重合的。铜鼓被认为是古滇青铜文化中最具特色的器物。我们不难发现，铜鼓从被认为的神物、人们崇拜的对象、巫觋手中的法器、祭祀的礼器重器、财富和地位的象征，经历着使用流行地域族群文化因素的融入而变化发展。然而抛开地域和族群文化因素的影响，就铜鼓本身器形的变化、发展以及铜鼓形衍生器物的出现是受到使用地区特定族群原始巫术意识的影响，更具体地说，是受到传递这些宗教意识的巫觋群体的影响。这一时期，巫觋文化的影响渗透到人们生活、生产的各个领域及社会意识形态的方方面面。早期铜鼓所展现出的文化特色正是古滇时期巫觋文化特色。通过对铜鼓的研究我们也可以更加明晰，在巫术较为盛行的古滇社会，巫觋是身份地位最为显赫的人群，他（她）们占据着氏族部落中的绝大多数财富，是人们权威的精神领袖，同时也是某一特定文化（巫觋文化）的传承者。

越南出土的万家坝类型铜鼓

Wanjiaba-style Bronze Drums Excavated in Vietnam

阮文好 / 越南考古研究院 研究员

[摘要]

本文通过对越南发现的16面万家坝型铜鼓进行描述、分析等研究，提出了可分5个不同式别，指出铜鼓的年代大致从前4世纪至1世纪，探讨了铜鼓的来源，认为越南发现的万家坝型铜鼓与东山铜鼓是平行的，但和东山铜鼓没有根源关系。

[关键词]

越南　万家坝型铜鼓　式别　年代　来源

Abstract

The thesis aims at analyzing the 16 Wanjiaba bronze drums found in Vietnam, divides them into five different categories and points out that the existence of bronze drums lasts from 4th century B.C. to 1st century A.D. The paper researches the origin of bronze drums and draws a conclusion that these Wanjiaba bronze drums are parallel to Dongshan drum but has no internal relationship with it.

Key words

Vietnam; Wanjiaba-type bronze drum; Categories; Time; Source

自从1932年松林铜鼓出土时迄今为止，时间将近80年，和松林鼓相似的铜鼓在越南出土了16面。和东山铜鼓相比，此数字显得太悬殊。由于其型制及纹饰和中国云南省出土的万家坝型铜鼓是很相同的，笔者把它们列入万家坝类型铜鼓来研究。

一

万家坝型铜鼓在越南的发现和分布

在越南，万家坝型铜鼓已发现16面：其中有9面为出土物，分别为老街省2面、安沛省1面、富寿省2面、河内3面、清化省1面。另有7面铜鼓属传世品（据说也是在老街省、安沛省地带出土的）。现按其出土情况和铜鼓的造型、纹饰等方面资料，分别介绍如下。

（一）与其他类型铜鼓伴随出土的铜鼓（2面）

1. 老街11号铜鼓（93LC Ⅺ）[①]

1993年，在老街市红河岸边的1座水唱土丘中出土，伴出有3面其他类型铜鼓（编号为93LCⅧ，93LCⅨ，93LCⅩ）和1件大型铜釜。现藏于老街省博物馆。

鼓面中心已残失，胸和腰部残失了一半；胸部鼓突，腰部呈喇叭形，矮足，有2个对称单耳。面径45、高37厘米。鼓面中心为无芒太阳纹（一块圆饼形），腰部有22条竖线分格，腰部下边还饰2条阳纹圆圈；胸、足无纹。

2. 老街12号铜鼓（93LCⅫ）[②]

1993年，在老街市一座和水唱土丘接连的土丘上出土的，伴出有2面其他类型铜鼓（93LCⅦ和93LCⅥ），还有一些其他铜器（铜奁1件，铜瓯1件，托盘1件，大盆2件和残提梁2块）。现藏于老街省博物馆。

此鼓已残缺很严重，只残留鼓面与鼓胸一部分，鼓胸特大，其形状和倒置的铜釜相似。面径28厘米。

（二）有其他文物伴随出土的铜鼓（3面）

1. 陶舍鼓[③]

1978年，福寿省三清县陶舍社，在地表下0.5米深处出土。伴随出土有铜盆、铜碗、铜碟、五铢铜钱、银手镯、银戒指、玛瑙珠、铁矛、铁剑和一些陶、瓷器。出土时鼓面上还放着1把长铜剑。现藏越南国家历史博物馆。

该鼓面小，鼓胸突大，腰部呈喇叭形，足矮，两对绳纹耳。面径36、高26厘米。鼓面中心突出1块圆饼形的无芒太阳纹光体，共有5晕，第1、4晕为6条平行阳纹

①② 范明玄：《越南，红河上流的古代文明中心》，《考古学》，1992年。

③ 阮禄、阮文宣：《陶舍出土一批文物》，《考古新发现》，1978年。

线；第2晕为主晕，饰有大尾巴四足动物，作逆时针行走。第3、5晕为锯齿纹。鼓胸饰几何形纹，依稀可辨有锯齿纹，足部素面无纹。

2. 上农鼓[①]

1981年富寿省三清县上农社，在地表下1米处出土，伴出一些铜器，如方銎斧、钺等。现藏富寿省博物馆。

该鼓鼓面稍微凹下，胸鼓大，腰喇叭形，矮足，有1对绳纹耳。鼓面上有3个小孔，通体素面（图一）。

3. 马芫鼓[②]

2000年清化省绍化县绍军社军龟乡马芫田地中距地表下1米深处出土，伴出有2件青铜短剑。现藏清化省博物馆。

鼓面中心突出1块圆饼形的无芒太阳纹光体，鼓胸往上鼓，腰部呈喇叭形，饰12条阳纹复线分成格子，胸、足素面。矮足，有2对绳纹单耳。面径38.5、高29.5、足径44、胸高11.5、腰高15、足高3厘米。

（三）无伴出物的铜鼓（4面）

1. 松林1号鼓[③]

1932年5月，河山平省（今河内）章美县美梁社松林乡淞林寺附近的田地里，在距地表下0.5米深处发现。现藏越南国家历史博物馆。

鼓面中心太阳纹16芒，芒线长短不一，外边有2条小绳纹，芒外1晕，为变形曲折双线纹构成4个卷曲套叠的四边形回纹，外圈有辐射线纹。鼓胸无纹饰。鼓腰由斜线纹带纵分成格，每格有栏栅形纹，上下组成天窗。鼓足饰回形雷纹。小扁耳2对。鼓身有双合范缝线，器表粗糙，有气孔。鼓面有多处破洞，鼓身严重残缺。该鼓面径52、高36、胸径63.8、腰径46.3、足径71.8、壁厚0.3厘米，重68.2千克（图二）。

2. 松林2号鼓[④]

1973年，在河山平省（今河内）章美县美梁社松林乡淞林寺松林1号鼓附近出

图一　上农鼓（2011号）

图二　淞林1号鼓（5731号）

① 范明玄、阮长期:《上农铜鼓》，《考古新发现》，1979年。

② 裴代论:《在清化省出土的一面新东山铜鼓》，《考古学》，2001年。

③④ 范明玄、阮文宣、郑生:《东山铜鼓》，社会科学出版社，1978年。

① 阮文光：《安沛前史与初史》，社会科学出版社，2004年。

② 武卒幸、郑生：《初步研究海背铜鼓》，《考古新发现》，2007年。

③～⑥ 2010年，本文作者在参观由研究与保护文物的科学教育文化中心在河内博物馆举办展览时看到并记录。由于各种原因，未能记录到铜鼓的尺寸、大小及重量。

⑦ 团英俊、黄春征：《两面无纹饰铜鼓》，《考古新发现》，2006年。

土，现藏越南国家历史博物馆。

此鼓仅存鼓面和鼓胸。胸鼓突出，胸大于面径，鼓面中心为16芒太阳纹，共2晕，第1晕为回纹，第2晕为叶脉纹。胸部无纹饰，腰饰回纹一晕。面径38、胸径46厘米。

3. 戊东鼓①

2004年之前，在安沛省文安县成东地区出土。现藏安沛省博物馆。

鼓面中心为12（13？）芒太阳纹，外围饰回纹，胸部往上鼓，无纹饰。腰部呈喇叭形，腰上部以6条互套“V”字形纵纹分格，每格下边为中心一段纵线的锯齿纹，腰下部为回纹，足素面无纹。足矮，2对素面耳。面径43.5、高31.5、胸径62、足径70厘米。

4. 海背鼓②

2005年，河内市东英县海背社海背村调和湖地区出土。现藏河内市博物馆。

鼓面中心太阳纹23芒，外围为四条平行阳纹线，鼓面小于鼓胸，胸部突出且无纹饰；束腰呈喇叭形，腰上部饰复线角纹纵向分四格，格下边为人形纹。腰最下边为菱形回纹，足部稍微高无纹，四只单耳，耳面无纹（图三）。

（四）传世的万家坝类型铜鼓

在越南，万家坝类型传世铜鼓共有7面，出土地点不明，私人收藏（研究与保存古物的科学、教育、文化中心——UNESCO中心）。

1. 10u:1号鼓③

2010年在河内博物馆展出。面小于胸，胸鼓突，胸最大径在中部，胸径大于足径，腰成喇叭形，足矮，有两个素面单耳。通体素面（图四）。

2. 10u:2号鼓④

2010年在河内博物馆展出。环面，胸鼓突，胸径小于足径，腰呈喇叭形，足稍微高，有两个素面单耳。通体素面。

3. 10u:3号鼓⑤

2010年在河内博物馆展出。环面，鼓面小于鼓胸，鼓胸圆突，胸径小于足径，腰部呈喇叭形，腰与足交界处折斜外撇，有两只素面单耳。通体素面（图五）。

4. 10u:4号⑥

2010年在河内博物馆展出。鼓面特小，胸部突出于中部，胸上部有小孔，束腰，胸与足不区分，连接呈喇叭形，胸径小于足径，有两个素面单耳。通身素面（图六）。

5. 10u:5号⑦

2010年在河内博物馆展出。鼓面特小，面径等于胸径四分之一，胸不鼓而往外折一尖折角；胸径小于足径，腰与足没有区分，呈喇叭形，有一对素面单耳。通体素面（图七）。

图三　海背鼓

图四　10u：1号铜鼓

图五　10u：3号铜鼓

图六　10u：4号铜鼓

图七　10u：5号铜鼓

6. 06u:1号鼓[①]

2006年团英俊、黄春征在越南考古新发现会议上报告。

鼓面特小，胸部鼓突，腰与足没区分，呈喇叭形，2个素面单耳。通体素面。面径12、高25、足径31厘米。

7. 06u:2号鼓[②]

2006年团英俊、黄春征在越南考古新发现会议上报告。

鼓面特小，胸鼓突，腰与足没区分，呈喇叭形，2个素面单耳。通体素面。面径12、高28、胸径30、足径32厘米。

①② 团英俊、黄春征:《两面无纹饰铜鼓》，《考古新发现》，2006年。

二

分式和年代

从总体来看，16面铜鼓有着明显的特点：鼓面从特小到较小，胸部突出，腰部较短，呈喇叭形；初期，腰与足不区分，往后足从腰分出来成矮足，有1或2对素面单耳。此类铜鼓纹饰简单，鼓面饰太阳纹，但光芒数量不等，有的无光芒，仅有1块圆饼形光体。鼓身纹饰也很少，只有少量回纹、锯齿纹、点头栉纹、人形纹等。唯一的写实纹饰为蜥蜴之类的爬虫，尖头，四足，扇形尾巴……这些特征，在每面铜鼓上表现不一，这可能是由于发展的时间不同所引起。根据形制的演变及纹饰的发展，笔者把16面铜鼓初步分成五式：

Ⅰ式：1面（10u:5号鼓）。

釜形铜鼓，鼓面特别小，胸部不突而往外折，尖折角，腰短，腰与足不分，呈喇叭形，有2个对称素面单耳。通体光素无纹。属年代最早的一种铜鼓。

Ⅱ式：3面（10u:4、06u:1、06u:2）。

似釜形铜鼓，鼓面特小，胸突出，腰高，腰与足不分，呈喇叭形，有2个对称素面单耳。通体光素无纹。

Ⅲ式：3面（10u:2、10u:3、10u:1）。

鼓面扩大，胸部鼓突，腰高，喇叭形；足与腰有分别，有2个对称素面单耳。通体光素无纹。

Ⅳ式：2面（马芫鼓、上农鼓）。

鼓面扩大，胸部鼓突，腰部呈喇叭形，足矮，有2个对称素面单耳。有的鼓面有太阳纹。有的腰上有纵线分格。

Ⅴ式：7面（老街11、12号鼓，松林1、2号鼓，陶舍鼓，成东鼓、海背鼓）。

鼓面扩大，胸部不大突出，腰部呈喇叭形，足矮，有2个素面单耳。鼓面上有的有芒太阳纹，有的无芒太阳纹，只有1块圆饼形光体。鼓面上和鼓腰出现几何形纹饰和写实性纹。几何形纹饰母题主要是锯齿纹、点头栉纹、人形纹、回纹；写实性纹饰主要是生存在山林地区的四足动物形象。

这一批铜鼓年代，现在还没有^{14}C年代作根据，但有9面铜鼓有伴出物，可作为其年代推测的根据。

Ⅰ、Ⅱ、Ⅲ式铜鼓年代，大体是在前4世纪至前2世纪。

前4世纪至1世纪是越南此类铜鼓存在和发展的时间。

Ⅳ式铜鼓年代，属于此式的2面铜鼓都有伴出东山文化铜器，如方銎斧、钺，短

表一　越南万家坝型铜鼓分式及年代表

式别	鼓号	年代
Ⅰ式	10u:5	前4世纪至前2世纪
Ⅱ式	10u:4、06u:1、06u:2	
Ⅲ式	10u:1、10u:2、10u:3	
Ⅳ式	马芜（Ma Nguoi）鼓、上农鼓	前1世纪
Ⅴ式	老街11、12号鼓，松林1、2号鼓，陶舍鼓，成东鼓，海背鼓	1世纪

剑等，其年代应是前1世纪。

Ⅴ式铜鼓年代，老街11、12号鼓和陶舍鼓都有伴出器物，有铜器、银器、铁器、玛瑙珠，特别还有五铢钱等，是汉式器物，Ⅴ式铜鼓年代可能是1世纪。

综上所论，可以看到越南发现的16面万家坝型铜鼓，可分5式。年代从公元前到公元后，历时数千年。由此，可将其列入表一加以解读。

三

铜鼓埋藏之特点

此类铜鼓，埋藏时往往成对地埋在一起或附近，李昆声教授在《论万家坝型铜鼓》[①]就这样认定，在这里，16面铜鼓中也有两个对偶埋葬的例子：一是松林1、2号鼓，二是老街11、12号鼓。松林1号鼓与松林2号鼓被分别埋在同一个地点，相距大约500米，这两面铜鼓是一大一小的，是公母之别，现代越南倮倮族在使用铜鼓时也是大小成对来使用，这种配偶均是纯种铜鼓。通过这个例子，可以认为铜鼓公母之别是真的。

但老街11号鼓和老街12号鼓情况就不同。老街11号鼓与12号鼓是万家坝型铜鼓，它们分别在两座相近的土丘上埋藏，但每面铜鼓还和另外类型铜鼓埋藏在一起。老街11号鼓和3面别的类型铜鼓（老街8、9、10号鼓）埋在一起，老街12号鼓和2面别类型铜鼓（老街6、7号鼓）埋在一起。这些铜鼓类型代表着不同民族，不同文化，与老街两个万家坝型铜鼓是同时期、同年代的。它们之间大小有别，如和万家坝型铜鼓相配，使用时会有规律性的音阶。但此例是不是有确切的意义？这种情况在云南万家坝型铜鼓发源地还没发现过。

目前，越南出土的16面万家坝铜鼓，虽然是个很小的数字，但它们代表着越南万家坝型铜鼓发展过程中早晚不同的各个阶段。目前，这5个发展阶段的5式铜鼓，说明其和东山铜鼓是平行的，但和东山铜鼓没有根源关系，其晚期铜鼓和东山晚期铜鼓共出。

① 李昆声：《论万家坝型铜鼓》，《云南考古学论文集》，云南人民出版社，1998年。

中国广西和越南北部发现的黑格尔 Ⅰ型铜鼓的比较研究

A Comparison of Heger Type Ⅰ
Bronze Drums Found in North Vietnam and Guangxi China

郑　生／越南考古研究所 研究员

[摘要]

本文主要把中国广西西林、贵县、桂平、田东等地出土的黑格尔Ⅰ型铜鼓（石寨山型铜鼓），与越南北部玉缕、黄下、沱江、古螺、庙门、玻龙等地出土的同类铜鼓比较，发现两国出土的这些铜鼓，其铜质虽不同，但器形、纹饰却比较相似，表明中越两国以铜鼓为媒介的文化交流在两汉时期已经存在。

[关键词]

中国　越南　黑格尔Ⅰ型铜鼓　两汉时期　文化交流

Abstract

The thesis compares the Heger Ⅰ bronze drums unearthed in Xilin, Gui county, Guiping, Tiandong of Guangxi, China with the congeneric drums unearthed in Ngoc Lu, Hoang Ha, Song Da, Co Loa, Mieu Mon and Pha Long Research shows that the drums differ in bronze material but they have similar vessel shape and ornamentation, which proves the cultural exchange based on bronze drums between China and Vietnam exists in Han dynasty.

Key words

China; Vietnam; Heger Type Ⅰ Bronze Drum; Han dynasty; Cultural exchange

1902年，黑格尔（F. Heger）将其发现的铜鼓分成四大类，分别是：黑格尔Ⅰ型、黑格尔Ⅱ型、黑格尔Ⅲ型和黑格尔Ⅳ型。黑格尔Ⅰ型铜鼓主要分布在中国的南部、老挝、泰国、柬埔寨、马来西亚和印度尼西亚。发现的黑格尔Ⅰ型铜鼓的年代大致为前500年到200年。

在中国南部和越南，黑格尔Ⅰ型铜鼓主要分布区域有两处：越南北部的东山文化地区以及中国云南的石寨山文化地区。总的来说，东山型铜鼓和石寨山型铜鼓在外形上相似，但在细部装饰图案上就有所区别了。

在广西，中国考古学家们也发现了黑格尔Ⅰ型铜鼓，其中有部分是出土的。它们可以帮助我们将古代广西以及广西周边地区历史文化全貌展示在世人眼前。在广西发现的黑格尔Ⅰ型铜鼓，还可以帮助我们了解它们的年代以及反映出广西与其他地区之间不同的文化交流，例如云南、贵州、广东还有越南北部。

在本文里，作者试图类比研究广西和越南北部出土的同类型铜鼓。

许多黑格尔Ⅰ型铜鼓出土于广西壮族自治区发现的几座墓葬之中：

（一）1972年7月，在广西西林县的普驮乡1座墓葬中出土了4面铜鼓

在西林，一座墓葬中就发现了4面铜鼓（图一）。这是1座二次葬墓，其中的棺具就是那4面铜鼓。墓里和墓外的土层中埋葬着超过400件的随葬品，而人类的尸骨则是埋葬在铜鼓之中。中国考古专家认为这座墓葬的年代应该是西汉早期（前206～8年）。

这4面黑格尔Ⅰ型铜鼓与越南北部几个地方发现的铜鼓相似，像是玉缕、黄下、沱江、古螺、庙门还有玻龙（图二）。我们将这些地方发现的铜鼓与西林出土的这4面铜鼓上的图形比较后发现：

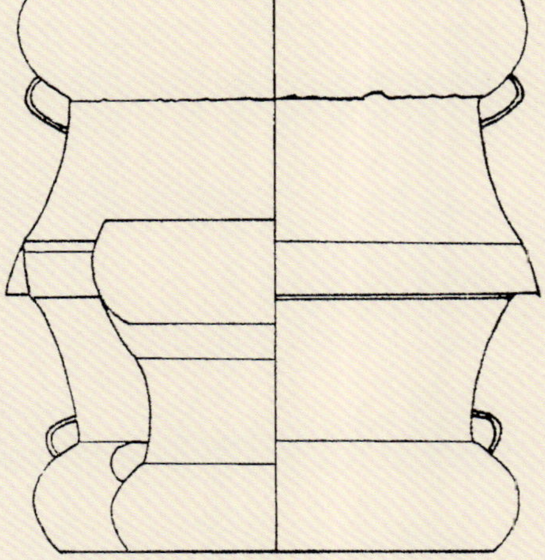

图一　广西西林普驮铜鼓葬式图

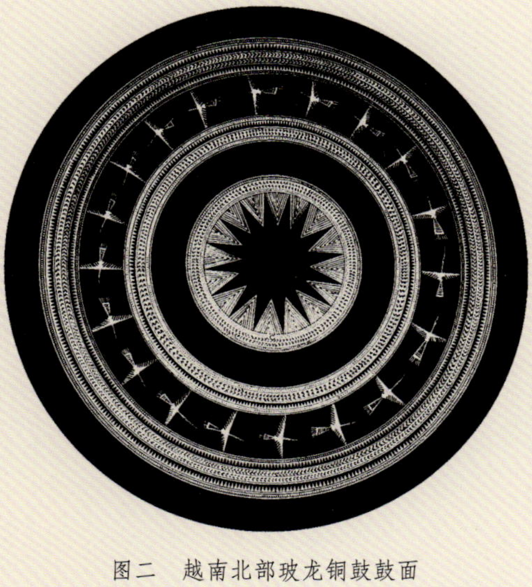

图二　越南北部玻龙铜鼓鼓面

西林铜鼓鼓面上装饰的鹭鸟纹与玻龙铜鼓上的鹭鸟纹相似，而羽人纹则与玉缕铜鼓上的羽人纹相似。特别的是，西林铜鼓上的鹿纹是包含母鹿、公鹿各1只，这与玉缕铜鼓还有庙门铜鼓上的鹿纹是一致的。西林铜鼓上半部分的划船纹和鱼纹则与部分玉缕铜鼓还有古螺铜鼓上的纹饰相似（图三）。

在对西林铜鼓进行研究的时候，洪声曾说过：西林铜鼓应该属于C类铜鼓，也就是说西林铜鼓出现得更晚一些，并且西林铜鼓应该比像Kham Chau铜鼓和Hop Pho铜鼓这类的A类铜鼓出现得更晚（黑格尔Ⅱ型），同样也比龙州和南宁出土的B型铜鼓出现得更晚（黑格尔Ⅱ型）。我们将西林铜鼓上的装饰纹饰进行分析，认为西林铜鼓、C型铜鼓（黑格尔Ⅰ型）和玉缕铜鼓以及古螺铜鼓的年代都比广西发现的黑格尔Ⅱ型（是指洪声所说的A、B型铜鼓）要早。

（二）在贵县西江流域出土的一号墓中发现了3面铜鼓[①]

在广西贵县出土的罗泊湾汉墓1号墓中，出土了3面铜鼓。M1:10号铜鼓装精美，鼓面上装饰的鹭鸟纹、划船纹还有羽人纹与越南北部的庙门以及Vu Bi出土的黑格尔Ⅰ型铜鼓上的装饰纹饰相似（图四）。

M1:11号铜鼓上装饰的划船纹和羽人纹与越南北部的Lang Vac和Quang Chinh出土的黑格尔Ⅰ型铜鼓上的装饰纹饰相似。

M1:13号铜鼓在铸好后就被毁坏，只有古人曾一睹它完整的面容。M1:13号铜鼓在铸好后被切割做成1面铜盘。铜盘的底部就是原本铜鼓的鼓面，有4只鹭鸟，与鼓面接合处作马蹄形铜足（图五）。M1:13号铜鼓的鼓面装饰的鹭鸟纹与越南北部的富维、Yen Tap和庙门出土的铜鼓上的装饰纹饰相同。

① 广西壮族自治区博物馆：《广西贵县罗泊湾汉墓》，文物出版社，1978年，25～34页。

图三　广西西林铜鼓与越南庙门铜鼓纹饰对比

图四　广西罗泊湾M1:10铜鼓与越南庙门铜鼓纹饰对比

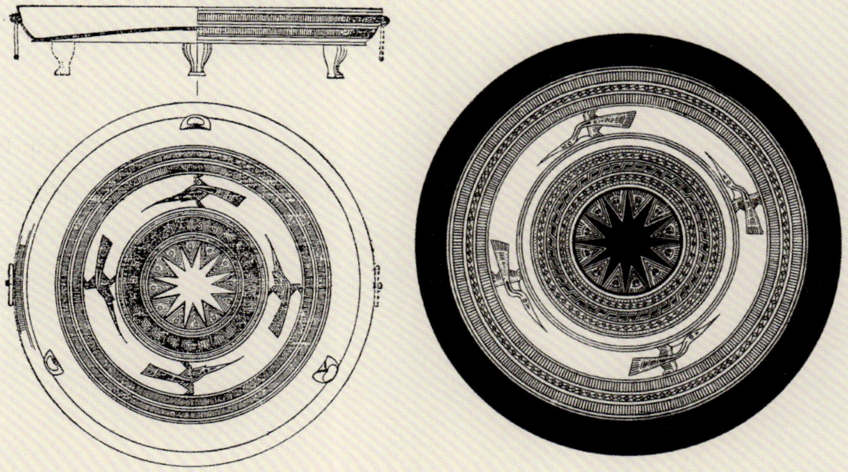

图五 三足案上的花纹与越南富维铜鼓面纹饰对比

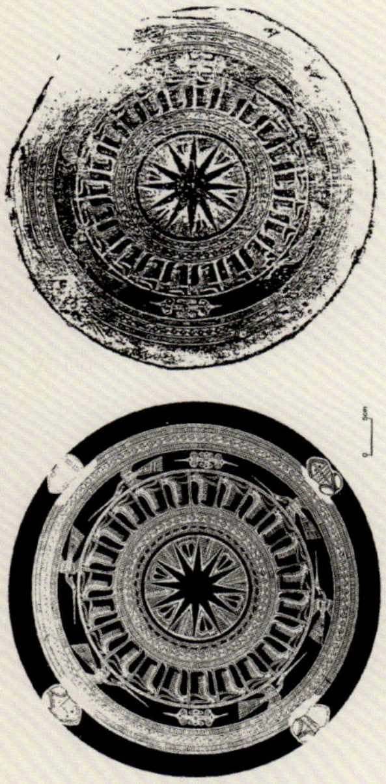

图六 广西桂平理村铜鼓与越南Da But铜鼓面上纹饰对比

对M1:10号铜鼓的合金成分分析发现，其主要成分是铜合金（其中含铜90.89%，锡11.5%）。M1:11号铜鼓同样也含有铜合金（其中含铜86.3%，锡14.5%）①。这些成分分析结果与越南北部出土的铜鼓的成分分析结果不同，主要是因为罗泊湾汉墓的铜鼓并不含有铅，而绝大多数的东山铜鼓中都含有铜、锡、铅。这是一个有趣的现象。

① 中国古代铜鼓研究会：《中国古代铜鼓》，文物出版社，1988年，184页。

（三）贵县铜鼓于1955年出土于广西贵县8号墓

除了前面提到的那些铜鼓之外，在广西桂平县（金田理村）还发现了1面铜鼓，而这面铜鼓与越南北部的NongGong、Da But 发现的铜鼓非常相似（图六）。这些铜鼓上的装饰纹饰以羽人纹、鹭鸟纹、花纹和几何纹为主。

将这9面铜鼓、在理村发现的铜鼓与在越南北部东山文化地区发现的铜鼓相比较，我们发现它们在装饰纹饰和形制上大体相同，我们推测中国的广西和越南北部的大部分地区在古代曾有过较为广泛的文化交流。除此之外，两个国家（特指广西和越南北部）在铜鼓的铸造方面也有很多相似之处，包括成分、和陶范模具等。

我们可以假设，两个地区在古代可能主要是通过水路或海路来进行文化交流。早在石器时代，广西的古人类和越南北部的古人类就已经开始文化交流了，并一直持续到青铜时代。在广西和越南北部发现的这些黑格尔Ⅰ型铜鼓所拥有的相似之处为我们证实了它们之间的密切联系。这样以铜鼓为媒介的文化交流应该在西汉至东汉时期就已经存在了。

老挝铜鼓的发现与研究

Discovery and Research on Bronze Drums in Laos

玛莱湾・考本玛 / 老挝国家博物馆 教授

[摘要]

本文主要对老挝沙湾拿吉省东帮矿山出土的大铜鼓进行描述，并介绍老挝国家博物馆收藏的部分铜鼓，探讨了铜鼓的保护与展示的设想。

[关键词]

老挝铜鼓　发现　研究

Abstract

This paper focuses on description to the bronze drum recovered from Xepon Mining Site in Savannakhet Province, Laos, and introduction to some part of bronze drums from the collection of the Lao National Museum, as well as the conception of their Conservation and display.

Key words

Bronze drums in Laos; Discovery; Research

一

老挝铜鼓

2008年1月，在老挝共和国沙湾拿吉省湄公河流域（南康河）附近的东帮矿山埋雷区一次常规扫雷行动中，挖掘出1枚金属物体。经探查发现这枚金属物体并不符合炸弹的一般形状。据考证，这是一面铜鼓，并且是老挝目前发现最大、最为完整的铜鼓之一。面径90、通高75厘米。鼓面太阳纹12芒，芒间翎眼纹，晕圈及纹饰模糊不清，锈蚀严重，依稀可辨的纹饰有勾连雷纹、同心圆圈圆点纹、鹭纹等，鼓面边缘为4个立蛙塑像，蛙头朝外股朝内。鼓面靠近太阳纹处有用铜线修补痕，铜钉17个，鼓胸饰两道锯齿纹间勾连雷纹、6只船纹（船上站立羽舞人、船下为大鸟）、游鱼等纹饰，鼓腰饰竖列切线同心圆点加锯齿纹夹勾连雷纹形，与横列切线同心圆点夹长尾动物构成横带，并分成8格，每格填入羽舞人。鼓腰下部饰7道纹饰，二弦分晕，第1、3、5、7晕为切线同心圆圈纹，第2、6晕为锯齿纹，第4晕为勾连雷纹。足部复线角纹。腰与足交接处用铜条外钉修补（图一～图六）。船纹表明铜鼓原本的主人与水有着重要的联系。通过对以上图案的分析，这面铜鼓反映出的很可能是东山人或类似东山当代社会文化。和在越南及中国其他铜鼓的出土方式一样，发现这面铜鼓的时候，它的位置是上下颠倒的。同时，与之相关的文物和这面铜鼓埋在一起。据此我们猜测，在历史上的某一时期，为了可以安全地保存这面铜鼓而将它藏于这个地方。围绕这面铜鼓的其他

图一　老挝最大铜鼓

图二　老挝最大铜鼓鼓面

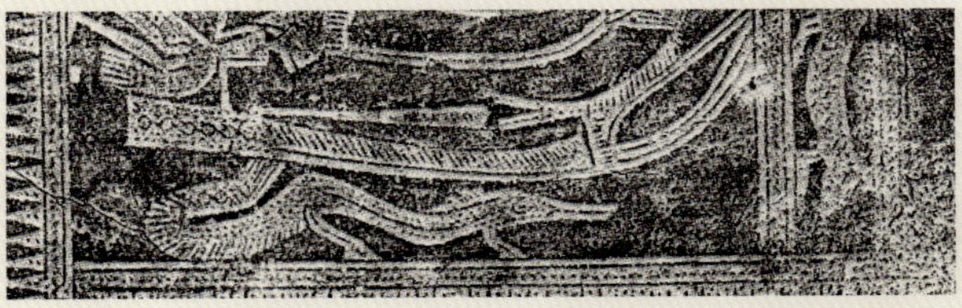

图三　老挝最大铜鼓鼓腰花纹——长尾兽（鳄鱼？）

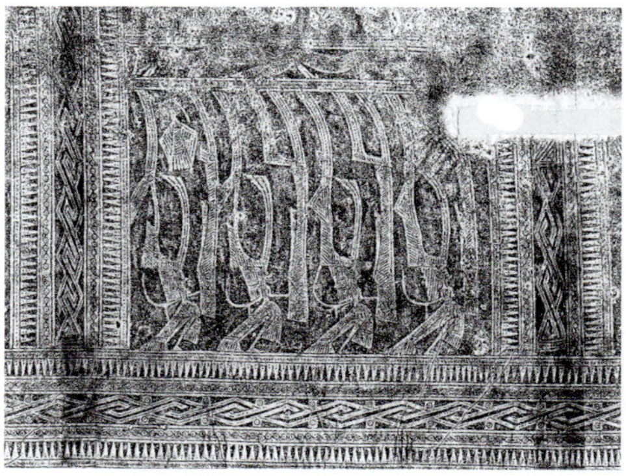

图四 老挝最大铜鼓鼓腰羽人纹

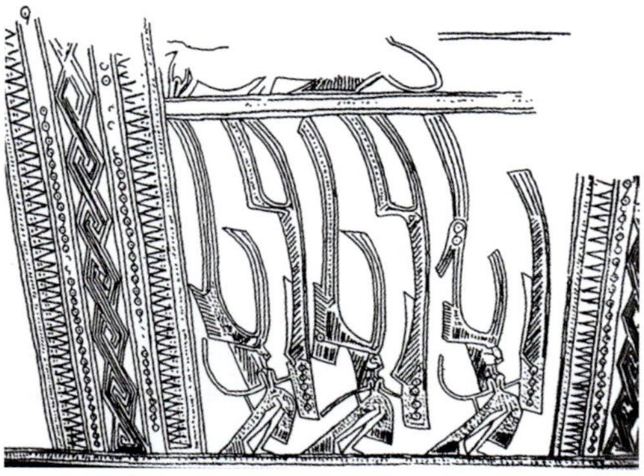

图五 老挝最大铜鼓鼓腰羽人纹

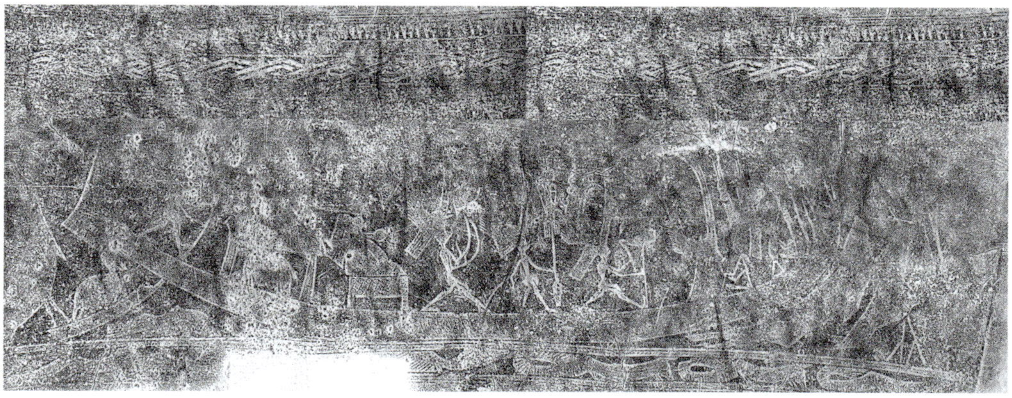

图六 老挝最大铜鼓鼓胸船纹

课题仍需进一步研究。在这里我们要感谢现今奥克夏纳矿业公司，MM集团及Lane Xang矿产公司的慷慨支持，因为他们的帮助使保存及展览这面铜鼓付诸实施（图七）。

与以上铜鼓相比，发现时间更早的另一面铜鼓被称为khongbarng。它出土于沙湾拿吉省，目前保存在老挝国家博物馆。

此铜鼓有4耳，其四周刻有太阳花（1株）和小青蛙（4只）图案，铜鼓外围装饰有象征着植物和动物的其他图案。为了即将到来的公众展出，铜鼓的清理工作正在进行当中。

国家遗产部部长Thongsa Sayavongkhamdy说："这面铜鼓高79、宽100厘米。它是第14面在Vilabouly区域Nongkadaeng和Meuangluang村庄之间的小溪附近发现的铜鼓。由于当地村民想将这面铜鼓保存在本地，当我们计划将它运往万象市的时候，村民们纷纷反对。于是我们向村民解释，这面铜鼓被许多泥土覆盖，如果不经过化学药剂清洁，在短时间内它就会生锈。最终村民们答应了我们的计划。"国家遗产部的考古学家在沙湾拿吉省发现了4面类似的铜鼓，其中在占巴塞省发现了3面，而在该省Khong区域一条河的旁边发现了另一面最大的铜鼓。

文物详细说明如下：

类型：

–黑格尔Ⅰ类型铜鼓

图七　老挝最大的铜鼓从矿山运出时的情景

出土时间地点：

–2008年1月，UXO队在南康河附近进行例行调查时发现并挖掘出土

处理：

– 现场用酒精对本体进行清洁

– 运往老挝国家博物馆

– 使用90%的异丙醇溶液加上蒸馏水进行再次清洁

– 同时使用羟基胺溶液进行细微的机械清洁

– 使用油墨拓印做记录

– 使用50%的异丙醇溶液再次清洁

– 在底部的小区域（控制区域）涂有丙烯酸树酯B72以做监测

建议：

– 继续监测防止进一步腐蚀

– 继续监测防止破裂处的尺寸扩大

储存：

– 将沙袋放置在铜鼓的不规则底部里以减小铜鼓断裂处的压力

– 提供干燥的环境

– 隔离污染物

上述发现的所有铜鼓均属于黑格尔Ⅰ型。通过对鼓身图案（包括羽人、平行四边形及复线三角形）的分析，我们得出以下结论：来自占巴塞省的老挝铜鼓和Sane铜鼓属于黑格尔Ⅰ类型铜鼓的早期亚型，而Don Tan铜鼓则属于黑格尔Ⅰ类型铜鼓的中期亚型。

研究对象：在占巴塞省发现的铜鼓

研究对象：在沙湾拿吉省发现的铜鼓

研究对象：在琅勃拉邦省发现的铜鼓

研究对象：在沙湾拿吉省Sepon村庄发现的铜鼓

以上铜鼓的鼓面由青铜及铜铸造而成，在世界范围内，这是一种较为领先的铜鼓铸造工艺技术。在中国南部、越南、泰国、老挝、缅甸、马来西亚以及印度尼西亚等国家和地区，就拥有以上这种工艺技术。在老挝的许多地区也发现了这样的铜鼓，具体包括：琅南塔省、乌多姆赛省、丰沙里省、川圹省、华潘省、沙湾拿吉省以及占巴塞省。目前，奥地利学者黑格尔先生将铜鼓分为Ⅰ、Ⅱ、Ⅲ、Ⅳ四个基本类型和三个过渡类型：

基本类型为黑格尔Ⅰ型、黑格尔Ⅱ型、黑格尔Ⅲ型、黑格尔Ⅳ型。

三个过渡型为Ⅰ－Ⅱ型；Ⅰ－Ⅳ型；Ⅱ－Ⅳ型。

今年年初，当地1位农民发现了1面铜鼓。由于铜鼓上沾满木炭和煤炭，铜鼓的顶部呈现出黑色。因此，这位农民就把它当做蒸煮罐使用了一段时间，之后他才发现这原来是1面铜鼓。出乎我们意料的是，铜鼓顶部表面的图案仍然十分清晰。一般情况下，铜鼓（鼓身）的顶部表面的保存完善与否十分重要，通过对它的分析可以判断出铜鼓的铸造日期，而这一部分也是最容易损坏的。目前，通过对其图案特征的分析，可以确定这面铜鼓属于黑格尔Ⅱ类型，其铸造日期大致在1或2世纪。但是关于这面铜鼓铸造的确切日期及其出土位置仍在进一步研究当中。在今后的工作中，希望能做到以下几点：

（1）如果可能的话，提供样品进行分析；

（2）通过机械设备移除一些腐蚀产物；

（3）检测青铜病；

（4）取拓片以描摹；

（5）使用50%的乙醇（或90度的酒精）进行清洁；

（6）将其存放于适当的展览容器中以提高其物理稳定性；

（7）继续研究准备有关铜鼓的老挝语及英语双语文本。

目前，这面铜鼓存放在Vilabouly办公区域的一间与Vilabouly电台相邻的房间内。房间内摆放有两个陈列柜，用来存放文物，主要包括铜器和瓷器。为了更加安全地存放这面铜鼓，可以将它单独放在陈列柜里，或者也可以放在已有的两个陈列柜里。在这之前，拓片和清洁铜鼓的工作必须完成。然而，目前由于这面铜鼓的物理性质仍处于不稳定的状态之中，我们认为最紧急的工作是应尽可能快地将它放进适合于它形状的柜子里。

二

博物馆对铜鼓的保护及展示

在对沙湾拿吉省的埋雷区进行常规清雷行动中发现了1面铜鼓。经过探查确认之后，它被运往老挝国家博物馆，并且作为未爆炸武器的1件重要物品来收藏，原因是起初它被认为是1枚炸弹。现在，连同包装箱的钥匙也已从矿业公司及沙湾拿吉省警察局转交给了博物馆。来自沙湾拿吉省的这面铜鼓向我们展示了获得新铜鼓或参观展览后的保存步骤：

- 在运送过程中，我们发现这面铜鼓的体积过大，以至于不能顺利地搬进存放室内。因此，我们搭建了一间临时存放室来存放这面铜鼓。

- 适当的文书工作：法律文件，贷款，送让契。

- 百分之百的相对湿度，温度和其他包括安保在内的环境因素应事先落实清楚。

- 老挝国家博物馆的法律文件。法定协议：以上这些重要文物都被视为老挝人民的共有财产。然而，关于所有权的法律文件还是需要具备。当博物馆接收文物的时候，出于保险目的，要详细记录文物当时的状况。根据老挝国家博物馆的一般收藏程序，所有与文物相关的遗赠文件、贷款文件、送让契、收据、博物馆要求的文件以及相片文书需要一一具备。

- 填写库存登记以及目录工作表。

- 情况报告（一种文物情况，签署及标注日期的记录文件）。

- 拓片。拓片工作是文物整理过程当中具有重要价值的一部分。通过比较分析，在拓片工作当中所发现的细节能够帮助我们解释文物背后所蕴藏的历史信息以及确定其铸造时期。

通过对这面铜鼓的拓片工作，判定这面铜鼓属于黑格尔Ⅰ类型，并且拥有接近2000年的历史。

铜鼓保存的基本条件如下：

- 在将这些文物放入主楼进行收藏之前，我们需要仔细检查这些文物可能带有的昆虫及真菌情况，因为这些昆虫和真菌极有可能感染损坏现存的其他文物。

- 以上原则通常适用于黏有污垢的文物。

- 如果存放的文物当中，有许多文物属于金属材质的话，那么，我们需要将这些文物进行分离，以防止相互之间发生化学反应，增加腐蚀的风险。

触摸文物：

- 触摸文物时，应戴上白色棉手套。

- 移动文物时，请使用托盘。文物的耳部是最脆弱的地方，严禁从耳部托起文物。

- 举起文物时，应用双手托住重心点的最低中心位置。

一些文物最脆弱的位置在于4个耳部支撑铜鼓的点，触摸时需谨慎。事实证明，若四个耳部的其中之一受到：

- 大比例的周期性潮湿腐蚀， 若湿度控制在最小限度，其稳定性可以保证。

- 在保存的过程中使用风扇和通风设备以最低限度地保持湿度。

– 铜鼓首次进行油污去脂的方法，采用50%的乙醇溶液混合蒸馏水。自来水通常包含腐蚀青铜的氯化物。

– 对腐蚀部分采用机械设备进行细微处理。

克木族铜鼓纹饰精美绝伦，其鼓膜上雕刻有4组累蹲蛙塑像，其中一些铜鼓的鼓身部分刻有浮雕。通过观察和测量，我们发现克木族铜鼓尺寸中等，鼓壁稀薄，统一厚度在1～2毫米。

这面铜鼓的图案反映了与东山文化有关的某一种文明或社会文化。其纹饰繁缛，整鼓密布精美的纹饰，并刻画以大鸟和鳄鱼形状。鼓身之上刻有一艘大船，表明这面铜鼓的主人与水有着重要的关系。

在这面铜鼓出土的现场，我们并没有发现与之相关的文物。当发现这面铜鼓的时候，它的位置上下颠倒。目前我们一致认为，在越南与美国的战争期间，这面铜鼓的主人为了安全地保存这面铜鼓，就将它从另外一个地方移到这里埋藏。具体转移的时间有可能是在19世纪60年代晚期或19世纪70年代早期，当时此区域正遭受着历史上著名的最为猛烈的空袭轰炸。

有关这面铜鼓的研究仍在进行当中。我们在此感谢现今奥克夏纳矿业公司及Lane Xang 矿产公司的慷慨支持，使保存及展览这面铜鼓付诸实施。

三

结　语

要确定这面铜鼓的铸造日期仍需进一步的深入探究。通过分析，我们发现，挖掘现场原有的铜或锡已被开采。目前，老挝缺乏足够的技术专家和设备来进行与之相关的其他研究工作，无论是进行现场斟探、整理档案还是记录情况，以我们仅有的资金来源，难以支撑以上工作的全面开展。

尽管我们的能力和资金有限，但是，就如何更好地保存铜鼓的课题，我们一直保持与世界上的其他专家进行交流。

在接下来的时间里，我们仍然会一如既往地开展保护铜鼓的研究工作，在这个领域的研究当中，让我们以及下一代走得更远。

越南高平省博物馆铜鼓

The Bronze Drums of the Cao Bang Provincial Museum, Vietnam

程能钟 阮光绵 / 越南考古研究所 研究员

[摘要]

本文通过对越南高平省博物馆收藏15面铜鼓的描述，并按照黑格尔铜鼓分类法进行了分类，认为其中有5面为Ⅰ型、6面为Ⅳ型、4面为Ⅰ-Ⅳ型鼓。其年代大约在前3世纪至15～16世纪。从而讨论铜鼓文化的发展，尤其是与中国广西铜鼓中的某一类铜鼓文化的联系。

[关键词]

高平铜鼓　类型　年代

Abstract

The accent of the paper is on description to the fifteen bronze drums from the collection of the Cao Bang Provincial Museum, Vietnam. Among them, according to Franz Heger's classification, there are five bronze drums of Type Ⅰ, six of Type Ⅱ, and four of Type Ⅰ-Ⅳ. The date could be from 3rd Century B.C. to 15th and 16th Century A.D., thus it's a discussion of the development of bronze drum culture, especially their correlation with a certain cultural form of bronze drum in Guangxi, China.

Key words

Cao Bang bronze drums; Type; Date

高平省是一个边境省份，位于越南北部，其北部与东北部和中国广西相邻，西面与越南宣光省和河江省接壤，南面毗邻越南北干省和谅山省。

根据考古资料表明，高平省历史悠久，其古老的传统文化一脉相承。

许多铜鼓出土于高平省。目前，高平省博物馆现存15面铜鼓，其中绝大多数的铜鼓是在19世纪80年代之前被发现。这15面铜鼓都是在生产劳动或征收房子时无意中发现的，而非通过正规的考古发掘。

在保乐县地区，私人房屋普遍都储藏有铜鼓。迄今为止，一些有关高平铜鼓的研究文献和出版物已纷纷发表，比如阮文宣（Nguyen Van Huyen 1987），卢江炮（Lo Giang Pao 1988，1994，1996，2001），程能钟（Trinh Nang Chung 2000，2009，Trinh Nang Chung，Ly Thi Tieu 2000，Trinh Nang Chung，Ha Thi Quyet 2001），李氏筱（Ly Thi Tieu 2000，2003），陈平（Tran Binh 2006）。但是，这些文章仅仅是对于某一类铜鼓展开的研究。

在本文当中，我们对高平省博物馆所收藏的铜鼓进行概述，并且总结出我们对这些铜鼓作出的初步研究成果。

一

铜鼓介绍

根据弗朗西·黑格尔及越南考古学家的铜鼓分类标准(Heger.F 1902；Pham Minh Huyen, Nguyen Van Huyen,Trinh Sinh 1987)，高平省博物馆所收藏的铜鼓可以分为以下三组：

（一）黑格尔I型铜鼓组

在高平省博物馆收藏的15面铜鼓中，其中有5面为黑格尔Ⅰ型铜鼓，即南光1号铜鼓（BTCB5707/KL432）、同灯铜鼓（BTCB21/KL21）、谷舍1号铜鼓（BTCB29/KL29）、本化1号铜鼓（BTCB1389/KL277）和鼓庞2号铜鼓（BTC23/KL23）。

类型1　东山铜鼓B组：1面铜鼓，也就是南光1号铜鼓。它于2004年在保乐县地区南光出土（Trinh Nang Chung，2009）。

该铜鼓背部平直，呈圆锥形。鼓面直径46、高29、足径49厘米。鼓面图案分为4个部分。第一部分：中央太阳纹12芒，芒纹尖锐呈三角状，芒间隐有“V”字形交替。第二部分：勾连雷纹，勾连同心圆圈纹，栉纹。第三部分：6只鹭鸟逆时针展翅环飞。第四部分：双道栉纹夹同心圆圈纹。鼓胸共5晕，1、3、5晕为锯齿纹，2晕为勾连同心圆纹，4晕为栉纹。在鼓胸及鼓腰之间刻有2道栉纹，夹稻穗纹带。根据刻在鼓身上的2道铸范，我们猜测该铜鼓是模铸造而成（图一～图三）。

类型2　东山铜鼓组，有4面铜鼓，分别是同灯铜鼓、谷舍1号铜鼓、本化1号铜鼓以及鼓庞2号铜鼓。

此组铜鼓具有以下特点：鼓面略微凸显，中央太阳纹10到12芒，芒纹尖锐呈三角状。根据鼓身及鼓面上的图案设计，这组铜鼓归类为东山铜鼓。同灯铜鼓纹饰以鸟展翅飞翔，作逆时针状环飞为主，其上图案主要为几何形图案，主要为圆圈切线纹、圆圈圆点纹、双行切线和典型人物图案。并且，此类铜鼓图案发展为新型Ⅳ和Ⅰ-Ⅳ型，即虚刻菱形纹以及钱纹的本化1号铜鼓。此铜鼓鼓面边沿有蟾蜍塑像，这表现在同灯铜鼓和本化1号铜鼓上铸有的单只青蛙和累叠青蛙。鼓身分为3个部分，比例相当。鼓足饰以三角纹。根据刻在鼓身上的双行线，该铜鼓是复型模铸造而成。

（二）黑格尔Ⅳ型铜鼓组

此铜鼓组有6面铜鼓，分别为鼓庞4号鼓（BTCB25/KL25）、鼓庞5号鼓（BTCB26/KL26）、鼓庞1号鼓（BTCB22/KL22）和陇内鼓（BTCB20/KL20）、蒙安鼓（BTCB 28/KL28）以及保乐鼓（BTCB27/KL28）。

根据形状和图案特征，此铜鼓组可分为以下几类：

类型1　包括4面铜鼓：鼓庞4号鼓、鼓庞5号鼓、鼓庞1号鼓和陇内鼓。

这类铜鼓刻有2道浮线，线条粗大。鼓面边沿超出鼓胸，中央太阳纹12芒，芒纹尖锐呈三角状。鼓身分为三个部分：鼓胸弯曲膨胀，鼓腰中部略微中空，铜鼓重心向足部倾斜。关于鼓面及鼓身的图案实例如下：

鼓庞5号鼓：同心圆、双行线、典型人物图案。

鼓庞4号鼓：圆圈纹、栉纹、异型游旗纹、绹纹（图四～图六）。

鼓庞1号鼓：同心圆、圈纹、栉纹、异型游旗纹。鼓面边沿立4只蟾蜍塑像，呈逆时针方向环列（图七）。

陇内鼓：钱纹、典型人物图案、编织篮图案、柠檬花图案。鼓面边沿有6只累叠蟾蜍塑像，大蟾蜍背小蟾蜍，以逆时针方向环列。

类型2　包括2面铜鼓：蒙安鼓和保乐鼓。

这类铜鼓刻有4道线条中等尺寸的浮线，鼓面边沿不超过鼓胸。鼓面中央太阳纹12芒，芒纹尖锐呈三角状。鼓胸明显突出，并将鼓身对半分成两个部分，逐渐往下收小。鼓身中部狭窄朝上，并刻有浮带纹，将鼓胸和鼓腰区别开。鼓面及鼓身的图案实例如下：

蒙安铜鼓：鼓面图案斑驳，按其上痕迹辨认为乳钉纹头部。

保乐铜鼓：同心圆、双行线、典型人物图案、雏菊线纹、乳钉纹头部、鱼骨图案。

（三）黑格尔Ⅰ-Ⅳ型铜鼓组

此铜鼓组有4面铜鼓，他们分别是鼓庞3号鼓（BTCB24/KL24）、谷舍2号鼓（BTCB30/KL30）、南光2号鼓（BTCB5706/KL431）和本化2号鼓（BTCB1363/KL276）。

这组铜鼓为中间形态的铜鼓，其主要特征如下：尺寸中等，鼓面外沿超出鼓胸，中央太阳纹12芒，芒纹尖锐呈三角状。鼓身分为3个清晰的部分，鼓胸弯曲，鼓足高耸向下倾斜。在鼓胸和鼓腰之间有两道合范线。根据刻在鼓身上的双行线，这面铜鼓是复型模铸造而成。

关于鼓面及鼓身的图案实例如下：

鼓庞3号鼓：同心圆圈纹、栉纹、乳钉纹、异型游旗纹、羽纹、绹纹（图八～图一〇）。

谷舍2号鼓：同心圆圈纹、双行线、典型人物图案、虚刻菱形纹、鱼骨图案。

南光2号鼓：树叶图案、乳钉纹、双行线、捆绳纹。

本化2号鼓：虚刻“V”形纹、钱纹、柠檬花图案、典型人物图案、编织篮图案、蜜蜂后部高翘飞舞。鼓面边沿立有6只蟾蜍塑像，按逆时针方向环列：3只单只塑像，3只累叠蟾蜍塑像，蟾蜍背部及底部刻有浮动曲折纹。鼓足铸有1只小鸭塑像。

二

铜鼓年代测定

作为越南铜鼓文化的一部分，高平博物馆收藏的大部分铜鼓都在无意中发现，并不是通过正规的考古发掘。这些铜鼓出土的时候，也没有发现任何其他的遗物同出。因此，测定这些铜鼓的年代非常困难。目前，通过文献资料和根据越南河江省、老街省和中国广西、云南的考古学家研究，我们初步得出以下的结论：

（1）在高平省发现的黑格尔Ⅰ型铜鼓组的铸造年代最为久远，然而铜鼓之间也存在着年代差异。通过比较图案和装饰的特点，黑格尔Ⅰ型铜鼓组的年代可以从以下内容中判定：

① 南光1号铜鼓在特征、形态和图案方面均与清化省永禄区的永宁铜鼓十分相似(Pham Huy Thong 1990：119)。根据《东山铜鼓》一书作者的观点，永宁铜鼓应归为东山铜鼓B组，并且属于东山文化(Pham Minh Huyen, Nguyen Van Huyen, Trinh Sinh 1987：28)。除太阳纹不同芒纹的特点之外，南光1号鼓鼓面图案的设计与中国广西西林发现的第283面铜鼓非常接近（广西壮族自治区博物馆1991：66），中国的考古学家将西林铜鼓归为石寨山类。

通过比较结果表明，南光Ⅰ型铜鼓的铸造年代在高平省是最早的，年代大约在前3世纪，它是东山文化的产物。

② 同灯铜鼓在许多特征上和以下的铜鼓十分相似，包括朗文铜鼓(安沛市)、纳

阳铜鼓（凉山市）、河江铜鼓等。根据纹饰和铸造工艺，同灯铜鼓属于东山晚期D类，年代判定在纪元早期。

③ 谷舍1号鼓和鼓庞2号鼓鼓面、鼓身设计的图案大部分符合传统东山铜鼓的特征，但是，因为谷舍1号鼓图案模糊不清，只能推测其年代大致在第一个千年。

鼓庞2号鼓中央太阳纹芒间的交替图案并非同一铜鼓组里面的孔雀羽毛，而是变成与河江省 BTHG.KL/Đ17铜鼓类似的菩提叶图案。这类佛教菩提叶主题采用的装饰图案，来自木、石、瓷器等由不同材质的器物上所饰的纹饰，根据上述判断，鼓庞2铜鼓的铸造年代可能在第二个千年。

④ 本化1号鼓刻印的图案如下：钱纹、柠檬花图案、编织篮图案。这些图案表明这面铜鼓的年代非常久远。柠檬花图案与陈—黎朝瓷器和石头上刻的主题非常相似。根据上述判断，本化1号鼓的铸造年代可能在15～16世纪。

（2）黑格尔Ⅳ型铜鼓组

与黑格尔Ⅰ型铜鼓组对比，黑格尔Ⅳ型铜鼓组在形态上略有不同，纹饰方面也进行了很多创新，东山铜鼓传统图案的数量也相对减少。鼓庞1号鼓、鼓庞4号鼓、纳阳鼓、蒙安鼓和保乐鼓鼓身及鼓面上普遍的纹饰图案包括：菩提叶图案、钱纹、编织篮图案、典型人物风格、雏菊线条纹、柠檬花图案、乳钉纹。这组铜鼓的铸造年代大约在第二个千年上半叶。

鼓庞5号鼓特征：传统的同心圆几何图案、双行线、典型人物风格。这些特征表明这面铜鼓的年代要早于鼓庞1号鼓、纳阳鼓、蒙安铜鼓组。它的铸造年代在第一个千年时期。

（3）黑格尔Ⅰ-Ⅳ型铜鼓组

黑格尔Ⅰ-Ⅳ型铜鼓组的形态与黑格尔Ⅳ型接近，但与其相比，这组铜鼓的图案纹饰反而和一些传统东山铜鼓的几何图案类似。鼓庞3号鼓和中国广西壮族自治区博物馆所藏的258号麻江型铜鼓十分类似。与河江省同一类铜鼓相比较，黑格尔Ⅰ-Ⅳ型铜鼓组包括：鼓庞3号鼓、谷舍2号鼓、南光2号鼓、本化2号鼓。这些铜鼓的年代可追溯至第二个千年上半叶。

三

对高平铜鼓的一些认识

（1）数据显示，黑格尔Ⅰ型铜鼓组有5面，黑格尔Ⅳ型铜鼓组有6面，黑格尔Ⅰ-Ⅳ型铜鼓有4面。至今仍未发现属于黑格尔Ⅱ和Ⅲ型铜鼓。

因此，如今高平省博物馆所收藏的15面铜鼓表明，高平省古代铜鼓文化发达。

迄今为止，这15面古代铜鼓的地域分布在高平省的四个区域（和安、保乐、保林、重庆），尤其是在保乐地区。除上述铜鼓之外，考古学家也在高平省发现了新铜鼓的线索，有望在该地区的更多地方发现更多的铜鼓，但下一步的研究尚未进行(Trinh Nang Chung，2009)。

（2）关于黑格尔Ⅰ型铜鼓—东山铜鼓，我们仅仅知道高平省是东山晚期Đ类铜鼓的聚集地。但是，根据对南光1号铜鼓(BTCB5707/KL432)的发现，我们知道高平省也是真正意义上的东山铜鼓分布的区域。随着在会安省、Nguyen Binh省和高平省铸造其他铜鼓的工具被发现，证明了上述区域也受到东山文化的影响。东山铜鼓晚期Đ类铜鼓是以东山文化命名，是东山铜鼓过渡到黑格尔Ⅰ-Ⅳ和Ⅳ型的一类铜鼓。

在高平省发现的黑格尔Ⅳ型铜鼓属于新类型的铜鼓，它们被视作东山型晚期铜鼓，恰恰和传统的东山铜鼓系列相反。在高平省存有大量的黑格尔Ⅰ-Ⅳ中间型铜鼓。通过高平省博物馆发现的铜鼓数量和民间收藏的铜鼓数量，这表明在古代高平省的族群非常喜欢使用黑格尔Ⅰ型晚期东山铜鼓和黑格尔Ⅳ和Ⅰ-Ⅳ型铜鼓。黑格尔Ⅳ和Ⅰ-Ⅳ型铜鼓主要出现在如倮倮族、Dao、Nung的少数民族地区以及越南北部山区（河江省、高平省），其中在越南北部山区的高平省发现了10面铜鼓。

尽管高平铜鼓有不同的类型，这些铜鼓之间仍存在共同特点：部分铜鼓中间有着相同呈圆形块状突起的太阳纹；部分铜鼓有钻孔；部分铜鼓有黑蓝相间的锈斑。黑格尔Ⅳ和Ⅰ-Ⅳ型铜鼓之间的铸造年代距离并不遥远，可能同存于某一时期，而黑格尔Ⅳ型铜鼓的铸造年代要晚于上述两者。

（3）在高平省，几乎大部分类型的铜鼓都共存于一个区域，甚至共存于一个公社，但这种情况在越南的鸿智、保乐地区的公社却十分罕见，这个现象值得深思。尽管如此，这一现象还是表明在高平省的居民与铜鼓有密切联系。铜鼓文化在高平族群的历史发展中存在了很长时间，其中倮倮人是其中的亮点。倮倮少数民族将铜鼓储存并且使用，并视为他们最为神圣的珍宝来看待。近期发表的人类学研究揭露了倮倮人掌握生产和使用铜鼓的时间有将近1800年。他们认为铜鼓是一种拥有超自然力量的物体，应与逝去的人一起埋藏。因此，铜鼓仅用于家中或家族中成员逝去的葬礼。可以看出，铜鼓被视为倮倮人的文化灵魂。我们认为，这种民族独特的文化应完好地继承并将之发展。

在高平省和北部山区省份（包括河江、凉山、太原、宣光、安沛和老街）还发现了黑格尔Ⅰ型晚期铜鼓、黑格尔Ⅰ-Ⅳ型中间型铜鼓和黑格尔Ⅳ型铜鼓。这些铜鼓表明，当东山文明结束的时候，山区少数民族仍继续发扬东山文化传统，并且在此基础上创造出类型独特的铜鼓。

（4）有迹象表明，在高平省的黑格尔Ⅳ和Ⅰ-Ⅳ型铜鼓与中国广西麻江型铜鼓组中的某一类铜鼓有着一定的联系。这个有趣的课题值得进一步深入研究。

图一　南光1号铜鼓鼓身

图二　南光1号铜鼓鼓面

图三　南光1号铜鼓鼓面墨线图

图四　鼓庞4号鼓鼓身

图五　鼓庞4号鼓鼓面

图六　鼓庞4号鼓鼓面墨线图

图七　鼓庞1号鼓鼓面墨线图

图八　鼓庞3号鼓鼓身

图九　鼓庞3号鼓鼓面

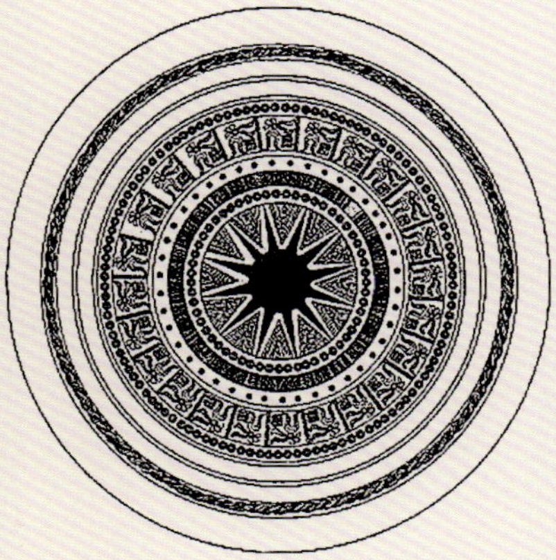

图一〇　鼓庞3号鼓鼓面墨线图

参考书目

广西壮族自治区博物馆:《广西铜鼓图录》，文物出版社，1991年。

弗朗茨·黑格尔:《东南亚古代金属鼓》，上海古籍出版社，2004年。

Lo Giang Pao:《 保乐发现的另一面铜鼓（高平省）》，《1988年考古新发现》，河内社会科学出版社，1988年，越南语版本。

Lo Giang Pao:《河江古代铜鼓与少数民族》，河内国际出版社，1996年，越南语版本。

Lo Giang Pao:《高平铜鼓》，《考古学》，2001年，越南语版本。

Lo Giang Pao, Nong Thi Duyen:《对河江和高平省铜鼓的探知》，《1994年考古新发现》，河内社会科学出版社，越南语版本。

Ly Thi Tieu:《论高平博物馆的两面铜鼓》，《2000年考古新发现》，河内社会科学出版社，2000年，越南语版本。

Ly Thi Tieu:《Ban Hoa铜鼓》，《2003年考古新发现》，河内社会科学出版社，2003年，越南语版本。

Nguyen Van Huyen:《Ngoc Khue铜鼓》，《1987年考古新发现》，河内社会科学出版社，1987年，越南语版本。

Pham Huy Thong：《越南东山铜鼓》，河内社会科学出版社，1990年， 越南语和英语双语版本。

Pham Minh Huyen, Nguyen Van Huyen, Trinh Sinh:《东山铜鼓》，河内社会科学出版社，1987年，越南语版本。

高平省人民委员会：《高平省专题》，河内国家政治出版社，2000年，越南语版本。

Tran Binh:《高平省Khau Trang村发现的两面铜鼓》，《2006年考古新发现》，河内社会科学出版社，2006年，越南语版本。

Trinh Nang Chung:《4月～5月份高平考古调查报告》，考古研究院文献所，河内，2000年，越南语版本。

Trinh Nang Chung:《 对高平省的史前考古概述》，科学会议主题：《与古代高平的相关议题》，考古研究院文献所，河内，2009年，越南语版本。

Trinh Nang Chung, Ly Thi Tieu, Ha Thi Quye:《高平省发现的铜鼓》，《2000年考古新发现》，河内社会科学出版社，2000年，越南语版本。

Trinh Nang Chung, Ha Thi Quyet, Ly Thi Tieu:《高平Coc Xa铜鼓》，《2001年考古新发现》，河内社会科学出版社，2001年，越南语版本。

广西铜鼓陈列的构思

The Conception on Bronze Drum' s Exhibition in Guangxi

吴伟峰 / 广西壮族自治区博物馆 研究员
潘 汁 / 广西壮族自治区博物馆 副研究员

[摘要]

铜鼓是具有广西历史和当代民族文化的代表性器物，也是中国南方民族及东南亚的文化载体。以铜鼓元素为主题的广西铜鼓陈列展览，全面展示铜鼓文化，诠释广西历史和民族文化的卓越成就，预期将带来良好的效益。

[关键词]

广西　铜鼓　展示　构思

Abstract

Bronze drum is a typical example of Guangxi historical and contemporary culture, as well as the carrier of the ethnic culture of southern China and South-eastern Asia. To organize an exhibition of Bronze drums annotating the outstanding achievements of Guangxi ethnic culture, a good social and economic effect could be anticipated.

Key words

Guangxi; Bronze drum; Exhibit; Conception

博物馆是国家或地区的历史文化缩影，是展示历史风貌和人文精神的窗口，是展现人文特色最有代表性的文化名片。构建有历史感、时代感和代表性的陈列展览，是博物馆最重要的工作环节。

广西壮族自治区地处祖国南疆，境内居住着壮、汉、瑶、苗、侗、仫佬、毛南、京、彝、水、仡佬、回等12个世居民族，有少数民族人口1711.05万人，占全区总人口的37.18%（2010年第六次全国人口普查数据），是我国人口最多的少数民族自治区。广西各族人民不仅创造了悠久灿烂和具有显著地域特色和民族特色的文化，使之成为整个中华民族璀璨夺目的文化殿堂的重要组成部分，而且在促进民族团结、维护国家统一、振兴经济发展等方面作出了重要贡献。

铜鼓可以说是广西民族文化的标志和象征，铜鼓在其漫长的历史发展过程中，与当地各民族的社会、经济、文化生活紧密地联系在一起，形成独特的铜鼓文化。铜鼓曾作为统治权力的象征，或作为祭祀用具和娱乐用具，广泛用于展示、集众、盟会、战阵、祭祀、娱乐、丧葬等场合。铜鼓又是一种综合艺术品，集冶炼、铸造、绘画、雕塑、音乐、舞蹈于一身，其独特的造型和丰富的纹饰，反映了铸造铜鼓的民族当时的经济状况、文化面貌和心理素质，堪称一部民族历史的百科全书。无论过去还是现在，铜鼓文化的影响都深深地触及当地人民的生活。同时，铜鼓也是中国南方各民族以及东南亚各国共同的文化载体，在以融合和交流为主题的历史发展进程中的作用及影响是重大而深远的。

一

陈列内容

广西铜鼓陈列展览，以一一展现这些元素为主旨，将以铜鼓文化为主线，来构建一个展现广西地方的历史文化、促进文化交流的平台，打造出厚重而亮丽的广西文化名片。广西铜鼓陈列内容主要可分为瓯骆遗风、鼓声悠远、人神共娱、炉火铸魂、艺术之光、盛世奇葩、南方神器、异彩纷呈等八个部分。

瓯骆遗风的主题是广西古代铜鼓文化，本篇以大型场景“花山岩画”开始，使人仿佛穿越时空，回到远古时代的西瓯、骆越时代，重温广西各族先民的生活情景。以文字、图片、模型、古籍抄本（复制）等来强调突出铜鼓的历史影响，用图表来说明在广西出土、发现的古代铜鼓的数量及分布情况。

鼓声悠远的内容是古代铜鼓探源。本篇着重展示古代铜鼓的起源，以文字、文物实物、复制品、模型、照片、油画等方式，叙述远古先民如何在日常生活中发现和使用铜鼓，通过铜釜与铜鼓的直观比较，说明由釜及鼓的演变过程。展出古代铜鼓的早期类型——万家坝型铜鼓文物及相关复制品。

人神共娱这一部分体现古代铜鼓类型及功能的发展变迁。本篇的重点在于通过文物陈列展示，来说明古代铜鼓的发展历程。一方面通过文物、文字说明、图表、纹饰展开图等阐释说明古代铜鼓的诞生期、成熟期、鼎盛期和衰落期的演变脉络，另一方面阐述说明古代铜鼓使用功能的变迁。共展出古代铜鼓的八大类型（两大系列）的古代铜鼓实物。

炉火铸魂展现铜鼓的铸造工艺。中国古代铜鼓的传统铸造技艺早在清朝后期（19世纪下半叶）失传，相对于古籍中丰富的有关铜鼓的记载，可谓极为贫乏。本篇根据最新的研究成果，通过文字、模型、照片、图表和实物等方法，复原古代铜鼓的铸造技术，并且再现了传统的铜鼓铸造工作现场，完成从造型、制范、刻花到合范、浇铸、成型等整个工艺流程。

艺术之光着重展示铜鼓的纹饰艺术。古代铜鼓不仅鼓形稳重大气，而且纹饰样式丰富，风格多变，生活气息浓郁。本篇通过实物、照片、拓片、绘图等形式来展示古代铜鼓的纹饰形式和绘画雕塑艺术，而且深入剖析这些艺术形式之所以产生的自然环境和各族先民生产生活方式的背景，以及它们所蕴含的民族文化内涵。

盛世奇葩的内容主要是广西当代的铜鼓文化。广西的壮族、瑶族、苗族、彝族等民族当中仍珍藏和使用铜鼓，至今已经历经两千多年的铜鼓文化仍在传承延绵，铜鼓文化的光辉依然闪耀光芒。为表现这些元素，本篇选取展出当代广西的壮、瑶、彝、苗四个民族在节庆和仪式上使用的铜鼓，并配以实景再现、照片、拓片、民族古籍文抄、音像等手段来实现。

南方神器体现了中外铜鼓的交流。铜鼓是中国南方和东南亚各国共同的文化载体。两千多年的铜鼓发展历史，是中国南方乃至东南亚地区各民族之间经济、文化交流的见证。各类型铜鼓之间，或有传承递变关系，或有互相影响关系。本篇通过对各地的铜鼓实物、照片、纹饰拓片、艺术风格、当代铜鼓习俗和数字图表的对照比较，总结异同，来表现中国与东南亚各国的文化交流史。

异彩纷呈是世界鼓文化的荟萃。和铜鼓一样，其他不同类型、不同民族使用的鼓作为礼乐器在人类精神文化生活中同样扮演着重要角色。本篇在广泛收集全国、全世界范围内的鼓文化及其相关表征物基础上遴选最有代表性的展品，展现世界性的形态不同、功能有别、风格迥异的鼓文化。这段内容可以不断增加，内容和形式都可以是未来时。

整个展览内容涵盖了古今中外铜鼓文化，重点突出广西铜鼓藏量之丰、铜鼓文化之盛。不但展示铜鼓文物本身，又顾及相关的民族文化、纹饰艺术、铸造工艺等背景知识，既有出土文物展览，又展现当代铜鼓文化，还扩展到世界的鼓文化。

二

展览形式

铜鼓陈列注重历史性、科学性、知识性、艺术性，传统文化与现代科技的结合，学术性与趣味性的结合，动态与静态展示的结合，广西、中国与世界的结合。展览内容丰富，寓情于景，声色俱佳，普及科学，参与性强，达到内容与形式的完满表现。

在陈列手法上，通过丰富的内容、多角度的视觉以及多样化的陈列形式，力争突破铜鼓展品单一性的局限，打破传统的通柜式陈列方式，达到学术性与通俗性、科学性与趣味性、艺术性与思想性的有机结合，提高铜鼓陈列的学术品位和艺术品位。铜鼓陈列应该通过借鉴吸收当今世界上最好的陈列理念，展览不仅要显示博物馆得天独厚的文化风采，而且要充分利用能够达到的科技成果，让人们在一种新时代的氛围中去追溯历史、体现民族文化与现代科技的结合，拉近观众与展品之间的距离，确保展览的水平不被快速发展的时代所淘汰。具体在展览中，在展品及图片的组合和表现手法上有所创新，运用声、光、电、多媒体等现代手段，具体采用导览系统、触摸系统、音像系统、声讯系统、自动模型、网上博物馆等形式。陈列要以人为本、寓教于乐，考虑观众的参与、娱乐等功能。面对散发着幽思古情的铜鼓，只要点击触摸屏上的不同类型的铜鼓图标，观众便能听到由远而近的铜鼓声；只要通过动画软件便可以体验、参与铜鼓铸造的乐趣。

广西铜鼓陈列的特色将力求体现在实景展出、技术再现、鼓乐演艺、产业创新等方面，博物馆里还有围绕铜鼓文化展开的艺术表演。用这几个方面的有机结合、联系来形成完整、新式的陈列体系，达到较高的陈列水平，建设一个有趣好玩的博物馆，带动博物馆社会效益和经济效益的发展。

三

潜在效益

目前，全国保存在各文博机构、高等院校、科研单位的铜鼓大约1500面。相比之下，广西迄今已发现从春秋晚期到清代末各个时期的铜鼓，种类齐全，收藏在全区各文博单位的铜鼓数量达到了610面，民间收藏和使用的铜鼓数量保守估计也达到1500面，总量超过2000面，广西的铜鼓拥有量为世界之最。关于广西地区铸造和使用铜鼓的记载，更是史不绝书，至今广西一些地区的壮、瑶、苗、彝等民族还在使用铜鼓。由此广西被冠之以“铜鼓之乡”、“铜鼓大本营”的美誉，绝非偶然。源远流长的铜鼓文化，凝聚着广西各族先民的聪明智慧，闪烁着广西文明历史的光辉。广西各民族共创造了丰富多彩的具有显著地方和民族特色的文化，是中华民族光辉灿烂文化的重要组成部分。

人类文明是在文化积累的基础上不断发展延续的，文化是人类或者一个民族的内核，而博物馆就是其中的一个重要载体。作为“聚地之神韵，集物之精华”的博物馆是人类文明的窗口、历史的缩影，是人们了解历史文化、启迪心智的教育场所，是树立国家与民族形象的标志，也是一种特殊的旅游资源，而铜鼓陈列是其核心内容。所以世界各国都非常重视博物馆的建设，视为体现文化底蕴和现代文明的象征。人民群众是历史的创造者，博物馆收藏的人类历史及环境的见证物属于全体人民所有，这就必然使博物馆必须具备公共性的属性。我们的祖先创造了历史，现代的每一个民众有权利了解自己的过去，自己民族的过去，自己国家的过去。博物馆是在自然文化遗产归全民所有的视野下建立的。

随着党中央西部大开发战略的实施和广西环北部湾经济区的开始建设，随着广西不断扩大的对外开放和各民族文化研究的深入与发展，建设一座集收藏、保护、研究和展示广西最具特色的民族文物——铜鼓的现代博物馆，充分展示铜鼓文化，是弘扬各民族悠久历史和灿烂文化，宣传广西、开发广西、促进广西对外开放、发展经济的迫切需要，是有效保存民族文物、抢救民族优秀文化遗产的需要，是广西民族学、考古学、历史学研究与对外部世界交流的需要，是对全社会进行爱国爱乡教育、增进各民族相互了解和团结的需要，是带动广西旅游业发展的需要，是落实党和国家抢救、保护、弘扬民族优秀传统文化政策的具体体现。广西铜鼓博物馆的建设以及铜鼓的陈列展示，是将目前分散于全区国有文博机构的铜鼓集中收藏，实施专业而有效的保护，进行全面、系统、深入的研究，向公众展示铜鼓的发展历史、铸造技术和艺术特点，并以此为主线，宣扬民族优秀文化，让国内外观众全面感受光辉灿烂的广西本土文化，共享我国文化遗产保护与研究的成果，共享当今中国公共文化事业繁荣发展。

广西拥有的世界第一的铜鼓数量，加之铜鼓历史悠久，种类齐全，分布广泛，精品荟萃，基于此，广西铜鼓博物馆也必将成为世界上独一无二的铜鼓专题博物馆，成为世界一流的铜鼓研究保护中心，打造一个精彩的铜鼓陈列展示，势必成为广西最具影响力的文化品牌之一。随着中国—东盟自由贸易区建设的不断推进以及泛北部湾经济区战略的实施，广西铜鼓博物馆的建设必将体现我区经济建设与文化事业齐头并进，为中国与东盟各国的文化交流提供新的空间与平台，有利于国家战略构建的顺利实施。

广西壮族自治区拥有5100多万人口，其中有少数民族人口共约1700多万，是我国人口最多的少数民族自治区。首府南宁市人口300多万，其中大中专学生和中小学生数量将近80万。这些数字都是未来广西铜鼓博物馆陈列展览的潜在观众群体。近年来随着一年一度的中国—东盟博览会永久落户南宁，随着中国—东盟自由贸易区建设的加快推进以及环北部湾经济区战略的实施，南宁已经成为承接中国大陆与东南亚国家的桥头堡，成为区域性的国际大都会。光临南宁的外籍商旅人士、旅游者、留学生逐年增多，仅2008年南宁市接待的国内游客更是达到了惊人的2000万人。在这种情况下，广西铜鼓博物馆的成立以及铜鼓陈列展览的推出可谓应运而生，必将为广大市民、游客提供绝佳的怡情之旅、文化之旅，成为宣扬民族文化、提高广西和南宁的知名度、拉动旅游经济的推动力。

广西全区由各级文博单位收藏的600多面铜鼓中，绝大多数都有残缺、破损的情况。原因不外乎两种，一是入库收藏时已经因年代久远等因素本来就已经锈蚀残缺严重，二是入库以后一直得不到科学的保护修复，导致病害更加严重。目前收藏保存在全区的各个文博机构库房里的铜鼓文物，几乎全部是自然堆放，远远达不到青铜器文物保护所需要的环境指数标准。极少数单位虽然可以修复铜器文物，但其技术水平仍停留在很低的水平上。这种情况对于号称“南国神器”的铜鼓文物来说，是非常令人担忧的。这种状况如果得不到根本性的改变，这类南方民族文化的最具代表性的器物很可能损毁在我们一两代人手中。因此，以广西铜鼓博物馆的建立为契机，通过铜鼓文化的陈列展示，呼唤社会各界的关注，成立铜鼓保护修复中心，加强铜鼓文物保护技术的研究，加大保护的力度，从根本上改变长期以来因技术落后、投入不足而造成的铜鼓文物缺损严重的局面，是一项功在当代、利在千秋的大事。广西的铜鼓研究起步较早，涌现出一批卓有成就的铜鼓研究专家，在国内外学术界有较大的影响。中国古代铜鼓研究会为这项研究做了大量的工作，取得了有目共睹的成绩。随着广西铜鼓博物馆的成立，该研究会也将落户于此，并以此为新的平台，其铜鼓研究必将达到一个新的高度。由此，广西铜鼓博物馆将成为集展示、研究和保护修复于一体的中心，在国内外学术界占有领先的地位。

通过陈列、表演、技术等，推动古代青铜文化、文物仿制、工艺品的创新发展，带动广西地方历史文化的发展和传承，同时也会推动相应文化产业的发展。铜鼓博物馆的建设以及铜鼓陈列的推出，必定会使铜鼓的文化影响力增大，也必定使铜鼓的地位更加重要，铜鼓的社会和经济价值也会大大提升。

国外、区外的一些地方也正在紧锣密鼓地加紧对铜鼓的研究，大力挖掘其本土的铜鼓文化，打造铜鼓文化品牌。就地域性和时效性而言，彼此间具有竞争性，所以广西铜鼓博物馆的建设以及广西铜鼓陈列的尽早问世具有相当的紧迫感。

第二部分

青铜文化研究

Part 2

Research on Bronze Culture

广西羊角纽铜编钟的研究

A Study of Bronze Chime Bells with Horn-shaped Knobs in Guangxi

黄启善 / 广西壮族自治区博物馆 研究员

[摘要]

本文通过对广西发现的羊角纽铜编钟进行了分类研究，分析了羊角纽铜编钟的形式、年代、命名、演奏等方面内容，提出了羊角纽铜编钟在中国南方金属打击乐器中的作用，从而探讨中国南方青铜文化的发展与传播，认为广西羊角纽铜编钟大约流行于战国至两汉时期，是古代西瓯骆越青铜文化的组成部分。

[关键词]

广西　羊角纽铜编钟　研究

Abstract

So far, 19 bronze chime bells with horn-shaped knob have been discovered in Guangxi. Without the lost 2 samples, the existed 17 samples principally spread in Guigang city, Rong county, Pubei county, Liuzhou city, gongcheng county and Xilin county. The paper will research on each bell by its origin, size, weight, decorative patterns and other contents. The Bronze Bells with Horn-shaped knob can be divided into 2 categories (A and B), and each category has 2 styles.

Several question will be discuss in this paper:

1. The scientific name: "Bronze chime bells with Horn-shaped knob" is considered appropriate.

2. The age: A category is considerably between BC 206 to AD 8. B category should be after BC rather than in the "Warring States" decades.

3. Performance: The bells should be placed on shelf to play instead of hanging by rope or hook when tested audio frequency. Thus there is an argument to the result of audio frequency test in the past.

4. Proprietary: Those bronze chime bells is considerably the percussion instrument belong to Ouyue and Luoyue nation, and in a great deal to play ensemble with bronze drum and cylindrical bronze bells with annular knob.

Key words

Guangxi; Bronze Chime Bells with Horn-shaped Knob; Study

羊角纽铜编钟是中国南方和越南北部地区古代青铜文化中一种最具有特色的打击乐器之一，它与这地区的古代铜鼓文化有着千丝万缕的联系，有人把它誉为一对孪生兄弟。广西位于中国南方，是一个以壮族为主的少数民族聚集地，悠久的历史和内涵丰富的民族文化，引起了世人的关注。这里发现一批古老的羊角纽铜编钟，同样备受学术界关注，一些专家对羊角纽铜编钟的发现、年代、音律等方面进行了研究。广西现已发现羊角纽铜钟19件，仅次于云南省，云南已有了专论①，但广西却没有专论。多数均散见各类论著中②，因此，本文拟对广西发现的17件羊角纽铜钟进行专门的整理和研究，并就羊角纽铜编钟有关用途和音频乐律的测试方式进行探讨，不妥之处请方家赐教。

① 黄德荣：《云南羊角纽编钟》，《四川文物》2007年第5期。

② 蒋廷瑜：《羊角纽铜钟初论》，《文物》1984年第5期。

一

发现概况

目前，世界上已发现羊角纽铜编钟64件，其中除了在越南发现14件外，其余50件在中国云南、广西、湖南、贵州、广东等地发现。广西目前发现的羊角纽铜钟已达19件，其中有2件已遗失，实有17件，主要分布于桂东南的贵港市、容县、浦北县，桂中的柳州市，桂北的恭城县，桂西的西林县等县市。具体发现数量统计于表一。

表一　广西发现羊角纽铜编钟数量统计表

序号	发现地点	发现时间	数量（件）	来源
1	贵港市郊	1964年	1	农民掘土发现
2	贵港市罗泊湾M1	1976年	1	考古发掘
3	容县龙井化村	1976年	4	掘土发现
4	浦北县大岭脚村	1974年	4	农民掘土发现
5	浦北县印刷厂	1984年	2	征集
6	浦北利县竹逵村	1986年	3	农民郭润光掘土发现已遗失2件
7	柳州市大埔镇	1982年	1	征集
8	西林县普驮铜鼓墓葬	1972年	2	考古征集
9	恭城县东寨村	1983年	1	农民刘厚藏掘土发现
合计			19	

从上表一可以看到一种现象，广西目前所发现的羊角纽铜鼓主要分布于桂东南、桂北、桂西和桂中等四个地区。

二

铜钟介绍

为了便于研究，在这里有必要对广西现有的17件羊角纽铜钟作一详细的介绍。

贵港羊角纽铜编钟，1件。为当地农民掘土所得，1964年，广西壮族自治区博物馆从贵县（今贵港市）农民手中购到，现藏广西壮族自治区博物馆，年代为汉代。该钟高22.2、底长15、宽9.5厘米，重1290克。器身上部对穿1个长方形孔，以便悬挂，孔长4.5、宽1.7厘米，顶部有1对外撇的羊角形纽。通体素面无纹（图一）。

贵港罗泊湾羊角纽铜编钟（土10821），1件。1976年在贵港市罗泊湾1号西汉早期木椁墓底下的东面器物坑内出土。伴随出土的还有192件青铜器，有兵器、乐器、食器、车马器等。而羊角纽铜钟和2件直筒形铜钟一起置放于三足铜案上的1件彩铜盆中。如图二，31号为羊角纽铜钟，29、30号为直筒形铜钟。

该羊角纽铜钟高19、底径横长14、纵宽8.1厘米，方孔长5.4～5.7、宽1.2～2厘米。重1500克。正面铸人面纹，人眼、鼻、口等面部隐约可见（图三）。

图一　贵港羊角纽铜编钟

图二　羊角纽铜钟与直筒钟放在盆中
（罗泊湾1号汉墓）

图三　贵港罗泊湾羊角纽铜编钟

大岭脚羊角纽铜编钟，4件。1974年，浦北县官垌公社平石大队大岭脚村农民于该村后背岭挖土时发现。一共出土4件。大小相似，钟身下部有一道菱形雷纹图案（图四），钟的尺寸、重量数据列于表二。

从表二可看到，浦北大岭脚4件羊角纽铜钟的高度几乎相等，如以56-3号钟的高度与最矮的56-2号钟相比，其高度相差6毫米，如果以4件从矮到高排列，它们与相邻之间的高矮落差为2、6、1毫米。从底部看，4件铜钟底横长完全相同，都是15厘米，纵宽有2件相同都是9.6厘米，其余2件分别是9.3、9.8厘米。从其比值看，4件铜钟的通高与口横长之比为1.63～1.66厘米，仅相差0.3毫米之内。通高与横宽之比为2.53～2.63厘米，相差仅0.1厘米。重量几乎相等。再从其造型观察，这4件铜钟的钟体、方孔、底部开口、羊角纽等造型几乎一样，由此可见，这4件铜钟当出某一铸铜工匠之手。同时，其钟声乐律、使用、携带等方面因素，都是铸铜匠师熟思之结晶。这4件铜钟当为1组4件的打击乐器。

表二　浦北县官垌公社平石大队大岭脚村4件羊角纽铜编钟数据表

编号	通高（厘米）	底横长（厘米）	底纵宽（厘米）	方孔尺寸（厘米）		重量（克）
				长	宽	
56-1	24.5	15	9.6	6.1	1.9	1330
56-2	24.3	15	9.3	5.7	1.6	1377
56-3	24.9	15	9.6	6.1	1.7	1552
56-4	24.8	15	9.8	5.5	1.5	1410

图四　浦北大岭脚羊角纽铜编钟

浦北印刷厂钟，2件。1984年在浦北县印刷厂仓库拣选出，现藏浦北县博物馆。其中：浦北57号羊角纽铜编钟，通高26.4、底部口长16.5、宽11.9厘米，穿孔长5.2、宽1.6厘米。重2000克。正、背面阴刻舞人、马图像（图五）。浦北58号羊角纽铜编钟。钟体残缺并被压扁，通高21.9、底长17.6厘米，宽度因压扁而不清，穿孔长5、宽1.4厘米。重548克（图六）。

恭城东寨羊角纽铜钟，1件。1983年广西恭城县莲花乡东寨村农民刘厚藏在其菜园内掘土时发现，该钟通高19.7、底口横长13.5厘米，底口纵宽8厘米，穿孔长4.8、宽1.7厘米。重350克（图七）。

利竹逵羊角纽铜编钟，3件，1986年浦北县福旺乡六寮利竹逵村农民郭润光在后背岭挖沟种木薯时发现，事后一个月，县博物馆才获悉消息派人调查，其中有2件已被郭之孙当废铜卖掉。余下1件，由县博物馆征回，该件羊角纽铜编钟编号为浦151号，通高19.2、底口横长12.2、底口纵宽7.9 厘米，穿孔长6.1、宽2厘米。重589克（图八）。

西林普驮羊角纽铜编钟，2件。1972年在西林县八达公社普合大队普驮粮站晒场西汉早期铜鼓墓葬中出土，钟身呈半截橄榄形，两件大小相同，平口，素面无纹，通高28、底长17.6、宽12.7厘米。上端开1个对穿的长形孔。孔长5.3、宽1.3厘米（图九、图一O）。

大埔羊角纽铜编钟，1件。1982年2月10日柳州市博物馆工作人员在柳州地区土产公司五里卡废旧三仓拣选，后经调查，此钟来自柳城县大埔镇，钟的一面有1个破洞，通体素面无纹，通高20.5、底口横长14厘米，底口纵宽4厘米，方孔长6、宽2.2厘米。重600克（图一一）。

图五　浦北县印刷厂57号羊角纽铜编钟

图六　浦北58号羊角纽铜编钟

图七　恭城东寨羊角纽铜编钟

图八　浦北利竹逵151号羊角纽铜编钟

图九　西林普驮羊角纽铜编钟

图一〇　西林普驮羊角纽铜编钟

图一一　柳州大埔羊角纽铜编钟

图一二　容县龙井化羊角纽铜编钟

表三　容县六王公社龙井化村4件羊角纽铜编钟数据表

容县库房编号	纽长度（厘米）	通高（厘米）	口横长（厘米）	口纵宽（厘米）	方形穿孔（厘米）		重量（千克）
					长	宽	
001200-1	3.7	22.7	10.3	9.8	2.0	1.4	1.425
001200-2	4.7	22.3	10.2	9.1	2.0	1.6	1.050
001200-3	3.3	22.7	10.3	9.2	1.8	1.1	1.295
001200-4	2.2	24.5	10.2	9.2	1.6	1.3	1.210

龙井化羊角纽铜编钟，4件。1976年在广西容县六王公社龙井化村出土，钟体形状和大小略有差异，其中001200-1、2、3号羊角纽铜钟的纽部呈“T”形。是否是羊角形的另一种表现。001200-4号羊角纽铜钟的纽部呈“鱼尾”状。4件羊角纽铜钟的面部饰S形云纹，底部饰9道密集的弦纹（图一二）。其尺寸和重量数据列于表三。

三

铜钟分类

从目前广西所发现羊角纽铜钟的造型、纹饰、重量等方面情况看，其钟体没有太大的变化，都呈半截橄榄形钟体，当然，有的钟体瘦高一点，有的则矮胖一些。而纽部羊角形有所变化。有的纽羊角上弯，有的纽羊角横直，为此，对羊角纽铜钟的分类已有几种不同的方法，如李纯一先生的“比值”分类方法，以通高与铣间之比值在2以内为Ⅰ型，2以上为Ⅱ型，Ⅰ型有平口和凹口之分。广西普驮西汉羊角纽钟、罗泊湾1号墓西汉羊角纽铜钟、浦北56-1号羊角纽铜钟被列为Ⅰ型二式。容县001200-4号羊角纽铜钟为Ⅱ型一式，001200-1、2、3号羊角纽铜钟为Ⅱ型二式。依据李纯一的比值分类方法，我们对广西这几件羊角纽铜钟进行了比值计算于表四。

表四　广西部分羊角纽铜编钟体的比值计算表　（厘米）

钟 号	通高	口横长	口纵宽	通高与口横长比值	通高与口纵宽比值	穿孔	
						长	宽
普驮钟1号钟	28.0	17.6	12.7	1.59	2.20	/	/
普驮钟2号钟	28.0	17.6	12.7	1.59	2.20	5.3	1.3
罗泊湾（土10821）	19.0	14.0	8.1	1.36	2.34	5.4~5.7	1.2~2.0
贵港1号钟	22.2	15.0	9.5	1.48	2.33	4.5	1.7
浦北大脚岭56-1号钟	23.0	15.0	8.3	1.74	1.40	6.1	1.9
浦北大脚岭56-2号钟	24.3	15.0	9.3	1.62	2.61	5.7	1.6
浦北大脚岭56-3号钟	24.9	15.0	9.6	1.66	2.59	6.1	1.7
浦北大脚岭钟56-4号钟	24.8	15.0	9.8	1.65	2.53	5.5	1.5
浦北印刷厂57号钟	26.4	16.5	11.9	1.60	2.22	5.2	1.6
浦北印刷厂58号钟	21.9	17.6	/	1.24	/	5.0	1.4
浦北利逵151号钟	19.2	12.2	7.9	1.57	2.43	6.1	2.0
龙井化001200-1号钟	22.7	10.3	9.8	2.20	2.31	2.0	1.4
龙井化001200-2号钟	22.3	10.2	9.1	2.19	2.45	2.0	1.6
龙井化001200-3号钟	22.7	10.3	9.2	2.20	4.47	1.8	1.1
龙井化001200-4号钟	24.5	10.2	9.2	2.4	2.6	1.6	1.3
柳州大埔1号钟	20.5	14.0	4.0	1.46	5.13	6.0	2.2
恭城东寨1号钟	24.5	13.7	/	1.78	/	/	/

从表四所列出的钟体高与口横长、宽比值数据看，广西普驮、罗泊湾M1：31号羊角纽铜钟和浦北56－1号羊角纽铜钟的通高与口横长比值为1.36～1.59，符合“李氏比值”分类法[①]，但他为什么把比值2.0作为Ⅰ、Ⅱ型分界线，没有更多的分梳。但从造型与普驮、罗泊湾、浦北56－1号羊角纽铜钟不甚相同的容县龙井化001200－4号羊角纽铜钟来看，其比值大于2.0，外观加比值，似乎划为Ⅱ型比较合适，因此，这种“比值”分类法应该说是有一定的科技含量，以数据说话。如何充分发挥科技作用同时又考量其物体表象等因素，是值得研究的。把“比值”分类法同考古学分类法结合起来，应当说是比较理想的方法，有人对全国38件羊角纽铜钟的通高与底横长比值作了分析，在38件羊角纽铜钟中，通高与底横长比值从1.28到1.84有34件，而这些羊角纽铜钟在外观上也比较相似。似乎归为同一类比较合适，在2.0以上有4件。而且这4件都是广西容县六王公社龙井化村出土的铜钟，仔佃观察这4件的羊角纽、钟身等造型确实与广西普驮、罗泊湾、浦北56－1号羊角纽铜钟不同。因此，本文将利用“比值”法进行分类，并引入考古学分类方法的理念，注重钟体造型的变化，综合分析各种原因，使分类处于比较合理的范围，现把广西的羊角纽铜钟中分作两大类型。

A型　13件，分二式。

Ⅰ式：4件。包括柳州大埔钟、浦北利逵151号钟、西林普驮钟2件，其主要特点：钟身上小下大，肩部明显上收，钮槽平坦且间距较大，羊角高伸长弯。钟体素面无纹。钟体与底口横长比值为1.46、1.59、1.78。落差0.2之间。但柳州大埔钟的钟体与口纵宽的比值为5.13。与上述羊角纽铜钟的比值落差较大，但造型仍无他异，故归此类。

Ⅱ式：9件。包括罗泊湾M1：31钟、贵港钟、东寨钟、浦北大脚岭56－1、2、3、4号钟和浦北印刷厂57、58号钟。其主要特点是钟体比较丰满，上下比较均匀，羊角较短，纽间较窄。钟体铸有纹饰，如菱形雷纹、人面纹等，钟体与底口横长比值在1.24～1.74，相差较大。方穿孔长4.5～6.1厘米，宽1.3～1.9厘米。比值在0.24～0.31。

B型　4件，分二式。

Ⅰ式：1件。容县龙井化001200－4号钟，其主要特点是钟体瘦高，羊角纽呈鱼尾状，穿孔小，长1.6、宽1.3厘米，几乎呈正方形，钟体底部饰9道弦纹。钟体与底口横长比值为2.4。

Ⅱ式：3件。容县龙井化001200－1、2、3号钟，其主要特点是钟体瘦高，纽部非羊角形，而且呈T状，穿孔长1.8～2、宽1.1～1.6厘米，几乎成为正方形，方孔小，与上述一类钟的大穿孔相比差别较大。钟体底部饰9道弦纹。钟体与底口横长比值为2.19～2.20。与一类钟的底口部比值在2.0以下形成明显的差异。

① 李纯一:《中国出土乐器综论》，文物出版社，1996年。

四

问题讨论

（一）关于羊角纽铜钟的命名

羊角纽铜钟是一种青铜打击乐器，其主要特征是中空，外形酷似半截橄榄核状，上小下大，纽部似羊角，下方有一长方形挂孔，侧面各有一条合范线。钟体多数为素面，个别铸有纹饰，一般饰有动物纹、几何形状纹和人面纹。对于羊角纽铜钟的命名，已有诸多叫法，目前能找到的文献资料是1933年罗香林在文史学研究所月刊第3期发表的《古代越族考》中，介绍了广东发现的羊角纽铜钟，他当时将其称之为“铜铎”①。1956年，云南省博物馆在晋宁石寨山发掘的6号墓中发现1件羊角纽铜钟，称为“大铜铃”②。1978年，广西文物工作队发表的《广西西林县普驮铜鼓墓葬》中称之为“钟”③。1984年蒋廷瑜先生在《羊角纽铜钟初论》中说：“根据钟纽的奇特，我们姑从俗称，把它叫羊角纽钟”④。1963年，越南黎文兰等人所写的《越南青铜时代的第一批遗迹》一书中认为是“象铃”，但在文中又说：“有一些人认为这些铃子是缚在象颈上的。铃的大小可能适于这种用途。但所有找到的铃子都没有铃铛，可能认为这是一种供敲打的铃更合适些”⑤。云南省博物馆黄德荣先生在《云南羊角纽编钟》中认为：“虽然称羊角纽铜钟较为贴切，只是这类器物多以数件一起用，故笔者认为用羊角编钟更合适一些”⑥。1985年，本文作者曾在《乐器》上发表文章，认为“因其钮形似羊角，而且所发现者绝大多数都相配成套，故名羊角纽铜编钟”⑦。至今，经过26年的资料发现和研究，我仍认为以“羊角纽铜编钟”命名为好，这个名称比黄德荣先生所命之名多一个“铜”字。这是根据我国馆藏文物定名的基本要求而增多了文物的质地，以别它质。正如潘郁生先生在《博物馆藏品数据库管理若干问题思考》中所说：“藏品定名的用词排序一般来说器物名称放在定名最后，它前面的修饰词是质地”⑧。因此，称“羊角纽铜编钟”比较好。理由如下：

（1）从发现的资料看，目前已在27处发现64件羊角纽铜钟，2～6件为组已有发现，而且还发现由小到大组成一套编钟的文物，如1975年，楚雄万家坝1号墓出土6件羊角编钟（图一三）。1989年，云南元江县牛街一农民锄地时发现1组羊角纽铜编钟，共4件，置于坑内，坑内未发现伴随物。1974年，广西浦北县官垌公社平石大队大岭脚村农民于该村后背岭挖土时发现4件在一起的羊角纽铜编钟（图一四）。1974年，广西浦北县官垌公社平石大队大岭脚村农民于该村后背岭挖土时一共挖出4件。大小相似。1987年11月，云南省新平县漠沙西尼河出土4件，形状基本相同，1941年越南兴安省发现4件套在一起的羊角纽铜编钟等。其组合如下表五。

① 罗香林：《古代越族考》，《文史学研究所月刊》，国立中山大学，1933年第1卷第3期。

② 云南省博物馆：《云南晋宁石寨山古墓群发掘报告》，文物出版社，1959年。

③ 广西壮族自治区文物工作队：《广西西林县普驮墓葬》，《文物》1978年第9期。

④ 蒋廷瑜：《羊角纽铜钟初论》，《文物》1984年第5期。

⑤ 黎文兰等人著、梁志明译：《越南青铜时代的第一批遗迹》，1982年，中国古代铜鼓研究会印。

⑥ 黄德荣：《云南羊角纽编钟》，《四川文物》2007年第5期。

⑦ 黄启善：《广西西林县出土的汉代羊角纽铜编钟》，《乐器》1985年第1期。

⑧ 潘郁生：《博物馆藏品数据库管理若干问题思考》，《博物馆与旅游——广西壮族自治区博物馆第二届学术研讨会论文集》，广西科学技术出版社，2010年。

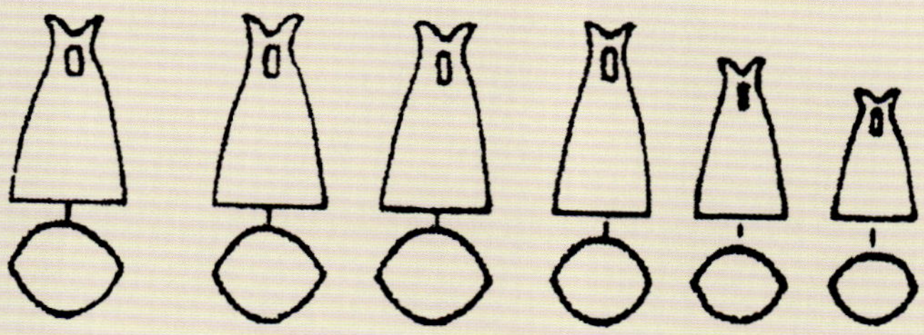

图一三　云南万家坝6件套编钟

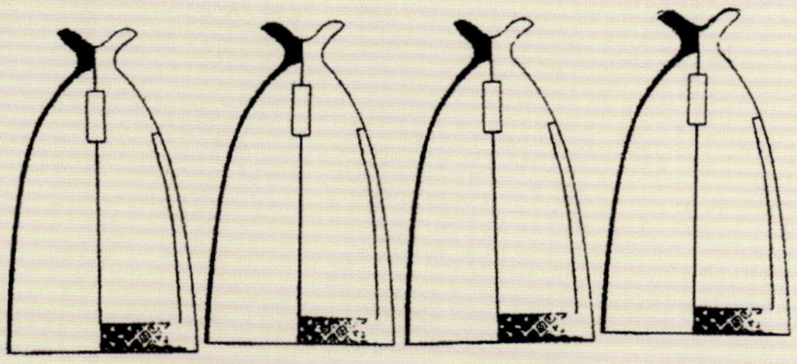

图一四　广西浦北4件套编钟

表五　羊角纽铜编钟成组情况表

地点	件数	单件为组	2件为组	3件组	4件为组	6件为组
云南楚雄万家坝	6					★
云南晋宁县石寨山	1	★				
云南新平县腰街细丫口	1	★				
云南新平县漠沙西泥河	4				★	
云南西畴县芦材村	1	★				
云南文物商店	1	★				
云南广南县小尖山	1	★				
云南元江县牛街	4				★	
云南麻栗坡新保寨	4				★	
广西贵港1号	1	★				
广西贵港罗泊湾M1:37	1	★				
广西西林	2		★			
广西浦北县大岭脚	4				★	
广西浦北县印刷厂	2		★			
广西浦北县利逵	3			★		
广西恭城县	1	★				
广西容县	4				★	
广西柳州大埔	1	★				
广州市博物馆	1	★				
湖南省长沙、衡阳	5					
贵州省安龙县停西乡	1	★				
贵州省安龙县文昌官	1	★				
越南北江	2		★			
越南兴安	4				★	
越南北部	2		★			
越南老街	6					★

从上表五可看到，除湖南省长沙、衡阳收集5件不明其组合外，其余组合有单件组、2件组、3件组、4件组、6件组等。其单件有12个，占实际总数的20.33%；2件组4处8个，占13.55%；3件组1处3个，占5.08%；4件组6处24个，占40.68%；6件组2处12个，占20.39%。如果把2件以上组合形式数量与实际总数之比，约占79.66%。由此可见，2件组以上组合形式占相当大的比例。因此，将铜钟命名为“羊角纽铜编钟”是比较符合实际的。

（2）从花山岩画中看，广西宁明花山岩画中，有4处绘有羊角纽编钟的演奏图像，其中有除了单件钟外，在宁明花山和宁明高山各有一处4件为套的羊角纽铜编钟演奏图像（图一五）。

（二）关于羊角纽铜编钟的年代问题

羊角纽铜编钟产生于何时，虽然文献没有记载，但考古发掘资料可以给予充分证明，经过科学考古发掘的云南楚雄万家坝M1号墓出土的羊角纽铜编钟，是目前已知此类钟中最古老的物件。经中国社会科学院考古研究所和北京大学历史系考古专业碳-14实验室对万家坝M1号墓的棺木测定，该墓葬年代距今2375±80年，相当于春秋晚—战国时期。正如黄德荣先生所说：“M1号墓的年代定在春秋晚—战国时期，它也就是A型羊角编钟的年代”[①]。在云南广南小尖山墓地和晋宁石寨山第6号墓出土的羊角纽铜钟，也被认为是战国至西汉时期的遗物。那么，广西羊角纽铜编钟的年代又如何呢？广西羊角纽铜编钟经过科学考古发掘获得只有1件，即贵港罗泊湾1号西汉早期墓出土的羊角纽铜编钟。该墓葬年代“为西汉初期，上限到秦末，下限不会晚于文景时期”[②]。其余羊角纽铜编钟都是未经过科学的考古发掘获得，但有的具有明显时代特征的伴随物可证。如广西西林县普驮铜鼓墓葬出土2件羊角纽编钟，伴随物均显示西汉初期特征，因此，把其列入西汉初期之物当是无疑。由此，本文将广西羊角纽铜编钟分为A、B两大类型，目的在于寻求其相对年代。

（1）A型Ⅰ式，包括柳州大埔钟、浦北利逵151号钟、西林普驮钟2件，其主要特点：钟身上小下大，肩部明显上收，纽槽平坦且间距较大，羊角高伸长弯。其中的西林普驮钟的年代，当与墓葬年代相同。至于柳州大埔钟，有的认为是“战国时期”[③]。但仔细观察对比，与云南广南小尖山战国至西汉墓地出土的羊角纽铜钟相似，广南小尖山钟的羊角纽上弯较多，而柳州大埔钟的羊角纽向上短斜，羊角弯度不大，而钟体与西林普驮钟完全一样，因此，把它归入A型Ⅰ式是比较合适，其年代与西林普驮墓葬的年代相当。

（2）A型Ⅱ式，包括罗泊湾M1：31钟、贵港钟、东寨钟、浦北大脚岭56-1、2、3、4号钟和浦北印刷厂57、58号钟。其主要特点是钟体比较丰满，上下比较均匀，羊角较短，纽间较窄。罗泊湾M1：31钟铸有人面纹、浦北大岭脚羊角纽铜钟身

① 黄德荣：《云南羊角纽编钟》，《四川文物》2007年第1期。

② 广西壮族自治区博物馆：《广西贵县罗泊湾汉墓》，文物出版社，1988年，89页。

③ 柳州博物馆：《柳州馆藏文物珍品》，广西美术出版社，2007年。

图一五　花山羊角纽铜编钟图画

图一六　浦57号铜编钟刻划纹

饰菱形雷纹，浦北印刷厂仓库拣选出，人物、巨兽纹等与云南新平县漠沙西尼河出土双菱形纹钟和麻栗坡八布乡江东村委会新堡寨村小组毛木树林处出土人面纹钟相似，而罗泊湾M1的年代为西汉初期。

（3）A型钟形体与广西宁明花山岩画中的羊角纽铜编钟图像也十分相似，浦北印刷厂钟体刻划舞人、马图案纹饰，与宁明花山的舞人、马图像也十分相似（图一六）。

（4）B型虽分二式，但其基本型是相同的，只在羊角纽形状上有别。整个体形与A型有很大区别，类似体形的羊角纽铜编钟，在目前已发现的60多件钟中是别具一格的，如羊角纽或直横或像鱼尾，穿孔长只有1.6～2厘米，与A型穿孔长普遍在5～6厘米形成了鲜明的对比。首先从穿孔看，穿孔已由原来的长方形变成近似方形，再从钟体看，钟体形似弹头，如此弦纹多见于两汉时期的青铜器上，尤其细致密集且较凸出的弦纹，在冷水冲、灵山型铜鼓鼓身上常见，依据各方面资料显示，这类钟似乎是接近衰落时期的产物，而不是"战国时期"①的遗物，有可能是西汉晚期至东汉时期的文物。这是目前所看到遗物的年代，当然，广西出现羊角纽铜编钟可能还早，因为广西宁明花山岩画已有羊角纽铜编钟演奏的画像，而宁明花山岩画的年代为战国至东汉时期，当然也有人认为"是在西周至唐代这段时间绘制的"②。羊角纽铜编钟最早在云南出现，尔后逐渐向周边扩散，因此，广西羊角纽铜编钟流行时间当晚于云南。

（三）关于羊角纽铜编钟的悬挂演奏问题

羊角纽铜编钟的悬挂方式直接影响其乐律，在先秦时期，钟类乐器多采用悬而击之，称"悬鸣"，手拿击之，称为"执鸣"，插入座架上敲击，称为"植鸣"。羊角纽铜编钟在演奏时采用那一种方法呢，李纯一在《中国出土乐器综论》中认为是"悬鸣"，并绘图示意（图一七）。

从图一七中看到，李氏推测的5种方式，一是绳子直接穿过方孔悬挂，二、三是缚其双角悬挂，四是绳子穿过方孔后再缠羊角根部悬挂，五是用金属钩勾住穿

① 广西文物管理委员会、广西壮族自治区文化厅：《广西文物珍品》，广西美术出版社，2002年。

② 梁旭达：《试论广西花山崖画的年代问题》，《广西博物馆文集》第二辑，广西人民出版社，2005年。

孔悬挂。李氏悬挂法与广西宁明花山岩画所画的羊角纽铜编钟架挂法不一样（图一八），是古人画不对还是李氏悬挂法不妥当？对此，我们作了一小实验，发现李氏悬挂法值得商榷。

（1）缚羊角悬挂法，从中国、越南目前所发现的羊角纽铜编钟看，每1个羊角纽铜编钟都有1个长方形穿孔。而且穿孔也很大，留着穿孔不用去缚羊角，似乎此法不妥。

（2）绳穿孔悬挂法，羊角纽铜编钟的穿孔都是长方形，长一般在3～6厘米，宽也有1厘米以上，云南万家坝M1出土的6件羊角纽铜编钟中，有1件是目前已发现的羊角纽铜编钟中最小的铜钟，但其穿孔长也和其他钟一样，长3、宽1.4厘米。如果用绳子穿，只需1个圆孔即可，无需那么大的长方孔，因此，绳穿孔悬挂法也是不可信的。

（3）勾孔悬挂法，用金属勾孔似乎也不妥，也不需那么大的方孔。因此，广西宁明花山崖画所绘的羊角纽铜编钟架挂法是值得信赖的。

（4）架挂法，我们的小实验是依据广西宁明花山岩画所绘的羊角纽铜编钟架

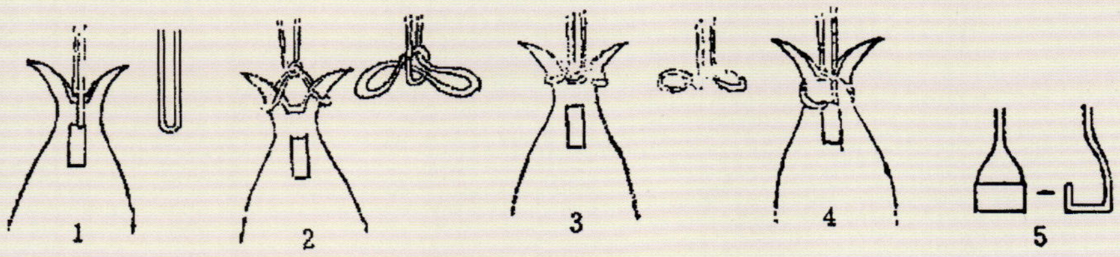

图一七　李氏悬挂羊角纽铜编钟示意图

图一八　花山岩画羊角纽铜编钟架挂图

图一九　小实验架挂图

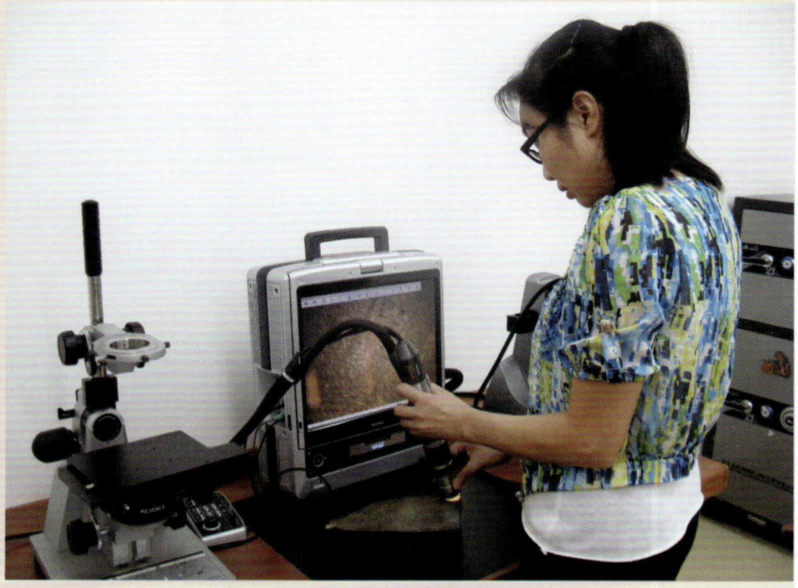
图二〇　羊角纽铜钟测试图

挂图来做的，用1块长方形木条穿过方孔并提起使钟体离地形同架挂（图一九），用小木棍敲击钟的正鼓点和侧鼓点，发现其声音与绳穿孔悬挂法或缚羊角悬挂法不一样，因此，过去用缚羊角悬挂法或绳穿孔悬挂法或勾孔悬挂法所测到的羊角纽铜编钟音频乐律结果是值得怀疑的，由于铜钟方孔穿了方木架条，其音频会有一定旋律散传到木架上，因而当我们敲击正鼓点或侧鼓点时，听到的声音比较圆润，不是钉当震耳的尖声。实验员还用基恩士VHX_600E数码显微镜对钟身进行检测，未发现敲击痕迹（图二〇）。因此，当时敲击时并非有人所说："因木棒敲击声音很沉闷而用金属棒"。但实验证明当时应是用质地较软的木棒作槌，如用金棒槌敲击，击点必留有金属棒槌击痕。而检测结果未发现击痕。

羊角纽铜编钟与铜鼓、环耳直筒形铜钟一起，作为古代金属打击乐器，这在广西花山岩画、广西罗泊湾汉墓、西林普驮汉墓、云南万家坝、石寨山、越南海防船棺墓等，都发现和证实羊角纽铜编钟与铜鼓、环耳直筒形铜钟在演奏时是合乐之器，因此，羊角纽铜编钟在演奏时当为架挂，尤其是多件套编钟，如果是绳挂或勾挂，敲击时钟体会摆动而影响击打。而架挂法则使钟体固定稳当，尤其是木架条插入钟体四方穿孔后，使钟身更加牢固，因此，羊角纽铜编钟架挂法是当时最理想的方式。

（四）关于羊角纽铜编钟的族属问题

对于羊角纽铜编钟的族属问题，前人已有所分析研究，如黄德荣先生在《云南羊角纽编钟》一文中认为："如果按照濮人的说法，云南羊角编钟的主人都是濮人。如果按照越人说，在云南部分地区（滇池地区的越人）也使用羊角编钟。不过无论持何种观点，句町国、居住在元江流域之主人的族属应是濮，这一点学术界无异词"[①]。由此可见，云南羊角纽铜编钟的族属当属濮族。而广西又如何呢？蒋廷瑜先生认为，"羊角纽钟可以视为岭南越族的一种特殊乐器"[②]。依据《史记·西南夷列传》载："西南夷君长以什数，夜郎最大；其西靡、莫之属以什数，滇最大"。可以认为"滇"族在靡、莫这两个族群中势力是最大的1个。1956年晋宁石寨山第6号墓中发现1件羊角纽编钟和1枚"滇王之印"金印，还出土了铜执伞俑、铜鼓、环纽编钟等大量青铜器。《史记·西南夷列传》还记载汉武帝元封二年（前109年）滇王尝羌内附，"赐滇王王印，复长其民"。这表明石寨山第6号墓主是一代滇王，反映了"其西靡、莫之属以什数，滇最大"记载的真实性。广西西部地区与云南、贵州为邻，源出云南省沾益县马雄山的红水河把广西、贵州、云南紧紧相连，使广西的越人与滇人、夜郎人既有物质交流又有文化交流，广西西林古为句町地，春秋战国时期句町部族的活动范围，《华阳国志·南中志》云："句町县，故句町王国名也，其置自濮，王姓毋，汉时受封至今"[③]到了西汉，句町开始设县，根据《汉书·地理志》，句町设县为汉武帝元鼎六年（前111年），而《汉书·地

① 黄德荣：《云南羊角纽编钟》，《四川文物》2007年第5期。

② 蒋廷瑜：《羊角纽铜钟初论》，《文物》1984年第5期。

③（晋）常璩著、严茜子点校：《二十五别史·华阳国志·九家旧晋书辑本》，齐鲁书社，2000年，59页。

理志》句町条下引应邵注说，句町县是“故句町国”。据此可知，先有句町国，后才有句町县，而句町国应由句町族而得名。西林普驮西汉铜鼓墓葬出土的2件羊角纽铜编钟的使用者为句町族是无疑的。而在广西贵港罗泊湾1号西汉墓葬出土了1件羊角纽铜钟，这是在骆越地域出现的，柳州、容县、恭城、浦北等地出土或征集到的羊角纽铜编钟，虽不能认定是墓葬或窖藏之物，但其在古时瓯、骆越族人居地出现，这无疑是古时瓯、骆越族人曾使用之物，因此，可以说广西发现的羊角纽铜编钟当属西瓯、骆越族人所执有。

五

结　语

广西发现羊角纽铜编钟数量仅次于云南，排列在世界上已发现的羊角纽铜编钟的第二位。因此，对广西羊角纽铜编钟的研究将有助于解决羊角纽铜编钟的产生、发展、衰落等发展历史过程，从而了解其用途、属族、音频乐律等方面情况。通过对广西羊角纽铜编钟的分析研究，我认为：

（1）广西羊角纽铜编钟的产生与云南是羊角纽铜编钟发源地有很大关系，两地近邻，往来密切，从云南传入广西。

（2）广西羊角纽铜编钟在广西流行时间应该是两汉时期，虽然宁明花山岩画的年代为战国至东汉，但广西目前考古发现的羊角纽铜编钟都是西汉时期，而有的把未经考古发掘获得的征集品定为战国文物是有所欠缺的。

（3）羊角纽铜编钟虽有单个出现，但不影响其称为“编钟”，因为“编钟”更体现其真正的用途，它不仅自身可编连多钟，而且还与铜鼓、环纽铜钟形成配套的合奏打击乐器。

（4）羊角纽铜钟最早在云南滇族使用，然后扩散周边，为西瓯骆越族所纳。

（5）羊角纽铜编钟的演奏方式是架挂法，而不是绳悬法或勾挂法。因此，过去运用不当悬挂方式测试其音频乐律等结果是值得怀疑的。综上所述，可以认为广西羊角纽铜编钟是骆越青铜文化的组成部分，曾经与铜鼓为伍，演奏一曲一曲幽雅动听的和谐之音。

广西古代社会进入青铜时代的时间问题

Discussion about the time of Guangxi Entering Bronze Age

蓝日勇 / 广西壮族自治区博物馆 研究员

[摘要]

本文从中国青铜时代的标准和特征出发，研究广西出土的先秦青铜器，认为广西古代社会进入青铜时代的时间为春秋晚期。

[关键词]

广西 进入 青铜时代 时间

Abstract

There were three theories on the academic problem of when Guangxi entered the Bronze Age, they are the late Shang and early Zhou Dynasties, the middle and late Western Zhou Dynasty and the late Warring States Period. According to the standards and characteristics of the Chinese Bronze Age, we researched the ancient bronzes which were discovered in Guangxi archaeological work and discovered that this region was still in the preliminary stage of the development of Bronze culture in the late Shang and early Zhou Dynasties, and until the middle of the Spring and Autumn Period, it also used Stone-mold in the Bronze casting, the process is very slow, by the late Spring and Autumn Period, not only some of the tombs' burial accessories were all bronzes, but also because the use of advanced Mud-mold casting technique to produce large containers, particularly, there appeared the combined Sacrificial vessel and Musical Instruments,such as the ancient cooking vessels, clocks and so on, it proved that at this time Guangxi had entered the Bronze Age.

Key words

Guangxi; Entering; Bronze Age; Time

在广西青铜文化的研究中，涉及本地何时进入青铜时代的问题已在多种论著中有简单提及。概括起来主要有三种说法：商末周初说、战国晚期说、桂西西周中晚期说。由此而见，关于这一论题，学术界目前还没有形成定论。笔者认为，这一问题先前之所以出现多种见解，除了缺乏专门深入讨论之外，个中原因可能还与各家采用的标准不同有关。所以，本文借此尚存的空间，以中国青铜时代的特征为标准，开展探讨，期为引玉之砖。

一

中国青铜时代的认知标准与特征

就世界范围而言，在人类技术发展的历史中，使用青铜兵器和工具的时代就称青铜时代。“青铜时代”首先由丹麦人克·吉·汤姆森提出使用，他在1816年被命名为国家博物馆首席馆长后，为了陈列藏品，将馆藏武器与工具按制作材料进行了分类，并依其材料划分出石器、青铜器和铁器三个相互衔接的时代。他在《北方古物指南》称“青铜时代”为“以红铜或青铜制成武器和切制器”的时代。汤姆森的学说后来被丹麦以外的欧洲其他国家如瑞典、德国、英国的一部分考古学家所采用。到19世纪中叶，由于史前考古的发现，不仅证实了划分三个时代的学说，同时欧洲的考古学家开始依照各国考古材料对三个时代的学说进行了修订与补充，先将石器列分为旧石器时代与新石器时代；接着，19世纪最后30年，由意大利考古学家提出，应在青铜时代前加进一个“铜石并用时代”。至19世纪末叶，此一建议已得到欧洲部分考古学家的赞同。“铜石并用时代”的提出并将这一个相对独立的时期从青铜时代中划分出去，可以使“青铜时代”的特征与此一名称更相符合。

西方考古学传入中国后，我国考古学者所采用的青铜时代的概念，也是强调青铜器在社会物质文化中所起的重要作用。如1955年出版的《原始文化史纲》书中的由容庚、张维持合著的《殷周青铜通论》就引用苏联学者M·O·柯斯文所下的定义：“青铜成为广泛传播的，制造工具、武器、器皿和装饰品的主要原料”。1980年出版的《中国大百科全书·考古学》分卷解释青铜时代是“以青铜作为制造工具、用具或武器的重要原料的人类物质文化发展阶段。”美籍学者张光直在其《中国青铜时代》一文亦明确指出，“我们所谓中国青铜时代，是指青铜器在考古记录中有显著重要性的时期而言的。而辨识那显著重要性的依据，是我们所发现器物的种类和数量，使我们对青铜器的制作和使用在中国人的生活里占中心地位的事实，不容置疑。”

世界各地进入青铜时代的年代有早有晚，欧洲和伊朗、土耳其、美索不达米亚一带在前4000～前3000年，印度及埃及在前3000～前2000年，非洲大约在前1000～公元初年，美洲到将近11世纪才出现冶铜中心。中国的青铜文化起源于黄河流域，青铜时代始于前21世纪，止于前5世纪。中国青铜时代的特征是“大量使用青铜生产工具、兵器和大量使用青铜礼器”[①]。

二

广西先秦青铜器发现概况

尽管中国内地在前3000年的马家窑文化中已出现青铜小刀，前2300年的齐家文化遗址中见到青铜镜，但广西出土的青铜器，年代最早的是商代晚期。而且只有两例。一是武鸣县马头公社全苏大队勉岭出土铜卣、铜戈各1件，二是马头公社那堤大队敢猪岩发现1件铜戈。勉岭出土的铜卣（图一），扁圆体，垂腹，纵向提梁，通体以云雷纹为地，饰三重花纹，商代晚期特征非常明显。又卣盖内阴刻一铭文，可译为“天”字或“子”字，同中原地区一些商末周初青铜器上的铭文很相近，因而该铜卣应为商末之物。勉岭及敢猪岩铜戈，在纹饰或造型上亦具有商代晚期的特征，时代相同[②]。西周的铜器，在广西先是零星发现，后才在墓葬有出土。零星发现计有横县镇龙浮雕饰铜钟，兴安县兴安镇田心砖厂铜簋，灌阳云纹铜钟和三角援铜戈，忻城大塘乳钉纹铜钟，宾阳、荔浦、陆川所出的3件铜罍[③]。墓葬出土西周铜器仅有两处，一处是武鸣县马头乡马头圩元龙坡，另一处为贺州市马东村。元龙坡墓地一次发掘清理古墓350座，随葬品较少，一般只有三四件，其中约三分之一的墓空无一物。随葬品以陶器为主，次为铜器、玉

① 马承源：《中国青铜器》，上海古籍出版社，1988年。

② 蒋廷瑜、彭书琳：《历史的足迹——广西历史时期考古手记》，广西人民出版社，2006年。

③ 梁景津：《广西出土的青铜器》，《文物》1978年第10期；广西壮族自治区博物馆：《近年来广西出土的先秦青铜器》，《考古》1984年第9期。

图一　铜卣

图二　铜尊

石器。铜器计110余件，有矛、钺、斧、匕首、镦、镞、圆形器、卣、盘、刀、凿、针、铃、钟（？）、链环。其中，矛21件，钺11件，斧23件，匕首3件，镦10件，镞10件，圆形器5件，卣1件，盘1件，刀12件，凿1件，针2件，铃5件，钟（？）1件，链环1件。这批墓葬的年代，发掘简报执笔者认为"上限在西周，下限在春秋时期"。但有学者认为更晚①。马东村共发现两座墓葬，1号墓仅出土1件铜罍，2号墓见随葬品7件，全是青铜器，为鼎、甬钟、矛、短剑、镞、钺和锛，数量皆各1件。这两座墓的年代，简报推断是西周晚期或春秋早期②。春秋时期的青铜器，零星发现的不多，迄今资料公布的有宾阳新宾下河凉水坪栉齿纹铜钟、南宁郊区那洪苏盘窃曲纹铜钟、宾阳芦圩铜钟。集中发现的仅有1例，即1971年在恭城县嘉会公社秧家大队收集到的33件青铜器，器类含鼎（5件）、罍（1件）、尊（图二）（2件）、编钟（2件）、钺（2件）、剑（4件）、戈（1件）、镞（5件）、斧（2件），还有车饰和尖状器各2件。此外，武鸣县马头乡马头圩元龙坡墓地出土的青铜器，当有一部分属春秋时期，待发掘报告出版时，定会有较清楚的知晓③。战国青铜器发现较多，出土地点亦多，而大多数的青铜器出自墓群。田东锅盖岭2座土坑墓发现铜器14件，包括鼓1件、剑2件、矛2件、镦1件、斧4件、叉形器3件。武鸣马头安等秧86座土坑墓出土器物205件，采集器物11件，其中青铜器86件，包括剑、矛、钺、镞、斧、刮刀、镯、钏、带钩、铃等。武鸣独山岩洞葬出土铜剑、钺、斧、矛、戈、镞、刮刀。宾阳韦坡村2座墓先后发现于1977年和1979年，收集铜器21件，含鼎、剑、矛、钟、斧、叉形器、刮刀等。象州下那槽战国墓，发现时间不详，采集铜器计3件，为矛、钺和人首柱形器。平乐银山岭110座墓，出土加上采集到铜器计400件，包括了鼎、盆、钵、勺、剑、矛、钺、戈、镞、镦、矩、斧、凿、刮刀、钻头、削、盖弓帽、铃、带钩、杖头饰等种类。1991年发掘的岑溪糯垌花果山14座土坑墓，出土铜器30件，分属剑、矛、锛、钺、斧、刮刀、削、镞、镦，另外，还于墓群所在地收集到铜器39件，器类基本同于墓葬所出，仅增加鼎和簏两种。2001年广西文物工

① 广西壮族自治区文物工作队等：《广西武鸣马头元龙坡墓葬发掘简报》，《文物》1988年第12期；李龙章：《广西右江流域战国秦汉墓研究》，《考古学报》2004年第3期。

② 贺州市博物馆：《广西贺州市马东村周代墓葬》，《考古》2001年第11期。

③ 广西壮族自治区博物馆：《近年来广西出土的先秦青铜器》，《考古》1984年第9期；广西壮族自治区博物馆：《广西恭城县出土的青铜器》，《考古》1973年第1期。

作队勘探贺州市高屋背岭古墓群，探出129座墓，试掘2座，证实为战国墓，出土文物50件，青铜器占48件，内中刀锯两用器、转角器、棺栓为首次发现①。

三

广西青铜时代问题的讨论

从上可见，广西最早的青铜器为商代晚期器，数量很少，皆是零星出土，无伴随物，当为窖藏品；因无伴随物，导致入藏的时间不明，性质欠清楚；它们的器型和装饰作风皆同中原同类器，可谓是中原传入的铜器；也由于埋藏情况不明，何时传入广西尚属未知。著名的勉岭铜卣，为何传到武鸣埋于当地，有专家学者作出如下三种推测：一是南方民族首领向商王进贡地方特产，商王将铜卣回赠给他们带回。二是南方民族首领在同商或商的附属国打仗时虏获了这件铜卣，作为战利品带回。三是商末周初中原战乱，失败的奴隶主南逃，把铜卣带到这里来②。这三种可能中无论哪一种成立，都说明铜卣是传来广西的，它同另外两件戈的出现，只能表明于商代末期或西周初年，中原的青铜器传到广西腹地，广西之有青铜文化始于此时，此时是广西青铜文化发展之初期。

广西零星发现的西周青铜器，在年代上，皆属西周中期和后期的器物，从造型和装饰看主要还是中原内地的风格。如忻城大塘铜钟，钟身饰乳钉纹，舞部饰兽面纹，鼓部正中饰窃曲纹，其造型与纹饰与长安普渡村西周墓出土的铜钟相似。又如荔浦、陆川出土的铜罍，器形呈“亚”字形，体现出西周时期同类器物的作风，立体兽耳装饰及其高圈足的做法，大同于四川彭县窖藏的西周铜罍。而且这种造型和装饰的铜罍，在内蒙古自治区亦有出土，现正在内蒙古自治区博物院历史展厅展出。武鸣马头元龙坡墓群出土的1件铜卣和铜盘，也皆是中原风格的器物。关于马头元龙坡墓群的年代判断，发掘简报以铜卣、铜盘作为主要依据，确定起止于西周晚期。另外是依据采集于部分墓葬中的木炭所作的碳-14测定获得的数据进行推论。如151号墓木炭碳-14测定的年代是距今2850±70年，从而认为内中有西周中期墓；又46号墓木炭碳-14测定的年代是距今2625±70年，相当于春秋中期。从而将这批墓葬推断为西周至春秋时期。但数百座墓中西周墓与春秋墓的各自数量，又春秋墓中哪些为早期哪些是中期，简报皆未能详分。不过简报中提到，“元龙坡墓葬出土的陶器中，有4件拍印变形云雷纹等几何形纹的陶器，与广西地区以往发现的春秋时期盛行的夔纹陶器相比，器形纹饰不大相同。”这样，这批墓葬中当有春秋早期的墓葬存在。因此，有学者认为这批墓葬是目前广西发现的时代最早的青铜时代墓葬。但笔者认为，墓葬的材料反映的青铜文化还没

① 广西壮族自治区文物工作队：《广西田东发现战国墓葬》，《考古》1979年第6期；广西壮族自治区文物工作队等：《广西武鸣马头安等秧战国墓群发掘简报》，《文物》1988年第12期；武鸣县文物管理所：《武鸣独山岩洞葬调查简报》，《文物》1988年第12期；广西壮族自治区文物工作队：《广西宾阳县发现战国墓葬》，《考古》1983年第2期；广西壮族自治区文物工作队：《广西象州县发现一批战国文物》，《文物》1989年第6期；广西壮族自治区文物工作队：《平乐银山岭战国墓》，《考古学报》1978年第2期；广西壮族自治区文物工作队等：《岑溪花果山战国墓清理简报》，《广西考古文集》，文物出版社，2004年；广西壮族自治区文物工作队等：《贺州市高屋背岭古墓群勘探与试掘》，《广西考古文集》，文物出版社，2004年。

② 蒋廷瑜、彭书琳：《历史的足迹——广西历史时期考古手记》，广西人民出版社，2006年。

有发展到青铜时代阶段。理由有三：其一，350座墓葬仅随葬110件铜器，平均起来3座墓才有1件，简报由于缺乏墓葬登记表，使读者不知有多少墓葬随葬铜器，而从简报所例举的墓葬中有2座墓随葬2件和3件铜器的情况看，无铜器的墓葬应该占绝大多数，这应该是社会上铜器还很稀少的体现，离社会大量使用还有相当大的距离。与此墓群时代相同又处于旁近乡镇的岜马山岩洞葬，随葬品就仅见陶器、石器、石子、玉器的情况可作进一步佐证。其二，出土的铜器中，以兵器为主，没有生产工具，更没有礼器。所谓“礼器”，1981年上海辞书出版社出版的《辞海》这样界定：“礼器，也称彝器。古代贵族在进行祭祀、丧葬、朝聘、征伐和宴享、婚冠等活动时举行礼仪所使用的器皿。指青铜器中的鼎、簋、觚、豆和钟、镈等。”简报中虽然说有1座墓发现1件钟体残片和3枚钉，但未发照片等资料，致读者难以确定。又位置不清，性质使人存疑。再是全国各地考古发现的铜钟资料，无论窖藏还是墓中随葬品，都是成套或成件出现，单埋1残片和3个断钉，不可思议。还有本处墓群出土的实物资料反映了当地当时青铜文化尚处于早期发展阶段，铜器的铸造技术是石范法，石范标本全是小件兵器之类的范具，排除了本地能铸造铜钟的可能。再是墓群唯一明确是出土的、属于中原传入的铜卣是完整器，又填土中不见铜钟的其他残片，这就可以肯定这里没有打碎大型铜器分埋或散撒于填土中的习俗。所以，它们很可能不是随葬品，属于扰混之物，或者属性有误。其三，铜器制造技术相当原始。突出的表现是出土的一批砂石铸范，计有完整、成套的双面范6副，单范能辨清铸造器形的6件，残碎的30多件，有的石范内有烧焦的痕迹，说明已经使用过。石范虽有质硬不易破碎可反复多次使用的优点，但缺点也十分明显，质硬加沉重很难制造大型范，又不易在上面雕刻精致的纹饰，所以石范只能铸造小件青铜器，而且多是素面，或是只有简单花纹的青铜器（图三）。而要铸造大件、薄胎和装饰复杂细致的青铜器，只有靠陶范铸造技术和失蜡法。元龙坡这批石范，分属“凤”字形钺、扇形钺、单斜刃钺、斧、镞、圆形器、叉形器等器物范，其中一些钺、斧、镞的范器，将墓中所出的这三类器分别放入，正好吻合，这只能说明在西周末到春秋中期以前的这一时段内，当地已有比较原始的青铜冶铸业。中国青铜时代初期的夏代，除了铸造青铜工具锛、凿、刀、鱼钩和青铜武器戈、戚、镞以外，最大的特点是还能铸造青铜容器爵、斝和鼎，从青铜铸造技术上谈，是掌握了先进的陶范法。以此对照，广西古代社会在春秋中期以前尚未跨入青铜时代。

贺州市马东村两座墓所出的8件青铜器，简报推断它们是西周晚期或春秋早期。笔者经查有关资料，觉得将年代定得过早。一号墓的铜罍定为西周器尽管有造型作依据，但罍肩部装饰的涡纹在恭城秧家铜罍上出现，应该是年代较晚的信息。二号墓的越式鼎，在湖南所出的春秋时期青铜器中多见。如资兴旧市春秋墓出的1件（图四），竖耳，侈口，圜底，袋腹，三高足，上部略粗，近似蹄足，内半空，下部较细，圆柱形，实足，在马东二号墓的越式鼎上完全体现。两者的区别点仅在，资兴旧市越式鼎腹部布满纹饰，上下饰曲折纹，中间一周圆涡纹变形夔纹相间，耳里面饰变形夔纹和龙蛇纹①。而马东越式鼎为素面无纹，按照中国青铜器在西周以后装饰逐渐简素的规律，马东越式鼎比旧市越式鼎为晚。旧市越式鼎为春秋早期，则马东越式鼎当属春秋晚期。中国考古学判断文化遗存的年代，传统的科学做法，是以年代最晚的现象来把握，因而贺州马东的铜器墓年代应和恭城秧家铜器墓一样，为春秋晚期。本文探讨广西青铜时代问题，便基于这两批铜器材料。

观察恭城秧家与贺州马东的铜器，它们的一个共同特点，是出现了鼎和钟。而鼎和钟正是中国青铜礼器中最重要的器物。古籍中所谓的"钟鸣鼎食"正是说明在先秦社会把鼎和钟分别作为贵族所使用的礼乐器的代表。在先秦社会，按《公羊传 · 桓公二年》何休注："礼祭，天子九鼎，诸侯七，大夫五，之士三也。"恭城秧家春秋晚期墓共出5鼎，看来应有组合。除鼎之外，古代使用青铜乐器，其等级制度的规定，也是很鲜明。所谓宫悬、轩悬、判悬、特悬，即天子用乐钟时可四面悬挂，诸侯三面悬挂，大夫两面悬挂，士一面悬挂。据研究，使用乐钟最少3件成编。恭城秧家春秋晚期墓仅出2件编钟，似有遗漏。查发掘简报，说到这批青铜器是公社社员在取土修路时发现，墓葬未经科学发掘，随葬品未完全取出仍有可能。还有是据群众反映和现场残迹观察得知，早在筑路取土前墓葬地表已经几次挖乱，被削去两米，这也可能是造成乐钟缺一的原因。又恭城秧家与贺州马东墓葬随葬的物品，全是铜器，表明社会上已大量使用青铜器。这种现象，已基本体现了中国青铜时代的特征。因此，笔者认为，广西古代社会是发展到相当于中原地区春秋晚期时才跨入青铜时代。

大量的事实证明，广西青铜文化是在中原青铜文化影响下发生的，自身缺乏原创动力，决定了广西青铜文化发展的缓慢性。从铸造技术层面上讲，中原内地在新石器时代开始使用石范，发展到至迟是夏代已换成先进的陶范。而广西地区，从算平南石脚山新石器时代晚期遗址发现的那件石范，因出在扰乱层中，又数量单一，引人疑虑可以不计，而那坡感驮岩所见到石铸范，时在距今3800～2800年范围内的

① 湖南省博物馆：《资兴旧市春秋墓》，《湖南考古辑刊》，岳麓书社，1982年。

图三　石范

图四　铜鼎

青铜文化阶段，证明广西地区在商周时期确实还在使用石范，可惜时到春秋中期，这种状况并没有得到改变。虽然目前广西没有发现先秦时期的冶铜遗址和铸造铜器作坊，但从恭城秧家铜器中4件越式鼎身上留存铸痕判断，广西青铜器陶范制造技术于春秋晚期得到使用，铸造技术上的长期落伍，应该是广西社会较迟跨入青铜时代的一种原因。当然，这种技术落后现象是社会落后的体现，有专家根据武鸣马头两个墓群的材料，分析那时瓯骆社会的性质，认为“随葬品数量不多，各墓之间差异不很悬殊，表明骆越人的社会生产力还比较低，他们跨入了阶级社会的门槛，但处于阶级社会的初级阶段，社会内部的分化、发展是极为缓慢的”①。

从上面介绍广西青铜器发现概况中可以看到，广西青铜文化从开始就伴随着中原青铜器的传入而来，在西周和春秋时期，都有从长江流域甚至黄河流域传入青铜器，而且在整个青铜器数量中，所占的比例比较大。进入青铜时代以后，在所看到的青铜器中，那些为广西本地铸造者，有的在造型与纹饰上明显仿自中原的青铜器，有的与中原的大同小异。新出现的器类，多仿周边的滇、楚、越。如春秋末期和战国时期的万家坝型及石寨山型铜鼓，源头为云南地区的铜鼓文化。再是广西青铜时代的青铜器，大型容器的组合缺乏地方性，如礼乐器，由中原编钟加楚鼎、越鼎来体现。所有这些，或许正是广西青铜时代的特点。

① 马头发掘组:《武鸣马头墓葬与古代骆越》，《文物》1988年第12期。

广西先秦青铜兵器反映的瓯骆方国武装实力

Ou-Luo Ancient Country's Armed Force reflecting from Unearthed Bronze Weapons on Guangxi in Pre-Qin Dynasty

郑超雄／广西壮族自治区博物馆 研究员

[摘要]

广西出土先秦时期的青铜器中，以青铜兵器最多，青铜兵器的大量出现，表明先秦时期瓯骆方国社会已有王权政治和军事武装力量。秦始皇在平定岭南战争中，之所以遭到西瓯、骆越方国的顽强抵抗，致使秦军以“伏尸流血数十万”的代价才能统一岭南地区，从出土先秦青铜兵器中窥视一斑。

[关键词]

青铜兵器　瓯骆方国　武装实力

Abstract

Most pre-Qin dynasty bronze wares unearthed in Guangxi are bronze weapons. The appearance of large number of bronze weapons proves that the Ou-Luo apanage owned empire and armed force. In the battle in Lingnan area, Qin shi huang faced the fierce resistance of Xiou and Luoyue, and occupied the lingnan area at the expense of thousands of soldiers. This can be inferred from the unearthed bronze wares.

Key words

Bronze weapons; Ou-luo states; Armed force

秦始皇在平定岭南战争中，之所以遭到西瓯、骆越方国的强烈有效的抵抗，说明当时的瓯骆方国都有一支训练有素的武装力量。武装的素质包括三方面，一是武装兵员的数量，并有较严格的军阶组织序列；二是灵活机动的战略战术；三是配备精良的武器装备。

当时西瓯、骆越方国的武装力量有多少人？很难作出确切的回答，我们只能从秦军的军队数量来推测。当时秦军共有50万分五路军，进入广西的有两路军，主帅尉屠睢在西路军指挥，是为主战场。若按每路军10万人算，那么最早进攻西瓯方国的秦军约有20万。第一阶段战役虽说西瓯军失利，但秦军并未能长驱直入西瓯腹地，而是被滞停在灵渠以北崇山峻岭地方，并相持三年之久。说明，西瓯方国的武装力量人数与秦军数量是相持平或是更多些。另外，汉武帝平南越国时，桂桂监居翁号召数十万人归降，此时距秦平岭南时间不远，由此推算，与秦军作战的西瓯武装至少在10万人至20万人。文献中说他们的组织中已有君、将，而在将之下应当还有其他军阶序列。因为秦军是组织严密的正规军队，与之对抗作战的西瓯军队，若没有相对应的组织和纪律约束，是无法与秦军对峙数年之久的。正因为他们有组织有纪律，并且有很优秀的指挥统帅，才能对秦军采取灵活机动的战略战术，达到克敌制胜的目的。他们依据丛林、河流、峻岭、烟瘴等地理环境，不与秦军搞阵地战，分散于丛林中，对秦军各个击破的战术应用得相当成功，致使秦军“伏尸流血数十万”。在战争中，人固然是很重要的，但是我们绝对不能忽视武器的作用。没有精良的武器装备，即使有成千上万不怕牺牲的勇士，也是很难取得战争的决胜权的。试想，如果西瓯方国仍处于野蛮社会，手持木器、石器与秦军作战，其后果就不堪设想了。进入战国时期，西瓯、骆越方国的青铜武器在数量和质量上都远远超过商周时期，下面我们选择几个主要墓葬介绍该时期的青铜兵器随葬情况。

平乐银山岭战国墓，共出土377件青铜器，最多的是兵器，其次是生产工具和生活用具。兵器中的剑、矛和工具中的斧、刮刀等，都有使用和磨损痕迹，有的经过长期使用，磨蚀很厉害，质地较好，锋芒仍在。兵器中以剑发现最多，共46件，出土于43座墓中，一般1墓1剑，只有3座墓分别出长、短剑各1把。出土时，一般纵放墓室中部，个别的横放在墓室头端。剑共有五种形式，最长的剑通长67.8厘米，最短的剑长13.5厘米，较多的剑一般长20～25厘米。Ⅰ式剑发现7件，长宽身，圆首茎，茎上有二道凸箍，有格。这式剑，在中原内地从春秋时代晚期到战国时代中、晚期都流行，尤以江淮流域的楚墓中出土最多，安徽淮南蔡家岗战国墓、湖北松滋大岩咀东周土坑墓都出土不少。据此推测，此式剑应是从内地传入的。Ⅳ式剑，35件。无格，折肩，剑身有脊。此式剑最常见，有明显地方特色。形体短小，多数无首，有首的则首茎分铸，首多覆钵形，少数为空圆首或首饰同心圆纹，有柄，全是扁茎，茎上有孔，有的茎上有朽木残迹，推测首柄与茎之间原有木柄衔接。此式剑应是本地铸造。铜矛39件，分别出土于32座墓中，大部分与剑共出，个别的墓出2件或3件，形制变化较大，共有6种之多。另外还发现铁矛3件，分别出土于3墓中。戈，仅发现1件。器身光亮，内平直、援上扬，援、胡、内均为利刃。内上横刻“江”、“鱼”二字，笔画纤细如丝，内的另一面也有细刻文字，但磨蚀严重，已无法认读。此戈应是外地传入。铜镞，170件，分别出土于41座墓中，一般每墓数件，多的10余件，M55最多，出22件，常与剑、矛共出。矢杆、矢箙均朽，除三棱形2件、条形1件外，其余均为双翼形。另外还发现有铁铤铜镞8件，分别出土于7座墓中，均三棱形，铜叶粗短，三刃聚为削锋，三面光平。铤圆柱状，有麻线缠绕痕迹。铜钺，8件。分别出土于8座墓中。Ⅰ式2件，双重肩，小方首，宽弧刃，此类器在广东德庆和四会战国墓中均有出土。Ⅳ式2件，扁圆首鉴，圆弧刃，两侧稍向外伸。外观与磨制石斧无异。以上均是墓葬出土的兵器，在这批墓葬发掘之前或发掘期间，人们在地表上也采集到一批兵器，计有铜剑3件，铜矛5件，铜钺7件，其中的靴形钺2件，此类钺在广东德庆战国墓、云南晋宁石寨山都曾有出土。铜戈1件，铜镞2件，铁钺2件[①]。

武鸣安等秧战国墓葬，出土青铜器86件，以兵器为主。其中铜剑15件，分别出土于15座中，其形式与平乐银山岭差不多，特别是具有地方特色的扁茎无格剑发现最多，共有9件。铜矛6件，其中1件上铸有“王”字，此类矛在广东同类墓中发现最多。钺2件，镞6件，分别出于5座墓内。铜斧共31件。此类器物从商周以来一直在骆越地区多见直到战国时期仍占主导地位，据此推测，斧在骆越方国内到战国时期仍有兵器与劳动工具的双重性质。而在平乐银山岭西瓯方国墓地内，仅发现7件斧，且形体较小，已无兵器作用，而作为纯的劳动工具。

武鸣两江乡三联村独山岩洞葬，是单独个体的墓葬，随葬器物也以兵器为多。计有铜剑4件，其中3件为扁茎无格，另1件仅见剑锋未明式样。铜钺2件，铜矛2件，其中1件上面铸有变体“王”字，铜戈1件，铜镞1件。恭城秧家春秋晚期墓出土的兵器有：铜钺2件皆靴形，铜剑4件，3件为扁茎无格形式，另1件为圆茎，圆首，窄格；铜戈1件，铜镞5件。田东县锅盖岭铜鼓墓中出土的青铜兵器：铜剑2件，均属地方产品，皆扁茎无格，铜矛2件，铜戈1件，铜斧4件。宾阳韦坡两座战国墓中，也以随葬兵器为主。其中1号墓出土铜钺2件，矛2件，斧3件；2号墓出土铜钺1件，铜叉形器1件（很可能属兵器类）。1991年和1998年，灵川县的海洋乡水头村、潮田乡富足村的岩洞里相继出土了一批战国时期的青铜兵器，富足村岩洞的青铜兵器有：戈1件，矛1件，骹的正面印铸有“王”字，铜钺2件，器身上铸印雷纹，镞4件。该岩洞在文物工作者发现之前，已有村民在洞内挖泥土，据传早年曾在洞内发现1件青铜长剑，1件青铜短剑以及砺石等，但已下落不明。水头村岩洞出土的青铜兵器有：铜钺1件，戈1件，矛1件，镖枪头1件，镞2件[②]。

① 广西文物工作队：《平乐银山岭战国墓》，《考古学报》1978年第2期。

② 灵川县文管所：《灵川两岩洞葬出土青铜器》，《中国古代铜鼓研究通讯》第十九期。

综合上述考古材料可知，瓯骆故地上，凡是发现有战国墓的地方，几乎都有青铜兵器。目前在广西境内，除河池地区各县少发现战国青铜兵器之外，其他地方几乎都有战国时期的青铜兵器。有些是出土于墓葬中，有些则是在河流中或是地表采集。采集的青铜兵器数量也不少，目前尚难完全统计。战国时期的青铜兵器品种中，诸如矛、钺、镞、戈在商周时期都已存在，而青铜剑则是新出现的兵器，据目前考古发现所知，青铜剑在广西地区最早发现于恭城秧家春秋晚期墓中，进入战国时期则大批量发现于墓葬中，它与矛一样，是西瓯骆越军队中的主要装备。考古学材料已表明，西瓯骆越部队用的剑早期有些是从楚国传进来的，但很快他们就学会了仿制，现在所发现的剑，绝大部分是地方产品。因此说，剑在瓯骆地区的出现，显然是受到周边地区的政治、军事和文化的影响而出现。

在我国，剑始于何时，目前尚无确切的考古材料可证。但在西周早期就已有剑实物了。甘肃灵台白草坡西周墓中曾出土有透雕龙纹鞘的剑，就是很好的实例。春秋晚期至战国是青铜剑最盛行的时代，汉代的铁剑流行后，青铜剑逐渐被淘汰。剑在北方地区，是贵族和兵士随身佩带用以自卫防身进行格斗、可斩可刺的兵器。《说文》："剑，人所带兵也，从刀佥声。"《释名·释兵》："剑，检也，所以防检非常也。又，敛也，以其在身时，横拱敛在臂内也。"在春秋战国时期，人们佩剑还有表示等级身份的意思。《考工记·桃氏》载士阶层的人，因所佩剑长短重量之不同，称之上制、中制、下制，而分别为上士、中士、下士所服。

瓯骆故地发现的铜剑，最早是春秋晚期，战国时期盛行，是在北方地区流行用剑的时间内出现的。因此，其用剑意识和用剑制度也或多或少受到影响。剑在瓯骆地区也明显有身份地位象征的作用，在贵族墓中往往都有几把剑陪葬，如恭城秧家春秋晚期墓出土4件不同类型的剑，武鸣独山岩洞葬也出现4件青铜剑，这些墓主的身份显然地位很高，他们有单独的墓地，高档次的随葬品多，这些都是他们生前所拥有的，他们的身份应是君、将一级人物。随葬剑的数量越多，就越显示他们权力、地位的显赫。

剑，除显示身份地位作用之外，更多的是武装士兵。平乐银山岭战国墓群中，铜兵器的随葬是很有规律的。剑、矛、镞三种兵器齐全的墓有25座；有矛、镞无剑的墓4座；有剑、镞无矛的12座；有剑、矛无镞的2座；只出一种兵器的有11座。此外，有8座墓出铜钺，1座墓出铜戈，1座墓出铁矛。出铜钺的墓，随葬品一般较丰富，常见铜钺，铜剑、铜矛、铜鼎同出。根据上述统计数字分析，这些随葬有青铜兵器的墓主，生前都是西瓯方国的武装人员，这些人员是有等级地位区别的。第一种等级的墓主是随葬剑、钺、鼎、矛组合器型。钺是征伐仗权性质的武器，鼎是权力地位的象征；剑，一方面表示身份地位，更重要的是具有防身自卫和刺击的实战作用。此类墓主应是直接率兵作战的将领甚至有君王一级的人物。第二种是剑、矛、镞组合形式，这类墓主因武器齐全，估计是方国中的武装骨干，或是相当于将以下的军官。第三种等级的墓主是仅随葬一种或是2件兵器的墓主，他们应是方国内的士兵。有等级差别即能说明方国的武装实体具有严密的组织形式，有严密组织的武装实体是有战斗力的团体。只有进入高级的文明社会才能具有这样的武装实体。春秋战国时期中原地区的步兵装备，一般也都是剑、矛、镞作为常见的装备，西瓯、骆越方国的步兵装备已接近中原地区步兵装备的水平。唯较差的是，瓯骆方国很可能没有骑兵。但骑兵在北方平原地区具有很大的威力，在广西崇山峻岭、林木茂密、河流交错地区就没有优势。

据统计，平乐银山岭战国墓群中，随葬有青铜兵器的墓共有47座，无兵器随葬但有生产生活用器随葬的墓共63座，其中有陶纺轮、生产工具、生活用具的37座。有陶纺轮的墓主应是女性，无陶纺轮又无兵器者可能是老年男性或未成年人。从上述数据看，西瓯方国内的老人、妇女、儿童是不列入武装人员序列的，即使是在全国抗战的紧急情况下，这些人也不参加对外战争，而青壮年男性就必须要参加战斗。平乐银山岭墓群共210座，就有47人是武装人员，这些比例在西瓯方国统辖的地域内应当具有普遍性，在骆越方国内也应相同。在这些武装人员中，有30座墓有兵器、生产工具、生活用具，这些墓主生前平时都应是亦兵亦农，即使是贵族也要参加或组织生产劳动，在战时则完全脱离生产劳动。另外有17座墓只见有兵器和生活用具。这些人，不管地位高低，估计都是职业军人，是方国的常备军。负责平时和战时的卫戍职责。优择青壮年男子作为武装实体构成分子，除增强武装实体的战斗力之外，进一步体现了国家机器稳固、强大并正常运转。它与现代文明国家运转模式并没有什么区别，只不过是运转节奏快慢而已。

值得提出的是，武鸣马头安等秧战国墓、两江乡三联村独山岩洞葬、灵川县富足村岩洞葬分别出土有铸印“王”字的青铜矛。“王”字形的青铜器在我国南方地区广为分布。在岭南地区以广东发现最多，主要发现于广东省粤西西江流域地区，集中在四会、广宁、德庆、封开、罗定等市县。这些市县都在西江流域，有的在主流两岸，有的在支流上。据初步统计，在这一地区发现有“王”字青铜器有34件，计有矛22件，人首柱形器2件，篾刀7件，斧1件。另外，在粤东地区的揭阳市和惠安县分别发现铜矛和甬钟上也有“王”字。在岭北地区，都是发现于楚、吴、越地区的湖南、浙江和江苏省。目前最北发现的1件“王”字铜矛在江苏省六合县，已经达到长江以北地区。岭北地区发现最多的是湖南省，据不完全统计有7件以上，除中部的邵阳出土1件铜矛之外，其余6件都发现于湖南省的北部地区，即湘江下游的长沙、宁乡和洞庭湖之滨的益阳。从岭北出土“王”字形符号青铜器来分析，吴越和楚国地区发现青铜矛大多数定为战国早期或春秋战国之交，极少数定为战国中期，属于战国晚期的没有发现，在岭南地区情况则相反，从数量来说属于战国晚期的比较多，属于战国早期的比较少。因此说印有“王”字青铜器是从岭北传来的，约在战国中期以后岭南地区才大量铸造。

关于青铜器上“王”字的意义问题，在学术界有不同的说法。有的认为是一种族徽，有的认为这是“王”字形符号，是青铜器铸造者的“族之标志”，还有的认为这是类似“王”字，即是我们现代概念中君王的意思。

岭南发现的“王”字形青铜器，特别是青铜兵器，很可能来源于浙江的越国，在已发现的越王剑和矛上都刻印有“王”字。越国兵器上铸印“王”字，其意义是占有的意思，即是铸印有“王”字的剑、矛都属于越王占有，甚至是这些兵器的拥有者，也属于越王的臣民，这是奴隶制国家王权政治的标志。越国在其鼎盛时期曾将这些印有“王”字青铜兵器作为礼品赠送给楚国，在湖北发现的越王剑及湖南等地发现印有“王”字兵器应当是越国赠送的礼品。但是也不排除在楚国灭越国以后所获的战利品。徐恒彬先生认为：“岭南地区没有与越国发生战争，不可能直接得到战利品。赠送与陪嫁的可能性存在，但无法找到有关的文字与实物资料，目前也无法说清楚。从出土的器物情况分析，‘越式矛’即A型矛，是从越国直接或间接从楚国传入的；B型矛有不少部分可能从楚地传入；其余多数的‘王’字符号青铜矛、篾刀、斧和人首柱形器等是受越国影响而在本地铸造。”[①]岭南地区铸印有“王”字符号的青铜器，说明此时期的王权观念已在该地区具有普遍意义，人们心目中已普遍出现了王权意识的向心力。铸有“王”字符号的青铜器并不是专指某一君王所拥有，而是抽象“王”的意义。抽象“王”权的出现进一步说明国家王权政治得到认同和巩固。

从具体的“王”到抽象的“王”思想理念的发展，是国家文明、国民素质进步发展的重要标志，因为具体的“王”是要消亡的，方国内的君王是有来有去，但国民却是永存的。因为某一具体的王死后，国民很可能涣散了王权政治意识，这是文明初期阶段的思想意识，进入高级阶段后，人们心目中有了“抽象”的王权理念，它就不受某一具体“王”存在与否的影响，这就是王权政治思想进步的表现。瓯骆地区出现有“王”字符号的青铜器，正是王权政治思想进步的物态表现。

军队是方国政权的支柱，平乐银山岭战国墓地仅仅是西瓯方国的一个缩影。我们不能说对抗秦军一二十万人，只有平乐银山岭那几十人的武装。如果是这样理解，无疑是以卵击石。平乐银山岭墓地的性质，只能说是西瓯方国的一个辖区，是否能说是方国的政治中心即相当于“国都”治地，目前尚难以回答。在这个辖区范围内，大部分武装人员仍要参加生产劳动，有极少部分人可能专职于戍守，维护辖区内的安全，保护居民们生产生活的正常运行。一旦有战事，君王就会发出指令，各辖区内的武装人员必须是有序地集结到某一地方，并由君王或是君王委任的“将”级人物统一指挥。在秦瓯战争的第一阶段中，由于西瓯方国仓促应战尚无完

① 徐恒彬：《论岭南出土的“王”字形符号青铜器——兼谈苍梧及西瓯国地望问题》，《广东省文物考古研究所建所十周年文集》，岭南美术出版社，2001年。

成战略集结，结果是国君译吁宋被杀害。紧接着是“皆入丛薄中……莫肯为秦虏，相置桀骏以为将。”这就是重新集结部队，重新确认统一指挥的将领，大大地加强了对抗力量。在西瓯方国内发现的青铜武器，同类器物的造型和尺寸都差不多，估计当时对武器的打造是有一定的定制，也就是说，尽管和平时期，方国的武装都以血缘为单位分散在各个驻扎点上，但是他们的武器装备则是统一的。恩格斯在谈到国家与氏族不同的第二个特点时说：“就是公共权力的建立，这个公共权力已经和那自行组织为一个武装力量的居民不直接符合了。这个特殊的公共权力之所以必需，是因为自从社会分裂成阶级后，居民自动的武装组织已经成为不可能的了。”①特殊的公共权力即是军队，成熟国家的军队是完全脱离生产劳动的。然而各民族军队的形成和发展并非统一模式。从表面上看，西瓯方国的武装仍是以血缘为纽带的独立单元形式，如平乐银山岭战国墓地和武鸣安等秧墓地都属于氏族性质的公共墓地，埋葬在这些墓地的墓主仍带有浓郁的血缘色彩。但是，一旦由整个方国集结军队的时候，这个武装实体就冲破了血缘、地缘关系，充分显示出“特殊公共权力”的特点了。在广东地区，由各种不同族群、不同文化背景建立诸多小方国，他们各自为阵，没有一个君王能统一各小方国，就很难集结大批量的军队与秦国对抗，所以很快土崩瓦解，这就是历史的客观事实。

① 恩格斯:《家庭、私有制和国家的起源》，《马克思恩格斯文选》两卷集（Ⅱ），人民出版社，1963年，317页。

广西汉代铜马研究

A Study on Bronze Horses
of Han Dynasty in Guangxi

陈小波 / 广西壮族自治区博物馆 副研究员

［摘要］

本文就广西出土的铜马，根据其形体特征和伴出的器物进行研究，认为这些马的役用类型有挽用型（包括重挽、轻挽两型）和骑乘型两种，以挽乘兼用的马为多；铜马的来源是来自我国的西北地区；铜马反映的是墓主的身份、地位、职业和财富等情况。

［关键词］

广西　汉代铜马　役用类型　铜马来源　墓主身份

Abstract

The article is mainly research on the bronze horses excavated in Guangxi Province. According to the body characteristics of the horses and the vessels which excavated with the horses, the author considered that the types of the horses are divided into two kinds: the draft horse (heavy draft and light draft) and the saddlebred. And most of them were combined the draft and saddle factions together. The bronze horses come from the Northwest area of China. They reflect the tomb owner's identity, status, profession and wealth, etc .

Key words

Guangxi; Bronze horse of Han dynasty; Application type; Source of bronze horse; Owner's identity of the tomb

在我国古代，被列为“六畜之首”的马是军事、交通的主要动力，有些地方还是农耕、运输的好助手，役用十分广泛。尤其在国防上，马更是强兵之源，占有十分重要的地位，被视为“甲兵之本，国之大用”①而深受历代统治者的重视。研究古代的马资料，对了解一个地区的军事、交通运输、经济文化的历史具有重要的意义。本文试就广西出土的汉代铜马，从其发现情况、形体特征、役用类型、马的来源及反映墓主的相关情况等方面进行探讨，提出一些个人看法。持论不当处，祈各方读者不吝指正。

一

铜马发现简况

考古材料显示，广西发现的铜马数量不多，目前只有寥寥可数的3处共4件马的个体：

第一处，西林普驮鎏金铜骑俑和鎏金铜马腿各1件。1972年7月，广西西林县八达公社普合大队普驮粮站西汉早期墓出土的这件铜骑俑，表面鎏金。马为昂首站立，马尾单独铸造，插入臀部之上的方孔中。马体膘肥壮实，昂首，竖耳，圆眼，张嘴，露牙，长颈，平身，翘尾，四足直立。背上置方形鞍，鞍上坐一骑士。骑士头戴武冠，身着袴褶，缚裤，束臂鞲，脚着靴，两手并举胸前，伸向马颈背，双目前视，两腿跨坐鞍上，勒缰策马，威武雄健。铜骑俑通高59、长61厘米（图一）。

① （唐）李贤等注、（宋）范晔撰：《后汉书·马援列传》，中华书局，1973年。

图一 西汉早期 西林鎏金铜骑俑
（1972年西林县普驮粮站铜鼓墓出土）

同墓出土的还有鎏金铜马腿、鎏金铜弓帽、流金铜盖弓帽、鎏金铜车饰、鎏金铜衔镳、兽头铜辖、鞋底形虎纹铜当卢、铜铃以及铜柄铁剑、铁铤铜镞等兵器。其中鎏金铜马腿的外观造型与鎏金铜骑俑的马腿有所不同，腿体略小，没有鎏金同骑俑的马腿粗大，肢体细长，腿节轮廓分明，蹄部有铁锈和细布纹。长13厘米[①]（图二）。

第二处，贵县风流岭铜马1件。1980年8月，贵县（今贵港市）风流岭31号西汉墓的车马坑内出土。出土时马的腹部虽被压坏，部分破碎，但整体基本完整。该铜马为雄性，分头、耳、身躯、四肢、尾等九段铸就后装配而成。装配的接头为子母口，有铆孔，以竹钉固定。马的体形高大，肌肉丰满，四肢刚健；昂头、竖耳、张嘴、硕身、翘尾，右前腿提起，作前奔嘶鸣状。眼、鼻、舌、唇残留有涂朱痕迹。马体高大，自足至耳高115.5、长109厘米，马背宽30厘米（图三）。在同一车马坑内还出土有铜俑和鎏金铜带辖车軎、鎏金铜刀形镳、鎏金铜环、鎏金铜圆帽形泡、鎏金铜兽面纹饰、铜衔、铜当卢、铜盖弓帽等马车的零部件，以及铜弩机、勾云纹环首铜削、铁戟等兵器。其中的铜俑为一络须老者，戴冠，身着长袍，披甲，高鼻，深目，两眼正视，面目端庄朴实。两腿跽坐，双手置于胸前，似原有持物。袍、甲上残留有涂朱痕迹。俑高39厘米，两侧间宽15厘米[②]（图三，前者）。

第三处，合浦风门岭铜马1件。2003年12月，合浦县风门岭26号西汉后期墓出土的这件铜马，出土时四腿虽有不同程度的锈蚀或压碎，但基本可复原，其他部位保存完好。铜马未表现生殖器官，性别不详。马分头、身、尾、四肢等七段，各段自铸后装配而成。装配的接头为子母口，无铆孔，但从接口的痕迹看，似曾用胶黏合加固。马腿与马身的接口处刻有较随意的动物纹样，纹样竖跨两个部位，作为铆合的标志。马为昂首站立，竖耳朝前，突眼圆睁，张口嘶鸣，长颈高竖，平腰直身，曲尾翘举。其体形虽不大，但肌肉结实，显得刚健有力。马背高50.8、通高94.8、总长98.8厘米[③]（图四）。

① 广西壮族自治区文物工作队：《广西西林县普驮铜鼓葬》，《文物》1978年第9期，47页。

② 广西壮族自治区文物工作队：《广西贵县风流岭三十一号西汉墓清理简报》，《考古》1984年第1期，59页。

③ 熊昭明：《合浦风门岭汉墓》，科学出版社，2006年，53、54页。

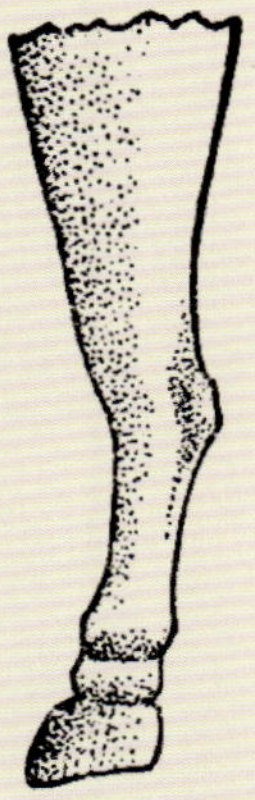

图二　西汉早期　西林鎏金铜马腿
（1972年西林县普驮粮站铜鼓墓出土）

图三　西汉　贵县铜马与铜跽俑
（1980年贵县风流岭31号墓出土）

图四　西汉后期　合浦铜马
（2003年合浦县风门岭26号墓出土）

以上3处共4件铜马的个体材料，都是西汉时期墓葬出土的实物，材料真实，年代准确，信息可靠。马的数量虽有限，但其直观逼真、形象生动的造型，以及同时出土的车、俑、武器等材料，都是研究西汉时期广西马的养殖历史、役用类型、马的来源以及雕铸艺术等方面的珍贵实物史料。

二

铜马性质及役用类型

众所周知，我国的畜马业出现很早，《诗经》中有关养马、牧马和驾驭马车的诗句就不少，《周礼・夏官》有“校人”掌国马之政，“辨六马之属”。所辨之六马分别是：繁殖用的“种马”，骑兵用的“戎马”，仪仗用的“齐马”，驿传用的“道马”，佃猎用的“田马”，杂役用的“驽马”。若按役用类型分，则有挽用型（包括重挽、轻挽两型）和骑乘型两大类型马。

所谓铜马，就是指以铜铸马的形象，早在汉代我国就很盛行铸造铜马。据《后汉书 · 董卓传》载：“悉取洛阳及长安钟虡、飞廉、铜马之属以充铸焉”。说明汉时的长安、洛阳等地就铸有不少铜马。从考古发现的铜马所见，汉人所铸的铜马既有如同1969年甘肃武威雷台汉墓出土的专作陪葬明器的铜车马①，也有像陕西汉武帝茂陵东侧一号无名冢从葬坑出土的作为相马用的“辩六马之属”的鎏金铜马式②。所谓“马式”，是指马的标准，马的模范，也就是相马用的标准模型。这种马式的铜马，还有文献记载西汉的东门京③、东汉的马援④等铸造的铜马式。墓葬用的明器铜马与相马用的马式铜马，由于用途的不同，其性质及役用类型亦各不相同。至于广西出土的这些铜马的用途及性质如何，现根据铜马的形体特征及其出土时的位置、伴出的器物等方面进行客观具体的分析，并作初步推断如下：

1. 西林普驮鎏金铜骑俑

由于出土铜骑俑的这座墓是以铜鼓作为葬具的二次葬墓，随葬品的原来位置已遭扰乱，被分散在铜鼓的周围或鼓内，缺乏第一次陪葬时器物原始位置的遗迹信息，因而无法从器物的位置进行考证，只能依相关的伴出物及铜马的形体特征进行分析推断。出土的这件铜马，有马鞍且有俑骑于马背的鞍上，表现的显然是役用类的骑乘型马。从马的形体特征看，其体高基本等于体长，整体身形略呈正方形，高头长面，颈部细长，鬐甲高，背腰短，前中后三躯接近相等，胸深长但较宽，四肢长，尾础高，也呈现出骑乘型马的形体特征。从伴出铁剑、铁镞等兵器推测，这位骑俑应是一名武士，也许就是当时军旅用的骑乘型“戎马”一类的形象。但从马的

① 高炜：《雷台汉墓》，《中国大百科全书·考古学》，中国大百科全书出版社，1986年，269页。

② 张廷皓：《西汉鎏金铜马的科学价值》，《农业考古》1985年第1期，137页。

③《汉书·公孙弘传》。

④（唐）李贤等注、（宋）范晔撰：《后汉书·马援列传》，中华书局，1973年。

四肢看，肢体粗大，蹄显厚重，也具有重挽型马的一些特征，属早期挽乘兼用的混合型马。

除鎏金铜骑俑外，该墓还出土有1件鎏金铜马腿，腿体比鎏金铜骑俑的马腿略小，造型也没有鎏金铜骑俑的马腿粗大，显然属另1个铜马个体的马腿。说明此墓第一次埋葬时还有1匹完整的鎏金铜马随葬，但拾骨后第二次埋葬时不知何故仅以1马腿代表这匹马的个体陪葬。从马腿的形象看，腿体细长，肥瘦适中，有“瘦见肉，肥见骨”的强健；飞节端正，膝高蹄轻，系短且直立，应属善于长跑的马腿形象，亦即骑乘型的马或适宜奔跑供驿用的“道马”类。与马腿同时出土的还有鎏金铜弓帽、鎏金铜盖弓帽、鎏金铜车饰、鎏金铜衔镳以及兽头铜辖、鞋底形虎纹铜当卢、鞋底形山羊纹鎏金铜牌饰、心形绵羊头鎏金铜牌饰以及铜铃等共216件车具，说明这件鎏金铜马腿原个体的铜马是拉车的轻挽型马。铜骑俑的骑乘型马与挽拉马车的挽用型马两种役用类型不同的马同一墓出土，说明当时的马匹已有较为明显的分工，即有拉战车的马和骑兵骑乘的马两种。但从外形特征看，这两匹马都属挽乘兼用的马。

2. 贵县风流岭铜马

从清理简报的墓葬平面图看，铜马放置在车马坑的南面近墓道处，车马器及铜俑主要集中在紧随铜马之后的车马坑北面，表明铜马、铜马车及铜俑是马车具配套的一个整体，其中的铜俑原来应是置坐于车上的1位驭手，是专职为墓主驾驭马车的车夫。遗物出土位置的布局就清楚说明，这匹马是挽拉墓主乘坐这辆马车的轻挽型马。从马的形体特征看，其体长大于体高，整匹马的体形呈长方形，肌肉发达，头稍粗重，颈部显粗，鬐甲偏低，背腰宽广，胸深宽，中躯长，四肢刚劲有力。这样的体征，既有轻挽型马的特点，也有骑乘型马的特征，亦应是1匹挽乘兼用的马。

3. 合浦风门岭铜马

从26号墓的平面图看，这件铜马并不出自外藏椁，而是单独放置在墓室椁门右侧的位置上，既无鞍具、车具及驭手的俑同出，也无骑士的俑和武器共存，说明这件铜马与上述两件陪葬用的铜骑俑和铜车马的明器不同，它既不是显示墓主身份地位的专用马车的马，也不属显示车驾骑乘仪仗阵容的“齐马”。从体形看，马的个体较高大，通高达94.8、总长达98.8厘米，估计原铸者的用意并不是陪葬用的明器，而是1件有特殊用途的铜马。从马的姿态看，该马伫立的姿势，与我国现存最古的唐代兽医著作《司牧按骥集》中所绘制的相马图的姿势相当。从鉴马的要求看，现代鉴定马匹外形的要求，首先是要使马处于伫立的静止状态，再用肉眼鉴定各个部位的发育状况，然后方可进行步样鉴定。正由于这件铜马具有相马的四足伫立的静止姿态的必备姿势，所以推断这件铜马可能是汉代“辩六马”之一的。从马放置的位置看，铜马一般都出自墓的外藏椁内，但这件铜马却移至室内，出自墓室的前端，单独放置在墓室椁门外右侧的位置上。这个特殊的“门外”位置，与西汉时期相马专家东门京铸的“铜马法”献给汉武帝时、武帝诏立于“鲁班门外”①（后改称“金马门”）的位置相仿，两马都是置于相同的“门外”，两者的性质应该相同，都是供学习观赏的“铜马式”；从铜马的外形看，马的体长大于体高，低身广躯，敦实强健；头稍重，鼻隆孔大；颈短粗，鬐甲较低，肩宽而略显短斜，胸廓深长且较宽；四肢短而健壮，显示出重挽型马的外形特征，应是1匹重挽型马的实用铜马式。

以上分析结果表明，广西的铜马有挽用型（包括重挽、轻挽两型）和骑乘型两大役用类型的马。其中以挽用型的马为主，骑乘型的马为辅，但大多实为挽乘兼备的马。由此可见，西汉时期广西的马属于挽乘兼用的混杂期。从西林铜鼓墓中同时出土有骑乘型马和轻挽型马的情况看，当时的马已有较为明显的分工，而这时广西的马匹正处于挽乘有别、定向繁殖的早期阶段。铜马的性质有陪葬用的明器马和相马用的马式两种。其中以陪葬用的车驾乘骑模型明器的马为主，只有个别属鉴别马体外形特征的重挽型铜马式。

① （唐）李贤等注、（宋）范晔撰：《后汉书·马援列传》，中华书局，1973年。

三

铜马的来源

广西发现的铜马数量虽不多，但造型逼真，高头前昂，咧嘴立耳，躯体雄浑壮健，曲尾高翘，四肢强劲有力，或动或静，形象生动。关于这些马的来源问题，是本地马还是外来马？从考古资料看，目前广西以至岭南地区发现的旧石器时代和新石器时代的遗址中，均无马的踪影。就是战国以前，广西有关马的形象或马的饰物也难得一见，可以说广西是无原始马种的地区。直到20世纪70年代初，在西林普驮西汉早期的铜鼓墓中发现铜马后，才结束了广西无马的历史。西汉以前无马的史实表明，广西地区不是马的原产地，出土西汉时期的这些铜马应是从内地传来的马。而我国内地传统上有九大养马区，地点分别在东北、西北和西南等地。广西出土的这些铜马到底来自上述三处的哪一方？这个问题值得考究。

首先，从贵县风流岭出土的铜马看。该马形体高大，肌肉丰满，四肢刚健，高头昂首，咧嘴竖耳，曲尾翘举，右前腿提起，作前奔嘶鸣状，是1匹拉车的雄马。与铜马一起出土的还有1件高鼻、深目、颌下有须的“胡人”驭手铜俑，而“胡人”是中国古代对西方和北方各民族的泛称，表明这位“胡人” 驭手是来自我国的西北地区。那么，与之同出的铜马无疑也是来自这一地区。

其次，从西林普驮出土的鎏金铜骑俑看。著名考古专家蒋廷瑜先生认为，这件鎏金铜骑马俑，其马雄浑健壮，四肢粗壮有力，马尾单独铸造插入臀部上方的方

图五　西汉骑马俑对比图
1. 广西西林鎏金铜骑俑　2. 陕西咸阳杨家湾陶骑俑

孔，骑士身穿裤褶，脚穿靴，双腿跨坐鞍上。其造型、作风都同陕西咸阳杨家湾西汉前期墓中出土的陶骑马俑（图五）十分相似[①]，加上骑士脚穿的长筒靴，与北方游牧民族喜欢着雪地靴的习惯也较一致，说明这匹马和俑都是来自陕西地区，与贵县风流岭铜马一样也是来自我国的西北养马区。

既然西林、贵县出土的铜马都是来自西北的养马区，估计合浦风门岭出土的这匹铜马以至广西的种马，可能基本上都是来自这一地区。

① 蒋廷瑜:《西林铜鼓墓葬与汉代句町国》，《考古》1982年第2期。

四

铜马反映墓主的情况

广西的铜马都出自墓葬，多为随墓主埋葬的明器，对了解墓主的身份和地位具有重要意义。而铜马与墓主的关系，又与铜马出土时的遗迹遗物有关。铜马出土时伴出的遗迹遗物的不同，反映墓主的情况也有所不同。

比如西林普驮的鎏金铜骑俑，出土铜骑俑的这座墓为二次葬墓。死者的骨骸用“珠襦”裹殓，以四面互相套合的铜鼓作葬具。出土后，墓主的骨骸和牙齿经广西医学院解剖教研室鉴定，证实是1位25岁左右的男性。墓内出土的400多件随葬品中，有铜柄铁剑、铁铤铜镞等高品质的武器，有耳杯等高档的食具，有六博棋盘等高雅的娱乐用具，还有大量高品位的玉石、玛瑙等配饰。随葬品的数量多，种类繁，制作精，品位高，表明墓主生前是1位身份显赫、地位较高、且有领兵权的统治者。另外，该墓还出土有代表另1马个体的属轻挽型马的鎏金铜马腿，以及1套装饰华丽的铜马车构件。这件鎏金铜马腿的马当是挽拉这辆华丽铜马车的马，而这辆马车应是墓主乘坐的专用车。至于鎏金铜骑马俑的骑士，其头戴武冠，上身穿裤褶，下体缚裤，束臂鞲，脚穿靴，威武雄健，应是负责护卫墓主安全的贴身乘骑卫士。那装饰华丽的马车和雄健的乘骑卫士，就是显示墓主既有“专车”待遇，也有贴身骑士护卫的显赫统治者，成为反映墓主身份和地位的标志性实物。

另外，关于这座铜鼓墓墓主的族属及身份问题，在此顺便谈点个人看法。从墓中出土的实物看，这位墓主虽然埋葬在汉代句町的所在地，但他也许不是南方少数民族的人，更不可能是句町族的首领，而有可能是1位来自西北或中原地区、带兵南下征战的军旅要员。主要依据有三：

（1）从毁鼓作葬具看。铜鼓，是我国古代南方少数民族使用的一种重器、乐器，是统治权力、地位、财富的象征，用以集合部众、发号施令、指挥作战，并作为祭祀、赏赐、进贡的重器。文献记载：“有鼓者极为豪強”（裴渊：《广州记》）；“有鼓者号为都老，群情推服”（《隋书·地理志》）；“鼓声宏者为上，可易千牛，次者七八百。得鼓二、三，便可僭号称王”（《明史·刘显传》）。可见，古代南方少数民族都普遍尊重和珍视铜鼓。尤其这座铜鼓墓所在地的古句町国遗民，至今还把铜鼓当成祖宗基业之标志、后代命脉之所出、精神心灵之所在、感情愿望之寄托[①]，体现了珍视铜鼓的传统。但是这座墓的埋葬者却不以为然，既不是把铜鼓作为显示权力、地位或财富的陪葬品，也不是把铜鼓当做祖宗基业、后代命脉、精神情感的寄托，而是把铜鼓作为埋葬污秽腐嗅尸体的葬具。这一做法，简直就是把铜鼓视为“废物”来利用，从传统观念看似有蔑视以至亵渎铜鼓的意味。需要特别指出的是，这座墓不仅用四面相互套合的铜鼓作葬具，而且为了埋葬的需要还不惜将其中两面完整的铜鼓毁坏，锯成上下两截或截去鼓身的大部，把南方民族珍视的铜鼓毫不吝惜地毁掉，明显是一种蔑视铜鼓的行为。从史料看，凡是蔑视甚至毁坏铜鼓的，一般都不是铸造或使用铜鼓的南方土著民族。比如东汉伏波将军马援将在交趾获得的骆越铜鼓熔铸为马式[②]；贵县罗泊湾一号墓将1面铜鼓锯下鼓面改制成三足案[③]。这些不珍视不爱惜甚至毁坏铜鼓的人，都是来自北方的中原人。这座墓既然损毁两面铜鼓，并以损坏的“废物”铜鼓用作葬具，表明墓主对铜鼓毫无感情，与南方土著民族尊鼓、颂鼓、爱鼓的情感迥异，应该也不是南方的少数民族，可能亦是来自北方的中原人。

（2）从骑俑及器物来源看。关于铜马的来源，前文已考证此马是来自西北地区。既然西林这件鎏金铜骑马俑的造型、作风与陕西咸阳杨家湾西汉前期墓的陶骑马俑相似，而且马背上这位脚穿长筒靴的骑士，与古代南方少数民族的跣足习惯截然不同，与北方游牧民族习惯穿的雪地靴却较为一致。加上同一墓出土的铜跽坐

① 兰天明:《句町文化壮族始祖布洛陀的渊源值得探究》，《2011年布洛陀文化学术研讨会论文集》，广西壮学学会，2011年，623页。

②（唐）李贤等注、（宋）范晔撰:《后汉书·马援列传》，中华书局，1973年。

③ 广西壮族自治区博物馆:《广西贵县罗泊湾汉墓》，文物出版社，1988年，38页。

图一　越南1号铜壶

图二　越南2号铜壶

2009年7月笔者在参观越南历史博物馆时在该馆陈列室看到1件镂孔圈足铜壶，觉得很眼熟，立即想起广西贺州汉墓和广州汉墓也曾出土过类似的铜壶，因而产生了研究兴趣。

一

镂孔圈足铜壶的发现

越南历史博物馆展出铜壶，有盖，直口，高颈，扁圆袋状腹，喇叭形镂空云纹高圈足，颈部外侧附麦穗纹半圆环形耳，耳根及中部各有缠丝纹短柱与器体衔接。盖顶圆隆，附三只柱状钮，盖沿饰麦穗纹。口沿平滑，卧刻汉字篆体铭文半圈，文曰："金镂壶一，容一石，名曰万岁第末十六"。颈、肩、腹均匀分布五道宽凹带弦纹，其间遍饰细小圆圈纹（图一）。

越南历史博物馆收藏镂孔圈足铜壶不止1件。2010年10月我再次参观该馆时，发现在原位置展出壶换了1件。此件铜壶没有錾刻汉字铭文，壶盖也不同了，盖面不是三柱状纽，而在盖顶中心设圆环纽，且系活动连环链，与颈部一环连接，颈下有一圈雷纹，腹中部有一圈勾连云纹，上下的纹饰锈饰不清，但没有原先那件铜壶那样的宽凹带弦纹，只有高圈足镂空云纹是相同的①（图二）。

① 2009年、2010年参观越南历史博物馆所见。感谢越南阮文好先生、丁丽玄小姐代为核实。

俑、六博棋盘[①]、耳杯、铜洗、车器、盖弓帽等主要的铜器，与甘肃、陕西以及中原地区同类器物亦相似，表明这些鎏金铜马、鎏金铜马腿、鎏金铜骑俑、车器以及大量的日常生活用器等，都是来自甘肃、陕西以及中原地区的。由此看来，这位墓主应该也是来自西北或中原地区的可能是带兵南征的1员武将；那位着雪地靴的骑士也许就是墓主从北方带来的擅长乘骑战术的贴身卫士。至于墓中出土有南方特色的葬具铜鼓，随葬品中也出有南方特色的素面羊角纽铜钟[②]、鞋底形虎纹铜当卢、鞋底形山羊纹鎏金铜牌饰、正面有双孔和背面有小乳突的乳白色玛瑙扣[③]、圆柱形或扁圆柱形玉管、球形或扁圆形红色玛瑙串珠等饰物，应是墓主在南方进军途中缴获的战利品。

（3）从“珠襦”殓葬看。在我国使用“珠襦”的情况比较特殊，《西京杂记》卷一就有“汉帝送死皆珠襦玉匣”[④]说，除表明“珠襦”、“玉匣”不是少数民族的首领使用而是汉人的帝皇所用外，也反映了汉帝、“珠襦”与墓主之间的关系。可见，当时能享受“珠襦”或“玉匣”的死者，其身份和地位并非一般。此墓既然用“珠襦”这种以珠缀串成的短衣包裹骨骸埋葬，除说明墓主是汉人外，还表明其葬制和身份地位之高。这位南征的青年将军死后，其尸体经历了第一次埋葬，再经拾骨二次葬才裹以“珠襦”而埋。如此显赫的地位，如此显见的北方人，如此特殊的毁“铜鼓”作葬具的二次葬，似与墓葬所在地的少数民族习俗无多少联系，墓主也不会是当地少数民族的头领，而是汉人。

又如，贵县风流岭的铜马。这件雄性的铜马高115.5、长109厘米，是广西目前发现的铜马中个体最高大雄伟的1具，它在墓中的车马坑内与整套装饰华丽的铜马车的零部件和1件高鼻深目的西北铜“胡人”驭手同时出土，表明这里的马、车、驭手是1组配套齐全的车马整体；这匹铜马就是专门挽拉这辆马车的刚健雄马；这套车马器和驭手与墓主都是来自我国西北地区的。从墓中同时出土有4件同弩机、6件铁戟和1件带漆鞘勾云龙虎纹环首铜削等先进且高等级的兵器推断，这位墓主应是一位来自西北地区、拥有相当军事实力、级别也相当高的军事首领；这辆马车就是象征墓主出行、带兵、行军或指挥作战时专用的车马模型，是1件专门用作陪葬的车马明器，与其他享有“专车”待遇的军政统治者和大户人家一样，死后都有车马随葬。比如1969年甘肃武威雷台秩比二千石的张姓将军夫妇墓出土的铜车马仪仗俑和马踏飞鸟铜像[⑤]，以及贵州兴义当地郡县官吏、土著大姓或汉族地主墓出土的铜马车[⑥]等，与他们陪葬铜车马的性质相当，都是用以显示墓主统治者的身份地位显赫和享受“专车”待遇而制作并随葬的。

再如，合浦风门岭的铜马。前文已说过，该马出土时是单独放置在墓室椁门右侧的位置上，无鞍具、车具、驭手俑、骑士或武器等同出，表明这匹马不是军用的骑乘型或拉单人马车的轻挽型的马，而是挽拉载重马车的重挽型的铜马式。这种铜马的铸造不是为了陪葬，而是为了鉴别和挑选适用于挽拉负重马车的马的标准模型

① 灵台县文化馆:《甘肃灵台发现的两座西汉墓》，《考古》1979年第2期，图版柒。

② 云南省博物馆文物工作队:《云南省楚雄等万家坝古墓群发掘简报》，《文物》1978年第10期，图版贰，3。

③ 云南省博物馆:《云南晋宁石寨山古墓群发掘报告》，文物出版社，1959年，115页，图版壹壹伍，1。

④（梁）吴均:《西京杂记》（卷一），四部丛刊子部，上海涵芬楼按江安傅氏双鉴楼藏明嘉靖孔天胤刊影印。

⑤ 高炜:《雷台汉墓》，《中国大百科全书·考古学》，中国大百科全书出版社，1986年，269页。

⑥ 卢兆荫:《贵州西部汉墓》，《中国大百科全书·考古学》，中国大百科全书出版社，1986年，150页。

铜马式样。它的出土，反映了墓主生前可能是1位擅长相马术的畜牧专家。该墓除出土铜马外，还出土有铜黄牛2件、铜狗2件、铜池塘1件、铜鹅6件、铜鱼1件、铜青蛙2件等。据此推测，墓主生前可能是1位相士，他不仅相马，可能还相牛、狗等家畜，并从事畜禽和水产的养殖并取得了成功，积累了不少财富。从其丰富而珍贵的金串饰、银指环、银碗以及大量金铜畜禽动物等随葬品看，这位墓主并非一般人，如果不是掌马政畜禽、管池沼水产的高管要员，至少也是1位靠相马牛等家畜技术和从事畜禽水产养殖而富甲一方的大户人家。由此可见，铜马的出土不仅反映墓主高级别的身份和地位，还反映墓主生前从事的职业和财富的拥有。

五

结　语

广西出土的铜马数量虽少，只有3处4件马个体，但意义重大。西汉铜马的发现，结束了广西无马的历史。马匹初传广西时，马的役用类型有挽用型（包括重挽、轻挽两型）和骑乘型两种。其中以挽用型马为主，骑乘型的马为辅，但西汉时期的马大多为挽乘兼备的马，是广西畜马史上挽乘兼用的混杂期。马的来源，主要来自我国西北的养马区。所见的铜马，有的挽拉墓主专用的华丽马车，有的背上跨坐着护卫墓主的骑士，有的是墓主生前相马用的铜马式。有铜车马陪葬的墓主，多为北方南下的军政要员；蔑视并破坏铜鼓的墓主，基本都不是南方少数民族的人。出土的这些铜马，是反映墓主身份、地位、职业和财富的重要实物史料。

镂孔圈足铜壶研究

A Study on Bronze Pots
with openwork and round foot

蒋廷瑜 / 广西壮族自治区博物馆 研究员

［摘要］

本文展示了越南北部、广东广州、广西贺州出土的10件镂孔圈足铜壶，它们都是西汉南越国时期的。其共同特点是：直口，短颈，扁圆袋状腹，喇叭形高圈足，颈部外侧都有1对半环形附耳。它们的外部轮廓与岭南越族特有的陶匏壶极为相似，可能是由陶匏壶发展变化而来的。这种铜壶都出在南越国时期中下级官吏的墓葬中，代表了所有者的一定身份地位。

［关键词］

镂孔圈足铜壶　南越国时期　中下级官吏

Abstract

This thesis introduces 10 "Piercing-bottom Bronze Pot" of Nanyue kingdom during the Western Han dynasty that unearthed in North Vietnam, Guangzhou of Guangdong province and Hezhou of Guangxi province. What they all have in common is: straight mouth, short neck, oblate-bag belly, flaring high-ring foot and a couple of semicircular handles outside the neck. The 10 bronze pots' outlines are similar to gourd-shaped pottery pot that especially owned by Yue people of South of the Five Ridges, and might be changed and developed from gourd-shaped pottery pot. This kind of bronze pot were all found in lower-level officials' tombs of Nanyue kingdom for representing the owner's status.

Key words

Piercing-bottom Bronze Pot; Nanyue states' period; Lower-level officials

图三　贺州铺门高寨铜壶

在越南清化省博物馆也曾展出2件镂孔圈足铜壶，据越南考古研究院阮文好先生从说明牌得知，这两件铜壶是该省绍化县绍原社出土的。

广西贺州铜壶是1976年在贺县铺门河东高寨汉墓出土的，通高31、口径13、腹径31厘米。也有盖，直口，高颈，扁圆腹，喇叭镂孔高圈足。颈外侧有一对半环耳，盖顶设半环纽，与越南历史博物馆2号铜壶相似。壶身合范缝特别清晰。颈、肩、腹共有5道宽凹带纹，颈部饰三角垂叶纹，其他部位饰大面积的凸点纹。足上镂孔双“S”形云纹图案6组[①]（图三）。

广州镂孔圈足铜壶发现也不止1件。

最早是1955年在华侨新村玉子岗1座西汉前期墓中发现的，已残，盖面有三角形纹、圆圈纹和点线纹图案，盖沿有耳横出，已断，圈足作直条形镂空[②]。

1957年在华侨新村竹园岗1座西汉前期墓发现1件较完整镂孔圈足铜壶，腹下部断裂成两半，器体颇大，高43、口径14.4、腹径36.6、圈足径33厘米。缺盖，器形为直口，短颈，鼓腹，圜底，圈足如喇叭筒形。器身、底部及圈足间都有范铸痕，虽经打磨，但仍有条痕。器耳附于颈部，上半作圆环形，至中段各有短柱与颈壁贴合，耳根弯曲，有缠绳纹及卷涡纹，侧视则耳部曲线与颈肩间之曲线相应。在环耳内各有1个指环状的鼻，饰有叶脉纹。耳是穿绳提取用的，鼻是穿绳系盖用的。器身有三周纹带：近口沿一周为摺带纹，上下有四线旋纹相间；肩部一周以正中为界，分成左、右两组，两组纹样相同，是对称排列的勾连雷纹，上下以小点弦纹带相间；腹部一周分两组，下面的一组也是勾连雷纹，上面一组为绹纹，上下也以小点弦纹带相间。圈足上半镂空，作三角形孔。这类图案花纹，和两广地区古代铜鼓的花纹装饰风格极相类似，在西汉前期墓出土的铜提桶中也有相同的纹样[③]（图四、图五）。

① 广西壮族自治区文物工作队等:《广西贺县河东高寨西汉墓》，《文物资料丛刊》4，文物出版社，1981年。

② 广州市文物管理委员会，广州市博物馆:《广州汉墓》，文物出版社，1981年，131、132页。

③ 广州市文物管理委员会、广州市博物馆:《广州汉墓》，文物出版社，1981年，131、132页。

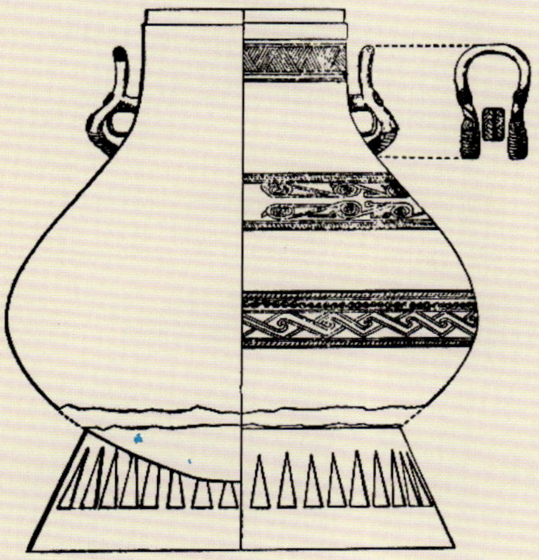

图四 广州华侨新村竹园岗“李嘉”墓铜壶

图五 广州华侨新村竹园岗铜壶

1982年7月在三元里瑶台柳园岗11号墓出土1件，短颈，直口，鼓腹，圜底，广圈足如喇叭筒形，上部镂空作三角形孔。颈部附双耳，耳的上半作圆环形，高于壶口，用以系绳提取；下有1双线形鼻，用作穿绳固盖。壶盖为木制，平口实心，唇内有1深凹槽，与壶口相套。盖面微隆，髹黑漆，上附4个扁平兽形纽。器颈和腹部各饰一周雷纹，上下各以绹索纹相间。通高26.4、口径8、腹径16.7厘米①（图六）。

1958年广州西村增埗广州冷冻厂工地1座西汉中期墓出土的镂孔圈足铜壶，原有木盖，颈、肩和腹部各有图案纹带一周：近口沿一周为摺带纹，上下有双线旋纹相间；肩部一周是带双切线的圆圈圆点纹，其上是双线弦纹，下为折线纹带；腹部一周为勾连雷纹，上下各为一周双线弦纹相夹的切线圆圈圆点纹带；圈足作云纹镂空，两耳相对的两边各有1道纵向合范痕，通高38、腹径32厘米②（图七）。

1983年冬在香港举办穗港汉墓出土文物展览，出现1件镂孔圈足铜壶，是香港艺术博物馆的藏品，据传原出广州东山，为著名文物收藏家杨铨先生旧藏。这件铜壶，缺盖，器体雄伟，高51厘米，子口，短颈，附双耳，耳的上半作圆环形，另有一个双巴小环纽，颈、肩和腹部各有图案纹带一周：近口沿一周为摺带纹，上下有双线旋纹夹绹索纹相间；肩部一周是勾连云纹，其上是双线弦纹夹绹索纹，下为双线弦纹夹折线纹带；腹部一周为勾连云纹，上下各为一周双线弦纹相夹的切线圆圈圆点纹带；圈足作镂空云纹③（图八）。

据以上粗略统计，到目前为止，所知镂孔圈足铜壶至少已有10件，出土地点包括广东广州、广西贺州和越南清化，都在岭南的古代越人地区。黄展岳先生称之为“越式铜壶”是正确的④。它们的共同特点是：直口，短颈，扁圆袋状腹，喇叭形高

① 广州博物馆、香港中文大学文物馆：《穗港汉墓出土文物》，1983年，50页。

② 广州市文物管理委员会、广州市博物馆：《广州汉墓》，文物出版社，1981年，227页。

③ 广州博物馆、香港中文大学文物馆：《穗港汉墓出土文物》，1983年，54页。

④ 黄展岳：《论南越国出土的青铜器》，《铜鼓和青铜文化的新探索》，广西民族出版社，1993年。

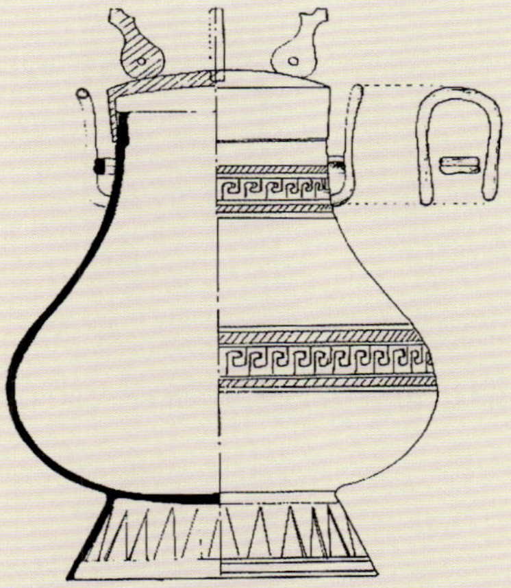
图六　广州柳园岗铜壶

图七　广州西村增埗铜壶

圈足，颈部外侧都有一对半环形附耳。它们的外部轮廓与岭南越族特有的陶匏壶极为相似，可能是由陶匏壶发展变化而来的。镂孔圈足铜壶内部的差别是，越南4件铜壶和贺州铺门铜壶、广州东山铜壶的圈足镂孔卷云纹，广州的另3件铜壶的圈足镂孔三角齿纹。越南1、2号铜壶和贺州铜壶都有铜盖，其他几件铜壶缺盖，其中柳园岗的1件有木盖，估计缺盖的铜壶原来也应该是有木盖的。盖的装饰也有些差别，越南历史博物馆1号铜壶盖顶有3只柱状纽，而2号铜壶和贺州铜壶盖顶中心是半环纽，广州柳园岗铜壶木盖是扁圆兽形纽。纹饰也有一些差异，越南1号铜壶盖沿饰麦穗纹，颈、肩、腹在宽凹带弦纹间遍施细小圆圈纹；越南2号铜壶颈下有一圈雷纹，腹中部有一圈勾连云纹；贺州铺门铜壶颈部饰三角垂叶纹，其他部位饰大面积的凸点纹；广州竹园岗铜壶近口沿有一周摺带纹，肩部有两组对称排列的勾连雷纹，腹部上面是绹纹，下面是勾连雷纹。广州柳园岗铜壶颈部和腹部各饰一周雷纹，上下以小点弦纹相间，腹饰雷纹。但整个纹饰风格都与岭南地区古代铜鼓花纹接近，所饰附耳则与岭南地区汉代特有的铜桶极为相似。

图八　广州东山铜壶

二

都是前2世纪的物品

广州竹园岗墓是1座有墓道的分室木椁墓，在广州汉墓中是规模最大的一种，随葬品陶器、铜器都很丰富，陶器组合物既有鼎、盒、壶、钫等仿铜“礼器”，又有瓮、罐、瓿、匏壶、双联罐、四联罐、格盒等地方色彩浓厚的本地传统陶器，这种随葬既有地方色彩陶器，又有汉式仿铜礼器的墓葬，是岭南地区典型的西汉前期墓。陶瓠壶虽然是西汉中期以后流行的陶器，但此墓的陶瓠壶矮胖，是最早的类型，陶器表面拍印的纹饰也是地方色彩浓厚的几何纹，所出铜镜是西汉前期流行的变形兽纹铜镜。由此可以断定此墓是西汉前期的墓葬。

广州柳园岗墓墓坑长4、宽3、深6米。葬具为一棺一椁。随葬器物共101件，以漆、木器为主，其余为铜器和陶器，漆器有奁、耳杯、盆、碟、盒、钫、壶等，木俑24件，木剑12件，左侧置木鸠杖1根；陶器有罐、瓮、瓿、熏盒等；还有青釉原始瓷小碗、罐各1件。木椁的结构形制与长沙战国至汉初的相类似。出土的陶罐、陶瓿、漆钫、漆壶的器形、纽饰，与长沙楚汉墓所见的很雷同，可确认其年代是西汉初年，即南越王国时期。

贺州高寨一号墓原报告把它归到西汉后期。这座墓是带斜坡墓道的竖穴土坑木椁墓，墓坑平面呈“凸”字形，坑内用原坑土回填，墓壁经夯打，光滑平整。墓室长4、宽2.1、高0.7米。墓室上下铺有0.6厘米厚的薄炭层。墓底中部偏北置铜镜、镜扫、珠饰等随身器物。据残存棺材漆皮范围推断：棺是纵陈于椁室中部。棺室东北角置2矛头，排成“×”形。室东有铜盆、陶灯各1。墓室后部随葬品有铜壶、陶鼎、陶甗、陶罐、陶壶。从墓葬形制和随葬品组合的情况看，与广州西汉中期墓类似，特别是从其侈口，直颈，深腹，圜底，圆柱足，附半环耳，盖如覆钵的陶鼎来看，也是西汉中期以前的。因而这座墓可以重新确定其年代为西汉中期，不可能晚到西汉晚期。

越南清化省博物馆展出的绍阳镂孔圈足铜壶，说明牌上标注为“冯原文化铜壶”。冯原文化是越南红河中游新石器时代晚期文化，这时青铜文化刚刚萌芽，不可能铸造像铜壶这样大而精美的青铜器，只有在东山文化时期才有这种铜器出现，因此这种铜壶只能是东山文化时期的产物。有的学者认为镂孔圈足铜壶是战国时期楚文化的遗物，是中原内地传来的，其实在整个楚文化分布区也没有见到类似的铜壶。即使到了前1世纪，中原内地也没有这类铜壶。我们知道，铜壶是汉代使用十分广泛的盛酒器，类型很多，与镂孔圈足铜壶最相近的是铜圆壶。铜圆壶有的也是平口，短颈，深圆腹，喇叭形高圈足，但不同的是，铜圆壶多是侈口，有的颈较长，一般颈部没有附耳，而在腹部有铺首衔环，圈足不镂孔[①]。两者之间的区别一看可知。说它们受到中

① 吴小平:《汉代铜壶的类型学研究》，《考古学报》2007年第1期。

原铜壶的影响是可以的，但绝不是从中原内地传来。从上面的论述来看，这种镂孔圈足壶只见于岭南南越国势力范围之内，就在南越国存在的前2世纪。

从越南1号铜壶铭文来看，此类铜壶自铭为“金镂壶”，并刻有容量和编号。这种在铜器上刻镂计容计重铭文的做法也是西汉前期的作风，广西贵港罗泊湾西汉前期墓随葬的多件铜鼎、铜桶上都刻有这种铭文。

镂孔圈足铜器除了铜壶以外，还有铜瓿、铜扁壶、铜碗，也只见于岭南越人地区。如越南越溪船棺出土的镂孔圈足瓿（瓶），小口，口部近旁有一对倒“U”字形的直立附耳，附耳两边对称，其中各套1个小耳环以便绑盖。瓿盖顶部稍稍隆起，瓿身溜肩，为两边稍扁的球形，下部较上部宽大，平底，附稍微外撇的圈足，圈足镂刻匀称的三角形孔；越南越溪铜碗（盅）也是镂孔圈足器，碗广出口沿，圜底，有微外撇的圈足，圈足上镂刻排列整齐的梯形孔①。广州柳园岗11号墓出土1件铜瓿，圈足也镂梯形孔，出土时还保留木盖，说明附耳是用于穿绳提取用的，鼻用于穿绳系盖。广西贵港罗泊湾汉墓出土1件铜蒜头扁壶，壶口为六瓣蒜头形，短颈，宽肩，两肩有衔环铺首，扁腹，长方形足，足部镂三角形孔②。

由此可见，器底带镂孔圈足（或方足）的做法是前2世纪岭南越式铜器中比较流行的一种做法。这种镂孔艺术到西汉后期衍变成錾刻花纹还保留在一些铜器上，如广西兴安石马坪西汉晚期墓出土铜扁壶，直口，子母口，溜肩，扁圆腹，长方形圈足，盖顶和肩两侧均有半环纽，以活链相接，錾刻花纹布满全身，盖顶是菱形纹、锯齿纹，颈部刻双凤，腹中部刻鳞状羽毛纹，口下、上腹和足部刻锯齿纹。广西合浦堂排西汉晚期墓出土2件錾刻花纹铜盒，广西合浦风门岭26号墓出土的长颈壶、活链扁壶，广东广州横枝岗汉墓的铜盒的圈足（方足）上都錾刻有这种锯齿纹。

① 〔越〕黎文兰、范文耿、阮灵：《越南青铜时代的第一批遗迹》，河内科学出版社，1963年。中文版由梁志明译，中国古代铜鼓研究会印，1982年。

② 广西壮族自治区博物馆：《广西贵县罗泊湾汉墓》，文物出版社，1988年。

三

物主为南越国中下级官吏

广州竹园岗墓在华侨新村竹园岗南面近岗顶处。随葬品陶器、铜器都很丰富，墓室全长7.26、深4.3米，正西向。两室均前窄后宽，平面如两个梯形相接。前室最宽2.2、后室最宽2.98米。墓穴中的填土用原坑土掺沙，墓道全填黄沙。墓道是阶梯式的，每级高0.1～0.15米，深约0.3米，是在广州汉墓中规模最大的、结构较复杂的木椁墓。随葬物多丰富，在后室放置了三堆：陶器数量最多，堆叠在后室的末端，计有瓮、罐、瓿、壶等和铜鼎共77件；后室前右侧有壶、瓿、釜、盉、鍪等铜器，还有陶桶1件，陶鼎、陶盒、陶釜各成对；左侧除铜方盘、铜卮、石暖炉外，还有成堆陶三足盒和许多彩绘漆器残片。

在前室的有陶壶、陶钫、陶盒和铜壶，左侧处还有滑石鼎和铜铙。前后室之间有1支铁矛。棺的位置有铜镜、玉璧、玉印和玉佩饰。棺位左边还有器表染殊砂的双联罐1件、四联罐2件、熏炉1件、铜镜、铜卮各1件和铜冒形器1对。在棺前置铁釜、玉杯和陶匏壶各1件。其中有1件四耳陶瓮肩部印有“常御”2字，有3件陶罐肩部印“居室”2字。

这样规模大、随葬品相对丰富的墓，墓主绝非一般平民百姓。陶器戳印铭文来看，“常御”应是官署名。这种官署，文献虽然未载，但从汉人喜用“常”字代替“长”字的情况看，陈直认为“常御”就是“长御”，南越国的常御相当于汉朝的长御，常御是南越国后宫的女官①。麦英豪认为，“常御”戳印或刻划在陶瓮、陶罐、陶壶等储容器上，大概是主管赵氏皇家起居馐膳事宜的官署，把常御定为官署名较为切合②。后来他又认为“常”“尚”通假，“常御”也就是“尚御”，常御实是南越国中少府所属尚方、御府的合称，“是取掌王室服饰、车驾、用具、玩好的机构”③。“居室”也是官署名，《汉书·百官公卿表》记载，少府属官有“居室”官令丞，西汉初年的居室令是执掌诏狱的主要官员之一，同时也主管一部分陶器（如瓦）的监制。3件陶罐肩上打印“居室”戳印，可知该陶器的监造者为南越国的居室令，职掌同于汉制。该墓还随葬1件玉印，覆斗纽，印面正方形，刻白文“李嘉”2字，应是墓主私印，可以推知墓主是南越国居室令丞李嘉。

广州柳园岗墓随葬陶器全属地方特色的器形，墓主在葬仪上仍保持自己的南越风习。随葬大量漆器：奁、耳杯、盆、碟、盒、钫、壶等，还有立俑、跪坐俑等木俑24件，木剑12件，木鸠杖1根，陶器瓮、罐、瓿、熏盒，青釉原始瓷器碗、罐等。其中有1件陶瓿两耳部打印“臣辛”2字戳印，墓主自称为“臣”，也应是南越王国中的中、小级官吏。椁盖上有箕踞而坐断发文身的木俑，似为拱卫墓主而设的守墓人。从随葬红漆的木鸠杖来看，墓主还是1位年逾70岁的长者。汉代崇尚尊老，对年满70岁的老人“授之以王杖，哺之以糜粥。八十九十，礼有加赐”。据《续汉书·礼仪志》记载，这种王杖长九尺，“端以鸠为饰”，一般称之为鸠杖。从汉代有关的律令得知，这种鸠杖有时相当于符节，持鸠杖的老人可以自由出入于官府；打骂持鸠杖的老人被视为大逆不道，会受到惩罚。持鸠杖者也可视为有特殊权力的人。

广西贺州高寨1号墓是1座带斜坡墓道的竖穴土坑木椁墓，墓室长4、宽2.1、高0.7米，原有漆棺椁，虽然规模并不很大，随葬品也不甚丰富，但它所葬的位置却是汉代封阳故城近郊，在它的南边就是长13、宽8米的金钟大墓，那是1座随葬“左夫人印”玉印的南越国侯王墓④；与高寨1号墓处在同一墓群的4号墓也出土过“如心”金印、“须甲”玉印，玉龙、玉珮、玉璧和代表一定权力身份的铜桶，墓主也应是南越国时期中下级官吏。

其他镂孔圈足铜壶出土情况不明，估计也是出在类似墓中。用镂孔圈足铜壶陪葬应是南越国时期中下级官吏的特有时尚，镂孔圈足铜壶在当时代表了拥有者的一定身份地位。

① 陈直：《汉书新证》，天津人民出版社，1979年，470页。

② 广州市文管会：《广州淘金坑的西汉墓》，《考古学报》1974年第1期。

③ 广州市文物管理委员会、广州市博物馆：《广州汉墓》，文物出版社，1981年。

④ 广西壮族自治区文物工作队、广西贺县文物管理所：《广西贺县金钟一号汉墓》，《考古》1986年第3期。

广西荔浦县双江镇永吉村墓葬出土青铜器

Bronze Wares Excavated in Tombs at Yongji Village, Shuangjiang Town on Lipu County in Guangxi

覃　芳　李　珍／广西文物考古研究所 研究员
黎福金／荔浦县文物管理所 馆员

［摘要］

2010年1月，广西荔浦县双江镇永吉村大塘屯发现一批青铜器、陶器和石器，一些青铜器的形制是目前广西地区没有发现过的，其年代大约在春秋晚期或战国早期。这批青铜器的出土，对研究岭南地区青铜文化有着重要意义。本文主要介绍此座墓葬出土的遗物，并探讨与周边文化的关系。

［关键词］

荔浦　青铜器

Abstract

In January of 2010, a number of bronze wares，pottery and stoneware are found in Yongji village in Shuangjiang town of Lipu county in Guangxi. The shape and style of some of these bronze wares is unprecedented, which can date back to the Late Spring and Autumn Period or Early Warring States Period. The discovery of these bronze wares is significant to the research of bronze culture in the south of the Five Ridges. The thesis aims at introducing the relics unearthed in this tomb and researching their relationship with surrounding culture.

Key words

Lipu county; Bronze wares

一

前 言

2010年1月，广西荔浦县双江镇永吉村大塘屯村民韦礼达在建沼气池时，发现了1座古墓葬。墓葬应为竖穴土坑墓，出土的遗物有青铜器、陶器、石器等共60多件。由于被转卖，最后征集回来的文物有56件，包括青铜器有剑、钺、镞、斧、矛、凿、戈、刮刀、镦及2块铜渣等，陶器只有1件曲折纹陶瓿，石器1件为砺石。据村民反映，同时出土的还有2件铜鼎及1件铜盆，另外有1件陶器被打碎填路，1件青铜器太残被扔掉，但都找不到残片。村民还反映双江镇派出所1副所长拿走了4件保存完好的青铜器，后来经多方做工作，实际追回了3件，铜斧、铜钺、铜剑各1件。虽然剩余文物至今仍没有追回，但此墓出土的遗物很丰富，现将荔浦县文物管理所征集回来的文物作介绍。

二

出土遗物

1. 青铜器（共55件）

（1）剑，5件。可分三式。

Ⅰ式，2件。标本M1：20，扁茎，无格，茎上有两穿孔，刃平直，截面呈菱形，中脊不明显。长22.8、宽3.2厘米（图一，1）。标本M1：57，扁茎，无格，茎上有两穿孔，刃平直。长条形，中脊明显。长22.5、宽2.5厘米（图一，2）。

Ⅱ式，2件。标本M1：17，扁茎，无格，茎叶不分明，茎上有一穿孔，中脊凸起，从茎部一直到剑锋尖部。长19.9、宽2.7厘米（图一，3）。标本M1：21，扁茎，无格，茎叶不分明，茎上有一穿孔，中脊凸起，从茎部一直延伸至剑锋尖部。剑锋狭长，锋部尖锐，器身残断。

Ⅲ式，1件。标本M1：22，扁茎，无格，茎上无孔，刃平直，茎叶不分明，中脊凸起，从茎部延伸至锋尖。两侧底平，剖面略呈“十”字形，已残断。长21.5、宽2.9厘米（图一，4）。

（2）矛，5件。可分四式。

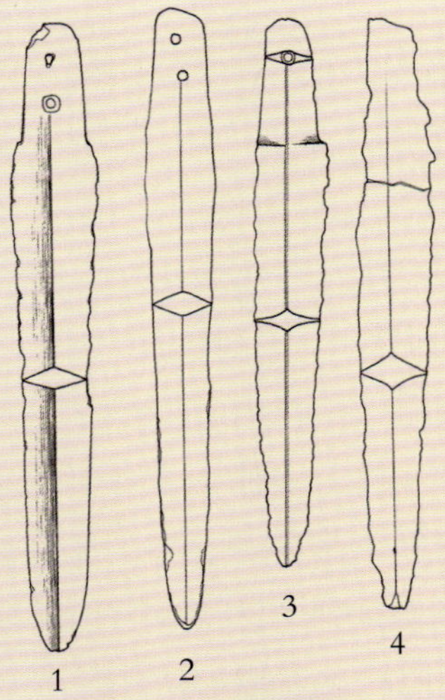

图一　铜剑
1、2. Ⅰ式　3. Ⅱ式　4. Ⅲ式

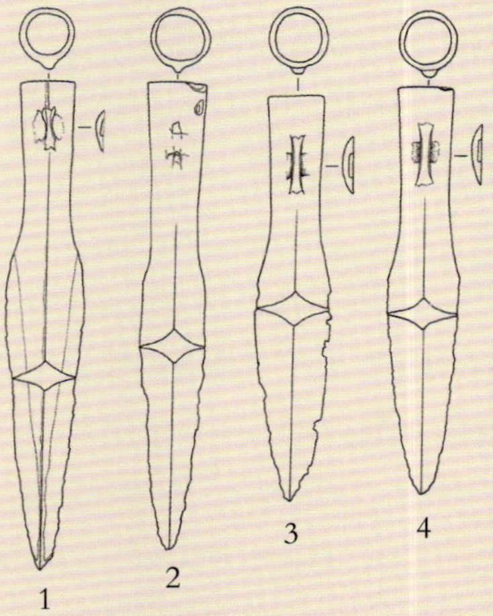

图二　铜矛
1. Ⅱ式　2. Ⅲ式　3、4. Ⅳ式

Ⅰ式，1件。标本M1：19，圆銎，长骹长叶，呈灰黑色，锋锐利，截面呈菱形，中有脊。筩上有1纽，纽残；筩部有1对穿孔。基本完整。

Ⅱ式，1件。标本M1：13，圆銎，銎内残留有朽木。长骹，呈灰黑色，锋锐利，中脊凸起很甚，筩上有1纽。长20.1、宽3.3、銎径2.3厘米（图二，1）。

Ⅲ式，1件。标本M1：14，圆銎，长骹短叶，骹叶几乎等长。筩上有1纽，筩部有1对穿孔。基本完整。长19.3、宽2.8、銎径2.5厘米（图二，2）。

Ⅳ式，2件。标本M1：15，圆銎，銎内残留有朽木。短骹短叶，骹叶几乎等长。中脊凸起。保存完好。长16.8、宽3.2、銎径2.5厘米（图二，3）。标本M1：16，圆銎，銎内残留有朽木。短骹短叶，骹叶几乎等长。筩上有1纽。保存完好。长16.8、宽3、銎径2.3厘米（图二，4）。

（3）斧，7件。可分为三式。

Ⅰ式，4件。标本M1：1，方銎，銎微内凹，銎部正面有纹饰。体形较大，束腰，宽刃，刃呈弧形。保存完整。长16、刃宽6.2、銎口长4.1、宽1.9厘米（图三，1）。标本M1：59，方銎，銎微内凹，銎部正面有纹饰，但锈蚀不太清楚。体形较大，束腰，宽刃，刃呈弧形。器身布满蓝色铜锈，保存完整。长13.7、刃宽6.5、銎口长4、宽2厘米（图三，2）。标本M1：4，方銎，銎微内凹，体形较大，束腰，宽刃，刃呈弧形。保存完整。长14.5、宽6.1、銎口长3.7、宽1.8厘米（图三，3）。标本M1：5，方銎，銎微内凹，体形较大，束腰，宽刃，刃呈弧形。保存完整。长12.8、宽5.4、銎口长3.8、宽1.9厘米（图三，4）。

Ⅱ式，1件。标本M1：6，方銎，銎微内凹，体形较小，腰微束，长条形，平刃，刃微残。长7.2、宽2.2、銎口长2、宽1.3厘米（图三，5）。

Ⅲ式，2件。标本M1：7，銎呈六菱形，銎微内凹，体形较小，腰微束，长条形，平刃，刃残。长7、宽2.7、銎口长2、宽1.2厘米（图三，6）。标本M1：9，方銎，銎残，体形小而短，腰微束，弧刃。长5.5、刃宽3.4、銎口长2.7、宽1.4厘米（图三，7）。

（4）钺，7件。可分三式。

Ⅰ式，1件。靴形。标本M1：12，长方形銎，直口，銎部较长，銎部饰有云纹。一侧肩上有倒刺，圆刃。保存完整。长9.8、刃宽11.8、銎口长3.5、宽1.7厘米（图四，1）。

Ⅱ式，2件。铲形。标本M1：2，椭圆形銎，銎稍长，平直刃，无纹饰。微残。长13.4、刃宽7.7、銎径5.5厘米×2.5厘米（图四，2）。标本M1：10，椭圆形銎，銎部较短。保存完好。长10.5、宽7.4、銎径4.5厘米×2厘米（图四，3）。

Ⅲ式，4件。凸字形。标本M1：3，长方形銎，銎微内凹，銎部有兽面纹饰，锈蚀模糊，銎内有朽木痕迹。平肩，平刃。长7.7、刃宽6.8、銎口长3.7、宽2.6厘米（图四，4）。标本M1：11，长方形銎，銎较长，銎微内凹，肩微斜，平刃，刃宽大。保存完好。长9、刃宽7.7、銎口长3.5、宽1.5厘米（图四，5）。标本M1：8，长方形銎，銎较长，銎微内凹，銎内有木屑。体形较小，斜肩，平刃。长5、刃宽3.2、銎口长2.2、宽1.2厘米（图四，6）。标本M1：58，长方形銎，銎微内凹，銎部有兽面纹饰，銎部较长。平肩，平刃，刃宽，刃部稍

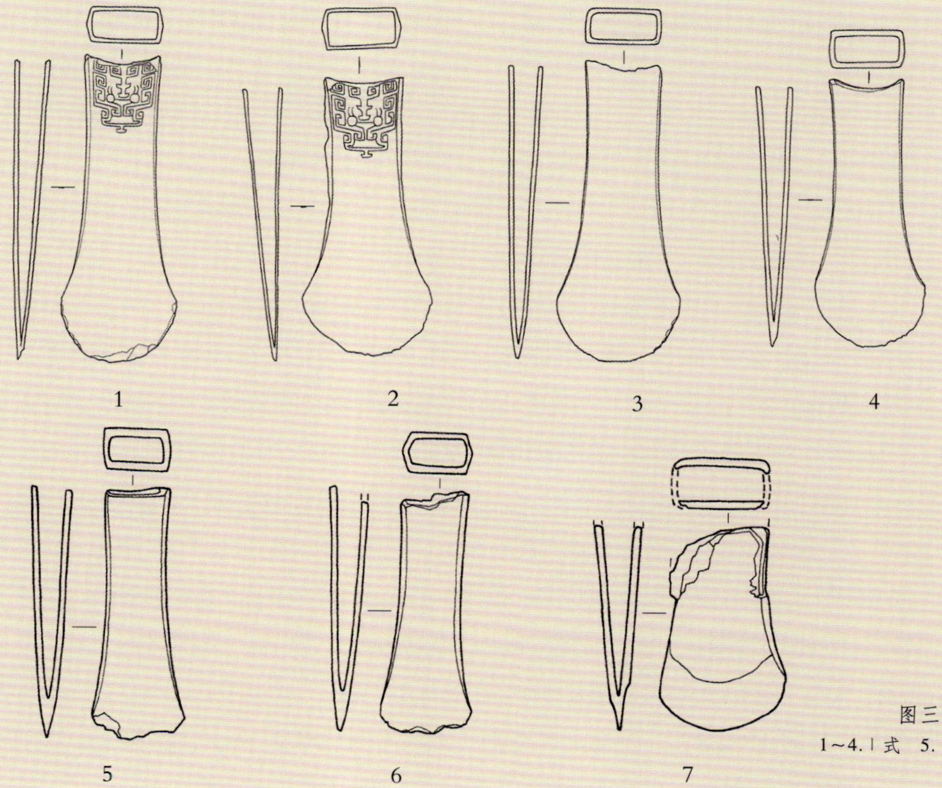

图三　铜斧
1~4. Ⅰ式　5. Ⅱ式　6、7. Ⅲ式

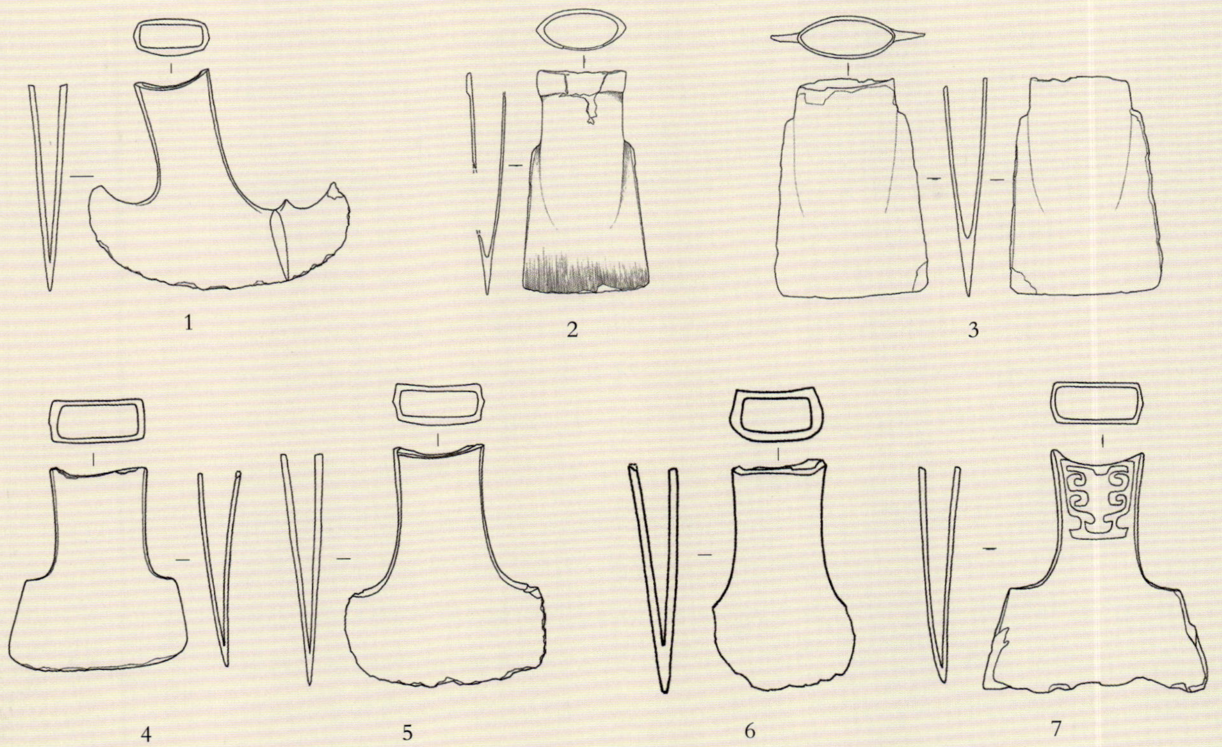

图四　铜钺
1. Ⅰ式　2、3. Ⅱ式　4～7. Ⅲ式

残。长8.4、刃宽7.8、銎口长3.2、宽1.4厘米（图四，7）。

（5）凿，3件。可分三式。

Ⅰ式，1件。标本M1：23，圆銎，銎内有朽木，器身呈圆管状，凹刃，保存较好。长9.2、直径1.9厘米（图五，1）。

Ⅱ式，1件。标本M1：24，方銎，銎内有朽木，器身呈条行，上大下小，平斜刃。长9.8、銎口长2.2、宽1.4厘米（图五，2）。

Ⅲ式，1件。标本M1：26，六菱形銎，銎下部呈方形，銎微残。器身呈条形，上大下小，平刃。长8.5、宽1.5厘米（图五，3）。

（6）戈，1件。

标本M1：27，器身光亮，内平直，平援，援、胡、内均为利刃，共有4穿，内上有1穿，阑侧有3穿，长援微昂。保存完整。长18.5、高8.4厘米（图六）。

（7）柱形器，2件。可分二式。

Ⅰ式，1件。标本M1：51，顶部呈房子状，身部为长方形，上大下小，中空，底穿，两侧各有1长方形穿孔，器身正面及侧面各有1不规则穿孔。长21.8厘米（图七，1）。

Ⅱ式，1件。标本M1：52，顶部呈房子状，两头微上翘。器身呈长方形，上大

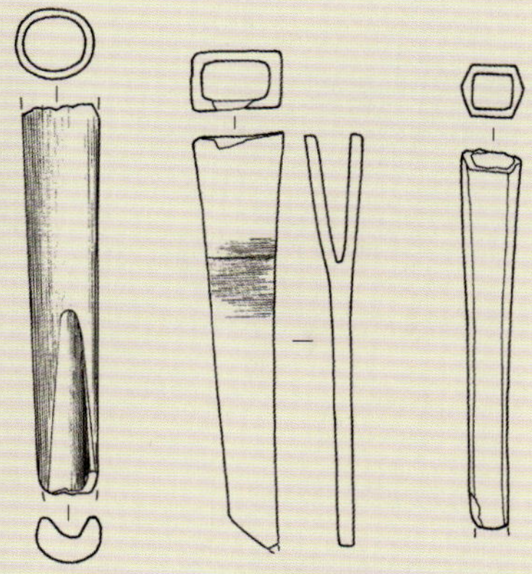

图五　铜凿
1. Ⅰ式　2. Ⅱ式　3. Ⅲ式

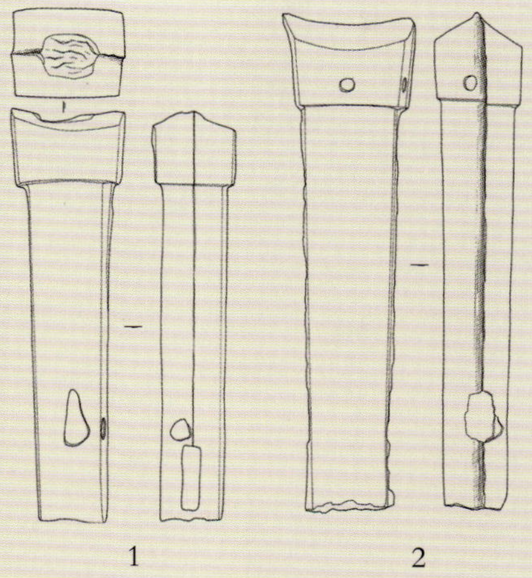

图七　铜柱形器
1. Ⅰ式　2. Ⅱ式

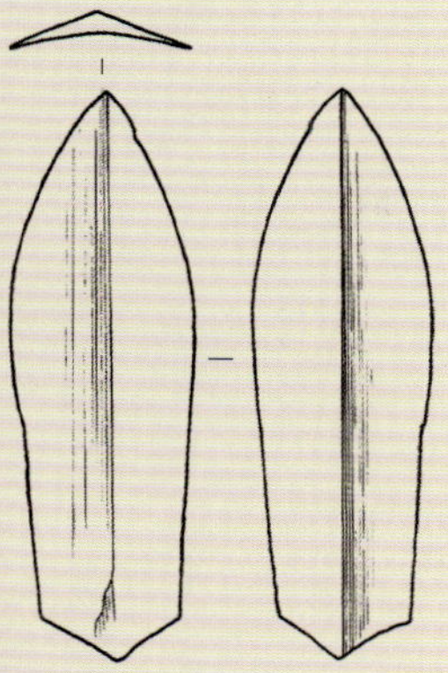

图九　铜刮刀

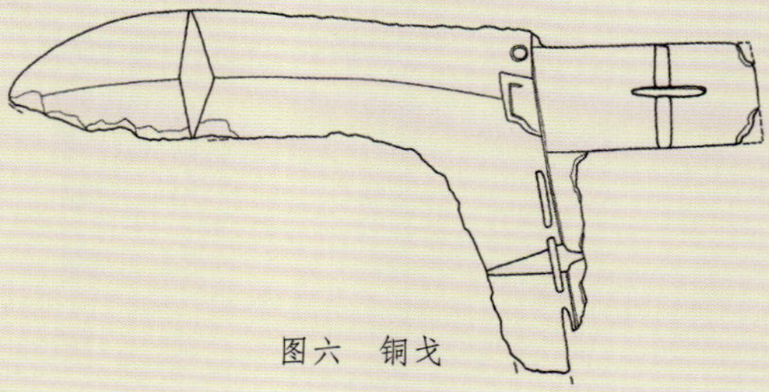

图六　铜戈

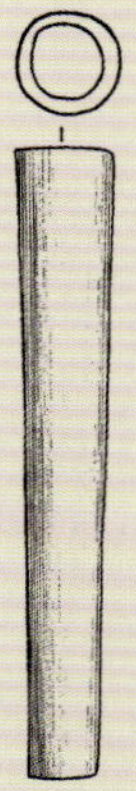

图八　铜镦

下小，中空，底穿。顶部正面及两侧均有圆形小孔1个，只有后侧没有。器身两侧有1长方形孔，后侧及一侧有各有1不规则穿孔。与Ⅰ式大致相似，只是Ⅱ式体形较长，顶部有圆形穿孔，而Ⅰ式没有。长24.6厘米（图七，2）。

（8）镦，1件。

标本M1：25，圆管状，中空，内有残留朽木。上端大，下端小，封底。长10.3、直径1.7厘米（图八）。

（9）刮刀，1件。

标本M1：18，呈灰黑色，质地坚硬，剖面略似人字形，竹叶形，器身向上翘，背有脊，两刃前聚成锋，后部平。长8.7、宽2.7厘米（图九）。

（10）镞，24件。

形体上没有很大的差别，均长身，尖翼，凸脊，刃呈斜线，前聚成锋；倒刺较长，微外扬，铤较长。身长在6～7.5厘米（图一〇）。

（11）铜锭（渣），2块。

平面呈椭圆形，表面都有绿色铜锈。标本M1：53，重3600克。标本M1：54，重2900克。

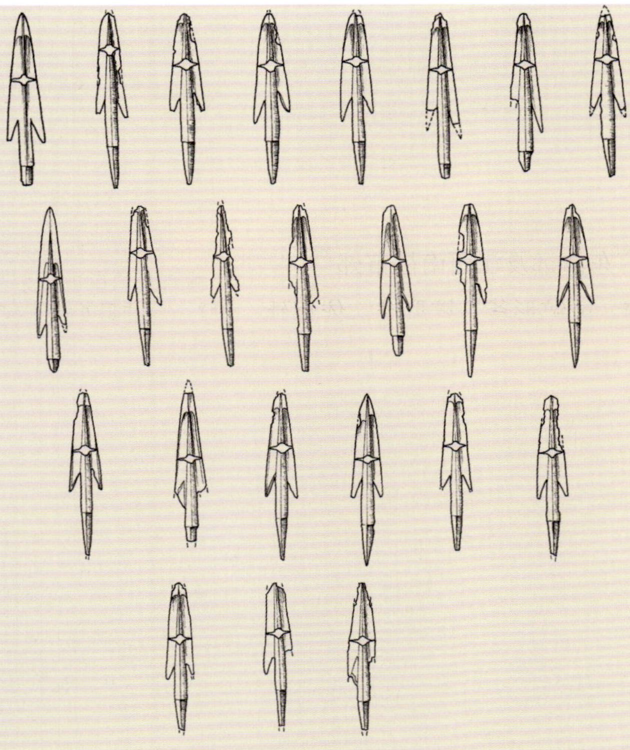

图一〇　铜镞

（编号第一排28～35，第二排36～42，第三排43～48，第四排49～51）

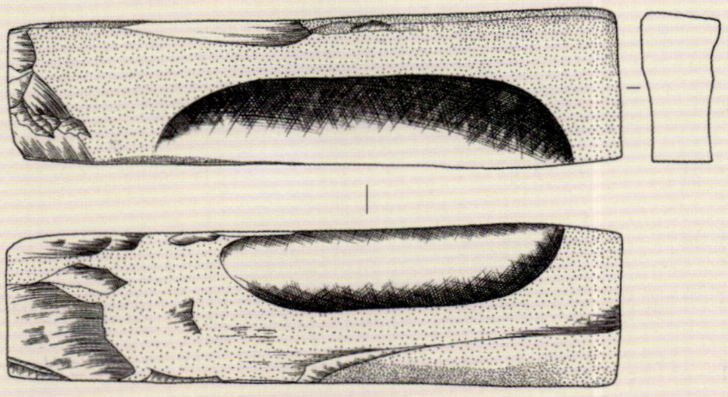

图一一　砺石

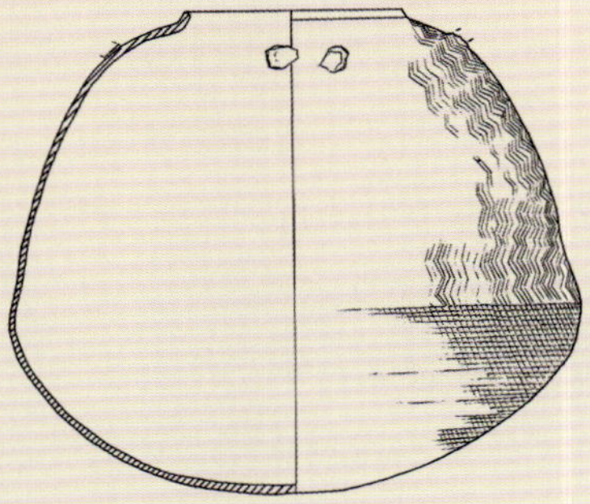

图一二　陶瓿

2. 石器（1件）

砺石，1件。标本M1：55，呈长条形，四面磨光，四面由于使用过，均内凹。长20.5、宽5.5、厚2.6厘米（图一一）。

3. 陶器（1件）

陶瓿，1件。标本M1：56，圆唇，敛口，圆肩，肩部有3耳，但已残，鼓腹，圜底。肩部及腹部饰有曲折纹，底部饰拍印菱格纹。器形较大，原应有盖，可能丢失。高26.5、口径12.2、腹径31.8厘米（图一二）。

三

结　语

这批青铜器未经正式的考古发掘，缺乏出土地层及清晰的墓葬形制，器物上也没有明确的铭文可资考证，因此，判断这批文物的年代比较困难。墓葬出土的铜戈、扁茎无格剑、靴形铜钺、铜斧与广西恭城秧家出土[①]的相似，广西恭城秧家青铜器的年代在春秋晚期。出土的青铜剑，都为扁茎无格剑，这类剑在平乐银山岭发现最多，宾阳韦坡、武鸣安等秧、独山、岑溪花果山等地都有发现，广东罗定背夫山、清远马头岗、罗定南门垌、广宁铜鼓岗等地也有发现。扁茎剑在中原、江汉和吴越地区也有少量发现，但此剑在湖南和岭南流行，时间也早。出土的铲形钺，在广西目前还没有发现，而在湖南衡阳、耒阳灶市[②]、广东清远及江西南昌市郊[③]、萍乡市田中古城遗址出土的铲形越相类[④]，有些称之为铲，或铲形斧、铲形钺，依蒋廷瑜先生意见，称为铲形钺比较合适。而发现这些铲形钺的墓葬、遗址，年代都在春秋晚期。出土的铜刮刀，与平乐银山岭战国墓出土的相似[⑤]。出土的靴形钺，肩上有倒刺，这种形制的钺目前在国内没有发现。柱形器为岭南地区所独有，始铸于春秋时期，终于战国。对于柱形器的用途，有人认为是棺架上的柱头饰，有些人认为是礼器，是仪仗的杖头饰物。这种器物出土的比较少，在广西的象州县罗秀乡军田村那曹屯出土1件[⑥]。综合这些因素，这批青铜器的年代在春秋晚期，或战国早期，对研究广西甚至岭南地区青铜文化有着重要意义。

荔浦县双江镇永吉村大塘屯墓葬出土的遗物，绝大部分为青铜器，其组成主要以兵器为主，部分青铜器里残留有朽木，说明是实用器；出土的铜锭（渣），目前没有测试，但不管是铜锭还是铜渣，说明当时成熟的冶铜业已经出现。而墓葬中大量青铜器的出现，也说明冶铜业、铸铜业相当发达。如果此墓葬出土遗物像村民说的还有2件铜鼎，随葬品应是剑、钺、鼎、矛组合器型。钺是征伐仗权性质的武器，鼎是权力地位的象征；剑，一方面表示身份地位，更重要的是具有防身自卫和刺击的实战作用。此墓主应是直接率兵作战的将领，甚至还掌握青铜的冶炼及铸造技术，墓主人的身份与地位是比较高的。

附　记：本文的编写得到了广西文物考古研究所、桂林市文物工作队、荔浦文物管理所的大力支持，并得到蒋廷瑜、彭书琳、潘郁生等研究员的指导，在此深表谢意！本文的绘图由张小波完成。

① 广西壮族自治区博物馆：《广西恭城县出土的青铜器》，《考古》1973年第1期。

② 李龙章：《湖南两广青铜时代越墓研究》，《考古学报》1995年第3期。

③ 彭适凡：《江西地区出土商周青铜器的分析与分期》，《中国考古学会第一次年会论文集》，文物出版社，1979年。

④ 萍乡市博物馆：《江西萍乡市田中古城遗址调查简报》，《考古》2011年第2期。

⑤ 广西壮族自治区文物工作队：《平乐银山岭战国墓》，《考古学报》1978年第2期。

⑥ 广西壮族自治区博物馆：《近年来广西出土的先秦青铜器》，《考古》1984年第9期。

广西左右江流域早期青铜文化遗存的认识与研究

A Review on the Early Bronze
Relics in Basins of Zuo Jiang and You Jiang in Guangxi

何安益 / 广西文物考古研究所 副研究员

[摘要]

本文通过借鉴广东早期青铜文化研究领域的成果，分析广西左右江流域早期青铜文化遗存文化特征，通过与周边文化比较，将其初步划分三组三期，理清该区域早期青铜文化遗存发展脉络，认为该区域早期青铜文化大致相当于中原的商中晚期至西周早中期，尽管可能受到广东的影响，但因区域文化传统差异，有自身的特点。

[关键词]

左右江　早期　青铜文化遗存　分期　断代

Abstract

Referring to the research on Guangdong early Bronze Culture, the paper analyses the cultural characteristics of Bronze Culture of Guangxi Zuojiang and Youjiang river basin. Compared with surrounding culture, the Bronze Culture of Zuojiang and Youjiang river basin can be preliminarily categorized into three groups, each representing three periods. Still, the paper combs its development traces and holds the idea that the bronze culture in this region roughly equivalent to middle-late period of Shang dynasty and early-middle period of Western Zhou dynasty. Although it is influenced by Guangdong, it has its own characteristics owning to traditional regional culture differences.

Key words

Zuojiang and Youjiang river; Early time; Bronze relics; Stages; Division of history into periods

一

前　言

早期青铜文化遗存，顾名思义，是对新石器时代末期向青铜文化过渡阶段相关考古遗存的概称，是青铜文化萌芽阶段的定义。因文化传统存在地区差异，中国各地区早期青铜文化出现时间并非一致，不同区域青铜技术发展水平也极度不平衡，从而形成具有明显区域特征的早期青铜文化，特别是岭南地区，相当于中原的夏商之际，仍处于史前末期，而至商中晚期至西周早期，受中原青铜文化影响，开始出现中原式青铜戈，但更多的是小件青铜制品，不见大件青铜器，此时，岭南开始步入青铜文化萌芽期，其尽管与史前存在差异，但还使用石器，甚至还大量使用夹砂陶器，其文化发展的滞后性和区域特色显著，而至西周中晚期以降，岭南较多出现青铜制品，且出现大件青铜器，青铜文化发展开始步入另外发展阶段。因此学术界倾向于把岭南的商中晚期至西周早期划入早期青铜文化阶段，但因区域环境和时代发展关系，个别区域或可能晚至西周中晚期，其中包括了广西西南部地区的左右江区域。

从广西公开发表属于商中晚期至西周早中期的相关材料年代可知，该时期的遗存分布比较广泛，但经过科学发掘不多，材料的系统性存在不足，与此相对应，其研究状态总体上仍处于材料积累和构建阶段。虽然如此，广西通过多年的工作及研究的深入，局部区域目前已发掘多处经确认属于该阶段的文化遗存，且较集中分布在左右江流域，如广西右江流域的岜马山和敢猪岩岩洞葬、那坡感驮岩遗址第二期、左江流域的龙州更洒岩洞葬等，这些遗存的年代以及所出土器物组合特征具有早期青铜文化特征，而除了该区域，广西其他区域因材料分散且多未经发掘，其文化面貌还难以做出准确判断。

由此，笔者通过分析左右江区域的早期青铜文化遗存，谈谈个人看法，如有不妥，敬请指正。

二

岭南早期青铜文化遗存基本认识

根据考古材料可知，岭南早期青铜制品普遍认为是受中原青铜文化影响产生，但因岭南固有的文化传统，青铜文化的产生与发展与中原不同，并不能完全按中原标准衡量。对此，苏秉琦先生指出“岭南有自己的青铜文化，有自己的夏商周”[①]；蒋廷瑜先生通过研究石戈，认为岭南石戈产生于青铜文化萌芽时期，是当地文化发展的结果[②]。两位先生的研究成果实际均指出了岭南青铜文化的发展和模式有别于中原地区。从出土遗物情况看，岭南早期青铜文化阶段最具时代特征的是石范和石戈出现，当是该类器物于本区域长期石器工业传统，地方特征突出，并由此产生符合本区域石器文化特征的小件青铜制品，如博罗横岭山墓地所见青铜锛为有段[③]，与本区域的有段石锛一致，此类锛在属于浮滨文化阶段的福建墓林山[④]遗存也见有出土。此外，浮滨文化还见有出土青铜戈、铃、矛[⑤]，其中戈具有中原文化因素，广东饶平浮滨文化墓葬也出土过青铜戈，李伯谦先生认为此青铜戈属浮滨文化铸造，时代相当于中原的商末至西周初[⑥]，但浮滨文化出现实质性青铜制品可能是受到中原商文化的影响产生。

虽然如此，岭南青铜技术发展既有别于中原地区，也与临近的湖南、江西也存在不同；另外，岭南内部各区域发展状况也存在较大差异，发展极度不平衡，如岭南早期青铜文化阶段，广东盛行几何印纹的泥质硬陶或原始瓷器，器类丰富，但同时期广西仍流行使用夹砂绳纹陶器，器类单一，体现内部文化差异，但这种差异实际上仍没有脱离岭南的文化大传统，该传统卜工先生概括为石器的长过程、珠江的大传统、聚落的多形态、地域的三大块[⑦]。

在岭南传统文化背景基础上去理解岭南的早期青铜文化并展开区域研究总结，广东的研究成果具有参考意义，如李岩先生通过研究，把广东早期青铜文化遗存归纳为三个类型：粤东的浮滨、粤北的石峡中层、珠三角的村头，通过分析他们之间的相互关系，认为石制品中的石范和石戈与陶器中的尊、凹底器、带流器是广东早期青铜文化遗存标志性器物群[⑧]；杨杰先生则把广东早期青铜文化遗存划分为粤东、粤西、粤北、粤中四个区域，但从总体文化面貌看，粤西、粤中、粤北可以归入一个大文化区域，粤中区是文化主流；粤东可独立划分一个区域[⑨]。据其研究，广东在该时期的陶器普遍流行圜底、凹底、平底和圈足，石器如戈、“T”字形环、凹刃锛、璋，青铜器为器形小而简单的斧、锛、凿、铃和鱼钩，以斧为主，流行砂岩质石范，属于青铜器铸造的初级形态[⑩]。

浮滨文化、石峡中层类型、村头类型，其时代大致相当于中原的商中晚期至西周早期，该时间段属于广东早期青铜文化发展阶段，同时也应是岭南地区早期青铜文化发展阶段，而相当于中原的夏末商初，则属于岭南地区新石器时代发展末期。商中晚期至西周早期的岭南地区，受中原文化影响，最早出现青铜文化特征器物是石戈和石范，而从范模看主要为小件青铜器，青铜容器或礼器铸造技术仍无法铸造，这是岭南地区早期青铜文化发展基本现状。同为岭南地区的广西，与广东相比较，两地存在千丝万缕联系，而上述的研究成果既可以作为认识岭南地区早青铜文化的基础，也

① 苏秉琦：《中国文明起源》，生活·读书·新知三联书店，1999年。

② 蒋廷瑜：《岭南出土石戈探微》，《南中国及邻近地区古文化研究》，香港中文大学出版社，1994年。

③ 广东文物考古研究所：《博罗横岭山——商周时期墓地2000年发掘报告》，科学出版社，2005年。

④ 福建省博物馆：《福建云霄墓林山遗址发掘简报》，《东南文化》1993年第3期；陈兆善：《“浮山类型”研究》，《福建文博》1997年第1期。

⑤ 陈兆善、杨丽华：《虎林山遗址》，海潮摄影艺术出版社，2003年。

⑥ 李伯谦：《关于岭南地区何时开始铸造青铜器的再讨论》，《考古》2008年第8期。

⑦ 卜工：《岭南文明进程的考古学观察》，《历史人类学学刊》第三卷第二期，2005年；《文明起源的中国模式》，科学出版社，2007年。

⑧ 李岩：《广东早期青铜时代遗存述略》，《考古》2001年第3期。

⑨ 杨杰：《广东早期青铜文化试析》，《华夏考古》2010年第3期；《岭南地区青铜时期文化研究》，社会科学出版社，2011年。

⑩ 杨杰：《岭南地区青铜时期文化研究》，社会科学出版社，2011年。

可在此基础上加以辨别，当可作为我们认识广西早期青铜文化遗存的标准之一。

三

左右江早期青铜文化遗存的分布及内涵

（一）遗存的分布情况及文化面貌

根据考古材料，广西也发现有石范、璋、石戈等岭南早期青铜文化阶段典型断代器物，其中牙璋、石范、石戈共存的文化遗存目前仅在那坡感驮岩遗址[①]出现；出土石范地点见四个地点，除感驮岩外，还有平南石脚山[②]、灵川定江新岩洞[③]、武鸣马头元龙坡墓地[④]，其中属于本文研究区域的为感驮岩和马头墓地；而牙璋唯有那坡感驮岩个例。石戈在多个地方见出土，这些地点中包括了左右江区域的那坡、武鸣、龙州县、大新县、田阳县[⑤]，大新的石戈为出土，龙州和田阳所见石戈出土地点不明确，那坡感驮岩和武鸣的岜马山岩洞葬则经过科学考古发掘，岜马山岩洞葬属于随葬品，而感驮岩石戈不是原生地层出土[⑥]。左右江流域的早期青铜文化遗存中，那坡感驮岩遗址作为个例，文化面貌清楚，可以此为标尺，把该区域具有相似特征的文化遗存置于同一框架内开展研究。从材料可知，与感驮岩第二期文化遗存文化面貌接近的有岜马山岩洞葬[⑦]、敢猪岩岩洞葬[⑧]、更洒岩洞葬[⑨]、元龙坡早期墓葬[⑩]等，这些文化遗存年代上大体属于商中晚期至西周初，仍属于岭南地区早期青铜文化的时间范畴。

1. 感驮岩遗址第二期文化遗存

位于那坡县城厢镇的后龙山感驮岩洞穴，该遗址的文化堆积共分五层，可划分三期二段，其中第一期和第三期不属于本文讨论的范围，在此略去。第二期文化遗存为该遗址的第二层和第三层文化堆积及以下开口遗迹，出土文化遗物以陶器为主，也有石器和骨器。陶器以夹砂陶为主，有少量的泥质陶，纹饰种类多样，绳纹占主流，典型器型为罐、壶、簋、纺轮等，而磨光的高领圈足壶、簋、双耳圈足小罐为主要典型陶器；石器为斧、锛、凿、装饰品、石范等，其中所见凹刃的凿和锛比较有特色；骨器有铲、锥、簪，其中出土1件骨质牙璋。石范和骨牙璋均为该期最具时代特色的器物。墓葬葬式流行仰身直肢。

需要说明的是，该遗址发掘前仅洞外保留部分原生堆积，而洞内堆积已完全被破坏后形成次生堆积，感驮岩遗址大多数文化遗物为次生堆积所得，有石戈、石凿、石范、石镞、石锛、陶纺轮、大量陶片等，其中石戈在原生堆积未见出土，但

①⑥ 广西壮族自治区文物工作队等:《广西那坡县感驮岩遗址发掘简报》2003年第10期；韦江等:《浅析那坡感驮岩发现的石范》，《中国古代铜鼓研究通讯》第十六期。

② 郑超雄:《壮族文明起源》，广西人民出版社，2005年，173页。

③ 莫志东:《浅析灵川出土的铸铜石范》，《中国古代铜鼓研究通讯》第十七期。

④ 广西壮族自治区文物工作队:《广西武鸣马头元龙坡墓葬发掘简报》，《文物》1988年第12期；韦江等:《武鸣元龙坡墓地》，《中国文化遗产》2008年第5期。

⑤ 蒋廷瑜:《岭南出土石戈探微》，《南中国及邻近地区古文化研究》，香港中文大学出版社，1994年。

⑦～⑨ 广西文物考古研究所等:《广西先秦岩洞葬》，科学出版社，2007年。

⑩ 广西壮族自治区文物工作队:《广西武鸣马头元龙坡墓葬发掘简报》，《文物》1988年第12期。

根据次生堆积的文化遗物与第二期对照，并结合原生地层，基本可确认所出土的石戈和凹刃的石凿和锛属于第二期。

2. 岜马山岩洞葬

位于武鸣县城东北陆斡镇覃内村南的岜马山天然洞穴内。随葬品有陶器、石器、玉器、小石子。陶器均为夹砂陶、素面，器表打磨光滑。火候较高，大部分器表陶色不匀。器类有圈足壶、圜底罐、釜、双耳小罐、纺轮等。石器均为磨制石器，以磨光的凹刃凿、锛、戈等生产工具和兵器为主。玉器数量较少，仅见镯。

3. 敢猪岩洞葬

位于武鸣县马头乡那堤村山敢猪岩的一个天然洞穴内，随葬品有陶器、石器、玉器、骨器、铜器、海贝等100余件，以陶器和玉石器为主。陶器均为夹砂陶，以夹细砂为主，陶色有红、红褐、橙黄、灰黑、黑等几种，以红褐、灰黑和黑色为主。器表多素面，少量饰细绳纹。以圜底器和圈足器为主，三足器极少，只发现1件锥状足，双耳器物流行。器型有壶、釜、罐、钵、豆、盘、篮、纺轮等，以双耳小罐、壶为主。石器磨制光滑，部分为玉质。器类有锛、凿、钺、刀等，装饰品为玉质，有玦、镯、环、璜等，凹刃的锛和凿特征突出。青铜器过去曾采集到1件青铜戈。

4. 更洒岩洞葬

位于龙州县逐卜乡三叉村谷更屯更洒山天然洞穴内，有陶器、石器。陶器均为夹细砂、夹炭陶，不见泥质陶。陶色以灰黑、红褐色为主，也见有少量灰褐、灰陶。火候普遍较低，器壁较薄。纹饰绝大多数为细绳纹，仅见1片为刻划纹。绳纹装饰风格一般为竖向、斜向，以竖向为主，腹部纹饰比较规整细密，底部错乱，饰纹方法为竖向、斜向滚压而成。陶器制作方法均为泥片贴塑，口和领部有轮制痕迹；绝大多数陶器器内和器表领部和肩上部抹有一层细泥浆，有的抹平且抛光。陶器有圜底器、圈足器，以圜底器为主，另见有1件平底器。器型有罐、圈足壶、碗、杯等。圈足壶和鱼篓形罐比较有特色。玉石器器形较小，计有斧、锛、凿、玦等，未见凹刃的凿或锛。

5. 元龙坡墓地

位于武鸣县马头乡马头圩元龙坡顶上，该墓地共发掘350座，均为长方形土坑墓葬。出土随葬器物1000 多件，随葬有陶器、青铜器、玉石器，出土的石范和青铜器具有特色。54 座墓无随葬品,随葬品一般为3～4 件, 最多不过10余件,差别不明显。陶器以夹砂灰陶为主,其中又以粗陶为多，夹砂陶占陶器总数的99%以上，器类绝大多数为圜底，有少量圈足、平底器，种类有釜、罐、钵、壶、碗、杯、纺轮等，器表多经打磨，素面为主，也有绳纹、云雷纹、弦纹、蓝纹和方格纹，还见有彩绘陶。铜器种类有盘、卣、矛、钺、斧、剑、刀、镞、针、圆形器、凿、镦、铃、钟、链环等。玉器有环、钏、玦、管饰、穿孔玉片、坠子、扣形器、方形玉片、镂空雕饰、凿等。石器有范、砺石等。

本区域除以上地点外，龙州八角岩和武鸣敢刀岩岩洞葬，也大致属于早期青铜文化遗存，只是二者材料略为简单。

（二）各区域遗存内涵分析

从上可知，左右江区域早期青铜文化遗存陶器主要流行夹砂，圜底、圈足为主要器类，少量平底器，三足器不流行，流行绳纹和磨光素面陶；器型流行敞口圜底罐、圈足壶、簋、双耳圈足罐、杯、纺轮等。石制品流行锛和凿，装饰品盛行，个别遗存出土石戈、石范等，骨器最重要器形为牙璋。在这些器物中又以圈足陶壶、陶簋、双耳罐、凹刃的凿和锛具有特色，也是主要的器物组合，青铜器有戈、矛、钺、斧、镞等。当然，他们之间既有联系，也有差异。

第一，从右江流域的感驮岩遗址第二期分析，早晚两段存在共性和差异，主要体现在陶器上，石器和骨器总体差异不大。

陶器共性是二者均以夹砂为主，流行绳纹，有少量的篮纹、附加堆纹、刻划纹，唇部流行拍印的花边口，器类以圜底圈足器为主，不见三足器，主要器型均有高领罐和纺轮。差异是早段以中绳纹为主，有少量网格纹。而晚段虽以中绳纹为主，但粗绳纹数量也较多，细绳纹基本消失，附加堆纹细小，新出现彩绘和刻划戳印彩绘复合纹，磨光陶增多。早段陶器主要器形比较简单，杯形罐和钵为本段独有。晚段出现少量的平底器，杯形罐和钵消失，出现大敞口高领罐、圈足壶、簋形器、盆、杯等器类，圈足壶、簋形器、带耳器物、衬花工艺具有特色。石器均流行斧、锛、镞，早段见有双肩、树皮布拍和石范，晚段不见，但新出现矛，且石器的加工技术细腻，个别石器还出现刻划符号；均流行使用骨器，但晚段见有牙璋而早段不见。

除上述特征外，该遗址的第二期早晚两段不同程度受外来文化影响，但总体而言土著性较强，依然属于本区域文化传统，具有区域特色。

如早段所见的树皮布拍，本区域史前末期少见，但该类器物在环珠江口广泛存在，时代也较早，且时间延续长，从新石器时代中期至西周初均有发现，同时该区域在商周时期常见石范，其中香港路湾出土石范年代上限大致属于商中期[①]。晚段近似喇叭口的大敞口圜底高领罐，其敞口及领部特征比较特殊，这类器物与本区域的更洒及该遗址二期早段、弄山存在个别差异，而与福建虎林山[②]有相似之处，而同时该段所见的陶杯、圈足壶、凹刃石器也与其同类器物相似[③]，但从二者的文化面貌看，漳州浮滨文化阶段与感驮岩二期晚段的迥异，却出现个别相似因素，可能不是偶然。除陶器外，该遗址的石戈也应是受到外来文化影响，直内无阑戈见于粤东榕江流域[④]和珠三角，且以浮滨文化特征显著，浮滨文化大量存在的凹刃器形制在感驮岩也有，只是材质和加工技术存在不同。

晚段陶器所见的衬花工艺装饰，不见于广西其他文化遗存，广东也不见，但在

① 杨耀林：《深圳及临近地区先秦青铜器铸造技术的考察》，《考古》1997年第6期。

② 陈兆善、杨丽华：《虎林山遗址》，海潮摄影艺术出版社，2003年。

③ 陈兆善、杨丽华：《虎林山遗址》，海潮摄影艺术出版社，2003年；陈兆善：《“浮山类型”研究》，《福建文博》1997年第1期。

④ 广东省博物馆等：《广东大埔县古墓葬清理简报》，《文物》1991年第11期；揭阳市文化广电新闻出版局：《揭阳考古(2003～2005)》，科学出版社，2005年。

云南的新光遗址[①]、石佛洞遗址[②]、越南冯原文化[③]等均见到，根据目前研究可知，该类装饰主要来源于西南地区，可能受到云南的影响，这种证据在该遗址并不是孤例，如该遗址还发现粟米，显然与本地常见稻作农业风格不同，而与西北旱作农业有关，经云南传入到那坡。再有骨牙璋，也具有西南文化因素，该器物在广西属于个例，其形制与金沙遗址和三星堆遗址相比除材质大小不同外，形状十分接近，但从金沙遗址多见小牙璋的特征看，并不排除来源于金沙遗址可能，况且，在金沙遗址同时还见到与感驮岩二期相类似的凹刃凿[④]。

与本区域相比较，早段常见的敞口圜底陶罐和双肩石器特征与弄山岩洞葬类似，而晚段的圈足陶壶和陶簋形制特征与更洒、敢猪岩、岜马山岩洞葬相似，双耳圈足罐在敢猪岩也常见；同时，晚段的双耳圈足罐和陶杯器形特征也见于顶蛳山第四期[⑤]；再有，早晚两段凹刃石凿见于史前时期的百色革新桥[⑥]以及岜马山和敢猪岩。

总体而言，感驮岩早段陶器纹装饰以及双肩石器特征，与史前末期接近，也与更洒接近，体现文化传承性；而晚段的陶石器特征则与岜马山、敢猪岩相似。

第二，左江流域的更洒岩洞葬流行绳纹和刻划装饰以及敞口圜底罐、双肩石器，与那坡感驮岩二期早段、弄山岩洞葬、顶蛳山第四期相似，但更洒的陶器流行圈足壶和簋，与感驮岩二期晚段、岜马山、敢猪岩形状基本相似，只是更洒的陶壶和簋装饰绳纹，与上述三个地点略有不同，但簋的大小与感驮岩二期晚段有差异而与敢猪岩相似，与此三遗存比较，更洒不见凹刃的石锛和凿，此外该遗存所见的鱼篓形陶罐，前述的三个地点不见，本区域的新石器时代晚期也不见此类罐，但在元龙坡墓地见有类似陶罐，在福建昙石山遗址M120随葬的罐[⑦]也与其较接近，只是二者时代和空间均相差较远。广东区域在横岭山墓地见有，但该器底部为凹底。显然，更洒所见鱼篓形罐作为个例，其来源是否为本地或外来就目前资料均难以寻找到考古证据。另外，该遗存的双肩石器，在左右江区域多见于新石器时代晚期遗存，早期青铜文化阶段，仅见于感驮岩二期早段。

第三，武鸣河流域敢猪和岜马山岩洞葬的陶器普遍流行素面磨光，器型流行壶、簋、双耳器，石器流行凹刃的凿和锛及装饰品，不见双肩。二者所见陶器总体特征与该区域的弄山岜旺岩洞葬存在区别，与感驮岩二期早段也略有差异，但与更洒和感驮岩二期晚段相似；石器接近感驮岩二期晚段。敢猪岩的陶豆特征与深圳屋背岭商代墓葬所见相似[⑧]，而杯不见顶蛳山和感驮岩二期晚段的敞口斜腹小圈足杯，其双耳圈足特征比较独特，或与双耳器在该遗存流行有关；另外，在敢猪岩偶见三足器，而该类器物主要流行于距今4000年左右的弄山和岜旺岩洞葬以及感驮岩遗址第一期，红水河流域也见，其时代属于史前末期，显然与本文讨论的时代阶段存在差异。再有，敢猪岩过去还采集到青铜戈。敢猪岩所体现的文化面貌呈现多元化和复杂性，或许与该岩洞葬内部之间可能存在早晚关系，只是由于埋藏环境局限，难以区分。

① 云南省文物考古研究所等:《云南永平新光遗址发掘报告》，《考古学报》2002年第2期。

② 云南省文物考古研究所等:《耿马石佛洞》，文物出版社，2010年。

③ Han Van Khan. Van hoa Phung Nguyen. Ha Noi: Nha xuat ban Dai hoc quoc gia Ha Noi, 2005.（韩文恳:《冯原文化》，河内：河内国家大学出版社，2005）。

④ 成都市文物考古研究所:《成都金沙遗址Ⅰ区“梅苑”地点发掘一期简报》，《文物》2004年第4期。

⑤ 中国社会科学院考古研究所广西工作队等:《广西邕宁县顶蛳山遗址的发掘》，《考古》1998年第11期；李珍:《邕宁顶蛳山贝丘遗址》，《中国文化遗产》2008年第5期。

⑥ 广西壮族自治区文物工作队:《广西百色市革新桥新石器时代遗址》，《考古》2003年第12期；谢光茂:《百色革新桥石器制造场遗址：罕见的史前石器“生产线”》，《中国文化遗产》2008年第5期。

⑦ 福建博物院:《闽侯昙石山遗址第八次发掘报告》，科学出版社，2004年。

⑧ 广东省文物考古研究所等:《深圳屋背岭发掘报告》，《考古学报》2004年第3期。

第四，关于元龙坡墓地，从目前学术研究状态可知，对该墓地的年代各有表述，有认为该墓地年代上限可至商晚期，也有认为是战国晚期，而简报认为是西周春秋时期，虽比较笼统，但简报结论仍获得多数认可。事实上，从简报材料所知，该墓地当存在早晚关系，只是当时没有把各墓葬细分，从而形成目前的学术争锋。

从元龙坡墓地碳-14的测年数据看①，多个数据接近距今3000～2800年，而个别数据则接近距今2600年以下，可知元龙坡墓地可划分早晚两期。早期墓葬的年代应大致属于西周早中期，晚期墓葬应大致属于西周晚期至春秋时期，时代早晚的划分，可与随葬品特征相对应。

根据简报，所见的陶器均以夹砂陶为主，质地差，陶色和素面磨光为主的装饰特征，与本区域岜马山、敢猪岩、感驮岩二期晚段文化遗存接近，但出现云雷纹和戳印方格纹，呈现新的变化，应是受到外来影响。器形以圜底、圈足为主，与本区域岩洞葬相似，器形也是如此，如报告中提及的Ⅰ式碗，与该区域岩洞葬所见陶簋相似，而M235随葬的陶壶从形制看，口部较大，矮胖，双耳，与顶蛳山第四期圈足罐相似，这类罐在感驮岩二期晚段和感猪岩见有，因此称之双耳圈足罐或更能体现其特征，深腹罐则与更洒的鱼篓形罐接近，同时元龙坡墓地所随葬的玉质凿也与左右江商时期文化遗存玉质凿相同。由此可知，元龙坡墓地陶器与该区域在早期青铜文化阶段大致相似，明显不同于云南和广东。当然元龙坡墓地器物特征也吸收了外来因素，出现新面貌，但并没有受到太多影响，更没有受到广东的印纹硬陶或釉陶器文化强烈冲击，区域文化传统依然突出，与感驮岩二期、岜马山、敢猪岩陶石器关系密切，有文化传承关系。因此，元龙坡墓地与该区域早期青铜文化阶段陶器呈现的文化关系表明，以该类器物为代表的墓葬年代或略早，上限至少能达到西周早中期。

元龙坡墓地所随葬的青铜器，主要为矛、斧、钺、镞、镦、刀等小件青铜器，这些青铜器在福建和广东商末西周初的文化遗存也见有出土，如福建虎林山M19随葬有戈、矛、铃，墓林山见有铜锛；广东博罗横岭山墓地第一期，随葬有斧、锛、矛，而第三期的风字形斧与元龙坡所见相似②，其中第一期年代大致相当商周之际，第三期大致相当西周中晚期。另外在环珠江口地区，多见属于斧、钺、镞、鱼钩、刀等石范，其年代上限可达商中期③。由此可知，商末周初的广东,小件青铜器已比较普遍存在，而元龙坡墓地虽然与之相距较远，但从感驮岩二期晚段、更洒、岜马山、敢猪岩所见圈足壶以及感驮岩的刀范、敢猪岩青铜戈可知，在商末周初，广东先秦文化与左右江区域实际已经展开交流，因此元龙坡墓地在西周早中期出土青铜小件应该成为可能，当然，与广东相比，其形制上与之存在差异，但是并不能完全否定青铜技术初创性，该墓地随葬较多石范应是原始青铜技术的反映。总体而言，左右江区域出现青铜制品可能晚于广东，年代当晚于浮滨文化和横岭山、环珠江口青铜制品年代上限，结合本区域其他早期青铜文化遗存文化特征，元龙坡墓地年代上限也可达到西周早中期阶段，这也大致符合该区域早期青铜制品的发展演变关系。

① 中国社会科学院考古研究所:《中国考古学碳-14年代数据集（1961～1991年）》，文物出版社，1992年。

② 广东文物考古研究所:《博罗横岭山——商周时期墓地2000年发掘报告》，科学出版社，2005年。

③ 杨耀林:《深圳及临近地区先秦青铜器铸造技术的考察》，《考古》1997年第6期。

元龙坡墓地青铜制品出现时间虽晚于广东，但所见双肩双斜刃青铜钺、桃形和桂叶形铜青镞具有本地特色，其他区域少见，这类器物明显属于本地铸造，并非外来影响，这可从出土青铜镞与石范范模一致可证明；另外从双肩双斜刃铜钺源流可知，该类器物与本区域史前的双肩不对称石斧形制大致接近①，不对称石斧广东少见，而云南②、广西左右江和红水河区域③比较多见，表明区域文化的共性，该类器物一般认为源于云贵高原，但是从云南所见早期青铜制品形制看，见有段锛，而不是双肩双斜刃铜钺，与广东和福建类似，但与元龙坡墓地所见显然存在差异，究其原因，可能与早前阶段石器文化传统有关。从整个华南、西南的夏商时期文化遗存看，有段石器主要分布在云南、贵州、广东、福建，而左右江区域少见，但双肩石器常见。同时，从云南和左右江区域早期青铜文化遗存面貌可知，尽管感驮岩二期晚段见有云南衬花陶器因素，但该类陶器风格并没有广泛影响左右江，而云南常见的平底器也没有在该区域广泛流行，即使如前所说双肩不对称钺，其早期形制似乎也并非来自于云南，从云南的双肩石器分布区域看，主要分布在滇东，但其年代多在距今3000年左右，而双肩不对称钺年代可能更晚；而在广西，双肩石器年代最早出现在新石器中期，不对称双肩石器在弄山岩洞葬已发现有④，从该遗存的文化面貌可知，属于史前末期，大致距今4000年，显然早于云南，也就是说，不对称形双肩石器极有可能来源于广西本地的双肩石器，由此可知，元龙坡墓地所见不对称双肩青铜钺应有其文化传统。

根据以上可知，元龙墓地出现青铜制品虽然晚于广东，但鉴于元龙坡墓地的陶器、小件青铜器特征体现的广西左右江的区域特色，且与该区域其他早期青铜文化文化遗存具有文化的传承性，同时鉴于该区域文化发展的延迟性，该区域的早期青铜文化遗存年代下限或可划至西周早中期，因此可把元龙墓地早期阶段墓葬归入本区域早期青铜文化阶段，其中M19、M61、M63、M144、M151、M215、M224、M270、M273、M237、M316、M235等墓葬或可作为代表。但鉴于简报所见资料不全，目前仍难以作出准确判断。

（三）左右江区域早期青铜文化遗存的年代

关于左右江区域所见早期青铜文化遗存的年代问题，该区域早期青铜文化遗存有多个碳-14测年数据，其中那坡感驮岩第二期文化遗存有四个，分别为距今3815±50年、3463±50年、3131±50年、2883±50年⑤；敢猪岩岩洞葬人骨测年数据为距今3245±35年，木炭标本两个，分别为距今3160±35、3105±40年⑥，样品总体稳定，也符合该遗存的文化面貌，因此该遗存的年代大致距今3200～3000年，从邕马山的文化内涵与敢猪岩相似可知，其年代应与敢猪岩接近。元龙坡墓地均为木炭标本，共九个数据，除了BK86056数据年代明显偏晚外，其余最早的为距今3230±100年，最晚的为距今2530±100年，如前面分析，其早段当距今3000～2800年。

就以上所见的测年数据，感驮岩遗址的第一个数据属于螺壳样品，所见测年数据与其他数据相比存在较大误差，综合该遗存文化特征，第二期的年代上限当距

①③④⑥ 广西文物考古研究所等：《广西先秦岩洞葬》，科学出版社，2007年。

② 杨帆等：《云南考古（1979～2009）》，云南出版集团，2010年；汪宁生：《云南考古》，云南人民出版社，1980年。

⑤ 广西壮族自治区文物工作队等：《广西那坡县感驮岩遗址发掘简报》，《考古》2003年第10期。

今3400年左右比较合适；而最后一个测年数据则偏低，从该遗址二期晚段文化遗物特征可知，继承了前段的部分文化特征，陶器仍存在绳纹刻划纹，这些特征在敢猪岩岩洞葬和岜马山岩洞葬基本不见，不过三者存在共同的器物组合，如夹砂的陶圈足壶、簋以及双耳罐，另外三者陶器均流行素面磨光，石器方面流行凹刃的凿，体现文化面貌的共性。由此可知，感驮岩第二期后段年代下限当不晚于敢猪岩岩洞葬年代上限，因此第二期的年代当距今3400～3000年。更洒岩洞葬从文化面貌特征可知，与感驮岩第二期前段相似，其年代应相当。据以上测年数据，并结合左右江流域所见的早期青铜文化遗存的文化面貌分析，其年代上限应该不早于距今3400年，下限约距今2800年，大致相当于中原商中晚期至西周早中期。

从以上对左右江各遗存分析可知，该区域的各早期青铜文化遗存中，尽管文化共性和相互关系比较清楚，但他们之间的差异也是存在，而根据各遗存的文化面貌共性大致可以把左右江流域早期青铜文化遗存分为三组：第一组为更洒岩洞葬和感驮岩二期早段，第二组为感驮岩二期晚段、敢猪岩、岜马山，第三组为马头墓地早期墓葬。

四

广西左右江区域早期青铜文化遗存的分期

（一）左右江区域的早期青铜文化遗存文化分期

目前所见的左右江早期青铜文化遗存中，仅发掘一个遗址，其余均为墓葬，随葬品虽然丰富，但除元龙坡墓地外，其余墓葬保存一般，且发掘时已经凌乱，相互间地层叠压关系证据不足，各文化遗存的联系主要是依据器物组合特征，而元龙坡墓地则因材料公布不够完整，各墓葬具体内涵不明。笔者根据上述各文化遗存的文化特征及相互关系，并参考相关测年数据，将左右江流域的三组早期青铜文化遗存相对应分为三期。

第一期，以第一组为代表，龙州八角岩也可归入该期。该期主要文化特征是陶器流行装饰绳纹和刻划纹，少量抛光，口沿多为素面抛光，器类流行圜底和圈足，不见三足，典型器型有杯形罐、敞口罐、圈足壶、簋、钵，所见鱼篓形罐特殊，而圈足壶的颈部与肩部相接处为弧状，壶和簋装饰绳纹。石器平面为梯形，截面多为椭圆形，流行双肩，石器的选料比较广泛，制作技术精细不一，以磨制为主，还存在少量打制石器，磨制有局部磨光，残留疤痕，也有通体磨光后抛光，器类主要为斧、锛、凿、研磨棒，刃口以弧刃为主，偶见简单的窄面凹刃凿，骨器主要为铲、锥、簪，出现石范和树皮布拍，但不见青铜实物，装饰品简单，主要为玉质的镯和玦。

第二期，以第二组为代表，敢刀岩岩洞葬可归入此期。该期主要文化特征是陶器流行夹砂，以素面抛光为主，少量装饰绳纹，刻划纹不流行。器类流行圜底和圈足，出现平底器，双耳器和圈足流行，典型器物有敞口罐、高领罐、圈足壶、簋，新出现双耳罐、杯、豆、碗等，壶和簋多为素面磨光。石器制作规整精细，选料讲究，多为玉质，以通体磨光抛光为主，平面呈梯形，截面多为长方形，不见双肩，刃口多为直刃或斜直刃，部分弧刃，器类主要为锛、凿、石戈，斧不流行，凹刃凿常见，新出现凹刃锛，其刃面加工细致，既有窄面，也有宽面，装饰品较第一期丰富多样，出现牙饰件和海贝。骨器类型与第一期接近，但新出现牙璋，并开始出现戈一类的青铜制品。

第三期，以第三组为代表。陶器粗糙，以夹砂陶为主，火候低，器类以圜底为主，有部分平底，圈足较少，装饰素面磨光为主，出现仿青铜装饰风格的云雷纹，敞口罐与前两期相似，但圈足陶壶与前两期相比，形状特征已存在较大差异。石器类型简单，主要为石范，不见双肩和凹刃器，玉器较多出现，玉凿与第二期相似。小件青铜制品较多出现，主要以斧、矛、镞、钺等为主，具有本地特色，代表新的变化。

根据上述的分期，可知左右江流域的早期青铜文化遗存主要以第二期为主，陶器组合为圜底敞口罐、圈足壶、双耳器、簋、杯、纺轮等，石器为石范、戈、凹刃凿或锛等(图一)。总体而言这类器物组合与该区域的史前末期以及春秋战国时期均存在较大差异，从第一期至第三期之间关系看，相互之间既有联系，又有差异，体现该区域从商中晚期至西周早中期的文化发展演变过程。依据主要器物组合关系，其发展演变主要存在三点，一是陶器的变化，从各期特征看，细绳纹从早至晚逐渐减少以至消失，至以素面磨光为主，制作技术从复杂至简单粗糙，逐渐退化；圈足由低矮向高足发展，足跟从近直至外撇；双耳器从早至晚逐渐流行；类型从多样至简单，具体而言，第一期器类单一，主要装饰绳纹和刻划纹，以敞口罐、圈足壶、簋为主；第二期主要装饰绳纹，但素面磨光大量出现，器类多样性，新出现豆、杯、双耳罐，圈足的壶和陶簋盛行；第三期的陶器器类趋于单一，夹砂陶步入没落，纹饰装饰以素面为主，新出现云雷纹、斜方格纹。二是石器的变化，第一期以斧和锛为主，第二期以锛和凿为主，第三期仅见凿，总体而言从早至晚双肩石器和石斧逐渐不流行，凹刃器由少渐增多后又消失。玉质装饰品从早至晚越来越流行；三是青铜制品从早至晚，逐渐成熟，第一期出现石范，但不见青铜制品实物，第二期开始出现中原式青铜戈，第三期出现具有地方特色的小件青铜制品实物。

（二）与周边的文化关系

根据左右江区域早期青铜文化遗存典型器物可知，陶圈足壶和簋，石器的戈、凹刃石凿和锛、石范，骨器的牙璋等特征显著（图二），其中圈足壶造型与三水银州的H22③：2圈足罐[①]、河宕遗址甲M1：3圈足罐[②]、南沙鹿颈村M1：1圈足罐[③]、高要茅岗的Ⅲ式罐造型特征类似[④]，这类陶器除广东外，在福建虎林山也见有类似的圈足壶[⑤]，

① 广东省文物考古研究所等:《广东三水市银洲贝丘遗址发掘简报》，《考古》2000年第6期。

② 广东省博物馆等:《佛山河宕遗址——1977年冬至1978年夏发掘报告》，广东人民出版社，2006年。

③ 广州市文物考古研究所:《广州南沙鹿颈村遗址的发掘》，《广州考古五十年文选》，广州出版社，2003年。

④ 杨豪、杨耀林:《广东高要县茅岗水上木构建筑遗址》，《文物》1983年第12期。

⑤ 陈兆善、杨丽华:《虎林山遗址》，海潮摄影艺术出版社，2003 年。

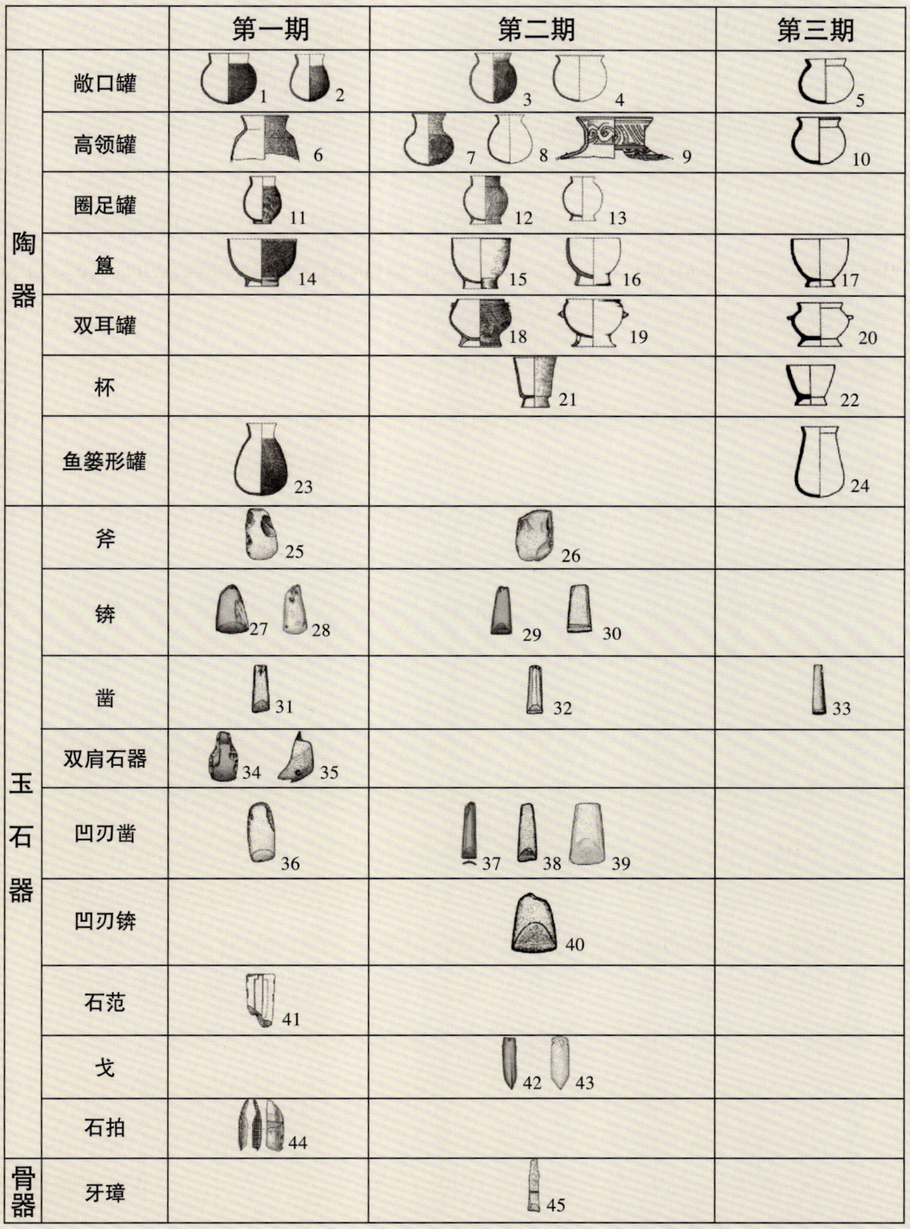

图一　广西左右江区域早期青铜文化遗存典型瓷器物对比图

说明：1、2、11、14、23、27、31、34. 采自更洒；3、6、7、9、12、15、18、21、25、26、28、35、36、39、41、43、44、45. 采自感驮岩；4、8、13、29、42. 采自岜马山；5、10、17、20、22、24、33. 采自元龙坡；16、19、30、32、37、38、40. 采自敢猪岩

从年代可知，广东所见较早，而鉴于地缘关系，左右江区域所见的圈足壶原型可能来自粤北或珠三角可能性更大，根据李岩先生的研究认为，石峡文化乌骚岭类型已影响广西东部[①]，显然，类似于左右江区域商时期的圈足壶来自于广东并非没有可能。陶豆和簋，特别是豆，广东比较普遍，但簋可比较遗存不多，目前在岭南地区仅见于左右江流

① 李岩：《对石峡文化的若干再认识》，《文物》2011年第5期。

域和横岭山墓地[1]，福建昙石山遗址也见有[2]，不过其造型与左右江所见存在差异，而横岭山墓地第二期的陶簋造型与左右江比较相似，从其形制而言，陶簋或是从本区域的陶碗发展过来；第二期的大敞口高领罐虽与浮滨文化相似，但器身造型和装饰风格与本区域史前末期所见的釜和罐一致，体现文化的传统性。由此可知，从福建、广东、广西左右江区域，商中晚期至西周初均出现类似器物组合，当是文化共性，更是文化的相互交融，这种文化共性及互动关系的存在，在其他器物方面也有诸多体现。

石器方面，第一期文化所出现的石器组合及个别器物，如方格纹树皮布石拍、石范、凹刃器等，与该区域史前文化传统不同，而该类器物共同出现在一个地层单位中，既与本区域早前文化存在较大反差，或可表明是外地传入，与相近区域比较，可发现与广东东部沿海地区的比较接近。树皮布拍在广西除感驮岩外，目前仅见于百色革新桥[3]和马山尚朗岭遗址[4]，云南则有较多发现，形式多样，但其年代上限均不早于距今4000年[5]，而该类器物在广东的环珠江口地区均有较多发现，因此感驮岩所见树皮布拍的来源可能

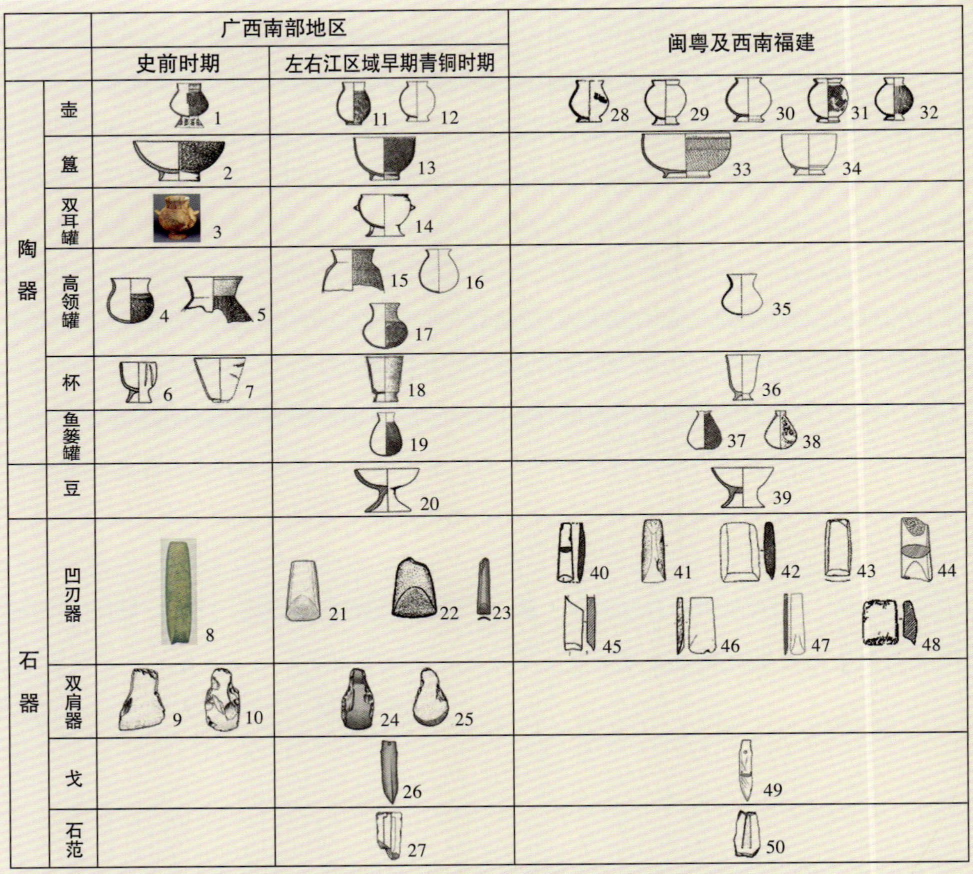

图二　左右江区域早期青铜文化遗存陶石器与周边比较

1、2、4、6、9. 采自弄山（从报告陶碗，此为便于比较）　3、7. 采自顶蛳山　5、10、15、17、18、21、27. 采自感驮岩　8. 采自革新桥　11、13、19、24、25. 采自更洒　12、16、22、26. 采自岜马山　14、20、23. 采自敢猪岩　28、40. 采自广东石峡　29. 采自广东茅岗　30. 采自广东银州　31. 采自广州鹿颈村　32、35、43. 采自福建虎林山　33、37. 采自广东横岭山　34、38. 采自福建昙石山　36. 转引《浮山类型研究》　39. 采自广东屋背岭　41、49、50. 采自《揭阳考古》　42. 采自广东大埔　44 采自云南文山壮族苗族自治州　45. 采自成都宝墩　46、47. 采自成都梅苑　48. 采自江西吴城

① 广东文物考古研究所：《博罗横岭山——商周时期墓地2000年发掘报告》，科学出版社，2005年。

② 福建博物院：《闽侯昙石山遗址第八次发掘报告》，科学出版社，2004年。

③ 广西壮族自治区文物工作队：《广西百色市革新桥新石器时代遗址》，《考古》2003年第12期；谢光茂：《百色革新桥石器制造场遗址：罕见的史前石器“生产线”》，《中国文化遗产》2008年第5期。

④ 广西壮族自治区文物工作队等：《广西马山县六卓岭、尚朗岭新石器时代遗址发掘报告》，《广西考古文集》第二辑，科学出版社，2006年，188～205页。

⑤ 邓聪：《史前蒙古人种海洋扩散研究》，《东南文化》2000年第11期。

与革新桥和尚朗岭无关。而第二期所见的石戈和骨牙璋，也具有强烈的外来文化影响因素，从石戈看，显然从广东传入，而骨牙璋则具有金沙的因素。

对于凹刃石器，第一期仅见凹刃凿，刃面窄而浅，第二期开始较多出现玉质条形或梯形的凹刃锛和凿，刃面宽而深，制作精细，锛的平面为梯形、截面为长方形为主，个体大小不一，总体较小。该类器物除了广西外，在广东、福建、成都、云南以及东南亚均见有①，江西也见有②，表明文化大传统。广东和福建主要见于浮滨文化，江西为吴城文化、云南分布在文山壮族苗族自治州（以下简称"文山州"），年代也大致属于商末西周初。江西、福建、云南绝大多数为梯形凹刃锛，少量为凹刃凿且选材不一，以砂岩和页岩为主，大部分个体较小，刃面简单随意，制作粗糙，浮滨文化见有长度超过20厘米的凹刃凿，刃面较宽而深，四川凹刃凿主要见于成都的金沙和三星堆遗址，该区域流行玉质凹刃凿③，器身较长，刃面加工细腻，通体磨制且抛光。广西除左右江流域外，柳江流域的宜州六桥岩和鹞鹰山岩洞葬也见有凹刃的锛和凿④，但二者的文化面貌与武鸣河的岩洞葬具有较多共性，或可能是文化同源，年代当相差不远。另外在左右江的百色革新桥遗址也有发现，见报道均为凿⑤，而且其年代属于新石器时代中期，该遗址的凹刃凿与本区域的早期青铜文化遗存所见存在差异，与浮滨文化、吴城文化、云南文山州也存在差异，不过其形制及制作技术特征与金沙遗址十分相似。

关于凹刃凿或锛的起源问题，从广东区域看，目前材料见于粤北的石峡遗址第三期的M47见有出土凹刃凿⑥，该期的年代大致距今4000年左右，粤中的佛山河宕遗址第2层也见出土凹刃凿⑦，其年代与石峡遗址第三期大致相当，由此可知广东目前所见凹刃锛或凿，最早年代也不过在夏商之际或略早。从成都平原区域看，出现凹刃石器最早的地点为四川新津县宝墩遗址D型凿⑧，根据研究可知，宝墩遗址属于宝墩文化的第一期，其年代距今4500～4200年⑨，云南较少发现，其形制或是受广西影响。由此可知，无论从成都平原，还是广东所见较早时期的凹刃石锛或凿，其年代大致在距今4000年左右同时出现，均为实用器，器形较小，出土数量较少，或是偶然为之，制作技术及使用材料与后期所见相差甚远。而革新桥所见凹刃石凿的年代与广东、成都相差太远，但从革新桥遗址石器制造场内出土共存物中，见有石拍、研磨器等⑩，特别是石拍，广东出现最早，之后向西南地区以及东南亚传播，西南地区出现时间较晚，相当于史前末期。显然，革新桥遗址凹刃凿的年代与目前已认知的该类器及其共存器物出现时间并不一致，是否属于本地起源仍有待更多证据。鉴于感驮岩遗址见有与浮滨文化石戈、陶圈足壶及杯相类似特征器物以及具有与金沙遗址相似特征的牙璋形制特征，左右江区域早期青铜文化遗存中所见到的凹刃锛或凿可能是浮滨文化与金沙文化的二者结合体。

总之，左右江区域从青铜文化各期文化特征看，第一期与本区域的新石器时代末期相似，如第一期的陶器夹砂绳纹以及刻划装饰风格、敞口的釜和高领罐特征，石器的双肩、长形或梯形的斧和锛均具有强烈地方文化因素，体现文化传统。而第二期已与史前末

① 周志清：《金沙遗址出土凹刃玉凿形器初步研究》，《成都文物》2003年第4期；云南省考古研究所等：《云南边境地区（文山州和红河州）考古调查报告》，云南出版集团等，2008年。

② 江西省文物考古研究所等：《吴城——1973至2002年考古发掘报告》，科学出版社，2005年。

③ 成都考古所：《金沙考古发现——走进古蜀都邑金沙村》，四川出版集团，2006年。

④ 广西文物考古研究所等：《广西先秦岩洞葬》，科学出版社，2007年。

⑤ 广西壮族自治区文物工作队：《广西百色市革新桥新石器时代遗址》，《考古》2003年第12期；谢光茂：《百色革新桥石器制造场遗址：罕见的史前石器"生产线"》，《中国文化遗产》2008年第5期。

⑥ 广东省博物馆等：《广东曲江石峡墓葬发掘简报》，《文物》1978年第7期。

⑦ 广东省博物馆等：《佛山河宕遗址——1977年冬至1978年夏发掘报告》，广东人民出版社，2006年。

⑧ 中日联合考古调查队：《四川新津县宝墩遗址1996年发掘简报》，《考古》1998年第1期。

⑨ 李明斌：《略论新津宝墩遗址的分期》，《华夏考古》2001年第1期。

⑩ 广西壮族自治区文物工作队：《广西百色市革新桥新石器时代遗址》，《考古》2003年第12期；谢光茂：《百色革新桥石器制造场遗址：罕见的史前石器"生产线"》，《中国文化遗产》2008年第5期。

期存在较大差异，陶器中所见圈足壶、陶簋与石制品的凹刃锛和凿、石戈、石范的特征与东南沿海的福建、广东存在相似性，具有海洋文化因素。尽管如此，左右江流域早期青铜文化阶段的发展模式与东南沿海有所不同，该区域地方土著文化因素体现更强烈。

（三）各期的断代

该区域第一期出现石范，表明已出现青铜技术，而比较周边区域，广东浮滨文化所见的青铜制品，其绝对年代均不早于距今3500年，最早也不过距今3349年[①]，环珠江口所见石范年代也不早于距今3400年。另外，从云南地区看，目前确切所见的早青铜文化遗存为大理银梭岛遗址[②]和剑川海门口[③]，青铜制品出现的绝对年代也是不早于距今3500年。可知无论广东或云南，最早出现青铜文化制品的年代大约距今3400年，当是广东和云南新石器时代末期向青铜文化过渡的时代分界线，广西介于两地之间，应该不会例外；其次，左右江流域出现早期青铜技术，当不是本地产生，而是受到周边文化影响，特别是广东。从陶器观察，圈足陶壶似乎与珠三角所见关系密切，而根据河宕遗址第一期墓葬年代可知，其绝对年代距今4000～3200年；最后，该区域第一期的陶器和石器虽然受到外来文化的影响，但从器物类型学看，与史前末期既有共性又有差异，部分特征虽继承了本区域的史前文化，文化发展具有相承性，但二者之间差异也比较明显，二者之间或有缺环。综合以上，第一期的年代上限距今3400年，而该期文化出现广东商时期的文化因素，从文化传播角度，第一期的年代下限当晚于广东同类遗存年代上限；另外，第一期的文化特征与敢猪岩以及感驮岩第二期晚段相比较，应不晚于敢猪岩，再从感驮岩第二期晚段数据看，两个炭化稻米测年数据也存在明显矛盾，因此第一期的年代下限约距今3200年，第一期的年代大致相当于商中晚期。

第二期的绝对年代。如前面论及，该期文化各个单位所体现的文化面貌具有一致性，总体差异不大，其时代应该基本接近。从感驮岩第二期晚段的测年数据看，年代跨度较大，且炭化稻米数据之间的误差，当不可取，而所见陶壶、凹刃凿和锛与敢猪岩、岜马山基本一致，虽然也存在个别差异，但只是内部早晚之间的相互关系，与整体文化面貌相比，可以忽略。而与第一期相比，虽继承部分文化特征，圈足陶壶和簋继续沿用，却存在较大风格转变，石器技术也是如此。因此该期的年代上限当不超过第一期年代下限，或可与第一期下限接近。属于第二期测年数据中，扣除部分存在的误差，该期的年代大致距今3200～3000年，大致相当于商晚期。

第三期是以元龙坡墓地早期墓葬为代表，所见测年数据上限可知，与敢猪岩所见测年数据存在冲突，从陶器特征看，二者文化面貌虽然相似，但元龙坡所见陶器比较简化、粗糙，显示夹砂陶器的没落，而敢猪岩与那坡感驮岩第二期晚段的器物组合、陶石器工艺均相似，其年代上限应接近第二期；另外元龙坡墓地已经开始出现比较成熟的青铜技术，品种增加，显示新技术的开始广泛应用，如前所述，笔者认为第三期的年代上限当距今3000年，下限约距今2800年，大致相当于西周早中期。

① 广东省博物馆等：《广东大埔县古墓葬清理简报》，《文物》1991年第11期。

② 云南省文物考古研究所等：《云南大理市海东银梭岛遗址发掘简报》，《考古》2009年第8期。

③ 云南省文物考古研究所等：《云南剑川县海门口遗址第三次发掘》，《考古》2009年第8期。

五

余 论

至此，本文通过对左右江早期青铜文化遗存的辨识梳理，并根据广东相关的研究成果，对左右江流域早期青铜文化遗存划分三组三期，该类遗存的时代大致介于商中晚期至西周早中期。从各期文化特征看，第二期是左右江区域早期青铜文化发展重要阶段，所见文化遗物特征突出，时代性和区域性明显。当然，本文对左右江区域目前所见的早期青铜文化遗此的分期和断代，未完全解决的所有问题，如第一期尽管与该区域的新石器时代末期文化面貌存在诸多相似特征，二者的年代上限和下限比较接近，但差异性也是存在，可能存在缺环，第一期出现的石范，当代表该区域新技术的出现和应用，揭示青铜技术的萌芽，有别于史前时期的石器技术；同样在第二期与第一期以及第二期与第三期也是如此，而从第三期看，已经较多出现小件青铜器，其原因如何仍有待于我们进一步思考。从第三期的文化面貌所体现的特征可知，青铜文化开始在该区域得到长足发展。根据横岭山墓地西周中晚期出现青铜鼎和甬钟大件青铜器，元龙坡墓地西周晚期至春秋时期，则出现青铜卣和盘，表明岭南青铜文化大致在西周晚期至春秋时期迈入新的阶段，也就是说，从现有考古学证据而言，商中晚期至西周初和西周晚期至春秋时期可能是岭南青铜文化发展重要分界线，商中晚期至西周初岭南区域出现青铜文化萌芽，而至西周晚期至春秋时期则是青铜文化开始进入发展期。

总之，广西左右江流域所见的早期青铜文化遗存的文化特征可知，总体上承袭岭南文化大传统，并以第一期和第二期为代表，流行夹砂陶和石器，区域特色明显，与广东同时期的文化遗存相比，既有共性，也有差异。共性方面，该时期两地均有符合本区域文化传统的典型断代器物组合，出现凹刃石器、石范、石戈、骨牙璋等；差异方面主要是二者的典型断代器物陶器不同，左右江区域主要为夹砂陶，装饰绳纹或素面，为圜底或圈足的圈足壶、簋、双耳小圈足罐等，而广东主要为泥质的各类几何印纹硬陶或釉陶的尊、凹底器、带流器等一类标准器物，这种差异主要是小区域环境中史前文化发展不同形成，左右江区域深受本地史前末期文化的夹砂陶影响，广东几何印纹硬陶风格并未对左右江区域产生实质性影响，这种情况直到战国时期才有所改变，主要原因当是地理环境的相对封闭以及区域文化传统。但不管是广东或广西，在早期青铜文化阶段，岭南的两大区域均出现符合自身小环境发展的典型器物群，当然左右江流域早期青铜文化遗存中，鉴于其地理位置特殊性，处于云贵高原、东部沿海、越南北部三方包围的三角地带，其发展过程中自受到多方面文化因素影响，形成区域特色，但从文化面貌看，主要是来自于广东，成都平原和云南影响并没有占据主流，或许暗示该区域的早期青铜文化是受到广东影响下产生，并吸取多方面因素，最后殊途同归，促使社会复杂化，促进社会文明的进步。

解读祥云大波那木椁铜棺

Interpretation on the Bronze Coffin with Wooden Outer Coffin at Dabona on Xiangyun in Yunnan

李铁军 / 云南省博物馆 志愿者

[摘要]

滇西地区青铜时代墓葬，是云南青铜文化中重要的组成部分，在云南青铜文明中占有重要位置。本文试图通过对祥云大波那木椁铜棺墓葬的一一解读，以小见大，加深对滇西青铜文化的认识和了解。

[关键词]

墓葬结构　随葬器物　铜棺冶铸　青铜纹饰

Abstract

The tombs of Bronze Ages in the western Yunnan is an important part of Yunnan bronze culture, and plays a significant role in the Bronze Civilization of Yunnan. This thesis interprets the bronze coffin with wooden outer coffin of Xiangyun Dabona, Yunnan, discribe the bronze culture of western Yunnan from a detail, and lead to a better understanding of this ancient culture.

Key words

Tomb's structure; Funerary objects; Manufacture of bronze coffin; Patterns on bronze wares

（二）家畜和家禽模型

占了17件中的15件（另2件是房屋模型），比例较大，且“六畜”品种齐全，表明滇西地区的先民已有了对“五谷丰登，六畜兴旺”的祈求[①]。战国西汉时期，原系怒江、澜沧江河谷游牧民族的“昆明”人，沿澜沧江支流进入洱海区域，其中部分成为当地的农业定居民族，但畜牧业在他们的经济生活中仍占有较大比重。该墓葬中出土的成套“六畜”模型，就反映了这部分“昆明”人农、牧并举的生产状况[②]。恩格斯曾指出：“家畜的驯养和畜群的繁殖，创造了前所未有的财富的来源，并产生了全新的社会关系。”由此看来，墓主生前是把这些家畜、家禽作为财产看待的，并有了较发达家畜（禽）养殖业[③]。

（三）墓中的铜鼓造型较原始，具有早期铜鼓的特征[④]

鼓面仅有简单的四角光芒，四周无晕纹；胴、腰、足三段分明，素面无纹，足部外侈。其出土时鼓面向上，无烟痕，器身有孔不能作炊具，鼓内壁无纹饰，伴出乐器有钟、葫芦笙等。这些情况，说明此时铜鼓已彻底脱离炊具，独立出来成为一种专门的乐器了[⑤]。值得注意的是，同时出土的1件铜釜敞口鼓腹、小平底，颈腹之间有双耳外，底有烟熏痕迹。铜釜倒置过来看，与铜鼓十分相似。而差别在于底面直径较小，且足边无折棱。故清理报告中认为：“过去，对铜鼓形式来源于何物，颇多揣测，迄无定论，此式铜釜之出现，又增添了一个值得注意的线索。”1974年冯汉骥先生在《云南晋宁出土铜鼓研究》一文中，通过对出土的铜鼓和铜釜的进一步对比指出：“从早期铜鼓的形制来看，它似乎是一种实用器（铜釜）发展而来”，使认识更加明确具体。1975年，在楚雄万家坝M1、M23发掘出土了5具原始铜鼓。当时它们皆倒置着，且部分鼓内壁有花纹，其中四面的外壁还有很厚的烟炱，显然是烹煮食物留下的痕迹，而内壁花纹则主要用于美化。这些现象都清楚地表明了铜鼓与铜釜之间的亲缘关系，并对铜鼓起源于何地、何物等重大学术问题，提供了有力的实物证据[⑥]。如此年代既早、流行于春秋至战国初期、又最原始的铜鼓类型，到2007年2月止，总共出土了62面，多数分布在我国，越南和泰国有少量发现[⑦]，后被考古界定名为万家坝型铜鼓，它们都与铜釜很相似。而铜釜又是由相同形状的陶釜——云南青铜时代流行的一种炊具（锅）——演变而来。它的来历甚至可追溯到距今3500多年前、大理白族自治州宾川县白羊村新石器时代遗址出土的陶釜[⑧]。陶釜不仅是日用品，还可充当如鼓类一样的打击乐器。因此，由“炊具而兼乐器”的陶釜演变为铜釜，再变成原始铜鼓，也是很自然的事[⑨]。

（四）此墓未出现铁器

没有货币，也没有像晋宁石寨山那样的金、银、珠、玉和漆器等。主要随葬品

① 云南省文物工作队：《云南祥云大波那木椁铜棺墓清理报告》，《二十世纪大理考古文集》，云南民族出版社，2003年。

② 张增祺：《中国西南民族考古》，云南人民出版社，1990年，27页。

③ 张增祺：《滇西青铜文化初探》，《云南青铜器论丛》，文物出版社，1981年，104页。

④ 云南省文物工作队：《云南祥云大波那木椁铜棺墓清理报告》，《二十世纪大理考古文集》，云南民族出版社，2003年。

⑤ 席克定、余宏模：《试论中国南方铜鼓的社会功能》，《古代铜鼓学术讨论会论文集》，文物出版社，1982年，164页。

⑥ 王大道：《云南铜鼓》，云南教育出版社，1986年，78页。

⑦ 李昆声、黄德荣：《再论万家坝型铜鼓》，《考古学报》2007年第2期。

⑧ 王大道：《云南铜鼓》，云南教育出版社，1986年，80页。

⑨ 王大道：《云南铜鼓》，云南教育出版社，1986年，84页。

滇西地区有着悠久的历史和古老的文化，在云南青铜文明中占有重要位置。著名的祥云大波那木椁铜棺墓就是其中最具代表性的墓葬之一。1964年3月初，在大理白族自治州祥云县城东南30公里的云南驿坝子，1个名叫大波那的汉族、白族杂居的大村落里，考古人员对该墓进行了清理①，经放射性碳-14测定为：前6世纪末—前4世纪中②，也即战国时期（前475～前221年）。祥云大波那铜棺，是我国目前发现的唯一一具保存完好的铜铸棺材③，也是云南出土青铜器中最大的1件。那么，它在云南青铜文化的发展中地位如何？有何值得后人探究的东西？这正是本文通过学习，要尝试着去一一解读的问题。

一

墓葬结构

祥云大波那木椁铜棺墓葬为长方形竖穴土坑墓，与云南青铜时代常见的墓穴并无区别④。也许是当时人们头脑中视死如生，灵魂不灭，死后仍要在阴间生活的观念根深蒂固，所以将木椁和铜棺都做成当时颇为流行的“井干”式和“干栏”式房屋结构，形成外椁和内棺的式样。

（一）木椁即外棺——“井干”式房屋结构

这是用圆形或方形木料层层交叉堆砌，构成房屋底架和墙壁的一种特殊建筑形式⑤。因其转角处的木料均相交出头，与“井上四交之干”的形状相同，故称“井干”式⑥。井干式住房的特征：为一方桶式结构，即从地面开始用四根木料搭建成“井”字形式样，再向上层层垒叠，构成四壁合围的居室。

祥云大波那墓的木椁，是先用初加工的长约5米的四根木料，平排在墓底，再在巨木两侧和两端的交接处开出榫口，之后将木料相互迭架套接成一个方形框架，与“井干”式房屋建筑的墙壁相似⑦。据考古资料证实：我国中原地区商代后期至秦汉时期的棺椁就有“井干”式结构；汉初的一些宫苑建筑也是这种形式。云南从战国至西汉初普遍流行这种建筑。有的直接建在地面上，有的建在“干栏”式的底架上，形成两者的有机结合。祥云大波那墓中的木椁，就是建在地面上的较典型的“井干”式建筑结构形式。到了近现代，除森林较多，木材资源丰富的民族地区，如东北地区的鄂伦春和达斡尔族，西南地区的独龙族、普米族和摩梭人等仍在使用外，其他地区已基本没有这种建筑了⑧。

① 云南省文物工作队熊瑛、孙太初执笔：《云南祥云大波那木椁铜棺墓清理报告》，《二十世纪大理考古文集》，云南民族出版社，2003年。

② 张增祺：《云南冶金史》，云南美术出版社，2000年，19页。

③ 黄懿陆：《滇国史》，云南人民出版社，2004年，第269页：“据20世纪70年代的考古发现，在今广西西林县普驮曾发现鎏金铜棺葬和铜鼓葬，据说与句町王有关。”（句町国地属牂牁郡，西汉元鼎元年，即前111年置。与益州、越嶲、永昌郡同归属于汉代四郡一都尉。句町故地与滇国故地山水相连，同族同源同地域）。经请教云南省博物馆黄德荣教授得到确认，因是发掘出土在“文革”期间，铜棺已遭到破坏，仅留残片。此棺长2、宽1米。为实用葬具。

④ 张增祺：《云南建筑史》，云南美术出版社，1999年，39页。

⑤ 张增祺：《云南建筑史》，云南美术出版社，1999年，40页。

⑥ 黄懿陆：《滇国史》，云南人民出版社，2004年，225页。

⑦ 云南省文物工作队熊瑛、孙太初执笔：《云南祥云大波那木椁铜棺墓清理报告》，《二十世纪大理考古文集》，云南民族出版社，2003年。

⑧ 张增祺：《云南建筑史》，云南美术出版社，1999年，47页。

（二）铜棺即内椁——“干栏”式房屋结构

其主要特征是“上设茅屋，下豢牛豕”①。具体为房屋建在桩柱上；正脊两头翘起并长于屋檐，即所谓的“长脊短檐”式；屋顶作两面坡式结构等特点②。据考古发现，最早的“干栏”式房屋建筑遗存，是发现于前4800年左右的浙江余姚河姆渡新石器时代遗址③。而在云南则是在距今3000多年的剑川海门口早期青铜时代遗址发现的④。这种建筑在多雨潮湿，又多虫兽的南方是非常实用的。所以，至今仍普遍分布在我国的江浙赣、两广和云贵川、台湾等省区。云南的傣、壮、布依和傈僳等民族的民居建筑，至今依然保持着这种远古遗风⑤。祥云大波那出土的铜棺，即是形状如“干栏”式建筑的结构。铜棺重约257千克，长2、宽0.6、高0.64米，用七块铜板拼合而成：底板向上的一面有凹槽和榫眼，用以对应四壁（即四块铜板）的榫头。安装时板壁上较长的榫头可穿过榫眼直落地面，形成“干栏”式房屋的底柱（即铜棺的12支脚）。使棺底与木椁间保持一定距离，以防地下水对棺底的侵蚀。这与现实生活中“干栏”式房屋的防潮功能是一样的。顶盖用两块铜板对合成“人”字形屋脊状，且长于壁板和底板，如长脊短檐的“干栏”式住房屋顶⑥。

二

随葬器物试析

墓内随葬器物丰富，共110件。其中铜器105件、陶器5件。包括锄、锛等农具和两件一套似刀状器的纺织工具；矛、剑、啄、钺等兵器；釜、杯、尊、勺、豆、箸等生活用具和铜鼓、葫芦笙、钟乐器；还有房屋模型，猪、牛、羊、马、鸡、狗等成套“六畜”模型及一些形状各异的饰物⑦。从随葬器物看，呈现以下特点：

（一）生产工具

以锄类最多共8件，锛1件，部分还有使用过的痕迹，证明是实用物。它们的发现，说明当地的农业生产已发展到了一定水平。生活用具中除豆和箸外，没有汉式器物，且铜箸是云南目前所见最早的筷子实物⑧。而如尊、杯、勺、匕⑨等器物，虽是汉名，但在器型上远不如中原的同类器物丰富，且有华美的纹饰，而是更多地融入了地方特色，样式简单古朴而无纹饰。此外还有“干栏”式房屋模型。这些器物不仅表明当时已处于比较定居的农业社会，还说明边疆云南与中原地区的经济文化交流已是事实。

① 张增祺：《云南建筑史》，云南美术出版社，1999年，48页。

② 黄懿陆：《滇国史》，云南人民出版社，2004年，226页。

③ 辞海编辑委员会：《辞海（历史分册·世界史·考古学）》，上海辞书出版社，1979年，314页。

④ 肖明华：《剑川海门口青铜时代早期遗址》，《二十世纪大理考古文集》，云南民族出版社，2003年，203页。

⑤ 李昆声：《云南文物古迹》，云南人民出版社，1984年，32页。

⑥ 张增祺：《云南建筑史》，云南美术出版社，1999年，53页。

⑦ 云南省文物工作队：《云南祥云大波那木椁铜棺墓清理报告》，《二十世纪大理考古文集》，云南民族出版社，2003年。

⑧ 李昆声：《云南文物古迹》，云南人民出版社，1984年，142页。

⑨ 马承源：《中国青铜器》：“匕是挹取食物的匙子。”在中原地区的“考古发现中，匕常与鼎鬲同出。”上海古籍出版社，2003年，155页。

是铜器[①]，占了随葬器物总数的95%。据昆工冶金化学系化验室对各类铜器所做化学分析结果表明，当时滇西地区对合金成分的掌握还不成熟。与石寨山（滇池区域）出土的铜器相比较，两者有较大的差别[②]（表一）。

通过对以上表格的分析对比，可以看 出三个不同[③]：

第一，晋宁石寨山的6个数据中，含铜量高于85%的只有1个；而祥云大波那的10个数据中，除3个外，含铜量都高于85%。说明前者的合金工艺已臻成熟，后者尚处于不太完善的阶段。

第二，在石寨山的青铜器中，锡含量最高达20.07%，最低为6.04%；铅含量最高达21%，最低为0.39%；且每件青铜器的铅锡含量均在9%以上，最高者达28.15%。而大波那青铜器中，锡含量最高为16.34%，最低仅为0.16%；铅含量最高为2.89%，而低者仅为零；每件青铜器的铅锡含量大都在9%以下，最低的仅0.19%，最高的也不超过17%。可见前者为高铅锡青铜器，后者为低铅锡青铜器，有的甚至是红铜器。特别值得注意的是，在石寨山出土的青铜器中，铜剑、斧等兵器的含锡量都较高，其平均值约为15.79%，符合硬度的要求；铜鼓含锡铅量约15%～28%，既要有一定的硬度，使其音域宽广声音洪亮，也需要相当的韧性，使之在频繁的击打中不易破损；铜镯的含锡量较少，一般为6.04%，更具有韧性，长期使用也不致破碎。这些都说明了，古滇池区域的工匠们，已能根据青铜器的不同用

① 云南省文物工作队：《云南祥云大波那木椁铜棺墓清理报告》，《二十世纪大理考古文集》，云南民族出版社，2003年。

② 张增祺：《滇国与滇文化》，云南美术出版社，1997年，90页。

③ 张增祺：《云南冶金史》，云南美术出版社，2000年，27页。

表一　晋宁石寨山与祥云大波那青铜器合金成分比较一览表

出土地点	器物名称	合金成分（%）				总和	材料
		铜	锡	铅	铁		
晋宁石寨山	铜鼓	82. 95	15 .07	0. 55		98. 57	锡青铜
	铜鼓	69. 9	14 .3	14 .4		98. 6	铅锡青铜
	铜斧	82. 21	12. 81	1. 74	0. 31	97. 07	锡青铜
	铜剑	76. 18	20. 07	0. 39		96. 64	锡青铜
	铜柄铁剑	81. 53	14. 5	0. 84	1. 52	98. 39	锡青铜
	铜镯	87. 38	6. 04	3. 8		97. 22	铅锡青铜
祥云大波那	铜锄	92. 9	0. 19			93. 09	红铜
	铜釜	97. 5	0. 16	0. 6	0. 14	98. 4	红铜
	铜锛	94. 2	3. 71		0. 2	98. 11	锡青铜
	铜矛	93. 79	2. 35	0. 62		96. 76	锡青铜
	铜钟	79. 96	16. 34	极少		96. 3	锡青铜
	铜葫芦笙	97. 63	1. 32	0. 52		99. 47	红铜
	铜圆环	79. 6	14. 75	2. 89		97. 24	铅锡青铜
	铜棺	89. 6	5. 02	2. 25		96. 87	铅锡青铜
	铜匕	84. 13	13. 69			97. 82	锡青铜
	铜马	93. 8	1. 92	1. 12		96. 84	红铜

注：该表格未完全引用原文，只选用了其中两处青铜器出土地点即：滇池区域的晋宁石寨山和滇西地区的祥云大波那的材料。表格的后两栏是笔者所加。

途，决定加锡的多少，对青铜器合金成分已有了较准确的认识。与古代中原地区青铜合金的“六齐”[①]之说相近[②]，这对边远地区的工匠来说实属不易。

第三，滇池区域和滇西地区青铜器合金成分的差异，显然和当地冶铸工艺水平的高低有关。当时滇池地区的滇国居民主要从事农业生产，经济、文化都比云南其他地区要进步；而滇西地区的“昆明”人仍处于农牧并举的生产发展阶段，其生产水平远不及滇池地区。

三

铜棺的铸造

青铜铸造技术是我国古代文明发达的重要标志之一。云南出土的一些春秋战国时期的青铜器，如晋宁石寨山的铜鼓、祥云大波那的铜棺等，都表明了这一时期云南地区已普遍地掌握了陶范铸造技术。铜棺的铸造反映了战国时代的云南冶炼工艺已达到了较高水平，铜手工作坊也有了较大的规模[③]。

这是1具用“地坑范铸造法”制成的铜棺，具体铸造的方法是[④]：在空地上挖出1个形状、大小、厚薄和铸件一样的坑，经平整夯实后，将预先制好的板状铸范（即陶范），包括形成榫眼的泥心和支钉，平铺在坑底，板上的花纹必须向上。然后，用若干坩埚将铜液连续不断地注入范腔中，待铜液冷却后，即可撤范取件。这样大型的铸件，不但要求铸范强度既高透气性又好，且只能1范1件，不能重复使用；还要若干熔炉和坩埚连续不断地浇铸，加之铜板上的纹饰又如此繁缛精细，铜棺的“人”字形坡顶一面就有124平方米，难度之大可以想见。7块铜板分别铸成后，将榫眼和铜楔斗拢，1具铜棺就拼合成功了。以当时较简单的生产工具和简陋的生产条件，要营建和完成这样一个庞大的工程，需要较长时间和较固定的作坊来保证，因此，一个定居的社会条件就是必需的[⑤]。

四

青铜器上的纹饰

“滇西类型”的青铜文化，很少装饰成分。即使是出土铜器数量颇多的楚雄万家坝古墓群，仍是品类少，纹饰简单。到了祥云大波那等地古墓时期出土铜器才品类渐多，纹饰也略有可观[⑥]。如：铜钟的挂柄有半环状“人”字辫纹组，钟体布满了

①② 马承源:《中国青铜器》，上海古籍出版社，2003年。

③ 曹献民:《云南青铜铸造技术》，《云南青铜器论丛》，文物出版社，1981年，203页。

④ 张增祺:《云南冶金史》，云南美术出版社，2000年，46页。

⑤ 云南省文物工作队:《云南祥云大波那木椁铜棺墓清理报告》，《二十世纪大理考古文集》，云南民族出版社，2003年。

⑥ 李伟卿:《云南民族美术史》，云南美术出版社，2006年，50页。

蛇形雷纹，口沿饰一道卷云纹；铜棺除底板外更是遍体密布纹饰：对合成“人”字形屋脊状的两块顶盖饰有三角形纹图案，两侧板饰回纹，头足挡板则饰以鹰、燕、虎、猪、蜥蜴等飞禽走兽，造型古朴生动，纹饰富于装饰效果；铜杖头上雕铸有两豹相抱的立体形象；通体呈四棱锥体锋锐无刃口的鹦鹉形啄，将饰物与器物浇铸在一起，颇具匠心；还有“六畜”模型和饰有蟾蜍的圆牌饰等[①]。由此可见，大波那出土器物上的纹饰，已包括了平面的、立体的、抽象的、具体写实的、装饰性的以及肖形的等多种不同手法，可视为滇池类型铜铸艺术的先驱[②]。

除此之外，这些青铜纹饰还有祭祀功能。据载，绝大多数中外学者，在对商周青铜器上的动物纹饰的文化内涵研究后认为：这些纹饰“具有宗教上和仪式上的意义”，是“人的世界与祖先及神的世界之沟通的媒介”。原始社会人们曾把动物奉为神灵和图腾祖先。早期奴隶社会仍维系着这种信奉。因此，奴隶主用动物形象来显示自已超世间的权威神力，是很自然的。也就是说，青铜器上的动物纹饰是图腾崇拜的遗存。而把铜棺的头足挡板，看做是远古先民巫术中常见的“符图”，用以“护身避邪”、“镇魔压邪”、“遣神役鬼”，与景颇族寨门上刻的龙齿锯纹、傣族的文身、汉族的门神[③]等都具有异曲同工之妙。《左传·宣公三年》进一步指出青铜器上的动物纹饰还有“使民知神奸”、“协于上下以承天体”的作用，即青铜器上的形象，可以使人知道哪些动物是助人的神，可助人通天地，而哪些动物则对人无助无益[④]。在铜棺头足挡板上，共有九种动物38只，其中老鹰占了14只为1/3强，燕子11只、老虎5只，其他8只。这仅仅是巧合吗？我们知道，鹰是充满传奇色彩的猛禽。千百年来，鹰一直被人类所神化，它不仅寓意着勇敢和威武，更象征着武力和皇权。我想这是否至少可以说明，来自滇西北高原峡谷的“昆明人”，是将高原猛禽老鹰视为他们最重要的保护神和勇敢、威武的象征。而属候鸟的燕子，常随季节变化而迁徙。这是否与先秦时期昆明人“随畜迁徙，毋长处”的游牧生产、生活方式相似？尽管到了秦汉时期，大部分昆明人已迁至金沙江以南及滇池区域以西区域，生产、生活方式也由原来的“随畜迁徙”，逐步转化为以农、牧业相结合的定居形式[⑤]。但他们遥远记忆中的祖先故地，颠沛流离的迁徙经历,都是这个民族难以忘怀的“历史情结”,当然,也包括与他们生产、生活息息相关的燕子等自然物和纷繁世事。何况燕子在以农业为主的定居民族中，又是象征春天来到春耕在即和祈雨祈年、祈求风调雨顺的吉祥之鸟呢。这是否是两种文化习俗碰撞的表现？在多民族的中国，这种难以忘怀的民族“历史情结”，常常会通过史诗、民歌、神话、故事、图画甚至服装刺绣等形式代代相传，铭刻在心永志不忘。

据考古资料，湖南长沙马王堆M1出土的西汉帛画和长沙楚墓出土的绢帛画也即非衣(“T”字形的旌幡类帛画)，都有蛇龙盘桓，对天、人、冥（也有说是水界）三界时空作有联系的分割和导引。专家认为，和马王堆等古墓一样，祥云大波那铜棺上的纹饰也有着类似的作用[⑥]。在棺上覆盖，刻绘图画，或以“神路图”导引亡灵轮

① 云南省文物工作队：《云南祥云大波那木椁铜棺墓清理报告》，《二十世纪大理考古文集》，云南民族出版社，2003年，203页。

② 李伟卿：《云南民族美术史》，云南美术出版社，2006年，51页。

③ 刘稚、秦榕：《宗教与民俗》，云南人民出版社，1991年，121页。

④ 陈荣富：《宗教礼仪与古代艺术》，江西高校出版社，1994年，73页。

⑤ 张增祺：《滇国与滇文化》，云南美术出版社，1997年，41页。

⑥ 邓启耀：《宗教美术意象》，云南人民出版社，1991年，110页。

回三界，在云南各族中也很常见，在独龙族创世纪神话中就讲道，人们在“第一次面临死人的事时，都不知所措，他们聚在一起商量说：‘这个人应该再活回来’，四脚蛇跑出来告诉人们说：‘人死了应该用土埋’”。在祥云大波那铜棺的头足挡板上就刻绘有这类怪异的爬虫类动物[①]，这正是云南边陲的少数民族先民，对诸多动物图腾崇拜的遗存，他们死后也期望这些“神灵”能护佑、导引亡灵获得重生。西双版纳的克木人至今就保留有对18种动、植物的氏族图腾崇拜的习俗[②]。

综上所述，云南青铜器以它特有的蛮荒气息和质朴形制而异于中原，他们铸铜鼓以感天通灵，铸铜棺以送魂压邪，铸铜芦笙以迎生赛神……[③]这些正是青铜器所要传达给后人的宗教信息；再从滇西地区古代民族分布状况，从墓中出土的极其丰富的随葬品，包括诸多象征权力、地位和财产的铜鼓、铜钟、权杖[④]、酒器、餐具、“六畜”模型和豪华巨大的铜棺葬具等，进一步印证了墓主身份的非同一般，他应是“昆明人”某部落的“君长”、“邑君”之类的人物，他们是云南历史上最早出现的剥削者。祥云大波那文物的发现，说明至少在云南这一地区，已建立了奴隶制。奴隶主不仅生前追求大量财富，死后还要继续占有。墓葬的奢华及随葬品的精美丰富，真实地反映了奴隶主的卑劣和贪欲[⑤]。总之，祥云大波那木椁铜棺墓所涉及的有关滇西青铜文化的诸如社会发展状况、墓葬形制、冶金铸造、铜铸艺术等方面，对后人认识其在云南青铜文化发展中的位置、作用，为云南地区的考古和民族历史的研究所提供的资料，都有着不可忽视的重要意义。

① 邓启耀：《宗教美术意象》，云南人民出版社，1991年，122页。

② 刘稚、秦榕：《宗教与民俗》，云南人民出版社，1991年，142页。

③ 邓启耀：《宗教美术意象》，云南人民出版社，1991年，130页。

④ 李昆声：《云南文物古迹》，云南人民出版社，1984年，33页。

⑤ 马曜：《云南简史》，云南人民出版社，1983年，25页。

中国南方青铜工具的发现及研究
——再论海南青铜文化及其相关问题

Discovery and Research on Bronze Implements of South China
—Rethinking about Bronze Culture in Hainan and other Questions

涂高潮 / 海南省博物馆 研究员

[摘要]

文章用大量旁证材料论证了海南昌江等地出土、原定名为“青铜环形器”的器物实为青铜圆锯或圆形锯，这一研究成果将海南青铜文化的研究提高到一个新的层次；作为海南青铜文化主体的生产工具中主要的品种青铜圆锯的定名，不仅是对该类器物名称的“拨乱反正”，更重要的是还原其本来面目，使海南青铜生产工具的种类更丰富、可供研究的实物更多。类似的青铜器在云南、广西两地的发现，表明中国南方（滇、桂、琼）青铜文化的发展脉络、承继关系、文化传播、民族交融存在着千丝万缕的联系。

[关键词]

中国南方　青铜工具　发现研究　海南青铜文化　相关问题

Abstract

The article, with the massive evidence, has proved the unearthed places such as Hainan Changjiang. Originally named "the bronze ring", the bronze ware actually was a bronze circular saw. This research promoted the study of Hainan bronze culture to a new level. Denominating the bronze circular saw the majority of Hainan bronze culture, it not only accurately identifies the appellation of this sort of bronze ware, but also reverts such wares to original appearance. These discoveries make the types of bronze ware producible tool more affluent and abundant, and bring out more practicalities for study. The similar bronze wares were dug in Yunnan and Guangxi. It presented that in south China (Yunnan, sweet osmanthus, fine jade) the developing direction, the continuation, the cultural diffusion and the national amalgamation of the bronze culture were closely connected.

Key words

Southern China; Bronze implements; Discovery and research; Hainan's bronze culture; Relative questions

海南的古代文化在经历了昌江南阳溪洞穴遗址和三亚落笔洞洞穴遗址的旧石器时代文化之后，又经历了以陵水大港村遗址为代表的新石器时代文化。而海南古代文化的历史长河中青铜时代文化没有缺席已经是不争的事实。正是由于海南青铜时代文化的存在以及它对海南新石器时代文化与铁器时代文化的链接，使得海南古代文化中的旧石器时代、新石器时代、青铜时代和铁器时代能够完整地串联起来。

如果说之前部分学者对海南是否存在青铜文化尚有些疑问的话，当我们对海南这些年出土的青铜工具等文化遗物及其相关遗址的田野调查和发掘资料进行深入分析后，其最终结论应该是可以肯定的：海南古代文化中确实有青铜文化的一席之地，而海南的文明发展史中也确实经历了一个相对长的青铜时期，远不是部分考古或文化学者所说的海南没有青铜文化、或只有青铜文化因素；海南青铜时代是海南古代史中的重要组成部分，而不仅只是海南历史长河中的一个匆匆过客。

海南古代文化中确实有青铜文化的一席之地，而海南的文明发展史中也确实经历了一个相对长的青铜时期，这从海南出土的青铜圆形锯就可以清楚地看出来。海南昌化江流域的乐东、昌江、白沙、东方等地出土的青铜圆形锯已经是相当发达的青铜文化的象征，其成熟的铸造工艺、不同的锯型锯式、多种组合的使用方法以及铜锯上优美的花纹装饰，无不透出其成熟的意味。而这种海南常见的生产工具到目前为止很少见于国内其他同时期的青铜文化遗址，就是在中国整个青铜时期，圆形青铜锯也极少见。没有交流或贸易的迹象、也就没有可模仿的对象。海南多个地方出土的青铜锯如果不是舶来品，其来源唯一可以解释的是海南青铜文化时期的自我创造！制造出一件经过多种工序后而完成的青铜工具绝不是平地惊雷、一蹴而就那样简单，它是当时社会政治、经济、科学、文化发达的结晶。试想一下，如果没有相对发达的农耕经济基础和先进的磨制石器技术积累，又怎能具备制造出青铜生产工具的客观条件；再如果没有社会的大量需求和相当成熟的文化创意，又如何能激发那些能工巧匠的创造欲望?

当大汉天子的金戈铁马在西汉武帝元封元年（前110年）平定南越，跨过琼州海峡在海南创设珠崖，儋耳二郡、实行封建式的统治时，我们就应该清楚地知道，建郡之前的海南岛已经具备了相当的经济基础。如若不然，西汉王朝也不必举大军进军儋琼。

王克荣先生曾经在1987年第1期《海南黎族苗族自治州民族博物馆馆刊》（《海南岛的主要考古发现及其重要价值》）一文中将“青铜文化遗址和遗物”与“石器时代文化遗址和遗物”并列，表明海南的青铜文化确实存在。虽然王先生是将海南岛出土的所有青铜器：如青铜斧、青铜锅以及铜鼓和铜锣统统归纳到海南青铜文化的范畴（其中的铜鼓和铜锣可能是汉代以后的遗物），但是他将其中的青铜斧等生产工具作为海南青铜文化的主要遗物的表述是比较准确的。

其实，海南岛上出土的青铜生产工具远不止昌江七差尼下遗址和乐东九所新庄两地出土的青铜斧。笔者曾经在1997年中国南方及东南亚地区古代铜鼓和青铜文化第四次国际学术讨论会上就《海南青铜文化及其相关问题》的讨论中除提到过这两件青铜斧外，同时还列举了海南近年考古发现的其他青铜工具，如东方广坝昌化江西岸台地和昌江七差大仍遗址出土的青铜刀，昌江七差大仍遗址和白沙青松新丰遗址出土的青铜环形锯等。

经过仔细观察，《海南青铜文化及其相关问题》中提到的海南东方广坝昌化江西岸台地和昌江七差大仍遗址中出土的环形青铜刀实际上也应该是一种空心圆形锯。这从以下几个方面可以得到印证。

一般来说，刀者，体厚。刀体不大，差别较小，小者寸余，大者三尺，以长度在一尺左右者居多。直刃或弯刃。刀体多由刀背或刀脊向刀刃渐薄。有长条形尖头单面直刃、长条形尖头双面直刃、长方形平头单面直刃以及弯条形尖头单面直刃等。其用途以作生活用具为主，生产工具为辅，是用来切、割、斩、削、刺、砍的工具。鉴于刀的用法多为切、砍、割、削、挖等特性，它的着力点必须在一个方向，使力点则是由上向下、或由后向前，以由一个方向向另一个方向用力而形成的能量完成其对物体的分割，来实现其使用的目的。所以，刀应该是一面刃、另一面则是着力点，其形状亦应是以一面刃的形式出现。而锯者，直刃或圆刃。刃面有齿。有长条单面刃和圆形刃两种。体薄。锯体远较刀体为大。锯体大小不等，长短区别亦较大。小者三寸或近尺，大者过米，最长的条锯则达数米。以作生产工具。主要用来分割大型木材和石材。条形锯对物体的切割以来回拉动锯体实现力量的转换而将物体分割开，而圆形锯对物体的切割则是以旋转锯体实现力量的转换而将物体分割开。

海南东方广坝和昌江大仍出土的青铜钏形刀的形体是圆形（或称为扁体环形），它的用法正是以切割的形式出现，其着力点在整器的中心，使力点也在整器的中心并以旋转的方式实现用力的转换。

如果上述说法能够成立，那么在海南西部地区出土的青铜环形器应该都归类为青铜环形锯。又由于这些锯齿的形态差别明显，其用途显然不会一样，因而使我们得出一个清晰的结论：那就是海南出土的青铜锯已经达到了一个相当成熟的高度——此种青铜器是一种多式样、多类别组合的多用途的生产工具。

经过反复研究和对比，可以肯定地说，海南昌化江流域出土的青铜环形器，就是青铜圆锯！为什么将青铜环形器原定名更正为青铜环形扁体锯呢？现在我们回过头来具体分析一下海南东方、昌江、白沙等地出土这批青铜器。这些出土的青铜器，正面似环，横截面扁薄，其形体呈扁体、圆形、中空。全器成环状圆形。外缘环一周锯齿，锯齿分尖头齿（有三角形齿和针形齿两种）、平头齿（即方形齿），锯齿不完整，残、断、缺、破等现象严重。好部光滑。内缘突起无磨损痕迹，使中间的空出部分更是便于穿插柱状物以支撑整个器体。内圈的握柱部分厚于外圈的锯齿部分，是锯齿厚度的三倍。内圈的锯体部分保存完好，外圈的锯齿因磨损而变薄。表面铸饰辫纹。根据锯齿有两种不同形态：即平头齿和尖头齿，可以看出，这些青铜圆形锯是通过其中间的柱心的旋转而产生能量来完成对所切割对象的切割任务的。而不同形式的锯齿显然与其切割不同对象有关。

从锯刀切割材料的方式来看，外缘有平行线纹的平头齿锯所切割对象应该多为质地比较细腻、坚实的材料。因为这尖锯刀，其齿间距极小，仅相当于金属物质的伸缩缝，所以这种锯齿的锯在切割材料时的伸缩范围受到限制。而具有三角形锯齿的锯，由于其齿间距较大，其切割的对象应该是质地粗松、含水量较大的物质。

众所周知，生产工具是生产力的重要组成部分。一切社会的进步首先体现在生产工具的进步上。中国各个历史发展阶段的递进无不都是证明了这一点。

在石器时代，人类首先是学会了利用天然石块作狩猎工具，猎杀野兽、捕获鱼类，以此手段获得人类自身生存所必需的食物。而当人类在不断的生产实践中发明和创造了用人工把天然石料加工成石材进而加工成石器，并将之用于狩猎、捕鱼、农耕、纺织等广泛的生产和生活活动中时，社会就进化到了新石器时代，人类也因之进入了文明时代。当新石器时代的生产工具发展到一定的成熟阶段，新材质的生产工具就应运而生。

青铜时代是新石器时代之后人类进步的产物。人们制造的生产工具，由原来使用的天然石质材料发展到使用金属材料。由于金属材料的韧性、金属材料的锐利程度以及金属材料的可回收等诸多特性，使当时以青铜这种金属材料制造的器物，逐渐进入人们的生产和生活领域。由于青铜器的生产工序远较利用天然材料制成的器物的生产工序复杂得多，难得多。所以，当生产力中的重要因素生产工具由天然石材变成了金属材料时，其给社会经济的发展、对人们的生产生活以至于对战争的进程，都将产生了极大的影响。而当金属材料普遍地用于社会的各个方面时，用青铜材料制造的生产工具和生活用具注定要成为人类社会政治经济文化生活的主角，并主宰社会的各个方面，其社会的生产力和生产关系也会发生根本的变化。

通常地讲，石质生产工具的获得比较容易，是因为制造石质生产工具的制作流程比较简单，取材也方便。海南岛上石材种类丰富，广泛分布的花岗岩石质材料是在距今4.4亿年前到2.3亿年前的晚古生代形成的花岗岩石层，其他还有火山岩石、砾岩石、油页岩石、燧石、麻石和片石等。海南现在已经发现的石器生产工具中，旧石器时代的石质生产工具多用燧石打制而成；新石器时代及以后的石质生产工具则多用花岗岩石、砾石、片石、麻石和油页岩石经打制成型后再进行磨制加工而成。海南各地历年来出土了大量的石质生产工具，其跨越的年代涵盖旧石器时代、新石器时代、青铜时代、铁器时代。由此可见，海南制造石质工具取材容易、制作工序简单、工艺并不复杂、技术难度也不高。

而制造青铜材质的生产工具则远比制造石质的生产工具复杂得多。一件青铜工具制作必须经过一系列的生产工艺及生产流程，包括选矿、冶炼、制模、铸造、成型、打磨抛光加工等。以选矿而论，在今天的现代科技条件下，看起来也许很简单。但是，在四五千年前，则不是那么容易的。当长期使用石质材料的人们在生活中感觉到石质生产工具远不能满足人们的全部生产需要和生活需要时，强烈地需要有一种比石质生产工具更能解决生产或生活难题时，金属材质的生产工具就必然会出现。在这种强烈的社会生产和人们生活需求的前提下，人们开始尝试着将金属矿产进行挑选或精选。而纯度高、易提炼、熔点低、矿藏资源分布广泛的优质铜矿便自然而然地出现在人们的面前，成为人类开始冶铸金属生产工具和生活用具的首选金属。如果说，选矿只是生产金属材质用具和器皿的最起码、最容易解决的工艺难题的话，那么金属材料的冶炼无疑是制造青铜器的全部工艺流程中难度最大的。

选矿和冶炼是青铜器制造的两个基础环节。海南铜矿十分丰富，是海南有色金属矿藏比较丰富的品种。这些著名的铜矿多集中在海南岛西部和南部，如保亭的响水铜矿、摩天岭铜矿，白沙的松涛铜矿、琼海的烟塘梅岭铜矿、定安的翰林铜矿和昌江的石碌铜矿等。

在古代社会，铜矿的冶炼方法通常称作氧化矿还原熔炼法。冶炼铜矿石时，是将矿石与木炭放在冶炼炉中进行冶炼。由于这些矿石是氧化矿，因此这种冶炼被称作氧化矿还原熔炼。虽然目前只发现春秋时期的炼铜竖炉，用竖炉冶炼铜矿，能持续加料，持续排渣，间断放铜，从而加快了冶炼速度，提高了冶铜的生产效率。

当冶炼铜矿、铸造出青铜器的各项技术和条件成熟，所铸造的青铜器能够满足社会经济生产生活等各个方面时，社会的形态也随之进入了较之新石器时代发达得多的青铜时代。

而海南出土的青铜圆形锯，其铸造和使用者在铸造初期必然对海南当时所具备的技术条件和经济基础有比较清楚的认识和了解，方能铸造出如此复杂的先进生产工具。像这样复杂的生产工具，在生产技术和经济基础落后的新石器时代是无法完成的。它必定是在社会发展到一定程度、经济基础相对雄厚的前提下完成的，一个经济发展程度相对成熟的社会必须要经过一个相当长的发展过程，才可能具备相当成熟的青铜铸造技术铸造出生产工具中的高级类型——组合式生产工具。

中国青铜时代经历了两千多年的发展。在这个相当长的社会发展进程中，随着青铜时代社会经济的不断发展，中国的青铜工具也经历了一个由简单到复杂、由低级到高级、由单一用途到多种功能的复合用途的过程。

从甘肃齐家文化出土的青铜刀，我们可以看出萌芽时期青铜铸造工艺的原始和落后。而从河南二里头出土的青铜器，我们也可以清楚地看到即使是处在夏代的都邑内，使用的青铜器仍然呈现出较原始的现象。如二里头出土的青铜器胎子轻薄、空隙大、气泡多，表面粗糙，呈现出青铜器时代初期青铜铸造技术的落后状态。经过一段时间的发展和进步，到了商代二里冈时期、青铜器的铸造水平才有了长足的进步。而当历史的年轮到达商代晚期以及后来的西周，中国青铜器的铸造水平迅速提高，有的青铜器的华美程度甚至达到了登峰造极的地步。

从青铜礼器和生活用器铸造水平的不断进化，使我们有条件了解到中国青铜容器的发展脉络。相对于青铜容器，中国的青铜生产工具铸造水平肯定同样地经历了一个从简单到复杂、从单一品种到多品种、从单一品种的单一类型到一个品种的多个类型的发展轨迹。海南昌江、白沙、东方等地出土的青铜圆形锯也正好证明了这一点。

青铜容器（包括礼器和日用器）与青铜工具构成了中国青铜时代的物质基础。虽然今天的人们所看到的出土青铜器中，青铜容器的数量较青铜工具大得多，这是我们不能否认的事实。但是，鉴于青铜容器的使用方式与青铜工具的使用方式完全不一样这个特点，我们同样认为，在中国的青铜时代，当时铸造的生产工具不会比生活用具少。这从当今生活中的生产工具与生活用具数量的比例中也能看出来。

如果纯粹从器物学的角度来分析，昌江、东方、白沙等地出土的青铜圆形锯（原名为圆形锯齿形器）与今天仍广泛地使用在物体切割方面的生产工具——合金钢圆形锯有异曲同工之处（图一、图二），可以说几乎完全一致。所不同的只是昌江等地出土的锯是在青铜时代用青铜材质铸造的，而当今日常生产或生活中使用的锯是现代用合金钢材质制成的。如果器型无二，仅材质不同，由此我们可以大胆地推断：海南昌江、白沙、东方等青铜时代遗址出土的青铜圆形锯就是当今社会广泛使用的合金钢材质的圆形锯的始祖，它们有着直接的发展承继关系。可以这样说，海南出土的青铜圆形锯是目前中国发现的年代最早的圆形锯。

人们的社会生活除了人与人之间的交际、交往、交流外，更多的是要生产生活所必需的产品或用品。而人类在生产这些产品和用品时，必然需要通过人使用生产工具这个媒介来实现、来完成。

海南青铜文化以生产工具、生活用具为主，作为生产工具的青铜圆形锯，从其先进的式样来看（与现代圆形锯相似），它一定经历了一个相当长的发展演变过程；而从其严重磨损的程度分析，可以肯定这类工具的消耗量是很大的。

由此，我们得出一个结论：海南出土的青铜圆形锯很少见于大陆两广及云贵川地区。它是海南青铜时代物质文化的一个突出特征，正是由于这些具有鲜明个性、独特文化现象的先进青铜工具的发现，足可证明海南青铜时代不仅存在，其延续的时间还相对较长；海南青铜文化的特征明显，而且相对发达。

在两广及云贵川地区，虽然类似海南青铜圆形锯出土极少，但与之型式相近或相像的锯齿形青铜圆形器也时有出土，如云南大理洱海东岸金棱岛出土的春秋战国时期“齿轮形铜镯”等。据此，我们也可以说，海南青铜圆形锯的出现在南方地区应该是有它们的必然性的。虽然我们一时还难以说海南的青铜圆形锯与上述地区的类似青铜工具是同一个文化系统，但至少说明海南与两广及云贵川地区在东周到西汉这一历史时期文化上的依存、交流关系。

图一　海南出土青铜圆锯（上排为平齿锯、中排为三角齿锯、下排为尖齿锯）

图二　现代合金钢圆形锯

海南古代青铜器的来源

——“舶来品”说质疑

The Source of Ancient Bronze Wares in Hainan —An Argument to the "Foreign import" Theory

李 勃 / 海南师范大学文学院 教授

[摘要]

考古发现和古籍记载表明，海南岛古代曾有各种青铜器。其来源，学术界大都认为是“舶来品”。对此说法，笔者甚难苟同。考诸史志，海南古代青铜器当多属本岛产品。

[关键词]

海南岛 古青铜器 来源

Abstract

According to many archaeological discoveries and ancient articles, there once existed various bronze wares in ancient Hainan island. Tracing back to the source, archaeological circles conclusion is different. In author's opinion, those ancient bronze wares found in Hainan island should be local product.

Key words

Hainan island; Anctient bronze wares; Source

关于海南岛古代青铜器的来源，学术界虽然大都认为是“舶来品”，但目前尚无专文进行探讨。因而，研究本课题，对于了解海南岛古代冶炼技术发展史，对于探索和宣传海南岛的古代文明，对于了解海南岛先民们建设海南的历史贡献，对于提高海南各族人民的自尊心和自豪感等，无疑都有重要的学术价值和现实意义。

一

1950年以来海南发现的古青铜器

所谓青铜器，即采用铜、锡、铅、铁等合金制成的各种器物。1950年以来，先后在海南岛各地发现了一批古代青铜器，有铜环、锅锅（釜）、铜鼓、铜斧、锅锣、铜爵、铜剑、铜箭镞等。如王克荣先生的《海南岛的主要考古发现及其重要价值》[①]、丘刚先生的《海南古遗址》[②]、王育龙和高文杰先生的《海南古代墓葬》[③]等记载。可以划分为以下八类：

（1）属于国家一级文物的战国时期的青铜环形器10件。据海南省文物考古研究所编写的《海南省近五十年文物考古工作述》一文：“1994年，昌江县燕窝岭出土9件战国青铜绳纹环型器。铜环外径8.7～11.4、环宽1～2、厚0.2～0.3厘米，外缘为齿状，齿长0.25～0.7厘米，环面有6～8圈绳纹，器重50～125克(同样器物80年代中期在东方市曾出土1件)。该类器物用途不明，在海南乃至国内尚属首次发现，有很高的研究价值。因我省青铜文化遗存发现甚少，又缺乏明确的地层关系，为此，除铜绳纹环形器可疑定为战国器物外，目前还少见相当于中原殷周之际的遗迹和遗物。”[④]关于这批铜环的发现和鉴定情况，丘刚先生在《海南古遗址》一书里介绍较为具体：“20世纪90年代初，昌江县七差乡燕窝岭的村民在山坡上耕种时，陆陆续续挖出了几件从未见过的一种环形金属器物。器物上面的图案很细密，如绳子一圈圈紧密盘结，最外边一圈呈齿轮状……1994年11月，国家文物局专家鉴定组到海南各地巡回文物鉴定时，确认这种器物为战国时期的青铜环形器，并定级为国家一级文物。这种造型奇特的器物在海南乃至全国尚属首次发现，而它在2000多年前的战国时期作什么用途，至今仍是一个谜团。”[⑤]笔者认为，该铜环疑是古代本岛黎族先民妇女首饰所用的铜环。如《岭外代答》卷2《海外黎蛮》载：“黎装椎髻徒跣裸袒，而腰缭吉贝，首珥银钗，或铜或锡……其妇人高髻绣面，耳带铜环，垂堕至肩。”

（2）汉代以前的铜锅（釜）12件。详见《海南岛的主要考古发现及其重要价值》[⑥]、《海南省近五十年文物考古工作述》[⑦]、《海南古遗址》[⑧]、《海南文物记事》[⑨]等。

①⑥ 王克荣：《海南岛的主要考古发现及其重要价值》，《海南大学学报》（人文社会科学版）1988年第1期。

②⑤⑧ 丘刚：《海南古遗址》，海南出版社，2008年。

③ 王育龙、高文杰：《海南古代墓葬》，海南出版社，2008年。

④⑦ 海南省文物考古研究所：《海南省近五十年文物考古工作述》，《新中国考古五十年》，文物出版社，1999年。

⑨ 沈志成、沈艳：《海南文物记事》，海南出版社，2008年。

（3）汉代以来的青铜鼓12件。详见《海南岛的主要考古发现及其重要价值》①、《海南文物记事》②、《海南省近五十年文物考古工作述》③、郝思德和黄兆雪先生的《从民族学材料看黎族与骆越族的关系》④、《海南古遗址》⑤等。

（4）汉代的铜铃、铜钟（件数未详）。详见《海南百科全书》彩色插图第1页⑥。

（5）古代铜锣多件。详见《海南岛的主要考古发现及其重要价值》⑦、《海南文物记事》⑧等。

（6）秦汉以前的青铜斧多件。详见《海南岛的主要考古发现及其重要价值》⑨、《海南古代墓葬》⑩、《海南百科全书》彩色插图第1页⑪等。

（7）青铜箭镞多件。详见《海南古代墓葬》一书⑫。

（8）海南民间收藏的各种古代青铜器。近年来，海南民间收藏的各种古代青铜器也不断出现，其中较为重要的有以下三种：一是4000年前的青铜爵1件⑬，二是春秋战国时期的青铜古剑1把⑭，三是千年双耳花瓶青铜器1件⑮。

可以肯定，以上青铜器只是海南岛古代青铜器的极少部分，还有很多尚未被发现。

二

古籍记载的海南古青铜器

据现存古籍记载，海南岛古代曾有各种青铜器。其中属于礼器的有铜镬，属于乐器的有铜鼓、铜钟、黎金、铜锣等，属于饰物的有铜环、铜钗、铜圈等，属于兵器的有铜铳、铜飞枪、矮将军、竹节长颈破落户、碗口、赛将军、大将军等，属于祭器的有铜爵、笾、豆、簠、簋、钘、登、尊等，属于宗教神器的有铜佛像、铜狮、铜豸等。兹列举如下：

（一）属于礼器的有铜镬

如文渊阁《四库库书》之《太平御览》卷757《器物部二·镬》和《渊鉴类函》卷383《器物部二·镬》俱载："《朱崖传》曰：朱崖大家[有]大铜镬，多者三五百，积以为货。"考"《朱崖传》"也作"《珠崖传》"。据《隋书》卷33《经籍志二》载："《珠崖传》一卷，伪燕聘晋使盖泓撰。"此又见宋人郑樵《通志略》卷66《艺文略第四》等。《朱崖传》是现存最早记载海南岛情况的地方文献。该书早佚，其内容散见于《太平御览》卷757《器物部二·镬》和卷820《布帛部七·纻》及卷973《果部十·龙眼》、《初学记》卷8《岭南道第十一》、《御定渊鉴类函》卷383《器物部二·镬》和卷335《州郡部二·岭南道》及卷366《布

①⑦⑨ 王克荣：《海南岛的主要考古发现及其重要价值》，《海南大学学报》（人文社会科学版）1988年第1期。

②⑧ 沈志成、沈艳：《海南文物记事》，海南出版社，2008年。

③ 海南省文物考古研究所：《海南省近五十年文物考古工作述》，《新中国考古五十年》，文物出版社，1999年。

④ 郝思德、黄兆雪：《从民族学材料看黎族与骆越族的关系》，《首届黎族文化论坛文集》，民族出版社，2008年。

⑤ 丘刚：《海南古遗址》，海南出版社，2008年。

⑥⑪ 李克：《海南百科全书》，中国大百科全书出版社，1999年。

⑩⑫ 王育龙、高文杰：《海南古代墓葬》，海南出版社，2008年。

⑬ 张洁、侯宏亮：《海口发现4000年前青铜爵》，南海网，2008年7月31日；新华网，2008年7月31日。

⑭ 张洁：《海口发现春秋青铜古剑》，《南国都市报》，2008年6月7日。

⑮ 张永生、钱兵：《千年青铜器藏身海口民间》，《商旅报》2008年4月9日；彭桐、陈笑闻：《海口晚报》2008年4月10日。

帛部二·布》、《说郛》卷61下著录晋人郭义恭《广志》等。考东晋十六国时期以“燕”字为国名者，有前燕、后燕、西燕、南燕和北燕，前四燕的统治者均为鲜卑族，惟北燕的统治者为汉族。五燕中唯南燕（398～410年）为东晋所灭。又据《通志略·艺文略第三》载：“《南燕录》五卷，记载慕容德事，伪燕尚书张铨撰。《南燕录》六卷，伪燕中书郎王莀撰。”由此可知，所谓“伪燕盖泓”之“伪燕”，显然是指南燕。其“伪”字当为东晋或南朝人所加。所谓“伪燕聘晋使”，意谓到东晋访问的南燕使者。南燕盖泓能够撰《珠崖传》，说明他出使东晋时曾游历珠崖（即今海南岛），当是经实地考察和掌握第一手资料后才撰成此书，而绝对不是仅凭传闻记述而成。这也说明《珠崖传》所记当时海南岛情况当属实。这里所说的“大铜镬”，虽未提及其形状和作用，但既然“多者三五百”，则知其显然不是炊器，而是礼器，当作为财富、地位和权力的象征。所谓“朱崖大家”，显指海南岛的黎族先民首领。既然“朱崖大家”有“大铜镬”，“多者三五百”，说明当时黎族先民大小首领都拥有数量不等的“大铜镬”。据《水经注》卷36《温水注》引晋代王氏《交广春秋》说：晋代海南岛黎族先民“可十万余家”，则全岛黎族先民各级首领所拥有“大铜镬”之总数量，至少当有数千。

（二）属于乐器的有铜鼓、铜钟、黎金、铜锣等

这方面的记载很多,诸如：

《舆地纪胜》卷124琼州《景物下》“铜鼓岭”条载：“在文昌县。俗传民得铜鼓者，验之，乃诸葛武侯征蛮之钲。因以名之。”[①] 此又见《宋本方舆胜览》卷43琼州《山川》“铜鼓岭”条[②]。

按：诸葛武侯征蛮之地与今两广和海南岛无涉，所谓“乃诸葛武侯征蛮之钲”，此显误传。

《大明一统志》卷82琼州府“铜鼓山”条：“在文昌县东一百里。俗传民尝于此山得铜鼓，因名。”[③]

《大明一统名胜志》卷10《琼州府·文昌县》载：“铜鼓山……后人于此掘得铜鼓，因以名山。”同卷《儋州》载：“蚂蝗山，在州东三十里，以形似得名。相传汉时屯兵于此，土人常掘得铜鼓、钲、铛等物。”[④]

正德《琼台志》卷5《山川上·文昌县·山类》“铜鼓山”条载：“在县东一百里青蓝都。古传诸獠铸铜为大鼓，悬于庭中，置酒以招同类。来者若富家女子，则以金银钗扣鼓，竟留以答主人。若仇杀相攻，则击此鼓，到者云集。后遗瘗此山，乡人掘得之。”又卷6《山川下·万州·山类》“铜鼓山”条载：“在州西十里。昔人曾于此掘得铜鼓。”又卷9《土产下·器用属》载：“铜鼓，诸州县时掘得之。详林泉生《铜鼓记》……黎金，似铜鼓而匾小，上三耳，中微具脐。黎人击以为

① （宋）王象之：《舆地纪胜》，江苏广陵古籍刻印社，1991年，939页。

② （宋）祝穆：《宋本方舆胜览》，上海古籍出版社，1991年，392页。

③《大明一统志》（下册），三秦出版社，1990年，1258页。

④ （明）曹学佺：《大明一统名胜志》，见《四库全书存丛书·史部一七〇册》，齐鲁书社，1996年，294、297页。

号。”又卷42《杂事·皇朝》载：“铜鼓出南方，林泉生《记》及余《铜鼓岭辨》已及之。至今乡曲往往挖得之，形各不同。永乐中，万州土官王惠起黎兵，挖引多辉溪水，得一鼓，长三尺，面围五尺，凸二寸许，沿边皆科斗，各衔线抵脐，束腰豸尾，若今之杖鼓。击之，声如鹅鹳，闻数十里。凡鼓形声，未有如其怪远者。”此又见万历《琼州府志》卷12《杂志·遗事》。

嘉靖《广东通志初稿·琼州府》之《山川·文昌县》“铜鼓山”条载：“在县东一百里。古传诸獠铸铜为大鼓，悬于庭中，置酒以招同类。来者若富家女子，则以金银钗扣鼓，竟留以答主人。若仇杀相攻。则击此鼓，应者云集。后遗瘗此山，乡人掘得之。”[①]此又见嘉靖《广东通志·琼州府》之《山川·文昌县》“铜鼓山”条[②]。

嘉靖《广东通志·琼州府》之《杂事》“铜鼓”条载：“永乐中，万州土官王惠起黎兵，挖引多辉溪水，得一鼓，长三尺，面围五尺，凸二寸许，沿边皆科斗，各衔线抵脐，束腰豸尾，若今之杖鼓。击之，声如鹅鹳，闻数十里。凡鼓形声，未有如其怪远者。”[③]

《古今图书集成·方舆汇编职方典》卷1373《琼州府部》之《琼州府山川考一·文昌县》“铜鼓岭”条载：“在县东六十里青蓝都。古传诸獠铸铜为大鼓，悬于庭中，置酒以招同类。来者若富家子女，则以金银钗扣鼓，竟留钗以答主人。若仇杀相攻。则击此鼓，到者云集。后遗瘗此山，乡人掘得，因以名岭。”又卷1374《琼州府部》之《琼州府山川考二·万州》“铜鼓岭”条载：“在州南五里。昔人掘得铜鼓，故名。”[④]

清初屈大均《广东新语》卷16《器语·铜鼓》载：“故永乐中，万州土官黄惠，于多辉溪中得一铜鼓，长三尺，面宽五尺，凸二寸许，沿边皆科斗，各衔线缕抵脐，束腰豸尾，若今之杖鼓然者。击之声如鹅鹳，闻数十里……文昌、万州亦有铜鼓岭，皆以掘得铜鼓而名。”[⑤]

清人程秉钊《琼州杂事诗》载：“铜鼓山，在定安城东六十里。山势雄峻，下有龙神庙，相传诸獠瘗铜鼓于此。乡人发得之，因以名山。”见周伟民、唐玲玲辑纂《历代文人笔记中的海南》[⑥]。

道光《琼州府志》卷43《杂志三·金石》“铜鼓”条载：“永乐中，万州土官王惠起黎兵挖引多辉溪水，得一鼓，长三尺，面围五尺，凸二寸许，沿边皆蝌蚪，各衔线抵脐，束腰豸尾，若今之杖鼓。击之，声如鹅鹳，闻数十里。”又“府学宫铜鼓”条载：“其制若圆墩，而空其下。高尺有四寸，四围八尺六寸，两旁缀耳，高可二寸。满鼓回字花纹，极工致。面平，周衔线抵脐。凡八围，每围线三条。身凡二十一围，每围如面之线。”又“天宁寺铜鼓”条载：“款云：大明成化十二年，广州府番禺县客人李福通铸造。”又“昌化县铜鼓”条载：“明天启五年，邑人获之，藏峻灵王庙中。面围二尺六寸，中空，旁缀两耳，面有蛙凡四。通体厚二分，其色白。惟脐间缺损，击不成声。”又“感恩县铜鼓”条载：“在真武庙中。国朝嘉庆二十五年，西郊河畔农民垦土得之。鼓高一尺八寸，围二尺有八寸。面有四蛙，左右各缀耳如环。周身线纹细致，斑驳陆离。击

① 《嘉靖广东通志初稿·琼州府》，海南出版社，2006年，14、15页。

② 《嘉靖广东通志·琼州府》，海南出版社，2006年，272、273页。

③ 《嘉靖广东通志·琼州府》，海南出版社，2006年。

④ 《古今图书集成》，中华书局、巴蜀书社，1986年。

⑤ （清）屈大均：《广东新语》，中华书局，1985年，437页。

⑥ 周伟民、唐玲玲辑纂：《历代文人笔记中的海南》，海南出版社，2006年，170页。

之，其声冬冬。”又同卷“定安县谯楼古钟”条载：“姚应甲《定安古钟记》略：铜钟古色，光莹可爱，纽之蒲牢，一足微缺。考铸之日，镌明永乐九年，铸之人邑令吴君定实，重凡三百余斤。初置谯楼上，叩之声闻至郡。”又“郡城隍庙铜钟”条载：“旧在谯楼上，后楼废，移庋城隍庙内。款铸‘大明正统元年，海南卫指挥佥事信官张玉、石玉等仝琼州府知府程莹捐资铸造，计重二千三百二十斤’。钟高五尺，周身铸有八卦纹。”①

民国《琼山县志》卷14《金石志·唐宋元明》“谯楼铜钟”条载：“款云：海南卫指挥佥事信官张玉、石玉等同琼州府知府程莹发心各出俸资，命匠人新铸禁钟一口，计重二千三百二十斤，永充在本卫府楼中开鸣晓昏，专为禁动，镇军民而康泰，保卫府以平宁，雨旸时若，国泰清安。大明正统元年岁次丙辰夏四月吉旦。共九十七字……其钟今在府城隍庙，高五尺，大三十余围，有八卦纹环绕之。”又“府文庙铜鼓”条载：“其制圆若轮而空其中，高尺有四寸，径二尺八寸，围八尺四寸，两旁缀耳高一尺二寸。满鼓回字，花纹极工致，面平。周衔线抵脐，凡八围，每围线三条。身凡二十一围，每围如面之线。重五十余斤。无制造年代，相传与礼器同时所铸。考文庄《祭器碑记》文，无言及铜鼓，则非同时所铸可知。然确是代遗器，尤可宝贵。”又“天宁寺铜鼓”条载：“款云：‘广州府番禺县客人李福通喜舍资财，铸造铜鼓一面，在于琼州天宁寺大洪宝殿，永远供俸，祈愿佛日增辉、风调雨顺、国泰民安者。时大明成化十三年三月吉日造。’共六十六字环鼓面旁边。”② 以上又见民国王国宪《琼崖志·金石志》之“铜鼓一”、“铜鼓二”、“谯楼铜钟”、“府文庙铜鼓”、“天宁寺铜鼓”、“莫氏宗祠铜鼓二”、“临高铜鼓”等③。

文渊阁《四库全书》之雍正《广东通志》卷52《物产志》载：“黎金，形似铜鼓而匾小，上有三耳。黎人击之，以为号。”

清人李调元《南越笔记》载：“琼州有黎金，似铜鼓而匾小，上三耳，中微其脐，黎人击之以为号，此即锴也。古时蛮部多以铜为兵，以铜为器，富者鸣铜鼓，贫者鸣锴，以为聚会之乐。”此又见《广东新语》卷16《器语·铜鼓》。

光绪《崖州志》卷113《黎防志一·黎情》载：“崖州黎……最贵蛤锣，豪强之家有以数十牛易一锣者。”

民国许崇灏编著《琼崖志略》第四章《琼崖居民·黎族·嗜好》载：“黎人嗜好极少，然亦不能绝无……富者爱好古代铜鼓、铜锣，以鼓缘、锣柄有虾蟆形者为上品，真伪新旧均有考证。每鼓或锣之价，可值数牛至十余牛不等。若有四虾蟆以上者，则非百牛不办矣。”

（三）属于饰物的有铜环、铜钗、铜圈等

如：《桂海虞衡志·志蛮》载：“黎，海南四郡坞上蛮也……蛮皆椎髻跣足，插银铜锡钗，妇人加铜环，垂堕至肩。”④

① （清道光）《琼州府志》（第四册），海南出版社，2006年，1927、1928、1948、1949页。

② （民国）《琼山县志》（第二册），海南出版社，2004年，764、777、791页。

③ （民国）王国宪：《琼崖志》，《琼志钩沉（三种）》，海南出版社，2006年，59～67页。

④ （宋）范成大：《桂海虞衡志》，《说郛三种》（第六册），上海古籍出版社，1988年，2874页。

《岭外代答》卷2《外国门上·海外黎蛮》载："黎装椎髻徒跣裸袒，而腰缭吉贝，首珥银钗，或铜或锡，首或以绛帛彩帛包髻……其妇人高髻绣面，耳带铜环，垂堕至肩。"①

《文献通考》卷331《四裔八·黎峒》引石湖范氏《桂海虞衡志》曰：黎人"皆稚髻跣足，插银铜锡钗……妇女绣面高髻，钗上加铜环，耳坠垂肩。"

《诸蕃志·海南》载："黎，海南四郡岛上蛮也。……其人椎髻徒足，插银、铜、锡钗，妇人加铜环，耳坠垂肩。"②

万历《琼州府志》卷8《海黎志·黎情》载：黎人"椎髻徒足，插银、铜钗，花幔缠头腰，戴藤六角帽。妇人高髻，钗上加铜环，耳坠垂肩，衣裙皆五色吉贝。"③此又见康熙《琼州府志》卷8《海黎志·黎情》、道光《琼州府志》卷20《海黎志·黎情》、康熙《崖州志·黎情》等。

《古今图书集成·方舆汇编职方典》卷1389《广东黎人歧人部汇考一·汉》载："其去省地远、不供赋役着为生黎……椎髻徒足，插银、铜、锡钗，花幔缠头腰围，戴藤六角帽。妇人高髻，钗上加铜环，耳坠垂肩，衣裙皆五色吉贝。"

近人徐珂编《清稗类钞》之《服饰类·黎人之服饰》载：黎人"儿童耳垂大环，或银或铜，以为美观，亦随贫富为之，既婚则无。"④

民国《海南岛志》第三章《人民·附黎苗俸伎》载："黎女均穿耳，戴铜圈，小者径寸，大者五六寸。四差黎女每耳多至18圈，圈径五六寸，两耳窗孔大盈寸。各铜圈于耳前后另用小圈束之，置于头上，望之如戴铜丝帽然。约计两耳之铜圈重量，都10两以上。"⑤

（四）属于兵器的有铜铳、铜飞枪、矮将军、竹节长颈破落户、碗口、赛将军、大将军等

如：正德《琼台志》卷42《杂事·皇朝》载："铜鼓出南方……顷文昌人挖得一铜铳，长筒匾腹爹底，响亦七八十里，其声雄震而拽余如霆。"此又见嘉靖《广东通志·琼州府》之《杂事》"铜鼓"条。

正德《琼台志》卷18《兵防上·兵器》载：明代海南卫(明代海南岛最高军事机构)及其所属内外各千户所,都按规定以铜或铁制造飞枪、矮将军、竹节长颈破落户、碗口、赛将军、大将军、铁猫、枳马丹、竹节神炮、手铳等各种兵器。

万历《琼州府志》卷7《兵防志·兵器》也载："卫所军器，各有定制，迄后因时损益。洪武初，府设军器局，以大使、副使各一员领之……工匠募之于民，日银三分，军匠副之。国初颁降门城器械附图：竹节长颈破落户、大将军、赛将军、矮将军、飞枪、长颈破落户、枳马丹、碗口、铁猫、竹节神炮、神炮……"以上兵器亦分为铜火器和铁火器两种。由此可以推知，明代以前驻岛军队也当自制铜兵器和铁兵器。

① （宋）周去非：《岭外代答》，上海远东出版社，1996年，35、36页。

② 《诸蕃志（外十三种）》，上海古籍出版社，1993年，40页。

③ （明万历）《琼州府志》（上册），海南出版社，2003年，410页。

④ 徐珂编：《清稗类钞》（第2册），海南国际新闻出版中心、诚成文化出版有限公司，1996年，2156页。

⑤ 民国陈铭枢总纂：《海南岛志》，海南出版社，2004年，143、144页。

（五）属于祭器的有铜爵、笾、豆、簠、簋、铏、登、尊等

诸如：

万历《儋州志·地集·学校志·祭器》载：明万历年间儋州学祭器有："铜香炉五个，铜花瓶四个，大铜爵七十一个，小铜爵六十七个，磁爵一个，铜簠五个，铜簋十四个，锡铏十七个，锡簋三十一个……"[①]此又见康熙《儋州志》卷2《学校志·祭器》。

康熙《琼州府志》卷9《艺文志·记》收录明代裴崇礼《元大德间吉阳军军学正齐孟坚铸铜爵记》载："朱崖学庙祭器，有古铜爵五……刻云：'大元大德丁未，吉阳军学学正齐孟坚造公用祭器。'凡二十字。计至今日，一百七十一年矣。"[②]此又见康熙《崖州志·艺文志》[③]、乾隆《崖州志·艺文志》之《文庙铜爵记》。

乾隆《崖州志》卷4《学校志》载：清代崖州学以铜制造的"祭器"和"乐器"有：铜酒樽三个、铜爵一百四十九个；铜编钟一十六口、特编钟一口。

道光《琼州府志》卷38《艺文志二·记》收录明代丘濬《琼州府学祭器记》载："琼郡学祀，旧有祭器，久而废坏弗备。成化辛卯，广东按察副使丰城涂君伯辅奉玺书来饬兵备。下车之始，未遑他务，首市铜鸠工，博考古图像，按其制之。其为器，爵百四十而奇一，笾七十有二，豆如笾之数，簠、簋各四十有四，铏十有二，登五，尊三，总其凡三百九十有三。事费一出于官，而民弗与知。以明年春二月上丁，将释奠于先师。"从"市铜鸠工"可知，以上祭器皆以铜为之。又卷43《杂志三·金石》"府学祭器碑记"条载："成化辛卯，广东按察副使涂棐市铜鸠工，博考古图像，按其制制之。其为器，爵百四十而奇一，笾七十有二，豆如笾之数，簠、簋各四十有四，铏十有二，登五，尊三，总其凡三百九十有三。郡人丘濬有记。见《艺文志》。"此又见民国《琼山县志》卷14《金石志》"府学祭器碑"条。以上又见民国王国宪《琼崖志·金石志》之"府文庙铜祭器"、"文庙铜祭器"、"莫氏宗祠铜龙炉"等。

（六）属于宗教神器的有铜佛像、铜狮、铜豸等

诸如：

民国《琼山县志》卷14《金石志·唐宋元明》"天宁寺铜佛"条载："案：佛高六尺有奇，大三尺，尊严端重，铸法甚工。惜无款识，不知年代，询之寺僧，相传以为前代所存。考寺创于宋而元明因之，观明初重修碑记，无一语及铸佛事，则佛为宋时旧物无疑。"又卷16《金石志· 明清》"海氏宗祠铜狮铜豸遗器 "条载："案：高二尺许，重二十余斤，不铸年月，为明代所留遗。海氏子孙世世相传，以为忠介公时所造，至今春秋祀事，敬为陈设。可见世家宗器，数百年犹宝用之，名贤之遗泽孔长也。"此又见民国王国宪《琼崖志·金石志》"海氏宗祠铜狮铜豸"条。

此外，还有金属所制的"古礶"。如清王士祯《香祖笔记》卷8载："琼州黎峒

① （明万历）《儋州志》，海南出版社，2004年，115页。

② （清康熙）《琼州府志》，海南出版社，2006年，201、202页。

③ （清康熙）《崖州志》，海南出版社，2006年，与乾隆《崖州志》合一册，55页。

有黎长统之，必符、王二姓乃得立。黎长家有古礶，传为祖先所遗，非陶非石。天欲雨，则先鸣；官军将入山，则大鸣。”（文渊阁《四库全书》本）

所谓“礶”，古同“罐”。既然“非陶非石”，则显然是采用铜、铁金属所制。

三

海南岛古代青铜器的来源——“舶来品”说质疑

从上述可知，海南岛古代曾有各种青铜器，那么，这些青铜器究竟是本岛生产、抑或是从岛外传入呢?

关于海南岛古代青铜器的来源，学术界大都认为是舶来品。诸如:

关万维先生的《琼州文化》说：“黎族不谙冶铜，更不从谈起铜鼓。”（辽宁教育出版社1998年，第3页）

丘刚先生的《海南古遗址》第二章说：“迄今在海南出土的青铜釜，大多分布在海南岛的西部或北部如临高、儋州等沿海，而且这些地带都是海南岛距大陆较近的区域……这些青铜釜很有可能就是汉朝军队从大陆带来的行军炊具……由于海南本地铜矿甚少，目前在海南尚未发现有明代以前冶铜业存在的物证。在海南出土的10余件北流型、灵山型铜鼓，可以推断全是从大陆两广地区传入的。”又第七章说：“从已获得的考古材料和历史文献来看，从史前时期经秦汉一直到唐宋时期，海南的社会历史发展是极其缓慢的。直到今天，海南发现两汉时期的遗址并不多……同时，从秦汉到唐宋漫长的历史阶段中，除海南岛环岛四周外，其余大部分地区仍处在原始社会阶段……尤其重要的是，海南直到明代以前都没有发现青铜冶炼遗址。”“迄今为止在海南岛各地发现的青铜釜、铜鼓和青铜环形器主要是舶来物……是否可以得出这样一个结论：海南岛历史发展进程中不存在青铜时代。”

又郝思德、王大新先生的《海南考古的回顾与展望》说：海南“汉代考古除对部分遗址和墓葬进行发掘外，最重要的是发现了一批青铜器。”“考虑到当时海南岛较为落后的生产力水平以及目前仍缺乏青铜文化的考古材料，尤其是未发现有冶铜业存在的实物证据，因此，还难以推定这些大型青铜器是在海南本地铸造的。根据有关史料的记载，西汉初期平定南越和东汉初期征交趾时，汉朝军队曾途径海南岛进行征战，这批青铜器也有可能是当时军事活动所带来的。”①

又《海南古代墓葬》一书说：“海南岛青铜鼓是来源于两广地区的文化传播。它虽发现于海南岛，但并不说明海南岛就是制造生产的地方，因为这里既不具备铜鼓矿料的来源，也没有发现铜鼓铸造遗址。有学者推测，极有可能是西汉时期平定南

① 郝思德、王大新:《海南考古的回顾与展望》，《考古》2003年第4期，294、295页。

越或东汉初期征战交趾时汉朝军队在海南岛进行军事活动时流下来的遗物。”

从上述可知，学术界认为海南岛古代青铜器都是舶来品的理由，可归纳为以下四点：

一是由于海南岛的社会历史发展极其缓慢，生产力落后；二是由于海南岛的铜矿资源甚少；三是由于目前海南岛尚未发现明代以前的青铜冶炼遗址；四是这些青铜釜很有可能就是汉朝军队从大陆带来的行军炊具。

若按照以上说法，则海南岛古代冶炼技术发展史完全属于空白。然考诸史志，此说诚难令人信服。主要理由有六：

其一，早在先秦时期海南岛居民已与祖国大陆有一定的经济文化交流，中原文化尤其是青铜文化已在岛上有所传播。考古资料表明，早在1万年，“三亚人”已定居在海南岛上。当时岛上既然有了人类活动，则必然要和外部世界有所交往。相传先秦时期，本岛居民与中原王朝已有友好交往。如南朝梁代萧绎《金楼子·兴王篇一》载：“尧乃老，使舜摄行天子政，巡守得举用事……绥耳、贯胸之民来献珠虾。”①这里的“绥耳”，即“垂耳”、“缓耳”、“儋耳”，指古时海南岛的土著居民。如南朝梁代陆倕《石阙铭》序云：“南服缓耳，西羁反舌。”《后汉书·文苑传上·杜笃》也云：“连缓耳，琐雕题。”唐人李贤注：“缓耳，耳下垂，即儋耳也。”

又万历《广东通志》卷2《藩省志二·事纪一》载：“周武王十有三年，初定南海为藩服（原注：《通历》：王既灭殷，乃正九服彻法，以南海地在东南扬州之裔，定为藩服，乃经土地而并牧其田野，以距于海）。十有四年，初通关旅，儋耳入贡。”②以上说明，早在先秦时期，本岛居民已归向于中原王朝，并与之有一定的经济联系。

又上文已提及，目前唯独在海南岛发现了战国时期的青铜环形器10件，这虽然不能直接证明战国时期海南岛居民已掌握了青铜冶铸技术，但至少可以说明：当时本岛居民与祖国大陆已有一定的经济文化交流，中原文化，尤其是青铜文化已在岛上有所传播，本岛居民很早就已了解青铜文化。青铜器品种众多，其体积有大有小，形制有简单和复杂。既然早在先秦时期本岛居民能够与中原王朝发生友好关系和中原文化已在岛上有所传播，既然本岛居民很早就已了解中原青铜文化，则他们仿造或自制一些体积小和形制简单的青铜器，看来并非难事。

其二，秦汉时期海南岛与古代“铜鼓产地”主要地区的社会发展状况大致相同，而且岛上的居民大都来自祖国大陆，难道他们没有制造铜鼓的智慧或能力?目前我国学术界一般认为，古代“铜鼓产地”，即我国南方和西南方以及越南、缅甸等地区。如张荣方先生《什么是铜鼓？它是怎样流传的？》一文说：“铜鼓，是我国古代南方少数民族地区的特有文物，初由用作炊具的铜釜发展而来，后成为号令部众的权力象征，或作为祭祀、赏赐、进贡的重器。”“我们说铜鼓的发祥地是我国云南滇池以西地区。铜鼓从铜釜分离出来成为专门乐器，大概在前7世纪左右，相当

① （南朝梁）萧绎：《金楼子·兴王篇一》，《百子全书》（第四册），岳麓书社，1993年，3012页。

② （明万历）《广东通志》（卷2），见《四库全书存目丛书·史部一九七》，齐鲁书社，1996年，43页。

于中原地区的春秋时代。当时生活在那里的民族是濮族。濮族首创铜鼓，然后向东南西北方向传播。从现在资料看，铜鼓分布稠密的地区有四大块，即我国云南滇池地区，两广南部云开大山区，越南北部和中部偏北地区以及缅甸的掸邦地区。这些地区的民族在很长时期内都使用铜鼓。”[①] 以上说法基本上代表了我国学术界关于古代铜鼓产地和使用地区的观点。此外，我国很多古籍也记载上述地区生产和使用铜鼓，详见《后汉书》卷54《马援传》及唐人李贤注、《隋书》卷31《地理志下》、《通典》卷184《州郡十四·古南越·风俗》及卷187《边防三·南蛮上·獠》、唐人刘恂《岭表录异》卷上、宋人周去非《岭外代答》卷7《乐器 门》“铜鼓”及“铜”条、宋人陈旸《乐书》卷125及卷159、元人马端临《文献通考》卷148《乐考二十一·夷部乐·南蛮》、明人方以智《通雅》卷30、清初屈大均《广东新语》卷16《器语·铜鼓》、近人徐珂编《清稗类钞·种族类》“苗族黎族”条等。

古代“铜鼓产地”的居民几乎都是南方少数民族，既然他们都会铸造铜鼓，为何海南岛的居民不能铸造铜鼓？难道海南岛社会落后及其居民智力低下吗？考诸史志，事实并非如此，这从以下两点可以说明：

一是中原王朝在海南岛设立地方政权的时间与“铜鼓产地”的主要地区大致相同。据史载，秦始皇三十三年（前214年），平定南越地（即岭南地区，包括今两广、海南岛和越南等），开置南海、桂林和象三郡，并征发五十万人戍守五岭，与越人杂居[②]。从此，中原文化开始大规模在岭南地区传播。秦代，雷州半岛属象郡地[③]，则距雷州半岛较近的海南岛也当隶属于象郡。又据明正德《琼台志·风俗》载：“秦以水德王，其数用六，今琼人行使铜钱犹用六数，以六文为一钱，六十文为一两，六百文为一贯。又田禾以六把为半担，十二把为一担，亦用六数。皆秦旧俗也。”这也说明秦朝文化即中原文化对海南岛社会的深刻影响。到秦末汉初，海南岛属南越国[④]。汉武帝元鼎六年（前111年）灭南越国，在其境内分置南海、苍梧、郁林、合浦、交趾、九真、日南、珠崖、儋耳等九郡。其中前七郡辖区范围，几乎都属于古代“铜鼓产地”。后二郡都在海南岛上，二郡共辖十六县[⑤]。现考知其具体县名的有14县，即瞫都、山南、玳瑁、珠崖、紫贝、苟中、儋耳、至来、九龙、临振、乐罗、颜卢、永丰、顺潮[⑥]。汉武帝时能够大规模在海南岛建立地方政权，这也说明在此之前秦朝和南越国对本岛已经有所经略和中原文化已在岛上广泛传播。可以想见，早在前110年，西汉中央政府就已在海南岛建立众多的地方政权和进行直接统治，推行封建教化，难道可以说本岛社会历史发展极其缓慢吗？

至于古代盛产铜鼓的“西南夷”之地（主要在今云、贵二省），汉武帝时也先后在该地区设置犍为、牂牁、越嶲、益州、武都、沈黎、汶山七郡[⑦]。由此可见，海南岛与“铜鼓产地”的主要地区大致同步进入文明社会。

这里需要说明一点：以往学术界有一种较为流行的说法认为，汉元帝初元三年（前

① 张荣方:《什么是铜鼓?它是怎样流传的?》,《中国历史三百题》，上海古籍出版社，1989年，175～177页。

② （汉）司马迁:《史记》卷6《秦始皇本纪》及注、卷113《南越列传》。

③ （唐）杜佑《通典》卷184《州郡·古南越》海康郡雷州；《旧唐书》卷41《地理志四》雷州；《太平御览》卷172《州郡部十八·岭南道》。

④ （汉）班固:《汉书》卷6《武帝纪》、卷7《昭帝纪》、卷95《南粤传》。

⑤ 《汉书》卷64下《贾捐之传》。

⑥ 李勃:《海南岛历代建置沿革考》，海南出版社，2005年，30～43页。

⑦ 《史记》卷116《西南夷列传》。

① 李勃：《汉元帝罢珠崖郡后海南岛之归属考》，《中国边疆史地研究》2009年第1期，117～126页。

② 李勃：《海南岛历代建置沿革考》，海南出版社，2005年，第二章至第八章。

46年）罢珠崖郡后,海南岛完全成为化外之地，直至南朝梁武帝时，中央政府才重新在岛上设立地方政权。其实，此说有悖史实。实际情况是：汉元帝虽罢珠崖郡，但并没有放弃海南岛，仍在本岛北部设立朱卢县，改隶于治所在雷州半岛徐闻县南的合浦郡。时合浦郡的最高军事长官都尉的治所也驻朱卢县①。西汉以后，大陆中央政府或局部政权仍一直在岛上设立地方政权，如：东汉时在岛上设立朱崖县,并在永平十年(67年)复置儋耳郡；三国时期吴国在岛上设置朱卢、珠官二县，归交州珠崖郡（治所在徐闻县）直接管辖，又遥领于蜀汉交州刺史；两晋时期在岛上设置毒质、珠官二县，归交州合浦郡管辖。其时到东晋访问的南燕使者盖泓曾游历海南岛，然后撰有《珠崖传》一书；南朝时期宋齐梁陈四个封建王朝都在岛上设立地方政权，其中宋朝置朱卢、珠官二县，归珠崖郡（治所在徐闻县）管辖；齐朝沿置朱卢县，归越州合浦郡管辖；梁朝置崖州、珠崖郡及义伦、朱卢等县，归广州都督府管辖；陈朝因之。从隋朝开始，中央政府不断加强对本岛的统治和管理，设置的统治机构越来越多，如隋炀帝大业六年（610年）在岛上设立珠崖、儋耳、临振三郡和十四县（舍城、澄迈、颜卢、武德、琼山、义伦、毗善、昌化、吉安、感恩、宁远、临川、延德、陵水），三郡均直属中央政府，并督于扬州司隶刺史；唐朝先后在岛上设置三都督府（即崖州都督府、琼州都督府、镇州都督府）、七州（即崖、儋、振、琼、万安、镇、忠）和二十六县（即舍城、澄迈、颜城、文昌、临机、义伦、富罗、昌化、吉安、感恩、涔阳、落场、宁远、临川、延德、吉阳、落屯、琼山、曾口、颜罗、容琼、乐会、万安、富云、博辽、陵水），隶属于岭南节度使等②。大量的史实表明，汉元帝以后，中原文化在海南岛的传播不是中断，而是不断加强。

二是海南岛的主要居民大都来自祖国大陆，汉武帝时已有11万余汉人定居在海南岛上。海南岛是个移民岛，世居岛上和人数较多的居民是汉族，其次是黎族，苗族和回族只占极少数。岛上的汉人祖先都是历代先后从祖国大陆各地迁移来的。汉人迁居本岛当开始于秦朝统一岭南之时，至西汉时期逐渐增多。据《汉书》卷64下《贾捐之传》载：儋耳、珠崖二郡，“合十六县，户二万三千余。”这些民户，显然都被编入西汉政府户籍，属于所谓“编户齐民”。每户若以五口计算，则有11.5万人。西汉时期，一般只有汉族才被编入政府的户籍，这些民户当多数是秦代以来从大陆迁移来的汉人。这并非凭空臆测，而是有充分的理由和证据可以说明：

第一，秦代应当已有部分汉人迁入海南岛。如《汉书·高帝纪》载：“前秦时徙中县之民南方三郡，使与百越杂处。”唐人颜师古注：“中县之民，中国县民也。”即中原地区的汉人。所谓“南方三郡”，指秦代在岭南地区所设立的南海郡、桂林郡和象郡。又，南朝刘宋裴駰的《史记集解》引徐广曰：秦朝遣“五十万人守五岭”。见《史记·秦始皇本纪》注。所谓“五岭”即岭南地区。海南岛在岭南之域内，在这“五十万人”中，应当有一部分到达本岛。

第二，汉武帝元封元年（前110年）在海南岛开置珠崖、儋耳二郡和十六县，说明在此之前岛上显然已有许多汉人定居或本岛已经具有大规模建立地方政权的一定基础。此后，为加强岛上的统治力量，汉朝必定再从大陆迁移一批汉族军民到本岛来驻守和开发。

第三，西汉统治阶级根本不把岛上的土著居民当人看待。史书对此屡有记载，诸如《汉书·贾捐之传》载：贾捐之称海南岛的黎族先民为"骆越之人"，"父子同川而浴，相习以鼻饮，与禽兽无异"，"其民犹鱼鳖"。《汉书·地理志下》载："自初为郡县，吏卒中国人多侵凌之。"《三国志·吴书·薛综传》载："珠崖之废，起于长吏睹其好发，髡取为髲。"《太平御览》卷373引《林邑记》载："朱崖人多长发，汉时郡守贪残，缚妇女割头取发。" 这些情况表明，汉朝派驻海南岛的吏卒根本不把岛上的黎族先民当人看待。由此可以想见，在西汉统治阶级眼里，那些"与禽兽无异"、"犹鱼鳖"的黎族先民，难道会被编入西汉政府的户籍里吗?

第四，从海南岛黎族归化的历史可以推知，西汉时期能够主动归化而被编入政府户籍的黎族先民必定有限。秦汉以来，由于汉人大量迁入本岛，黎族先民被迫向山区迁移。他们由于长期生活在深山老林里，交通闭塞，与外界缺少交往，因而使其社会发展极其缓慢。宋代汉族统治阶级开始把黎族人民划分为熟黎和生黎两种。如《宋会要辑稿·蕃夷五》之43载："其服属州县者为熟黎，其居山峒无征徭者为生黎。"此又见《宋史·蛮夷传三·黎洞》。又《文献通考》卷331《四裔八·黎峒》说："蛮去省地远，不供赋役者名生黎。耕作省地，供赋役者名熟黎。"此又见《岭外代答》卷2《海外黎蛮》、《桂海虞衡志·志蛮·黎》。由此可知，所谓"熟黎"，意谓被编入政府户籍、服从政府管辖并且承担政府赋役的黎人。所谓"生黎"，意为散居在远离州县的山沟里，不入政府户籍，不服从政府管辖，不向政府提供赋役的黎人。由"生黎"转变为"熟黎"，不是在短时间内仅凭暴力就能实现的，而是需要经过漫长的招抚和感化的历史过程。历观载籍，海南岛黎族大批归化，当开始于北宋。如《岭外代答》卷2《海外黎蛮》载："昔崇宁中，王祖道经略广西，抚定黎贼九百七峒，结丁口六万四千，开通道路一千二百余里。自以为汉唐以来所不臣之地，皆入版图。官僚皆受厚赏。淳熙元年（1174年），五指山生黎峒首王仲期率其旁八十峒、丁口一千八百二十人归化。"至清代仍继续归化。如《嘉庆重修一统志》卷452琼州府一《山川》"黎峒"条载："本朝德威所至，黎人向化。雍正八年，琼山、定安、陵水、崖州诸生黎二千九百四十六人，相率愿入版图。"① 但直至中华人民共和国建立前夕，在五指山黎族中心地区还保留着一种原始社会组织形式，叫做"合亩"。"合亩"制成员就相当于古时不服王化、不供赋役的"生黎"。由此可知，早在汉武帝时，能主动归化而被编入西汉政府户籍的黎族先民，显然只是凤毛麟角。

第五，汉武帝末年岛上有很多"善人"（即汉人）。据《后汉书》卷116《南蛮

① 《嘉庆重修一统志》（第29册），中华书局，1986年，23165页。

传》载：“武帝末，珠崖太守会稽孙幸调广幅布献之，蛮不堪役，遂攻郡杀幸。幸子豹合率善人还复破之，自领郡事，讨击余党，连年乃平。”所谓“合率”，意为纠合并率领。所谓“善人”，本指平民。如《后汉书》卷4《孝和孝殇帝纪》载：延平元年七月，“贪苛惨毒，延及平民。”

唐人李贤注：“平民，谓善人也。”孙豹依靠“善人”的力量，才把黎族先民的暴动镇压下去，这说明当时岛上“善人”人数很多。而这些“善人”，显然都是汉人，而绝对不是黎族先民。不然，难道他们会帮助孙豹镇压同类？

以上理由或证据足以说明：当时岛上“二万三千余”编户当为汉人无疑。人脑是文化的最重要载体，文化可以随着人口的转移而转移。祖国大陆各地的汉人迁居本岛后，不仅为开发本岛增加了劳动力，并带来了先进的生产技术，而且不断改良岛上的人口素质，促进本岛社会的加快发展。西汉时期岛上既然有11万多汉人，可以肯定，其中不乏世代擅长冶铸技术的能工巧匠。

至于本岛黎族居民，我国学术界大都认为是由古代越人或骆越的一支，在秦汉以前从两广大陆渡海到本岛来发展而成的[①]。若按此说法，则更有利于探讨本岛铜鼓等古代青铜器的来源问题：既然留居在两广原地的越人都能够铸造铜鼓，难道迁居本岛的越人反而不会铸造铜鼓？难道具有开拓进取精神、勇敢渡海到本岛来的越人都是弱智者？如果说黎族先民的智力水平难以胜任铸造铜鼓的工艺技术要求，那么，难道来自大陆的本岛汉人也都没有铸造铜鼓的能力吗？难道本岛汉人的智力都远远不如古代“铜鼓产地”的各少数民族吗？

其三，史籍记载表明，早在西汉前期海南岛土著居民已掌握了兵器的冶铸技术。如《汉书》卷28下《地理志下》载：“自合浦徐闻南入海，得大洲，东西南北方千里，武帝元封元年略以为儋耳、珠厓郡。民皆服布如单被，穿中央为贯头。男子耕农种禾稻、苎麻，女子桑蚕织绩。亡马与虎，民有五畜，山多麈麖。兵则矛、盾、刀，木弓弩，竹矢，或为骨镞。”所谓“男子耕农种禾稻、苎麻，女子桑蚕织绩”，意即“男耕女织”，这是中国封建社会小农经济的生产方式,其形成的基本条件是铁犁、牛耕的逐步普及和封建土地私有制的确立。这也说明当时本岛大部分地区已发展至封建社会。所谓“兵则矛、盾、刀”，意为兵器有矛、盾、刀。这说明当时岛上的土著居民早已懂得冶铸技术，即利用铜或铁来铸造矛、盾、刀等各种兵器。西汉时期，因汉朝统治阶级在岛上实行暴政，迫使黎族先民连年不断地进行起义，多次痛击南下镇压起义的汉朝军队，使汉朝的人力、物力都遭到了惨重的损失。如《汉书·贾捐之传》记载汉元帝时丞相于定国曾这样说：“前日兴兵击之连年，护军都尉、校尉及丞凡十一人，还者二人，卒士及转输死者万人以上，费用三万万余，尚未能尽降。”黎族先民能够多次打败装备精良的汉军，这也说明他们能够制造兵器，而且其自制的兵器非同寻常，足以和汉军的武器相抗衡。试想，在距今约2200年

① 陈永龄:《民族辞典》“黎族”，上海辞书出版社，1987年，1209页；《辞海·民族分册》“黎族”、“骆越”，上海辞书出版社，1982年，35、149页。

的西汉前期，岛上的土著居民既然已掌握了兵器的冶铸技术，难道不会制造铜釜、铜鼓等青铜器吗？难道可以说海南岛的社会发展极其缓慢和生产力落后吗？

史书记载，古代本岛黎族自制的铁器最著名的是"黎刀"。如《桂海虞衡志·志器》载："黎刀，海南黎人所作。刀长不过一二尺，靶乃三四寸，织细藤缠束之。靶端插白角片，长尺许，如鸥鹨尾以为饰。" 此又见《说郛》卷62上、《古今说海》卷11、雍正《广东通志》卷52《物产志》等。既然"黎刀"为"黎人所作"，则说明"黎刀"系由黎人自制，而非购买。古代本岛黎族人民既然能够铸造精良的"黎刀"，难道不会铸造青铜器吗？事实并非如此，请看以下文献记载古代本岛黎族也会自制青铜器：

清人赵慎畛《榆巢杂识》载："琼州附属昌化县黎地产石碌铜，为黎人检挖，贩作颜料。更可煎炼作铜，制器亦甚坚良。"近人徐珂编《清稗类钞·矿物类》"石碌矿"条也载："琼州昌化之黎地产石碌矿，黎人检挖之，贩作颜料，且可煎炼作铜，制器亦甚坚良。"以上两书所记相同，这说明古代海南岛黎人曾采挖昌化县石碌铜矿，不仅贩卖作颜料，而且也用来冶铸青铜器。这是古代海南岛黎人冶铸青铜器的明确记载。

又《清稗类钞·种族类》"苗族黎族"条载："苗族、黎族在湘、蜀、黔、滇、两粤之间……其人被服缯纩，好歌舞，挟巫蛊之术，好铸铜鼓，所用兵器，为弓、矢、刀、矛、剑、盾之属。"黎族主要聚居在海南岛，可见该书作者在这里也肯定海南黎族人民会铸造铜鼓和各种兵器。

试想，既然古代本岛黎族人民也会冶铸铁器和青铜器，难道本岛汉人不懂得青铜器冶铸技术？由此看来，上文《朱崖传》所记"朱崖大家"拥有"三、五百"的"大铜镬"，当为本岛黎族先民自制产品或聘请本岛汉人工匠到黎区为其制造，因为黎区有制造青铜器的丰富的矿产资源（详下），而不可能是舶来品。不然，难道古代黎族先民的大小首领都拥有雄厚的财力可以从岛外进口数量庞大的"大铜镬"吗？

其四，海南岛蕴藏着非常丰富的铜矿等矿产资源。史籍和方志等记载表明，海南岛的铜矿等矿产资源不是甚少,而是非常丰富。诸如：

《清史稿》卷23《德宗本纪一》载：光绪十四年（1888年）春正月庚申，"开广东昌化石碌铜矿。" 卷23《德宗本纪二》载：光绪二十四年（1898年）秋七月丙午，"命三品卿衔胡国廉总理琼崖垦矿事。"又卷124《食货志五·矿政》载："……锡，则广东儋州，广西南丹土州、富川、贺县。（光绪）九年，诏各省煤矿招商集股举办。自是，云南、四川均设招商及矿务局，贵州设矿务公商局，山西设矿务公司。粤东琼州之铜矿，浙江宁波之铅矿皆率招商集股开办。"

又《德宗光绪实录》卷251载："光绪十四年正月庚申，两广总督张之洞奏，琼州昌化县境内大艳山，开采石碌铜矿，凡贩运出琼州海口者，请自光绪十四年起，三年之内，山税及关税厘金概行暂免。”[①]

又《光绪朝东华录二》载：“光绪十二年九月丙午，张之洞奏：琼州一府孤峙海南，黎巢其中，民环其外……至铜铅各矿，皆在黎境。”

又《光绪朝东华录三》载：“光绪十四年二月甲申，张之洞等奏：琼州府昌化县境内大艳山，《府志》名峻灵山，多产铜及石碌，故亦名为石碌山。前经香山职员张廷钧招集股分，购备机器，前往开采，业经奏明在案。查石碌为矿苗所结，下有铜矿，精华上溢，融为石碌。每石碌百斤，佳者可炼铜十余斤至二十斤不等，其不能炼铜者卖作颜料。兹查大艳山地近黎境，道路既远，瘴疠犹重，出产虽佳，工费甚昂。现在黎境甫通，矿务创始，倘无确利可图，必致观望自阻。惟有减轻成本，始足以徕商贩而惠民黎。兹拟将昌化石碌及铜斤，凡贩出琼州海口者，自光绪十四年起，三年之内，所有山税及关税厘金概行暂免。俟开采所销大旺，再将税厘酌量抽收。其余琼属五金等矿，如有集资开办，亦即一律办理，暂免税厘，庶几通商惠工，利兴而岛民裕矣。”从“每石碌百斤，佳者可炼铜十余斤至二十斤不等”可知，石碌山铜矿石的铜含量极高。

又《光绪朝东华录五》载：“光绪三十四年七月丙午，农工商部奏：琼崖矿产饶富……胡国廉前请办儋州那大等处锡矿，亦经臣部核准量予变通有案……臣等公拟仰恳天恩俯念琼崖事体重要，明降谕旨，特派大员督办琼崖垦矿事宜，以重事权，并请饬下两广总督饬劝业道及琼崖道实力保护，并由臣部随时稽查，遇事维持，俾策全功而收实效……上谕：农工部奏筹议华商创兴琼崖地利事宜，酌拟办法一折。着派三品卿衔胡国廉总理琼崖垦矿事宜。其有关涉地方他项商民利害事务，应会同地方官妥善办理。余依议。”

又《清实录·德宗实录》卷594载：光绪三十四年（1908年）七月丙午，“谕内阁……用副朝廷轸念炎黎至意。又谕农工商部，奏筹议华商创兴琼崖地利事宜，酌拟办法等语，着派三品卿衔胡国廉总理琼崖垦矿事宜。其有关涉地方他项商民利害事务，应会同地方官妥商办理。”[②]

又清人赵慎畛《榆巢杂识》载：“琼州附属昌化县黎地产石碌铜，为黎人检挖，贩作颜料。更可煎炼作铜，制器亦甚坚良。嘉庆三年，疆吏奏将此铜充粤局鼓铸，遂不复采运滇铜矣。”此又见近人徐珂编《清稗类钞·矿物类》“石碌矿”条。这条资料表明，海南石碌铜产量大，从清嘉庆三年（1798年）起，由“粤局”即广东省有关官府组织开始开采，石碌铜完全满足广东鼓铸的需要，不再采运云南铜。

又道光《琼州府志》卷44《杂志》附录《同治五年阖呈请封禁昌化石碌山全案》载：昌化县石碌山，“该处出产铜碌，均属黎峒”。“今该监生林腾汉串通外国人，径赴昌化县黎峒诸山，并无执照，而招工开采铜碌。”所谓“铜碌”，即铜矿石。这说明清代昌化县石碌铜被外国人非法招工开采。

① 唐启翠辑录点校：《明清〈实录〉中的海南》，海南出版社，2006年，270页。

② 《清实录·德宗实录》第59册，中华书局，1987年，858页。

又民国《海南岛志》第十五章《矿产》载：“本岛矿产未经详细勘查，然已发现者，则五金矿藏俱甚丰富，尤以金矿及铁矿前途为有希望。”同章第三节《铜矿》载：海南岛主要铜矿区有四处：五指山藤满峒矿区、昌江石碌山矿区、崖县回风岭矿区、澄迈石鼓岭矿区。第四节《铁矿》载：“本岛铁矿有赤铁、褐铁、磁铁、含锰铁多种。赤铁产崖县喃咪独田，定安南牛，陵水阪头岭、七弓岭等处。褐铁、锰铁产崖县西路第四区。磁铁产澄迈西峰、定安羊角。” 第五节《锡矿》载：“本岛之儋县西玢、感恩麻姑岭、乐会总溪口及黎区喃唠峒等处皆产锡矿，就中以西玢之矿曾一度开采。” 第六节《铅矿》载：“本岛铅矿多为方铅矿，中含银质，故又称银铅矿。发现甚多，兹择其重要者概述之。”

又民国陈植《海南岛新志》第八章第五节《矿业》载：据民国二十四年琼崖视察团经济组职员矿区调查结果表明：“本岛矿产尤以锡、铁、铜、铅、锑、金、银等矿为大宗”。其中铜矿分布在全岛六县十二处，即：乐会县一，陵水县一，崖县三，昌江县二，澄迈县一，定安县三，五指山附近一。其中重要铜矿区是：五指山附近之藤满岭（峒）矿区，昌江县石碌铜山及金牛岭矿区，崖县之回风岭矿区，澄迈县之石鼓岭矿区。又第九章第六节《矿业》载：“本岛矿产，据日人调查，具有金、银、铜、铁、锡、钨、硅、铅、水晶等各种矿产，就中以铁为最富。”[①]

又《海南百科全书·总述》“海南”条说：“至1997年，发现海南岛矿产有88种，占全国已发现矿产168种的52.38%；已探明有工业储量的矿产67种，占全国已探明矿产168种的有工业储量的矿产152种的44%。”又《地理》“金属矿产”条说：“海南省金属矿产主要有铁、钛、锰、铜、铅、锌、铝、钼、镍、钨、锡、金、银、铌、钽、锆、镓、镉等19个矿种，产地97处。其中有大型矿床8处，中型矿床21处。”

诸如此类，不胜枚举。以上记载至少说明以下三点：一是海南岛蕴藏着非常丰富的制造青铜器所需的铜、锡、铅等矿产资源，遍布全岛各地；二是古代本岛黎族曾检挖贩卖，也用来冶铸青铜器；三是从清朝嘉庆三年（1798年）以来，或由官府开采或招商集股开采，或被外国人非法招工开采等。矿产资源是自然形成，并非古无而今有。由此可见，学术界所谓“海南岛的铜矿资源甚少”，显然有悖史实。

其五，西汉前期大陆各地都已普遍使用铁器，至汉武帝时和东汉时期南下海南岛的汉朝军队不可能带来早已过时的青铜釜炊具。据张荣芳先生等著的《南越国史》一书说：“考古发现，中国最早的人工铸造铁器属于春秋时期，而战国时期铁器使用已经较为普遍……秦统一岭南后，随着大批中原人南下，许多铁器才在岭南普遍使用。西汉时期的墓葬遗址中出土的铁器数量急剧增加。据不完全统计，属于南越国时期的铁器就已出土700余件。出土铁器的品类有农具、手工业工具、炊具、武器和杂具等。与农业有关的铁器种类有锄、锸、铲、镰、镢、斧、凿、锤、锛、削、刀、弯刀、劈刀、铲刀等。这一大批品类丰富的铁器发现，使我们对南越国铁

① （民国）陈植：《海南岛新志》，海南出版社，2004年，135～142、209、210页。

器的推广与使用有了感性的认识。”①

又据练铭志先生等著的《广东民族关系史》一书说：“据《广州汉墓》载，西汉前期墓出土铁器156号件，器形可辨的110件，其中生产工具45件……南越王墓出土的资料比上述更进一大步。该墓出土铜铁工具共124件，其中铁工具120件，占总数的97%。铁器工具中，农业的有锄、锸、镢和镰刀，手工业的有斧、锛、锤、凿、锛、劈刀、刮刀和锉等。……尽管铁器使用的上限仍有不同意见，但至迟在西汉前期，至少在今广州一带，铁器工具已占据主导地位，并普遍应用于农业和手工业生产领域。秦末至西汉，铁器骤然大量出现，当与秦始皇平定岭南及其后大批中原人入粤有关。部分铁器为本地铸造。”②

按上所说，既然战国时期中原地区已普遍使用铁器，既然南越国时期（前204～前111年）和西汉前期岭南地区也已广泛使用铁器，那么，可以推知，到汉武帝元鼎六年（前111年）汉朝军队消灭南越国后南下海南岛时所带来的炊具，应当是铁锅，而不可能是早已过时的青铜釜。考西汉军队大批进驻海南岛主要是镇压本岛黎族先民起义，时间在汉武帝末年（前87年）至汉元帝初元二年（前47年）间③，东汉军队大批进驻海南岛主要是马援率兵平定交趾二征起义时到达本岛安抚响应起义的黎族先民，时间在建武十八年至二十年（42～44年）间④，这时候汉朝军队所使用的炊具更不可能是青铜釜了。由此观之，海南岛所发现的青铜釜显然不是汉朝军队的炊具，况且其形制也不适宜用来煮饭和炒菜，而应当是本岛土著居民使用的器物，疑为《珠崖传》所记“珠崖大家”喜爱的“大铜镬”。

其六，史实表明，古代本岛曾有青铜冶炼遗址，但已遭破坏。从上文《榆巢杂识》和《清稗类钞·矿物类》“石碌矿”条所记可知，既然古代黎族曾检挖昌江县石碌铜矿“煎炼作铜，制器亦甚坚良”，则说明古代本岛必定有青铜冶炼遗址不疑，其遗址应当主要集中在石碌矿区或其附近。因为矿石笨重，加之古代交通闭塞，难以外运。但由于石碌矿区先后历经清代广东官府开采和招商开采、清代外国人非法招工开采、抗日战争时期日本抢夺开采、1950年以来我国政府长期开采等，由此可知，该地的古代青铜冶炼遗址显然早已遭受彻底破坏。至于历史上分布在本岛其他地区的青铜冶炼遗址，因规模小和历史悠久，也当全遭人为破坏。试想，在20世纪50年代，海南岛和全国各地一样大炼钢铁，遍地高炉林立，但现在几乎已看不到任何有关痕迹。何况距今2000多年前在地表上的青铜冶炼遗址，安能完好地保存下来？此外，海南省的考古工作起步较晚，况且考古发现又多属偶然性，可以肯定，埋藏在海南岛地下的古代青铜器（如“大铜镬”、“古罐”等）还有大量的尚未被发现。

以上理由和证据可以说明海南岛所发现的古代青铜器当多属本岛产品。

① 张荣芳、黄淼章：《南越国史》，广东人民出版社，1995年，184页。

② 练铭志、马建钊、朱洪：《广东民族关系史》，广东人民出版社，2004年，89～91页。

③《汉书》卷7《昭帝纪》、卷8《宣帝纪》和卷64下《贾捐之传》；《后汉书》卷《南蛮传》。

④《后汉书》卷1下《光武帝纪下》卷54《马援传》和卷116《南蛮传》；《舆地纪胜》卷124琼州；《诸蕃志》卷下《海南》。

湖北随州出土西周噩国青铜器研究

A Research on E State (in the western Zhou Dynasty, 11th century-771 B. C.) Bronze Wares Unearthed in Suizhou, Hubei

阮文清／湖北省博物馆 研究员
冯少龙／湖北省文物考古研究所 研究员

[摘要]

湖北随州新发现的一批噩国青铜器，器型有鼎、簋、甗、尊、卣、爵、觯、彝、罍、盉、斝、盘等。器物造型及纹饰都与西周中心地区宗周成周的青铜器相一致，有些器物上的纹饰精美程度甚至超过了宗周成周青铜器，其中扉棱兽首面纹尊、兽首面纹提梁卣、噩侯方彝造型典雅，纹饰精美，是西周青铜器中难得一见的精品。大量重要的噩侯青铜器在湖北随州安居出土，解决了历史学考古学关于“噩国”历史地理上的千年悬案。这批青铜器的发现，对于探讨和研究西周时期湖北地区的历史文化，具有极高的历史价值、艺术价值和科学价值。

[关键词]

随枣走廊　西周　噩国　青铜器

Abstract

A batch of the E state's bronze wares were newly discovered in Hubei Suizhou, whose shapes include ding, gui, yan, zun, you, jue, zhi, yi, lei, he, jia, plate, and so on. Their shapes and patterns are the same as the styles and features of the bronze wares that were unearthed at the Western Zhou' central area, Zongzhou Cheng Zhou. The perfect degrees of patterns in the some of them even exceed the bronze wares of Zongzhou Cheng Zhou. These bronze wares, such as zun with gibbous wale and animal faces patterns, you with animal faces patterns and girder handle, the Marquise E square yi, whose shapes are elegance and patterns are graceful, are infrequent fine works and representative works with the most historical value and artistic value among the Western Zhou bronze wares. The unearthing of lots of important the Marquise E bronze wares at Hubei Suizhou Anju, has solved an unsettled historical and archeological question over thousands years at the aspect of the E state's historical geography. The discovery of this batch of bronze wares has extremely high historical value, artistic value and scientific value on the discussion and research about historical culture on the Hubei area during the period of the Western Zhou Dynasty.

Key words

Suizao corridor; Western Zhou dynasty; E state; Bronze wares

一

如果有人要问，近年来，湖北西周时期考古最为重要的发现是什么？回答肯定是：随州两次出土西周早期数百件青铜器。欲究原因，大概是随州地处湖北北部,正位于淮河流域与长江流域交接地带的随枣走廊，北面的桐柏山是淮河的源头，南面的大洪山南邻汉水，地理通达，真可谓西通宛洛，南达吴越，地当荆豫要冲，遏阻襄汉咽喉，是周王室俘金掠铜的重要通衢。这里山水秀美，土壤沃腴，物产丰盛。这里人文荟萃，历史悠久。历山炎帝神农故里，是华夏苗裔心目中的圣地。又随州因随国而得名，随国或称曾国，是周王室宗姓封国之一。20世纪70年代末期，一次神奇的考古发现，使得全世界的目光聚焦在中国湖北随州擂鼓墩：1座特大型东周时期古墓——曾侯乙墓被发现发掘。墓中件件套套的珍奇国宝，破土而出，令世人为之震惊。出土文物有大量精美的青铜礼器、漆木器、金银器、珠玉器及各类乐器、车马兵器和纺织服饰等。最引人注目的是墓中出土的曾侯乙编钟汇成百钟之势，音律互补，共同构成了一曲中国先秦古乐的传奇。大量精美的文物展现了鼎盛时期曾国文化的辉煌成就。学术界称誉曾侯乙墓出土文物与文化成就：是青铜铸造史上的创举，是纺织史上的突破，是美术史的奇葩，是音乐史上的绝响，是天文史上的界碑。这诸多方面的成就代表着当时中国乃至世界文化的最高水平。

无独有偶，就在人们已经习惯将随州看作古老曾国故地的时候，在这片土地上，又有两次惊人的重大考古发现，使得本已习惯的考古学文化研究中的传统意识、观点和体系都需要面临重新认识。一是2011年1月，在随州市淅河镇蒋家寨村叶家山发现两座西周早期贵族墓[①]。一号墓出土方鼎、斝、簋等文物数十件，其中青铜礼器、兵器共30多件；二号墓出土青铜器、原始青瓷、玉、陶器等20余件珍贵文物，其中青铜器共有9件，两墓中出土如此巨量的青铜器在湖北考古史上较为少见。2011年，湖北省文物考古研究所对该墓地进行了钻探和发掘，共发现西周墓葬60余座，出土大量的西周时期的文物。其中新发现的青铜器达百件以上，而且在许多青铜器上有铭文。从已发布的新闻照片中，可以看到新出土有一些湖北过去没有发现过的西周青铜器器物，如分裆鼎（鬲鼎）、觥等。由于这批资料尚未发布，在本文中仅作发现介绍，期待着资料早日发表。

另一次重大考古发现是在随州安居羊子山出土的一批有噩侯铭文的青铜器。本文将重点介绍这批青铜器。

安居地处随州市西约15千米，这里是发源于桐柏山的㵐水与发源于大洪山的涢水交汇地带，在㵐水岸边的东北部，有1座安居古城遗址，有学者认为是曾国的都城

① 《西周原始青瓷首现随州淅河叶家山》，《湖北日报》2011年1月15日。

所在①，楚国历史上的那位“我有敝甲，欲观中国之政，请王室尊吾号……而王加位我自尊耳，乃自立为武王熊通”，就是死于征伐随国的旅途，而地点明确，就是死在这溠水岸边。安居古城外的西边有桃花山，西南边有羊子山。这一带的地下密集地分布有西周至汉代的墓葬。20世纪70年代以来，在此地有一些重要的考古发现。时代为西周时期的考古发现主要有如下几次：

1975年，在羊子山发现西周早期的噩国青铜器，器型有兽面纹鼎、簋、鱼父乙爵、噩候弟曆季尊各1件②。尊上铭文为“噩侯第曆季作旅彝”，与上海博物馆藏“噩候卣”铭文完全相同。

1979年，桃花山发现2座西周晚期墓葬，出土青铜器、玉器、漆器等。M1出土青铜鼎2件、鬲4件、簋4件、壶1件、盘1件、匜1件、车马器144件及残玉器、漆器等。M2出土铜鼎4件、簋1件、鬲4件③。墓葬的年代是西周晚期，这器物的国别与族属与曾国器相关，已经收录在《曾国青铜器》一书中④，本文不再细述。

1980年，在安居羊子山发现墓葬1座，编号M1。墓中出土青铜器18件⑤，其中铜礼器有鼎、簋、爵、尊、觯各1件，卣2件以及戈等。铭文器有“戈父辛爵”和“子父癸觯”。墓葬的时代是西周早期。

2007年11月，因盗墓贼盗掘未遂，在安居羊子山墓地抢救性清理墓葬1座，编号羊子山M4。出土青铜器27件，器型有方鼎、圆鼎、簋、甗、罍、盉、盘、提梁卣、尊、斝、觯、爵、方彝等。其中多有铭文，记明为噩国铜器，时代属于西周早期，具有相当重要的学术价值⑥。

① 石泉：《古代曾国——随国地望初探》，《武汉大学学报》（社会科学版）1979年第1期。

② 随州市博物馆：《湖北随县发现商周青铜器》，《考古》1984年第6期。

③⑤ 随州市博物馆：《湖北随县安居出土青铜器》，《文物》1982年第12期。

④ 湖北省文物考古研究所：《曾国青铜器》，文物出版社，2007年。

⑥ 随州市博物馆：《随州出土文物精粹》，文物出版社，2009年。

二

羊子山发现的西周早期青铜器3批共49件。发现器物类型较为齐全，器型有鼎、簋、甗、尊、卣、爵、觯、彝、罍、盉、斝、盘等。几乎囊括了西周青铜器的全部器型。以下将择其典型器物进行叙述。

（一）鼎

食器。鼎往往具有特别的涵义，代表着江山社稷。在祭祀天神、地祇、先祖等重大礼仪中，鼎供奉牲肉、簋供奉食粮，是最重要的祭器。《周礼》对鼎的使用有特别严格的规定，其数量与组合标志着主人的身份、地位。有方鼎、圆鼎之分别。

1. 方鼎

方鼎是商周时期流行的主要礼器器型，方鼎上多有铭文。出土的方鼎在造型和纹饰上与陕西、河南等地西周早期器物极其相似，极可能就是“舶来品”。

“噩中”方鼎　2007年随州安居羊子山4号墓出土。通高35.4、口长25.6、口宽19.9厘米。器体作长方形，带盖，附耳，四柱状足。器口折沿方唇，直壁深腹，平底。盖上四角饰有竖立状的扁体龙形，龙首向下，龙嘴及龙足触底，龙尾内卷，形成扉棱状。盖中有拱形纽。盖面拱形纽的两边，对称的饰有云雷纹底的兽首面纹。兽首面纹图像的构图与西周早期的“白□卣”盖上的纹饰及陕西临潼博物馆收藏的周武王时期的“利簋”上的纹饰基本相同，主体图案是由兽首上的额、角、眉、眼、鼻、耳等构成。在盖纽下饰有一蝉纹。口沿外两侧附对称的方形体弧顶耳。西周早期的方鼎上着附耳的器物不多。在器腹的四隅有凸出的钩状扉棱。腹部上饰有兽首面纹，纹样与盖上兽首面纹基本相同，差别在于图案中间是以扉棱为鼻额。四足直立，足上部饰兽首面纹，中间起扉棱。足中部有弦纹，足底部微微粗涨，似有蹄足之状。盖内阴刻有两行六字铭文：“噩中乍宝（尊）彝”。该器造型厚实庄重，纹饰繁缛，形制及纹饰特征皆为西周早期之风格，故其铸造年代亦应是西周早期（图一）。

兽首面纹方鼎　2007年安居羊子山4号墓出土。通高26.9、口长18.4、宽12.5厘米。器体为长方形。折沿平口，无盖。直耳直腹，腹较浅，平底。四柱状足，足体较高。腹部饰以云雷纹地的兽首面纹，中间以扉棱为兽首面纹的鼻额。器腹四隅有扉棱。足上部饰兽首面纹，兽眼似为“臣”字形。兽首中间起扉棱。足中部有弦纹，足底部微微粗涨，似有蹄足之状。器物造型接近于西周早期的德方鼎，只是该器物显得较为粗糙一些，应是西周早期的铸器（图二）。

2. 圆鼎

龙形兽体纹鼎　2007年安居羊子山4号墓出土。器高43.3、口径33厘米。其造型特征是折沿上翘，方唇，沿面上有方体直耳。深腹圜底，口部内敛，下腹浑圆外鼓。上腹部饰以

图一　“噩中”方形鼎

图二　兽首面纹方鼎

三组云雷纹衬地的兽体纹。兽体纹以扉棱作为额鼻中脊，亦凸脊为界分。纹饰图案中的兽体左右平面展开。在兽体的尾后，各有一只倒立状的龙纹。亦可以将主体图案视作为由左右两只形体相同的侧视造型的龙体，头部相接相融形成一个全新的构图，其特征是一首双身的奇异造型。这种纹饰学术界过去称为饕餮纹，现在多称 “兽面纹”。

该器上的兽体纹与上海博物馆收藏的西周成王时期“德鼎”上的“兽面纹”几乎完全相同。器下腹素面。腹下三柱足，足微微内敛。足上部较粗，浮雕有以扉棱为额鼻的兽首面纹。该处的纹饰图案是由兽首及面部的器官眼、鼻、牙、耳、额、角等构成，而无兽首之外的构造，故称之兽首面纹。兽首面纹下有三道凸弦纹。足中部稍微内束，足下部有外展，似呈蹄足状。该器造型规整，制作精美，庄严稳重，胎体厚实。此器形制特征与大克鼎相似，只是腹部较之稍深，下腹更圆。这种形制应该是西周早中期颇为流行的造型，从器物形制与纹饰特征综合分析，推断此器的年代应是西周早期（图三）。

云雷羽翎兽体纹鼎 1980年安居羊子山1号墓出土。器高20、口径16.6厘米。器为折沿直耳，沿面微外垂，方唇。腹较深，圜底近平。口部内敛，下腹外鼓。三柱状直足，足较高。在器上腹饰有以云雷纹和羽翎状纹构成兽身的兽体纹。这种纹饰在商代晚期至西周早期的青铜器上十分的常见。该器无论是造型还是纹饰都具有明显的西周早期青铜鼎的特征，与2007年安居羊子山4号墓出土内卷角兽面纹鼎相比较，其时代应该稍早一些（图四）。

（二）簋

簋是青铜礼器组合中最主要的器物之一，也是最为常见的器物，簋为盛食器，造型亦有多种样式，有圈足簋、方座双耳簋、方座四耳簋等。

图三　龙形兽体纹鼎

图四　云雷羽翎兽体纹鼎

图五 方座双耳簋

1. 方座双耳簋

2007年安居羊子山4号墓出土。通高27.6、口径21厘米。器形是西周早期流行的上圆下方式样。上为圆形器体，下有正方形高座。侈口、深腹、腹下部外鼓，圜底。高圈足下连方形高座。器腹两侧有对称的半圆环耳，环耳下有长方形垂珥。半圆环耳体上的装饰造型较为复杂，有三个各自独立又相联系的立体装饰体所组合。环耳上部竖立有弧面牌状的兽体纹，兽体纹由对称的两条龙纹组合而成。在牌状兽体纹的下面是一个圆雕状的兽首，兽体纹弧面牌状体又形成了圆雕兽首头顶的双角。兽首仰面冲前，左右张开大大的耳朵，宽眉圆眼，翻卷的蒜头形鼻。脸面有几分像人的面目。而宽大的口中吐出长舌，舌头翘起，嘴两侧露出獠牙，显露出兽性十足的凶恶面孔。兽首后是圆颈成为了半圆耳的部分耳体。兽首的下面是一只圆雕的凤鸟。兽首翘起的长舌又恰好构成了凤鸟的冠。凤鸟体形呈弧状，构成半圆环耳的下部。凤鸟头部为长喙回钩形，圆眼圆睛。鸟身为短颈凸胸，双翅贴体，尾端上翘。尾翼向后舒展，下侧一翼呈直折回卷形贴在垂珥体上，形成了局部的浮雕效果。凤鸟的双腿亦作立状浮雕在垂珥上。在这小小的半圆环耳体上，兽体纹弧面牌状体、圆雕兽首和圆雕凤鸟浑然一体，尤其是局部的巧借手法的娴熟应用，兽体纹弧面牌状体被作为了圆雕兽首的双角；圆雕兽首的翘舌又成为凤鸟的冠，这些都是那么的自然和谐，没有丝毫生硬的感觉，真可以说是匠心独运，妙不可言，体现出古代工匠已经具有了十分高超的艺术造诣。这耳体上的装饰造型完全可以称得上是古代艺术品中的精妙之作，透射出十分强烈而又神秘的艺术魅力。要仔细地欣赏和品味其中的奥秘，还需要下一番工夫才行（图五）。

2. 方座四耳簋

2007年安居羊子山4号墓出土。通高28.8、口径21.5厘米。圆形器腹方形座。折沿平口，腹较浅，圈足较高，几乎与器腹等高。器口及腹部上饰对称的四个半圆形耳。耳环下有长条形的垂珥。环耳体为简略形圆雕兽体。器腹上饰有浮雕状的冏纹，冏纹形似旋转的火轮。圈足体上饰兽首面纹。方座上饰兽首面纹，兽首面纹以四隅角为额鼻中心。造型和纹样与之相接近的器物，见于著录的是陕西宝鸡市博物馆收藏的西周□伯四耳方座簋。其造型更为精致而前者显粗糙，显得更原始一些。安居出土这件器物明显缺盖（图六）。

3. 直棱瓦纹簋

2007年安居羊子山4号墓出土。通高13、口径18.3厘米。圆体深腹，圜底近平，高圈足。敞口沿外侈。腹部对称饰兽形附耳，耳下有垂珥，垂珥呈钩形。腹上部饰兽体纹，兽首部凸鼻圆眼，反卷角，兽体由云雷纹组成，左右展开。兽体上端以羽纹为兽脊。这种纹饰流行于商代晚期至两周早期。下腹部满饰竖立状的瓦棱纹。圈足部素面无纹。附耳上的兽形简化的两周模糊不清，器官难以辨识（图七）。

（三）甗

甗是西周时期最为常见的炊器，也是重要的礼器。器形有方形、圆形之分。羊子山出土器为圆甗。

羽状角兽面纹甗

2007年安居羊子山4号墓出土。通高51、口径31.6厘米。圆形。造型为甑鬲连体，甑为敞口方唇，口沿上竖绹体环耳。弧壁深腹，腹下部内收缩与鬲口形成束颈状。甑腹内

图六　方座四耳簋

图七　直棱瓦纹簋

图八　羽状角兽面纹甗

图九　噩侯弟曆季尊

以心形箅格为小平底，箅体与甑体用环相套。鬲为小口，斜肩，高裆柱状足。甑体上部饰云雷纹地兽体纹。兽体有对称的侧视龙纹组合而成。中间的额鼻部起凸棱，形成一首双体的兽体纹。下腹饰蕉叶状的兽面纹。鬲体上是以足为中心的兽面纹。其纹饰图案与同墓所出的四耳方座簋方座上的纹样相似。在西周早期的铜甗上多有此类纹饰，是十分流行的式样。如江西博物馆藏应鉴甗、辽宁博物馆藏黄伯矩甗、陕西宝鸡纸坊头鱼伯墓出土的甗等诸多器物上的腹与足部都是以这种式样装饰的（图八）。

（四）尊

1. 噩侯弟曆季尊

1975年安居羊子山出土。通高19.8、口径25.1厘米。器体呈椭圆形。喇叭形口，颈较高，腹微鼓，高圈足。腹及圈足上有凸弦纹。器腹一侧有龙形半圆鋬。龙形下有垂珥。器腹内底有铭文："噩侯弟曆季作旅彝"（图九）。

2. 扉棱兽首面纹尊

2007年安居羊子山4号墓出土。通高34.5、口径25.1厘米。喇叭形敞口。长颈微束，深腹稍鼓。圈足部较高，分为上下。器体圆形。器体上以对称的钩形扉棱界分为前后相同的两个图案组合单元。颈部正中有圆雕兽首。兽首头顶有展开的羽毛状的双角。半圆形双耳张开。面部器底清晰可辨，突出的口中吐出翻卷长舌。兽首造型与同墓所出土的提梁卣器口上的相同。兽首后连接的浅浮雕节状兽体。节状兽体为左右对称，组合为一首双身的形象，再向上翘起形成一个圆角方形的构图。在双身尾部中间有扉棱。兽体纹两侧有焦叶状的龙纹。龙体亦作节状。腹上饰浮雕兽首面纹。翻卷双角，蚕形眉，臣字眼，眼中圆睛凸起，中有圆瞳孔，蒜头大鼻。翻卷的獠牙，口中吐出向上翻卷的长舌，长舌为扉棱。宽大的嘴中露出獠牙。花叶形的双耳凸起，器体上

图一〇　扉棱兽首面纹尊

图一一　噩侯提梁卣

的纹饰与同墓所出的基本相似。圈足较高，为两个台阶。圈足上部饰一首双身的节状龙纹，龙纹体似雷纹回卷，尾端呈爪状（图一〇）。

（五）卣

1. 噩侯提梁卣

2007年安居羊子山4号墓出土。通高30.4、口径11.4～15厘米。器体呈圆体，平口承盖。盖沿内敛，呈束颈状。盖面隆起，顶上有筒形纽。盖面上有凸弦纹，弦纹外侧饰双身兽体纹，兽首居中呈高浮雕状，两侧有双身，为侧旋的变形龙纹，龙纹体为云雷纹。纹样整体为一首双身，由兽首与左右两个对应的变形龙纹组成。器身的口部明显内敛，颈腹浑然一体，无明显界限。腹下部外鼓，高圈足。颈部饰双身兽体纹，纹样与盖上纹饰相同。圈足上有凸弦纹，颈部有环纽，纽中套拱形提梁，提梁由两条兽体构成，兽首铸雕出耳、眼、鼻、嘴等，头顶上有一对圆锤状的粗角。兽体向后翻拱，尾部连成一体。兽体上满饰云雷纹。该器的造型纹饰都与上海博物馆藏保卣相接近，在纹饰上较之简单一些，其时代应为西周早期所铸之器，在盖内有阴刻铭文“噩侯作旅彝”（图一一）。

2. 兽首面纹提梁卣

2007年安居羊子山4号墓出土。通高49.5、口径12.1～15.2厘米。器呈扁体圆形。有盖，盖沿竖壁成圈形，沿上盖面隆起。盖顶以圆雕兽首的头颈为纽。兽首顶有翻卷双侧的羽状角。兽首造型与同墓出土的扉棱兽首面纹尊上的造型相同，口吐长舌作翻卷状。

盖上有左右对称的向下作伏冲卧状的龙纹，龙首圆头棱眼，上唇翻卷为尖钩，下唇两侧左右分开贴于平面。龙体起伏为扉棱，以龙纹扉棱界分前后单元图案。盖面饰口吐长舌为扉棱的兽首面纹，纹样与扉棱兽首面纹尊上的相同，翻卷形成尖形獠牙。在盖沿体上饰有圆首曲体的节状龙纹，龙尾凸出为扉棱。

平口承盖，颈腹一体，深腹，腹下部外鼓，高圈足。腹两侧有凤鸟形的扉棱界分左右，腹体上部正中饰圆雕兽首，兽首形同扉棱兽首面纹尊上的。腹中部饰内吐长舌翻卷状的兽首面纹，纹饰造型与器盖上的纹饰相同。圈足上饰内卷涡形角的一首双身兽纹，造型与扉棱兽首面纹尊上的相同。在器体口部外的两侧有环纽套接拱形提梁。提梁下端为圆雕兽首。兽首上生有粗壮的角。角部的后方为圆柱体，向上渐细。而柱体上方衍生出一只单头双喙的鸟首。鸟头呈扁体，中有圆眼，两侧留有钩状的喙，鸟头之上饰三尖的冠，好似公鸡的花冠。如此怪异的造型，在青铜器中较为罕见。兽首半月形眉，棱形眼，宽长的大嘴，露出三角形的排齿。口中吐出长卷舌。兽首后颈粗壮。

上连覆鳞纹的扁体成为提梁的下段部分。在提梁的中段，生出一圆雕兽首。兽首体后联成覆羽状扁体提梁。在提梁顶上凸起有圆钩形的扉棱。

在器盖内有铭文："作宝彝"。提梁卣是西周时期十分流行的器物造型，而纹饰如此纷繁复杂图案的并不多见。其造器形纹饰相似的器物在保利博物馆馆藏中有一件，被称之为神面纹提梁卣，是保利博物馆的镇馆之宝。随州出土的这件在品相上要更胜一筹（图一二）。

（六）爵

饮酒器，亦是作为礼器组合的器物之一。

云雷纹爵

2007年安居羊子山M4出土有三件，纹饰造型相同。通高20.5、流至尾长17.1厘米。长嘴圆腹。翘角尖尾，半圆长流。口上有帽形柱，柱上似蘑菇形。深腹直壁，圜底。腹下三刀形足。腹部一侧有兽首吐舌状的半圆鋬。腹中部饰连珠纹边饰的云雷纹带。该器与陕西灵台白草坡M1出土的铜爵的造型和纹饰基本相同。二者都具有西周早期同类器物的特征（图一三 ）。

（七）觯

饮酒器。

子觯

2007年安居羊子山4号墓出土。通高18.6、口径8.5～10.5厘米。器体呈扁圆形。器口之上有盖。盖隆起，盖顶有圆柱体的拱形纽。盖上有弦纹带中饰联珠纹，中间带饰云雷纹。器口外侈，颈部内束，腰腹弧壁，下腹外鼓。高圈足，圈足上有弦纹带中饰云雷纹。颈腹间纹饰与盖上纹饰相同，弦纹形成带圈，上下带圈中饰球状的联珠纹，中间带圈饰云雷纹。在盖内及器腹底内有相同的阴刻铭文"子"字，故名子觯（图一四）。

图一二　兽首面纹提梁卣

图一三　云雷纹爵

图一四　子觶

（八）彝

盛酒器。

噩侯方彝

2007年安居羊子山4号墓出土。通高60.1厘米。器体呈扁方形体，造型规整，而纹饰相当繁缛。有盖，盖形呈四面斜坡拱背状，似屋顶形。盖顶背上竖立扁方柱，柱上端栖一对昂首相向的尖喙凤鸟。鸟体上部为圆雕状，身体下部连铸在一起，鸟足爪浮雕在方柱之上。鸟背有钩形扉棱，似为凤鸟的冠。主柱两侧的盖顶端有似鸟喙回首衔翘尾状的扉棱，好似屋脊的两端翘角。

盖上四面坡之间有钩形对称肩棱界分。盖上坡面部饰有浮雕状的兽首面纹，兽首面器官清晰明朗，脸膛宽展。兽首上有对称的内翻角。兽面凸眉，眉上有小棱似蚕，眉下有臣字形眼，圆睛中有圆圆的内凹为小瞳孔。鼻部凸圆。兽嘴似张开状，两侧回卷，形成尖角状，似为兽嘴中的獠牙。兽首面上最突出的是一对花瓣状的兽耳，向两边高高翘起，形成了高浮雕的效果。在兽首面的额中至鼻尖有尾端似鱼尾的扉棱。兽嘴中吐出扁长翻卷伸展向上的长舌，前端分叉为回钩状，长舌上伸至兽首的额头，以此长舌构成了兽首额。

器体为平口直颈，颈较高，斜肩，深腹，高圈足。颈、肩部四隅及器腹中间起扉棱，颈部饰有侧视浅浮雕的凤鸟纹。肩部饰有火轮状的囧纹及倒竖状的变形凤鸟纹。肩部宽面上有圆雕状的兽首为纽，纽体较为粗大。兽首造型为翻卷的双角左右展开，形似绵羊的犄角，角体上方呈钩形扉棱，而角体上面浮雕有龙，龙体与兽角浑然一体，好似兽首是以龙为角。兽面上眉毛为双层弧形。臣字形眼，眼中圆睛圆瞳。鼻形似蒜头，鼻孔清晰可辨。小小的两耳平展，耳面上有丁子形凹。兽嘴中左右露出粗长的尖牙，好似象牙。口中吐出长舌，向上翻卷，尾部回卷，尾端叉形展开，似象鼻的鼻尖状。该兽首从侧面看好似大象卷鼻露齿，怪就怪在兽首上的大而卷的双角，是大象头上没有的。

在窄面的肩部中亦铸有圆雕形的兽首造型。最为引人注目的是兽首上的一对粗壮的圆柱花形角。顶端中有圆珠位于花瓣之中。兽首两目清晰，兽额及鼻尖嘴唇中部凸棱翘起。双目圆瞪，双耳展开，兽嘴向下作吞食状，弧形圆柱体被吞咬入兽嘴中，圆柱体背上有凸起的窄脊。下有卷尾，形成垂珥，圆雕兽首与被吞食的圆形兽体构成环纽耳，环纽中套有圆形环。

器体的四隅皆为钩形扉棱。上腹部饰有兽首面纹，纹饰与盖面上式样相同。体形大一些。下腹部饰兽体纹，由两只侧视龙纹组合而成，额至鼻间有扉棱。高圈足，圈足上饰有圆雕状的兽首，连接的是浮雕状的左右双体兽身，连接兽首尾的是凸出形成叉状兽尾，兽尾又作为了圈足部的扉棱。器底中悬挂有铃，铃内有小舌。盖内有刻铭："亚侯作厥宝尊彝"（图一五）。

（九）罍

盛酒器。

亚侯罍

2007年安居羊子山4号墓出土。通高30.9、口径13.9厘米。器体圆形，有盖，盖呈覆豆形，筒形圆纽。盖面隆起状，盖饰有凸弦纹，形成带圈，带圈中饰浮雕火轮状的囧纹。器身为侈口，束颈，颈较高，圆肩深腹。高圈足。腹下部明显内收。在肩部上饰两道凸弦纹，凸弦纹带圈中饰以火轮状的囧纹。肩部有对称的牛首吐长舌形的环纽，环纽套有圆环。盖内刻有铭文："亚侯作旅彝"（图一六）。

图一五　亚侯方彝

图一六　亚侯罍

图一七　双线尖形纹盉

图一八　扁体牛首錾斝

图一九　噩侯盘

（一〇）盉

亦为盛酒器。

双线尖形纹盉

2007年安居羊子山4号墓出土。通高30.3、口径13.5厘米。器上有盖，盖隆起。顶上有半环纽，盖上饰弦纹，盖后侧有半环纽套连錾上方。器口外侈，短颈内束，斜肩鼓腹，分裆高足。足微呈蹄形。器前有翘起的管形流，后侧有兽形錾柄。錾上兽的面目模糊不清，器腹及足腹部有双线尖形纹饰，颈肩部有二道弦纹（图一七 ）。

（一一）斝

温酒器。

扁体牛首錾斝

2007年安居羊子山4号墓出土。通高30.2、口径19.1厘米。侈口方唇，束颈，颈较高，广肩鼓腹，分裆，高柱足直立。口沿上有对称的帽形柱，柱伞圆形，伞上有圆凸顶。伞面上雕刻涡纹。斝体素面。在颈部与腹部上附有半圆形錾手，錾手扁方体，上端为一牛首形。牛首扁方体，牛嘴下连长弧形錾体，似从牛嘴中吐出的长长的牛舌（图一八 ）。

（一二）盘

盥洗器。

噩侯盘

2007年安居羊子山4号墓出土。通高10.4、口径34.8厘米。圆形，敞口。平折沿，方唇，深腹。圆底近平。高圈足，圈足底端明显外侈。腹部饰有双体兽纹。兽体由云雷纹构成，兽脊上有羽状纹。圈足上饰有两道凸弦纹。盘腹内底刻铭：“噩侯作旅彝”（图一九）。

三

众所周知，湖北是以“鄂”为其简称。传统观点认为，湖北地区被称之为鄂，应该是从东汉三国以后开始的。其实不然，湖北与鄂的关系可以用源远流长一词来形容。“鄂”与噩有着非常之密切的关系。西周早期噩侯青铜器在湖北随州出土，可以说，湖北称鄂的历史是十分悠久的。噩，是一个非常古老的氏族，姞姓。商代时已受封立国。在甲骨文中多有“噩侯”的记载。“贞，令口从噩侯伐儿方受……”，“……令方从噩侯寇周”。在《史记·殷本纪》中记载有商纣王时“以西伯、九侯、噩侯为三公”，结果是三公中的九侯、噩侯被杀，西伯被囚。但还是可以看出商代时噩侯的地位相当高。商代的噩地并不是在湖北，而是有可能在桐柏山北的河南沁阳，甲骨文中记载历代商王常到噩地田猎。西周时期，噩与周王室的关系时好时坏，若即若离。关于噩与周王室的恩怨情仇，在出土的西周青铜器铭文中有较为清楚的表述。噩侯簋有铭刻：“噩侯作王姞媵簋，王姞其万年子子孙孙永宝”。证明噩曾经一度与周王室通婚。噩侯驭方鼎铭文：“王南征，伐角、僪，唯还自征，才坏。噩侯驭方内醴于王，乃祼之，驭方友王，王休宴，乃射。驭方佮王射。驭方休阑，王宴，咸酓。王窺易驭方玉五瑴，马四匹，矢五束，驭方拜手稽首，敢对扬天子丕显休赉，用乍尊鼎，其万年子孙永宝用”。而在这个时期，噩的都城应该南迁至桐柏山南的湖北随州。噩器的大量出土，反映出西周早期时，噩国的核心区域应该是在随州的溠水与涢水的交汇地带。随州羊子山出土的青铜器群是“噩”国器，噩为姞姓，噩侯曾为商纣王的三公之一，后臣服于周王室，在周初被移封到随枣走廊，曾经是周王室的依靠力量，又曾经一度成为带领东夷势力反叛周王室的主力。噩的力量非常强大。周王室先后两次动用大量的军队“西六师、殷八师”才将之打败。这一史实在禹鼎铭文中有很明确的记录。应该是在被周王室打败后，其实力已经大大削弱，又被楚国乘虚而入，鄂国更是江河日下，一蹶不振。其核心区域的影响力在西周晚期就为曾国所代替。

在以环绕大洪山为核心的区域发现了大量曾国青铜器，曾国为姬姓，曾国在该地区的兴旺时代是西周晚期才开始，可能是在该地区中以噩为首的方国或是被灭或是被逼迁移后，曾国是在噩国移居于湖北东部的鄂州后才得以迅速壮大起来，成为了西周晚期周王室在这一区域的重要代表。

湖北因是楚国的核心地区，也有以楚地而自称。其实楚国与鄂国的关系也非常密切，西周中期，楚君熊渠曾经大肆的讨伐鄂地。熊渠是楚国西周时期的具有传奇色彩的一位重要人物，也是楚国第一位发力开疆拓土、颇有作为的楚君，熊渠的事迹在史书中有较多的记载。主要的功绩是："熊渠生三子。当周夷王之时，王室微，诸侯或不朝，相伐。熊渠盛得江汉间民和，乃兴兵伐庸、杨粤，至于鄂。"关于三处的地望，争议较大，目前由于新资料的出土，鄂为西鄂已经基本得到认同。熊渠甚至自封其子为王，皆在江上楚蛮之地。虽然后"及周厉王之时，暴虐，熊渠畏其伐楚，亦去其王"。但可以理解为从此这里皆为楚所实际控制。楚国从西周中期开始就牢牢地掌握了对噩的控制权，以至于鄂国或鄂族成为了楚国的附庸，后来直接成为了楚国的封君"鄂君"，有两件重要的文物可以证实，这就是"鄂君启"车节和舟节。

尽管在春秋时期也有如《左传·隐公六年》所载："翼九宗五正顷公之子嘉父，逆晋侯于随，纳诸鄂，晋人谓之鄂侯。"可以理解为：嘉父此时来到随地，招纳散居的鄂人聚集，而被晋人称之为鄂侯。应该说此鄂侯非彼噩侯，完全是两码事。

王国维先生曾经考订楚国一度以鄂为郢，近人也有持这种观点[①]。在清华简楚居中记载有楚昭王曾经以"鄂郢"为居[②]，就是说以鄂为都。证实了鄂郢存在的史实。

① 殷崇浩:《楚都鄂补》，《汉江考古》1984年第1期。

② 清华大学出土文献保护中心:《清华大学藏战国竹简（壹）》，中华书局，2011年。

四

湖北是周王室与蛮夷和南淮夷进行冲突的重要缓冲地带，这里既是周王室严加控制的势力范围，又是征讨蛮夷的前沿阵地。湖北地区是周王室早期控制较为牢固的地区。至少可以从青铜器的发现情况这一点上得到证明，青铜器表现出中原特征可以用同出一范来形容。湖北西周青铜器的发现很自然地让人联想到华夏集团、东夷集团、苗蛮集团之间的关系。虽然湖北的尤其是鄂东地区与淮夷地理上更接近，毕竟在湖北地区的西周封国都是与周王室有相当密切的关系，他们主要来源于早期的中原的华夏集团，与东夷集团和苗蛮集团来说还是在文化上更先进一些，主要是受到宗周文化的影响更大一些。通过对这批西周青铜器的器物组合、器形特征、装饰纹样诸多方面的综合观察，就总体风格上是与西周核心区域的宗周和成周地区的文化面貌基本相同和同步的。

湖北这批新出土的西周青铜器纹饰上的特征与风格，也与中原和周原出土青铜器上的纹饰风格基本一致，有许多纹饰几乎是完全相同的，这与湖北西周青铜器在器类、组合和造型与中原、周原青铜器完全相同的特点相一致。但不可否认的是，湖北出土的一些西周青铜器在纹饰图案式样上，比中原、周原青铜器更为繁缛，甚至可以说更为精美。尤其是西周早期的青铜器特别突出。在器物的表面装饰有造型类似写真的动物头首形象，在写真的基本特征上，又突破性地创造出与自然物种相异的动物形态，有形的怪异造型隐含的是让人难以理解的诡异的含义。使人不由自主地对之产生一种对神灵的敬畏感。纹饰风格上的这种特色，在周原出土的青铜器中少见。

纹饰的特点突出表现为在纹饰的写真性和高浮雕效果上。兽首面上具有明显的人面器官的特征，尤其是眼、鼻的特征与人的眼和鼻是完全相同的。再就是对于细部的刻画非常精确到位，如眼睛的眼皮、眼眶、圆睛、瞳孔都表现得层次分明，可以用栩栩如生来形容，也正好符合饕餮亦人亦鬼的特点。其实在人类文明的幼年阶段，在艺术作品中经常可以看到有半人半兽的，这种现象不仅在中国、在亚洲普遍存在，在欧洲、非洲和美洲也都普遍存在，应该是一个世界性的历史现象。在这些浮雕写真的形象，无法去用一种自然界中存在或曾经存在过的动物来定位和确定其名称。动物的神形与神性是可以相互转换的。同样，人与动物、与神也是可以相互转换的。对于动物的神奇怪异进行一种超自然的组合创造，绝非只是为了获得审美效果，一定是有其更深层次的含义。

青铜器是物质文明的重要标志，同时从中透射出时代的文化精神，有幸鉴赏这造型典雅，纹饰繁缛华贵，制作精良考究的古代青铜器珍品，就宛若进入一种诗情物语境界，好似读诗经中的风、雅、颂，这青铜文化中的风雅颂，更显得琳琅满目，精彩纷呈，绚丽多姿，美轮美奂，显示出独特的艺术魅力。青铜器中所蕴含着的德与美，真可谓令人叹为观止。

器物的造型突出的是器用功能，而其器物外表上的纹饰装饰表现出更为独到的文化特质。从出土文物上观察，其铜器制作十分精美，在纹饰上甚至远远超过了曾侯乙墓出土铜器的纹饰。就器物的纹饰精美程度而言，其艺术价值、工艺价值更高。这些文物和科学考古资料，对于探讨和研究西周时期湖北地区的历史文化，具有极高的历史价值、艺术价值和科学价值。

中国南方青铜器上羽人船纹图刍议

Brief Research on Boat Patterns with Feathermen on Bronze Wares of South China

周志清 / 成都文物考古研究所 副研究员
李晓帆 / 昆明市博物馆 副研究员

[摘要]

南中国地区长期以来一直处于华夏的边缘地带，其独特的青铜文化由于其特殊的地理位置散发出多元与复合的文化特征，它是中国青铜文化中一朵壮丽的奇葩。羽人船纹图是流行于南中国地区战国至汉代一类较有区域族群特色的青铜器装饰图案，图案构思巧妙，纹饰繁缛，铸造精美，是一种独特的叙事图画。战国晚期至西汉中期是此类题材最为活跃的时期。此类图案主要出现于铜鼓和铜桶的腰部，羽人与船纹是其图案的中心，其主要是作为礼器的装饰纹样出现的。

[关键词]

人物叙事画　南中国　羽人　船纹图　铜桶

Abstract

The region of Southern China has always been considered to be on the peripheries of China. Because of its particular geographic location the Bronze Age cultures in this region are exemplary of this complex and multifaceted tradition. The immortal boat pattern was a popular and perhaps ethnically distinctive form of Bronze decoration in Southern China from the Warring States to the Han dynasty. Its composition is ingenious and was skillfully cast and they are unique forms of narrative decoration. This design was most actively used from the late Warring States to the mid-Western Han.

This immortals and boats design is most commonly present on the waist of bronze drums and buckets of which it forms the center and appears to have been used as a decorative scheme for ritual objects. It is a design which exclusively characterizes the bronzes of Southern China and Southeast Asia and prevalent in the regions inhabited by the ancient Kingdom of Yue: central Yunnan, Southern Guangxi, and Northern Vietnam. It was of special ritual for the locals in adapting to the environment and it embodies the assimilation of man and environment. It also indicates that because of the particular geographic configuration of Southern China there was frequent exchange and interaction with surrounding regions. There was probably recognition of shared ethnic identity between groups and the shared pattern of immortals and the boats points to the fact that they likely shared common religious beliefs.

Key words

Character narrative drawings; Southern China; Feathermen; Immortals and boat design; Bronze buckets

南中国地区[①]古代青铜文化中的青铜器以其独特的造型、鲜明的民族特点、繁缛的装饰而成为中国青铜文化大家园中一朵壮丽的奇葩。而在该地域出土的铜鼓和铜桶上我们可以经常发现人物叙事图画的纹饰，即以人物为中心的写实性叙事图案。这些人物叙事图画，人物刻画形象生动，栩栩如生；画面完整，表现了一个完整的活动过程。这使得那些因缺乏史书记载而被淹没于历史尘土之下的先人的活动场景得以复活，为中国古代广博和多元的青铜文化增添了新的个案材料，再现了当时的活动场景，对于复原当时的社会形态、生业和生产方式提供了鲜活的“图画”资料。西南地区青铜时代遗存中常见的铜鼓和铜桶是叙事图案最为常见的载体之一。船纹图是其中常见的装饰题材，根据目前的材料，其流行的时代大致在战国时期出现，西汉时期是此类题材最为活跃的时段，东汉以后衰落[②]。关于船纹图认识主要有几种说法，国外学者多认为是一种祭祀仪式[③]，国内学者多认为是龙舟竞渡习俗的写照[④]，也有部分人认为古人越渡海洋的历史写照[⑤]，笔者认为这些说法既有合理之处，又难免缺失，需要针对不同背景的船纹图作具体的分析，才可理解其背后意义。羽人船纹图是船纹图中最常见的图案，它的出现有着其特定的环境。

青铜桶又名铜筩，因其体形呈圆桶形，口部有对称贯耳，又名提桶，上大底小，多有器盖。根据目前的考古资料，该类铜器在中国境内仅见于南中国的两广地区和云南三地，其他地区则不见。云南呈贡天子庙41号墓所见的铜桶，时代为战国中期，而个旧黑玛井出土的铜桶则为东汉初期。五牛盖铜桶（天子庙M41：103）[⑥]，圆形盖，盖面铸有铜鼓鼓面特有的晕圈，盖面中央铸鼓形圆台，圆台上焊接四头立起的瘤牛（原应有五头，出土时残缺一头），牛身似披挂有某种装饰物。盖两侧有对称贯耳一对。桶身高，子母口，口沿有对称吠犬形耳一对，与盖耳对应。桶底平，下焊有三足。桶身铸有十二晕，主晕二组，上组为羽人（因其人身用鸟羽装饰而得名）竞渡船纹图（图一，1），间以水鸟纹；下组用斜格纹、同心圆纹纵分六格，每格铸有瘤牛、水鸟，每格图像各不相同，这两组主晕图像为写生式图像，图像刻画得栩栩如生，具有强烈的写实感。主晕上下和中间纹饰间以锯齿纹和同心圆纹。口径29、底径49.5厘米。

广州南越王墓铜筩（B59）[⑦]，子母口，复耳。桥形外耳，内耳为贯耳。器身有四组纹饰带，口沿和器足处有三组几何形纹带，这三组纹饰均以勾连菱形纹为主，上下缀以弦纹、点纹和锯齿纹等。器腹中部的一组为主晕，装饰有羽人船纹图，各船间以水鸟，一共四只船，形象大同小异。船身修长呈弧形，两端高翘像首尾。首尾各竖2根祭仪用的羽旌，中后部有船台，台下置1鼎物，中前部竖1长杆，杆上饰羽，下悬木鼓。每船有羽人5名，一人持弓执剑，第二人立于船台上，一手持鞋形钺，另一手执首级。船台前三人，头一人持弓执剑，第二人坐鼓形座上，左手执棒击鼓，右手执一物，第三人左手执裸体俘虏，右手持短剑，船尾1人划桨。每只羽人

① 本文所指的南中国地区特指主要是西南夷地区、两广及东南亚地区北部紧邻中国的区域。

② 蒋廷瑜：《古代铜鼓通论》，紫禁城出版社，1999年。

③ 松本信广：《表现古代传说中的车与船》，《东亚民族文化论考》，1958年。

④ 汪宁生：《试论中国古代铜鼓》，《考古学报》1978年第2期；蒋廷瑜：《古代铜鼓通论》，紫禁城出版社，1999年。

⑤ 梁钊韬：《西瓯族源初探》，《学术研究》1978年第1期。

⑥ 昆明市文物管理委员会：《呈贡天子庙滇墓》，《考古学报》1985年第4期。

⑦ 广州市文物管理委员会等：《广州汉墓》，文物出版社，1981年；广州象岗汉墓发掘队：《西汉南越王墓发掘初步报告》，《考古》1984年第3期；广州文物考古研究所：《广州文物考古集》，文物出版社，2003年。

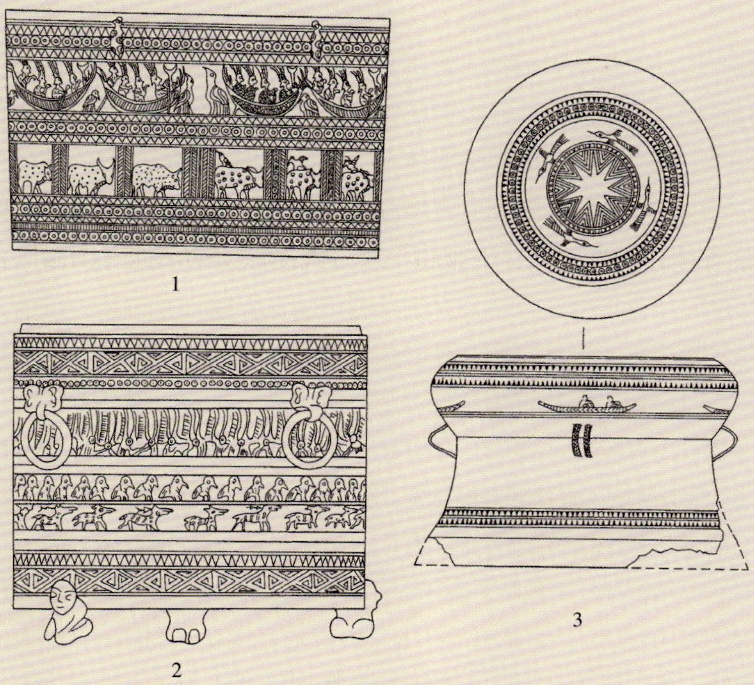

图一 羽人船纹图案

1. 天子庙（M41：103） 2. 英国格拉斯哥博物馆藏铜奁 3. 石寨山铜鼓（M3：3）

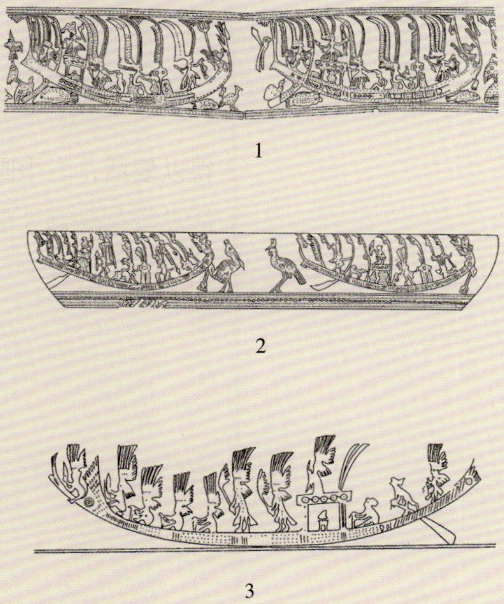

图二 船纹图案对比图

1. 南越王墓铜筩（B59） 2. 越南玉镂1号鼓 3. 会理3号鼓

船纹图上还装饰有水鸟、海龟、海鱼（图二，1）。

越南出土的青铜器上人物叙事图画主要出现于越南北部东山文化时期（前5世纪～1世纪，即中国的战国至东汉初），主要见于铜鼓和铜桶两类器物。其早期铜鼓如约丘鼓、鼎乡鼓等铜鼓胸上装饰有四组船纹，船上有裸体、椎髻、执桨的人物三至八人。船间有鸬鹚一至二只，腰部分成纵格，内填牛纹或空格。此类人物叙事图画人或物构图简单，风格朴素自然。而该地区中期以玉镂1号鼓为代表，船纹图装饰繁杂，构图精致，画面丰富。鼓胸上装饰有四组船纹，每船绘有四至七个头戴羽冠，腰上装饰尾羽的羽人，船间饰有鸬鹚、鱼等。腰部纵分为几格，内填徒手、执斧、执盾、执矛和执杖的羽人①（图二，2）。而在越溪和东山出土的铜桶上也装饰有与铜鼓上相同的人物叙事图画②（图三）。

从上述青铜桶和铜鼓上的写实性的人物叙事图画可以看到其器身上刻画的均是羽人船纹图，羽人是整个叙事画面的主体，不同的羽人在其中扮演着不同角色，水鸟、船、海鱼等共同营造事件发生的活动场景乃是在水面之上，而头带高耸羽冠，下着羽毛短裙，跣足的羽人构成了事件活动的中心，他们均以大江或大海和湖泊为进行仪式活动的舞台，渲染出其对大自然神秘莫测的困惑及祈求人外力量（extra-human power）或超自然（supernatural）力量的福佑。

① 黎文兰等：《越南青铜时代的第一批遗迹》，河内，1963年，梁志明译本，1982年，中国古代铜鼓研究会出版；梅原末治：《安南清化省东山出土的桶形铜器》，《东亚考古学论考》，东京，1944年，413页；阮文煊，黄荣：《越南发现的东山铜鼓》，越南历史博物馆，1975年，梁志明译。

② 云南省博物馆：《云南晋宁石寨山古墓群发掘报告》，文物出版社，1959年。

羽人是流行于南中国地区古代青铜文化中青铜器上常见的一种纹饰，它广泛出现于西南地区和两广地区青铜文化中的铜鼓、铜桶、铜钺上。其中铜鼓是该类纹饰最常见的器物载体，从目前南中国地区古代青铜文化的情况看，船纹图主要流行于石寨山型铜鼓的盛行时期（前5世纪～1世纪），特别是其中晚期。此类纹饰本身有一个发展和演变的过程，在石寨山型中期铜鼓上，即战国晚期至西汉早期，其特点是船身浅狭，首尾装饰得像鸟首和鸟尾。人物少，羽人身上装饰较为简单，头上羽毛不甚突出，多为裸体、椎髻。整个人物叙事图画面单一，画面结构不复杂。这类船纹图给人的视觉印象总体上构图简单，人物的活动场景更接近于生活，画面欢快和活跃，其主题主要是捕鱼图和行舟图，宗教仪式化的东西少见。它反映了中国南方地区，特别是铜鼓和铜桶流行的百越地区江河湖沼众多，水产丰富，在其先民的生业形态中，渔猎业是其农耕经济的一个重要组成部分，是其居民适应其生存环境的一种生活常态。石寨山M3：3，鼓胸上为锯齿纹带，下为四组船纹，船纹上的人像多模糊，每船有隐约可见者的裸体、椎髻人像，船身狭长（图一，3）[①]。石寨山M15：7，鼓胸中部装饰四组船纹，每船上有三个裸体、椎髻的人像。李家山M24：42A，鼓胸饰有四组船纹，船身浅狭，首尾装饰像鸟首或鸟尾。船上有四至五人，除个别短发外，余皆椎髻，除一人披衣外，余皆裸体，头上都没有装饰羽毛，各自执桨划船。船的前后绘有鱼、鸬鹚等动物。李家山M24：42B，鼓胸中下部饰有四组船纹，船身狭长呈弧形，首尾装饰得像鸟首和鸟尾。每船上有四个头戴羽冠、裸体、划桨的人；腰上部装饰立牛和羽人舞蹈图（图四，1）。石寨山3-796铜鼓鼓胸下部环绕装饰四组船纹，船身狭长呈弧形。每船上有四人，皆裸体，椎髻垂发，船首和船尾高翘起似鷁首和鷁尾[②]（图四，3）。

① 云南省博物馆：《云南晋宁石寨山古墓群发掘报告》，文物出版社，1959年；云南省博物馆工作队：《云南江川李家山古墓群发掘报告》，《考古学报》1975年第2期；云南省博物馆：《云南晋宁石寨山古遗址及墓葬》，《考古学报》1956年第1期。

② 云南省博物馆：《云南晋宁石寨山古墓群发掘报告》，文物出版社，1959年；云南省博物馆工作队：《云南江川李家山古墓群发掘报告》，《考古学报》1975年第2期；云南省博物馆：《云南晋宁石寨山古遗址及墓葬》，《考古学报》1956年第1期。

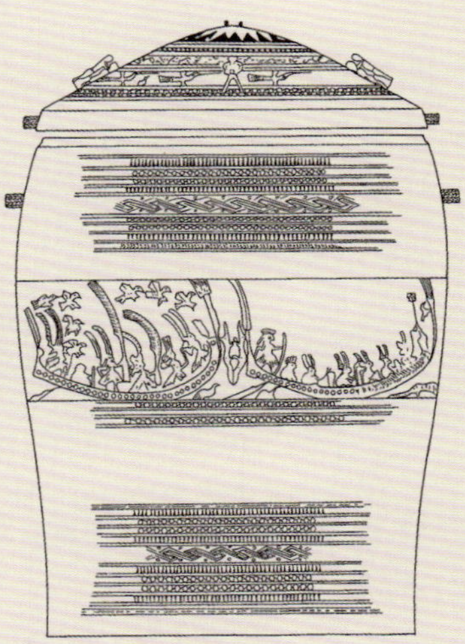

图三　越南越溪和东山铜桶上羽人图案

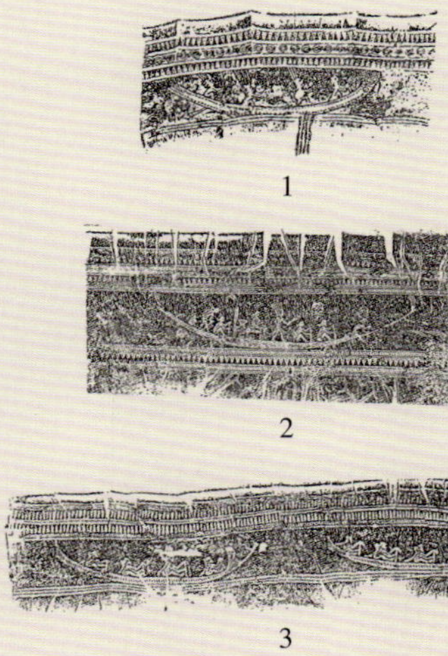

图四　铜鼓船纹图案
1. 李家山铜鼓（M24：42B）　2. 石寨山3-796铜鼓
3. 广南M1号鼓

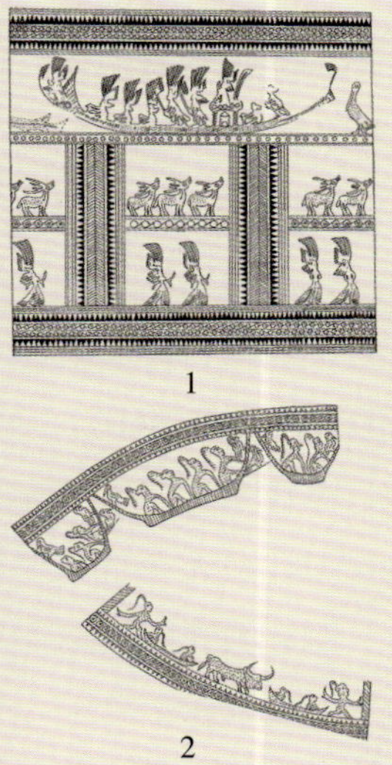

图五　铜鼓船纹图案
1. 广西西林土280号鼓　2. 石寨山铜鼓
（M51：58）

石寨山型晚期（西汉中晚期至东汉初）铜鼓上的船纹图构图繁芜，船身狭长，装饰复杂；船身上人物较多，多为装饰繁缛、戴着高耸羽毛的羽人形象；水鸟、鱼、牛等动物共同构成了一个叙事画面，而其画面表现的人物活动场景多庄严肃穆，俨然宗教祭祀仪式活动，其主题主要是竞渡和祀河图。如石寨山M1：58，鼓胸下部饰有六组船纹，船短而深，首尾不分，船首和船尾翘起，各立一鸬鹚，水面上也绘有鸬鹚；每船上有二至四人，皆裸体、椎髻，髻后插一根羽毛。鼓腰纹饰分为两部分，每部分二组船纹，船间有牛、鸟及舞人[①]（图五，2）。广南M1号鼓，鼓胸中部饰有四组船纹，船身狭长呈弧形，首尾装饰得像鹢首鹢尾，中后部有一船台，台后树起祭仪用的羽旌，每船上有七、八、九人不等，除执羽者披尾饰外余皆裸体、椎髻。其中台前第一、第四人头戴羽冠，下身披着前短后幅长的尾饰，执羽仪向水神致敬。第五人作于台上击鼓，第七人髻插双羽掌舵，其余划桨。这四条船形态各异，第一条船，鼓置于台下，司鼓悠然抱膝而坐；第二条船，鼓置于台前，司鼓抱膝蹲坐；第三条船，司鼓执起鼓槌准备击鼓；第四条船，司鼓奋力作击鼓状，表现了当时祭祀水神时连续活动场景的再现。鼓腰纵分为十四格，格中有羽人和剽牛等画面[②]（图四，2）。广西西林土280号鼓，鼓胸中部饰有六组船纹，船身颀长呈弧形，首尾高翘像首尾，装饰华丽。中后部有一船台，台背树起一排羽旌，台下置一鼎形物。每船上有八、九、十一人不等，船上人物除个别外，皆戴羽冠、椎髻，后缀饰羽翼。其中高立于船台的一人头戴高耸的羽冠，别着宽袖及地长袍合掌垂袖，似为祭祀仪式的主持者。其中船上立者为上裸、腰系两羽翼，坐者全裸、划桨。船间有鸬鹚或鱼纹。鼓腰分为十二格，每格分为上下层，上饰鹿纹，下饰舞人。此类船纹图均有较高的船台，装饰华丽，船体较大，人物形象有其社会角色分层的明显差异，并有依仗用具点缀其中（图二，3；图五，1）。会理3号铜鼓，鼓胸饰有六组船纹，船短而浅，底部平直，首尾不分，朴素无饰。船上有二人至四人，皆椎髻，髻后插羽毛或用斜纹布巾束发，皆身着短衣裤，执桨划船。鼓腰分别装饰鸬鹚、鸬鹚老鹰、鸬鹚水牛、鸬鹚牛鹰等画面[③]（图二，3）。从人物的活动场景观察，其当与某类祭祀河神活动相关。

英国格拉斯哥博物馆收藏的铜桶（原文名为“铜奁”[④]），盖身缺失，子母口，形体大，形状呈圆桶形。平底，底部有三足，每足为光头、大眼、高鼻、跪坐的裸体人身构成。口沿下有带悬环的铺首四个。通高51厘米。器身遍布纹饰，共有四组纹饰，每组纹饰之间用三弦纹隔开，装饰手法如同铜鼓上的晕圈。纹饰从上至下有两组几何形纹带，这两组纹饰均以双勾连菱形纹为主，间以锯齿纹、同心圆纹、圆点纹，器腹中部有两组主晕，中间以三弦纹分割开来，第一组为变形羽人纹，大眼、头上羽毛极长；第二组分为上下两组，间以双弦纹分割，上组为鸟纹，同向排列，大嘴，大眼，宽尾，下组为鹿纹，分为雄性和雌性，错落而饰（图一，2）。

① 云南省博物馆：《云南晋宁石寨山古墓群发掘报告》，文物出版社，1959年；云南省博物馆工作队：《云南江川李家山古墓群发掘报告》，《考古学报》1975年第2期；云南省博物馆：《云南晋宁石寨山古遗址及墓葬》，《考古学报》1956年第1期。

② 云南省博物馆：《云南晋宁石寨山古墓群发掘报告》，文物出版社，1959年；云南省博物馆工作队：《云南江川李家山古墓群发掘报告》，《考古学报》1975年第2期；云南省博物馆：《云南晋宁石寨山古遗址及墓葬》，《考古学报》1956年第1期。

③ 广西壮族自治区文物工作队：《广西西林普驮铜鼓墓葬》，《文物》1978年第9期。

④ 黄得荣：《英国格拉斯哥收藏的晋宁石寨山青铜奁》，《云南文物》1997年第2期。

这件铜桶的抽象的变形羽人纹，呆板的动物形象，推测为石寨山晚期的作品。西汉晚期以后在滇池区域、越南北部、广西南部基本上不见此类纹饰的踪影，它与强势汉文化对南中国的百越地区的经略相关，伴随着西汉中央王朝对西南夷地区的拓殖而消失。作为百越中西瓯、骆越等越人标示物的铜鼓船纹图也逐渐失去其生存的空间，其象征意义逐渐弱化。

以上青铜桶和铜鼓上的人物写实性图画均以羽人为人物中心的船纹图，它形象生动地再现了当时人类活动的场景，在展现其发达的渔猎经济和高超的江河驾船技术同时，带我们随着那翱翔的飞鸟跨越时空区隔，置身于那远古神秘的聚落之中，去感受祭祀仪式尊严与凝重。而那些头戴高耸羽冠、身披尾羽的羽人，其举手投足仿佛像空中翱翔的飞鸟。而羽人活动的舞台则是船身和船底狭长呈弧形的木船，首尾装饰成鸟状。长喙并戴有短蓑冠，像鷁首和鷁尾，人与鸟巧妙地融合在一起。这是当地居民适应其生存环境生态足迹，是人与自然和谐发展的产物。羽人船纹图是南中国和东南亚地区青铜文化中特有的装饰图案，其流行地区为云南中部、广西南部和越南北部古代越人传统的居住区，是当地居民适应其生存环境的一种独特的仪式诉求，体现了人与自然的融合，同时也反映出南中国地区由于相近的地理或环境，人群的交流与互动频繁，古代族群之间可能有着共同的族群认同或族群记忆，羽人船纹图或许是他们有着共同信仰传统的体现。

人与自然的关系是自人类自出现以来，便一直是萦绕其头脑中且挥之不去的疑惑，远古时代，人类在与自然的抗争中，面对大自然的神秘莫测，人类往往感到孤立无援，对大自然的神秘充满了敬畏，人们认为超自然的神秘力量的存在，万物有灵论便成为其原始信仰的源泉，为了与大自然达到和谐，为了娱神、媚神以求保佑自己和福佑子孙，原始的祭祀礼仪活动便成为其生活中一个最为重要的组成部分，原始巫术礼仪活动孕育而生，作为礼仪活动中的宗教实践者——巫师相应产生，在早期人类社会中由于他们具有超自然的个人经历体验而能够直接从神那里获取力量并与之交通①。巫师作为生死世界沟通的媒介，一些神灵化的动物或植物常常成为其沟通神灵的助手②。动物是早期人类亲密的朋友，也是渔猎时代人类获取动物蛋白最主要的来源，其与人类之间的密切关系不言而喻，万物有灵信仰在早期人类社会的广泛流行，使得许多动物成为巫术礼仪活动中最重要的助手，在早期人类社会中，此类神灵动物则由于地区和时代的差异性而呈现出多样性。

①② 张光直:《商周青铜器的动物纹样》，《中国古代艺术与政治——续论商周青铜器上的动物纹样》，《中国青铜时代》，文物出版社，1986年。

水是地球上人类和许多生物赖以生存的基本要素之一，它与人类之间的关系也最为密切。而人类对水资源认识的局限性以及对其“神秘力量”的恐惧，对江河湖泊中的水充满了向往与敬畏，为了自己和子孙的生存发展，面对神秘莫测且生机勃勃的江河湖泊，人类很早就围绕江河湖泊产生了各种各样的原始宗教仪式活动，以祈求万世之幸。古代南中国地区河湖密布，池沼广袤，水产丰富，《后汉书·西南夷传》云滇池地区："有盐池田渔之饶，金银畜产之富"；森林茂密，动植物种类繁多，为该地区的人类生存的持续性发展提供了理想的空间。中国南方地区曾广泛流行有祭祀河神的习俗，在早期人类社会中，它在当时人们生产与社会活动中扮演着十分重要的社会角色，而在祭祀仪式活动中充当人神沟通媒介的鸟人化的羽人则是这些原始礼仪活动的实践者——巫师。《楚辞·九歌·河伯》："与女游兮九河，冲风起兮横波……与女游兮河之渚……波滔滔兮来迎，鱼鳞鳞兮媵予。"王夫之注："河伯，河神也。四渎视诸侯，故称伯。楚王有疾，卜曰：'河为祟。'昭王谓其非境内山川弗祀焉。昭王能以礼正祀典，故已之，而楚国固曾祀之矣。"《河渎神祠》："铜鼓赛神来，满庭幡盖徘徊，水村江浦过风雷，楚山如烟开。"《送客南归有怀》说："瓦樽留海客，铜鼓赛江神。"反映的正是祭拜河神的场景。

羽人在中国南方古代社会中特殊的象征意义赋予其特定的话语意义，中国特别是南中国地区普遍存在着太阳崇拜，鸟崇拜成为该地区最为常见的崇拜形式，作为神鸟化身的羽人是其人格化的体现，他广泛出现于原始祭祀礼仪活动中，是巫术活动的实践者[①]。巫师是巫术活动中生死世界沟通的媒介，神灵化的动物则往往是其沟通神灵的助手，巫师的出现深刻影响早期人类生活的方方面面。因此，船纹图中羽人乃是某种祭祀礼仪活动中的巫师，其整体画面乃是一场巫术活动的场景再现，记录了墓葬主人的精神和灵魂世界。作为原始宗教活动的实践者——巫师的身份随着时代的演进也悄然而变，"国之大事，在祀在戎。"战争和祭祀是早期部落社会中最重要的两件事，这二者的主持主要为部落社会中的巫师或头人，随着时间的推移，世俗权力和神权在分层化社会中的不断结合，巫师和部族统治者悄然混为一体。而作为"神权"符号载体的青铜器因其特定的时空语境而具有同样的符号意义，在烟火缭绕的祭祀仪式活动中作为神器而被人们顶礼膜拜，在早期人类分层社会中成为其拥有者身份和地位的象征物，变成强势阶层的"重器"，象征着财富和权威，强化了统治阶层的强势地位。《隋书·地理志》云："有鼓者，号为都老，群情推服。"铜鼓和铜桶长期以来在所流行的族群中一直具有特殊的符号意义，而此类青铜器仅见于大中型墓葬等具有明显的社会分层或结构分层的物化空间中，又是其意义延伸的例证。

透过对上述材料的梳理，我们认为装饰有羽人船纹图的青铜器（主要为铜鼓和铜桶）最初的功能主要是作为礼器出现的，而非后来所谓实用的容器、葬具、酒器、贮贝器[②]等。此类纹饰主要流行的时代是在石寨山中晚期（即战国晚期至西汉中期），西汉晚期以后，伴随着西汉中央政府对西南夷地区的拓殖，此类纹饰随同其主人掩埋于历史的尘埃之中。羽人船纹图主要流行的中心地区是云南的滇池地区、广西南部和越南北部地区，在广东、四川南部、贵州西南等地发现的此类纹饰可能主要是族群移动或文化互动交流所致。而在滇池地区和越南北部红河地区交界地带

① 周志清:《羽人与羽人舞》,《江汉考古》2001年第1期。

② 黄展岳:《铜提桶考略》,《考古》1989年第9期。

的个旧、蒙自等地冶炼遗址的相继发现，为我们认识两地文化和东南亚国家或地区间古代文化互动和族群之间的移动提供了思考的契机，并对流行于该地区同质青铜器的产源地、制作、贸易等相关的探讨打下了坚实的基础。云南境内个旧、蒙自自古以来就是著名的铅、锡矿产区，《汉书·地理志》载："贲古，北采山出锡，西羊山出银、铅，南乌山出锡。"今人考证古贲古，即位于现在的个旧、蒙自、建水一带。从地理上看它处于越南红河三角洲与滇池区域的中间地带，其青铜文化因素中具有两地青铜文化中一些共同的因素[①]，同时该区域还具有一些两广沿海古代文化中所常见的文化因素，该青铜文化的主人可能与两广地区古代骆越、西鸥、南越有着紧密的联系，其族属极有可能属于百越系居民。黑玛井古墓群和冲子坡冶炼遗址等发现的青铜器可作为当地在东汉时期发达的冶炼业和活跃的商品经济缩影，反映出其青铜冶炼技术和商品交易应在很早以前就已经存在。经鉴定西南地区青铜文化中的青铜器的铅含量偏高[②]，这同滇池地区、广西南部和越南北部地区出土青铜器的合金成分极为相似，反映出当时西南地区青铜冶炼技术中的一个重要特色。对中国南方青铜时代羽人船纹图的分析有助于南中国地区和东南亚地区古代文化之间人地互动关系的研究，同时也昭示我们对于该区域古代文化因素的探讨必须将其置于一个宏观的叙事环境中予以讨论。

① 周志清：《浅析云南元江流域的青铜文化》，《考古与文物》2009年第3期。

② 北京钢铁学院冶金史研究室：《贵县罗泊湾一号墓出土的五件铜器鉴定报告》，《广西贵县罗泊湾汉墓》，文物出版社，1988年；戴宗品、张忠凯：《个旧冲子坡冶炼遗址发掘简报》，《云南文物》1998年总第46期。

柳州博物馆馆藏几件青铜器的研究

A Research on Bronze
Wares Collected in Liuzhou Museum

刘 文 / 柳州市博物馆 副研究员

[摘要]

本文对20世纪80年代柳州博物馆征集、出土的青铜编钟、青铜匕首、青铜角器、青铜剑、青铜钺等青铜器进行描述。探讨了这些青铜器年代、来源以及青铜文化发展内涵，提出了这些青铜器有来自中原和本地铸造的可能。

[关键词]

馆藏 青铜器 研究

Abstract

This article makes a through inquiry into the age, spread of Bronze Chime bells, Bronze Dagger, Bronze Vessel, Bronze Sword, Bronze Yue-poleaxe ect historical relics that were collected by Liuzhou Museum or unearthed in 1980s.

Key words

Museum's collections; Bronze wares; Study

图一　横山编钟

一

横山青铜编钟

1985年10月，广西区建五公司二处五工段倪迪昭、李春光两位师傅在柳州市太阳村镇横山边路经挖墙基工地发现一样东西，经谢浩然干部知道后报告了柳州博物馆，笔者前往工地见到两位师傅又看到了那件出土的青铜编钟，他们立刻就问我，这是什么东西？我说这是古代的青铜编钟，是古代文物。接着我向他俩了解东西的来历时，他们说："这个是一个很巧而有趣的事，有一天，我们俩从这个工地走，偶然间就看见了这个东西，两人说这是什么东西？从来没有见过，感觉到这个东西很古怪，我们俩商量后，就把它拿到了我们住的工棚里，之后，放到了我们的床底下，没想到晚上睡觉时做了一场噩梦。第二天，我们就把它拿到工棚外面门口去放了，过程就是这样。"后来，我跟他俩解释，这不会是有什么不祥之兆，这个是编钟，是文物，它是古代的打击乐器，用小木槌击奏。为了宣传保护文物，我还和他们说，1978年夏，文物考古工作者在湖北省随州市西北擂鼓墩的地方，发掘了一座战国时曾侯乙墓，出土的文物其中有65件一套青铜编钟，为打击乐器，重2500公斤。1981年夏，在擂鼓墩又出土了文物，其中有36件一套青铜编钟。在太阳村横山边这里发现唯一的1件编钟，这个位置又没有墓葬的迹象，这可能是当时由于战争或者什么原因遗失在这里的。后来他们听完后就没有什么害怕的了。横山出土的编钟是距地表1.4米深处挖出的，残重16斤，断面呈椭圆形，为合铸，高39.5厘米，甬间方纽中有一孔两面共有不完整的36个枚，钲间有三角变形蝉纹、篆间有斜角雷纹饰（图一）。

二

渡村出土的青铜器

1986年4月，柳州市柳江县进德乡渡村村民刘锦章三兄弟在利用水稻田改为鱼

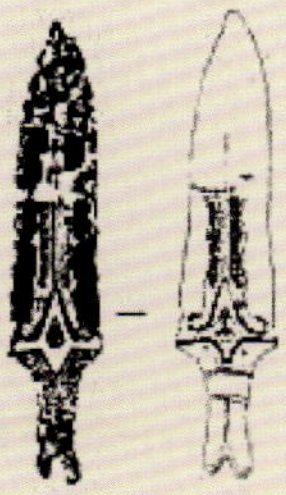

图二　渡村匕首

图四　喇叭形器

图三　渡村编钟

图五　渡村编钟

塘、挖至地下深约1米时，三兄弟每人挖出1件古代青铜器，1件云雷纹编钟、1件人面纹匕首、1件似喇叭形器。

匕首　进格处铸短线纹，呈“八”字形排列，两面短线纹中间各饰一人面纹。格呈“V”形，扁茎、茎端为钳形，茎两侧有鸟纹，通长23.2厘米（图二）。

编钟　甬长5.9厘米，中空，与钟体相通，断面呈椭圆形，有干和一残耳，旋已脱落。舞作两面坡形，饰云纹，篆及隧部饰云雷纹，征中间饰双线“S”纹，36个枚为旋纹。钟壁较厚，内腔有音脊，一面近枚处有四条竖脊线。钟体较短，通高27.8厘米（图三）。

喇叭形（原定无名器）器　正中为一柱状，饰12组纹饰，有弦纹、竖线纹和卷云纹等。1994年11月，江西省博物馆馆长、江西省考古研究所所长彭适凡及江西省博物馆周广明先生到柳州博物馆看到馆藏的这件喇叭形器之后，他们说，这个器物从来没有见过。认为这是国内不可多见的南方器物，其变形龙纹等精致的纹饰也是不多见的，至于它作何使用的、是何种器物，大家认为至今还是个谜（图四）。

2010年11月，柳江县文物管理所向渡村村民刘锦芳同志收购了1件与1986年同时出土的几件青铜器中的1件编钟，该钟通高24.1厘米，甬长5厘米，中空，与钟体相通，断面呈椭圆形，有旋，有干，干为一扭曲双绳索纹，旋中有凸旋纹两道，两面各18个枚，枚作双叠圆台状，正面1枚残断，每组3枚（图五）。

三

馆藏征集的青铜器

我馆馆藏有全国罕见的完整青铜角（形如牛角）器，说起这件器物的来历，那就要从改革开放的1978年秋季说起，那时博物馆为了保护文物增加文物藏品，成立了文物保护小组，决定到柳州地区仓库的总仓第三仓建立文物拣选点，当与该库的同志接触时，据他们说，以前从这废旧库中往外调走很多各种废旧金属到一些冶炼厂，总仓的废旧金属很多都是从柳州各县调来的。我们博物馆为了文物不外流失，后来又在市废旧收购部门开始定时间，每星期去一次，之后，每月去一至两次看有没有属于文物的。没多久，我们（包括市内废旧部门）就分头去。1983年，我在三仓库粗选堆里偶然发现一件奇怪的从没有见到过的一件像牛角一样完整的青铜角形器，青铜角通长20、口径7.2×6.6厘米。体饰云雷纹、人字纹和三角纹（图六）。多年来，在此还拣选到有青铜兵器的斧、钺、剑等。

钺　2件。柳州柳江县成团发现。长身弧刃，有肩，肩以下内收成銎，銎下部稍残。通高7.9、刃宽6.6厘米（图七）；柳州来宾县（今来宾市）征集，椭圆形身，弧刃，身上部内收成銎，銎呈扁圆形，口部呈弧状，銎及刃部稍残。通高9.5、刃宽6.7厘米（图八）。

斧　2件。大的一件来自柳州市鹿寨县黄勉乡。小的来自武宣县（隶属来宾市）。皆椭圆形銎，长身有肩，刃作弧形。大的通高8.8、刃宽7厘米（图九）。小的銎口、刃部稍残，通高6.9、刃宽6厘米（图一〇）。

变形蝉纹剑　1件。地点不明，扁茎、无格、茎上有孔。剑身有脊，断面呈菱形，身茎交界处呈斜向内收，两面两侧有凹翼及不规则椭圆形凹纹，剑身通体留有锉痕，茎端断折。长15厘米（图一一）。

四

青铜器的分析

柳州古时为百越之地，在周朝时中原文化已传播至此。据《诗经·大雅》记：“周朝时，江汉之浒，王命召虎，式壁四方，彻我疆土，匪疚匪棘，王国来极，于

图六　青铜角形器

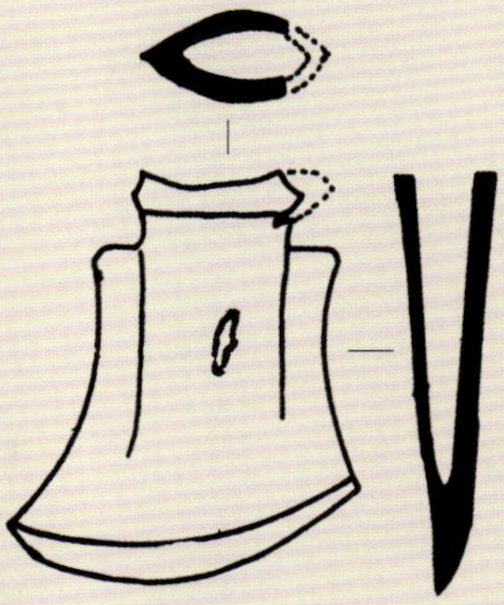

图七　成团铜钺

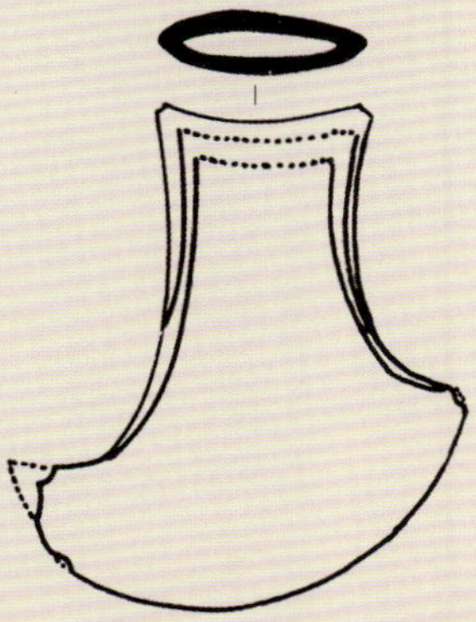

图八　来宾铜钺

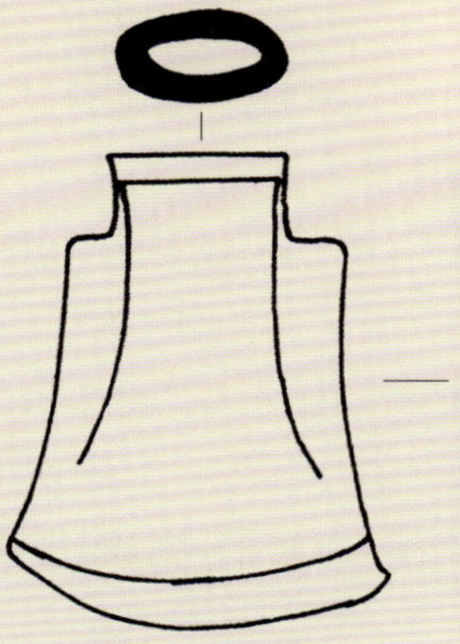

图九　黄勉铜斧

图一〇　武宣铜斧

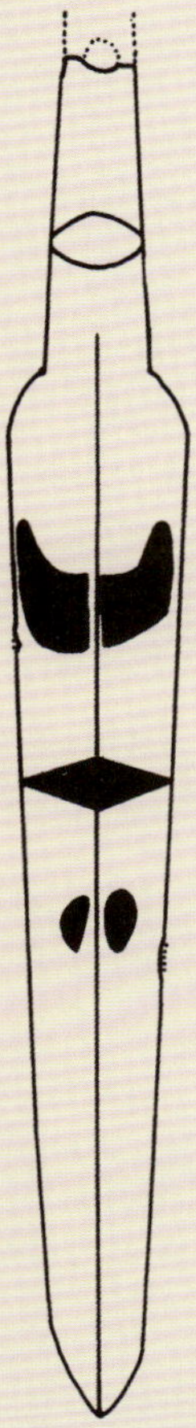

图一一　变形蝉纹铜剑

疆于理，至于南海”[①]。从柳江县出土的青铜器与有关记载来看，西周之前中原文化已与属百越地区的柳州有较密切的联系是无疑。直至秦始皇统一后的有关记载，柳州贡给朝廷（秦朝）的物产据《柳州府志·物产》载：“秦皇利越之犀、象、珠玑……柳（柳州）虽无可喜之物，而羽毛华实裨于核者亦所不乏”[②]。从这些记载来看，柳州应该可以说是从周朝时由北往南开辟的其中一条路线。

（1）从渡村出土少有的两面纹青铜匕首来说，中原至今未有发现，应是南方地区少数民族的特殊器物，可能为某个少数民族的族徽。编钟饰有云雷纹及双线“S”纹，这件编钟的雷纹等纹饰为中原等地出土的一些青铜礼器常见的一种纹饰。但是甬与内腔相通，正面有纹饰。喇叭状青铜器也为少见，其用途不明，可能也为广西百越族所铸造。但又有中原出土的青铜器的卷云纹、环带纹（似变形龙纹），环带纹盛行于西周中、后期。根据这些特征，时代约为西周中后期。“西周中期的钟，有干、旋、枚者，惟甬仍中空与内腔相通。”[③]

① 《诗经·大雅》，上海古籍出版社，1987年。

② 王锦:《柳州府志·物产》，卷十二，页一，乾隆二十九年出版。

③ 陈梦家:《西周铜器断代》，《考古学报》1956年第3期。

2010年柳江渡村出土带绳索形耳编钟，绳索形在武鸣县马头乡元龙坡147号墓出土于二层台上的铜卣，提梁作绳索状，提环饰牛头纹，扁圆腹，圈足。口盖及腹部饰夔纹。元龙坡墓葬中出土的铜卣、铜盘是可供比较的依据，对墓葬的断代具有重要意义。容庚先生认为，铜卣皆属西周前期以前之物，西周后期以后未见其器。在元龙坡部分墓中采集到的木炭标本，经北京大学考古系碳-14测试最早为距今2960±85年，最晚为距今2530±100年，上限为西周，下限在春秋时期[①]。“1963年在陕西长安县沣西马王村出土一件器身椭圆，有盖，盖有圆纽，圈足，口两侧有半环耳连以绹索提梁，中间为浮雕式的饕餮纹，两侧为云纹，上下围小圆圈纹，圈足饰变形饕餮纹。卣口、盖及腹部饰变形窃曲纹，可断为西周中晚期。”“田东大岭坡出土1件甬钟，高56、宽33.5厘米，重25千克，直筒甬，甬上有旋，旋上有干，钟体有36个乳钉状的枚，枚长有景，正面钲间、篆间布满精细的勾连雷纹和云纹，舞部于部也有精细的几何图案花纹，隧部饰夔龙纹，但是背面无纹饰。这种形制的甬钟在中原地区流行于春秋时期，正面有纹饰，背面无纹饰是岭南越式甬钟的特点”[②]。

1971年11月间，广西壮族自治区恭城县加会公社秧家大队的社员在秧家附近取土修路时，发现了一批青铜器。鼎5件，1式1件。圆口，沿下微束，附耳，深腹，圜底，马蹄足。耳内外、口下、腹部饰蟠虺纹各一道，腹部间以绳纹二道，腹下饰三角纹一道，膝上器饕餮纹，纹饰工整。通高55.5、口径57、足高20厘米。初步认为，这批青铜器的“年代属于春秋晚期或战国早期”[③]广东四会鸟旦山战国墓铜鼎1式，盘口内边缘有一对半环耳，做成绳状[④]。经分析与上述对比，柳江县这件铜钟除有枚、纽为绳索形外，没有繁缛的纹饰，正反为素面，我认为也应为岭南越式范围，从没有繁缛纹饰的钟来看，有可能已开始走向衰落，纽为绳索形，这一特征与中原青铜文化有着渊源关系。此钟年代应较晚，大约为春秋至战国时期较恰当。

（2）从征集少有的青铜角器来说主要纹饰有云雷纹、三角纹等。这种纹饰也是中原出土的一些商周青铜器中主要的纹饰，经故宫博物院杜廼松先生定为西周，该器物应为礼器（酒器）。以兽角饮酒乃一种古老的习俗。“我国古代饮酒用角之证。云南丽江纳西族在宴会时仍保存用牛角饮酒之俗。在云南弥勒、宜良等地彝族（撒尼人）他们过去也是“俗嗜酒……以角为杯”。在四川凉山及滇东北等地彝族之中，直到今日仍能见到这种牛角杯的实物”[⑤]（图一二）。以这些文字记载，有可能为南方少数民族铸造所用，那是哪个民族用的呢？还有现在所知的有贵州黔东南的苗族有身着盛装的苗族姑娘手捧雕刻精美图案的牛角盛满自家酿米酒对客人来到以“拦路敬酒”的习俗”[⑥]。

（3）太阳村横山出土的编钟，钲间饰有三角变形蝉纹、篆间饰斜角雷纹。“甬中空，与内腔相通，甬间方钮中有孔。饰有蝉纹是早期安阳殷墟出土的鸢卣的提梁上”[⑦]。之后，是商周青铜器纹饰之一，但那时的蝉纹头眼身纹齐全，四周填云雷

① 广西壮族自治区文物工作队:《广西码头元龙坡墓葬发掘简报》，《文物》1988年第12期。

② 蒋廷瑜:《桂岭考古论文集》，科学出版社，2008年，26、63页。

③ 广西壮族自治区博物馆:《广西恭城县出土的青铜器》，《考古》1973年第1期。

④ 广东省博物馆:《广东四会鸟旦山战国墓》，《考古》1976年第2期。

⑤ 林声:《试释云南晋宁石寨山出土铜片上的图画文字》，《文物》1964年第5期。

⑥ 力强:《奇特的迎客礼——拦路》，《民族画报》1987年第3期。

⑦ 容庚、张维持:《商周彝器通论》，文物出版社，1984年，137页。

图一二　贵州苗族拦路敬酒

纹，花纹繁缛，还有一种带有蝉足，也填云雷纹。盛行商至西周[①]。该钟的蝉纹已简化，与广西恭城县秧家出土的甬钟蚕纹饰有近似之处[②]，时代应为春秋晚期，该钟正面有纹饰，背面无纹饰，笔者根据蒋廷瑜先生与一些甬钟研究对比，认为这钟有岭南越式甬钟特点。但该钟又不为圆筒式，但又存在有一种南北文化的融合。

（4）征集的一把两面两侧有凹翼的青铜剑，在剑身铸有凹槽，在襄阳山湾东周墓有出土[③]。而在湖南长沙浏城桥一号墓出土藤柄铜矛凹槽相似，身铸凹槽但为蝉纹。该剑为变形蝉纹，时代约为春秋晚期至战国早期。

（5）征集的来宾青铜钺与桂林平乐银山岭报告图三八钺、鹿寨黄勉的斧与银山岭图三八钺[④]。与此相类似及长沙浏城桥一号墓图版拾叁，1木柄铜斧相似。该铜斧约为春秋中期至战国时期[⑤]。

① 金石：《青铜器》，《文物》1977年第7期。

② 湖北省博物馆：《襄阳山湾东周墓葬发掘报告》，《江汉考古》1983年第2期。

③ 湖南省博物馆：《长沙浏城桥一号墓》，《考古学报》1972年第1期。

④ 广西壮族自治区文物工作队：《平乐银山岭战国墓》，《考古学报》1978年第2期。

⑤ 湖南省博物馆：《长沙浏城桥一号墓》，《考古学报》1972年第1期。

五

中原青铜文化的传播探讨

从以上青铜器分析，不乏为中原文化的传播至南方百越民族的文化融合而百越民族又有独自发展。青铜文化的传播首先为黄河流域传播至长江流域的湖南后进至广西。1974年1月于武鸣县码头乡全苏村勉岭山麓出土一件铜卣，有提梁，有盖，器体呈椭圆形，下有圈足。通高40厘米，腹径横24厘米，纵19.4厘米，重10公斤。器表呈灰黑色，是所谓“黑漆古”。盖和身上四周都有高耸的扉棱，通体以云雷纹为地，饰三重花纹。盖面和腹部都是浮雕式的兽面纹，目、眉、耳突起，目似圆球，眉如卧蚕，眉尖突出器体外。盖的边缘、颈部、足部各装饰夔纹一圈，夔身上又饰以勾云纹。盖顶有纽，纽由6只蝉纹合成瓜棱形。提梁像一把弯弓，背面由两两相背的夔龙组成三角纹带，三角内又填饰蝉纹。提梁两端作成牛头形。全器构图严谨，刻镂精工。卣盖内有阴刻铭文“天”族徽。从造型、纹饰来看，与湖南宁乡王家坟山晚商戈卣很相似，不仅器形相同，连盖侧和腹侧所饰的扉棱、犄角均相同，只是戈卣所饰主要纹饰为凤鸟纹，勉岭卣腹部所是水牛角兽面纹。也与安阳殷墟出土的鸢卣近似，鸢卣提梁似蝉纹，两端作兽首形，遍体饰饕餮及夔纹，盖器内铭文各一字。因此可断为商代晚期，在广西铜器中还有是带有绹索形提梁卣及绳索形纽的编钟，装饰有变形蝉纹铜鼎、编钟等，这些都是北方青铜文化的南传影响无疑。在广西的北部、中部、南部皆有西周青铜器出土，从这些出土的器物来说至少在商代晚期或在这之前中原青铜文化传至广西。传播的路线，笔者认为应是由广西北部—中部—南部。

在广西出土铜钺有多种形状，如斜刃钺、梯形钺、靴形、双肩铲形、扇形、凤字形、圆刃形、荷包形。这些青铜器都富有浓厚的地域性。我国铜钺的出现大约在殷代。1952年，中国社会科学院考古研究所等单位在郑州市人民公园附近的殷代遗址出土有似几字纹饰、平肩、斜刃的铜钺①。1982年在山西蓝田县泄湖兀家崖三队社员平整土地发现西周墓葬，其中墓中出土1件内呈方形，刃作弧形，援两侧有透雕虎形装饰，虎形头部接近阑处各有一穿的青铜器②。1975年岗上公社台西大队褚志书捐献1件1972年在藁城台西村出土商后期饕餮兽面纹铁刃青铜钺③。以钺的解释，《说文解字》：“钺，大斧也。”西周时代的虢季子有“赐用钺用征蛮方”，古文献内也常见有关钺的记载，如《史记·殷本记》：“赐弓失斧钺使征伐”。广西发现的钺在受中原的影响，但也有仿中原青铜纹饰，如广西恭城县秧家大队出土的銎部饰雷纹靴形钺，时代为春秋晚期或战国早期④。最早在广西武鸣县马头乡元龙坡西周—春秋时期墓葬出土有钺等青铜器，同时有用红砂岩雕凿而成的双斜刃“风”字形钺、单斜刃钺等。另在灵川县发现有两面凿成“风”字形铜钺石范⑤。1962～1965年间，湖南省博物馆从长沙废铜仓库拣选的有16件铜钺，其中1件带三角纹；Ⅱ式与广西平乐银山岭报告图三三铜钺饰三角纹有相似之处，有异同。长沙拣选的10余件铜钺很可能为广西越族范围，在楚文物中是未见的⑥。本文征集的属“风”字形铜钺，形制与广西灵川县新岩遗址发现的铜钺石范形制相同，从广西发现的一些铜钺来看，应为地方所铸。

① 安至敏:《郑州市人民公园附近的殷代遗存》，《文物参考资料》1956年第3期。

② 樊维岳:《蓝田出土一组西周早期铜器》，《考古与文物》1987年第5期。

③ 河北省藁城县文物管理处台西考古队:《文物》1977年第6期。

④ 广西壮族自治区博物馆:《广西恭城县出土的青铜器》，《考古》1973年第1期。

⑤ 莫志东:《浅析灵川出土的铸铜石范》，《中国古代铜鼓研究通讯》第十七期。

⑥ 高至喜:《湖南发现的几件越族风格的文物》，《文物》1980年第2期。

广西百越青铜文化的探讨

Discussion on
Baiyue Bronze Culture in Guangxi

覃国宁 / 柳州市博物馆 副研究员

[摘要]

广西的青铜文化颇具地域特色，本文通过对广西出土的石范、青铜器的研究，通过诸多的考古资料及其丰富的青铜文化内涵，探讨百越青铜文化的发展历程，从而深刻地揭示广西百越青铜器在艺术、工艺、造型、纹饰等方面所蕴含的民族文化特色。

[关键词]

广西百越　青铜文化　探讨

Abstract

The Guangxi bronze ware is distinguished by the splendid Baiyue folk culture. It's a bright pearl and in the ancient Lingnan area and its inexhaustible cultural and material wealth is to be discovered. The thesis aims at researching a large amount of archaeology material and abundant cultural intension of Guangxi bronze ware, revealing the characteristic culture, art, handicraft, shaping and ornamentation. Therefore, it is significant to explore and discover the bronze ware.

Key words

Baiyue of Guangxi; Bronze culture; Research

在青铜器研究领域里，广西的青铜器颇具地域百越民族文化。众多的考古资料证明，广西百越青铜文化是中国古代青铜文化艺术宝库中的一颗熠熠生辉的明珠。广西出土的西周浮雕饰大铜钟、西周云雷纹角形杯、西周兽耳变形蝉纹铜罍、西周人面纹铜剑、西周喇叭形铜器、春秋“告”铭提梁铜鼎、春秋兽首柱形铜器、战国人面纹铜剑、战国靴形钺、汉代人面纹羊角纽钟、汉代人面纹、云纹鎏金铜棺、汉代羽人竞渡纹铜筒、汉代牛拉橇饰变形羽人纹铜鼓、汉代蛙负田螺饰“四出”钱纹铜鼓、汉代漆绘竹节纹提梁铜筒、汉代漆绘铜盆、汉代六博铜棋盘、汉代人形铜吊灯、汉代干栏式铜仓、汉代羽人铜灯、汉代动物雕饰池塘、新莽悬山顶干栏式铜仓等等杰出青铜艺术品，特别弥足珍贵，其文化、工艺、技术、造型、纹饰独具百越民族文化特色。给后人留下了取之不尽的文化艺术，无论岁月如何流逝，无论多少年过去，它的影响一直深入人心，给人以深刻之印象。这是广西古代百越族以无比智慧创造的并引以骄傲的卓著的璀璨绚烂的青铜精粹。一部广西史，满怀岭南情，广西是百越青铜文化的主要发祥地。据《汉书》记载：“自交趾至会稽七八千里，百粤杂处，各有种姓”。也就是说，从今天长江以南的沿海省份，直到越南北部的广袤地区，都曾是古越人生息繁衍的沃土。相传，越人的君王是大禹的后裔。夏后帝少康的儿子被封在会稽，看守祭祀大禹的陵墓。几千年来，绵绵瓜瓞繁衍成大大小小的古越民族：春秋时期有于越，战国时期有扬越，汉代有瓯越、闽越、南越、骆越，三国时期有山越……在中国历史上，此隐彼现，星罗棋布，史学家称“百越”。西瓯和骆越是“百越”中的两大重要支系。西瓯越人生活在今天广西西江中游及灵渠以南的桂江流域；骆越人聚居于今天广西的左右江流域、越南的红河三角洲及贵州省的西南部。历史上的瓯骆之地，地处亚热带，拥江临海，气候湿热，生息在这里的古越人“文身断发，以避蛟龙之害”，瓯骆越人创造了独具地域民族特色和无限魅力的青铜文化。

广西百越地区出土的锈蚀斑驳的青铜器以独特的外表及古朴典雅的造型、繁缛富丽的纹饰向人们展示着青铜文化的悠悠历史，承载着历史和沧桑的文化遗产，向人们讲述着广西百越族先秦时期祖先们的智慧、勤劳和勇敢。从广西田野考古发掘出土的文物资料来看，早在旧石器時代，广西地区就已经有了人类活动的文化遗存。进入新石器时代以后，广西的考古发现更是丰富多彩，陶器也开始出现。最能够体现瓯骆地区文化特色的，还是在本地出土的印纹陶和青铜器。广西地区的青铜文化同岭南其他地区一样：部分器物是直接从中原传入的；至于本地铸造的青铜器物，尚且吸收了比邻的滇、楚文化因素，制作精美、构思奇特、纹饰繁复，独树一帜。只是相较于中国其他青铜文化区，发展较为缓慢。春秋時期，以铸造简单的钺、剑、矛、弩机、镞等兵器和斧等生产工具为主。战国时期，则有铜鼓、人面纹铜剑等珍贵器物。1971年在广西恭城县加会发现的春秋晚期墓葬和1974年在广西平乐银山岭发掘的战国中晚期墓葬，都出土了大量青铜器和陶器。其中，扁茎短剑、双肩铲形钺及帶有水波纹、米字纹、刻画符号的陶器都是极具地域特色的。随着与中原地区经济、文化交流的增加，越人使用的器物，无论是器形还是纹饰，都出现了多元文化的意韵。其中，以状似短靴而得名的“靴形铜钺”最具代表性。钺，本是中原地区的青铜兵器，而靴形钺的独特造型，则鲜明地反映出中原文化与地域文化的交流、融汇。秦、汉时期，战事频仍。为避战乱，一些中原汉人迁徙移居岭南“与越杂处”，他们带来先进的文化和生产技术，促进了广西的社会进步。广西地区墓葬出土的先秦時期的青铜器，不仅品类丰富，而且数量较大，有炊器、酒器、乐器、兵器、工具等。所以对广西百越青铜文化的进一步发掘、整理和研究，至今仍存在着重要的现实意义。

一

具有一定规模的冶炼遗址

截至目前为止，广西的田野考古已发掘了一批西周、春秋、战国墓葬，但是，却尚未发现有西周、春秋、战国时期的冶炼和铸造遗址。现今发现的广西北流铜石岭遗址，乃为广西汉代的冶铜遗址。其范围2平方公里，已发掘出14个炼炉。出土文物有铜锭、炉渣、鼓风管、矿石等。1978年，通过考古发掘，在铜石岭冶铜遗址的山腰上，还发现采矿坑道，由于坑道塌方堵塞，考古人员无法进入。据说大约在20世纪60年代，广西壮族自治区地质局第六地质队在铜石岭调查时发现7个古矿井，并清理了3个古矿井，矿井深达20多米。矿道内残留有木头支架和铜石矿。经当时冶金部矿冶研究院对铜矿石化验分析，硅孔雀石含铜量为2.85%，孔雀石含铜量高达46.25%。“这种矿石，只要同木炭一起加热，就可以还原出铜来”。该遗址年代，经中国社科院考古研究所对出土的木炭进行测定，距今1910±90年，相当于西汉时期。

二

出土的青铜器石范

（一）商代石范

1. 那坡感驮岩石范

3件。1998年，广西文物工作队在那坡县城附近的感驮岩遗址进行考古发掘，在商代文化层中发现3件铸铜石范。其中第一件石范，编号为AT01，石范呈长方形，粉红砂

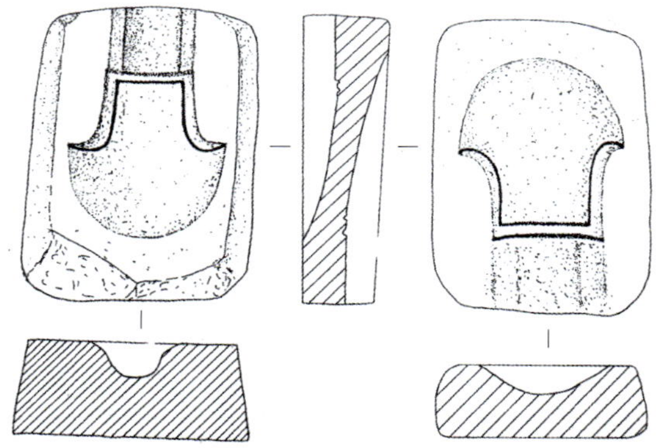

图一　双面铸铜钺石范

岩，长3.5、宽2、厚0.8厘米。背面凹凸不平，正面磨平，残留铸铜范模型，因残破严重，铸造器形难以辨认。第二件石范，编号为BT08，石范呈长方形，灰白色砂岩制成，长7、宽3.5、厚1.2厘米，背面呈弧形，正面磨平，有一个椭圆形的浇铸口，石范里面存在黑色浇铸残留。所铸之器似为刀类铜器。第三件石范，编号为AT36，长方楔形，一头大一头小，粉红砂岩，长4.4、宽3～4、厚1.8～2.2厘米，为小型工具的銎部之范芯。

2. 平南石脚山石范

1件。20世纪60年代发现，被认为是“商代遗物”。

（二）西周石范

1. 武鸣元龙坡石范

较完整的有6件。残碎的30余件。均为红砂岩质。计有双斜刃钺、单斜刃钺、扇形钺、斧、镦、镞、圆形器等铜器的石范。范呈长方椭圆形，正面磨平光滑，浇注口椭圆形。其中铜镞石范，内凿3件镞箭模型，由此可见，一模可铸造3支镞。石范还可以反复使用，大大提高了生产率，也反映了广西青铜文化已进入了发展的时期。

2. 灵川县新岩石范

5件。1993年，灵川县定江镇聚田村农民在新岩洞中取土，发现了石范，其中有铜钺石范4件，铜斧石范1件。伴随出土还有铜渣等，由此可见，此处可能是制造铜斧、铜钺的遗址。

（1）双面铸铜钺石范　3件。其中有2件残碎，但可复原。较完整的1件，长方形，长10.6、宽8、厚3.2厘米。系黄褐色砂岩制成。石范两面凿刻有风字形铜钺范模。浇注口呈椭圆形。这些石范至少一次可浇铸2件铜钺。从铜钺石范模型看，所铸的铜钺为风字形，钺身上部两侧呈弧形上翘，圆弧形刃。銎首扁圆形，銎身有一道凸棱（图一）。

（2）单面铸铜钺石范　1件。长方形，长8、宽6.7、厚3.5厘米。系用褐色细砂岩制成。石范正面凿刻铜钺模型，所铸铜钺也呈风字形，钺身上部两侧呈弧形上翘，圆弧形刃。銎首扁圆形，銎身有一道凸棱。石范背面弧形，打磨光滑。

（3）单面铸铜斧石范 1件。呈不规则的长方形，长8.9、宽8.8、厚3.2厘米。系用粉红色砂岩制成。石范正面凿刻铜斧模型，斧首扁圆形銎，斧身稍长，呈矩形，刃部圆弧形。石范背面呈弧形，打磨光洁。

三

独具特色的青铜器

大量的文献和考古实物资料业已证明，广西百越先民早已开启了灿烂的文明。而在文明起源和发展过程中，青铜器的铸造代表了当时广西社会的最高生产力和科技发展水平，促进了本地区农业、畜牧业、手工业和文化等多方面的进步与发展。广西百越青铜文化不仅深受中原地区青铜文化和滇、楚文化的影响，并且许多青铜艺术品多彩多姿，颇富地域百越民俗特色，具有重要的历史价值、艺术价值、科学价值和收藏价值，在中国和世界文化宝库中有着永恒的魅力，例如：

西周夔纹提梁铜卣 通高28.5、底径13.2×16.4厘米。圆垂腹带盖，盖顶有扁圆形捉手，盖面饰夔纹；颈部饰夔纹、弦纹，且腹部两侧有绳索纹提梁，圈足。现藏南宁市博物馆。

西周云雷纹角形杯 高21、口径 6.6×7.2厘米。器呈黄牛牛角状，两侧有范痕，器身图案用弦纹和几何纹隔开并分四个层次，其纹饰依次为云雷纹、云纹、云纹和三角纹。现藏柳州市博物馆。

西周兽耳变形蝉纹铜罍 通高39.5、口径20、腹径30厘米。鼓腹，圆形直口，短颈，带盖，盖顶有三环纽和圆形捉手，腹部饰变形蝉纹，其两侧有兽耳，圈足。现藏广西壮族自治区博物馆。

西周人面纹铜剑 体长23、刃宽4.6厘米。锋尖锐，叶形，体短，脊起棱，近格处脊上饰人面纹，扁茎呈丫状。现藏柳州市博物馆。

西周喇叭形铜器 高8.8、直径16.2厘米。器呈喇叭花状，握为圆棒形，其上饰云雷纹、蛇纹、弦纹等几何纹饰。现藏柳州市博物馆。

春秋“告”铭提梁铜鼎 通高28.5、口径23.5厘米。盘口，附耳被扭丝形提梁勾着，短颈，垂圆腹，内壁有“告”铭，平底，半圆形三足。现藏广西壮族自治区博物馆藏。

战国人面纹铜剑 体长39、刃宽6.2厘米。锋锐，刃部略宽为弧形，起脊，在脊上近格处饰有人面纹，扁茎。现藏柳州市博物馆。

战国靴形钺 高4.5、刃长5.5、刃宽2厘米。器呈靴形，素面。銎口圆。现藏柳州市博物馆。

汉代人面纹羊角纽钟　高19、底径8.1×14厘米。器呈半橄榄形，下大上小，顶部两侧各有一个外侈的角，上部中间有一长条形镂孔作穿，面饰人面纹。现藏广西壮族自治区博物馆。

汉代羽人竞渡纹铜筒　高47、口径63厘米、底径厘米。体呈筒形，腹部饰羽人纹、竞渡纹、几何纹等，且腹部两侧还饰有条状蛙形耳。（南宁藏家）

汉代牛拉橇饰变形羽人纹铜鼓　高59、面径82.4、足径83.5厘米。其圆形束腰中空，面沿四蛙、两蛙间各有一牛拉撬圆雕像，呈逆时针环列，鼓面饰太阳纹十二芒、变形羽人纹、变形翔鹭纹、弦纹；胸部凸出鼓面往下收敛成束腰，胸饰圆圈纹、弦纹、波浪纹及变形船纹；腰饰两对辫纹扁耳、一对环耳及变形羽人纹、同心圆圈纹、弦纹、波浪纹、几何纹；胫部渐大，饰菱形纹、弦纹、三角纹、几何纹，足外侈。现藏广西民族博物馆。

汉代骑士饰变形羽人纹铜鼓　高66.2、面径87.7厘米。其圆形中空，面沿四蛙，蛙间立圆雕乘骑和水鸟各一件，饰太阳纹十二芒，芒间坠形纹、变形羽人纹、变形翔鹭纹。鼓胸饰相背的船纹，辫纹扁耳两对。现藏广西民族博物馆。

汉代蛙负田螺饰“四出”钱纹铜鼓　高67.2、面径133.7、足径124.9厘米。其圆形中空，鼓面突出鼓胸，面沿六蛙负田螺顺时针环列，面饰太阳芒纹、晕间叠印“四出”钱纹、弦纹；肩、腰、胫部满饰成组的弦纹，肩腰部是两对扁耳，胫部一侧饰一圆雕虎。现藏广西玉林市博物馆。

汉代漆绘竹节纹提梁铜筒　通高42、口径14、底径13厘米。体修长呈竹筒形带盖，即面铸竹节纹，且漆绘有人物、鸟兽、植物等图案。腹上部还饰铺首连接有链的套环提梁。现藏广西壮族自治区博物馆。

汉代漆绘铜盆　高13.5、口径50、底径44.5厘米。折沿口，圆浅腹，且腹上有对称的四个铺首衔环，平底。其内壁及面分别饰漆绘鱼纹、龙纹和人物、奔马、禽兽图案。现藏广西壮族自治区博物馆。

汉代六博铜棋盘　高9、长30厘米。盘面为长方体,其面饰有阴刻的几何线条纹，“T”字形四足。现藏广西壮族自治区博物馆藏。

汉代跽坐人俑铜吊灯　俑高13.5、灯盘口径9.5厘米。人俑跽坐着，且双手扶着搭至腿上的圆形浅腹灯盘，故此，灯盘仅铸一足，另外，人俑前额有一环纽套着垂直的环链，其上有钩用于悬挂。现藏广西昭平县文物管理所。

汉代干栏式铜仓　通高37.3、面阔79.3、进深42.7厘米。悬山顶，仓作长方体，门前左右有护栏，平底。现藏广西壮族自治区博物馆。

汉代柿蒂纹人形足铜盘　高7.5、面径37.5厘米。盘心用阴线细刻秀美的柿蒂纹间二鹿二凤纹，然后依次为弦纹、云锦纹、菱形纹、三角纹，风格富丽华美而纤巧；三足作人形蹲踞承盘状。现藏广西壮族自治区博物馆。

汉代动物雕饰池塘 1件，近正方形，开口宽，往下略有收分，至底每边收分1.6厘米。开口前后长54.8、左右宽52.4、高7.6厘米。后挡板上方有两排水口，圆形，其中一个有榫头堵塞。池中有圆雕凤鸟、鹅、鱼、青蛙等多群动物模型。凤鸟4只作站立状，低首翘尾，头上有翎，毛羽阴线刻画自然流畅；鹅6只，其身体浑圆，肥胖可鞠。颈背及腹部用长短线和片状阴线细刻羽毛。6只鹅之形状，一种颈部伸直，头向前张望，另一种颈部弯曲至背部，作梳理羽毛状。鱼1条，其唇、眼、鳃、鳍、尾部及鳞片等用阴线刻画。青蛙2只，其形制大小有些许差别，造型较抽象，头三角形，柱状目凸出，不同的部位之间用阴刻斜短线分隔。现藏合浦县博物馆藏。

汉代龙首三眼长方形铜灶 通高72、上宽23、下宽27、灶高18厘米。体呈长方体，头部饰龙首，长方体上饰有三眼，上置三个铜釜。现藏广西壮族自治区博物馆。

新莽悬山顶干栏式铜仓 通高54、面阔58、进深42厘米。悬山顶，仓作长方体。正面精雕细刻人形、凤鸟、兽面、虎细线刻纹以及兵器戈等；左面装饰树形灯、人形、羽翎细线刻纹；背面装饰树形羽翎、凤鸟、虎、小兽细线刻纹；右面装饰龙凤细线刻纹；正面有一扇方形门，有藕节四柱足。现藏合浦县博物馆藏。

广西考古发现的百越青铜器很多，以上仅列出具有代表性器物。

四

青铜制作工艺的探讨

广西百越青铜器上的纹饰装饰，饱含着自然、生动、奔放、纯朴、野性、温柔的个性，体现了广西古代百越先民的智慧和高超的制作工艺以及独特的思维方式。流传下来的各种纹饰装饰，数量多、种类多，形式各异，其蕴藏着深厚的、浓郁的百越民族之风格特征和文化内涵，宛若诠释着岭南古老百越族历史优美画卷的精美篇章，是我们今天了解广西地域社会状况及百越族先民文化特征和发展的重要依据，体现了广西古代百越人的无穷的创造力和对美的执著追求，这种别具风格的纹饰，直到今天仍然散发着强烈的艺术魅力，具有高度的审美艺术价值。

（1）从纹饰装饰内容来看，广西所发现的青铜器纹饰有兽面纹、凤鸟纹、夔纹、云雷纹、龙纹、蛇纹、重环纹、云纹、蟠螭纹、蟠虺纹、人面纹、蝉纹、变形蝉纹、几何纹、锯齿纹、人物、画像纹、弦纹、羽人纹、蛙纹、太阳纹、同心圆纹、栉纹、翔鹭纹、鱼纹、云锦纹、回纹、勾连云纹、复线交叉纹、乳丁纹、船舶纹、缠枝花纹、瑞兽纹、柿蒂纹、螺旋纹、虺纹、山字纹、波浪纹、网纹、绹纹、绳纹、铺首纹、象纹、猴纹、牛纹、羊纹、熊纹、舞人纹、四神规矩纹、云山海兽纹、虎纹，树形纹、羽翎纹、五铢钱纹、“四出”钱纹、铭文纹等。这些纹饰题材多数取自本区域的自然、人文、动植物等，既反映了民族青铜文化的特点，也显示了民族精神的寄托。如独占鳌头的广西铜鼓，其古朴雄奇，体积硕大，铸造精湛，造型别致，题材众多，纹饰繁缛富丽，有着浓郁的地域风貌，蕴藏着深厚的民族文化内涵，现藏广西民族博物馆。这些非常可贵的铜鼓，题材形式各异，纹饰多姿多彩，争奇斗艳，如有大自然神圣的光明之源——太阳芒纹，是祈求幸福吉祥的纹饰；变形羽人竞渡船纹，则再现了广西古代百越人有头插羽毛和赛龙舟的民族习俗。此外，乘骑、牛拉橇、喂马饰、蛙饰、鸭饰、龟饰、田螺饰等圆雕，再现了当时的物质生活和农耕的状况，而鱼纹、翔鹭纹、鸟纹、水波纹等，亦折射了广西古代社会美丽无比的大自然风光。这些史实和丰富的社会背景，能够装进一件件铜鼓青铜乐器、礼器之中，流芳青史，不能不说这是古代广西百越人艺术创造的辉煌。当然，这些铜鼓艺术品，深刻地体现了古代广西贵族的政治意愿和审美情感。

（2）从青铜器的类型来看，广西所发现的百越青铜器，种类繁多，器型各异。有西周时期的尊、罍等酒器，钺、戈、矛、刀、镞、匕首、镦等兵器，钟、铃等乐器以及斧、凿、盘、针、链环、喇叭形器、圆形器、角形器等。春秋时期有食用器、酒器、兵器（戈、钺、剑、镞）、乐器编钟、工具斧、兽首柱形器等。战国时期有食用器鼎、盆、钵、勺，酒器有尊、盉、罍，乐器有鼓、钹、钟、玲、羊角纽钟，兵器有剑、矛、钺、弩机、镞、戈、匕首，工具有斧、锛、凿、刮刀、削、钻头、锯片以及带钩、手镯、钏、兽首柱形器、杖头饰、码角器、盖弓帽等。西汉时期有食用器鼎、釜、鍪、甑、锅、甗、簋、盒、碗、钵、盆、勺，酒器有壶、钫、盉、魁、樽、鐎斗、杯、卮、案，乐器有鼓、钟、铃，兵器有剑、矛、镞、弩机、戟、刀、弹丸，工具有斧、铲、削，水器有盘、三足盘、鉴、方匜、洗、筒桶，车马器有镫、铃以及臼、杵、俑、镜、镜刷把、牌饰、扣饰、屋、仓、灯、灶、井、镇兽、铺首环、马、牛、狗、鸟、鹅、鱼、青蛙、池塘、熏炉、博山炉、带钩、印、尺、环、熨斗、弓帽、盖弓帽、五铢钱等。东汉时期有食用器鼎、釜、锅、盆、鉴、簋、钵、筷子、盒、碗、小碟、勺、豆，酒器有壶、鐎斗、樽、杯，兵器有剑、矛、刀、弩机、镞、镦，乐器有鼓、钟、铙、铃，工具有削，水器有洗、盘，车马器有镫以及博山炉、灯、镜、镜刷把、尺子、鸠杖、戒指、顶针、带钩、手镯、簪、匽、钉、三脚架、印等。

(3)从青铜器铸造工艺来看，广西出土的百越青铜器，制作精良，工艺高超。

从目前考古发现的石范来看，广西最早在商代已能制造青铜器，正如蒋廷瑜先生在《试论岭南早期青铜器铸范》一文中所指出的那样：“众多石范的出土，一方面说明岭南地区在距今3000年前就有自己的青铜铸造技术，另一方面又说明这种铸造技术相当原始，而且1000多年没有明显的变化。”由此可见，广西的青铜文化历史悠久，源远流长。正如黄启善先生在《广西青铜文化研究》一文中指出“广西青铜文化尽管受中原青铜文化的影响，但它在发展过程中，自始至终，都带有浓厚的民族文化色彩”。如独具地域民族特色的神秘的人面纹羊角纽钟、铜剑，是人们在劳动中逐渐产生并追求的结果。广西出土的战国人面纹铜剑、汉代人面纹羊角纽钟，乃国之珍宝，其人面纹装饰精美细腻，独具地域风貌，是古代广西百越地区的标志性文化之一。它是人体的图腾崇拜？或是有“人通天神”的寓意？疑惑是纪念祖先的理念？还是人丁兴旺的向往？这些无不撩拨着人的情感，引发人们无限的想象。这是古代百越民族文化的结晶，反映了他们对人丁兴旺和幸福生活的无限向往，寄托着自己的审美理想。不同的地域有着不同的审美标准，人面纹青铜剑、羊角纽钟也体现青铜文化由北向南风格的衍化和出新，标志着百越文化青铜器逐步趋向创新和臻善。

尤其是精雕细刻的錾刻花纹工艺，更是广西青铜文化的精髓，为百越地区先民所独创所仅有的。正如蒋廷瑜先生所说：汉代錾刻花纹艺术，源自岭南，“尤其是广西东南部，应是汉代錾刻花纹铜器的制作中心和主要生产地”[①]。柳州市博物馆馆藏——汉代柿蒂纹铜盘所装饰的图案就是用錾刻花纹来装饰的。盘高6.3、直径37.8厘米；盘底纹饰繁缛富丽，盘中上刻柿蒂纹，周围依次装饰鸟纹、雁翎、弦纹、三角纹、云锦纹等，兽形三足。综观广西各市博物馆及文物管理所所藏汉代青铜器，一定数量的汉代錾刻花纹青铜器的发现，不仅拓展了人们对我国古代錾刻纹青铜器分布的认识，并且细致生动的描绘方式所折射出的广西百越汉代社会的生活内容的艺术画面和生动活泼的审美情趣，是研究广西汉代历史和社会形态的宝贵的丰富资料。广西汉代的青铜艺术，是广西百越先民智慧的结晶，是我们祖先留给我们的一份珍贵遗产，以科学的态度分析和继承这份珍贵的文化遗产，将对我们了解中华民族悠久的人类文明历史进程和精神文化内容有着特殊的重要性。

① 蒋廷瑜:《汉代錾刻花纹铜器研究》，《考古学报》2002年第3期。

五

青铜文化与民族文化的融合

广西古代百越地区不仅有着一派绿水青山和旖旎无限的风光，更有着独特的民族习俗。特别令人瞩目的西周人面纹铜剑、西周云雷纹角形杯、战国靴形钺、汉代人面纹、云纹铜棺、汉代干栏式铜仓、新莽悬山顶干栏式铜仓、汉代羽人竞渡纹铜筒、汉代羽人纹乘骑铜鼓、汉代划船纹栉纹铜鼓、汉代羽人翔鹭纹铜鼓、汉代羊角纽钟等，都是十分珍贵的反映百越地区民族文化的典型实物资料。

虽然现在早已时过境迁，许多不同的种族也已变异融合，但是，我们仍然能够通过上述丰富的考古实物资料了解到百越族独特的风俗风貌和文化。如西周人面纹铜剑的辫发之像；西周云雷纹角形杯的牛角杯饮酒习俗；汉代干栏式铜仓、新莽悬山顶干栏式铜仓的干栏式建筑模型也是显著的主题，其再现了百越族的居住建筑习俗；汉代羽人竞渡纹铜筒装饰的羽人纹，即头戴羽毛饰物，亦为历代百越族的普遍爱好；汉代羽人纹乘骑铜鼓的乘骑反映了戎装骑士、骑马与马的造型，这也表明了百越族人极善养马，在汉代马是他们所钟爱的财富，家马已成为主要乘骑，而骑马亦是其民族之风俗；汉代划船纹栉纹铜鼓的船纹，可见竞舟之俗；汉代羊角纽钟为伴奏乐器，是广西古代百越族乐队演奏的主要形式。耐人寻味的是，广西出土了数百件历代铜鼓，而铜鼓是乐器及重要礼器，毫无疑问，祭祀铜鼓，跳铜鼓舞，是其百越民族喜闻乐见的舞蹈形式之一，其民俗功能有铜鼓崇拜、以鼓求雨、作葬具、祭祖、祭神、祈求丰收等方面。

不同的地域，有着不同的居住民族及其风俗文化。事实证明，华夏文明事实上也是在广泛吸收周边民族文化的基础上发展起来的，它又通过民族与文化互动融合将中原文明传播到周边民族地区。广西百越族创造了优秀的青铜文化艺术，而其风俗文化之影响也是巨大而深远的。

六

结　语

综观广西百越地区上古的青铜艺术，堪称祖国多民族文化艺术中一颗耀眼的明珠。所以深刻地揭示广西百越青铜文化、艺术、工艺、造型、纹饰独具地域民族特色文化，是广西文物研究者任重而道远的责任，而对于它的进一步发掘、整理和研究，至今，仍存在着重要的现实意义。

广西铜器珍品简论

A Brief Review of Precious Bronze Wares in Guangxi

何英德 / 桂林博物馆 研究员

[摘要]

广西铜鼓在世界数量最多，堪称世界一流。笔者通过精选国家一级文物，通过铜鼓、麒麟铜尊、铜针等一些比较珍贵的文物，以事实说明广西并非南蛮之地，从商末周初至战国汉代，广西铜器不乏珍品，通过微型研究，让精湛的铜器制作技术在我国科技史上占有一席之地。

[关键词]

翔鹭纹铜鼓　麒麟铜尊　铜针

Abstract

The South China's Guangxi Autonomous Region has rich cultures and long history as well as abundant cultural relics of ethnic groups, especially renowned for bronze drums. The Guangxi bronze drums could rank at the first in the world on its quantity and quality. The author here tries to prove that Guangxi is not a barbarous place through studying the precious cultural relics like bronze drums, bronze wine vessels decorated with Chinese unicorn and bronze needles, all of which are under national protection. There are quite a few treasures of Guangxi bronze drums dating back through the late Sang Dynasty to the early Zhou Dynasty, the Warring Period to the Han Dynasty, which could parallel with the national bronze drums. It aims to help Guangxi people to regain their national confidence and self-esteem through this micro study. Guangxi is an autonomous region with various minorities and Guangxi people have been brave, diligent and intelligent since long ago. Guangxi should obtain its own position in the cultural history of China's minorities. And the superb skills of making bronze drums are important components in the scientific history of our country.

Key words

Bronze Drum with Flying-ardeidae Pattern; Kylin-shaped Bronze Zun; Bronze needle

广西地处岭南，商末周初至战国汉代就有青铜器而且精品也不少，本文例举几件青铜器来略谈广西青铜文化在我国青铜文化中的地位。

所谓青铜时代，就是指掌握青铜冶炼和铸造技术广泛制作和使用青铜时代；中国青铜文化起源于史前时期。文献记载的黄帝铸鼎，蚩尤作铜兵就是对那个时代人们走向青铜时代门槛的经典代表。岭南青铜时代起源于商末周初，虽然没有中原青铜时代、西南三星堆时代的青铜器那么突出，但也不乏有些青铜精品，也折射出岭南商末周初青铜文化的繁荣。尤其是进入战国汉代，岭南文化的青铜器的铜鼓、羊角纽钟以及其他铜器可以反映青铜铸造的几种主要工艺，这些工艺有范铸法（如石范）、失蜡法、错金银工艺、镶嵌红铜工艺等。中国古代青铜器的形制演变分为五期。第一期：发祥期，即夏至早商。第二期：勃兴期，即晚商至周初。第三期：规范和鼎盛期，即西周早中期。第四期：持恒和衰落期，即西周晚期。第五期：转型期，即春秋、战国及其以降[①]。故岭南青铜器精品按照中国古代青铜器的分期应归到第三或第五期比较合适。

一

民族瑰宝——翔鹭纹铜鼓

翔鹭纹铜鼓，现收藏于广西壮族自治区博物馆，该鼓鼓面小于鼓胸，胸部膨大凸出，腰部收缩为圆柱形，足部扩张，大于腰，面径56.4、通高36.8、足径67.8厘米，在铜鼓分类中属石寨山类型。鼓面中心有太阳纹十二芒，芒外七晕圈，饰栉纹、勾连雷纹、翔鹭和锯齿纹，主晕为十只衔鱼飞翔的鹭鸟。鼓身九晕圈，饰有锯齿纹、圆圈纹、龙舟竞渡和羽人舞蹈图案。第四晕圈在胸部，饰有六组羽人划船纹，船头向右，每船六人，其中三船的划船者全戴羽冠，另三船各有一人裸体；船头正下方有衔鱼站立的鹭鸶和花身水鸟，水中有游动的鱼。第六晕圈在腰部，饰八组羽人舞蹈纹，间隔以绳纹、锯齿纹、同心圆圈纹带。每组二至三人，舞人头戴羽饰，下身系展开的羽裙，两臂外伸，五指张开，掌心向外，上身向后倾斜，两腿叉开，作翩翩起舞状。舞人的上空有一或二只衔鱼的翔鹭。鼓足一侧卧刻隶书“百廿斤”（铜鼓重量，实测为30750克）。1991年1月，经全区馆（所）专家审定认为：翔鹭纹铜鼓出自西汉时期墓葬，时代准确，是此类铜鼓断代的标准器。铜鼓保存完好，纹饰清晰，构图严谨，图案精美，工艺水平很高，是石寨山型晚期的代表作，定为一级藏品[②]（图一）。

大家知道铜鼓起源于云南，后来逐渐传到广西，并在广西得到了进一步发展。

① 张辛:《中国古代青铜的礼学观察》，《中国文物报》2004年7月20日。

② 李伟东、潘郁生:《民族瑰宝——翔鹭纹铜鼓》，《广西日报》2006年11月2日。

图一　翔鹭纹铜鼓

铜鼓集冶炼、铸造、绘画、雕塑、音乐、舞蹈于一身，是南方古代民族特有的综合艺术品。铜鼓文化源远流长，融合政治、经济、文化于一体，两千余年绵延不绝，直到今天，我们仍可在许多民族村寨领略到它的奇异风采。

铜鼓是西瓯、骆越的重器，他们不仅用铜鼓伴舞节乐，还曾把它作为权力和财富的象征，舍生忘死地去追求它和占有它；又把它视为“神器”，以为它有消灾赐福的功能，对它顶礼膜拜，让它主宰祸福。广西不仅拥有种类最齐全、数量最多的铜鼓，而且还拥有世界上最大的铜鼓，是当之无愧的“铜鼓之乡”。

铜鼓分万家坝、石寨山、冷水冲、遵义、麻江、北流、灵山、西盟共8个类型[①]。目前世界上仅存2000多面馆藏铜鼓，东兰县有传世铜鼓612面。为全球民间收藏铜鼓之最。东兰县的民间藏鼓、护鼓、养鼓、祭鼓、埋鼓、请鼓、赛鼓、舞鼓之风依然盛行，被誉为铜鼓文化的“活化石”[②]。

1995年11月，经国家文物局全国一级藏品专家确认组研究决定，认为这面贵县罗泊湾一号墓出土的翔鹭纹铜鼓，对研究古代少数民族历史、文化有特别重要的意义。翔鹭纹铜鼓，现在学术界似乎众口一词定为“翔鹭纹”，其实将它定为翔鹭纹的文化定位范围太窄，不一定反映出该地区文化的历史真实面貌，倒不如定为“仙鹤纹”更为科学，更为恰当。因为上古“仙鹤纹”的崇拜是环太平洋文化区的文化现象。例如东南亚各国以及北到辽东半岛、朝鲜、韩国，甚至日本都有这么一个古老的大同小异的“仙鹤变新娘”的历史传说，这些地区存在的这一历史传说，它的故事梗概是这样的。从前一个男子赶圩归来，在路上碰到一只从天上掉下来受伤的仙鹤，男人将它抱回家抚养。结果当他每天外出的时候，仙鹤马上变成一个姑娘，帮男人织布。有一天，男人突然转回家中，看见仙鹤拔出自己的羽毛来给自己织布，便就有“仙鹤变新娘”的历史传说，此后仙鹤变成了男人的妻子。如果将“仙

① 浙江省博物馆:《鼓声悠远——广西瓯骆文化遗粹》，文化艺术出版社，2007年，73页。

② 刘昆、李静:《陈耀灵与首家民间铜鼓博物馆》，《光明日报》2011年4月19日。

鹤纹”放到南环太平洋文化区当中去考虑，这样仙鹤纹比翔鹭纹解释更为科学，更为恰当，更为符合历史事实。因为仙鹤的传说可以追溯到2000年前的汉代，刚好与铜鼓历史上的花纹时代更为适合。因为这种有长长的嘴、长长的脚的鸟，尔说为鸟，吾说为鹤，很难说清楚，笔者以为定为仙鹤纹更符合科学的结论，也更便于还原它原来的历史真面目。

再如西林粮站铜鼓墓出土的四面铜鼓大小互相套叠，编号为208、281、283号的铜鼓也同样是精品！

280号鼓，是四面铜鼓中最大的一面。出土时已被从胸腰相接处截断，套在最外一层，面径77.5、高52、胸径85.6、腰径71、足径90厘米。纹饰精美，鼓面13晕，中心太阳纹16芒，芒间填斜线，第2、3、4晕为勾连点纹带，第5晕为勾连云纹，第6晕素面，第7晕饰20只翔鹭，逆时针旋转飞翔，构成一个美丽的流动花环，第8、3晕为勾连圆点纹、锯齿纹夹勾连圆圈纹；鼓胸上部与鼓腰下部饰6组船纹，每船有8至11人，在船台前者戴羽冠，其余均项髻，其中立者上裸，腰系两幨，坐者全裸，划桨；船间有鸬鹚或鱼，显示船在水中的环境；腰部被圆点纹、锯齿纹夹羽状纹纹带纵向分隔成12格，每格又被勾连圆圈纹带横格成上下两层，上层饰鹿纹，每格有鹿2只或3只，公母相配，昂首嗷嗷；下层饰羽人舞蹈纹，每格2人，均戴羽冠，腰系吊幨，摆手扭腰；腰下部饰圆点纹、锯齿纹夹勾连圆圈纹。一级文物，现藏广西壮族自治区博物馆。

281号鼓，是四面铜鼓中次大的一面，完整无损。面径72、身高49、足径83.3厘米，鼓面纹饰已锈蚀，只见中心太阳纹14芒，芒间饰斜线角形纹。鼓身纹饰也已锈蚀，隐约可见胸部有船纹，腰部有翔鹭纹和羽人舞蹈纹，羽人也头戴高羽冠，腰系吊幨，摆手扭腰而舞，羽人头上的翔鹭则展翅冲天而飞；在鼓胸的上下部和鼓腰的分格间饰锯齿纹、同心圆纹、羽状纹组成的纹带。一级文物，原藏广西壮族自治区博物馆，1989年调藏中国国家博物馆①。

贵县罗泊湾一号汉墓是1976年6月发现的。对于墓主的身份和族属问题，只能根据墓葬的形制和规模、出土器物的种类和数量及其形制和纹饰等推断。目前主要有三种意见：一是认为墓主“可能是北方来的汉族官吏”（以下简称“汉族说”）；二是认为罗泊湾一号汉墓和二号汉墓是“西瓯君夫妇墓”（以下简称“西瓯说”）；第三是“认为应是南越国分封于当地的异姓诸侯”，而且“应为骆越的首领人物”（以下简称“骆越说”）。对于墓主的身份，三种意见都认为是当地一个地位很高的统治者，而对墓主的族属，则意见分歧较大。笔者同意汉族说，认为墓主应是南越王派到当地的北方来的身任武职的汉族高级官吏。析是地名，在今河南，一说是番禺省，在今广州。可以看出罗泊湾一号汉墓墓主不过是把铜鼓当成是日常的一般生活用具，不具权力和地位的含意，罗泊湾一号汉墓墓主不可能是当地土著居民骆越

① 广西西林县委宣传部、广西西林县博物馆：《句町遗韵》（内部），12、13页。

的首领人物，而是来自北方的汉族高级官吏。“是越女从夫姓”罗泊湾一号汉墓人殉棺盖上刻写的“胡偃”和“苏偃”，“胡偃”、“苏偃”不是殉葬越伎的本名，而是墓主人以中原地区惯用的人名为他的越族奴婢取的名字。正是由于殉人的越族成分和她们的汉族名字“透露”了墓主为汉族的“信息”[①]。

西林县在汉代属句町，句町设县是在汉武帝元鼎六年（前111年）。从句町在汉代的活动情况来看，他们至迟是在战国时代，或许在“庄蹻王滇”之前就到了云贵高原。到汉代，句町的活动地域已包括现在云南的富宁和广西的西林、隆林、田林、百色、凌云一带。

1969年冬，西林县政府修筑西林至田林的公路。12月15日下午，一个民工举锄落地碰上一件硬器，发现地下有异常的响声，像是敲铜鼓的声音，便兴奋地喊道：“我挖到宝了。”公社领队和公路指挥部的同志次日到工地观看铜棺。只见铜棺为长方形，长约2、宽约0.66、高约0.7、棺板厚0.17米，内外表面全部鎏金，棺上镶有虎头、人面、云纹，十分漂亮。铜人面具8个，只收回5个，此外还收回虎头1件，玉环1件，破碎玉环4件，4个跪俑以及不少的玉管和玛瑙。从普驮铜鼓墓出土的最有价值的文物就算是铜骑马俑和六博棋盘了。其中的四个铜俑和六博棋盘是典型的中原造型风格，这四个铜俑和六博棋盘现珍藏于广西壮族自治区博物馆，每个俑的高度大约在10厘米，都着宽袖长裙，双膝跪地地向后而坐，是秦汉时代最流行的装束和坐姿。那么在随葬品中，四个铜俑反映的是什么场面，它们是做什么用的呢？专家分析认为，四个俑呼三喝四的造型，正是对弈六博棋的情景。

据考证，六博传入广西时，是在贵族阶层人员中首先展开的一种娱乐，因此用六博铜俑和棋盘随葬的墓主人，地位是很高的。而在该墓葬中发现的四面铜鼓更能说明这一点。铜鼓是我国古代南方兄弟民族的珍贵重宝，在《隋书·地理志》中说：“有鼓者号为都老，群情推服”。用铜鼓给死者做葬具，自然更是不寻常的事。那么这个墓主人到底是什么身份的人呢？据记载：得鼓二、三，便可潜号称王。就是说有两、三面铜鼓，你就可以当一个地方王了，所以这有四面铜鼓陪葬的墓，因为它的规格很高，应是句町王的墓葬。

铜骑马俑，四个铜俑和六博棋盘已被国家文物局全国一级藏品专家确认组定为一级藏品[②]。

考古学上，两广地区受云南地区文化影响最大最明显的莫过于船纹铜鼓了。在南越王墓中出土有9件大小不一的铜提筒，一般认为是骆越人的盛酒器，其中一件提筒腹部共绘有4只船纹，每只船内有6人，其中5人均头戴羽冠，身穿羽裙，动态大同小异。羽人船形纹饰在两广云贵等地出土的青铜器特别是铜鼓的发源地在云南中部偏西地区。在滇池地区成熟。同时沿着巨川大河向南、东、北三个方向流传。影响到我国南方和东南亚一大片古老的民族地区。我国当时存在的1400多面铜鼓中，只

① 邱明：《略论罗泊湾一号墓墓主的族属》，《广西文物》1987年第1期。

② 李伟东、潘郁生：《神秘的西林普驮铜鼓墓葬》，《广西日报》2006年12月18日。

有27面饰有船纹，在越南还有13面船纹铜鼓。借助于伴出物和考古研究的成果，可知船纹铜鼓出现的年代上限在战国前期。下限在西汉末。船纹的分布情况是：云南晋宁9面、江川3面、文山、广南、金平、麻栗坡、云县、腾冲各1面；广西西林、贵县各2面；四川会理及贵州赫章各1面。

国外的船纹铜鼓，大都发现于越南北部，基本上分布在红河三角洲，越南的近邻老挝等也偶有发现。与南越王墓时代大体相当或略早。认为船纹反映的是小船而非大船，一般只有4至6人，何大之有？是内河船而非渡海船。云南是铜鼓及船纹的发源地，南越王墓出土的骆越人的船纹铜提筒，充分反映出滇文化对南越国的影响[①]。

另外，广西发现的青铜钺有双肩铲形，凤字形，短鞋形，斜刃形，单斜刃形，靴形等多种形式[②]。尤其是靴形铜钺，是与浙江省的靴形钺有关联的。它源于浙江省长兴县博物馆馆藏的商代几何纹青铜钺[③]。宁波博物馆也有一把战国青铜靴形钺，与广西出土的靴形钺有惊人的相似，所以我认为：青铜钺应源于浙江一带，而后传到广西。由此可见，东瓯文化的南传，西瓯文化当中有一些东瓯文化的因素，可以窥探出民族迁徙的蛛丝马迹。

我们从民族古文献资料来考证一些与铜鼓有关作用问题，例如：《壮族麽经布洛陀影印译注》的《麽送方》篇有这么一段话："一天（铸）一面两面（鼓），就成铜鼓口宽大（倒装：就成宽大的一口鼓），就成铜鼓口外翘（倒装：就成向外翘的一口铜鼓）……敲你（指铜鼓，下同）挡鬼妖茅草（茅草中的鬼妖），敲你吓鬼神柴(树中的鬼神)，敲你讲给布道，敲你报给仙人。"这段话的意思是：一天造出一到两面铜鼓，铜鼓的鼓面宽大，鼓身向外翘出，人们敲铜鼓来挡住茅草中的鬼妖，吓跑树中的鬼神，敲铜鼓给布道（道公或麽公）知道，给仙人知道。《壮族麽经布洛陀影印译注》的《布洛陀造方唱本》："跟随唢呐和号角，人哪个办喜事大（大喜事），就吹号撑旗，做礼箩或做礼担，撑旗及吹唢呐……吹唢呐号角过路。"这段话的意思是：哪一家办大喜事，就请来唢呐手，挑着装礼品的担子，跟着唢呐和号角上路。《壮族麽经布洛陀影印译注》中的《铜源歌》："摇次铜铃第一，莫让头领压制地方，莫让王（地方首领）压制村寨；摇次铜铃第二，稻谷畲地给（长）齐肩，稻谷水田给（长）齐额头。" 这里说的是摇了两次铜铃，第一次摇铜铃是不给地方首领压制地方，第二次摇铜铃是祈求稻谷丰收。从这些麽经的话语中看出，古时候的壮族民间铜乐器，在当时是有作用的[④]。此墓的墓主人应是汉族或骆越西瓯君主？我们从布洛陀的《麽送方》的话中可以窥见一斑。从布洛陀的麽送方中的内容来看，此面铜鼓应似乎与壮人先人或多或少也有一点关系。

《史记》、《汉书》记载，在岭南早期发生的三件重大历史事件，一是秦始皇发50万"楼船之士"统一岭南。二是原秦将赵佗在汉高祖四年（前203年）在岭南的桂林、南海、象郡建立南越国，南越国传五世共93年。三是汉武帝元鼎六年（前111

① 周永卫:《南越王墓银盒舶来路线考》，《考古与文物》2004年第1期。

② 广西第三次文物普查领导小组办公室:《广西第三次文物普查基础知识读本》，广西科学出版社，2008年，47页。

③《中国博物馆志·浙江卷》，文物出版社，2010年，47页。

④《收藏》2009年第10期，封面图解。

年）派楼船将军等灭南越，攻陷南越都城番禺，汉兵“纵火烧城”，广西出土的青铜器应放到当时发生的历史事件当中去考虑，才能得出准确的历史答案。

二

春秋战国 —— 麒麟铜尊

麒麟铜尊，1991年广西贺县沙田乡龙中村岩洞墓葬出土，现藏广西壮族自治区贺县博物馆。这件铜尊张颌露齿，双目圆睁，双耳、双角直立。角呈圆柱形，饰蝉纹，内侧面各分出一支角，与长颈鹿形状类似。鼻梁和鼻孔用卷云纹、涡纹勾出。背部开椭圆形口，有盖，盖前端有双耳套链，与颈背环纽相连。盖面浮雕盘蛇，蛇身饰三道鳞纹，居中蛇首昂起形成盖纽。器颈部和腹部饰变形兽面纹，衬以雷纹地。器尾为一直立攀附的龙，单角，圆眼张吻，身饰葵叶形凹鳞纹。内底平，下承以四兽足。足外圆内弧。高53.7、长48、宽24厘米（图二）。此器器形和纹饰风格均受到中原文化影响，但形体更加矮壮，盖上浮雕盘蛇及尾部饰龙均属罕见，表现出浓厚的越文化特征，此器曾入选1993年中国文物精华展[①]。

麒麟铜尊可与山西西翼城大河口西周墓地出土的铜鸟形盉相媲美。在西周至春秋早期墓地中，该墓地规模之大，保存之好，时间之长，规格之高在全国罕见，

① 韦浩民：《贺江：昔日繁华耀岭南》，《广西日报》2010年8月5日。

图二　麒麟铜尊

从多方面提供了周代墓葬制度的重要信息。今后大凡研究周代墓葬制度，大河口墓地的材料是必不可少的。该墓地出土青铜器甚多，铜器铭文显示，这是一处名“霸伯”的宗族墓地，“霸伯”史料不载，可补史缺①。

麒麟铜尊虽然不是墓地出土，但也是非常重要的。据说麒麟铜尊是夜间农民守花生，见到一只白狐狸进洞，他们进洞追狐狸才发现的，不知确否？

三

武鸣先秦铜针

骆越，是战国秦汉时期聚居于桂西、滇黔东部及中印半岛东北部地区的一个土著民族。1958年10月间，在广西武鸣县马头乡发掘的一处西周至战国时期的墓葬，铜针出土于编号为101号西周墓底的西南角（该墓室长2.1、宽0.6、深0.7米），针长2.7厘米，分针身、针头两部分。针身扁薄，呈长方形，长2.2、宽0.6、厚0.1厘米。在针身的一端有长仅0.5厘米的针尖，针尖根部略粗，呈锥状；尖端极为锋利，铜质较好，出土时表面仍有光泽感（其中1件出土时已残断）。此件铜针虽然还没有进行文物定级，但是它的级别应该是相当高的，笔者认为起码是二级以上。先秦时针灸医术已在中原地区广泛施于临床，但目前所见史料，中原文化的大量传入岭南是从秦以后才开始的，很难设想先秦时期地处偏僻的桂南地区已经使用了先进的针灸医术。《战国策·赵策二》载：“被发文身，错臂左衽，瓯越之民也。”“瓯越”，即广西的古代居民西瓯、骆越。马头骆越墓地出土的2枚铜针，由于当时的经济及文化水平还比较落后，针灸医术可能还未出现，而铜针的形制也不适用于针灸，所以，将铜针用于针灸的可能性不大。相反，从文献记载来看，居住在桂南一带的骆越民族和其他各地越人一样曾盛行文身习俗，而用于文身的工具也曾是一些针具之类的器具，与墓葬出土的这两枚铜针属同类器物，而铜针也适宜于作这种细致的文身工具。这两枚铜针是文身工具的首次发现，对今后进一步研究百越民族的文身习俗提供了实物依据②。今天位于南太平洋中的岛国西萨摩亚的西萨摩亚人现在还喜欢进行文身，文身的人一是爱美的，对人体起到美化的作用；二是社会地位的标志。

广西出土文物与馆藏文物大约34.7万件，我们从34.7万件抽了几件珍贵文物来阐述，翔鹭纹铜鼓是大件文物，战国麒麟神兽铜尊属中型文物，铜针属小件文物。这些文物都是广西文物当中的精华之精华，珍品中的珍品。例如翔鹭纹铜鼓，它牵涉民族来源的问题；麒麟铜尊牵涉民族来源的问题；铜针牵涉我国针灸起源的问题，这些文物都非常之重要，说明广西并非南蛮之地，也曾出现许许多多的文物精华。

① 青岛市博物馆：《青岛博物馆新定级的九件一级文物》，《中国文物报》2011年8月3日。

② 黄云忠：《武鸣马头先秦古墓出土铜针初考》，《广西民族研究》1986年第2期。

汉代青铜博山炉的审美内涵

The Beauty inside Bronze Bo Shan Stoves in Han Dynasty

陈桂芬 / 桂林文物工作队 副研究员

[摘要]

本文通过中国汉人精神信仰的视角，综合一些文献资料的记载以及出土的一些实物珍品的记述，对汉代青铜博山炉的造型风格、工艺结构、功能价值等特点进行阐述和分析，从而揭示其丰富的审美内涵，并从侧面反映汉代经济贸易的发展与工艺美术的繁荣。

[关键词]

汉代　博山炉　审美内涵

Abstract

This article describes and discusses the modeling style, the manufacturing structure, the value of functions and other characteristics of the bronze Bo Shan stove from the Han Dynasty. The article is trying to see through the spirit and the belief of the Han Dynasty's people in order to discover the abundant beauty inside the ancient manufactures. Therefore, we could comprehend the boom developed Han Empire's economic trade and the prosperity of the manufacturing art in a particular way.

Key words

Han dynasty; Bo Shan stoves; Aesthetic connotation

喜香是人类的天性。熏香的习俗在我国起源很早。最初是热带地区的居民为驱臭除秽而焚烧香料。《周礼·秋官·剪氏》记载，当时人们直接熏烧草本植物类香草而还没有熏炉。专为燃香而制作的熏炉“始于约公元前五至三世纪的春秋战国时期”[①]，但考古发现的春秋战国时期的熏炉屈指可数，汉代熏炉则不胜枚举，全国各地都有发现，地域分布极其广阔。其数量之多，品种之丰富，设计之精巧，是其他朝代的熏炉无法比拟的，其中以青铜博山炉最为著名。

在千姿百态的汉代青铜器种类中，青铜博山炉以其丰富奇特的造型、华美绚丽的纹饰、精湛先进的铸造技术而在汉代铜器艺术中独树一帜，具有较高的历史价值、艺术价值和科研价值。

西汉时期上层社会中流行熏香。相传，汉武帝嗜好香熏，也信奉道教。道教信仰神仙，以追求长生不老之道为最高信仰。道教传说东方海上有仙山名“博山”，汉武帝即命人专门模拟其形做了一类造型特殊的香炉——博山炉。最初的博山炉是用青铜铸造的。虽然在博山炉之前已经有了熏炉，但都不像博山炉那样特点鲜明，使用广泛，影响久远，所以人们也常将博山炉推为香炉的鼻祖。《洞天清录·古钟鼎彝器辨》称：“古……无香炉，惟博山炉乃汉太子宫所用者，香炉之制始于此。”[②]

博山炉出现以后，陈设在室内，朝夕相见，人们希望其在实用的同时，给人以美的享受，于是又刻意追求它外观的精美。匠人在设计制作熏炉时，千方百计地对其进行美化，别出心裁地对其进行装饰。原本是属于功能性的日用品，越来越多地透出审美内涵。博山炉因此又成为了室内精美的陈设品与皇家贵族的奢侈品。当时富贵人家用其熏香房屋、衣物，制造芳香氛围，改善室内环境。汉代时用香熏烤衣被是宫中的定制，并且有专门用香熏烤衣被的曝衣楼。汉代蔡质所著的《汉官仪》中，就有关于熏炉熏炙衣物的记载：“女侍史洁衣服，执香炉烧熏。”[③]

史籍记载：两汉时期，华美的青铜博山炉在皇室和贵族中非常盛行，并一度成为上层贵族“沉静身心”的精神愉悦之物而备受追捧，是皇家贵族居室文化的重要组成部分。它兼具实用与美观的特点，具有极高的使用价值与艺术观赏性。本文拟对其丰富的审美内涵进行浅析。

汉代青铜博山炉的审美内涵是多方面的、综合的。本文拟透过汉代特定的时代精神信仰的视角，从造型风格、工艺结构、功能价值等方面对汉代青铜博山炉的审美内涵进行阐释。

① 钱东汉：《日照香炉》，上海文艺出版社，2009年，9页。

② （宋）赵希鹄：《洞天清录》，见《四库存书》第871册，上海古籍出版社，1987年，14页。

③（东汉）蔡质：《汉官仪》，见（刘宋）范晔、（唐）李贤：《后汉书》，中华书局，1965年，1411页。

一

造型艺术美

博山炉的形制，颠覆了前代铜器的造型，特立独行，与汉代的精神信仰相关联。汉代在我国古代人类的生命意识的发展史上，处于一个特殊的阶段。西汉初年，汉文帝、汉景帝以道家思想治国。道家是中国春秋战国时期诸子百家中最重要的思想学派之一。道家思想的特征之一，是幻想通过各种养生修炼得道成仙从而长生不老、长寿不死，反映在汉代人的实际生活中就是非理性的神仙信仰思想在社会群体中占据着重要的地位。汉武帝时期博山炉的兴起正是这种神仙信仰思想在当时现实生活中的一种反映。而道家的美学思想，其审美追求和生命追求是直接同一的。博山炉的造型艺术特征与功能价值特点恰好是汉代人鲜活的生命意识活动的一种样态反映。

从史料记载可知，春秋战国时期出现了神仙家，秦汉时期的神仙家称为方士。汉代由于方仙道思想的流行，人们多向往长生不老的仙境。《史记·武帝本纪》中就有汉武帝派术士求长生不老仙方的记述。青铜博山炉自汉武帝时期首创后，官府和民间竞相仿效。特别是西汉中期以后，随着对外交流的加强，贸易业的发展，陆上“丝绸之路”和海上“丝绸之路”的活跃，东南亚、南亚及欧洲国家的一些香料传入了中国，可用炭火熏烤的龙脑香和苏合香等固体香料增加，博山炉更为盛行，并在人们的日常生活中处于重要的地位，熏香成为了一种风尚，平民百姓用之熏蚊除湿，杀菌辟秽，净化环境；皇家贵族用之熏衣洁被、制造馨香氛围，显示尊贵。由于博山炉在汉代皇室和贵族中备受推崇，一些青铜博山炉成为了这个时期铜器中的上乘之作，它们以匠心独运的设计、玲珑精致的造型、精湛高超的工艺体现了汉代社会经济的发展和工艺美术的繁荣。

“所有的艺术形式都可以被视为与现实世界相对应的象征世界”。“象征”是一种符号，一种具有意符特征的符契或表征。“象征”正是博山炉造型风格的特色。

博山熏炉主要由炉盖、炉身和炉座组成，有的带圆盘形托座。炉体呈青铜器中的豆形。炉盖高而尖，镂空，呈层叠的山峦之形，其间雕有人物、飞禽走兽、奇花异草等纹饰，其形状象征传说中的海上仙山——博山，因名博山炉。博山炉构思巧妙，当炉腹内熏烧香料时，袅袅香气从镂空的错落有致的山形炉盖中飘逸而出，氤氲缥缈的香气与炉盖上雕饰的山峦造型相映成趣，让人犹如置身云雾缭绕的蓬莱仙境，令观者悠然神往。此外，博山炉香熏不仅具有杀菌、防霉的功用，还具有辟秽、驱邪的象征意义。

汉代博山炉所反映的神仙思想意识，具有鲜明的时代特征。博山炉设计的主题是“升仙”，这与汉代“方仙道”的流行密切相关。也正是由于“方仙道”的流行，中国美术史在汉代的一个重要发展是创造了一大批与神仙信仰有关的象征符号，包括仙人、仙山、仙境、仙兽等，博山炉的造型风格正是这些象征符号的体现。

据《史记》等典籍记载，东海之上有三座仙山，名曰“蓬莱”、“方丈”、“瀛洲”，山上有仙人居住，楼阁宫阙均为黄金白银建造，还有灵丹妙药，人食之可长生不老。“未至，望之如云。及到，三神山反居水下”。由此可知，传说中的神仙境界是虚无缥缈的。博山炉的造型设计与传说中的仙山形象相似。仙山形象大致可分为东海仙山与西方昆仑仙山两大系统。博山属于东海仙山系统。博山炉的整体造型象征出没于海上的仙山幻境。其底部的承盘象征波涛汹涌的大海；炉身与炉盖铸成层叠的山峦形象，其间铸有各式形状的镂孔，熏香时缭绕缥缈的香雾从镂孔中飘逸而出，极具仙山意境。炉体上雕刻的龙腾、虎跃、马奔、熊走、狗窜、豹扑、羊叫、鹿鸣、猴戏、凤翔、雁飞等各种动物形象，象征了仙界的勃勃生机。由此可以看出，汉代博山炉的造型风格具有极强的象征意义，生动地反映了当时方仙术士对海上仙山胜境的幻想与向往，是对当时具有“方仙道”信仰人士渴望长生不老死后成仙心理的一种体现，蕴含着丰富的思想情趣和审美内涵。

老子认为“道”是化生宇宙万物的本源。而“道”是“有”和“无”、“虚”和“实”、“有限”和“无限”的统一。这种观念也体现在汉代青铜博山炉的设计艺术中。博山炉的造型是现实生活中幻象世界的具象组合，在虚境向实境转化的时候，意与象开始融合，情与境形成统一，最后形成具有审美意义的感性形象。古籍对博山炉有许多记载，（汉）刘向《熏炉铭》：“嘉此正器，崭岩若山；上贯太华；承以铜盘，中有兰绮，朱火青烟。”（汉）李尤《熏炉铭》：“上似蓬莱，吐气委蛇，芳烟布绕，遥冲紫微。”（宋）吕大临《考古图》载:“香炉像海中博山，下盘贮汤使润气蒸香，以像海之四环。”类似记载还有很多。这些诗词描述了博山炉独特的造型艺术风格和特殊的审美形态。汉代青铜博山炉的造型是人们把主观情感和审美理想与现实生活相结合的体现，它能营造一种怡情逸性的高雅意境，具备一种造型艺术美。

二

装饰艺术美

汉代青铜博山炉的审美内涵不仅仅表现在其外观造型上，其形体的基本结构与外部装饰技艺也是其艺术价值不可分割的重要组成部分。

审美的形式观念与实用观念密不可分。人的主观情感意识与器物的实用价值相结合达到主客观的统一而产生美。汉代青铜博山炉造型虽千姿百态，但按器型的差异，大体分为带承盘的博山炉和不带承盘的博山炉以及有执柄的博山炉。它们均具有象征意义，是想象的仙山境界的缩影。仙山大致可分为东海蓬莱仙山与西方昆仑仙山两大系统。带承盘的博山炉：承盘象征大海，炉体象征海上仙山博山。不带承盘的博山炉，炉体也象征仙山。从设计思想上讲，汉人认为仙山除海上有之外，陆上也有。西方昆仑仙山即是。因此，汉代人认为不去海上仙山去陆上仙山也可以成仙。如（汉）上华山镜铭："上华山，见神人，食玉英，饮澧泉，得天道，物自然，驾飞龙，乘浮云，白虎引，直上天，赐长命，保子孙。"[①]（汉）善铜镜铭："汉有善铜出丹阳，杂以银锡清而明。朱爵玄武顺阴阳，八子九孙治中央。东上太山见神人……"[②]因此，博山炉也不一定都要有承盘以象征大海。此外，带承盘的博山炉，承盘象征大海只是人们观念上的意象。实际上，带承盘的博山炉，承盘还有特殊的作用。因为博山炉熏香时会产生香灰，设置承盘，可保持环境的清洁、物品的干净。"在汉代的香品中，有干燥的草本植物、树脂类的龙脑香、苏合香等香料。草本植物的茅香干燥之后就是可燃物，为了能充分燃烧，通常在炉身的底下设有通气孔。有的设计炉身较浅，炉盖隆起，而且在炉盖上备有数层镂孔。这类熏炉的容积较大。同时为了容纳自进气孔落下的灰烬，通常设有承盘"。此外，盛盘盛水，还可以降低博山炉熏香时炉体的温度。因此，承盘除具有象征意义外，还具有功能价值，是功能价值与审美形态的和谐统一。

汉代，由于经济的发展，其科学技术也空前繁荣。汉代的青铜工艺，在战国的基础上又向前发展了一步，装饰技艺方面显得更加丰富娴熟。对称、均衡、循环等美学构式的运用，动物、植物、人物等物态的刻划，大海、山峦、楼阁等景观的描摹；写实、夸张等手法的渲染，透雕、浮雕等技艺的应用……使青铜博山炉有着虚实相衬、灵动多变、纹饰优美、结构精巧的特色。正如（汉）刘歆《西京杂记》载："长安巧工丁缓者……作九层博山香炉，镂为奇禽怪兽，穷诸灵异，皆自然灵动。"（唐）徐坚《初学记》卷二十五引《咏香炉》古诗曰："四座且莫喧，愿听

①② 钱志熙：《两汉镜铭文本整理及文学分析》，《中华文史论丛》2009年第1期。作者根据刘体智编的《小校经阁金石文字拓本》以及冯云鹏、冯云鹓编的《金石索·金索》辑录。

歌一言。请说铜炉器，崔嵬像南山。上枝似松柏，下根据铜盘。雕文各异类，离娄自相连。谁能为其器，公输与鲁班……”

此外，有的青铜博山炉烟气镂孔设计成圆形、三角形、菱形或花边形等多种几何形状；有的镂孔从外观看不出，熏香时却是香气袅袅，景象朦胧，极具神秘氛围。有的炉座铸造成龟负凤、龟负鹤等象征吉祥与长寿的动物形象。寓意深刻的动物形象的运用、绚丽多姿的自然景观的装饰、灵活多变的铸造技巧的应用，使汉代青铜博山炉具有特殊的装饰艺术美，并以其独特的结构与装饰引发人们的审美联想，具有神秘性和迷惑力。

三

古诗赋铭美

我国古人很早以前就总结出“缘物起情”、“因物起兴”、“拟容取心”等深刻的审美规律。无论是从文献记载，还是从考古发现，皆可以看出博山炉的确是非常精美的实用艺术品。博山炉造型华美多姿，又与人们的生活起居有着紧密联系。因此，形态各异、巧夺天工的博山炉，不仅以其出色的技艺在工艺史上飘出缕缕清香，而且以其独特的韵味潜入了文人雅士的诗句赋铭中，在文学史上也留下袅袅余香，以至于今天我们还能看到许多自汉代以来咏叹博山炉的文学作品。

（齐）刘绘《咏博山香炉诗》：“参差郁佳丽，合沓纷可怜；蔽野千种树，出没万重山。上镂秦王子，驾鹤乘紫烟；下刻蟠龙势，矫首半衔莲。傍旁伊水丽，芝盖出岩间；复有汉游女，拾羽弄余妍。荣色何杂糅，缛绣更相鲜；密度或腾倚，林薄香芊眠。掩华终不发，含熏未肯然；风生玉阶树，露湛曲池莲。寒虫飞夜室，秋云没晓天。”①

（梁）昭明太子《铜博山香炉赋》：“禀至精之纯质，产灵岳之幽深，般倕之妙旨，运公输之巧心。有蕙带而岩隐，亦霓裳而升仙。写嵩山之巃嵸，像邓林之阡眠。于时青烟司寒，红光翳景。翠帷已低，兰膏未屏。炎荧内曜，宓芬外扬。似庆云之程色，若景星之舒光。信名嘉而器美，永为玩于华堂。”②

（陈）傅绰《博山香炉赋》：“器象南山，香传西国；丁缓巧铸，兼资匠刻。麝火理朱，蓝烟毁黑；结构危峰，横罗杂树。寒夜含煖；清霄吐雾。制作巧妙，独称珍俶。气氤氲，长若春；随风本胜千酿酒，散馥还如一硕人。”③

（梁）元帝萧绎《香炉铭》：“苏合氤氲，非烟若云。时秾时薄，乍聚还分，火微难尽，风长易闻，孰云道力，慈悲所薰。”④

①～③（唐）徐坚:《初学记》卷二十五·器物部（上）。

④（唐）欧阳询:《艺文类聚》卷七十·服饰部（下）。

对博山炉进行描述和歌咏的作品还有很多。上述诗词不仅是对博山炉精致的造型、美丽的形象生动传神的描写，同时也是对博山炉香熏的特殊功用淋漓尽致的赞美，描述了博山炉熏香时香烟缭绕的迷人意境，体现了中国传统美学范畴“意境”内涵之“情境交融”、“形神兼备”的美学价值。文人墨客对博山炉的赞赏，实质上也是对熏香习俗含意深远的文化内涵的一种表述，是博山炉功能价值内涵美的体现。这些引人入胜的诗词赋铭，描述了博山炉的美丽与超凡，体现了博山炉的造型艺术美和内在功能价值美，具有特殊的史料价值。读之，人们得到感官的愉悦和情操的陶冶，进而产生有益于身心健康的审美感受。文人雅士对博山炉香熏形与神、情、境的礼赞，为博山炉审美内涵的表现提供了独特的欣赏平台，体现了博山炉功能价值与艺术价值的完美统一，彰显了博山炉丰富的审美内涵。

四

南北特色美

相对于北方而言，汉代熏香的风气南方更加盛行，博山炉在南方发现也较多，这与南方特殊的气候环境和汉代南方地区港口贸易的繁荣有关。南国水乡，万山重叠，森林茂密。卑湿之地，潮气很重，蚊虫猖獗，瘴疠流行。居室、衣服、被褥容易滋生真菌。“地卑山近，衣润费炉烟”。熏香可以驱虫、杀菌、除湿、防霉、辟秽。此外，博山炉出现在西汉时期，与当时的燃香原料和人们的生活方式有关。西汉之前，人们使用茅香，即将薰香草或蕙草放置在豆式香炉中直接点燃，虽然香气馥郁，但烟火气很大。汉武帝时期，由于贸易业的发展，特别是自西汉中期开始，海上贸易日趋繁盛，南方的港口贸易日渐繁荣，龙脑香、苏合香等进口香料增加，刺激了熏炉的发展。人们将香料制成香球或香饼，放置熏炉中，下置炭火，用炭火的高温将这些树脂类的香料徐徐燃起，香味浓厚，烟火气又不大。因此，出现了形态各异、巧夺天工的博山炉，熏香之风日渐兴盛，熏炉也日渐增多，并在人们的生活中占据重要地位。熏炉不仅是人们生活的日用品，室内精美的陈设品，也是逝者的随葬品。已挖掘的汉墓，许多都有熏炉随葬。墓主人的地位越高，随葬的熏炉就越多越精美。“西汉后期，人们需要的熏炉数量骤增，仅广州地区发掘的400多座汉墓中，就有一半墓葬出土有熏炉”[①]；广州西汉南越王墓随葬的熏炉就达13件之多，其中青铜熏炉11件；河北满城西汉中山静王刘胜夫妇墓，也随葬了8件精美的熏炉，而且全为青铜熏炉。由此可见，在汉代，熏炉进入了它的鼎盛时期，并在人们的生活中处于越来越重要的地位。一些青铜博山炉成为了这时期熏炉中的精品。在出土

① 钱东汉:《日照香炉》，上海文艺出版社，2009年，9页。

的汉代青铜博山炉中，最为华美而珍贵的是1968年河北省满城汉墓一号墓出土的错金博山炉和二号墓出土的骑兽人物博山炉。

一号墓（刘胜墓）出土的错金博山炉（M1：5182）为不带承盘的博山炉。该炉“炉身似豆形、作子口、盖肖博山。炉身的盘和座系分别铸成后用铁钉铆合。通体错金。纹饰流畅自然，线条有粗细之分，细者犹如毫发。炉座圈足错金，作卷云纹。座把透雕，作三龙腾出波涛翻滚的水面以头托炉盘状。炉盘错金作流云纹，线条极为活泼流畅，炉盘上部和炉盖铸出高低起伏、挺拔峻峭的山峦多层。炉盖山势镂孔。山峦间神兽出没，虎豹奔走，小猴蹲居在高层峦峰或骑在兽身上，猎人肩扛弓弩巡猎山间或正在追逐逃窜的野猪，小树点缀其间，刻划了一幅秀丽的自然山景和生动的狩猎场面，而且在细部又加错金勾勒渲染，使塑造的景色更觉生意盎然。”①

满城M1：5182错金博山炉不仅造型优美，而且精工细琢，匠心独具，纹饰华丽。特别是错金技艺的运用，使器物更为华美，色彩对比更为强烈、纹饰线条更加鲜明，艺术形象更为生动。它集实用性与观赏性于一体，不仅体现了汉代工匠杰出的艺术技巧，同时折射出汉代青铜博山炉独特的审美内涵，具有很高的艺术价值和实用价值（图一）。

二号墓（窦官墓）出土的骑兽人物博山炉（M2：3004），为带承盘的青铜博山炉。其“整体雕镂精细，造型优美。由炉身、盖和底盘三部分组成。底盘折沿，浅腹，平底，上饰鎏银同心圆纹四周和一组柿蒂纹。炉盘中部为一骑兽力士。力士上身裸露，下身着短裤，腰间束带，腰带前垂，屈膝骑在伏兽上，左手撑于兽颈，右手擎托炉身，造型矫健、有力。兽跪卧，昂首，张口欲噬。颈部前伸做挣扎状。兽体下有一支钉，安插于底盘上的小圆孔中，圆孔的位置稍偏于一侧，孔径0.8厘米。炉身子母口，圆鼓腹，底部有一小圆座和力士的右手铆接在一起。炉壁饰宽凸弦纹一周，并有鎏银流云图案，但已模糊不清。炉盖透雕，分为上、下两层。上层铸出重叠的上峦，流云四绕，在云山之间有虎、熊出没、虎、羊相斗，人兽搏斗以及人物驱使牛车等场面。下层铸龙、虎、朱雀、骆驼以及草木、云气等纹饰，形象生动、逼真”②。

满城M2：3004骑兽人物博山炉构思新颖，造型优美，工艺精巧，其结构与装饰，充满浪漫情怀和大自然之美，体现出一种人与自然共生、神话与现实交错、抽象与写实并存的艺术风格，极富艺术感染力和实用价值，是实用与美观、功能与装饰的完美统一，为汉代青铜博山炉中的上乘之作，是一件达到高度审美内涵的铜器艺术珍品（图二）。

广西汉墓出土的熏炉也极为丰富。历年来发掘的汉墓中，仅合浦汉墓出土的铜熏炉就有16件，陶熏炉更多。合浦汉墓出土的16件青铜熏炉中，除“九只岭M5：48，底部无托盘，似为特例”③外，其余均为带托盘的青铜熏炉。2003年风门岭出土的青铜博山炉（M26：128）“由炉体、炉盖及托盘三部分组成。盖有镂孔，

①② 中国社会科学院考古研究所、河北省文物管理处：《满城汉墓发掘报告》（上），文物出版社，1980年，63页。

③ 富霞：《广西合浦出土汉代青铜器的初步研究》，《广西考古文集》（第四辑），科学出版社，2010年，390页。

饰博山草叶纹及云纹，炉体呈豆盘形，口微敛，子母口，腹部中间有一道凸棱，上部一圈网纹，下部羽纹、倒三角纹。盖顶与炉口之间有活链相连，喇叭形座足亦饰博山草叶纹及云纹，下与承盘相连。座足底有柱，与盘铆合。盘为广口，折沿，中腹内折，下腹收分为假圈足，底微内凹，中央有小孔与炉底座相铆接。托盘口沿刻一周三角纹。炉径6.2、托盘口径13.4、通高11.5厘米”[①]（图三）。

2001年合浦县九只岭东汉墓出土的1件铜熏炉（M5：48）则为无托盘的博山炉。“由盖、炉身、底座三部分组成。炉盖呈圆锥体。顶有展翅凤鸟形纽，纽下有四个圆形气孔，孔径0.45厘米。盖面作重山形，上刻芭蕉叶图案，叶面上刻兽面纹，下刻两组相对的龙形图案，边缘有叶状纹，盖缘饰两周图案，上为连续的三角形纹，下为弦纹。盖与炉身用子母扣合，炉盖与炉腹各有一半圆形耳，中有一圆孔，以链索相连，已锈断。炉腹上部有一周凸弦纹，将炉腹的图案分隔为上下两部分：上部为一周菱形纹，下部上为六条同向的龙形图案，下为一周弦纹。底座下部为一中空的圆锥体，上部为一托起炉腹的铜柱，铜柱与锥体的顶部相连。另外，在中空的圆锥体内有一直径0.8厘米的铜柱，上接圆锥体的顶部，下似为底部的一个支座。底座刻有同向的四条龙形图案，托起炉腹的铜柱的中部有一周圆形突起，通高19.5厘米。”[②] 广西合浦汉墓出土的青铜博山炉中大多数是非常精美的艺术珍品。它们的总体特征是：造型优美，工艺精巧，纹饰典雅，有地域特色，凝聚着汉代能工巧匠的聪明才智，承载着汉代文明的丰富信息。虽然距今已有约两千年的历史，仍给今天的我们以艺术美的享受。另外，1981年陕西省兴坪豆马村茂陵1号陪葬墓出土的错金银竹节铜熏炉（图四）也非常精美。

① 广西壮族自治区文物工作队、合浦县博物馆：《合浦风门岭汉墓——2003～2005年发掘报告》，科学出版社，2006年，73页。

② 广西壮族自治区文物工作队、合浦县博物馆：《广西合浦县九只岭东汉墓》，《考古》2003年第10期。

五

结　语

综上所述可知，汉代青铜博山炉的审美内涵是丰富多彩的。造型风格、工艺结构、功能价值三者之特征构成其审美内涵的注解。虚实相生、形神兼备、意境浑朴的特点构成其艺术形象整体性的美感。

汉代青铜博山炉以其理想的审美形象和深邃奇妙的文化意蕴彰显了其丰富的审美内涵，它们不仅具有绮丽的造型艺术美，而且具有丰厚的内在价值美。它们优美的造型、精巧的结构、特殊的功用能唤起人们无限的遐思，让人们在熙攘的俗世中感受幻象世界的美妙与神秘，享受俗世的逍遥与淡泊，使心灵意境得到美好的升华。它们跨越了时空的界限，给人们以永恒的美的感受和启迪。

图一　错金博山炉（满城汉墓出土）

图二　错金博山炉（满城汉墓出土）

图三　铜熏炉（合浦风门岭26号汉墓出土）

1

2

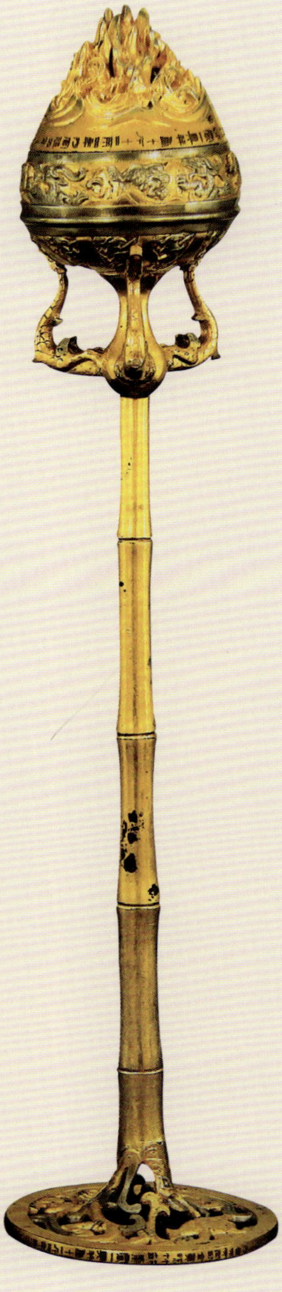

3

图四 鎏金银竹节铜熏炉（西汉，陕西兴平市出土）
1.盖部 2.足部 3.全身

羽纹铜凤灯与图像巫术符号

Phoenix-shaped Bronze Lamps and Symbols of Magic Images

闫玲君 / 广西师范大学 硕士研究生

[摘要]

本文从艺术源于巫术的角度出发，结合相关考古及文献资料，考察了羽纹铜凤灯艺术造型的象征意义。本文认为羽纹铜凤灯的艺术造型是一种图像巫术符号，其功能是用于避邪。

[关键词]

羽纹铜凤灯　图像　巫术符号　避邪

Abstract

Based on relevant archeological findings and literature, this paper has made an investigation into the symbolic meaning of the ornamental mould of the Phoenix-Shaped Bronze Lamp, from the perspective that arts originate from witchcraft. This paper assumes that the ornamental mould of the Phoenix-Shaped Bronze Lamp is a kind of image witchcraft symbol, whose function is to exorcise evil spirits.

Key words

Phoenix-Shaped Bronze Lamp; Image; Witchcraft symbol; Exorcise evil spirits

羽纹铜凤灯，1971年出土于广西合浦县望牛岭1号汉墓。根据墓葬的规模和随葬品的特征，考古人员推测这是西汉晚期合浦地区的郡县官吏或合浦地方豪强的墓葬[①]。

羽纹铜凤灯出土时共2件（图一），器形、大小完全相同，高33、长42、宽15厘米。灯形似凤鸟，通体錾刻羽毛。凤背上放置着灯盘；凤嘴衔喇叭形灯罩，正好罩在灯盘上方，灯罩上刻异兽，做回头张望之状；凤颈伸高向后弯转，与灯罩、腹腔相通；凤的腹腔中空，可以贮水，以容纳烟尘；凤尾下垂及地，与站立的双足保持器身平衡（图二）。羽纹铜凤灯造型优美、设计精巧、实用环保，既展示了汉代岭南地区流行的錾刻花纹铜器的精美，也反映了当时中国青铜灯铸造工艺的高超水平，是广西地区出土的西汉铜器中的精品，现藏于广西壮族自治区博物馆。

根据蒋廷瑜对此类錾刻花纹铜器的研究，其流行时间上起西汉中期，下至东汉晚期[②]。因此，羽纹铜凤灯的铸造时间应与其墓葬时代相近，大致为西汉中、晚期。

在汉代，中国美术史有了一个重要发展，即创造了一大批与神仙信仰相关的象征符号——仙山、仙草、仙兽等[③]，它们表现的不是现实世界的动物或植物的形象，而是以动物或植物为符号或象征的神话、巫术世界的艺术形象，有其深层的寓意和神秘的象征[④]。这类象征符号曾在汉代美术中大量涌现，同样，在岭南地区出土的汉代錾刻花纹青铜器上也没例外。那么，以凤鸟为主体形象设计的羽纹铜凤灯的艺术造型的象征意义是什么？笔者试就这个问题做一些探索。

① 广西壮族自治区文物考古写作小组：《广西合浦西汉木椁墓》，《考古》1972年第5期。

② 蒋廷瑜：《汉代錾刻花纹铜器研究》，《考古学报》2002年第3期，296页。

③ 巫鸿：《汉代道教美术试探》，《礼仪中的美术：巫鸿中国古代美术史文编》，生活·读书·新知三联书店，2005年，461页。

④ 李泽厚：《美的历程》（修订彩图版），天津社会科学院出版社，2002年，88、89页

一

汉代凤鸟的避邪功能

自古以来，凤就被人们视为一种神鸟、瑞鸟。卜辞中就有“帝使凤”的记载，

图一　羽纹铜凤灯

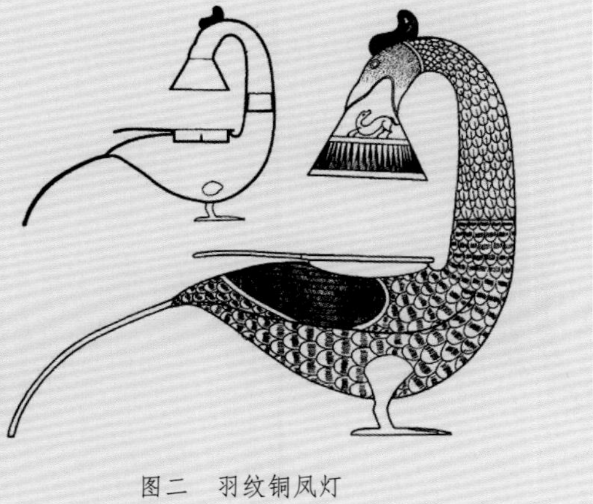

图二　羽纹铜凤灯

因甲骨文中“风”与“凤”同，可知在当时凤已经被视为上帝的使者[①]，其祥瑞观念由来已久。《说文》云：“凤，神鸟也……出于东方君子之国，翱翔四海之外，过昆仑、饮砥柱，濯羽弱水，莫宿风穴，见则天下大安宁。”《山海经·南次三经》云：“丹穴之山……有鸟焉，其状如鸡，五采而文，名曰凤皇。首文日德，翼文日义，背文日礼，膺文曰仁，腹文曰信。是鸟也，饮食自然，自歌自舞，见则天下安宁。”《礼记·礼运》云:“麟、凤、龟、龙，谓之四灵。”

在汉代，凤鸟通常被称为“朱雀”[②]。《春秋演礼图》中说：“凤为火精，在天为朱雀”。它不仅被人们视为祥瑞的象征，还作为驱逐邪恶，把守墓门、棺柩以保护死者不受鬼蜮侵扰的保护神。因此，汉代匠师常在壁画、画像石、瓦当、铜镜等上绘制凤鸟图像以示吉祥和避邪，如汉代四神铜镜上就可见到“青龙白虎辟不祥”、“朱雀玄武顺阴阳”的铭文。汉代画像石、画像砖上的凤鸟图像也非常多。以河南南阳方城东关汉墓出土的门扉画像石为例（图三），其上刻展翅欲飞的凤鸟，中刻两眼圆睁的铺首衔环，下刻执长矛向前刺的门神神荼[③]。根据《拾遗记》的记载：“尧在位七十年……有祗支之国，献重明之鸟……状如鸡，鸣似凤……能搏逐猛兽虎狼，使妖灾群恶不能为害……其未至之时，国人或刻木，或铸金，为此鸟之状，置于门户之间，则魑魅丑类自然退伏。”一些考古学家推断：汉画像石墓中，墓门铺首之上所刻对称鸟兽，其鸟具冠展翼，若凤凰者，即取义于“重名鸟”，认为它具有驱退凶鬼魑魅的功能[④]。并且，神荼、辅首衔环在汉代的功能都是用于避邪，与凤鸟刻在同一画像石上，也能说明凤鸟在汉代是具有避邪功能的。

① 巫鸿：《三盘山出土车饰与西汉美术中的“祥瑞”图像》，《礼仪中的美术：巫鸿中国古代美术史文编》，生活·读书·新知三联书店，2005年，164页。

② 易思羽：《中国符号》，江苏人民出版社，2005年，241页。

③ 郭太松：《试析汉画中的凤鸟》，《河南省文物考古论集》（第二辑），中州古籍出版社，2000年，275、276页。

④ 濮安国：《凤纹装饰》，中国轻工业出版社，2000年，19页。

图三　河南南阳方城东关汉代画像石凤鸟图

二

羽纹铜凤灯与图像巫术符号

在观察羽纹铜凤灯时，我们不能忽略一个细节。虽然此灯整体是作凤鸟造型，但它刻画了两种动物的形象：凤与兽。这两种动物之间似有某种联系，我们不可以切割开来看。昂首回头、大嘴张开的凤鸟形象，与衔于凤鸟口中灯罩上扭头张望的兽的形象构成了一副完整的图画，画面定格的内容似乎告诉了我们：一只象征美善、祥瑞的凤，正在追逐、吞食四散奔逃的象征凶鬼魑魅的怪兽。因为凤是一种神鸟，“以琅玕果为食”，不吃兽；凤此刻衔兽于口中，我们不妨大胆猜想：凤将吃兽，此兽或许为妖兽。

这种图像组合让我想到了著名的西班牙阿尔塔米拉洞穴壁画《受伤的野牛》，一种以图式助猎的图像巫术符号。原始的审美观往往与宗教巫术相关联，如欧洲史前的美术作品大都不是现代人所说的纯粹的艺术品，而是一种兼具艺术和巫术意义的作品。事实上，在中国的史前艺术作品中也出现过很多这种图像巫术符号，比如，内蒙古阴山岩画中就表现了带有箭头标记的鹿①。因为，在原始人看来，事物的形象与实体间具有某种不可言喻的神秘的同一性，若欲得到某种对象或某种结果，只需将他们以形象的方式诉诸画面，那就保证可以达到预期的目的了。也就是说，原始先民们认为，通过绘制动物的图像便可以控制现实中的猎物，杀死这些图像便杀死了这些动物。这种图像已不再是一种自然的符号，而是一种文化符号，是一种具有巫术法力的诅咒图像。

至新石器时期以来，人们就已习惯了使用特定的巫术灵物来达到辟邪、预知和通神等目的，并出现了用神秘图像控制鬼神或辟邪的巫术②。如河南濮阳西水坡仰韶文化时期遗址就曾发现塑有“龙虎”蚌图的大墓，其中较为典型的是M45。墓主人是一个壮年男子，遗骨在墓室中间，墓主骨骼两侧用蚌壳精心摆塑了一龙一虎图案③。一些学者认为这幅“龙虎”蚌图是四神早期图像④。所谓“四神”，是中国古代人们认为的方位神——青龙、白虎、朱雀、玄武，它们象征东、西、南、北四方。在汉墓中，四神主要是起镇守四方、驱邪除鬼、保卫墓主灵魂以及护送墓主升仙的作用。也有些学者认为，“龙虎”图案与道教中流传的道士借助龙、虎、鹿等交通工具，上天入地、拜见神明、制御精怪的观念有联系⑤。总之，无论它是象征着四神，起镇守四方、驱除邪恶的作用，还是为了永葆墓主的神通，都能说明这幅图案是被赋予了巫术法力的，它是一种图像巫术符号。

此外，比较有象征性的还有关于“夏铸九鼎”的传说。《左传·宣公三年》记载：“昔夏之方有德也，远方图物，贡金九牧，铸鼎象物，百物而为之备，使民知神、奸。故民入川泽山林，不逢不若，螭魅魍魉，莫能逢之。”其意大致是说：夏初统治者曾用方国进贡的青铜铸成九鼎，并将远方各种物像铸在鼎上，目的是让民众了解神灵、鬼魅的相貌，使民进入川泽山林，就不会遇到不合适的神，山魈鬼怪，不致加害⑥。夏王铸九鼎，解除了古人们生存和发展中所面临的最主要的灾难。由此可见，九鼎的神奇之处不在于它是否被用作祭器，而在于鼎上铸的奇异的物；“铸鼎像物”的作用也不仅是为知神奸、别善恶，更主要是为了禁不若，即用一种“模拟巫术”的办法，通过控制敌人的图像来控制敌人⑦。明人田艺蘅在《玉笑零音》中说：“周旦作《金滕》以祈天命，君子以为咒诅之媒；夏铸鼎像以辟神奸，后世遂有厌镇之术。”

汉代流行“仙道”思想。在仙道思想的巫术中，祈祷吉祥、避邪、预防灾祸的咒术非常盛行⑧。汉墓中的凤鸟又被人们视为能驱逐邪恶、保护死者灵魂的保护神。这更让我肯定灯罩上的兽形动物可能就是人们想象创造出来的凶鬼怪兽的形象，而羽纹铜凤灯艺术造型的象征意义在原理上与“铸鼎象物”也应是一致的，其功能都是通过这种图像来控制鬼怪以达到辟邪的目的。与此类似的图像还有：商代

① 孙新周：《中国原始艺术符号的文化破译》，中央民族大学出版社，1998年，13~15页。

② 胡新生：《中国古代巫术》，山东人民出版社，1998年，6、7页。

③ 濮阳市文物管理委员会等：《河南濮阳西水坡遗址发掘简报》，《文物》1988年第3期。

④ 李学勤：《西水坡“龙虎墓”与四象的起源》，《中国社会科学院研究生院学报》1988年第5期。

⑤ 张光直：《濮阳三蹻与中国美术史上的人兽母题》，《文物》1988年第11期。

⑥ 张光直：《中国青铜时代》，生活·读书·新知三联书店，1999年，433、444页。

⑦ 赵世超：《铸鼎象物说》，《社会科学战线》2004年第4期。

⑧ 邢富华：《从洛阳出土文物看汉代朱雀》，《太原大学学报》2002年第12期。

图四　河北满城汉墓出土的铜朱雀衔环杯

有凤鸟去怪人头的玉雕，战国青铜器上也有凤鸟抓鬼魅的形象[①]。湖南长沙出土的战国帛画《人物夔凤图》，根据郭沫若的研究，其画面的内容是：一个善良美丽的女性，在代表正义与和平的凤鸟同代表邪恶与灾害的独脚夔的斗争中，祈祷凤鸟获得胜利[②]。另外，满城汉墓出土的朱雀衔环杯（图四），也刻画了一只耸立于怪兽背上的朱雀，口衔圆环，展翅欲飞。朱雀脚下的兽匍匐着，昂首张口，似不堪重负做挣扎状[③]。这些图像都描述了凤鸟降服凶鬼怪兽的场景。

① 马承源：《中国青铜器研究》，上海古籍出版社，2002年，365～368页。

② 王逊：《中国美术史》，上海人民美术出版社，1989年，38页。

③ 中国社会科学院考古研究所、河北省文物管理处：《满城汉墓发掘报告》（上册），文物出版社，1980年，265页。

三

结　语

综上所述，笔者认为羽纹铜凤灯的艺术造型构成了一种图像巫术符号，其目的是为达辟邪之意。以其随葬，是替墓主镇妖辟邪，祝吉化凶，以保墓主在冥府平安生活。羽纹铜凤灯的艺术造型所蕴含的巫术思想，对于研究西汉美术史、宗教思想史均有重要的价值。

第三部分

青铜科技保护研究

Part 3

Research on Technological Conservation for Bronze Wares

广东博罗横岭山先秦墓地出土西周铜鼎的修复研究

Restoration for Bronze in Pre-Qin Period Tripods Unearthed from Henglingshan Cemetery on Boluo, Guangdong

莫永昇 / 广东省博物馆 馆员
莫　鹏 / 广东省博物馆 研究员

[摘要]

广东博罗横岭山先秦墓地是2000年度“全国十大考古新发现”之一，其出土的青铜器不仅展示了广东先秦时期丰富发达的文化内涵，而且对研究和认识广东青铜时代的考古学文化和推动对古缚娄国的研究和探讨等具有十分重要的意义。该墓地出土的西周铜鼎不但是本次考古发掘出土体形较大的青铜饪食器之一，而且又是广东地区出土数量不多的西周时期青铜器，所以就显得格外珍贵，但由于泥土的砸压和化学物质的腐蚀，西周铜鼎出土时腐蚀氧化和破损都相当严重，不利于日后的陈列、研究和保管，为保护修复好该青铜鼎，修复人员在科学检测分析的基础上，通过缓蚀处理、浸透加固、封护、黏接、修补复原等技术手段，最终把其修复保护好。

[关键词]

铜鼎　修复　研究

Abstract

Henglingshan Cemetery from Pre-Qin Period is one of Top Ten Archaeological Discoveries in 2000. Bronze ware unearthed from this place not only displays rich culture from Pre-Qin Period in Guangdong, but also makes a great significance in study of archeological and cultural issues in the Bronze Age as well as the deeper research into the Ancient Fulou. With large body, the tripod boasts itself among the small proportion of bronze vessels unearthed from Guangdong. However, because of soil crushing and chemical corrosion, the tripod suffered from serious oxidation and damage when it was unearthed, which was not conducive to future exhibition, research and storage. Based on scientific tests and analysis, the staff eventually restored the tripod by means of corrosion processing, soaking reinforcement, sealing protection, bonding, patching, etc.

Key words

Bronze Tripod; Restoration; Research

一

引　言

2000年间，广东省文物考古研究所为配合广州至惠州的高速公路建设，在广东的惠州市博罗县境内横岭山发掘了一处大型的先秦时期墓地，首期在8500多平方米的范围内共发现商周时期墓葬300多座，出土了一批陶瓷、青铜、玉石器等精美文物，这是迄今为止广东考古发现和发掘的同类墓葬中数量最多、出土器物最精美、品种最为丰富的青铜时代墓葬群，为研究广东的青铜文化时代、构建广东先秦史提供了宝贵资料。因此，该墓地被评为2000年度“全国十大考古新发现”之一。横岭山先秦墓地出土的130多件青铜文物是该墓地重要的文化遗存资料之一，它不仅展示了广东先秦时期丰富发达的文化内涵，而且对研究和认识广东青铜时代的考古学文化问题和推动对古缚娄国的研究和探讨等都具有十分重要的意义。

但这些青铜器在地下埋藏期间，由于受到各种化学物质的侵蚀和石头、泥土的砸压以及人为的破坏等，出土时破损和腐蚀氧化都极为严重，很多都出现有掉渣、开裂、酥粉等现象，给考古人员对这些青铜器的研究造成很大的影响，也不利于日后的展示和收藏。编号为M201∶1的西周铜鼎是该墓地本次考古发掘出土体形较大的青铜饪食器之一，由于其纹饰精美，保存较为完整，加上广东地区出土的西周时期青铜器数量不多，因此就显得格外珍贵。为了及时保护好这件西周铜鼎，我们优先对其进行了修复处理。

二

西周铜鼎形制及其残破状况

西周青铜鼎出土于广东博罗横岭山先秦墓地第201号墓的中部，编号为M201∶1。该鼎口径20.4厘米，最大腹径18.8厘米，腹深9.1厘米，通高22.4厘米，重1350克；形制为侈口，沿上立一对方形耳，浅腹略垂，圜底较平。三足呈半环形，中空，根部较粗，足端外撇。双耳和三足呈五点式分布，腹底三足之间有三角形凸起。三足下部二次补铸，外则包铸一层。腹部纹饰带由涡纹、回首夔龙纹、四瓣目纹组成，雷纹做地纹。三个四瓣目纹位于三足之上，三道铸缝在中间，两侧上下略有错位。三足根部呈兽头状，补铸部分将兽嘴、鼻遮住，只露两眼和嘴角。鼎底部残留有烟炱痕迹[①]。

① 广东省文物考古研究所：《博罗横岭山——商周时期墓地2000年发掘报告》，科学出版社，2005年，170、171页。

图一　修复前的铜鼎

图二　修复前的铜鼎残破状况（局部）

出土时，器壁较薄，铜胎腐蚀氧化较为严重，内外表层形成有一层厚0.8～1.5毫米不等、表面翠绿色里面蓝绿间粉绿色的氧化层膜，氧化层膜有大幅脱落的情况；器腹上部纹饰处因锈蚀残缺有口径最阔为高1.3厘米×1.8厘米左右的破洞一个；一鼎腿脱落，鼎腿脱落后鼎腹底部露有破洞一个，破洞断口有一向鼎腹外壁延伸长度为2.3厘米的裂缝，并有微小的向外变形情况，鼎腿曾被考古现场人员用“502瞬间快速胶黏剂”黏接复位，但由于黏接工艺处理不当已再次脱落，脱落后由于胶体和原来未清洗干净的泥土占位以及原断口向外变形的原因，造成如再次直接黏接会出现鼎腿错位变形的情况；另一鼎腿下部离足尖2.3厘米处断离，断口呈氧化铁红褐色，但仍能与上部断口相连接；断落的足尖现存碎片中线的右边因锈蚀而完全残缺，左边自上而下断裂成两块，两块碎片接缝及边缘部位有残缺；鼎的口沿部位自上而下有一长度为1.8厘米左右的裂缝；鼎的一方形立耳左边中间部位完全断裂（图一、图二）。

三

检测分析

为能科学地对该铜鼎开展保护与修复工作，在处理前对器物进行必要的检测分析工作，检测内容主要是该铜鼎各种合金含量情况及锈蚀产物物相结构，目的是通过检测分析来了解该铜鼎是否已受到氯化物的侵蚀，为下一步的防锈、除锈、加固和修补复原工作提供必不可少的科学分析数据。

由于该西周铜鼎具有十分珍贵的历史、文化、艺术价值和不可再造这一特性，因此，检测分析工作必须依据相关的法律法规要求，按照“最大保护”和“最小干预”

的原则，选用一些对器物无损伤的或是采样量极其微少、不会对文物本体造成危害或影响其外观的分析方法来进行检测。综合当前国内外在青铜文物检测分析工作上所取得的成功经验，结合我们所观察到的该青铜鼎的实际情况，在检测分析工作上我们先后分别采用“扫描电子显微镜/X-射线能谱联用仪（SEM/EDS）”、“D/max-3A衍射仪（XRD）”、“X射线能量色散谱仪” 和“硝酸银检测法”等科学仪器和手段对该青铜鼎的合金元素成分、物相、金相组织和氯化物进行检测分析。

（一） 合金成分检测

为避免因检测采样对青铜鼎造成破坏，检测分析选取了该青铜鼎腐蚀损坏最为严重而且又不会影响将来修补复原的残破断落鼎腿部位，从鼎腿足尖碎片处选取两个金属部位及其中一个检测部位表面的腐蚀氧化层进行。

检测点1：在碎片上选取一约0.5平方厘米的面积作为检测点，该检测点表面有厚达约1.2毫米左右的腐蚀氧化层，腐蚀氧化层从表面到里面分别是：首层是黑色烟垢层，二层是灰白色色层，三层是粉绿色层，四层是虽已腐蚀氧化成暗红褐色但尚有金属光泽的金属芯。检测部位是去除了表层腐蚀氧化层后的金属芯表面，利用中山大学检测中心配置的“扫描电子显微镜/X-射线能谱联用仪”对该部位进行了检测，检测结果见图三。

检测点2：利用中山大学检测中心配置的“扫描电子显微镜/X-射线能谱联用仪”对从检测点1表面取下来的腐蚀氧化层产物进行检测，检测结果见图四。

检测点3：在靠近检测点1旁边的两块碎片之间断面上选取一段长约1厘米的截面作为检测点。该检测点除断面两边表层有腐蚀氧化层外，中心部位是已腐蚀氧化成暗红褐色但尚有金属光泽的金属芯，我们对这一部位抛光后利用广东工业大学实验研究中心配置的“X射线能量色散谱仪”进行检测，检测结果见图五。

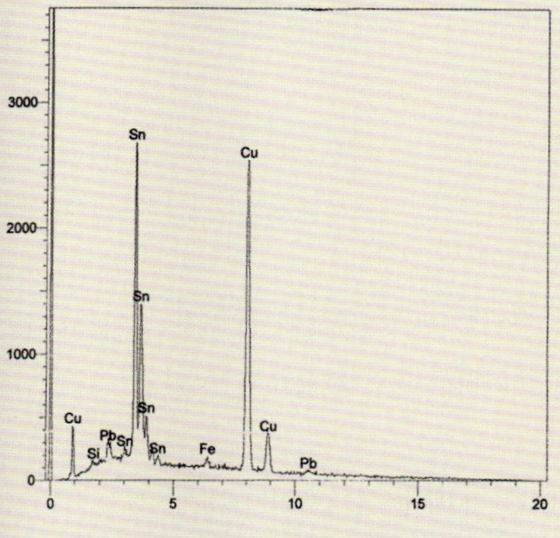

图三 检测点1的主要合金成分谱图

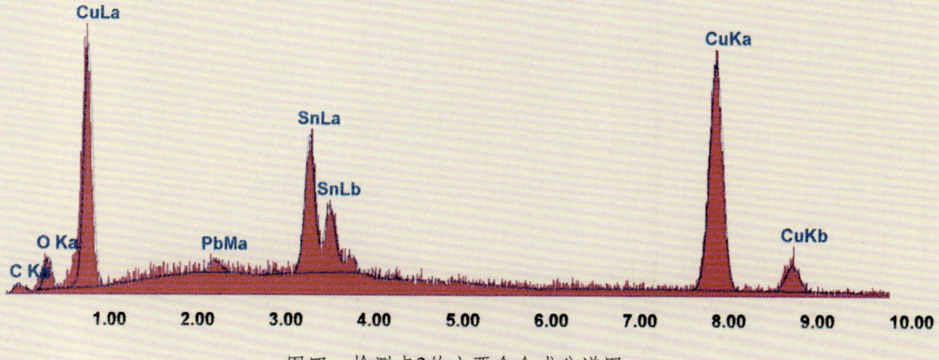

图四 检测点2的主要合金成分谱图

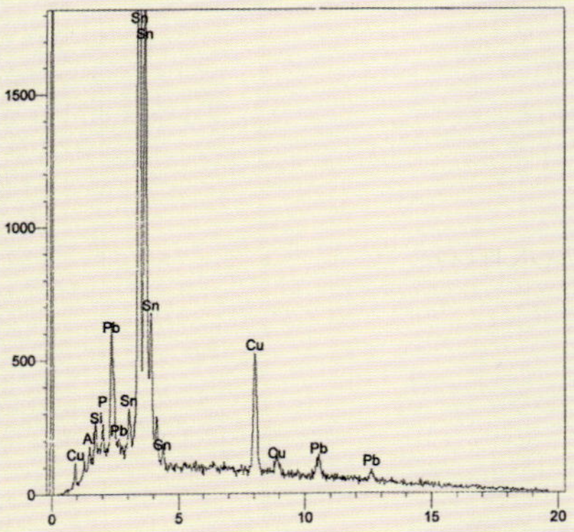

图五　检测点3的主要合金成分谱图

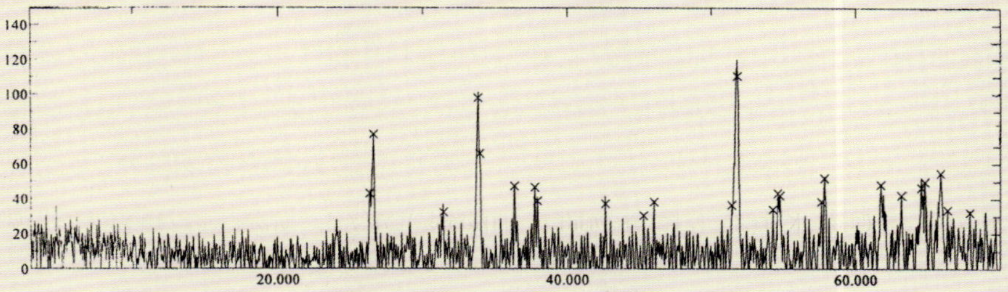

图六　鼎腿足尖碎片断面锈蚀产物物相检测谱图

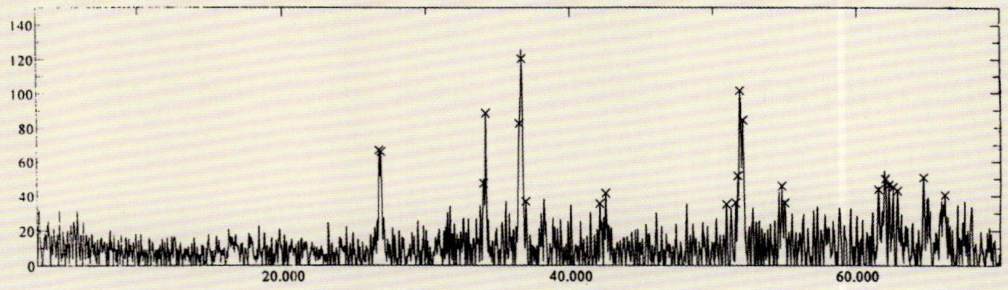

图七　鼎腿残碎片锈蚀产物物相检测谱图

（二）锈蚀产物物相检测

锈蚀产物物相检测共从该青铜鼎上选取了两个样本，其中：1号样本是来自于该青铜鼎鼎腿掉落的一片残碎片，残碎片约1.2 平方厘米，已全部腐蚀氧化成粉绿偏白色；2号样本选自于青铜鼎断落足尖的碎片断口横截面，该横截面腐蚀氧化极为严重，颜色呈暗红褐色。

检测选用的仪器是中山大学检测中心配置的“D/max-3A衍射仪（XRD）”，检测结果见图六、图七。

（三）金相组织检测

金相组织检测点与检测点3同一部位，其合金的显微组织显示为：块状初析相（平滑状）+ 细密共析体，不属于铸态组织（图八、图九）。因此，检测结论认为，从显微组织来看，该残片很可能经过均匀化热处理后快速冷却，抛光未浸蚀表面仅可见少量气孔。利用广东工业大学实验研究中心配置的“X射线能量色散谱仪”对块状初析相、细密共析体分别进行测定，其主要成分见图一〇、图一一。

（四）铜鼎出土时周边泥土检测

此项工作主要是检测墓坑里铜鼎出土时附近泥土的酸碱度和有否氯化物的情况。具体做法是：首先将泥土捣碎，用纯水溶解并用玻璃棒搅拌匀混，再用滤纸进行过滤，把混杂在泥水中的泥末、沙石、杂物隔除干净后装进玻璃杯内，然后用“酸碱度计”测量其酸碱度。接着用吸管吸浓度为5%的硝酸银溶液滴进澄清后的泥水中，并观察水中有否白色物质（硝酸银）沉淀，如有白色沉淀物就说明泥水中存在有氯化物。通过检测，铜鼎出土时周边的泥土酸碱度结果pH值为6.4，属弱酸性，泥水中也没有氯化物沉淀反应。

（五）检测结果分析

“扫描电子显微镜/X-射线能谱联用仪（SEM/EDS）”和“X射线能量色散谱仪”检测是属于半定量检测，它能够检测出化学元素序列中排列在第11的钠(Na)以后的所有元素，如果青铜文物上的锈蚀产物存在有氯元素的话，氯（Cl）在化学元素序列中排列第17，所以，它就一定能够作为青铜器的合金元素之一而被检测出来。“D/max-3A衍射仪（XRD）”则是根据物质晶体的衍射效应来测定晶体的内

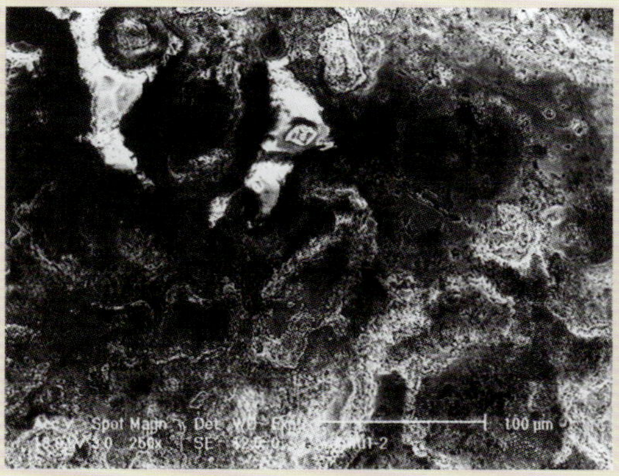

图八　足尖断面铜芯合金显微组织（250x）

图九　足尖断面铜芯合金高显微组织（1000x）

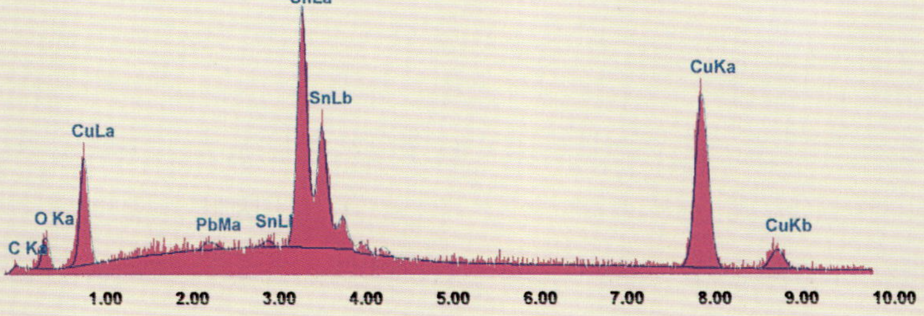

图一〇　足尖断面铜芯显微组织中细密共析体主要合金成分

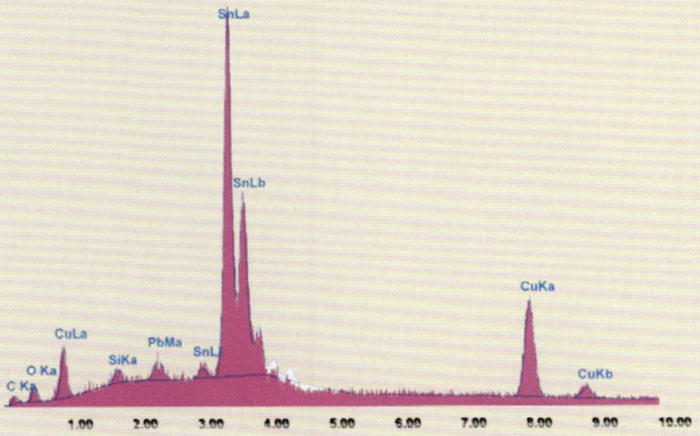

图一一　足尖断面铜芯显微组织中平滑块状相主要合金成分

表一　各检测点的主要合金成分　(%)

检测点	铜(Cu)	锡(Sn)	铅(Pb)	氧(O)	铁(Fe)	硅(Si)	磷(P)	铝(Al)
一	59.48	36.95	2.44	/	0.86	0.27	/	/
二	76.08	13.69	8.29	/	/	0.74	0.7	0.5
三	74.406	20.612	1.777	3.205	/	/	/	/

表二　检测点显示的主要锈蚀产物物相

样本名称	颜色	物相结果
1号样本	粉绿偏白	$Cu_2(CO_3)(OH)_2$（孔雀石）、SnO_2（锡石）
2号样本	暗红褐色	$Cu_2(CO_3)(OH)_2$（孔雀石）、SnO_2（锡石）

表三　检测点显示的不同显微组织主要合金成分　(%)

组织区域	Cu	Sn	Pb	Si	O	C
平滑块状相	34.09	59.43	2.83	0.57	1.64	1.44
细密共析体	58.38	37.17	1.26	/	3.19	0

部结构和鉴别晶体的物相，从而确定被检测样品的物质组成（表一～表三）。所以，作为结晶物质的氯化物，如果它存在于青铜器锈蚀产物上的话，就一定会以氯化亚铜（CuCl）和副氯铜矿、氯铜矿[$Cu_2(OH)_3Cl$]等氯化合物的“相”而被检测指示出来，但如果被检测的样品中氯离子（Cl^-）是以单质或其混合物存在于青铜器锈蚀产物上的话，指示出的则是“元素”。以上三项金属成分和锈蚀产物物相检测数据中都没有显示出该西周铜鼎的铜芯部位、铜芯与表层腐蚀氧化层交接处、铜芯表层的锈蚀产物及铜鼎出土时周边的泥土存在有氯元素和氯化合物。因此，该青铜鼎虽然腐蚀氧化极为严重，锈蚀层呈粉化状况，但还没有受到氯化物的侵蚀。

四

缓蚀处理与封护加固

从检测数据可见，该西周铜鼎并没有受到氯化物的侵蚀，因此，铜鼎的保护工作主要是今后的防锈问题和渗透加固。根据青铜文物锈蚀机理的研究，防锈问题通常只需要在青铜器的表面涂上一层树脂薄膜，使其与空气中的氧和水分隔绝起来，就能达到封闭保护的作用。但经长期观察，发现在青铜器的防锈上只单纯采用封护办法保护青铜器并不理想，因为青铜器在日常利用过程中，封护膜一旦受到损伤，空气中的氧和水分等物质又会与青铜器的基体接触而继续受到有害物质的腐蚀氧化，而且，潜藏于青铜器上的氯化亚铜（CuCl）实际上也是很难被树脂封闭住。但如果在进行封护处理前，先进行缓蚀处理，使其表面形成一层金属保护膜，然后再作封护处理，实行双重防护，就能有效地防止青铜器继续受到有害物质的腐蚀破坏。因此，对该铜鼎的防锈处理工作采取缓蚀与封护相结合的防锈处理方法。

根据目前国内外在青铜文物防锈处理工作上所取得的成功经验，该青铜鼎采用“苯骈三氮唑（BTA）乙醇溶液”作为缓蚀处理的材料，浓度选定为3%。缓蚀处理通常是要采用浸泡的办法，但考虑到该铜鼎鼎腹上部器壁较薄，腐蚀氧化较为严重，锈蚀层表面虽有一层光滑的层膜，但层膜下的锈蚀层并不坚硬，如采用液体浸泡的办法，浸泡时间的“度”如果把握不好，浸泡液中的有机溶剂就会造成器表表面腐蚀氧化层脱落，甚至造成器壁较薄部位因洞穿而损坏，前期的试验证实了这一点。所以，该铜鼎的封护和加固处理采用涂浸的办法，用毛笔蘸“苯骈三氮唑乙醇溶液”淋涂于青铜鼎的表面，使其与铜离子交替结合而形成一层类似高聚物线状结构形式、不溶于水的金属配合物透明覆盖膜——“苯骈三氮唑铜”，从而有效地隔断铜及铜合金与各种腐蚀介质的接触，使铜鼎得到保护。为促进青铜鼎中铜离子与缓蚀剂中的苯骈三氮唑充分反应，加快表面金属保护膜的形成，涂浸前先将青铜鼎放置在恒温干燥箱中加热至40℃左右再进行涂渗，涂渗五遍后将其放置在密封的玻璃器皿中约20多小时，等缓蚀剂充分反应后，用无水乙醇将凝聚在青铜器表面没有反应完全的缓蚀剂擦除干净，即进行封护处理。由于封护和加固采用的材料都是稀释后无色透明高分子材料，因此，该青铜鼎的封护处理是采用与加固处理两道工序同步完成的办法进行。青铜器封护和加固所使用的材料比较多，其中的Paraloid B72聚丙烯酸高分子材料是由甲基丙烯酸甲酯和甲基丙烯酸乙酯共聚而成的有机化合物，它不但具有无色、透明、折光性小的优点，而且还具有良好的渗透性和耐候性，因此，它是目前世界文博界公认的在青铜文物保护方面有着诸多优点的加固封护材料。经反复比较和试用，该青铜鼎选用英国产的“Paraloid B72”来作为表面封护和渗透加固材料。图一二、图一三、图一四是该墓地出土青铜器采用“Paraloid B72”进行表面封护和渗透加固前后效果对比照。

表面封护和渗透加固使用的“Paraloid B72”浓度，在前期的配方选择上分别配制了1%、2%、3%、5%四种配方，试验所见，如浓度太高，渗透效果不好，而且折光性较高。浓度大低，涂渗的次数要相对增加，才能累积足够的胶体进行加固。经权衡再三，最后确定分别选用浓度为2%和5%两种“Paraloid B72” 胶液进行封护和渗透加固处理。操作时用毛笔先在已形成有金属配合物透明覆盖膜的青铜鼎表面蘸涂三遍2%的“Paraloid B72”浸透加固液，最后再淋涂二遍5%的“Paraloid B72”浸透加固液，每淋涂一遍“Paraloid B72” 浸透加固液后要待其干透后再淋涂第二遍，这样周而复始，青铜鼎的表面就形成有一层无色、透明、耐老化和耐候性好、凝结时间快、凝结后不会产生光泽的封护膜，铜鼎器身的硬度也得到加强。

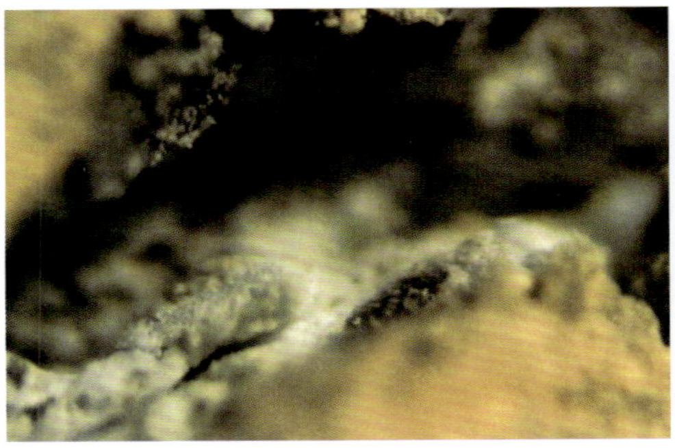

图一二　渗透加固前观察到的状况(15x)

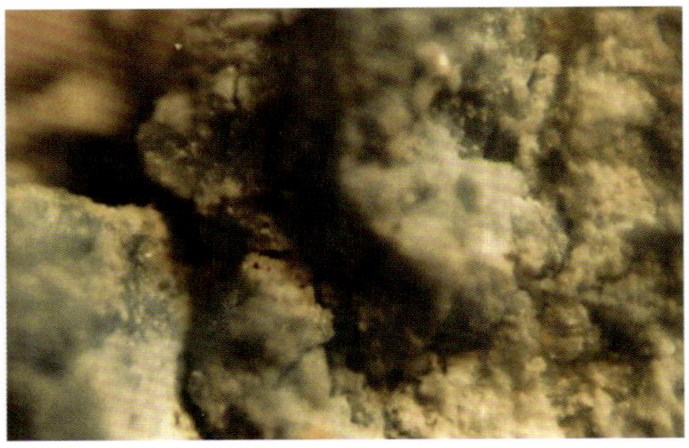

图一三　渗透加固前观察到的状况(10x)

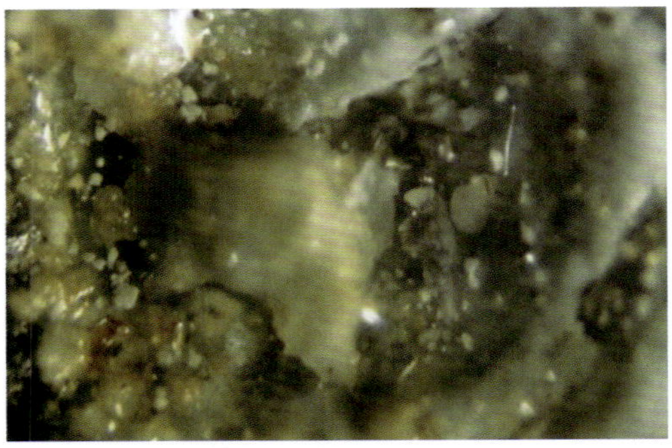

图一四　渗透加固后观察到的状况(15x)

图一五　碎片黏接复位后的铜鼎

五

补配复原工作

完成缓蚀和加固封护处理后，就可以根据该铜鼎各残破缺损部位的实际情况进行修补复原工作（图一五）。由于青铜鼎器壁厚薄不均匀，锈蚀又十分严重，因此，修补复原工作必须要采取传统工艺与现代科学技术相结合的方法进行。工艺上是传统的，材料上则是现代科学技术的成果，如补配材料的使用上，传统工艺通常是用金属材料进行补配，但该铜鼎的补配则使用质轻的高分子合成树脂材料进行补配。西周铜鼎的修补复原工艺过程如下：

1. 器腹上部纹饰处残缺破洞的补配复原

（1）由于破洞不大，从该鼎其他纹饰部位选取与破洞处相同或基本相同的纹饰用橡皮泥把它印制成阴模取下，印制时要注意与残缺口周边原有纹饰相接自然；

（2）将印制好的橡皮泥阴模涂上脱模剂，然后再用环氧树脂、固化剂、填充剂和颜料色粉等按配方比例及需要的色泽混合均匀调配成环氧胶泥，将其填注在已涂了脱膜剂的阴模范块上；

（3）待填注的环氧胶泥凝固后，除去橡皮泥胶模，制成环氧树脂补配件坯形；

（4）将环氧树脂补配件从铜鼎的内面垫托在破洞处，并对接好铜鼎器身上的纹饰，然后将残破洞口的形状描画在环氧树脂补配件上，并用刀具修整成与破洞口形状一致的补配件；

（5）最后用环氧树脂、固化剂、填充剂和颜料色粉等按配方比例及需要的色泽调配成胶黏剂将环氧树脂补配件黏接到残缺的破洞处，完成破洞的修补工作。

2. 该铜鼎考古现场修复时黏接错位的鼎腿调整复原修复工作

（1）用有机溶剂丙酮溶液将原黏接鼎腿时使用的“502瞬间胶黏剂”溶解后从鼎底分离脱落下来，并将两边接口处的黏胶和泥土彻底清除干净；

（2）鼎底与鼎腿连接处的破洞边缘出现的微小向外变形，采用手钳钳压加扭压办法进行矫形复位；

（3）然后根据鼎身的色泽用环氧树脂、固化剂、填充剂和颜料色粉等调配成黏合剂，将鼎腿重新定位进行黏接。

3. 断裂并有残缺的鼎腿修复工作

（1）用按比例调配好的环氧树脂胶黏剂将断落的碎片按原位黏接复原好；

（2）用橡皮泥从鼎腿的内侧把残缺部位垫托固定好，再按配方比例和需要的色泽调配好环氧树脂胶泥从鼎腿的外面把残缺的部位填补抹平；

（3）待填补的环氧树脂胶泥凝固后除去鼎腿内壁垫托的橡皮泥，然后用刀具修整好补配部位的形状，完成该鼎腿的修补复原工作。

六

表面修饰处理

西周铜鼎修补复原工作完成后，就可以进行最后一道工序，对修补复原部位进行表面修饰处理，这道工序在传统工艺上称为“做假”。对于这道工序，近二三十年来有着两种不同的看法，一种认为，对于修复补配的部位应不作任何修饰处理，原有的部位就是原有的颜色，新的修复补配部位要与原有的部位在色泽上有着明显的区别，以免给研究人员和观赏者造成混淆，这种处理效果称之为“考古修复处理方法”；另一种认为，从人们的审美观出发，对于修复补配的部位应根据补配件周边原有器物氧化腐蚀后的锈色情况，用矿物质颜料调胶黏剂在补配复原的部位上进行随色加以掩饰，使之与周边部位的锈色相协调，看不出修复补配的痕迹，不影响其外观的美感。同时，这种观点还认为，在现代高科技仪器面前，修复补配部位不管修饰得如何与原有部位协调逼真，都会原形毕露，丝毫不会影响专

图一六　修复后的铜鼎

业人员对它的研究，这种处理效果过去称之为“商业修复处理方法”，现在称之为“陈列修复处理方法”，这种处理方法实际上是青铜器修复传统工艺的一门“绝活”。

广东省博物馆早在20世纪70年代中期，根据时代要求和器物形状的不同，提出第三种处理方法，叫做“陈列研究处理方法”①，该处理方法的特点就是“内外有别”，凡是观众能看到的修复补配部位都必须要加以修饰，让观众看不出其修复补配过的痕迹，给观赏者美的享受。而观众看不到的部位（内部）则不作任何的修饰，让研究人员透过该部位就可以了解该文物修复补配前的状态。考虑到该青铜鼎的器形是侈口浅腹形和今后陈列展出的需要，该铜鼎修复补配部位其表面采用“商业修复处理方法”进行修饰，用黏合剂调非水溶性的矿物颜料粉根据修复补配部位的周边原来器物表面的颜色，通过点、涂、弹、压、贴等工艺方法，使修复部位的颜色与周边原有器物表面的颜色互相协调，浑然一体，毫无修复补配过的痕迹，完成该西周青铜鼎的修补复原工作，给观赏者美的享受（图一六）。

① 莫鹏：《中国青铜文物修复传统工艺的继承和发展》，《中国博物馆》1999年第3期；《东汉陶水田模型的修复研究》，《岭南考古论文集》（1），岭南美术出版社，2001年，167～179页。

七

结　语

广东博罗横岭山先秦墓地出土西周铜鼎自21世纪初修复保护至今已有多年，经观察未发现有出现变化的情况和迹象，说明在修复过程中所采取的方法和步骤是正确的。

本文所研究的仅是该青铜鼎的修复问题，其实，该青铜鼎还有许多问题尚需作进一步的研究，如铜鼎的铸造工艺问题、锈蚀机理及其保护问题等。先秦时期由于岭南地区交通的不便利，经济文化的落后和生产力水平的低下，其铸造的青铜器与中原地区也有所不同，不同的青铜器在不同的地理环境影响下就会产生不同的锈蚀情况，这些都十分值得我们去作深入的研究和探讨。对该青铜鼎的研究，是对“岭南地区出土先秦时期青铜器锈蚀机理和保护方法研究”的前奏和开端，我们冀望这一课题的研究能得以顺利开展。

拉曼光谱在青铜文物腐蚀产物研究中的应用

The Application of Raman Spectroscopy
in Research on Corrosion Products of Bronze Relics

吴　沫 / 广东省博物馆 馆员

［摘要］

拉曼光谱测试技术由于具有多种优点而适合对青铜文物不同部位的腐蚀产物进行针对性分析，有助于为确定青铜文物保护方案提供重要依据。本文通过近年国内已完成的研究案例说明拉曼光谱应用于青铜文物保护研究的成果、优势和局限性。

［关键词］

拉曼光谱　青铜文物　腐蚀产物　文物保护

Abstract

Raman spectroscopy technique has many advantages for component analysis on the different parts of the corrosion products of bronze relics. The test results can help to provide important evidences for bronze relics protection program. In this paper, the applications, advantages and limitations of Raman spectroscopy in study on corrosion products of bronze relics in recent years in China were reviewed and discussed.

Key words

Raman spectroscopy; Bronze relics; Corrosion products; Relics protection

一

引 言

青铜器在世界各地都有出现，它的诞生宣告人类迎来了一个新的文明时代——青铜时代。青铜文物是对古代人类灿烂的青铜文化和青铜器制作技术发展的见证，具有极高的历史、艺术和研究价值①。古代的青铜器在长期深埋地下的情况下通常已与埋藏环境建立起相对稳定的化学平衡关系，然而在经发掘出土后，其腐蚀速度反而加速②。因此，研究青铜文物的腐蚀产物和腐蚀机理，是对其采取行之有效保护措施的首要任务，也是目前青铜文物保护研究的发展趋势。拉曼光谱分析技术由于具有取样量小（也可无损）、无需对样品的特别制备、空间分辨率高、可进行微区分析、抗干扰强且使用方便快捷等优点被不断应用于青铜文物的腐蚀产物研究中，有助于揭示青铜文物表面的处理工艺和追溯腐蚀产物的形成过程，进而为确定青铜文物保护方案提供重要依据。本文拟通过近年国内相关的研究案例说明拉曼光谱在青铜文物腐蚀产物研究中的应用优势和局限，以期拉曼光谱在青铜腐蚀研究中能得到更充分和完善的利用。

① “青铜文物保护新技术研究”课题组:《青铜文物保护研究现状及发展趋势》，《殷都学刊》2004年第3期。

② 胡星明、毕建洪:《青铜文物腐蚀与保护研究》，《安徽大学学报》（自然科学版）2007年第4期。

二

应用案例

1. 春秋至战国时期青铜矛的测试

云南楚雄万家坝古墓群为春秋中晚期至战国初期的墓群。杨群等利用英国Renshaw公司的MKI1000型的显微共焦拉曼光谱仪，对该墓群中出土的1件青铜矛进行了无损的拉曼光谱分析，发现这件青铜矛中部淡绿色腐蚀区的产物主要为碱式碳酸铜，青铜矛尖处锈蚀产物主要为氧化亚铜（Cu_2O），并通过对青铜矛刃部和矛尖部截取的少量样品进行的电子探针测试，结果指出这件铜矛的矛身和矛尖部位的内部成分相差很大。矛身以纯铜为主，还有少量Sn和Si元素，矛尖则含有Cu、Sn、Zn、Fe、Si、C和Al共7种元素，且其中的Zn、Fe、Sn元素的含量相对较高，推测这件青铜矛在加工时采用了立式浇注法。由于Sn、Zn、Fe的比重大于Cu，在浇注时降落得较快，因此得以在矛尖处富集；而矛尖表面相对富集的SnO_2也对矛尖部位起到了抗腐蚀的作用。值得注意的是，由于样品矛尖处SnO_2的拉曼光谱极弱，因此在测试中未能发现SnO_2的拉曼光谱①。

2. 元代青铜镜的测试

王怡林等利用英国Renshaw公司的MKI1000型的显微共焦拉曼光谱仪，对云南省禄丰县黑井石龙村后山火葬墓出土的1件元代铜镜的表面绿色和黑色腐蚀区进行了拉曼光谱分析，发现两区域内的腐蚀产物都主要是碱式碳酸铜。其中，铜绿区域还测得氧化亚铜（Cu_2O），并利用电子探针对铜镜表面和内部进行了成分分析，测得铜镜本体是含铜量较高的低锡青铜合金，铜镜表面则除了含铜的氧化物外，还含有较大比例的Fe、Si、Al的氧化物。由于其中铁、硅的重量百分比都接近15%，铝的重量百分比接近5%，所以推测这枚元代铜镜可能在表面镀了一层铁铝合金。这种铁铝合金既能起到防腐蚀的作用，其造价成本又相对较低②。

3. 西汉青铜块和元代青铜残剑的测试

成小林（2004）利用美国Thermo Nicolet公司的Almega型共焦显微拉曼光谱仪，对1件元代青铜残剑上的锈蚀物进行了无损的原位分析，发现青铜剑上绿色和蓝色锈蚀物分别为两种碱式碳酸铜$CuCO_3 \cdot Cu(OH)_2$和$2CuCO_3 \cdot Cu(OH)_2$，即孔雀石和蓝铜矿；对1件表面覆盖有黑色腐蚀物的西汉青铜小块的腐蚀区进行原位分析，测到腐蚀产物为氧化铜CuO；另对1件含有多层腐蚀产物的元代青铜残片进行显微形貌观察和结构分析。发现这一金属残片表层约有3～4层的分层结构：最外层呈绿色，厚度不均，测得腐蚀产物为碱式氯化铜$CuCl_2 \cdot 3\,Cu(OH)_2$；第二层呈褐红色，结构较致密，测得腐蚀产物为氧化亚铜Cu_2O；第三层呈亮灰白色，结构疏松，未能检测出锈蚀产物，后经扫描电镜分析发现这层的Cu和Cl元素含量较多；第四层则为青铜基体③。

4. 战国墓出土青铜器的测试

位于湖北省襄樊地区的九连墩1号、2号墓为战国中晚期“大夫”级别的两座楚墓，于2000年经抢救性发掘共出土包括礼器、乐器、生活乐器、车马器等上千套文物。罗武干等（2007）利用法国JY公司LABRAM-HR型激光显微共焦拉曼光谱仪，对其中1号墓出土的几件青铜器表面的锈蚀产物进行了拉曼光谱分析。发现样品表面的蓝绿色锈蚀物中，绿色锈蚀物主要为孔雀石，即碱式碳酸铜$CuCO_3 \cdot Cu(OH)_2$，部分为蓝铜矿$2CuCO_3 \cdot Cu(OH)_2$，即另一种碱式碳酸铜$Cu_2CO_3 \cdot Cu(OH)_2$；蓝色锈蚀物主要为蓝铜矿，另有一些浅绿色锈蚀物则为副氯铜矿$Cu_2(OH)_3Cl$。由于青铜器在能接触到O_2、CO_2、H_2O、Cl^-及硫化物的环境中，易形成呈疏松颗粒粉末状的副氯铜矿，与水、氯气、氯离子等接触后可进一步锈蚀青铜器，因此建议清除青铜器表面的副氯铜矿，并将青铜器尽量保存在不与O_2、CO_2、H_2O、Cl^-及硫化物接触的相对封闭和稳定的环境中④。

5. 登州博物馆馆藏青铜器的测试

山东省蓬莱市登州博物馆新馆于2000年建成对外开放，其库房保藏的青铜器

① 杨群、王怡林、张鹏翔等：《拉曼光谱对古青铜矛腐蚀情形的无损研究》，《光散射学报》2011年第1期。

② 王怡林、杨群、张鹏翔等：《元代铜镜腐蚀情形的拉曼光谱研究》，《光谱学与光谱分析》2001年第1期。

③ 成小林：《共焦显微激光拉曼光谱在青铜锈蚀研究中的应用》，《文物保护与修复纪实——第八届全国考古与文物保护（化学）学术会议论文集》，2004年，46～52页。

④ 罗武干、秦颖、王昌燧等：《九连墩楚墓青铜器锈蚀产物的拉曼光谱分析》，《岩矿测试》2007年第2期。

① 李涛、秦颖、罗武干等：《古代青铜器锈蚀产物的拉曼和红外光谱分析》，《有色金属》2008年第2期。

自2004年以来开始出现腐蚀加快的现象，并在短短2年时间里有近半数的器物锈蚀严重，出现淡绿色粉状锈蚀物，甚至部分器物出现穿孔和掉渣现象。李涛等利用LABRAM-HR型显微共焦激光拉曼光谱仪，对其中的商代铜鼎、西周铜簋、西周铜鼎、西周铜釜、宋代铜镜、铜方鼎（年代不详）等10件锈蚀严重的铜器进行采样分析。发现这批样品中不同颜色的锈蚀产物分别是：蓝色物质为蓝铜矿，绿色物质为孔雀石和氯铜矿，淡绿色物质为副氯铜矿，白色物质为白铅矿和方解石，淡黄色物质为黄铅钒；对青铜器破坏最为严重的粉状锈蚀物主要是氯铜矿和副氯铜矿，而且其细小颗粒可随空气漂浮和流动“传染”其他铜器。因此，建议尽快隔离已感染“粉状锈”的器物，并对其采取除锈和除氯化物的保护措施。研究者同时对部分样品还进行了傅里叶变换红外光谱测试和X射线荧光光谱分析，分析结果证实了拉曼光谱测试的准确性①。

三

应用优势

从上述测试研究案例可以看到，拉曼光谱在青铜文物腐蚀研究中存在几项较为明显的优势。所以当我们对青铜文物的腐蚀产物作以下相关研究时，应优先考虑采用共焦显微拉曼光谱仪进行分析。

1. 有腐蚀物图谱供鉴别

研究的案例显示，对腐蚀产物中的孔雀石、蓝铜矿、氧化铜、氧化亚铜、氯铜矿、副氯铜矿、白铅矿、黄铅钒采用拉曼激光进行测试，可得到具有鉴定意义的图谱。其中，同为碱式碳酸铜的孔雀石和蓝铜矿，与同为碱式氯化铜的氯铜矿和副氯铜矿，都有相应的特征谱峰可作甄别。

2. 作原位测试无需取样制样

对于部分高度或厚度不超过拉曼光谱仪显微物镜聚焦点至样品台间距的样品，可进行原位的拉曼光谱测试，无需取样和制样。

3. 取样量少

对于体积较大或形制较复杂的青铜文物不便进行原位测试、而又不便刮取较多腐蚀产物时，可用针尖挑取一丁点腐蚀产物即可进行拉曼光谱测试。

4. 微区能准确定位，作多点测试

对于存在多处颜色不同、结构不同腐蚀区域的青铜文物，即使腐蚀区域面积很小，由于显微拉曼光谱仪的空间分辨率可达1～2微米，因而都可利用拉曼光谱仪的聚焦激光光斑准确定位，进行多点测试。

5. 可观察多层腐蚀物形貌并可逐层准确定位分析

在可进行原位拉曼光谱分析的前提下，对于存在多层腐蚀产物的青铜文物，可利用拉曼光谱仪的显微镜对样品的腐蚀区域进行逐层的形貌观察，并可利用聚焦光斑对每层区域准确定位后再进行相应的成分分析。

四

局限性

拉曼光谱仪对于青铜文物腐蚀产物的分析虽然具有以上五个方面的优势，但也存在一定的局限性。因此，当涉及以下情况时，可考虑借助其他分析仪器进行补充测试。

1. 对部分拉曼光谱不敏感的腐蚀产物的测试

从以上研究案例看，拉曼光谱并非对所有腐蚀产物有效，如对硫化铜和硫化亚铜就难以测试到具有鉴定意义的光谱①。硫化物的出现多被认为和微生物腐蚀有关②。如果青铜文物在缺氧环境中腐蚀速度仍然很快，就需要考虑青铜器可能受到微生物腐蚀，而相关的硫化物产物用拉曼光谱则很难检测到，就需考虑采用X射线粉晶衍射仪或X射线荧光光谱仪等进行测试。

2. 对文物的合金含量做定量分析

由于拉曼光谱分析的结果主要以显示特征峰为主的谱图，对于不同成分的含量常常难以做定量分析，故如果需要对青铜文物的合金含量做定量分析时，需借助电子探针等测试仪器作补充测试。

3. 研究腐蚀产物与环境间的关系

拉曼光谱测试主要是针对青铜文物表层的腐蚀产物作成分分析，以帮助逆推青铜器发生腐蚀的可能机理，从而制定相应的保护措施。然而，青铜器的腐蚀涉及极为复杂的过程，与青铜器所在的具体环境密切相关③。因此，当需要研究青铜文物腐蚀产物与其所在的土壤、空气或水间的具体关系时，就需要借助其他的化学模拟实验。

① 成小林:《共焦显微激光拉曼光谱在青铜锈蚀研究中的应用》，《文物保护与修复纪实——第八届全国考古与文物保护（化学）学术会议论文集》，2004年，50页。

② 张孝绒、郝新本:《微生物对金属文物的腐蚀作用》，《文博》1998年第2期。

③ 王菊琳、吕国诚，许淳淳:《青铜文物腐蚀研究进展》，《第八届全国考古与文物保护（化学）学术会议论文集》，2004年，97～105页。

略论青铜文物的保护与利用
——以柳州博物馆的实践为例

A Brief Discussion on Conservation and Development for Bronze Relics
—A Case about the Practice of Liuzhou Museum

韩玉燕 / 柳州博物馆 副研究员

[摘要]

本文从金属腐蚀学的一般原理着手，探讨青铜器的腐蚀机理及环境对青铜文物保护和利用的影响，针对青铜器腐蚀的三个过程，提出一些在保管、陈列和外展过程中应注意事项和防护措施。

[关键词]

青铜器　腐蚀机理　保护措施

Abstract

Based on the general principles of metal corrosion, this article explores the corrosion-mechanism of bronze and environmental influence for protection and use of bronze. Aiming at the three processes for bronze corrosion, it also gives a few suggestions about precautions and protective measures during storage, display and exhibition out of museum.

Key words

Bronze wares; Corrosion mechanism; Protective measures

中国的青铜时代大约从前2000年左右开始，历经夏、商、西周和春秋时代，前后15个世纪，青铜文化可谓源远流长。中国古代青铜器以造型优美、装饰富丽、铭文典雅、铸造精良等诸多特点，折射出它的灿烂辉煌，是中国举世闻名的重要文化遗产之一。它们对认识我国的文明特征，了解我国古代的历史、科技、汉字的发展演变和青铜艺术等，都有极其重要的价值。保留至今的青铜文物，历时千年，受到腐蚀不可避免，当今重要的是进行保护，合理利用，使其延年益寿。本文试从金属腐蚀学的一般原理着手，探讨青铜器的腐蚀机理及环境对这类文物保护和利用的影响，针对青铜器腐蚀的三个过程，提出一些在保管、陈列和外运过程中的注意事项和防护措施。

一

金属腐蚀的一般原理

在自然界中，大多数金属通常是以矿石的形式存在的。例如铜在自然界中多为硫化铜矿，其主要成分是铜的氧化物和硫化物，而铜的腐蚀产物——铜锈，其主要成分也是氧化物和硫化物[①]。可见，铜的腐蚀过程和其他金属腐蚀过程一样，都是回复到其自然存在状态（矿石）的过程。但若要从矿石中提炼金属，则需要提供一定的能量（如热能或电能）才可完成这种转变，所以金属状态的铜和矿石中的铜存在着能量上的差异，即金属单质比其化合物具有更高的自由能，所以金属具有放出能量而回到热力学上更稳定的自然存在形式——氧化物、硫化物、碳酸盐及其他化合物的倾向。显而易见，能量上的差异就是腐蚀反应的推动力，而放出能量的过程即是腐蚀的过程。伴随着腐蚀过程的进行，将导致腐蚀体系自由能的减少，故它是一个自发的过程[②]。

金属在一定的环境介质中经过反应恢复到它的化合物状态，这个腐蚀过程可用一个总反应过程表示：金属材料 + 腐蚀介质→腐蚀产物。它至少包括三个基本过程：① 通过对流和扩散作用使腐蚀介质向界面迁移。② 在相界上进行反应。③ 腐蚀产物从相界迁移到介质中去或在金属表面上形成覆盖膜[③]。

可见，金属文物的腐蚀是一个不可抗拒的自然现象，我们在保管和使用文物的过程中应该根据金属腐蚀的原理和腐蚀的基本过程加以保护，尽量减缓金属文物的腐蚀速度。

① 许并社、李明照等：《铜冶炼工艺》，化学工业出版社，2007年，1～3页。

②③ 南京化工学院：《金属腐蚀理论及应用》，化学工业出版社，1984年，2～5页。

二

青铜文物的腐蚀机理

根据金属腐蚀的三个基本过程：当青铜器长期暴露于空气中时或是埋藏在土壤里时，就和空气中的O_2、SO_2、H_2S、CO_2等气体接触，土壤里一般都是含有大量的Cl^-、SO_4^{2-}、CO_3^{2-}、OH^-等[①]。无论是露于空气中或是埋藏在土壤里，实际上就是一个和腐蚀介质接触的过程，腐蚀介质不断地向金属界面迁移，逐渐附着于金属表面，发生化学反应，产生锈蚀。青铜器的锈蚀产物主要有两种：一种是有害锈，一种是无害锈。无害锈是在正常环境中（常温常湿），锈蚀产物不再深入青铜基体。如CuO、Cu_2O、CuS、$Cu_2(OH)_2CO_3$等，这类锈既有审美的价值，又可作历史悠久的见证。但是有害锈则不然。其主要是因为土壤中的水和氯化物的侵蚀，会生成$CuCl$、$CuCl_2 \cdot 3Cu(OH)_2$。

$CuCl$是主要的腐蚀产物之一，极不稳定，其化学反应式如下：

$$2CuCl + H_2O \rightarrow Cu_2O + 2HCl$$

Cu_2O层靠近点蚀孔，遇氧气，加上水，盐酸生成碱式氯化铜，其化学反应式如下：

$$Cu_2O + 2HCl + 2H_2O + O_2 \rightarrow CuCl_2 \cdot 3Cu(OH)_2$$

$CuCl$层本身可以转化为碱式氯化铜，形成新的盐酸，使$CuCl$层进一步扩展。反应式为：

$$4CuCl + 4H_2O + O_2 \rightarrow CuCl_2 \cdot 3Cu(OH)_2 + 2HCl$$

生成的盐酸在氧存在下又与铜反应生成氯化亚铜，反应式为:

$$4Cu + 4HCl + O_2 = 4CuCl + 2H_2O$$

如此反复，铜基体不断地腐蚀掉[②]。

粉状锈的危害极大，会像传染病一样在青铜器基体上蔓延开来，青铜器一旦染上这种有害锈，其蔓延和发展是难以抑制的，久而久之，粉状锈就会从青铜器基体上不断脱落下来，至使青铜器穿孔、溃烂甚至瓦解。因为锈体的密度远小于合金基体，当锈体形成后，使铜器表面变疏松。此时外界的氯离子及溶解氧更容易渗入基体，造成恶性循环。不仅如此，粉状锈还可以传染给其他青铜器。

① 南京化工学院:《金属腐蚀理论及应用》，化学工业出版社，1984年，196、197页。

② 廖原:《青铜文物锈蚀机理及有害锈转化剂的研究》，《文物保护与考古科学》2003年第2期。

三

青铜器有害锈的发现和控制

国内外学者对青铜病的产生做了大量的研究，发现氯离子的存在是形成粉状锈的关键，它的存在改变了铜的氧化途径，大大增强了铜的氧化趋势，加快了反应速度。特别是在pH值较低的环境中，碱性基团（OH^-）被消耗，锈化过程更容易进行，使粉状锈呈恶性循环发展。通过对青铜粉状锈跟踪观测发现，锈蚀首先从表面棱角处发生，如果将数件青铜器同置一室，不采取隔离措施，有害锈就会传染给其他无锈的铜器。因此作为青铜器保管员，要经常查看展厅和库房内的青铜器的表面是否有变化，发现生锈就要检测它是否是有害锈，我们可以取一点锈蚀的产物，将其溶于HNO_3中，然后再加入$AgNO_3$，若有白色沉淀物产生，将其溶液过滤掉，在白色沉淀物中再次加入HNO_3，白色沉淀不消失，说明白色沉淀为AgCl，由于Cl^-的存在，说明器物遭到了有害锈的侵蚀，需要及时处理。

为了防止青铜病的破坏，文物工作者和文物保护学者进行了长期的研究和实践，以寻求简便、完善的保护方法。青铜文物的保护可从两个途径入手：第一是控制文物存放的环境，比如库房和展厅的光、温度、相对湿度等，以降低文物腐蚀速度；第二是从文物本身着手，除去腐蚀产物、封闭、稳定腐蚀产物。此外，文物工作者和文物保护研究者也在不断研究更为有效的缓蚀剂和复合试剂，以取得更好的保护效果。

四

环境对青铜文物的影响

在金属腐蚀的一般原理中，我们已提到：金属文物的腐蚀是一个不可抗拒的自然现象。我们能做的是如何减缓文物被腐蚀的进程，环境因素是至关重要的因素。受环境的影响，文物在保存或展览时，甚至在进行保护处理时都会进一步老化，青铜文物易因氧气、温度、湿度、大气污染物或光线的作用发生化学或物理的变化。实验证明，仅仅温度一项的影响都是相当大的，物理和化学变化的速度会因温度的升高而增加，温度每上升10°C，化学反应的速率会增加一倍[①]。光照也是加速青铜文

① 〔加〕Nathan StoLow著，宋燕、卢燕玲等译：《博物馆文物保护与展览》，科学出版社，2010年，4、5页。

物老化的一个致命因素。库房里的器物置于囊匣中，并存放在密集柜里，基本上可以隔断光线的影响，与空气接触的范围也大大减小，光线的影响和氧化作用降到了最低；展厅因要对观众开放，免不了要受到光的照射，文物与空气也是充分接触。因此展出的器物较库房里存放的器物更易受到环境因素的影响，尤其是已经受到Cl^-侵害的器物。氯离子往往贯穿于青铜器的整个锈蚀层，仅是各层内含量有所不同。氯离子在基体金属一定深度形成腐蚀沟槽，在这些腐蚀沟槽内氯离子普遍存在，对腐蚀过渡区腐蚀沟槽内的氯离子的完全清除难度很大，因为这些沟槽已进入基体内一定深度，强行脱除必会损伤文物本体。现今采取的清除只是宏观上的清除，微观上不能清除的那些氯离子在适当的环境条件下还会与环境影响因素之间作用进而重新生成有害锈①。

① 铁付德、陈卫等：《古代青铜器的腐蚀及其控制研究》，《文物保护与考古科学》1997年第3期。

五

柳州博物馆馆藏青铜文物的保护措施

为了有效地保护青铜文物，合理控制保存环境，从而切断青铜病发生、发展的渠道，最大限度地降低青铜文物的腐蚀速率。柳州博物馆主要采取了以下的保护措施：

1. 文物入库前采取的防治措施

（1）建立完善的文物数据信息。首先是文献资料的收集，主要收集记载青铜器出土的有关报告、出土时的文物照片、出土地的埋藏环境资料、文物研究论著等。其次是保管资料，主要是青铜器出土后的保存经历、保养记录、库房保存环境等保管资料。入库文物现状资料也是必不可少的，对每件青铜器做认真观察，记录其腐蚀残损状况。有了以上的文物信息资料，我们可以做到文物保护心中有数。

（2）对新征文物，作一些必要的前处理。首先，适当清除伴随在新征器物表面的泥土、污垢、硬结物、可溶性盐类等有害物质，避免文物病害缠身。清除污染方法有：用蒸馏水清洗、机械法、溶液法、纸浆糊敷法等。

2. 有效控制文物保管环境

博物馆只是环境污染的受体，本身没有对环境污染源进行干预和控制的能力，我们能做的只是对博物馆环境进行控制，让文物保存环境达到合理状态。

（1）温湿度的控制

温湿度的剧烈变化，会破坏器物的内部平衡。高温、高湿的环境则是加速金属器物腐蚀重要的外在因素，低于50%的相对湿度，温度在15～25℃的环境对青铜器的保存较为适宜，柳州在整个春季和夏季都是高温、高湿的天气，因此，柳州博物馆在这两季主要是通过除湿机和空调机来控制库房和展厅的温湿度。

（2）光线的控制

人类赖以生存的自然光和人工光，对文物的保护却是有害的，在本文的“环境对青铜文物的影响”部分已作了阐述。另外，光线产生的热量会使化学反应加速，从而导致文物老化。我馆在青铜文物展示时尽量避免阳光和灯光的直射，使用柔和光线，通过感应技术减少光照的时间。库房也采取防光、避光的有效措施，铜器均放置于避光的密集柜中。

（3）有害物和粉尘的控制

文物库房大部分时间处于封闭状态，空气中的硫化物、氧化物、灰尘等有害物弥漫在器物的周围，这些腐蚀介质附着于器物外壁，通过对流和扩散作用向界面迁移，然后在相界发生化学反应。因此要尽可能减少硫化物、可吸入颗粒、灰尘与青铜器物表面的接触。所采取的措施是：在进入库房前，先经过一个风淋通道，在强对流风的作用下，清除入库人员身体从外界带进的各种颗粒和粉尘，库房内每间隔5～10米安装一台空气净化机，另外文物基本单独置于囊匣中，减少器物与空气的接触。

3. 经常对腐蚀产物进行分析

青铜文物入库或进入展厅后，我们还定期观察器物细微的变化。柳州是一个工业城市，也曾经是酸雨较为严重的城市，经过一段时间的治理，气候环境虽然有了很大的改观，但SO_2依然是主要的空气污染物，加之空气湿度较大和汽车尾气的大量排放等，对青铜器的保管保护都是不利的因素。定期对青铜器上的各种腐蚀产物进行成分和结构分析，以确定腐蚀产物对文物的危害性，从而采取去除腐蚀物或其他保护对策。

六

青铜文物外展的有效保护问题

随着经济的发展，社会公众对文化生活的需求也越来越高，博物馆藏品的出库展出的频率亦会增加，兄弟博物馆之间的相互联展、借展、巡展等也将是不可避免的展开，这随之会带来文物展品保护新的、更高的要求。这里仅谈青铜文物外展时在包装、运输、存储过程中应该注意的问题。

（1）青铜文物在纳入外展计划后于实施前，须对每一件器物的现状做详细记录，包括影像资料和文字说明，尤其是器物的薄弱部位需着重强调一下，说明在包装、搬运和运输中需要哪种类型的保护处理，以保证其旅途的安全。如果是巡展，在每站结束拆展时，都必须进行检查，并与原始记录比较，器物发生变化必须弄清原因，明确保护办法才装箱。

（2）青铜器的保护受温度、湿度、光的照射等因素的影响较大，因此在为外展设计包装箱时，除了包装设计和包装材料需要考虑防震之外，还要考虑温湿度的可控性。相对湿度的控制可以通过运输箱的材料和包装箱内的缓冲材料来实现，温度的控制主要依靠包装箱的缓冲材料或保持外部环境温度的方法达到目的。

（3）在装车和运输过程中,文物可能会因为冲撞、摇晃、震荡等因素产生机械性损伤，随着运输量的增大，机械损伤的概率也会增加，这一点必须由文物部门与运输部门很好沟通，说明重要性，引起装卸单位特别是装卸工人的高度重视，在装卸时小心轻放。如果文物随火车行李车厢走，还要请行李管理员一路予以关照，防止新上行李对文物箱的挤压和文物箱被当做行李错误下站，确保安全。当然，要做到这一点，托运方押运文物人员的思想重视、责任心强度和工作认真细致程度也至关重大。

另外，器物在运输完成后，拆开包装之前通常要在安全条件下存放一整夜或更长时间，如果文物是在温度和湿度相差过大的地区之间运输，在运输过程中包装箱可能会受到冷（或热）的侵袭，在这种情况下，国外的经验是将包装箱放在博物馆的温度条件下保存8小时或更久①。让包装箱内的器物逐渐适应房间的环境条件，以此避免因温差和湿度差别过大而加速青铜器表面的化学反应。还有空包装箱的存储也要讲究，展出结束之前，要提前一周把包装箱打开，置于博物馆的温度条件下，让包装材料与室内空气充分接触，否则，包装时缓冲材料的温湿度会出现不均匀的现象②，青铜文物也会因之受到影响。

综上所述，可以认为利用科学的保护手段是永久保藏和陈列展览青铜器的重要措施，也是弘扬青铜文化的前提。因此青铜器在除锈、封护、储藏环境、外展搬运等工作中，都必须加以重点保护，使其延年益寿、惠及子孙万代。

① 〔加〕Nathan Stolow著，宋燕、卢燕玲等译:《博物馆文物保护与展览》，科学出版社，2010年，64、65页。

② 〔加〕Nathan Stolow著，宋燕、卢燕玲等译:《博物馆文物保护与展览》，科学出版社，2010年，238～240页。

汉代铜镜除锈与修复保护的初探

A Brief Study on Rust Removal, Restoration and Conservation for Bronze Mirrors of Han Dynasty

邓任生 / 广西壮族自治区博物馆 副研究员

[摘要]

青铜器文物修复与保护是目前每个文物工作者的一项工作和任务，本文介绍青铜除锈的几种方法及保护修复的相关问题，进一步分析和探讨，并对这些问题提出相应保护措施。

[关键词]

青铜器除锈　修复　保护

Abstract

Now protection and restoration of Bronze ware is a work and task for each worker which works for cultural relics. This Article main introduces several methods of removal of rust in Bronze ware and its problems about protection and restoration related. After further analysis and discussion, this article proposes protection measures corresponding.

Key words

Rust removal in Bronze ware; Restoration; Conservation

一

引　言

青铜器在我国历史文化中占有特殊的位置由于是合金的器物，在复杂的自然环境中会发生不同程度的腐蚀，尤其是地下出土的青铜器合金成分多样，埋藏环境不同，锈蚀层次多，成分复杂，其中有相当多的腐蚀产物为绿色的古斑，见证着青铜器悠久的历史，被称为“无害锈”，在常温常湿中，无害锈不再深入青铜本体，性质相对稳定，文物修复保护准则规定，原则上不要求去除，因此，这种锈蚀如果不影响纹饰、铭文等重要信息，要尽力保存，如果需要清除，可进行局部处理，有一种是浅绿色的氯化物，呈粉状，就像青铜器上的“恶性肿瘤”。其危害性在于腐蚀反应是在铜胎内向外表凸起使青铜器表面铜质膨胀。这种锈蚀极不稳定，而且容易扩散蔓延，致使器物畸形，纹饰剥落，铭文模糊，严重时整个器物粉化，酥瘫，完全毁坏。粉状锈还能侵害感染其他青铜器，能在青铜器自身和青铜之间相互“传染”。若一件青铜器患有粉状锈，将会威胁整个库房青铜器的安全，这就是“有害锈”。所以，把染上这种浅绿色粉状锈的青铜器称之为青铜病，俗称“青铜癌”，应及时予以彻底清除干净。

二

青铜器的除锈方法

绿色粉状锈是危害青铜器的有害锈之一，由于氯离子存在，空气中的青铜器在接触水分的情况下经常会发生水解，与氯离子反应从而产生氯化物，造成粉状锈的生成。因此，青铜器保护处理的第一步是尽量彻底去除氯离子，然后进行相关的隔离和水分处理，通常青铜器的除锈方法主要有三种，即机械除锈、化学除锈、电化还原法。

1. 机械除锈及操作方法

机械除锈包括手工挖除和借助微型电动机械工具除锈。

（1）手工除锈。即用手工挖剔、削切、刮磨、打磨等。工具有手术刀、刻刀、钢针、小铲、小锤、砂纸等，直接在器物上操作，细心地将粉状锈剔除。

（2）激光除锈。采用激光对青铜器孔洞深凹处的氯化物去除，具有准确、易行的特点，主要利用激光发出的巨大光能，在锈层表面上使表面温度迅速上升、相互作用时产生的光热、光化、光压等光学效应，从而将锈蚀层迅速烧熔，气化与本体分离，有效地把器物表面上的绿色有害粉状锈清除干净。

（3）超声波除锈法。采用超声波机械振荡波作用，发生高频冲击及振动液体，使青铜的粉状锈自然剥离，达到良好情况效果。

2. 化学缓蚀与封护处理

（1）缓蚀。即是阻止或延缓器物的病害的产生，目前基本采用缓蚀剂是用BTA缓蚀法。BTA也是苯骈三氮唑，它是一种很有效的青铜器缓蚀剂，为乳白粉末结晶，能溶于乙醇等有机溶液中。苯骈三氮唑与铜及铜合金形成不溶于水及部分有机溶剂的透明覆盖膜，生成膜比较牢固，能有效地隔断金属与腐蚀介质的接触，阻止腐蚀继续发展，使器物得到有效的保护。

（2）封护。是为了阻止环境因素，人为因素对器物可能造成二次损害，更有效地保护已修复好的器物不受侵害，对器物进行表面封护处理。一般使用无色透明、附着力强、抗氧化的封护材料。如丙烯酸树酯，聚乙烯醇缩丁醛、三甲树脂、聚甲基丙烯酸甲脂、微晶石蜡、硝化纤维树脂、有机氟树脂、有机硅树脂和Paraloid-B72等在20世纪70年代后期被国外应用作为基本的文物封护材料，至今Paraloid-B72已在国际上流行并得到广泛认可，它是由甲基丙烯甲酯和甲基丙烯酸乙酯共聚而成的有机化合物，能溶于多种有机溶剂。通常溶解在丙酮或二甲苯中以2%～10%的浓度应用。它无色透明，使用方便，常温下固化迅速，具有强度高、耐热、耐腐蚀性强、防真菌和一定的户外耐久性等性能。笔者曾对广西壮族自治区博物馆多件青铜器感染粉状锈后先以BTA缓蚀处理后，再以Paraloid-B72进行保护，经过多年观察，效果十分理想，尚未出现再次复发现象。所以此件汉代铜镜同样使用Paraloid-B72进行保护，使用8% Paraloid-b72丙酮溶液对汉代铜镜喷涂，做到有效保护。

三

修复保护计划与实施

根据铜镜的保存现状和修复保护原则（可逆性、兼容性和最小干预性），从历史研究、展览的角度出发，笔者以广西博物馆馆藏的一面汉代铜镜为例，介绍对粉状锈的处理方法。

（1）清洗。首先对铜镜上的土垢用脱脂棉蘸取无水乙醇湿润软化土垢，再用手术刀、钢针、小工具铲加以清除，在操作时需要认真细致，避免伤害器物。由于出土时铜镜已经断裂为数片，断裂面也需要认真清洗干净。对于质地坚硬的绿色锈层，其性质已趋于稳定，可保护内部金属免遭腐蚀，是一种古锈色的矿化层，成为该器物历史原真性不可分割的一个组成部分，不必去除并需要保留。铜镜经过表面处理后，浸泡在去离子水中，多次换水漂洗，铜镜经浸泡除氯后必须进行脱水处理，将铜镜各残片直接浸泡在乙醇溶液中，而后取出浸泡在丙酮溶液里进行脱水处理，达到对铜镜深层干燥。

（2）缓蚀。为了更加有效地阻止铜镜继续受腐蚀，减缓腐蚀发展的进程，在完成清洗程序后采用3%的BTA乙醇溶液浸泡的方法，而后将多余的结晶去除。

（3）黏接。在青铜器修复中所用的胶黏剂主要是环氧树脂，属于热固性树脂。它有黏接性强、固化收缩率小、耐化学介质性和稳定性好及工艺性能优良等优点。用环氧树脂黏接青铜器，对器物本身没有任何影响，可达到无损伤器物的原则。因此，环氧树脂是一种比较理想的黏接剂。笔者使用的是上海生产的双组分环氧树脂。操作时，首先给被黏接的碴口处涂刷15%B72作为可逆层。然后再向调和好的胶中加入矿物颜料与器物成和谐的颜色，对接好后进行黏接，放置6小时以上，黏接效果较好。

（4）封护。为了阻止环境因素、人为因素对器物可能造成的二次损害，更加有效地保护已修复好的铜器不受侵害，在完成以修复程序后，对其表面做封护处理。主要目的是在器物与大气之间形成一个隔离膜，以阻止可能出现新的腐蚀，选用的封护剂为2%的丙烯酸树脂（Paraloid-B72）进行表面封护。

（5）作旧。是文物修复工作的最后一道工序。虽然铜器经过以上几道工序修复原型已完整。但颜色尚不一致，所以要进行作色。笔者采用传统着色方法，运用抹、弹、点、画等手段进行作旧处理，使之与原器物和谐统一，达到文物修复保护的真实效果，完整地再现原有的神韵风采。

四

结　语

汉代铜器除锈与修复保护，综合了多种修复工艺技术和各种性能黏合材料完成。具体在操作中每个修复环节都是在成熟的理论方法指导下进行除锈与修复的，自始至终做到文物修复具有牢固、真实性并保证文物修复质量。总之，提高文物修复技术水平，不仅需要经过大量工作经验的积累，更重要的是需要我们从新技术和新材料的应用方法中去不断地探索和研究，以达到文物修复技术水平和要求。

浅论三十年来我国学者对古代铜鼓铸造工艺之研究和试验

A Brief Review on Chinese Scholars' Researches and Experiments for Bronze Drum Casting Process in the Last 30 Years

李欣妍 / 广西师范大学 硕士研究生

[摘要]

古代铜鼓铸造工艺的研究一直是铜鼓研究中的难题与薄弱环节，而自20世纪80年代开始，我国学者开始重视对古代铜鼓铸造工艺的研究，时至今日已经走过了三十年的历程。本文对我国学者关于古代铜鼓铸造工艺的三十年研究进行了梳理，并分为三个阶段对这些研究成果与不足进行了述评，以揭示古代铜鼓铸造工艺的未来研究方向。

[关键词]

古代铜鼓铸造工艺研究　成果　述评

Abstract

The researches to ancient bronze drum casting process is always a weak link in the bronze drum study. However, since the eighties of last century, Chinese scholars began to attach much significance to bronze drum casting process. Up to now, it has lasted for more than 30 years. This article combs Chinese scholars'researches of the ancient bonze drum casting process in the past 30 years, and discusses the achievements and shortcomings of these studies by dividing them into three phases, in order to reveal the future research direction of ancient bronze drum casting process.

Key words

Research of ancient bronze drum casting process; Achievements; Shortcomings

一百多年以来，众多中外学者纷纷致力于研究中国南方与东南亚各国的古代铜鼓，并取得了极大的成就，基本上理清了铜鼓的起源、年代、类型、族属、纹饰以及功能等基本问题。而古代铜鼓铸造工艺的研究则因史书记载不足以及考古实物材料欠缺，起步较晚，直到20世纪80年代我国学者才开始对其进行探讨，至今已走过了三十多年的历程了。时至今日，学者们的研究虽取得了一定的成效，但仍未完全摸清古代铜鼓的铸造工艺，尚留有一些亟须解决的谜团。因此，本文将这三十年研究成果划分为三个不同阶段：20世纪80年代、20世纪90年代以及最近十年进行述评，并在文中略抒己见。

一

古代用什么样的工艺铸造铜鼓？

20世纪80年代，是我国学者探索古代铜鼓铸造工艺的起始阶段，可以分为两个时期，以1985年为分界线，前期注重从铜鼓表面观察和我国铸造同类器物来推测铜鼓的铸造工艺，后期则更倾向于合金成分、调音规律等方面来探讨。

（一）铜鼓的铸造方法究竟是什么？

1981年，韩丙告先生提出铜鼓铸造方法可能有三种，即刮板法、木模法、失蜡法三种。他说“在发现的铜鼓中，上述诸法均有应用。铜鼓边壁有披缝的，为刮板法或木模法造型，无披缝为失蜡法造型。但绝大部分铜鼓的边壁有披缝。”[①]在铸造时，没有固定作坊，大部分是临时设场，随铸随用，而且一般采用鼓面朝下的浇注方法来保证鼓面上的花纹清晰、光洁。

在1982年召开的中国古代铜鼓研究会第一次学术讨论会，唐文元先生指出铜鼓的铸造工艺是夹铸垫片工艺，也就是说，在浇注铜鼓之前，在内模外范之间均匀地夹垫一些与所铸铜鼓壁厚相同的铜片或残铜钱，以保证铜液流畅，鼓壁通体匀称。而且可以省去失蜡法制作蜡模的繁复工艺，同时能较快地塑制内外范，工艺程序仅5道。这是中国传统的青铜铸造工艺在南方铜鼓铸造技术上的具体运用。这一论点新颖有力，“纠正了过去一些人认为鼓上的小疤块是铜块、铜钱未熔尽的残渣的错误说法”[②]。

在1983年12月27日至1984年1月2日举行的中国古代铜鼓研究会第二次学术讨论会，一些学者对铜鼓铸造工艺进行了深入的探讨，并在大会上作了内容丰富、观点新

① 韩丙告：《现代铜鼓及其铸造技术》，《现代铸造》1981年第4期。

② 中国古代铜鼓研究会：《古代铜鼓学术讨论会论文集》，文物出版社，1982年，15页。

颖的报告。此报告通过对100面广西、云南铜鼓进行成分分析及金相鉴定，他们发现铜鼓的金属材料为纯铜、铜、锡二元合金、铜、锡、铅三元合金；铜鼓皆由铸造而成；“铜鼓的合金成分、金相组织随着类型、时代、分布地区、社会形态及冶铸技术的变化呈现一定规律性变化。”[①]并认为：① 泥范法是铸造铜鼓的主要方法，占总数的91.2%。② 铜鼓生产从一鼓一范的单件生产，逐渐发展到基本定型的一范数鼓的生产，进而推测“在明清时代，可能已有专门生产铜鼓的作坊。”[②] ③ 铜鼓壁厚的变化趋势是面>胸>腰<足，这种设计比较合理，符合实用要求。④ 花纹制作方法灵活多样，运用巧妙。雕刻法用于复杂的花纹；印痕法、滚压法适用于制作简单的条纹饰。⑤ 铸件表面有无合范缝、铸件结构的繁简及花纹装饰的难易是判断其铸造工艺的具体依据。⑥ 古代铜鼓的铸造工艺大致经过四个步骤十二道工序。

与韩、唐两人观点相比，该报告对广西、云南铜鼓的铸造工艺的论述更加全面、系统、具体及深入。对于有无固定作坊，此报告与韩丙告看法不同，而这一问题有待考证。而唐文元所说的夹垫铸造工艺与此报告中的泥范法相吻合。

随后，黄增庆先生专门对壮族地区的古代铜鼓的铸造工艺进行了探讨，他指出壮族古代铜鼓的铸造合金成分，主要是铜，其次是铅、锡等，此外还掺杂有少量铁、锌等；壮族古代铸造铜鼓的金属材料有两种：铅锡青铜鼓、锡青铜鼓；“铜钱是壮族古代铸造铜鼓原料来源之一”，“铸造铜鼓有部分原料是采用铜钱熔化而铸造鼓的”[③]（这一观点值得商榷）；铜鼓多数是用范模铸造法一次浇注而成，这种范模用后一般即予毁弃，再做再铸；熔铸阶段，要经过调剂、精炼、灌注等三项手续，而用钱币铸鼓则不需经过调剂；壮族古代用泥模合范法铸造的铜鼓居多[④]；“冷水冲型”铜鼓鼓面的纹饰采用“蜡模合范法”。

在借鉴前人研究成果的基础上，吴坤仪、孙淑云对广西、云南现有的部分铜鼓的铸造工艺及金属材料进行了初步研究。铜鼓的铸造工艺包括造型方法、主附件的结合方法、花纹制作方法以及浇注方法。造型方法包括泥范法、失蜡法、泥范法与失蜡法并用三种；主附件的结合方法包括整铸法、浑铸法与分铸法；花纹制作方法包括刻纹法、印纹法与滚压法；浇注方法分为缝隙式浇注、顶注式浇注（分为中心顶注式浇注与鼓内壁中心顶注式浇注）。他们指出，广西、云南制作铜鼓所用的冶炼原料与其他地区存在一定的差异，铜鼓的合金成分随类型及时代的变化而变化，并认为“西盟型铜鼓均以失蜡法铸造而成，是铜鼓制作技术的进一步提高”[⑤]。该观点在后来遭到了其他学者的否定，他们认为只有晚期西盟型铜鼓是采用失蜡法铸造的，而早期西盟型铜鼓则是使用合范浑铸法的方法。其理由是“岭南地区发现的西盟型铜鼓被认为是较早时期的，鼓身上仍有合范痕，蛙等立体饰与鼓面等连成一体，而不同于缅甸、云南等地的晚期西盟鼓无合范缝，蛙等立体饰是在鼓铸后再连接上来的。说明前者是用合范的浑铸法铸成的，后者是用失蜡法铸好鼓后再连接上

① 范祖锜：《铜鼓研究学术讨论会述要》，《思想战线》1984年第3期。

② 北京钢铁学院冶金史研究室、广西壮族自治区博物馆、云南省博物馆：《广西、云南铜鼓铸造工艺初探》，《中国铜鼓研究会第二次学术讨论会论文集》，文物出版社，1986年，82页。

③④ 黄增庆：《壮族古代铜鼓的铸造工艺》，《广西民族学院》（哲学社会科学版）1984年第1期。

⑤ 吴坤仪、孙淑云：《中国古代铜鼓的制作技术》，《自然科学史研究》1985年第1期。

蛙等立体饰品。”[①]

这一个时期，学者关注的焦点在于古代铜鼓铸造工艺的造型方法。最初学者认为应是刮板法、木模法、失蜡法三种，接着有学者认为它是夹铸垫片工艺，后来学者们更倾向于泥范法、失蜡法、泥范法与失蜡法并用三种造型方法。

（二）铅同位素比值法的应用

有别于前期研究注重从铜鼓表面观察和我国铸造同类器物来推测铜鼓的铸造工艺，这一阶段的后期研究更注重从合金成分、调音规律来分析铜鼓的铸造工艺，在研究方法上力求创新。

1988年，姚舜安、万辅彬、彭子成三人开始运用铅同位素比值法对北流型铜鼓样品进行检测，发现“北流型铜鼓的数据全部落在北流以及周围几个县矿点的铅同位素比值所构成的区域内”[②]，并结合其他多方面因素来考虑，他们认为广西北流铜石岭遗址不仅是汉代冶铜遗址，还是铸造北流型铜鼓的遗址，而且是“迄今世界上找到的第一个铸造铜鼓的遗址”[③]。

1988年出版的《中国古代铜鼓》，是一部有关铜鼓的通论性专著，是在综合我国学者30多年来铜鼓研究成果的基础上写成的，是我国学者研究铜鼓的科学总结[④]。本书以一个章节的篇幅对我国古代铜鼓的铸造工艺进行了探讨，认为中国古代铜鼓的铸造方法有三种：泥型合范法、蜡模泥范法和失蜡法。其中冷水冲型、北流型、灵山型及部分石寨山型、遵义型和西盟型早期等体型较大的铜鼓大致采用了蜡模泥范法，该法结合了泥型合范和失蜡法的优点[⑤]。花纹的制作方法为刻纹法、板印法、戳印法和滚压法。铜鼓铸造工艺的发展反映了我国南方民族地区科学技术的不断进步，体现了古代南方民族的聪明才智，在古代冶金史上占有一席之地。与前面的研究相比，该书对我国古代铜鼓铸造工艺的进行了更为详细的论述，但并无自己的独创之处，更多的还是借鉴、吸收前人的研究成果。

为了推进铜鼓铸造工艺研究的深入开展，1986年至1991年，广西民族学院、中国科技大学和广西壮族自治区博物馆，对铜鼓矿料来源的铅同位素进行分析，通过确定铜鼓的矿料来源推断铜鼓的发源地。此次研究具有开创性意义，并取得了突破性成果[⑥]。研究者认为，铸造铜鼓的矿料分布区域相对集中，大体上可以分成两大区域，一个是以北流县铜石岭为中心的广西东南地区，一个是滇西—滇池地区—滇黔交界地区。

出于现实需要，广西河池地区民族歌舞团运用现代科学技术来仿制古代麻江型铜鼓，于1986年研制成功，外观虽似，但音色不佳。这种简单的仿制，对推动古代铜鼓铸造工艺的研究并无多大的裨益。正如作者所言，“铜鼓的铸造也还有许多问题，有待下一步解决”[⑦]。

① 陈文：《岭南地区铸造古代铜鼓略考》，《社会科学家》2000年第1期。

②③ 姚舜安、万辅彬、彭子成：《北流型铜鼓铸造遗址初探》，《考古》1988年第6期。

④ 蒋廷瑜：《铜鼓研究的科学总结——简评〈中国古代铜鼓〉》，《考古》1989年第12期。

⑤ 中国古代铜鼓研究会：《中国古代铜鼓》，文物出版社，1988年，225、226页。

⑥ 万辅彬、蒋廷瑜、韦丹芳：《铜鼓》，中国社会出版社，2008年，88页。

⑦ 张颖中、黄仲裕：《系列定音铜鼓的研究与铸造》，《乐器》1988年第3期。

由上可知，后期的研究工作是在前期研究工作的基础上进行的，它更注重团队合作、多学科交叉研究以及现实需要，其推断更为合理，成效更大。

这一个阶段基本上弄清楚了八大类型铜鼓的铸造工艺，归纳了铜鼓铸造工艺的一般流程，还发现了首个铜鼓铸造地点，开创了用铅同位素比值法来追溯铜鼓铸造地点的先例，划分了铸造铜鼓的两大矿料分布区域，并指出在明清时代，可能已有专门生产铜鼓的作坊。总的来说，20世纪80年代还是属于古代铜鼓铸造工艺研究的起步阶段。由于无前例可循，学者们只能从铜鼓表面观察和我国铸造同类器物以及合金来推测铜鼓的铸造工艺，推断及结论不一定正确。但毋庸置疑，前人的这些基础性研究工作为我们后来的研究打下了坚实的基础。

二

利用现代科技能重新铸出精美的古代铜鼓吗？

20世纪90年代，我国学者对古代铜鼓铸造工艺的研究步入了初期阶段。这一阶段仍是主要根据对铜鼓的直接观察、测量和现代化学分析、金相方法以及传统铜器铸造工艺来对古代铜鼓的铸造工艺进行探索，但更加注重从实践中探索，运用现代实验的方法来印证铸造工艺，检测前一阶段的研究成果，同时也纠正了过去因认识不足而导致的错误观点。如果说，80年代主要是从总体上把握我国古代铜鼓铸造工艺，进行推断，得出结论，90年代则注重运用现代科技来重铸铜鼓以检验这些推断与结论。

在这一阶段，对铜鼓铸造工艺的科学研究开始分两大区域进行，一是云南境内，一是广西境内。王大道认为，“云南铜鼓是采用‘泥范铸造法’和‘失蜡法’这两种方法铸造而成。鼓身有无竖直的合范缝，是判断铜鼓铸造工艺的重要依据。”①而彭子成等人通过对云南铜鼓和部分铜、铅矿料来源进行铅同位素示踪法研究，认为云南早期两类铜鼓的矿料主要来源于滇西和滇池地区，并由此可推测“云南的滇西和滇池地区是我国早期铜鼓的发祥地”②。

万辅彬教授则把现代物理技术应用在铜鼓研究中，对古代铜鼓进行了矿料来源的铅同位素考证、声学特性研究以及铜鼓调音刮痕探秘等，研究范围由小到大，由浅入深，获得了一批可喜的成果。

在1990年，他与其他学者一起继续运用铅同位素比值法，对广西三种类型古代铜鼓的矿料来源进行了考证。他们测试了95个样品，以充分的实验事实说明北流型和灵山型铜鼓的矿料来自北流铜石岭及其周围一带。广西出土的冷水冲型铜鼓铅同

① 王大道：《云南铜鼓》，云南教育出版社，1991年，44页。

② 彭子成、李晓岑、张秉伦、李志超、李昆声、万辅彬：《云南铜鼓和部分铜、铅矿料来源的铅同位素示踪研究》，《科学通报》1991年第8期。

位素分布场大致可分为三个区域[①]。1991年，万辅彬联合李世红、农学坚二人对出土于广西境内几种类型的大量铜鼓进行了考察研究，并作了声谱特性的测定，发现鼓面内部的刀凿痕迹应为古代铜鼓调音刮痕。这一看法不同于韩丙告说它是浇冒口的观点，而且更有说服力。

在1995年，为了复制“世界铜鼓之王”，万辅彬教授联合多位学者对世界铜鼓之王——北流型101号铜鼓作了细致的考察。考察结果认为：① 101号铜鼓的陶范由鼓面范，对半分型鼓身范和内范四者组成。内、外范均用刮板直接制作；内范为空心（正确与否，尚待考证，前面的学者则持内范为实心的看法）。鼓耳用蜡耳嵌埋法与铜鼓一次铸成。② 铜鼓表面纹饰均在外范上加工。③ 101号铜鼓的浇注工艺采用鼓面向下方式，两组缝隙式浇注系统，鼓足端为自然冒口。该观点纠正了前人认为101号铜鼓的浇注工艺是采用鼓面向下方式，缝隙式浇注系统，并在光体部设一冒口的看法。④ 垫片不仅可控制壁厚，还起着支撑内范、固定和稳定内范的作用。⑤ 101号铜鼓鼓足残缺的主要原因是铸造时浇注温度不够高以及鼓足部分缝隙浇口太薄；或是配料估算不足，铜液太少，导致最终未浇满。

紧接着，他开始尝试运用现代的科技进行了铜鼓的复制和仿制工作，以检验自己的推断。1995年，万辅彬教授领导的一个研究小组与广西壮族自治区博物馆、上海博物馆等单位合作，用陶瓷型模试铸出一面麻江型铜鼓，但效果不佳。之后，他们在广西民族大学组建了中国第一个铜鼓铸造实验室，继续开展麻江型铜鼓铸造试验。在后来长达三年多的时间里，他们投入大量的资金及人力，先后铸造了十几次，但仅铸出两面铜鼓，没有完全取得成功[②]。上述这些万辅彬进行的铜鼓铸造试验，由于没有前例可循，只能采用现代的技术与方法，结果也不尽人意。因此，他的一些推断，如认为北流型101号铜鼓的内范是空心的等，可能有待进一步考证。

纵观这一阶段的研究，比80年代有了长足的进步，研究古代铜鼓铸造工艺的局面已被打开。首先，现代科学技术，特别是现代物理技术的大量应用，使铜鼓铸造工艺的研究走上了科学研究的道路。其次，学者们通过考察与试验，探索了体大壁薄铜鼓的铸造工艺，进而来推测古代铜鼓的铸造工艺。再次，开始复制、仿制古代铜鼓，虽然采用现代的技术与方法，结果不甚理想，但总算迈出了大胆尝试的第一步。同时，纠正了前人的错误观点，如确定了鼓面内壁的凿痕或花纹为是调音的铲削痕而非浇冒口所在地。但需注意的是，这一阶段的研究仍存在其不足的地方。一些学者对于古代铜鼓的铸造工艺的把握仍停留在表面观测、理论推测、简单仿制的层面，实践认知仍有待提高与深化。

① 万辅彬、姚舜安、李世红、鲁冀邕、彭子成、蒋廷瑜：《古代铜鼓矿料来源的铅同位素考证》，《物理》1990年第3期。

② 吴伟峰：《壮族民间铜鼓铸造技术考察与研究》，《广西民族研究》2008年第1期。

三

成功铸造出形声俱佳的现代铜鼓

进入21世纪，学者们对于古代铜鼓铸造工艺的研究进入了一个科学总结的阶段。一方面，部分学者开始对过去二十年来的研究成果与不足进行了回顾总结与反思；另一方面，学者们归纳与总结了古代铜鼓铸造工艺的一般规律，并探索出研究的科学方法。此外，还注重理论与实践结合，在现代科学技术方法的启发下，成功地复制出形声俱佳的铜鼓。

万辅彬在《唐代以前广西冶铜铸铜成就概览》一文中指出，今天我们需要从现存铜鼓的实际考察着手研究古代铜鼓高超的铸造工艺。铜鼓的造型方法不同，工序也不同。如泥型合范法的工序包括制模型、翻外范、做芯范（内模）、合范、浇注、拆范及整理以及定音；失蜡法的工序则分为做芯范、做蜡模、制外范、化蜡、浇注拆范等几道工序。冷水冲型、北流型、灵山型及部分石寨山型等体型较大的铜鼓可能采用了蜡模泥范法，它结合了泥型合范法与失蜡法两者的优点，“工序与失蜡法大体相同，也是先做芯范，然后做蜡模，但不同的是不在蜡面上刻印花纹，而是在泥制外芯上压印花纹。”[①]同时他进一步分析了古代的铸造工艺，认为：① 制范面的泥料是经过研磨、筛选或淘洗的细泥配制成的。② 大多数铜鼓暴露有芯垫，冷水冲型、北流型、灵山型等采用方形芯垫。③ 北流型、灵山型、大多数冷水冲型浇口设在鼓测的范缝上，可避免顶注式浇注方法易产生冲击、爆范、氧化夹渣、气孔、砂眼和花纹损伤等缺陷。

他还指出万家坝、部分石寨山型和全部麻江型铜鼓是采用泥型合范法铸造[②]；失蜡法则在石寨山型M12：20号铜鼓和冷水冲型个别铜鼓上已有使用，但广泛运用失蜡法铸造的则是西盟型中、晚期铜鼓[③]。

蒋廷瑜先生对古代铜鼓铸造工艺的流程有了更简洁明了的概括。他指出，一般来说，每铸造一面铜鼓，都要经过4个步骤和12道工序。第一步为准备阶段，包括备料和整理场地两道工序。第二步为制范阶段，包括制模型、骨架、刮板，制内外范，制附件，刻花纹，干燥和烘烤内模外范等5道工序。第三步为合范浇注阶段，包括合范、焙烧预热和浇注等3道工序。第四步，修整和定音阶段[④]。

江渝则简要回顾了近一个世纪以来中外学者对中国南方和东南亚古代铜鼓铸造技术的研究，指出中国南方铜鼓的制造方法有泥型合范法、蜡模泥范法和失蜡法三种，三者铸造时各有不同。蜡模泥范法和泥型合范法的区别主要在于泥型合范要做模型，

① 万辅彬：《唐代以前广西冶铜铸铜成就概览》，《广西民族学院学报》（自然科学版）2001年第7期。

② 万辅彬、蒋廷瑜、韦丹芳：《铜鼓》，中国社会出版社，2008年，78页。

③ 万辅彬、蒋廷瑜、韦丹芳：《铜鼓》，中国社会出版社，2008年，81页。

④ 蒋廷瑜：《壮族铜鼓研究》，广西人民出版社，2005年，214页。

图一　越南民间泥范法铸铜鼓

图二　泥范铸铜鼓泥范外模

并且在做芯范的时候需要刮削泥模，刮削的部分正好是将来青铜溶液要填充的空间。蜡模泥范法和失蜡法的区别在于失蜡法是在蜡模表面刻印花纹而蜡模泥范法则在外范上刻印纹饰。而“大部分东南亚铜鼓，包括中国两广、云南地区的铜鼓采用泥型合范法或者蜡模泥范法的可能性更大。”[①]与当前我国许多学者不同的是，作者认为北流型、灵山型、大多数冷水冲型和部分麻江型铜鼓的青铜浇注口不在鼓侧的缝线上，而应该在鼓足上，并认为鼓身缝线不是合范线缝，它们的功能主要是装饰作用。另外，他还指出在铸造铜鼓时，应该先浇注附件，然后再和鼓身合铸。

陈文在其文章《岭南地区铸造古代铜鼓略考》中指出，西盟型铜鼓鼓身上多未有合缝痕，主要是用失蜡法铸造的。但西盟型早期铜鼓“应是用合范浑铸法一次铸成的，并非学术界认为所有的西盟型鼓都是用失蜡法铸造的。”[②]

黄启善观摩了越南民间铜鼓铸造的现场表演，并记述了越南工匠制范、合范、浇注、拆范、修补、打磨、抛光等铸造铜鼓的全过程（图一、图二）。他指出越南工匠“铸造铜鼓的技术，虽然运用了一些现代工具，但其制模造范的方法却是传统的制作方法”[③]。他认为，对其进行深入的考察与研究，有助于我们了解和研究古代铜鼓的铸造技术，早日破解我国古代铜鼓铸造工艺的难题。

吴伟峰先生回顾了前人研究古代铜鼓铸造工艺的理论与实践成就，指出今人新铸的铜鼓因内外范的间隙过大，导致其外观虽与传世铜鼓大致相同，但鼓壁太厚，重量太重，声音传不远。这一观点与一些学者把铜鼓声音传不远的原因归咎到调音机制方面的看法存在较大的区别，就目前而言该观点似乎更为合理。因为，河池市环江毛南族自治县上朝社区平治村板才屯韦启初、韦启叁兄弟，受到现代科技的启发，采用沙模铸造方法（即翻砂法）于2003 年成功铸造出形声俱佳的麻江型铜鼓，

① 江渝:《中国南方和东南亚古代铜鼓铸造技术探讨》，《考古》2008年第6期。

② 陈文:《岭南地区铸造古代铜鼓略考》，《社会科学家》2000年第1期。

③ 黄启善、党春宁：《越南民间铸造铜鼓的现场考察》，《广西博物馆文集》（第四辑），广西人民出版社，2007年。

图三　广西河池韦氏兄弟翻沙法铸铜鼓

图四　用翻沙法铸出来的铜鼓

2006年铸造了一面面径为110、高60厘米的大铜鼓。这些新铸造出来的铜鼓的音色、音质都比老铜鼓好，声音持续时间也比老铜鼓长，因此得到了壮、瑶族群众的认可（图三、图四）。因此，我们可以知道，目前越南还在运用传统的泥模合范法铸造铜鼓，广西地区则采用翻砂法铸造麻江型铜鼓，而江浙地区则采用失蜡法复制古代造铜鼓。

与20世纪90年代相比，近十年来更注重的是对前人研究工作的回顾与总结，理论方面并无多大的突破，但注意将理论运用到实践上，并运用现代科技成功地复制出形声俱佳、为少数民族所认可的铜鼓。可是我们仍要看到，古代铜鼓铸造工艺的谜团与难题仍存在，若要弄清楚古代铜鼓的铸造工艺仍需要继续努力。

四

结　语

自20世纪80年代至今，我国学者研究古代铜鼓的铸造工艺已经足足走过了三十年。回顾这三十年，可以说是一个探寻方法、进行推断、检验推断、得出结论、总结规律的研究过程。这一研究过程，体现了从分散到集中、自发到主动、单学科到多学科结合、理论到实践再到理论的特点。期间，取得了较大的理论成就，弄清楚了古代铜鼓铸造工艺的基本原理与具体工序，包括铜鼓制作的三种具体方法、鼓耳与鼓身结合的三种方法、雕刻铜鼓表面花纹的三种方法、铜鼓的合金成分、矿料来源与铜鼓调音机制等。在实践上，也取得了较大的突破，成功地复制出形声俱佳的铜鼓，开创了运用现代科技手段来恢复已经失传了的铜鼓铸造工艺，促进铜鼓文化的延续和发展的先例。还有，解决了部分的争议性问题。如确认了鼓面背部的刀凿痕迹为古代铜鼓调音刮痕，而非浇冒口所在地；不是所有的西盟型铜鼓都使用失蜡法，只有晚期西盟型鼓才是，而早期的铜鼓则采用蜡模泥范法。

未解决的争议问题，则包括铜钱是否是铸造铜鼓原料来源之一，铜鼓的内范有空心一说吗等。此外，学者们仅仅通过考察铜鼓表面及同类器物就认为泥模合范法是古代铸造铜鼓的最主要方法，笔者认为这个结论过于轻率。理由是：① 我国学者运用泥模合范法至今仍未成功复制铜鼓。② 目前在我国难以找到利用泥模合范法铸造铜鼓的痕迹，也没发现古代铸造铜鼓的泥范，而在今天的越南却得到保存？这是什么原因导致的呢？首先，有可能是失传了；其次，学者们可能没有掌握到泥模合范法的精髓所在；还有，我们是否可以怀疑古代中国根本就没有使用泥模合范法铸造铜鼓。可是如果没有使用该法，那么又会使用什么方法呢？是韦启初、韦启叁兄弟采用的翻砂法吗？还是在中国冶金史上占据绝对地位的陶范法呢？若能回答这个问题，那么我们研究铜鼓铸造工艺中存在的许多谜团都能迎刃而解了，因此这应是我们今后研究的重点方向。

一言概之，过去三十年来我国学者关于古代铜鼓铸造工艺的研究，只能说是部分揭秘了古人铸造铜鼓的工艺，还没有把握住古代铜鼓铸造工艺的奥秘与方法，难以依循古法来铸造铜鼓。

附　记：本文在写作过程中，得到黄启善导师的精心指导，并提供了本文插图照片，在此表示衷心的感谢。

第四部分

其　他

Part 4

Research on other Topics

青铜记忆刻录瓯骆文化印记

Bronze Wares
have Recorded Ou-Luo Culture

肖　君 / 广西壮族自治区博物馆 副研究员

[摘要]

最能体现瓯骆文化自身发展特点的是这一地区的青铜文化，为了让古老的文物更贴近现实的观众，合理调用讲解元素，通过对先秦及秦汉时期瓯骆区域文化中青铜文物的梳理，解读瓯骆文化的丰富内涵。

[关键词]

青铜文物　识读　瓯骆文化　共性目的

Abstract

The most representative culture in Ouluo culture is bronze culture. To shorten the distance between ancient antique and audience, we should make the best of explanation, classify the bronze ware in pre-Qin dynasty and Qin-Han dynasty and let audience understand the rich content.

Key words

Bronze relics; Record; Ou-luo culture; Common purpose

西瓯和骆越是战国至汉代百越族群中活跃在岭南的两大部族，广西西江中游、桂江流域以及广西左右江流域等地，是现代壮族也是古“瓯骆”人的聚居地。因其所处的自然环境和特定的生产方式，创造了独特的物质文化和精神文化，具有浓厚的地域特色。现今广西所拥有的个性强、弹性大、创生性好的文化空间及差异性文化特色的根基，早在瓯骆时期就已奠定了基础。正是这种历史的、地理的、民族的多元化，成就了中华文化统一性及多样性的鲜明特征。在中华文化的形成及发展过程中，少数民族作出了巨大贡献，博物馆应把保护和传承多元文化、促进多元文化和谐发展作为自己的终极使命。

以使用青铜器为标志的青铜时代，是人类发展史上的一个重要阶段。随着考古事业的发展，瓯骆故地多有新的考古发现，出土了数以万计的文物，其中最能体现瓯骆文化自身发展特点的是这一地区的青铜文化。从广西壮族自治区博物馆的“瓯骆遗粹——广西百越文化文物展”（以下简称“瓯展”）中，人们观赏到商至东汉时期精美的青铜器，面对这些饱含古人智慧并焕发出人文精神及时代风采的神圣器物，为了让古老的文物更贴近现实的观众，合理调用讲解元素显得尤为重要。作为一名资深的讲解员，笔者一直在思考讲解如何与时俱进的问题，广西壮族自治区博物馆的收藏与研究，不应只停留在“藏品说”及“文物价值”的体现上，本文尝试以青铜文物为触点，解读瓯骆文化的丰富内涵，并以此作为对讲解内容的拓展及与现代文化讯息融合的一个尝试，希望能达到文物讲解与本土文化宣传结合的目的。这是博物馆陈列参与者（包括博物馆管理者、工作者、观众等）实现共性目的（即参与者共同要求实现的目的）的最佳途径。笔者拟以此文作为探讨青铜文物讲解的引玉之作，求教于专家学者，请予批评指正。

一

瓯骆区域文化中的青铜礼乐器

青铜器的发明是人类进化史上的一大奇迹。中国青铜文化分布之广、范围之大是举世罕见的，青铜器出土的数量之多和历史之悠久也是独一无二的，工艺精湛、技术娴熟、内容丰富的中国青铜文化，是世界文化宝库中的精华。但是，提起广西古代的青铜器，人们大多只知道铜鼓，对其他种类的青铜器，由于缺乏记载而不甚了解，甚至产生了广西没有青铜文化的错觉。“瓯展”的展出，用翔实的史料拓宽了人们认识青铜文化的视野，让人们认识到广西也有自己独特的青铜文化。

青铜礼乐器是中国古代文明与礼制的象征。从本区域的青铜礼乐器发展态势，可以清楚地看到“俗化百越，礼教南疆”的文明进程。

1. 瓯骆地区发现的殷商式青铜礼乐器

青铜文化所反映的主要社会背景与时代精神是“国之大事，在祀与戎”。铸造和使用青铜器是阶级社会的重要标志。广西地区的古越人远在商周时期就已输入中原内地的殷商式铜器。早期的青铜礼乐器分别出自窖藏、遗址和墓葬。1974年出土于武鸣县马头乡的窖藏器“兽面纹提梁铜卣”，是商周时期典型的中原器物，既是盛酒的实用器也是礼器中的重器。其盖面、腹部、盖组、提梁等部位所装饰的兽面纹、蝉纹及牛头形的纹饰图案组合，综合反映了王权、国家与阶级意识。至于这面铜卣为何出现在瓯骆地区，有专家猜测，可能是赏赐、购买或交换而来，也有可能是战利品。虽然有多种可能，但中原青铜文化从商末周初始输入瓯骆地区并最终刺激其青铜冶铸业的发展是不争的事实。

广西地区的青铜文化是在中原文化影响下出现的，同时也伴随着中原青铜器的输入，因此中原青铜器在瓯骆青铜文化中占有相当比重，铜鼎就是其中之一。广西地区最早发现铜鼎是在恭城加会春秋墓中，而且一次出土五鼎，在瓯骆故地五鼎陪葬的仅此一例，说明墓主人身份非同一般。“瓯展”展出了其中三鼎，“蟠虺纹铜鼎”体现典型的“楚式鼎”风格，告铭提梁铜鼎及环耳铜鼎具有浅腹三足细长外撇等“越式鼎”的共同特征，其中“告铭提梁铜鼎”，器身铸有汉字铭文，由此可知，先秦时期汉字已传入岭南。

铸造青铜器是先进生产力的代表。据考证武鸣马头是骆越人活动中心，1986年，在武鸣县马头乡元龙坡发掘了384座西周至春秋时期墓葬，出土铜器等大批文物，同时出土了一批与中原内地的石质陶铸范不同的砂石铸范，这些砂石铸范大多数都留有浇注口，并且有使用过的痕迹。充分证明，广西地区至少在西周时期已跨入青铜时代，有自己的青铜文化。目前，广西春秋时期的青铜器出土范围已涉及20多个市县。这些墓地青铜文化的出现，标志着人类社会进入了文明时代。

2. 礼乐器仿制衍生品及越式器物

大量考古发现证明：“至迟在西周中晚期到春秋早期，广西的古越人已开始制造青铜器，而且产生了殷周式铜礼器的仿制品。”[①]装饰在青铜器上各种各样的纹饰，对研究当时的政治、经济、社会生活等都有极高的价值。在春秋晚期至战国早期的青铜器上，产生了中原内地青铜文化形制纹饰风格嬗变的特征。从形制和纹饰上看，有些器物为中原地区传入，有些则具有浓厚的地方色彩，应当是本地制作，特别是有些器物在制作上反映了本地与异地文化的融合，比如蛇蛙纹铜尊，造型体现中原风格，蛇斗蛙纹饰则具有浓厚的地方色彩，蛙与蛇是以种植水稻为生的瓯骆民族的图腾。如今，桂西壮族地区仍将青蛙看做是能促进人类、动物、植物繁殖力的女神而顶礼膜拜，并且每年都举行隆重的“蛙婆节”。尊是祭祀、宴饮演礼时的

① 谢崇安:《壮侗语族先民青铜文化艺术研究》，《中国壮学文库》，民族出版社，2007年，31页。

盛酒器，“蛇蛙纹铜尊”充分反映南北文化的交流与融合。同时期的青铜罍，造型与纹饰的制作较为精美，具有春秋晚期至战国早期的时代特征。

礼乐器的增多是中原内地商周礼制文化传入在青铜文化上的体现，礼乐器最常见的为打击乐器铜钟。铜钟在中原礼俗中用于宗庙祭祀，宗族宴享时演奏的打击乐器。由于悬挂方式不同，分为甬钟（斜挂）和纽钟（直悬），一般大小成编，配套使用，是商周以来盛行的打击乐器。在礼乐制度中，数量与悬挂方式具有贵族身份等级制度的标志意义。作为一种物质文化，西瓯地区流行甬钟，1971年恭城加会秧家出土的“兽面纹铜甬钟”，为西周时期常见类型，但其纹饰风格，与当地几何印纹陶器上的装饰花纹一脉相承，特别是“正面有纹饰，背面无纹饰则是岭南越式甬钟的特点。”[①]这种甬钟应当是春秋时期殷周式编钟的仿制品。

战国时期，广西地区出现了青铜羊角纽钟，羊角纽铜钟是具有地方特色的青铜打击乐器，被认为是受到中原内地殷周式编钟影响而产生的地方性礼乐器，与甬钟属同一类型。羊角纽钟流行于战国晚期至西汉初，岭南发现最多，在广西花山崖画上也有此型钟的图像。瓯骆地区应是这类钟的主要产地。羊角纽钟是与铜鼓同时产生并时常伴出的一种乐器，并且有的两者之间的纹饰相同。考古学上有“北鼎南鼓”的说法，表明铜鼓在一定的历史时期扮演着与北方权力象征的鼎一样的社会功能角色。有学者认为岭南地区经历了一个方国时期：瓯骆分属两个不同的方国，由于两者所接受的文化影响不同，因此西瓯方国以鼎、尊，骆越方国以铜鼓为权力象征。

春秋至西汉初年的两广地区墓葬中比较多见的典型越式器物是铜柱形器；作为棺具架柱头装饰使用，柱顶大多数装饰人首形或兽形。这种铜柱形器的形制、用法特殊，由于其青铜中含砷的特点完全有别于中原地区，加之伴出的夔纹陶遗存的青铜文化色彩，学术界大都据此认定岭南青铜时代有一个土著时期。

纵观早期青铜礼乐器在瓯骆地区使用及铸造情况来看，虽然受中原内地礼制文化的影响，但并未全盘接受，有轻礼器重实用器的倾向，显示出既封闭又开放的自成体系的区域文化特色。

二

从战国青铜器看瓯骆社会

战国时期铁器的出现促使中原地区青铜文化迅速衰落，在平乐银山岭战国墓葬中出土了相当数量的铁器，反映出中原先进生产技术首先通过湘桂走廊在西瓯地区推广的事实。铁锄、铁足铜鼎等是重要的实物例证。但就岭南地区而言，战国时期

① 蒋廷瑜:《右江流域青铜文化族属研究》，《桂岭考古论文集》，科学出版社，2009年，63页。

虽然已进入铁器时代，但铜器才刚刚开始广泛使用，因此战国时期是瓯骆青铜文化的一个重要历史时期。通过这一时期的青铜文化遗物，可以勾勒出当时瓯骆越人的历史文化风貌。

1. 亦耕亦战的方国社会

"国无他事，耕与战矣。"春秋战国时期，耕与战同样重要，不可偏废。西瓯、骆越的发展壮大，正是瓯骆人勤耕善战的结果。瓯骆聚居地由此成为广西历史上开发较早的地区，也成为较早与中原文化融合的地区。

"商周时期是岭南方国社会的初创阶段；春秋战国时期是岭南方国社会兴盛时期"[①]。广西出土的战国时代青铜器包括生活用具、生产工具、武器、乐器和杂器等，生活用器主要是鼎，生产工具主要是斧、凿、刮刀等。特别引人注目的是，平乐银山岭战国墓葬随葬品都是配套出土并且有一定的规律，生活用具是鼎、盒、杯配套。铜刮刀及环首铜削刀与铁锄配套，铜兵器是剑、矛、镞配套。凡是有铜兵器的墓不出陶纺轮，反之也一样，表明男女分工明确，没有陶纺轮的墓主人，应该是亦兵亦民的平民或贵族，有较强大的经济实力和军事战斗力。从平乐银山岭战国墓随葬品组合形式看，有明显的等级区分，墓主人的身份起码分三等：第一等级的墓主随葬剑、钺、鼎、矛组合器型，身份是将领或君王一级的人物；第二等级是剑、矛、镞等组合形式，相当于将以下的军官；第三等级的墓只随葬一种或两件兵器，应是普通士兵。有的墓主人既是武士，又是从事农业的生产者，还有些可能是西瓯社会中为数众多的耕战结合的平民，也可能是屯田的生产建设兵团的成员。

平乐银山岭战国墓群于1974年发掘，是战国中晚期西瓯人的中小型墓葬。这批墓葬具有明显的地方特点，比如墓底设置腰坑，应是商周墓葬的遗俗，但腰坑内放置陶器，则仅盛行于两广地区。随葬品基本组合是：铜兵器（或陶纺轮）+生产工具+生活用器。生活用器以陶器为主。墓中随葬品都是实用的生活器具、兵器和生产工具，而且都是配套组合出土，特色鲜明。在组合上以实用器为主，与其他地方重礼器的风尚不同。

2. 骁勇善战，民风彪悍

广西境内的百越民族既有共同的文化特征，也有差异，"以平乐银山岭战国墓为主体的遗存属西瓯文化，以武鸣马头先秦墓为代表的当属骆越文化。"[②]桂北、桂东的西瓯人接近楚，桂西地区的骆越人靠近滇，分别受到楚、滇文化的一定影响。

广西地区战国墓亦存在共同的文化特征，平乐等地战国墓葬群出土的青铜器中，以极富地域色彩的实用兵器为主，刀、钺、匕首、矛等具有浓厚的地域特色。铜匕首、特别是铜剑，形制独特，制作精良之程度，在全国也是很少见的，表现出骆越早期青铜文化较高的技术水平。

① 郑超雄、覃芳：《壮族历史文化的考古学研究》，《中国壮学文库》，民族出版社，2006年，307页。

② 蒋廷瑜：《西瓯骆越青铜文化比较研究》，《桂岭考古论文集》，科学出版社，2009年，83页。

青铜剑是新兵器，占的比例最大，它与矛一样，应该是瓯骆军队的主要装备。剑主要分为长短剑两大类，大多数是实茎剑。其中，长剑“圆首双箍铜剑”，是春秋晚期至战国在中原及楚地流行的剑式，各式短剑则受滇文化影响，圆首双箍铜匕首及云纹三角形铜匕首，无论从器型或纹饰上看地域特点都非常浓厚。早期的青铜剑以无格扁圆柄为主，有的有首，有的无首，共同的特征是：扁茎、无格、折肩、短身，有首的剑首与剑身分离，靠木片或竹片捆绑衔接，这种类型的剑属滇、黔、桂系统，应是本地制造。稍后一字形格的青铜剑盛行，形成地区性特点，其中“圆首一字格铜短剑”柄和身一次铸成，是受西部滇文化影响的产物。这些剑铸造精致，合金比例成熟，剑身上多有精美细致的阴刻图案。除铜剑外，平乐银山岭战国墓还发现一批配套兵器，其中扁茎短剑、双肩铲形钺、靴形钺等器物为当时南方百越文化所特有，而铜镞、铜矛的数量也不少，剑、镞、矛常在同一墓中共出，是“将”以下军官的组合形式。

剑在瓯骆地区也有身份地位象征的作用，像“人面弓形格云雷纹铜短剑”上装饰有人面纹，为王者之剑，是有身份和地位的人佩戴的。瓯骆故地发现的铜剑，最早是春秋晚期、战国时期盛行。平乐县银山岭战国墓群基本是一墓一剑，甚至有个别一墓两剑的，剑式非常丰富，体现了轻礼器重实用器、喜铸剑好使钺的地域特征。

值得一提的是最具越文化特征、兼具实用与礼用功能的越人铜钺。铜钺是古越人最典型的器物，渗入越人生活的方方面面，有学者认为，越人的得名，是因为使用钺著称的缘故，铜钺成为岭南越人重要的文化标志之一。瓯骆地区的铜钺流行于先秦时期，秦以后不再出现。瓯骆常见的是靴形钺，靴形钺常见于西南地区，用作兵器，瓯骆地区出土的靴形钺属于“圆踵形”，与云南等地的靴形钺在形制上有差异，地域特征明显。

铜钺的用途多种多样，在平乐县银山岭战国墓葬中占有一定比例，从铜钺的大小和铜钺出土时刃部都有砥砺使用的痕迹来看，大都是实用器，是身份的象征，大多数出现在第一等级的墓中。“瓯展”展出的铜钺有呈凸字形的还有梭形和椭圆形的，其中弦纹銎斜弧刃铜钺，为本地所产。瓯骆常用的“双肩铲形钺”很可能是木工用的一种刨铲工具。靴形钺可用作杀伐兵器和砍劈工具，有的靴形钺装饰华丽，可能作为仪仗用，或用于舞蹈，是方国文明的礼器之一。

史载秦始皇进军岭南，曾遭越人的顽强抵抗，首当其冲的是“西瓯” 军， 从“江虞”铭铜戈细刻的地名“江虞”二字中，可推断这件楚式戈可能是西瓯军从秦军缴获的战利品。通过这些青铜文物，能感受到浓厚的军事气氛及亦耕亦战的彪悍民风。

三

青铜盛世铸就瓯骆文化辉煌

“瓯骆故地既是中国南疆东西部地区的结合部，又是内陆与沿海地区的过渡地带。自古以来就是少数民族聚居的地区，古代文化有其特殊的历史渊源，在吸纳周边地先进文化的基础上，不断创新，形成独具特色的青铜文化。”[①]壮族是中国人口最多的少数民族。壮、瑶苗侗为主体的少数民族文化在广西的和睦相处、和谐共生，表明广西文化的兼收并蓄、多元共荣的文化格局的形成是有历史渊源的。地域文化与融合文化交相辉映正是“瓯骆”文化的主要特色。广西青铜文化的发展史，就是瓯骆文明进程的记录史。

1. 兼容并包的文化胸怀

秦、西汉时期，广西青铜文化在中原先进生产技术的催生下，逐渐进入鼎盛时期。1976年发掘的广西贵港罗泊湾一号汉墓，出土的青铜器是这个时期岭南青铜冶铸技术最高水平的标志。虽然对墓主身份认定仍众说纷纭，有说西瓯君者，有说桂林郡守或郡尉者，不一而足。但丰富多彩的随葬品，为研究广西汉代的物质文化提供丰富实物资料的同时，也为人们勾勒出壮族先民鲜明的文化底色。

罗泊湾1号汉墓出土的鼎、壶、杯形壶、蒜头壶、钫、盒、匜、勺等，与黄河流域战国晚期至西汉初期墓葬出土的相同，应是从北方传入的，羊角纽钟、铜鼓等器物与滇文化关系密切，盘口鼎、附耳铜桶、筒形钟等具有浓厚的地方特色，其中附耳铜桶是南越国时期岭南地区极富代表性的青铜容器，包括彩绘人物画像的铜筒、铜盆、铜灯、铜鼓改制的三足案等，这些器物多数属南越国桂林郡专用品，“从多件青铜器刻有‘布’字铭文来看，应是桂林郡首府‘布山’制造的。布山有专为郡府生产铜器的作坊，集中了当时最好的工匠。”[②]某些器物上的汉字铭文，提供了器物产地、流传地名以及度量衡的信息。

西林普驮铜鼓墓为广西地区首次发现的以铜鼓作为“二次葬”葬具的墓地，出土青铜器包括铜鼓、羊角纽钟、洗、耳杯、骑俑、跽坐俑、六博棋盘和各种牌饰。用铜鼓作葬具，除显示地位尊贵有财富外，还有鼓能通神、借神力保佑的意思。丧葬文化与铜鼓文化相交融，既表明了壮族及其先民是铸造铜鼓的主要民族，亦反映了铜鼓在超度亡灵中的功用。西林县在汉初为句町属地，墓主人是句町的统治者，出土青铜器代表了汉代句町的最高冶铸水平。透过广西贵港罗泊湾汉墓及西林县普驮汉墓出土的大量青铜珍品，可窥见当时的瓯骆文化既具有中原文化色彩及地方风

① 蒋廷瑜：《西瓯骆越青铜文化比较研究》，《桂岭考古论文集》，科学出版社，2009年，85页。

② 蒋廷瑜：《先秦两汉时期岭南的青铜冶铸业》，《桂岭考古论文集》，科学出版社，2009年，252页。

格，同时兼具楚、滇文化因素的多种文化杂糅的兼容并蓄的特征。

2. 开放、进取的民族精神

“壮族作为中国人口最多的一个少数民族，其民族心理中一个突出的特征是它开朗好学的性格。由于长期与汉族和其他民族杂居交往，深受汉族文化影响，壮族群众很少有狭隘民族意识和排外意识。”①

汉武帝元鼎六年（前111年）平定南越，将岭南3郡扩充为9郡，至此文化融合进入快车道，合浦是我国汉代对外贸易的重要港口，《汉书·地理志》载，武帝时已形成一条从合浦郡始发经东南亚通往印度、斯里兰卡的远航贸易航线，即“海上丝绸之路”。从1957年至今，仅在合浦县已抢救发掘汉墓800余座，出土文物万件。合浦汉墓的一个显著特点是，比较大的墓葬都盛行随葬青铜器，汉墓的随葬品中可以看到当时的青铜铸造工艺已达到很高的水平。

广西铜器中出现了两个比较有地方特色的品种——漆绘铜器和錾刻铜器。“漆绘铜器是一种器表以漆画装饰的青铜器，贵港罗泊湾1号汉墓出土的钫、壶、蒜头扁壶、杯形壶、提梁筒、盆等6种铜器，器表或以黑漆涂抹，或以黑漆和彩漆绘画，彰显富丽，最有价值的是漆绘铜盆和漆绘铜筒。”②铜盆的战争叙事画组画，似与传说中的越人“猎头”习俗有关，而漆绘铜筒的组画表现的是充满神秘宗教色彩的招魂升天图。西汉中期以后，在合浦、贵港、苍梧等中心城市兴起一种錾刻花纹工艺，这种在薄胎青铜器上用坚硬而精细的金属工具，采用錾凿和镂刻方式来制作铜器花纹，在其他青铜器上还未见到，“是岭南地区工匠对中国青铜器工艺的重大贡献”③。合浦汉墓出土的錾刻青铜器有水盘、酒樽、壶、食盒、魁、卮、杯、长颈壶、提梁壶、扁壶、熏炉、凤凰灯、席镇，包括盛食器、饮食器、灯具等居室用器，还有铜鸡、铜鸭等，铜凤灯是其中的精品。这些新兴的工艺品装饰技艺的流行，已不完全是高官贵族奢侈生活的时尚显示，更多的是对贸易需求的反映。

青铜模型明器西汉晚期出现最多的是铜仓，这些铜仓完全是以真实仓库为蓝本按比例缩小制作的，结构复杂，铸造工艺精巧。其中的“悬山顶杆栏式铜仓”让人们从一个侧面了解当时的房屋结构，也可能为干栏式建筑在越地流行提供证据，同时也可窥见海上丝绸之路”的开放繁荣；合浦汉墓中大量出土的铜仓，表明当时粮食储备相当丰富，为合浦周围聚集大量商人及手工业者创造了最根本的物质条件，也成为船舶补充给养的最佳中转站。东汉时期，在广西地区墓葬的随葬品中，形制独特的越式器已不常见，而专门用于陪葬的明器数量剧增，尤其是像庄园经济生活的井、灶、仓、圈及猪、狗、牛、羊、禽模型等大量出现，如合浦风门岭的铜牛、铜狗、铜鸟皆成双成对出土，形态栩栩如生，反映了当时“事死如事生”的厚葬风气的盛行及封建庄园经济的发展概况。

青铜冶铸业的出现，在科技史上具在里程碑的意义。中国古代青铜工艺在经过

① 李秋洪：《广西民族交往心理》，广西人民出版社，1996年，171页。

② 林强、蒋廷瑜：《贵港罗泊湾汉墓》，《中国文化遗产》2008年第5期。

③ 蒋廷瑜：《先秦两汉时期岭南的青铜冶铸业》，《桂岭考古论文集》，科学出版社，2009年，253页。

商至春秋时期的繁荣阶段以后，到秦汉时期已走向衰落。汉代青铜器已从先秦那种庄严、厚重、古朴的风格中变得轻便、灵巧，纹饰也崇尚简朴。而瓯骆地秦汉时期青铜铸造工艺却达到新高峰，最能代表当时青铜冶铸水平的当之无愧者为铜鼓，西汉以后的铜鼓已进入成熟时期，从铜鼓的造型来看，能灵活配比以铜锡铅为主的各种金属成分含量，使之构成不同特性的铜鼓，用来制作不同用途的铜鼓，体现了当时对金属中各种成分的科学配比达到了很高的水平。尤其是鼓面上的太阳纹、晕线纹、几何纹所表现的高超准确的葛圆技术和几何运算方法，更是令人惊叹不已。

秦汉时期岭南青铜器不但继续沿用先秦时期的范铸法，而且新采用失蜡法，失蜡铸造法能够铸造器型复杂、雕镂精细的铜器，在壮族地区则主要用于铸造铜鼓，以失蜡法铸造的器物玲珑剔透，有镂空的效果。

秦汉时岭南铜器铸造工艺的辅助工艺有焊接工艺、铆接工艺和套接工艺等，如罗泊湾1号墓用铜鼓改制的铜案采用了焊接工艺，还有采用榫卯套接工艺的“扶桑树形铜灯”，而铜马则采用了套接工艺。装饰工艺这时还出现了鎏金工艺，如西林普驮铜鼓墓的骑马俑、马蹄俑、各种牌饰、铜棺、面具等，表面都鎏金，除彩绘、錾刻工艺外，镂刻的“三兽铜镇”是镂刻工艺在錾刻花纹铜器上完美展现，更是岭南地区青铜器装饰工艺的突出成就。

透过这些青铜珍品人们不难发现瓯骆民族开放、吸纳的同时不故步自封及争取不断进步的可贵民族个性，在青铜文化中无处不闪现着学习、创新的进取精神。青铜器在中国古代文明史中占有非常重要的地位，回顾历史我们发现，当曾经千姿百态、灿烂辉煌的殷商青铜文化、地中海青铜文化、中亚青铜文化都已成为历史的追忆时，惟铜鼓文化至今仍活跃在历史舞台上，继续书写着西南少数民族的青铜文化奇迹。

“瓯骆”文化是中华民族灿烂文化的重要组成部分，“瓯骆”历史源远流长。就文化而言，广西以桂林山水文化、北部湾海洋文化和以壮瑶苗侗为主体的少数民族文化三大板块为主，三种不同形态的文化都共同具有兼容并包、开放进取的文化胸怀及鲜明的文化个性，使刚柔相济的广西文化独具魅力，是“瓯骆”文化的延续和发展。博大精深的青铜文化隐含着丰富多元的文化内涵，等待着我们一起去探寻。

从出土的青铜器试看梧州汉代的社会面貌

The Society of Wuzhou in Han Dynasty Revealed by Unearthed Bronze Wares

周学斌 / 杭州市文物考古研究所 助理馆员

[摘要]

本文简要介绍了梧州的地理位置与历史沿革，叙述了梧州汉代青铜器的出土情况，并以这些青铜器为视角并结合部分文献记载，尝试从三个方面描述当时的社会面貌：

[关键词]

梧州　汉代　青铜器　社会面貌

Abstract

This paper briefly introduces the geographical location and history evolution of Wuzhou, then describes the Han dynasty unearthed bronze wuzhou situation, and then to the perspective of bronze and combining with document account, try to part from three aspects of the society at that time described face.

Key words

Wuzhou; Han dynasty; Bronze wares; Social visage

图一　广西梧州地理位置示意图

一

梧州地理位置与历史沿革

梧州市位于广西壮族自治区东部，地处桂江、浔江、西江三水交汇之地，是广西著名的港口和口岸城市，素以“水上门户”著称。东与广东省肇庆市封开县接壤，南、西、北分别与广西的玉林、贵港、贺州市相邻。梧州地处广西山字构造的东南翼，东北高、西南低，北部多山，南部多丘陵，地理坐标为东经111° 51′ 14″～111° 40′、北纬22° 58′ 12″～24° 10′ 14″，市均海拔24米。属亚热带季风气候，夏长多雨，冬短无严寒，山多林密（图一）。

梧州是一座历史悠久的南方古城，古称苍梧、广信。考古发现表明，早在旧石器时代中晚期就有人类在这里繁衍生息。夏为荆南境，商周为百越地，秦统一岭南后在当地设桂林、南海、象三郡，梧州隶属桂林郡。汉高祖四年（前203年），赵佗在岭南建立南越国，梧州归属南越国管辖；汉高后五年（前183年），苍梧王赵光在此建苍梧王城，为梧州建城之始，至今已有近2200年的历史。

汉武帝于元鼎六年（前111年）平定了南越国之后，在岭南设南海、苍梧、郁林、合浦、交趾、九真、日南、朱崖、儋耳等岭南九郡，苍梧郡下辖广信、谢沐、高要、封阳、临贺、端溪、冯乘、富川、荔浦和猛陵等十县，相当于今之梧州、肇庆、贺州三市及湖南的道县、江华、江永等地，郡治所在地为广信，即今梧州。元封五年（前106年），全国置十三部（州），岭南属交趾刺史部，下辖苍梧等郡，广信是交趾刺史部治所。东汉沿袭西汉制，梧州仍称广信。

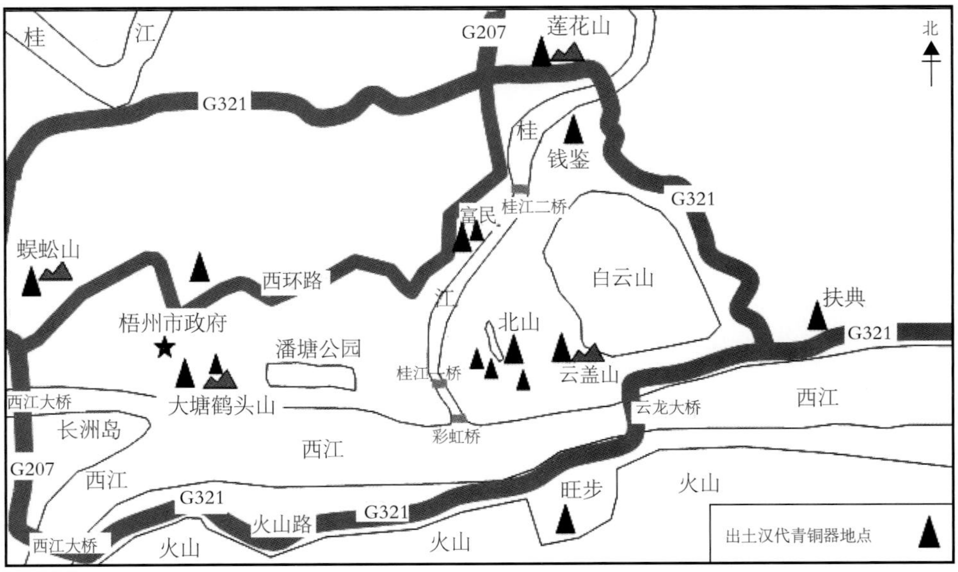

图二 梧州市汉代青铜器出土地点分布示意图

二

梧州汉代青铜器的出土情况

从现有资料来看，梧州的汉代青铜器基本上都是历年来在市区及市郊的汉墓中出土的，分布广泛，主要地点有旺步、龙新、大塘、白后村、富民、文化路、京梧、扶典、西堤路、罗山、莲花山、松山、北山、云盖山、崩山、南岸火山等（图二）。

梧州汉代青铜器的出土始于1956年河西白后村低山东汉墓的清理，此墓随葬铜弩机1件。至20世纪80年代初期，已出土汉代青铜器700多件，其中包括铜钱400多枚。

1958年，河西白后村低山汉墓出土汉代灯1件、剑2件；莲花山东汉墓出土鼎1件；罗山东汉墓出土鐎壶、弩机各1件；市郊东汉墓出土博山式熏炉、兽面铺首各2件，钵、樽、镜各1件；市郊汉墓出土印、带钩各2件，瓿1件；尤其在云盖山，发现的汉墓和出土的青铜器较多，三号墓出土东汉五铢钱2枚，五号墓出土东汉五铢钱6枚，六号墓出土东汉刀、剑各1件，还出土鐎壶3件，西汉墓出土器座2件，矛、樽、篹、盉各1件。

1959年1月，白后村低山东汉墓出土鉴1件。

1960年，莲花山东汉土坑墓出土壶1件。

1962年，河西二分厂低山东汉墓出土壶、提梁壶、四乳镜各1件。

1963年，河西二分厂低山东汉墓出土鐎壶、灯各1件，碗2件；蝶山八号汉墓出土东汉五铢钱154枚[①]。

① 余天佑:《简论梧州及周边出土的两汉钱币》,《西江经济社会》2010年第1期(总第23期，内部刊物)。

1964年，河西白后村低山西汉墓出土鼎、壶各1件；白后村东汉墓出土樽盖、规矩纹镜各1件；紫竹林汉墓出土洗1件；6月4日，万寿公社出土汉代昭明镜1件；7月，工人医院西汉墓出土五铢钱9枚；11月，市区出土矛1件。

1965年，白后村低山东汉墓出土提梁壶2件，壶、龙纹镜、灯、带钩各1件；木材加工厂松山东汉砖墓出土剑1件；莲花山东汉墓出土樽、碗、盒各1件；龙新蜈蚣山东汉墓出土棺钉3件；丝绸厂工地汉墓出土汉代碗2件，灯1件；1月30日，龙新三窝塘西汉墓出土鼎1件；3月4日，河西白后村低山砖厂出土东汉昭明镜1件；8月25日，河西白后村东汉墓出土鼎1件；10月，大塘1号东汉墓出土壶、提梁壶各2件，鐎壶、长颈瓶、仓模型各1件；10月14日，白后村低山东汉墓出土长颈瓶1件。

1966年，河西淀粉厂出土汉代规矩纹镜1件。

1969年，淀粉厂九龙山汉墓出土灯1件；河西崩山东汉墓出土碗1件。

1972年，市第九中学出土1件东汉“驾登龙”四神镜；市区还出土“长宜子孙”连弧纹镜、四乳镜各1件；旺步玻璃厂后背山旺步M1出土1件东汉铜尺；8月，旺步航运局船舶厂后背山东汉墓旺步M2出土碗3件，耳杯4件，筷条1双，洗、盘、龙凤纹方案各1件[①]。

1973年，市区出土汉代铜鼓、东汉规矩纹镜各1件；火山脚石油站宿舍出土碗1件；莲花山船机厂出土东汉盘、带钩、剑各1件；文化路汉墓出土勺1件；11月，大塘胜利酒厂鹤头山东汉长方形竖穴土坑墓鹤M1出土鼎、长颈瓶、洗、樽、熏炉、刷把、鐎壶、镜各1件，碗3件，鹤M2出土灯、樽、釜、甑、鐎壶、碗、镜各1件，盘5件，五铢钱33枚，鹤M3出土鐎壶、碗各2件，盘1件[②]。

1974年，富民纸箱厂后山出土铜镜1件。

1975年，河西二轻鞋帽厂后背山出土神兽纹四乳镜1件；6月，市区出土矛1件。

1976年，市区出土汉代矛、东汉碗各1件；市富民纸箱厂出土神兽纹镜1件；市石油站出土神兽规矩纹镜1件；7月，富民坊鬼儿头出土锅、三乳钉洗、碗、镜各1件，釜2件；12月，大塘鹤头山东汉墓鹤M4出土镜、壶、长颈瓶、案各1件。

1977年，扶典冷冻厂出土东汉樽、剑各1件；龙新百站仓出土汉代剑1件；市区修路时出土鐎壶1件；8月，河西淀粉厂出土东汉规矩纹镜1件。

1978年，莲花山船用机械厂东汉墓出土鐎壶、带钩各1件，碗2件，昭明镜3件；大塘鹤头山东汉墓出土碗1件；富民坊鬼儿头煤场出土东汉洗、剑各1件；旺步水厂发现三座东汉土坑墓，4月，旺步水厂M1出土洗、规矩神兽纹镜各1件，旺步水厂M2出土鐎壶、碗各1件，8月，旺步水厂M3出土碗、规矩纹镜各1件。

1979年，大塘鹤头山出土汉代带钩、矛各1件；扶典工农仓出土东汉碗、神兽纹四乳镜各1件；扶典冷冻厂出土东汉镜1件；富民纸箱厂出土东汉碗3件，盘2件；莲花山电筒厂出土东汉鐎壶1件；木材加工厂松山出土东汉镜1件。

① 梧州市博物馆：《广西梧州市近年出土的一批汉代文物》，《广西文物考古报告集》，广西人民出版社，1993年，406页。

② 梧州市博物馆：《广西梧州市鹤头山东汉墓》，《广西文物考古报告集》，广西人民出版社，1993年，407页。

1980年，北山后山东部出土西汉樽、杯各1件，大塘塑料研究所出土西汉盘、盆各1件，淀粉厂出土东汉印章、剑、镜、碗、樽、灯各1件，富民坊一建司出土东汉镜2件。

1981年，大塘塑料研究所出土东汉樽1件，纸箱厂出土东汉刀、带钩、甑各1件，9月，公安局东汉晚期砖墓出土鐎斗、镜各1件。

1982年，大塘标准件厂出土东汉碗、镜各2件，盘1件；市郊出土（废旧公司收回）碗2件；1982年10月23日，大塘龙山酒厂鹤头山东汉墓出土鐎壶2件，带钩4件，鼎、盘、饰件、龙凤纹筒①、釜、甑、提梁壶、铺首、碗、樽、镜各1件；11月2日，又出土东汉碗1件。

20世纪80年代苍梧县广平乡鐎金村出土汉代北流型铜鼓1件。

另外在梧州市第五中学汉墓出土东汉五株钱币200多枚；在鹤头山M7出土灯、三足案、樽、盘各1件，矛、戈各2件。

还有一部分具体出土时间、地点不详，包括新莽货布1枚，新莽货泉40枚；东汉碗、盘各1件，钵2件，镜9件，五铢钱25枚；汉代瓢、鸠形壶各1件，带钩2件。

① 黄贵贤、邝淑暖:《汉代龙凤纹针线筒》，《广西文物》1991年第2期（总第17期，内部刊物）。

三

梧州汉代的社会面貌

先秦时期，梧州为百越地区。与其他大多数百越民族一样，当时的人们以采集、捕捞、狩猎和原始农业为生。《史记·货殖列传》载：“楚越之地，地广人稀，饭稻羹鱼，或火耕而水耨，果隋赢蛤，不待贾而足。”这是一种严重依赖自然环境的自给自足的原始农业经济。秦始皇通过“秦瓯战争”于前214年统一岭南以后，随着灵渠的开凿、湘桂走廊和潇贺道等道路的修筑与开通，郡县制度的实施，军队的驻守和中原人的南迁，逐渐打破了百越地区原始落后的社会面貌。汉代，承袭并加强了秦代的各项制度，采取“和辑百越”的政策，进一步加快了梧州社会的发展进程。

（一）中央王朝统治的巩固

通过武力征服和一系列“和辑百越”政策法令的推行，汉王朝进一步巩固和加强了在岭南梧州地区的统治。

1. 武力征服，驻守军队

中原王朝统治岭南首先是以武力征服作为前提和保障的。“秦始皇三征岭南”，经历了越人的强烈反抗，但强大的秦军终归将岭南纳入了祖国的版图，掀开了梧州社会经济发展的新篇章。秦亡后，南海郡龙川县令赵佗起兵兼并桂林郡，建立南越国。汉武帝刘彻于元鼎六年出兵岭南，平定了南越国叛乱，使岭南重新回归中央。此后，汉王朝继续推行郡县制等政策法令。

为保障政策法令在越人地区的顺利实施，巩固在岭南的统治，汉王朝在当地驻守有大批军队。从梧州出土的汉代青铜兵器可以看到当时军队的一些情况。

首先是剑和刀。剑是古代贵族和战士随身佩戴的可斩可刺的短兵器，梧州共出土9件。均无首，多薄腊，从狭长，以扁茎厚格为主，也有少数圆茎有箍厚格剑。1977年，扶典冷冻厂工地出土的1件扁茎厚格剑，扁茎有圆形穿，可惜穿后部已残断，残长63.5厘米（图三，1）。刀是砍杀敌人的短兵器，梧州出土的2件均为环首刀。其中1981年纸箱厂出土的1件环首刀，锋尖、刀刃残缺，残长19厘米（图三，2）。汉代，随着冶铁技术的成熟，廉价、结实、锋利的铁质兵器已逐渐将铜兵器挤出了战争舞台，梧州汉墓中就出土有大量的环首刀等铁质兵器。据史料记载，铜剑、刀在汉代不仅是一种短兵器，也是一种身份等级的象征，具有一定身份地位的贵族或军官等才可以佩戴铜剑、刀。那么一把铜剑或刀所代表的就不止是一个兵卒了。所以这十多件铜刀、剑所反映的军队当不在少数。此外，梧州还出土有7件铜矛，基本上是狭叶刃，少数阔叶刃，骹呈圆形或矩形；2件铜戈，均为无阑直内式，戈柲已腐朽无存；2件弩，仅剩铜质弩机部分。弩是杀伤力强的远射武器，在当时应属非常先进的兵器。由此可见，当时驻守的军队数量不在少数，而且武器装备精良。

除兵器以外，1981年9月，公安局东汉晚期砖室墓出土了1件鐎斗。尖圆唇外折，口微敛，口沿内侧饰一周凹弦纹，弧腹，一侧带弯曲的扁条形执柄，圜底，三蹄足。口径10、通高8.2厘米（图三，3）。有学者认为鐎斗是随军用的炊器，“又称刁斗，汉晋时期的一种炊器，或用于军旅”①，从一个侧面反映了当时军队的情况。

① 马承源:《中国青铜器》，上海古籍出版社，2003年，299页。

2. “和辑百越”，广施恩信

前214年，秦始皇统一岭南后，不仅在当地推行郡县制，而且将南征的将士留下布防戍守，还将大批中原汉人迁居岭南“与越杂处”。这些措施使中原文化以空前的广度和深度传入瓯骆地区，客观上促进了汉越民族的融合。秦亡后，南越国王赵佗采取“和辑百越”的政策，尊重岭南人生活习惯，鼓励汉越通婚，引进中原先进生产工具，积极传播先进的汉文化，有效促进了汉越民族间的团结与融合，促进了当地社会经济的发展。

《苍梧县志》载：元鼎六年（前111年）“汉武帝平南越，以其地为广信县，置苍梧郡”。汉武帝平定南越后，设广信县，“……谓初开粤地宜广布恩信也”（《汉书》），以示对越人广施恩信。汉王朝不仅继承前代的郡县制，并采取了强化措施，将岭南重新划分为苍梧等九郡，细化管理；沿袭南越国“和辑百越”的政策，“以其故俗治，毋赋税”。这些政策的推行，巩固和加强了中央王朝在梧州的统治。

随着汉王朝在岭南统治的稳固和加强，作为苍梧郡治所在地的广信，社会趋于安

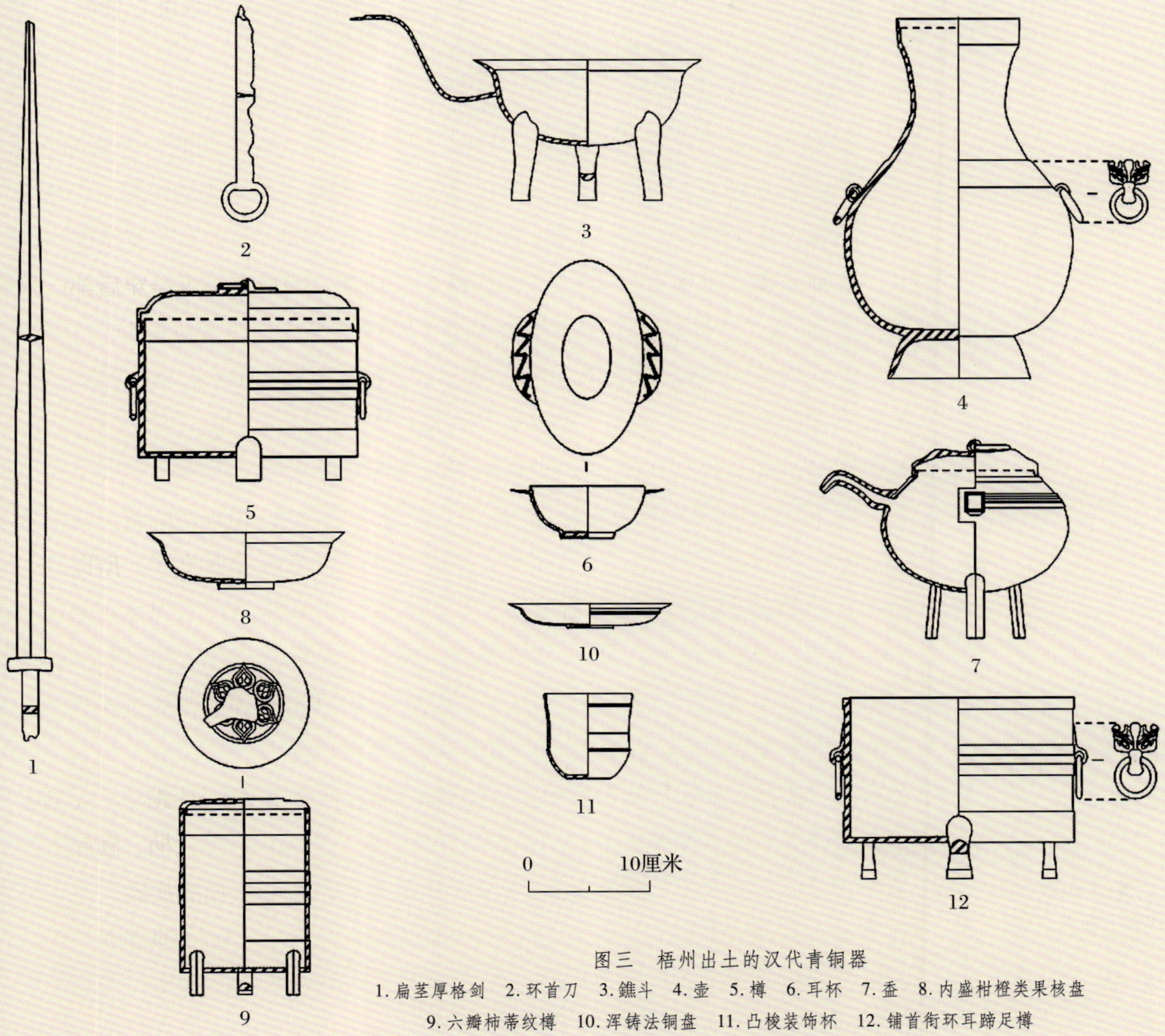

图三 梧州出土的汉代青铜器

1. 扁茎厚格剑 2. 环首刀 3. 鐎斗 4. 壶 5. 樽 6. 耳杯 7. 盉 8. 内盛柑橙类果核盘 9. 六瓣柿蒂纹樽 10. 浑铸法铜盘 11. 凸棱装饰杯 12. 铺首衔环耳蹄足樽

定，大批中原汉族人不断迁来定居，中原先进文化以空前的广度和深度传入，经济快速发展，生活水平提高，并“渐见礼化”。从梧州出土的汉代——尤其是东汉时期数量众多、器型多样、铸造精致、纹饰丰富的青铜器可以窥见梧州当时的经济和生活面貌。

（二）梧州汉代经济的发展

封建社会的经济发展一般包括农业、手工业和商业贸易三个方面的内容，梧州出土的汉代青铜器种类较多，好多器物保存情况较好，这为我们了解汉代的经济发展提供了宝贵的实物资料。

1. 农业

农业是社会发展的基础，也是封建社会最重要的经济活动。在梧州汉代墓葬中出土的一些青铜器内有稻谷、柑橙种子、板栗等，将这些农产品陪葬于墓葬中，说明当时不仅在中原，即使在偏远的岭南梧州，重农思想已经确立。

（1）粮食的充裕

粮食的充裕是农业发展进步的结果。梧州暂未发现汉代的铜质农业生产工具，不能直接看到当时农业发展的面貌，但从梧州出土的汉代青铜器所反映的酿酒业的兴盛和粮食储存技术的科学性，可侧面了解当时粮食的充裕，进而了解农业的发展。

大量酒器的出土揭示的是梧州酿酒业的兴盛。梧州出土的汉代青铜酒器有壶、樽、长颈瓶、耳杯、盉等种类，且数量相对不少。盛酒器壶有13件，有的带有提梁。1962年，河西二分厂低山东汉墓出土的1件口沿微残。盘口，束颈，圆鼓腹，上腹两周凸弦纹，附对称两个铺首衔环耳；平底，圈足外弧，饰一周凸弦纹。口径10.4、高29.2厘米（图三，4）。盛酒用的樽有12件，均呈圆筒形，腹壁有高有矮。1973年11月，大塘鹤头山M2出土的1件铜樽保存较好。盖顶有环纽，纽外饰有三周凸弦纹，腹壁竖直较矮，有三周扁平圈带装饰，两侧有铺首衔环耳；平底，下有三扁足。口径14、底径14、通高14.4厘米（图三，5）。饮酒用的耳杯有4件，1972年8月，旺步2号东汉墓出土的1件为椭圆形。两侧带弧形耳，耳上部饰有三线波浪纹，弧腹，平底，内底下凹，底下有椭圆形矮圈足。口径9.8～15、高4厘米（图三，6）。还有用于调酒的青铜器——盉，1958年云盖山西汉墓出土，盖顶有活环纽，盖与器身有活环纽相连；扁圆器腹饰有四条扁带形圈饰，腹侧有弧形流和一较直的鋬，中空；圜底，三足外撇。口径9.2、通高16.4厘米（图三，7）。装酒的长颈瓶有4件，1965年10月，大塘1号墓出土的1件东汉长颈瓶，有锈蚀，足残。圆唇，口近直，细长颈，扁圆腹，圜底近平，圈足外撇。器身饰有凹弦纹、三角斜线锯齿纹、龙凤纹和斜方格纹。口径2.7、高20.5厘米（图四）。这些酒器制作讲究，形制美观，可见当时酿酒业的兴盛。俗话说“酒是粮食精”，酿酒业的兴盛是建立在粮食充裕的基础之上的。

粮食储存技术的科学性也可在一定程度上反映粮食的充裕情况。1965年10月，大塘1号墓出土1件东汉青铜粮仓模型，制作精致，价值珍贵，现为梧州市博物馆收藏的一级文物。铜仓为干栏式，悬山顶，有瓦垄，屋顶破裂；与屋相似，室内不分间，前面中间开门，门有活环；平底，下有四圆柱承托仓体，有一足断；瓦垄与谷仓主体可分离。出土时仓内尚存大量的谷物，盖长40、宽32厘米，底长31、宽25.5厘米，柱高12、通高33厘米（图五）。我们虽不能从这件铜仓看出当时真正粮仓的大小和数量，却完全可推测出土当时粮食生产出现了大量剩余，需要用专用的粮仓来保存，可见当时粮食的充裕。粮仓为干栏式，这是适应梧州湿热的气候特征而采用的具有防潮功能的建筑形式。这种比较科学的粮仓建筑形式不太可能是一开始就采用的，应该有过一定时期的发展，换句话说，粮食充裕的状况已经出现了相当长的时间。

图四　铜瓶

图五　铜仓

（2）经济作物的栽培和家畜的饲养

经济作物的栽培和家畜的饲养主要反映在梧州汉代青铜器出土时器内残留的经济作物痕迹和器物的装饰上。

1973年11月，大塘鹤头山M2出土的1件铜盘，口沿微残。尖圆唇，敞口外折；浅腹微鼓，下腹急内收；圜底近平，矮圈足。出土时盘内盛放有柑橙类果核。口径16.4、高4.8厘米（图三，8）。同墓出土的1件铜碗，尖圆唇，敞口微外侈；深弧腹，圜底，矮圈足，底、足残。出土时碗内还有28颗板栗残迹。这些出土时器内残留的柑橙果核与板栗痕迹是梧州当时栽培此类经济作物的最有力的证据。

梧州出土的一些器物上装饰有柿蒂纹，多为四瓣柿蒂纹，也有六瓣的。1980年淀粉厂门前右侧出土的东汉铜樽，形体较小。子口盖残破一洞，分为两层，上层为平台，饰有六瓣柿蒂纹，下层内弧；器身直口方唇，腹壁竖直较高，口沿、中腹、下腹各有一周扁带圈带装饰，中腹圈带上有一周凸棱；平底，下有三扁足，截面近三角形。口径10.8、底径10.8、高16厘米（图三，9）。另外，1958年市郊和1973年11月大塘鹤头山M2出土的铜樽盖顶均刻饰有四瓣柿蒂纹，1件东汉“长宜子孙”铭文铜镜纽座上也有四瓣柿蒂纹。这些柿蒂纹饰应该是当时种植柿子这种经济作物在实物上的反映。

《西京杂记》记载，西汉初，南越王赵佗就曾将荔枝作为珍品进献给汉高祖，《三辅黄图》也载，汉“元鼎六年破南越，起扶荔宫”，从岭南移植荔枝，不难看出荔枝这种岭南名果在当时已经作为一种农副产品开始栽培。在梧州出土的汉代青铜遗物中虽然还未发现有荔枝的痕迹，但梧州当时种植这种水果也不是没有可能。

1958年，云盖山西汉墓出土的1件三羊铜樽，子口盖，口沿上部向内平收，平顶略下凹，正中为一活环纽，周围刻饰龙凤纹，其外凸起一周内缘高外缘矮的扁平圈带，圈带上等距饰三只立体羊，口、耳、眼、鼻及体上绒毛均刻饰清晰，呈卧状，头向环纽；直口圆唇，腹壁竖直较矮，口沿、上腹、下腹各饰一周扁平圈带装饰，中腹圈带上饰一周凸棱，两侧附有对称的两个铺首衔环耳；平底，下有三扁足，足面刻饰羊纹。口径23、底径23、通高22厘米（图六）。这件器物盖上的立体羊塑和足部刻饰的羊纹应该可以说明梧州西汉时期饲养有羊这种家畜。

2. 手工业

梧州汉代农业的发展为手工业的繁荣提供了基础，而手工业的进步突出表现在青铜业的发展上。

（1）数量大、器型多

梧州出土的汉代青铜器包括铜钱在内已达700多件，其数量之多，在同期的广西地级市中并不多见。这些数量丰富的青铜器基本上是实用器，可分为饪食器、酒器、兵器及其他日常用器等，具体器型包括鼎、碗、钵、釜、甑、盘、鐎壶、案、锅、盆、盒、鐎斗、勺、筷子、瓢、瓿、簋、樽、杯、盉、长颈瓶、耳杯、壶、提梁壶、剑、矛、刀、戈、弩机、镜、洗、灯、熏炉、鉴、刷把、筒、带钩、铺首、印章、尺、饰件、棺钉等，还有1件模型冥器干栏式铜仓模型。梧州汉代青铜器基本上出土于汉墓中，从墓葬年代和器型特征初步来看，西汉、东汉两个时期的区别比较明显。

梧州出土的西汉青铜器数量少，包括钱币在内一共才30件左右；器型种类不多，目前能明确为西汉时期的器物，三足器以兽蹄足为常见，有鼎、樽、杯、盉、提梁壶、簋、盘、盆、勺、矛、器座、钱币等，这些都是现实生活中的实用器物，目前还未发现专用于陪葬的冥器。

东汉是梧州青铜器最流行的时期，青铜器数量明显增多，包括铜钱在内共达600多件。这个时期的青铜器形制多样，相当一部分造型精致，带三足的器物多为扁足，兽蹄足少见。器体颜色以青绿色为主，均有不同程度的锈蚀。从用途性质看，绝大多数仍是实用青铜器，器型多样，根据其形制特征和用途及其数量多少，又可分为饪食器、酒器、兵器和其他器类及钱币五大类。饪食器有鼎、碗、钵、釜、甑、盘、鐎壶、案、锅、盒、鐎斗和筷条等，酒器有樽、长颈瓶、耳杯、壶、提梁壶等，兵器有剑、矛、刀、戈和弩机等，其他器类有铜镜、洗、灯、熏炉、鉴、刷把、筒、带钩、铺首、印章、尺、饰件、棺钉等，还有五铢钱币430多枚。专为陪葬铸造的模型青铜冥器——东汉干栏式铜仓也出现于这个时期。

（2）纹饰丰富

西汉时期青铜器的纹饰不多，基本上每件器物均有或凸或凹的弦纹，鼎、樽、盉、簋等器上有扁平圈带装饰，在樽和簋上有立体羊装饰，簋上还刻饰有三角斜线锯齿纹、龙凤纹样。

东汉时期青铜器的纹饰变得丰富起来，主要有抽象几何纹和各种动植物纹样等，几何纹包括弦纹、凸棱、扁平圈带装饰、竖线纹、斜线纹、三角斜线锯齿纹、菱形纹、连弧纹、规矩纹、波浪纹等，数量最多，广泛饰于各种青铜容器上，尤其是弦纹，梧州所出东汉青铜器基本上都有此种纹饰；动植物纹样包括龙、凤、神兽、羊、虎、鹿、熊、鱼及柿蒂等动植物形象，主要装饰于镜、樽、筒、釜、壶、提梁壶、鉴、鐎壶、案、长颈瓶、熏炉、尺等一些制作精美的器物上。个别器物上还有羽人纹、云纹和钱纹等。

铭文在东汉时期的部分青铜器上开始出现，除1件刻有“章和三年正月十日□□□□钱千二百”的铜碗外，其余均是铜镜，计有10多件，镜背有“朱氏”、“驾登龙”、“长宜子孙”等字样的铭文。

（3）铸造方法多样

梧州目前没有发现用于铸造青铜器的工具，但从出土青铜器的器型和装饰特征还是可以看出当时梧州青铜器铸造工艺的高超。

梧州出土的青铜器较为明确的铸造方法是范铸法。范铸法是出现最早、流行时间最长的一种青铜铸造工艺，其流程一般如下：先将做好的泥模倒置于座上敷泥分范，再匀刮器模形成空隙，然后灌注铜液，待铜液冷却后打碎外范，取出青铜器即完成。范铸法又可分为浑铸法、分铸法。

浑铸法是指用单范或多范一次浇铸而成。从器型特征看，梧州出土的东汉扁足铜鼎、碗、盘、洗、钵、釜、耳杯等器物即是用浑铸法一次铸造而成。如1973年11月鹤M2出土的1件小铜盘（图三，10），口沿微残，尖圆唇，敞口外折，近平沿；浅腹微鼓，饰一周凸棱，下腹急内收，矮圈足。口径13、高2厘米。器身无合范痕迹，应是浑铸法的产品。1973年11月鹤头山M1出土的铜鼎（图七），子口内敛，扁鼓腹，平底下有三扁足，器身至足部有三条垂直的铸痕，显然是用三分范浑铸而成。

分铸法用于铸造带附件器物。“青铜器大都为分铸，或称二次铸造”[①]。梧州出土的汉代青铜器，有的带活动的提梁，有的带活动的环耳或纽，有的带执柄或把手，有的带复杂的立体装饰。如1965年10月大塘1号墓出土的两件提梁铜壶，大小、形制相同，用数十个铜环串接而成的铜活链连接器腹与器盖，上部有半环形把手，便于外出携带；盖顶有圆环纽（图八）；同墓出土的1件铜鐎壶，衔环纽盖，与器身有活环纽相连，腹一侧带执柄（图九）等。这些器物都是一次浇铸不能完成的，需要用分铸法来二次铸造而成，同时反映了梧州汉代青铜器铸造技术的高超水平。

研究表明，汉代岭南已出现了失蜡法铸造工艺，此法“能够铸造器型复杂、雕镂精细的铜器”[②]。梧州出土的汉代青铜器是否有用失蜡法铸造而成的，还有待进一步的深入研究。

（4）装饰工艺精湛

梧州汉代青铜器的装饰比较丰富，主要包括弦纹、凸棱、扁平圈带装饰、竖线

① 马承源:《中国青铜器》，上海古籍出版社，2003年，510页。

② 蒋廷瑜:《先秦两汉时期岭南的青铜冶铸业》，《桂岭考古文集》，科学出版社，2009年，254页。

图六　铜樽

图七　浑铸法铜鼎

图八　分铸法提梁壶

图九　分铸法鐎壶

纹、斜线纹、三角斜线锯齿纹、菱形纹、连弧纹、规矩纹、波浪纹等几何纹，数量最多，广泛饰于各种青铜容器上，尤其是弦纹，梧州所出汉代青铜器基本上都有此种纹饰；另一种是动植物纹样，包括龙、凤、神兽、羊、虎、鹿、熊、鱼等动物和柿蒂等植物形象，主要装饰于镜、樽、筒、釜、壶、提梁壶、鉴、鐎壶、案、长颈瓶、熏炉、尺等一些制作精美的器物上；个别器物上还有羽人纹、云纹和钱纹等。从这些纹饰的特征来看，当时的装饰工艺按其时间先后可分为两类，一类是在器物铸成以前就已装饰的，另一类是器物铸成以后才装饰的。

凸棱、凸弦纹、扁平圈带装饰等应是铸造前就已装饰的纹饰，这种装饰普遍见于樽、碗、盘、钵、釜、鐎壶、锅、洗等青铜器上。1977年扶典冷冻厂出土的1件东汉铜樽，扁平圈带装饰较为集中。此器呈直筒形，腹壁较高。盖外观分两层，盖纽已残缺，使盖顶露出一洞；下层盖残破一洞，上部为一平台，子母盖口；直口圆唇，腹壁竖直较矮，腹部残破有两洞。口沿、中腹、底部各饰一周凸起的扁平圈带装饰，中腹圈带较宽，上有一周较窄的圈带；半圆形三足，近蹄形。口径10.8、底10.8、高16厘米（图一〇）。如1980年北山后山东部出土的1件西汉铜杯，口沿微残，口沿、腹部各饰一周凸棱，平底，口径7.3、高7厘米（图三，11）。

绝大部分精细的纹饰是在器物铸成以后装饰上去的，包括凹弦纹、竖线纹、斜线纹、三角斜线锯齿纹、菱形纹、连弧纹、规矩纹、波浪纹等几何纹样，龙、凤、异兽、羊、虎、鹿、熊、鱼、柿蒂等各种动植物纹样，还包括器物上的铭文。这些纹饰的制作工艺主要分为镂刻和錾刻两种工艺，有时独立使用，有时结合使用，尤其是錾刻花纹的青铜器极具岭南特色，錾刻花纹的汉代青铜器也是梧州最有代表性的古代文物种类之一。

镂刻工艺是在铜器铸成之后，用坚硬的钢刀直接镂刻而成，其特征是刻痕内窄而外宽，即剖面呈楔形。“凹弦纹、网纹等呈线状的纹饰，大多数是用钢刀直接镂刻的”①，梧州所出汉代青铜器基本上都有凹弦纹装饰，可见镂刻工艺在梧州汉代青铜器上运用之广泛。

錾刻工艺是用刃部长短不同的钢凿，一道一道凿刻，其特征是凿痕内外宽度基本一致，即剖面呈矩形。錾刻花纹的内容比较丰富，可分为抽象的几何纹样和写实的各种动物纹样两大类。梧州目前比较明确使用錾刻工艺的汉代青铜器主要是熏炉、灯、案、筒和长颈瓶等器类，较典型的有铜方案、熏炉和龙凤纹针线筒。1972年8月，旺步2号墓出土的东汉龙凤纹铜方案，呈长方形，四角各有一榫眼用以插足，足已失，口沿外折，沿上勾连“S”纹。案内纹饰分内外两区。内区正中刻一鼎，鼎内有鱼，鼎口溢出水花，左右各有一条面向鼎面而舞的龙，龙的上、下又各有一条鱼；外区饰龙、凤、神兽，四角各有一枝花树。围绕这些图案的是水波纹、菱形回纹、勾连“S”纹构成的纹带。图案富丽悦目，体现出我国汉代的美术设计和雕刻工艺已达到高度水平。长69.4、宽44、高2厘米（图一一）。1973年11月，大塘鹤头山M1出土的东汉铜熏炉，博山式。炉体呈青铜器中的豆形，上有盖，盖高而尖，镂空，作山峰重叠状，刻饰龙凤纹。盖顶立一凤，高冠昂首；两层山峰，每层四峰，交错排列，上层有三镂孔，下层四个镂孔；山峰下两周扁平圈带，间饰三角斜线锯齿纹。盖与炉身间有一活链相连，炉身以网纹和弦纹作底饰凤鸟纹。承柱矮细，下为喇叭口。底座为圆盘状，口沿外折，上饰一道凸弦纹和一周三角斜线锯齿纹。底盘微缺，平底。底盘口径17.6、高19.6厘米（图一二）。1982年10月23日大塘鹤头山汉墓出土的东汉龙凤纹铜筒，微残，子母口盖；直口，直腹，平底。盖面和紧靠盖面下的器身一侧各置一带孔扁圆纽，器身阴刻有龙、凤、虎和其他怪兽图案。口径3.5、高10厘米（图一三）。

“岭南地区，尤其是广西东南部，应是汉代錾刻花纹青铜器的制作中心和主要产地”②。錾刻工艺制作的繁缛精致的几何纹样和动植物图案，使器皿显得特别精美华丽，颇具地方特色，它不仅是梧州汉代青铜工艺精湛的代表，也是汉代梧州工匠对青铜制造业的一大贡献。

3. 商业贸易

秦汉以前，梧州社会中基本上没有什么商业贸易，“楚越之地……不待贾而足”。汉代，随着农业和手工业的发展，商业贸易经济日渐繁盛。“在汉代……苍梧郡的苍梧（今苍梧至梧州一带）……等都是广西当时最大的商贸都市”③。

① 蒋廷瑜:《先秦两汉时期岭南的青铜冶铸业》，《桂岭考古文集》，科学出版社，2009年，252页。

② 蒋廷瑜:《汉代錾刻花纹铜器研究》，《桂岭考古文集》，科学出版社，2009年，242页。

③ 梁旭达:《论广西秦汉时期的交通和商贸发展》，《广西考古文集》（第二辑），科学出版社，2006年，501页。

图一〇 扁平圈带装饰铜樽

图一一 錾刻工艺龙凤纹铜方案

图一二 錾刻工艺凤鸟纹熏炉

图一三 錾刻工艺龙凤纹筒

（1）大量青铜货币的出土是商业贸易发展最直接的证据

货币是商品交换的媒介，是商品交换发展到一定阶段的产物，它反映的是一种日常的商品交换关系。在“不待贾而足”的社会里，货币的存在是没有必要的，只有当时已经出现了商业活动才能解释梧州出土的青铜货币，而大量青铜货币的出土又是当时商业贸易发展最直接的证据。

西汉时期的货币较少，均为五铢钱，均为1964年7月梧州工人医院西汉墓出土；梧州出土的新莽时期的货币只有1枚货布和40枚货泉。可见此时以货币为媒介的商品交换活动虽已出现，但商业活动还不甚普遍。

东汉时期货币数量大增，均为是圆形方孔五铢钱。1958年，在云盖山三号墓东汉出土五铢钱2枚，五号墓出土五铢钱6枚；1963年，在蝶山八号东汉墓出土了五铢钱154枚；1973年11月，大塘胜利酒厂鹤头山鹤M2出土东汉五铢钱33枚；市第五中学汉墓中出土有五株钱币200多枚，另外，梧州市博物馆馆藏的25枚五铢钱，具体出土时间、地点已无从查证。大量青铜货币的出土足以证明东汉时期商业贸易的发展和繁荣。

（2）外来青铜器是商业贸易发展的又一个证据

在梧州出土的汉代青铜器中，有一部分器物，如蹄足圆鼎、蹄足樽、蹄足鐎斗、弦纹鉴等，带有鲜明的岭北风格，可能为岭北直接传入或当地仿铸的产品。1964年，河西白后村低山西汉墓出土的1件铜鼎，残缺，盖已失，圆形，敛口，三兽蹄足。1980年，北山后山东部出土的1件蹄足樽，呈圆筒形，盖已失。直腹较矮，口沿、中腹、底部各饰一周扁平圈带，中腹的较宽，上饰一周凸弦纹，上腹两侧附有铺首衔环耳一对；平底穿破，下有三个兽蹄足，一足缺失。口径19、底径19、高15厘米（图三，12）。1959年1月，白后村低山出土的鉴，口沿微残，圆唇，敞口外侈，口沿外侧饰一周凸弦纹；颈微束，弧腹，上腹有一周凸棱，上、下各饰一道凸弦纹，中腹对称附有一对铺首衔环耳，下腹内收；圜底近 平，内底下凹，圈足外撇。口径22、高12厘米（图一四）。

梧州出土的圆茎有箍铜剑、环首刀、铜戈、弩机等青铜兵器和铜镜也具有明显的中原风格。尤其是铜镜，达41件，均为圆形，有纽，宽缘，少数素面，大多饰有规矩纹、连弧纹或神兽纹，相当一部分还有铭文。从器物的造型和装饰来看，大部分应是岭北输入的产品，像梧州出土的1件神兽纹七乳镜，宽缘，圆纽，圆形纽座。外缘凸起，素面；内缘饰蟠螭纹，内、外各有一周凸弦纹。缘向内依次饰一周竖线纹、两周凸弦纹，弦纹间有“未央”等字样的顺读铭文，凸弦纹与纽座间饰有龙、凤、鹿等神兽纹、卷云纹及七乳。圆纽座向内依次饰两组内夹竖线纹的凸弦纹、蟠螭纹。直径18、缘厚0.6厘米（图一五）。这件铜镜完全是中原的风格。

虽然这些具有岭北风格的青铜器有一部分可能是当地仿铸的产品，也有一部分可能是军队、官吏或百姓因为自身需要或封赏当地越人而输入，但其中相当一部分应是通过商业贸易获得。无疑，外来青铜器是梧州汉代商业贸易发展的又一个证据。

（3）反映商业贸易的其他青铜证据

20世纪70年代出土的2件铜碗，从侧面反映了当时商品交换的发展深度。

1972年8月，旺步2号墓出土的1件铜碗，底部残破有1小孔。尖唇敞口，口沿外折；弧腹近直，下腹急内收，上腹一周凸弦纹，中腹有凸棱，凸棱上、下各有一道凸弦纹，下腹亦饰一道凸弦纹；平底，内底有一圈凸弦纹，外底刻有“章和三年正月十日□□□□钱千二百”铭文，直读，除部分铭文锈蚀外，清晰易辨；玉璧形圈足有三乳钉。口径23.5、足径12、高8.4厘米（图一六）。“章和三年”实为东汉和帝刘肇永元一年（89年）。1973年，火山脚石油站宿舍出土的1件基本完整，尖唇敞口，口沿外折；浅弧腹近直，下腹急内收，腹饰两道箍形凸棱；平底，内底中部饰五铢钱纹，边缘内凹；玉璧形圈足。口沿微残，外壁有锈蚀，青绿色；内壁光洁，保存较好。口径16.1、高6.3厘米（图一七）。

有人将以上铭文解读为此碗的价钱是一千二百钱，是否准确暂且不说，但将

图一四　铺首衔环耳圈足鉴

图一五　七乳神兽纹镜

图一六　“章和三年正月十日□□□□钱千二百”铭文铜碗

图一七　五铢钱纹碗

“钱千二百”刻饰于碗底、在碗上装饰五铢钱纹则足以说明“钱”的概念已深入人心，反映了人们对金钱的崇拜，可见商品交换的发展深度和商业贸易的繁荣。

（三）日常生活面貌

生活是指人于生存期间为了维生和繁衍所必须从事的不可或缺的生计活动。两汉时期，随着政治的稳固和社会经济的发展，人们的日常生活面貌也发生了根本的改变。

1. 衣、食、住、行

两汉时期，梧州地区农业发展、手工业进步，商业贸易繁荣，为人们的生活提供了物质基础，具体反映在衣、食、住、行四个方面。

（1）穿衣着装

《淮南子》卷一《原道训》：“九嶷之南，陆事寡而水事众，于是人民被发纹身，以像鳞虫；短绻不绔，以便涉游；短袂攘卷，以便刺舟，因之也。”讲的主要是先秦时期梧州人们披头散发，身饰纹案，穿衣着装简单朴素，以短衣短裤为主。

两汉时期保留下来的青铜带钩和饰件，反映了当时人们的衣着打扮发生了很大的变化。梧州出土有汉代的青铜带钩共13件，均为龙形带钩，下端有钉柱钉于皮带的一头，上端曲首作钩，用以钩住皮带的另一头，中间有钩体，侧视呈“S”形，首端截面呈圆形，尾端截面呈椭圆形，尾端较宽。如1982年10月23日大塘鹤头山东汉墓出土了4件带钩，形制相同，首、尾残断，长11.4、高2.6厘米（图一八，1）。1982年10月23日，大塘鹤头山出土1件铜饰件，微锈残。呈龙形，两条弯曲的长龙双头无尾，互相缠绕，龙头部位相对呈玦形。长21厘米（图一九）。制作精巧、造型美观的带钩与饰件在一定程度上反映了当时人们穿衣着装的华丽。

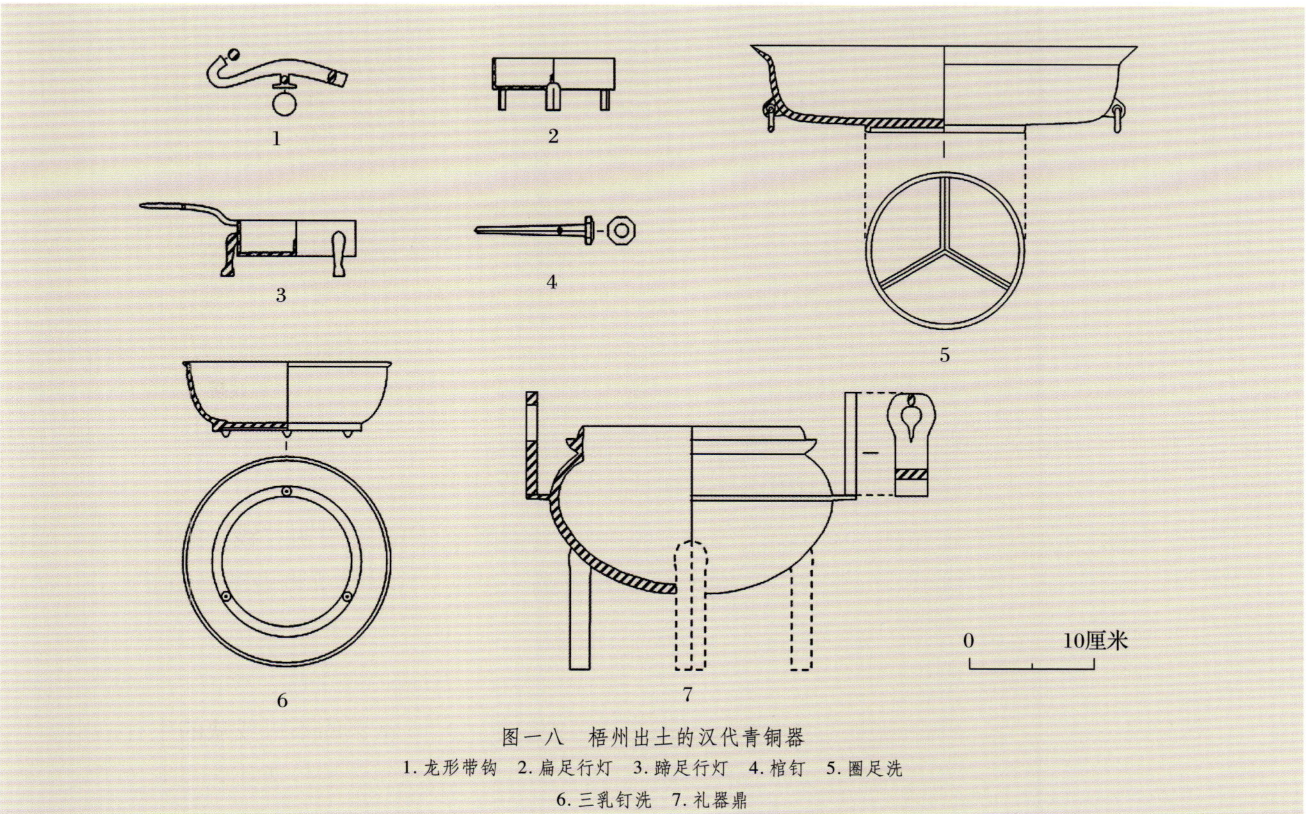

图一八　梧州出土的汉代青铜器
1. 龙形带钩　2. 扁足行灯　3. 蹄足行灯　4. 棺钉　5. 圈足洗
6. 三乳钉洗　7. 礼器鼎

（2）饮食

秦汉以前，“饭稻羹鱼……果隋蠃蛤”。两汉时期，随着农业生产的发展，人们的饮食生活有了显著的提高。

梧州出土的汉代青铜饪食器数量大，器型多，包括鼎6件、碗32件、盘14件、釜4件，甑、钵、案各3件，筷条1双，簋、盒、锅、盆各1件。鼎、釜、甑、簋、盒、锅是烹饪食物

图一九　龙形饰件

图二〇　铜铺首

的器皿，从其数量来看，鼎、釜、甑是比较常用的。碗、盘、钵、盆是盛放食物的器皿，以碗的数量最多，少数平底或玉璧形足，多为或高或矮的圈足。盘的数量也不少，均为尖圆唇，敞口外折，浅腹微鼓，下腹急内收。案、筷条也是古代进食过程中比较常用的器皿。这些饪食器大多制作精美，反映了当时人们饮食方式的进步。

1965年10月，大塘1号墓的东汉干栏式青铜粮仓模型出土时仓内尚存大量的谷物，说明当时人们的主要粮食是稻米，这种以米为主粮的饮食习惯一直延续影响到现代的梧州。1958年，云盖山西汉墓出土的1件铜樽，盖上等距饰三只立体羊，足面刻饰羊纹，可见羊肉已经进入了人们的碗盘之中；1973年11月大塘鹤头山M2出土的1件铜盘内盛放有柑橙类果核，同墓出土的1件铜碗内有28颗板栗残迹，1980年在淀粉厂门前出土的铜樽盖顶和1件"长宜子孙"铭文铜镜，纽座均刻饰有柿蒂纹，这些器物的出土明确揭示了当时人们饮食的多样化，除了以主粮解决温饱以外，还用羊肉、柑橙、板栗、柿子等副食调节饮食。

此外，梧州出土有大量汉代的青铜酒器，有盛酒用的壶、樽、长颈瓶和饮酒用的耳杯及调酒用的盉等，造型多样，表明了当时饮酒的盛行。

（3）居住

梧州现在已看不到汉代时期的建筑，出土的汉代青铜器为我们从侧面了解汉代的居住环境提供了一些线索。

1965年10月，大塘1号墓出土1件东汉干栏式青铜粮仓模型，制作精致，从此件器物的形制来看：首先，悬山顶房屋在汉代已经出现；第二，房屋已经使用瓦这种构件；第三，仓下有四柱承托，这是最具特色的一点，代表的是具有地域特色的干栏式建筑。干栏式建筑是指一种在木（竹）柱底架上建筑的高出地面的房屋，一般是用竖立的木桩或竹桩构成高出地面的底架，底架上有大小梁木承托悬空的地板，其上用竹木、茅草等建造住房。梧州地处热带、亚热带季风气候区，空气潮湿，具有防潮湿功能的干栏式建筑很早就在此产生。从平整光滑的仓壁来看，此时的干栏式建筑可能已使用砖或夯土砌筑墙体。

铺首呈兽首衔环之状，是门扉上的叩门、装饰之物，或作为古代一些器物上的装饰，中原地区早在商周时期就已出现。梧州出土的汉代部分青铜器，如樽、釜、壶等，器身饰有兽面衔环铺首装饰。另有单独的铺首3件，形制相同，均为饕餮纹兽面铺首。2件出土于1958年市郊东汉墓，形制、大小相同。额头竖起，两耳外翘，眼鼻清晰，两颊宽尖，长鼻，衔圆环。其中1件保存较好，通长22、宽13.5厘米（图二〇）。另1件是1982年10月23日出土于大塘鹤头山，环已断，通长9.5、宽9厘米。从这3件铺首的尺寸来看，它们应是门扉上的叩门、装饰之物，由此我们可以推测出梧州当时一些建筑屋门或院门的形象。

（4）出行

秦越战争期间开凿的灵渠与秦始皇统一岭南之后修筑的湘桂走廊和萌渚岭道，沟通了五岭南、北间的联系，为北人南下、南人北行创造了有利条件；梧州地处三江水口，沿桂江北上可至灵渠进而达至中原，沿浔江西行可至郁林、交趾、日南等郡，沿西江东下可至南海郡进而出海，可见其水陆交通之发达，出行之便利。

《越绝书·越绝外传记地传》载：“夫越性脆而愚，水行而山处，以船为车，以楫为马，往若飘风，去则难从”。可见在汉代，人们是以船为主要的交通工具。遗憾的是至今尚未发现具有船楫形象的青铜器。

灯的出现，延长了人们的活动时间，为人们夜间出行带来了光明。梧州出土有8件汉代的青铜灯，尤其是3件行灯，灯盘一侧有执柄，专用于夜间出行照明。1965年丝绸厂汉墓出土的1件行灯锈蚀严重。1969年淀粉厂九龙山出土的1件铜灯，盘壁略残。浅圆灯盘，直口，盘壁较薄，中央有圆柱状灯芯凸起，盘下三扁足，执柄已缺失。口径9.8、底径9.8、高4.5厘米（图一八，2）。1980年淀粉厂门前右侧出土的1件东汉铜灯，有残缺。浅圆灯盘，直口，壁直较薄，中央有圆柱状灯芯凸起，平底，盘下三蹄足。盘侧有向上弧起的执柄，截面呈椭圆形。口径9.4、底径9.4、高4.4厘米（图一八，3）。

2. “渐见礼化”

随着社会经济的发展和中原汉族移民的南迁，两汉时期人们的日常生活面貌不仅在物质层面出现了根本的变化，而且逐步在深层结构的精神文化层面出现了质的变化。正如《后汉书·南蛮西蛮夷传》所载：“使杂居其间，乃稍知语言，渐见礼化”。从出土的青铜器来看，具体表现在以下几个方面：

（1）厚葬习俗的传入并流行

梧州出土的汉代青铜器基本上是汉墓中的随葬品，我们第一眼看到的自然是当时的丧葬习俗。

汉代苍梧郡作为岭南九郡之一，富裕阶层云集，保留下来的汉代墓葬数量众多，其中相当一部分墓葬中出土有青铜器，包括鼎、碗、钵、釜、甑、盘、鐎壶、案、锅、盆、盒、鐎斗、勺、筷子、瓢、瓿、簋、樽、杯、盉、长颈瓶、耳杯、壶、提梁壶、剑、矛、刀、戈、弩机、铜镜、洗、灯、熏炉、鉴、刷把、筒、带钩、铺首、印章、尺、饰件、棺钉、铜仓模型等。其数量之多，在整个广西地区并不多见。尤其是其中的铜棺钉和铜仓模型，说明了人们对丧葬习俗的重视。1965年龙新三窝塘蜈蚣山东汉墓出土的3枚铜棺钉形制、大小相同，其中1枚残断。钉帽分两层，均呈正方形，上层尺寸大，下层缩小；钉身呈四棱锥状。全长10、帽宽2.3厘米（图一八，4）。1965年10月份出土于大塘1号墓出土1件东汉时期的干栏式铜仓模型，它是专为随葬而制作的模型冥器。这些汉墓中随葬的数量众多的青铜器物和专为丧葬而制作的铜棺钉、铜仓模型表明，汉代中原地区的厚葬习俗已传入了梧州地区并在当地流行开来。

丧葬制度属于上层建筑范畴，反映着一定的经济基础和社会政治制度。厚葬习俗的流行，尤其是随葬的数量众多的青铜器，反映了中原文化在梧州传播的深度和广度。

（2）生活方式的文明进步

随着社会经济的发展和中原先进文化的传入，两汉时期人们的生活方式逐步趋于文明进步。

洗是日常盥洗用具，犹如现在的洗脸盆，梧州出土有6件汉代的青铜洗。1976年7月出土的1件，直口，方唇较厚，直腹略外弧，下腹内收；内底下凹，玉璧形足较矮，下有三乳钉。口径18、高6.5厘米（图一八，5）。1978年4月旺步水厂工地出土的1件，口沿微残。敞口，尖唇，口沿外折近平，直腹略外弧，下腹急内收，腹部有对称两环耳，一环残缺；圜底近平，圈足。圈足中心向外伸出三条凸起的线段，将圈足平分为三个扇面。口径38、高8.4厘米（图一八，6）。

镜是古代照面的用具，梧州出土的汉代铜镜达41件，均为圆形，有纽，宽缘，少数素面，大多饰有规矩纹、连弧纹或神兽纹，相当一部分还有铭文。其中1件规矩纹四乳铜镜，宽缘，圆纽，复线方形纽座；外缘凸起，素面；内缘中部饰两道凹弦纹，弦纹外侧饰一周复线三角锯齿纹，内侧一周水波纹；缘向内依次饰一周竖线纹、凸弦纹，弦纹与纽座之间饰规矩纹、卷云纹和四乳。直径9.1、缘厚0.4厘米（图二一）。1959年1月白后村低山还出土1件铜鉴，也是用来照面的器具，不过器内要盛水。铜镜出现后，鉴的使用就开始减少了。

熏炉是汉代常见的熏香器具，也可用来熏衣、熏被以除臭、避秽，梧州出土有3件，全为博山式。均为高而尖的盖，镂空；承柱矮细，下为喇叭口；底座为圆盘状，口沿外折。1958年出土于市郊东汉墓中的1件，出土时盖缺，底座残，经修复后

图二一　规矩纹四乳镜

完整。盖上刻饰一周山峰，顶有圆环纽，口沿处一周扁平圈带装饰。炉身素面。口径6.6、底径6.6、海径16.6、高14厘米（图二二）。

这些盥洗、照面和熏香青铜器的出土反映了当时人们已不再“被发纹身”，开始对卫生状况及自身的形象给予了重视，表明了当时生活方式的文明进步。

（3）礼制的出现

在中国的青铜时代，奴隶制国家在建立了庞大的国家机器的同时，还建立了一套调整社会矛盾的礼乐制度，将其中“铸造技术精巧、气魄雄伟、造型优美、纹饰绚丽的青铜器定为青铜礼器”[①]。

在青铜礼器中，鼎是最重要的一种，是国家政权和个人社会等级的典型代表器物。《周礼·仪礼》记载，天子九鼎，诸侯七鼎，大夫五鼎，士三鼎。梧州出土的青铜鼎有6件，西汉时期的铜鼎有2件，均为圆鼎，敛口，蹄足。1964年河西白后村低山西汉墓出土的1件，严重残破。另1件为1965年1月30日龙新三窝塘西汉墓出土，子母口盖，顶有三个圆柱状突起，其间饰一周凸弦纹，中心有活环纽。鼎身敛口，圆形腹微鼓，上腹对称附有一对扁方形圆环耳，耳间饰一道箍形凸棱，平底。底部有三个简化的扁兽蹄足向外撇开，横截面呈三角形，内部为凹槽。口径17、高21厘米（图二三）。东汉时期的铜鼎有4件，均为三扁足，截面呈三角形。1965年8月25日白后村东汉墓出土的1件圆鼎，盖残失，下腹穿一洞。子口内敛，圆鼓腹，饰一周凸棱，腹两侧有竖耳，下方上圆环，底近平。口径14.2、腹径16、通高17.5厘米（图二四）。另外，1973年11月鹤头山M1、1982年10月23日大塘鹤头山汉墓各出土1件铜鼎，形制相似。1980年莲花山东汉墓出土的铜鼎，盖已失，身残破三孔，二足缺。子口内敛，口沿向外平折，束颈，扁鼓腹，上腹一周平边向外伸出，其上对称两竖耳，下方上圆环，平底。口径19、通高24厘米（图一八，7）。

① 蓝日勇:《骆越无国论》，《百越研究》，广西科学技术出版社，2007年，29页。

青铜簋也是重要的礼器，常在祭祀和宴飨时以偶数组合与奇数组合的列鼎配合使用。1958年在梧州云盖山西汉墓出土1件铜簋，制作精巧，纹饰华丽。盖顶微向上弧凸，中心有活环纽，残断；周围刻饰龙凤纹，外有三道凸弦纹，三道弦纹上等距饰三只立体羊，轮廓刻饰清晰，呈卧状，头向环纽；靠外侧的两道凸弦纹间有三角斜线锯齿纹；盖身饰满双线菱形纹饰，靠下部和盖沿各饰一道扁平圈带，间饰三角斜线锯齿纹。子母口，口沿处有一道扁平圈带装饰，下有一周三角斜线锯齿纹。弧腹，两侧附活环耳，下腹内收，圜底，圈足外撇，微残。口径22.3、通高13厘米（图二五）。

在梧州地区还出土有2件铜鼓。铜鼓是有鲜明地域特色的青铜器，首先是一种乐器，但在多数情况下是一种权力和地位的象征。1973年市郊汉墓出土，仅剩太阳纹鼓面残片。另1件是20世纪80年代在苍梧县广平乡螀金村出土，属北流型铜鼓，体积

图二二　铜熏炉

图二三　西汉铜鼎

图二四　东汉铜鼎

图二五　铜簋

大而沉重。鼓面饰太阳纹，太阳纹外有五道晕圈，上有四只立体蛙饰，鼓面大于鼓胸，呈“垂檐”式，胸部不甚突出，鼓胸、腰之间有四个环耳，鼓身遍饰云雷纹。面径88、残高40厘米，重约一百多斤[①]。

另外，汉代的壶、提梁壶、剑、刀、镜等青铜器，在一定条件下也代表着个人地位的尊卑上下，起着礼器的作用。

这些代表一定等级地位的鼎、簋、壶、提梁壶、剑、刀、镜、鼓等汉代青铜器，尤其是作为权力和地位象征的鼎、簋、铜鼓的出土，是礼制已深切传入梧州地区在实物方面的重要反映。

① 罗德振:《苍梧县发现汉代铜鼓》，《广西文物》1987年第2期（总第8期，内部刊物）。

四

结　语

综上所述，自西汉武帝设置苍梧郡以来，两汉时期梧州一直作为郡治所在地，随着中原地区人口的南迁、先进文化和先进生产方式的传入，农业、手工业、商业贸易得到了高度的发展，梧州已经成为中国岭南地区一个重要的政治、经济中心，梧州汉代的社会面貌发生了根本的变化。可总结如下：

（1）通过武力征服与“和辑百越”等一系列封建社会政策法令的推行，汉王朝促进了汉、越民族的融合，进一步巩固和加强了在岭南梧州地区的统治。梧州先是岭南九郡之一苍梧郡郡治所在地，后又成为全国十三部（州）之一——交趾刺史部的治所，名副其实地成为了岭南的一个政治中心。

（2）中原人口的南迁和先进生产方式的传入，促进了梧州经济的发展。两汉时期，梧州农业发展、手工业进步、商业贸易频繁，尤其是东汉时期，社会经济繁荣，已成为岭南的经济中心之一。

（3）随着政治的稳固和社会经济的发展以及中原先进文化的传入，人们的日常生活面貌也发生了根本的改变，衣、食、住、行各方面均有了显著的提高，生活方式趋于文明进步，明确尊卑等级的礼制出现，“渐见礼化”。

广西先秦古国研究综述

A Review of Research on Guangxi Pre-Qin States

陈虞添 / 广西师范大学 硕士研究生

[摘要]

本文主要介绍广西先秦古国研究情况，将其分三个阶段简要总结这些研究成果的特点，同时对这些研究文章进行分类概述，主要介绍瓯骆国的骆越名称探讨、瓯骆族源、关系、地理位置、社会性质、历史、青铜文化研究、与周边关系以及句町国的历史、文化、经济等方面研究成果，最后对广西先秦古国研究存在的不足及趋向提出自己的看法。

[关键词]

广西　先秦　古国　综述

Abstract

This paper describes the researches of Pre-Qin ancient states in Guangxi. The researches are divided into three stages. This paper makes a brief review of each stage and summarizes the characteristics of these research achievements. The theses of researches involved are classified and given overviews. These aspects are discussed in this paper: the discussion on naming Luo-Yue; the relationship between Ou and Luo; the ethnic source, geographic location, social nature, history, bronze culture of Ou-Luo; the relationship of Ou-Luo to the neighboring areas and research achievements of history, culture and economy of Gouding. And then this paper introduces my opinion on the problem and trend of researches on Pre-Qin ancient states in Guangxi.

Key words

Guangxi; Pre-Qin dynasty; Ancient states; Review

广西先秦的“古国”这一提法，见于郑超雄的《从古国到方国——壮族文明起源的新思考》[①]一文。该文根据历史文献、考古资料和苏秉琦先生提出的古国、方国、帝国的分期模式理论，论证壮族古代社会经历过古国、方国阶段。约在距今4000多年以前，岭南地区必有不少的古国实体。分布范围主要在湖南湘江流域及南部地区、广东的北部和西北部、广西的西北部和东部地区的苍梧古国与中原华夏集团尧舜禹古国同时存在。广东石峡文化遗址是古苍梧族所创造。桂南地区的石铲文化也应是桂南地区的古国文化遗存，其创造者是古骆越国先民。文章分三个阶段简要回顾广西先秦古国（西瓯、骆越、句町、苍梧等）研究情况。

第一阶段，20世纪50年代以前。这是研究西瓯和骆越的起始阶段。这一阶段的研究主要是以文献资料考证为主，西瓯和骆越都在研究百越的范围内展开，苍梧和句町在这一阶段较少论及，经过中外学者的研究取得了一些初步成果。

近代我国学者如梁启超、吕思勉、林惠祥、罗香林、徐松石等和外国学者如沙碗、鄂卢梭以及陶维英等对越与骆越的关系的看法。他们认为西瓯和骆越都属于百越系统。越人的分布颇广，从长江以南沿海、岭南、云南以及交趾等地，均有越人居住。越国建立在浙闽赣地区，都城设在绍兴，骆越（包括西瓯）分布在岭南西部和交趾。百越诸部名称很多，有于越、瓯越、闽越、南越、夔越、骆越等，统称为百越。越与骆越的民族渊源，同出于越。百越有着相同的风俗习惯，有着典型的器物铜鼓[②]。

第二阶段，20世纪50年代到20世纪末。这一阶段随着考古材料的不断发现和民族调查研究的陆续开展，为西瓯、骆越、句町等研究提供了丰富的材料。同时，其研究范围在扩大，涉及多方面，如对西瓯、骆越、句町的名称解释、族属族源、地理位置考证、社会性质、出土器物的研究、与周边地区的关系、宗教、文化、墓葬等。在方法上，有继续从文献资料方面入手的考证的文章，有单从考古学研究入手，有从民族调查来研究，也有从语言学的角度来研究。更多的是用多学科综合研究的方法来进行，如在考古学类型学、地层学和历史文献方面的考证基础上以及利用科学技术手段（如断代技术、金相分析等）为辅助来研究。另外，有一些专题性的研究也涉及这方面的内容。如百越民族史研究、铜鼓研究、壮学研究等都有论及。如百越民族史研究会编的《百越民族史论集》、《百越民族研究》中相关文章从史学角度论述瓯骆的发展历程。蒋廷瑜著的《古代铜鼓通论》一书中对西瓯和骆越也有论及。蒋炳钊主编的《百越文化研究》等论文集中都有对西瓯和骆越的论文。句町国研究肇始于20世纪80年代，最早发表这方面的研究文章的是蒋廷瑜先生发表的《西林铜鼓墓与汉代句町国》，其后有张世铨先生的《汉句町四题》和覃圣敏先生的《句町古史钩沉》等文章。

第三阶段，21世纪前10年。这一阶段是西瓯、骆越、句町研究的深入阶段，以跨学科综合研究和专题性研究为特点，表现在一些专题性研究专著的陆续出版。如郑超雄的《壮族文明的起源》和《壮族历史文化的考古学研究》从考古学和民族学等方面对西瓯和骆越进行

① 郑超雄：《从古国到方国——壮族文明起源的新思考》，《广西民族研究》2003年第4期。

② 石钟健：《试证越与骆越同源》，《中南民族学院学报》1982年第2期、第3期。

研究，广西文物考古研究所和南宁市博物馆编著的《广西先秦岩洞葬》，用考古学和人类学等方法从岩洞葬这一角度研究广西地区青铜文化及相关族属等问题，中共西林县委、县政府、广西文物考古研究所、广西历史学会合编的《句町国与西林特色文化》论文集，以句町为专题进行句町的历史、考古、民族文化等多方面的研究。而有关苍梧的研究相对较少，莫志东先生的《试论两广地区腰坑墓的族属及其文化特征——炎帝后裔苍梧部落南迁两广》[①]一文，认为两广地区腰坑墓是春秋末年到西汉初年聚居在两广地区的从陕西丹水地区南迁而来的炎帝后裔苍梧部落人的墓葬，腰坑习俗是苍梧部落聚居在河南、陕西南部时承袭商周文化的结果。另外还有一些文章零星论及有关苍梧古国的问题，在此不一一列举。

一

西瓯和骆越

西瓯和骆越的研究，除了历史文献中的记载，近代国内外也有学者在研究百越的论著中论及。石钟健的《试证越与骆越同源》[②]一文中介绍了我国近代学者如梁启超、吕思勉、林惠祥、罗香林、徐松石等和外国学者如沙碗、鄂卢梭、陶维英等对越与骆越的关系的看法，他们认为西瓯和骆越都属于百越系统。

新中国成立后，随着考古的不断开展，全国的考古事业蓬勃发展。在这一形势下，广西地区先秦时期的地下文物也相继出土，出土的考古材料为学者们研究西瓯骆越问题提供了十分有价值的材料。在20世纪70年代末开始，就有学者对西瓯和骆越相关问题进行探讨。20世纪80～90年代是西瓯和骆越研究热潮时期。学者纷纷在学术期刊上发表有关研究西瓯和骆越的文章。从20世纪80年代到21世纪前10年中的百越学术研讨会也有文章探讨西瓯和骆越问题。如百越民族史研究会编的《百越民族史论集》[③]、彭适凡主编的《百越民族研究》[④]、蒋炳钊主编的《百越文化研究》[⑤]等论文集中都有对西瓯和骆越的论文。

专著中也有论及西瓯和骆越问题。如张声震等编著的《壮族通史》[⑥]中相关章节从史学角度论述瓯骆的发展历程。蒋廷瑜著的《桂岭考古论文集》[⑦]中的先秦考古部分用考古学的方法研究西瓯和骆越的问题，他的《古代铜鼓通论》[⑧]一书中对这西瓯和骆越也有论及。还有《广西先秦岩洞葬》[⑨]也有对西瓯和骆越的论述。

1. 骆越名称探讨

关于骆越的名称和涵义，学者的观点不尽相同。“骆田说”、“骆马说“、“雒鸟说”、“马图腾说”等，以上各说大多从历史文献资料、考古材料、民族学材料和语言学方面的材料比较论证。

杨凌的《“骆越”释名新议》[⑩]认为骆(雒)越是中国古代岭南地区众多少数民族的

① 莫志东：《试论两广地区腰坑墓的族属及其文化特征——炎帝后裔苍梧部落南迁两广》，《炎帝与汉民族国际学术研讨会论文集》，2002年，77～85页。

② 石钟健：《试证越与骆越同源》，《中南民族学院学报》1982年第2期、第3期。

③ 百越民族史研究会：《百越民族史论集》，中国社会科学出版社，1982年。

④ 彭适凡：《百越民族研究》，江西教育出版社，1990年。

⑤ 蒋炳钊：《百越文化研究》，厦门大学出版社，2005年。

⑥ 张声震等：《壮族通史》，民族出版社，1997年。

⑦ 蒋廷瑜：《桂岭考古论文集》，科学出版社，2009年。

⑧ 蒋廷瑜：《古代铜鼓通论》，紫禁城出版社，1999年。

⑨ 广西文物考古研究所、南宁市博物馆：《广西先秦岩洞葬》，科学出版社，2007年。

⑩ 杨凌：《“骆越”释名新议》，《贵州民族研究》1989年第3期。

称谓之一。骆越的项髻之风，是将越贯以汉字“骆”、“雒”的真正原因。作者根据“骆、鬣”二字《说文解字》中诸多评方家的解释和越人的裸俗得出结论：骆(雒)越之为骆，取意于汉字，是一种隐喻，反映了汉族对少数民族项髻风俗的直观印象。谷因的《骆越之“骆”义何在》[①]一文赞同“马图腾说”，文章认为“骆”是整个越族的别称和前称，其所以称“骆”，是缘于对“骆马”的图腾崇拜。而“骆田”是指一种缺乏固定水源的稻田而言，不是越人名“骆”的原始。骆田之“骆”和骆越之“骆”两者涵义是不同的。

2. 瓯骆族属族源

西瓯骆越族属族源问题，论述骆越族属族源的文章较多，西瓯的文章相对较少，主要观点有：

（1）骆越属百濮族群，持此说的学者有范勇、王和平、何乃汉等学者。范勇的《骆越族源试探》[②]认为骆越属于濮僚系统的骆族先民，他的《试论骆越非越》[③]一文也论证骆越不属越族系统而属于濮僚系统。王和平的《浅论骆越族源及族属问题》[④]认为越南的东山文化应是古代骆越人的遗存。石寨山文化与东山文化的极端相似性，证明两地文化的创造者是具有很密切的亲缘关系的同一系统民族，石寨山文化与东山文化应是同一系统民族的文化，文章论证骆越是属濮僚系统民族。

何乃汉的《骆越非百越族群说》[⑤]认为百越和百濮都是对我国南方地区为数众多的少数民族的泛称。骆越族与邻近地区以至中原地区的民族，均有过密切的联系并产生过重大影响。骆越文化和滇文化有许多共同的独特的文化因素，骆越属百濮族群。

（2）骆越非百越，何光岳的《骆越的来源和迁徙》[⑥]论述骆人的起源，洛、雒、骆的名义和演变，雒人所创的《雒书》，骆人的南迁过程，骆越南迁交趾五个方面内容。文章认为骆越非百越的一支也不是广西土著民族。骆越是南迁的过程中不断与江南的越人群落融合形成了骆越。迁入广西时，骆越部族形成。战国末年，又因自福建西迁而来的西瓯侵入骆越之地，引起瓯、雒战争，西瓯占领了漓江、柳江流域，把雒越挤向西南，分布于今黔江、郁江流域，成为壮族的一支主要的先民。一部分南迁到越南的红河下游，成为越南的越（京）族的一支先民。潘雄的《骆越非我国南方诸族先民考》[⑦]考证骆越非我国南方诸族先民。作者认为越南族先民骆越生息在红河三角洲而中国南方民族先民西瓯则分布在西江流域。西瓯和骆越应属不同的民族系统。两者之间的地理分界基本上与今日的国界相似，在边境两侧有相互交错居住地。水、侗和布依等族先民与古骆越是没有族源关系的。骆越只能是现代南亚语系越语民族的先民。

（3）越与骆越同源，石钟健的《试证越与骆越同源》[⑧]根据大量文献和考古材料，从越与骆越的地理分布、物质文化、经济生产、风俗信仰、体质特征、语言、政治军事、晚近学者对这一问题研究成果等方面论述越与骆越同源。作者把浙闽地区古代的越人概称为“越”，岭西地区的西瓯、骆越人概称为“骆越”。 越与骆越在考古出土器物、经济生产方式、信仰、风俗习惯等都有相同的特点。越与骆越同源的最主要和最根本

① 谷因：《骆越之“骆”义何在》，《贵州民族研究》1993年第3期。

② 范勇：《骆越族源试探》，《四川文物》1985年第2期。

③ 范勇：《试论骆越非越》，《贵州社会科学》1986年第6期。

④ 王和平：《浅论骆越族源及族属问题》，《民族论坛》1987年第4期。

⑤ 何乃汉：《骆越非百越族群说》，《广西民族研究》1989年第4期。

⑥ 何光岳：《骆越的来源和迁徙》，《学术论坛》1988年第2期。

⑦ 潘雄：《骆越非我国南方诸族先民考》，《史学集刊》1984年第2期。

⑧ 石钟健：《试证越与骆越同源》，《中南民族学院学报》1982年第2期、第3期。

的原因是民族的亲缘关系（血缘关系）。

（4）骆越是本地土著人，广西学者大多数认为骆越是本地土著人，是壮族的先民，属百越系统的一支。张一民、何英德的《从出土文物探骆越源流及其分布》[①]认为广西地区实行屈肢蹲葬的原始居民是骆越先民，制作和使用石铲的人们也是骆越先民，制造和使用粤式铜鼓的是骆越民族的后裔——俚僚，操有壮侗语族的居民是俚僚的后二裔——壮、黎族及其他一些少数民族。同时，蹲葬、石铲和粤式铜鼓分布的地区就是骆越族大致的分布地区，其分布区域大致是在桂东南和粤西南等地。

张一民的《西瓯骆越考》[②]认为西瓯和骆越同是越人，西瓯、骆越是越族中两个不同的支系，西瓯、骆越属越族，可能是三苗的一支，非夏族。

张一民、何英德的《从广西铜鼓纹饰看壮族先民的心理素质及社会状况》[③]认为历史上的西瓯、骆越最初的祖先应是同一胞族或部落，这些胞族或部落的渊源应从百色盆地和左右江交汇处的范围中去寻找。以后随着时间的推移、人口的繁衍，逐渐形成西瓯、骆越两个部族。由于两个部族所处的地理环境不同，受各方面的影响不同，经济生活存在着一定差别，导致骆越部族形成了壮族南部方言。西瓯部族形成壮族的北部方言。这两大部族的组成当然并不排斥受东南越和西南濮的某些影响。正因为他们以土著为主又受到不同方面的影响，所以才形成了这两个系统铜鼓在花纹上的某些差异。

何英德：《广西南部壮族起源考》[④]认为广西南部壮族最早形成于左右江交汇处，尔后再不同程度地向四周进一步扩展，很可能有一支入越南与当地居民混合而成高山族、岱族、侬族，有一支东渡到海南岛，形成临高人，有一支经云南入泰国与当地居民混合形成泰族，有一支越过邕江北岸与桂中北地区居民混合形成西瓯。这些古人滚雪球的形式与石铲的分布疏密上正好成正比，但他们的渊源确是在左右江交汇处，如果再往上可往百色盆地中去寻找。

（5）西瓯族源复杂，梁钊韬的《西瓯族源初探》[⑤]根据历史文献资料和考古出土材料探讨西瓯族源问题。作者认为西瓯活动地方在贵县，西瓯的民族成分复杂，它包含古代骆越人、东瓯越人、复杂的倭人、楚人和中原人等。

3. 瓯骆关系

关于西瓯和骆越的关系，主要的观点有：

（1）西瓯与骆越是同一民族在不同时代的称谓。邱明的《西瓯骆越族称辨析》[⑥]认为“西瓯”与“骆越”是同一民族在不同时代的称谓。作者经过考证认为“西瓯”、“骆越”不是同族异称。西瓯和骆越是先秦至两汉时期居住在我国岭南地区的两个土著民族，他们同是百越族群中的两个支系。

（2）西瓯、骆越是岭南不同的部落或部落联盟。梁庭望的《西瓯骆越关系考略》[⑦]认为西瓯和骆越有密切关系，但并非同支异称。西瓯、骆越是岭南不同的部落或部落联盟。西瓯、骆越是壮族的先民，是构成壮族的两支岭南最重要的越人支系。西瓯是从骆

① 张一民、何英德：《从出土文物探骆越源流及其分布》，《中南民族学院学报》（人文社会科学版）1986年增刊。

② 张一民：《西瓯骆越考》，《民族学·民族史·地方史志文选》（乐生山房文集二），天马出版社，2005年，121～132页。

③ 张一民、何英德：《从广西铜鼓纹饰看壮族先民的心理素质及社会状况》，《民族学·民族史·地方史志文选》（乐生山房文集二），天马出版社，2005年，187～195页。

④ 何英德：《广西南部壮族起源考》，《壮侗语族民族论集》，广西民族出版社，1995年，44～50页。

⑤ 梁钊韬：《西瓯族源初探》，《学术研究》1978年第1期。

⑥ 邱明：《西瓯骆越族称辨析》，《云南民族学院学报》（哲学社会科学版）1995年第4期。

⑦ 梁庭望：《西瓯骆越关系考略》，《广西民族研究》1989年第4期。

越分化出来的农业集团，历史的发展，部分瓯与骆已融合为今天的壮人，另一部分则发展成为壮侗语族中的其他民族，广泛分布于黔、滇、粤及东南亚一些国家。

（3）瓯、骆既非同族异称，也非异地异族，而是同地异族。李秀国的《瓯骆关系新论》[①]用考古出土资料论述瓯骆是同地异族。骆越人一直基本上是持续独立地发展自己的文化，约在西周晚至春秋时期形成了自身的青铜文化。西瓯是东瓯越人从闽海南下西徙到粤西南和桂南一带，与当地的骆越人杂居而成。

（4）西瓯、骆越同源于古越人，是周秦及汉代主要活动于今广西地区的两个不同支系。张一民、何英德的《西瓯骆越与壮族的关系》[②]认为西瓯、骆越同源于古越人，是周秦及汉代主要活动于今广西地区的两个不同支系。今天的壮族是西瓯、骆越的后裔，西瓯、骆越也是其他一些少数民族(如广西境内壮侗语各族)的先民。

（5）西瓯、骆越是不同的两支原始族群。王明亮的《西瓯骆越三题》[③]认为西瓯、骆越是异族异称。西瓯主要是土著居民，可能有外来因素，如中原人、楚人、东部越人等，还可能融合一部分骆越人及南越人。西瓯、骆越出自同一祖先——“柳江人”或更早的古人类。西瓯、骆越是不同的两支原始族群，西瓯、骆越其中部分汉化了，部分融进了其他民族，部分则融合了其他民族成分，演变、发展成当今的壮族、布依族等现代民族。

4. 瓯骆地理位置

关于西瓯、骆越的地理位置有关研究瓯骆的文章大多有相关的论述。专门就两者的地理位置进行探讨的文章不多。主要看法有：

（1）西瓯在广西中部、西部、北部和贵州南部，而骆越在广东西部、广西南部、云南东部和越南北部的一些地区。

（2）先秦广西境内的西瓯在现今的桂林地区、梧州、贺州地区、玉林地区、桂平和贵港地区、柳州地区以及河池地区，南宁地区、钦州地区、崇左地区和百色地区则属骆越地。

（3）骆越族的主要活动地区是在广西西部的左、右江流域和越南北部的红河三角洲一带以至于海南岛。而广西东南的郁江、浔江沿岸以及广东西南的茂名等地，则是西瓯和骆越的杂居地区。梁敏的《论西瓯骆越的地理位置及壮族的形成》[④]认为西瓯在广西中部、西部、北部和贵州南部，而骆越在广东西部、广西南部、云南东部和越南北部的一些地区。他们的分界线大致是从广东西部肇庆、怀集一带往西，到广西梧州之后，循浔江、郁江往西到达南宁，再沿右江到达平果县，然后稍稍偏南，沿北回归线一直往西，到达文山苗族壮族自治州中部，分界线的西瓯跟目前壮语南、北方言的分界线大致相同。

（4）骆越民族的聚居地分布只在今越南北部。另外，西瓯和骆越的活动中心问题，在一些文章中也有论及。

5. 西瓯社会性质

西瓯社会性质的研究主要在观点有：一是认为战国秦汉时期，西瓯在原始社会解体之后绕过奴隶制度发展阶段而直接进入封建社会。二是认为战国时期西瓯社会仍处

① 李秀国:《瓯骆关系新论》,《中山大学学报》（社会科学版）1992年第1期。

② 张一民、何英德:《西瓯骆越与壮族的关系》,《广西师范大学学报》（哲学社会科学版）1987年第2期。

③ 王明亮:《西瓯骆越三题》,《岭南文史》1993年第3期。

④ 梁敏:《论西瓯骆越的地理位置及壮族的形成》,《民族研究》1996年第3期。

于原始社会军事民主制的末期，西瓯始终没有形成国家。

张一民、何英德的《西瓯社会经济形态初探》[①]认为西瓯部族在原始社会逐渐崩溃之后，没有经过奴隶社会而由商周时期的农村公社直接进入封建社会。因受中原先进的经济、政治、文化的强烈影响，使西瓯部族跨越了奴隶社会阶段而随着中原地区进入封建社会。战国秦汉时期，西瓯部族受到楚文化和中原文化的强烈影响，进入以自耕农为主的封建社会。杨琼的《战国时期西瓯社会性质探讨》[②]认为西瓯青铜文化受中原青铜文化的影响。战国时期西瓯社会仍处于军事民主制的末期，社会上已经产生了较大的阶级分化，但并不等同于奴隶制社会，西瓯始终没有形成国家。由于受外来影响和统治之故，西瓯社会进程是直接从原始社会步入封建制的阶级社会。

6. 瓯骆史

关于瓯骆史的研究，主要是论述两者的族源、地域和社会发展形态等，对西瓯和骆越是否产生了国家形态及两者的社会发展模式未展开探讨。

蒋炳钊的《关于西瓯、骆越若干历史问题的讨论》[③]认为西瓯、骆越均为百越民族中土著民发形成的不同支系。西瓯和骆越地区经过了漫长的原始社会，至春秋战国时期，已经处于奴隶社会，秦汉时向封建制转化，都是沿着人类社会历史的发展阶段前进。在进入阶级社会的过程中，生产力水平不断提高，同时受到中原和楚民族的影响和促进。西瓯地区接受汉文化和与汉人融合似乎比骆越地区快些。西瓯和骆越社会发展还存在不平衡，同一个民族内，地区之间也存在着差别。刘伟铿的《西瓯史考》[④]论述西瓯的主体来源于本土的原始人群，秦兵下岭南前西瓯形成，秦汉时西瓯国消失等方面。西瓯于战国末（约前323年）立国（组成母系氏族联盟），至前111年赵光降汉，被封为随桃侯，其间212年。当中属楚101年，御秦抗秦8年，属秦4年，被骆占封溪3年，在赵佗援助下打败安阳王立苍梧国96年。其中抗秦抗骆直至苍梧国后期控制疆域之扩大，为最雄壮的一幕。战争使西瓯从母系氏族社会跨进了奴隶社会。西汉末，西瓯、雕题、骆遗民大量融合到汉族中，其未融合到汉族中去的部分，东汉时起而造反。西瓯遗民变为乌浒蛮（苍梧蛮），雕题遗民变为鲛人，而骆国遗民，则称为蛮里、俚子。其活动地域已变得交叉纷纭。

7. 瓯骆青铜器研究

瓯骆青铜器的研究主要是根据出土的考古材料论述瓯骆青铜文化的产生、青铜铸造工艺、内涵以及其与周围地区青铜文化的关系等问题，还有论述瓯骆地区宗教性青铜器的种类、用途、文化内涵、社会功能及其在瓯骆青铜文化中的地位和作用等问题。

覃彩銮的《骆越青铜文化初探》[⑤]认为骆越和西瓯是战国秦汉时期活跃在我国岭南的一支越人。在骆越分布区内的青铜器多数出自墓葬，且有一定组合，是当时墓葬中最主要的随葬品，说明当时骆越地区已经广泛使用青铜器，骆越人已进入青铜时代。骆越青铜文化具有本地特征，同时也杂糅了大量的中原文化以及邻近地区青铜文化的因素。这一双重的文化特征，贯穿着骆越青铜文化的全过程。骆越青铜文化产生于春

① 张一民、何英德：《西瓯社会经济形态初探》，《中央民族学院学报》1990年第2期。

② 杨琼：《战国时期西瓯社会性质探讨》，《广西民族研究》1990年第2期。

③ 蒋炳钊：《关于西瓯、骆越若干历史问题的讨论》，《广西民族研究》1987年第4期。

④ 刘伟铿：《西瓯史考》，《岭南文史》1996年第4期。

⑤ 覃彩銮：《骆越青铜文化初探》，《广西民族研究》1986年第2期。

秋晚期，战国时期略有发展，旋即走向衰落。骆越青铜文化的产生发展乃至衰落是内地文化影响的结果。秦汉以后，骆越的青铜文化开始衰落。

覃彩銮的《试论骆越青铜铸造工艺及其艺术特征》[①]根据考古发现探讨骆越的青铜铸造工艺以及青铜器的造型和装饰艺术等问题。春秋战国时期，骆越才逐步进入阶级社会，并开始出现自己的青铜冶铸业。骆越工匠铸造青铜器的方法主要有内模外范铸造法、填范式铸造法、全范式铸法、套接式铸造法和失蜡法等五种。骆越青铜器的艺术创作，主要表现在造型和纹饰两个方面。骆越青铜器的造型艺术和装饰艺术，是骆越人民在制作青铜器的过程中创作出来的，并表现出浓厚的时代特征和民族特色，同时也受到汉文化影响。

陈大远的《西江青铜文化与岭南部族文化的探讨》[②]认为岭南部族文化是从旧石器时代发展而来的，西江与北江水系的民族文化属于同一类型，岭南先秦青铜文化中心在广东西江流域，“西瓯”和“南越”本是同一族属。文章主要论述西瓯的地域范围的变化、西瓯文化年代、西瓯与中原文化的联系、西瓯考古学文化、西瓯部族演变、西瓯社会风俗、西瓯军事等。

覃义生的《战国秦汉时期瓯骆宗教性青铜器探微》[③]论述瓯骆宗教性青铜器的种类、用途、文化内涵、社会功能及其在瓯骆青铜文化中的地位和作用等问题。文章认为骆越和西瓯在春秋战国至秦汉时期生活在今广西地区的居民主要是百越族群的一个支系。西瓯骆越民族的宗教性青铜器种类主要有乐器、面具、俑(包括人俑和马俑)、生活容器、兵器、祭器等。瓯骆人铸造的宗教性青铜器是围绕着敬神驱鬼、祛难求安这一神圣的活动所使用。其器具各具功能，各有用途，或单独使用，或组合配套，或作为乐器以娱神，或作为祭器以敬神，或用作法器以驱鬼辟邪，或用作陪葬品以慰亡灵。其青铜器一旦用于礼神驱鬼活动，除具有其自然属性的功能外，还被赋予神圣的灵性及功利观念。瓯骆人的宗教信仰及其功利的需要促进了青铜文化的发展与繁荣。

8. 瓯骆与周边关系

瓯骆与周边关系的研究主要有论述西瓯、骆越文化与中原文化的关系，骆越与“南岛语族”海洋文化的关系，骆越与海南岛临高人的关系，西瓯与海上丝绸之路的关系和西瓯与东瓯的关系等。

廖国一的《论西瓯、骆越文化与中原文化的关系》[④]论述西瓯、骆越文化与中原文化的关系。作者认为西瓯、骆越是百越民族中两个不同支系的民族。自商周以来，西瓯、骆越文化与中原文化的联系越来越深入，他们在各自独特的地方文化的基础上，进一步吸收了来自中原等地的以青铜器、铁器为代表的先进文化，如西瓯、骆越地区出土青铜器的器型、纹饰等有中原地区的风格，又具有浓厚的地方特色。与此同时，西瓯、骆越文化中的某些因素（如岭南地区的土特产），也传播到中原地区，为中原文化所吸收。

何英德的《骆越与“南岛语族”的海洋文化的关系》[⑤]论述骆越与“南岛语族”的海

① 覃彩銮:《试论骆越青铜铸造工艺及其艺术特征》,《贵州民族研究》1987年第1期。

② 陈大远:《西江青铜文化与岭南部族文化的探讨》,《东南文化》1993年第1期。

③ 覃义生:《战国秦汉时期瓯骆宗教性青铜器探微》,《广西民族研究》1999年第1期。

④ 廖国一:《论西瓯、骆越文化与中原文化的关系》,《民族研究》1996年第6期。

⑤ 何英德:《骆越与“南岛语族”的海洋文化的关系》,《百越文化研究》,厦门大学出版社，2005年，135～145页。

洋文化的关系。骆越与南岛语族海洋文化有密切联系。骆越地区与东南亚、欧洲等地有经济贸易关系。骆越文化的形成及精髓部分通过海上传播到亚洲、欧洲广大地区，影响极其深远。

詹慈的《试论海南岛临高人与骆越的关系》①从语言、地名、族源和民俗等方面考察海南岛临高人与骆越关系。临高人与两广骆越、俚人及其后裔壮族有深远的历史渊源。海南岛临高人是骆越、俚人的后裔，其族称的历史演变与古代广东西南部和广西南部的壮族是一脉相承的。临高人在铜鼓、房屋、“雕题之习”、服饰等方面与骆越人大体相同。

曾昭璇等人的《西瓯国与海上丝绸之路》②根据文献资料、考古出土材料和民族调查资料论证先秦海上丝绸之路的重镇可能是封开。先秦岭南小国甚多，西瓯国较大，文化也较发达。其社会已进入奴隶制阶段，西瓯国大致以西江中游为中心，其地南至广东茂名与骆越相错杂分布，北至平乐，东至广东西部，西及柳州。西瓯国的语言即今的壮语，受中原文化和楚文化的影响，西瓯国内由苍梧（由湖南迁入）和骆越等多民族组成，入西瓯古道有湘桂走廊和潇、贺连运，西瓯之地有西瓯人与骆越人苍梧人等混居，铜鼓创始于骆越人区。秦军桂江南下入西瓯首先立郡苍梧，汉苍梧郡治广信县即以封川江口区为主，今之梧州当时只为苍梧郡地。汉广信是岭南交趾部刺史治，即为管岭南的首邑，管治九郡。汉代发展外贸，以广信为中心分路入南海各港。

9. 骆越宗教

关于骆越宗教，主要从广西左江崖壁画和骆越地区墓葬来研究，论及的问题有骆越的多神崇拜和墓葬反映的宗教意识。

谈琪的《骆越人原始宗教祭祀的历史画卷——论广西左江崖壁画的族属、年代和内容》③认为广西左江及明江沿岸的壁画是属于壮族先民骆越人的作品。左江和明江流域的壁画反映的狗祭、以铜鼓作为祭祀器物、巫鬼等习俗与壮族的宗教祭祀习俗相同。左江壁画是壮族先氏骆越人进行宗教祭祀的情况的艺术表现。关于壁画的年代，其上限可追溯至战国时期，下限可推到两汉时期。左江流域崖壁画是反映左江流域壮族先民的祭雷神、祭河神、祭山神和祭祖先的原始宗教祭祀活动。

郑超雄的《武鸣先秦墓葬反映的骆越宗教意识》④认为武鸣元龙坡先秦墓葬体现了骆越人“灵魂返祖”宗教的观念。武鸣马头先秦墓葬朝向东的习俗，一是希望死者之魂升上东方天国栖息，二是希冀再生之意。元龙坡部分墓葬中用重石填压墓室是镇邪之用，打碎器物陪葬是给死者的散魂分用。船形墓和船形葬具的宗教意义：一是希望人死后仍过着生前的水上生活，二是作迎神之舟以渡亡魂升天，三是作送魂之舟。武鸣先秦墓葬中出土的陪葬石子与古代骆越人的占卜有关。武鸣先秦墓中出土的铜铃应是巫师所用法器。元龙坡的墓室内多有用火烧烤的现象与避邪观念有密切关系。

海力波的《左江崖壁画与骆越人之生殖崇拜》⑤认为左江崖壁画所处的地理环境与骆越人生殖崇拜中的水崇拜有关。左江崖壁画是骆越人却采用了大量的特定的象征

① 詹慈：《试论海南岛临高人与骆越的关系》，《中央民族大学学报》（哲学社会科学版）1982年第3期。

② 曾昭璇等：《西瓯国与海上丝绸之路》，《岭南文史》2004年第3期。

③ 谈琪：《骆越人原始宗教祭祀的历史画卷——论广西左江崖壁画的族属、年代和内容》，《广西民族学院学报》（哲学社会科学版）1988年第4期。

④ 郑超雄：《武鸣先秦墓葬反映的骆越宗教意识》，《广西民族研究》1994年第1期。

⑤ 海力波：《左江崖壁画与骆越人之生殖崇拜》，《民族论坛》1995年第3期。

符号来表现生殖器官和生殖行为。左江崖壁画反映骆越人以洞穴作为女阴象征的洞穴崇拜，以高山为男根象征的山崇拜。以妇女生育和女阴的象征的铜鼓崇拜，蛙崇拜是妇女生殖力的象征。广西东兰、凤山、巴马一带壮族民间的祭拜青蛙的节日就是壮族的生殖巫术的表现。左江崖壁画不仅是生殖巫术的表现，还是生殖巫术的结果，左江崖壁画半数以上都位于岩洞四沿，象征着由女阴中繁衍出众多的子孙。骆越人祈求由左江崖壁画中的生殖巫术给现实的繁衍带来良好的效果。

10. 瓯骆文化

瓯骆文化的研究主要从瓯骆地区出土器物中的刻划符号与古壮字的关系。有熊昭明的《广西先秦刻划符号刍议》①一文结合文献资料和考古材料论述广西先秦刻划符号的发展史及特点等。文章认为这种较为统一且富有地方特点的刻划符号，应是别于中原华夏民族和百越其他民族的义字和符号。从刻划符号可以推测银山岭战国墓是广西西瓯人的墓葬，马头安等秧战国墓葬是广西骆越人的墓葬，反映了西瓯和骆越族属的不同。先秦时期处于萌芽阶段的古壮字，在强大的中原文化的影响下，有的逐渐被融合，有的则被淘汰，而淘汰的这一部分文字正是今天所不能辨识的原因。

11. 瓯骆墓葬

瓯骆地区墓葬的研究，主要从考古出土材料论述瓯骆地区墓葬的年代、文化属性、社会性质、墓主族属及与邻近文化的关系等问题。

李龙章的《广西右江流域战国秦汉墓研究》②认为右江流域战国秦汉墓体现云南青铜文化和两广越族青铜文化的交汇和碰撞。右江上游的普驮墓除有汉文化因素外，主要受云南青铜文化因素的影响，两广越族青铜文化因素基本不见。右江中下游的锅盖岭、元龙坡、安等秧和独山等墓与普驮墓既有云南青铜文化的因素，也有两广越族青铜文化的成分。锅盖岭墓葬较元龙坡墓葬呈现的云南青铜文化色彩稍浓，右江下游的安等秧和独山墓葬呈现的越文化色彩要浓些，云南青铜文化的因素相对要少些。

容达贤的《广西平乐银山岭墓的时代与墓主》③论述广西平乐银山岭墓的时代与墓主。作者认为广西平乐银山岭墓群的主体部分（即早期墓葬）应该是秦平岭南时期的秦戍边吏卒墓。广西平乐银山岭墓群的墓葬形制及出土遗物反映的文化面貌总体特征与岭北地区的战国至秦时期楚文化相似。银山岭墓群中墓葬的葬具、形制和随葬品具有秦文化因素。广西平乐银山岭墓的墓主是被秦王朝统治者从岭北地区迁徙到岭南西瓯人居地充当戍卒的楚故地居民。

叶浓新的《武鸣马头古骆越墓地的发现与窥实》④认为马头元龙坡墓葬的时代，上限为西周晚期，下限在春秋时期。马头安等秧墓葬的年代应为战国时期。这两处墓地的主人应为同一民族。西瓯、骆越应是越人中两个不同的支系，马头元龙坡和安等秧两处墓葬应是壮族先民——骆越人的墓地。马头元龙坡和安等秧墓葬应是生活在这一地区的骆越氏族或部落的墓地，其社会性质是奴隶制的初级阶段，但在许多方面仍保

① 熊昭明：《广西先秦刻划符号刍议》，《广西民族研究》1993年第2期。

② 李龙章：《广西右江流域战国秦汉墓研究》，《考古学报》2004年第3期。

③ 容达贤：《广西平乐银山岭墓的时代与墓主》，《百越文化研究》，厦门大学出版社，2005年，394页。

④ 叶浓新：《武鸣马头古骆越墓地的发现与窥实》，《广西民族研究》1989年第4期。

持着氏族制度的传统。

蒋廷瑜的《从银山岭战国墓看西瓯》[①]根据考古材料和历史文献资料论述银山岭战国墓的特点、族属、社会面貌等问题。银山岭战国墓所反映的文化是百越文化的一部分。西瓯活动的中心在南越之西，骆越之北，楚之南，恰当今桂江流域和西江中游一带。银山岭墓所反映的社会性质是奴隶制，墓主人生前既是披坚持锐的战士，又是耕田织绩的农夫。西瓯社会发生根本变化是在秦统一岭南之后，特别是在汉武帝平定南越后，大部分西瓯人与汉人融合为一体，成为岭南越族中最早与华夏融合的一支。

蓝日勇的《试论罗泊湾一号墓墓主身份及族属》[②]从罗泊湾一号墓墓葬形制、出土木器中"私府"印文和人殉等方面论证墓主生前身份是诸侯或诸侯王。侯王封地在南越国境界内，是南越王国中央所封。今广西左、右江流域、邕宁县境一带，以及越南的北中部地区，是古代骆越族的聚居地域，骆民族应该是当地的主体民族。罗泊湾一号墓墓主为当地骆族的首领。

二

句町

句町国研究始于20世纪80年代，最早从考古学角度研究句町的学者是蒋廷瑜先生，他的《西林铜鼓墓与汉代句町国》[③]从考古学角度分析西林铜鼓墓葬品特征及年代。文章认为墓主人很可能就是句町族的首领，另外还论述了句町经济、政治、文化等方面。之后，张世铨的《汉句町四题》[④]研究句町的地理分布、政治、社会经济与周边关系等方面。覃圣敏的《句町古史钩沉》[⑤]一文主要论述句町的发展史，疆域范围、政治中心、族属、经济、水路交通、葬俗、宗教等方面。到90年代，学界论述句町问题的文章较少。21世纪前10年句町的研究日渐活跃起来，句町国及句町文化的研究成为学术研究的一个热点。2008年，在句町故地（西林）的首届句町国与土司文化研讨会成为一个热潮，国内知名的句町历史和土司文化研究的专家、学者共60多人与会探讨，会议共收录专家论文68篇，会后出版《句町国与西林特色文化》[⑥]一书。书中的文章研究句町的历史文化、政治经济、旅游开发等多方面的内容，研究重点是对句町名称的解释、地理位置的考证、句町的历史、句町族源、句町社会经济状况、句町国葬俗、句町宗教信仰、句町国与周边地区的关系等。由于历史文献中有关句町的记载较少，出土的考古材料为数不多，这是当前研究句町的局限。研究者大多是从历史文献资料中的一些记载，再结合考古出土文物和相关的民族调查等来进行。在研究方法上，有对历史文献的考证，如对句町地理位置的考证等，有分析考古出土文物，有的是使用语言学、民族学方面的方法来论证。

① 蒋廷瑜：《从银山岭战国墓看西瓯》，《考古》1980年第2期。

② 蓝日勇：《试论罗泊湾一号墓墓主身份及族属》，《广西民族研究》1986年第2期。

③ 蒋廷瑜：《西林铜鼓墓与汉代句町国》，《考古》1982年第2期。

④ 张世铨：《汉句町四题》，《民族研究》1983年第5期。

⑤ 覃圣敏：《句町古史钩沉》，《广西民族研究》1988年第3期。

⑥ 中共西林县委、县人民政府、广西文物考古研究所、广西历史学会：《句町国与西林特色文化》，广西人民出版社，2009年。

书中关于句町名称的探讨，主要有三种看法，① 是以学者何正廷为代表的观点认为按广南壮语来解释，句町含义有二：其一，"句町"即"九部联盟"或"多氏族部落联盟"之意；其二，句町"则是将首府建在"坡顶高"上面的国家。② 是认为"句町"一名有着越人命名的特色。以人名而言，越人之名常冠以"句"字。在人名地名前冠以"句"字，是越人的一种习惯。"句町"既以"句"字为冠，其王又"姓毋"，这种命名习惯正与越人同，故应视为越名。③ 是认为句町古国的解释是以红色藤蔓为图腾崇拜的国家。

句町地理位置在大多数论及句町的文章里或多或少都有所提及。研究主要集中在句町国的地域范围和句町国政治中心的位置两个问题上。句町国的中心位置这个问题上主要有两种看法，一是认为广西西林是句町国的政治中心，广西学者多持这一看法。另一看法是云南学者多认为现在云南的广南县是句町的中心。关于句町的地域范围的看法上，大多数学者都认为其地区范围在桂西北和滇东南，还有学者认为越南北部的一些地区也在句町国范围内。

句町的族源在其他研究句町的文章中多有论及，专就句町族源作研究的文章较少。主要看法有：① 句町族属百濮。② 句町古国的臣民是古代骆越族群的一员。③ 句町文化的族属有百濮和百越两大族系因素，而以百越族系为主。

句町的社会经济宗教信仰研究的论文不多，句町国社会经济的研究不是很深入。研究者大多从句町所处的地理环境、考古出土材料和交通条件等方面论述农业、手工业、与周边地区的经济关系等经济状况。句町的宗教信仰以多神崇拜为显著特点，崇拜的对象多，宗教活动形式也多种多样。

句町墓葬的研究主要以出土器物与周边地区出土器物的比较研究为主，如铜鼓等出土物，通过比较探讨墓葬年代、墓主人身份、族源、句町社会经济、句町与周边地区的关系等。

在句町国与周边地区关系的研究中，已有相关文章探讨句町与云南地区（漏卧、滇文化）的关系及句町与夜郎的关系。对于句町与其南面的越南地区和东面的骆越、西瓯的关系的研究较少论及。另外有蒋廷瑜的《夜郎句町比较研究》[①]认为夜郎和句町都是战国至汉代西南夷中两个毗邻的方国，它们之间的关系非常密切。它们在自身的发展过程中，互相碰撞，既有对抗，也有联合。句町和夜郎处在南越、滇和巴蜀之间，是这三大经济区域的枢纽地带。在经济方面，夜郎农业发达，生产工具先进（有铜器和铁器），手工业有冶铸、制陶、玉石加工业。句町高山畜牧业发达，农业则欠发达。此外，两者丧葬习俗相同或相近。考古出土文物方面有相同或相近的青铜器，如铜鼓、羊角纽钟、一字格剑、铜钺、铜戈、铜铁合制器等。

这些研究中，存在较多争议的是西瓯、骆越、句町的族属族源问题及其地理分布、社会性质等。关于族属族源问题，有学者认为骆越属百濮族群。也有认为骆越不是百越的一支，也不是广西土著民族，骆越是从黄河流域迁徙到广西地区的。

大多学者认为骆越是本地土著人，是壮族的先民，属百越系统的一支。关于西瓯族

① 蒋廷瑜：《夜郎句町比较研究》，《广西博物馆文集》（第四辑），广西人民出版社，2007年，111～116、316页。

源，梁钊韬先生认为西瓯民族成分包含古代骆越人、东瓯越人、复杂的倭人、楚人和中原人等。另一看法是认为西瓯属百越的一支，也是壮族先民。笔者认同西瓯和骆越均属越人的看法。句町的族源主要看法有：① 句町族属百濮。② 句町古国的臣民是古代骆越族群的一员。③ 句町文化的族属有百濮和百越两大族系因素，而以百越族系为主。对于句町的族源，第三种看法可从。西瓯和骆越的地理分布方面虽有诸多争议，但大多学者认为骆越族的主要活动地区是在广西西部的左、右江流域和越南北部的红河三角洲一带以至于海南岛。而广西东南的郁江、浔江沿岸以及广东西南的茂名等地，则是西瓯和骆越的杂居地区。这一看法可从。句町地理位置，研究主要集中在句町国的地域范围和句町国政治中心的位置两个问题上。句町国的中心位置这个问题上主要有两种看法，一是认为广西西林是句町国的政治中心。另一看法是云南学者多认为现在云南的广南县是句町的中心。笔者认为，由于种种原因古代人类活动存在迁移的可能，所以句町国的政治中心也可能随之转移，故广南、西林都有可能是句町活动的政治中心。关于句町的地域范围的看法上，大多数学者都认为其地区范围在桂西北和滇东南，还有学者认为越南北部的一些地区也在句町国范围内。对句町的活动范围，上述学者所论及的地区都有可能，每一个时期可能活动的地点不同，这有待考古出土资料来论证。

西瓯社会性质的研究主要在观点有：① 是认为先秦西瓯社会性质是奴隶制。② 是认为战国秦汉时期，西瓯在原始社会解体之后绕过奴隶制度发展阶段而直接进入封建社会。③ 是认为战国时期西瓯社会仍处于原始社会军事民主制的末期，西瓯始终没有形成国家。有关骆越的社会性质方面的探讨也有相关文章论及，认为骆越总体上比西瓯社会落后。笔者认为，由于现有的文献资料不足和考古出土材料尚不丰富，对认识其社会性质有很大的局限。

对于广西先秦古国的研究，从目前所取得的研究成果看，仍未有很大突破。研究西瓯、骆越的专著和文章较多，而句町和苍梧的相关研究还较少。西瓯、骆越、句町和苍梧社会性质、社会组织和精神层面的研究是将来研究的趋势。笔者认为，目前研究西瓯、骆越、句町和苍梧存在的不足主要在于文献资料记载不详，考古出土的资料不丰富。考古出土材料主要是墓葬遗物和一些采集的标本，而考古发现的遗址（如城址、居住房址、手工作坊、窑址等）十分缺乏。要进一步加深对骆越、西瓯和句町等岭南地区先秦古国的研究，一是加强田野考古调查和发掘来提供可靠的出土材料。二是引入科学考古的方法和技术来对广西先秦时期考古文化遗存的年代研究是十分必要的。三是以考古学、民族学等学科为基础，结合人类学、语言学和艺术学等学科进行综合研究。

附　记：还有很多与本文主题相关的文章没有收录在内，这是文章的一大遗憾。行文中不当之处敬请方家们批评指正。在文章的写作过程中得到黄启善、何英德、陈洪波等老师的指导，在此表示感谢！

从东山文化的多元因素看“瓯骆国”的形成

Perspective of the Formation of Ou-Luo
State from multi-factors of Dongson Culture

吴春明 / 厦门大学 教授

[摘要]

东山文化既有红河下游土著文化的延续，又表现为百越诸王国社会文化的直接交流与融合，以及“中心—边缘”、“中国—四方”政经关系框架下的周汉文明影响。根据中、越两国史籍，考古学上的铜荳、扪丘文化正值越南上古传说的“雒（骆）王”时代，也就是所谓“雄王”创立“文郎国”时期。东山文化进入青铜文化的鼎盛和铁器时代的初始阶段，形成了围城自重、割据一方、武力强大的边疆王国或民族国家，其主体延续了铜荳、扪丘等土著青铜文化基础，也吸收融合了西瓯、南越、滇越等百越其他支系及中原周汉文化因素的影响，体现了瓯骆建国的历史特点。

[关键词]

东山文化　多元因素　骆越文化　瓯骆国

Abstract

Ou-Luo had been recorded by Chinese and Vietnam historical documents as the first local kingdom in lower reach of Red River during last few centuries of B. C.. According to chronological, typological and comparing studies on the series of prehistoric archaeological cultures in this region, Dongshan Culture contains three different types of cultural traditions, the continuance of native culture of Red River as neltithic Phung Nguyen, bronze Dong Dau and Go Mun, the common sharing with Bai-Yue aboriginals in southern China, and the influence from Chinese Central civilization of Zhou and Han dynasties. The Bronze Dong Dau and Go Mun could be identified as Luo-Yue culture which had been misunderstood as “Hung Vuong” of legendary age of Vietnam. The early iron age Dongshan culture witnessed the development of Luo-Yue kingdom as a local authority and ranked society.

Key words

Dongshan culture; Multi-factors; Ou-luo culture; Ou-luo states

东山文化是红河下游的青铜文化盛期至铁器时代初期文化，距今2500～2000年，分布于红河下游及邻近的马（Ma）河、朱（Ca）河流域，以1924年法国远东博古学院在清化省东山村首次发掘到的一批含数百件青铜器的土坑墓而得名①。经过近一个世纪的考古调查和发掘，考古学者对东山文化的认识更加全面②。关于东山文化的性质及相关的骆越、瓯骆等民族史，学界有不同的看法，本文拟在东山文化内涵多元因素分析的基础上，尝试探索西瓯、骆越变迁与“瓯骆”形成的历史线索。

一

从东山文化的多元文化因素说起

东山文化的聚落遗址发现不多，除了河内西北15公里的古螺（Co Loa）城址外，普通的聚落遗址还有朱河河畔的义安省大湾（Dai Van）乡老盔遗址群（Lang Vac sites）的山顶（Xom Dinh）聚落。古螺城现存地面上的三重夯土城圈，城圈外分别环绕城壕，三重城壕与城内外的水系连成一体。发现有东山文化陶器、完整的东山铜鼓、铜鼓内盛放的铜犁和铜镞，秦汉时代特征的绳纹筒瓦、板瓦等遗存。

东山文化墓地有大量的发现，清化东山、贵嘴（Quy Chu）、富寿省的龙岔（Lang Ca）、道清（Dao Thinh）、海防省的越窠（Viet Khe）、河西省的曹村（Chau Can）、孙萝（Xuan La）、明德（Minh Duc）、河内市的富垄（Phu Luong）、安沛省（Yen Bai）的和民（Hop Minh）、义安省的老盔等都是东山文化的重要墓地。东山文化墓葬多竖穴土坑墓，其中越窠、曹村、孙萝、民都、富垄等墓地都发现独木船棺葬遗存，成为东山文化的重要特征之一。

内涵丰富、品种繁多的青铜器是东山文化的最大特色，有兵器与工具类、容器与用具类、装饰品、艺术品与乐器等。装饰纹样非常复杂，有席纹、复线三角纹、复线填点纹、“S”形纹、卷曲纹、螺旋纹、回纹等几何纹样，羽人舞蹈、武士征战、飞鸟走兽、舟船竞渡、太阳光芒、水波、绹索等写实具象图案，还有各种人物活动、动物形象的堆塑等。工具和兵器类占大多数，主要器型为斧、铲、镐、锸、犁、短剑（匕）、矛、戈、剑、镞、盾牌等。青铜容器、用具主要有提桶、壶、杯、带钩、铜镜等。青铜装饰品与艺术品也富有特色，主要有铜镯、脚护套、臂护套、项圈、带钩、人物和动物堆塑等，还发现有大量铜钟、铜鼓等特色乐器。

根据老盔、曹村等墓地的资料，东山文化的红陶、灰陶、褐色陶都比较粗糙，甚至火候都不及此前各阶段文化的陶器。除不少素面陶外，有拍印绳纹、条纹、方格纹、刻划水波纹、复线“S”纹、复线三角纹、平行斜线三角纹、戳印篦点纹等，

① 陶维英：《越南古代史》（下册），商务印书馆，1976年，300页。

② Lai Van Toi. Bronze Artifacts of Dong Son Culture at Co Loa (Hanoi). *Vietnamese Archaeology*, 2006(5). Charles Higham. *The Archaeology of Mainland Southeast Asian*. Cambridge University Press, 1989:192-203. Charles Higham. *Early Cultures of Mainland Southeast Asia*. Chicago:Art Media Resources Ltd. 2002:170-183. Peter Bellwood. *Prehistory of the Indo-Malaysian Archipelago*. Honolulu: University of Hawaii Press, 1997:269-271, 277-284. The Vietnam-Japan Archaeological Research Team. *The Lang Vac Sites*,Vol.1:1-156, 185-200. Basic Report on the Vietnam-Japan Joint Archaeological Research In Nghia Dan District. Nghe An Province. 1990-1991. The University of Tokyo,2004. Jeremy H.C.S.Davidson. Recent Archaeology Activity in Viet-Nam. *Journal of the Hongkong Archaeology Socitet*, Vol. VI(1975): 80-99, Hongkong, 1976.

这些纹样明显可在铜荳、扪丘文化中找到渊源。器型为圜底、圈足和少量平底器，不见三足和袋足器，主要有圜底类的宽斜沿束颈圆腹釜或罐、深腹圜底甗形器、钵，圈足类的束颈折肩罐或尊、深斜腹双耳提桶、敛口或侈口的斜腹碗、钵、簋、豆，平底类的束颈扁腹罐等。

东山文化位于华南与东南亚古代文化的交汇处，发展于东亚地区古代文化激荡、交流频繁的中国周汉时代，这一背景造就了东山文化内涵中明确的多元文化因素，既有鲜明本土的文化传统，更有许多外来的、尤其是周汉时期华南乃至中原的文化因素，与中南半岛的湄公河、湄南河流域同期文化关系也十分密切。

（一）红河下游土著文化传统的延续

东山文化是红河三角洲新石器、青铜文化延续发展的一个环节。该文化的石器、青铜斧、钺、铲等延续了冯原时代以来常形与有肩、靴形共出的传统。陶器群的总体特征仍是圜底的釜、罐、钵和圈足罐、钵、豆等，与冯原、铜荳、扪丘文化相比未有大变。青铜器、陶器上除了舟船竞渡、羽人、翔鹭等写实具象图案外，水波纹、回纹、绹索纹、复线填点、平行斜线三角纹、篦节纹、“S”纹等几何形纹样也是铜荳（Dong Dau）文化、扪丘（Go Mun）文化以来装饰纹样的延续发展①（图一）。

（二）东山文化与华南百越文化的共性

东山文化既与华南沿海百越各支系文化有共同的土著延续性，又表现在周汉时期瓯骆、西欧、南越、闽越等百越诸王国社会文化的直接交流与融合。

与华南沿海百越各支系文化共同延续的土著因素，比如有肩、靴形的石斧、铜斧、铜铲，几何纹、羽人竞渡纹与翔鹭纹等陶器和铜器装饰纹样，圜底、圈足的日用陶器群和铜器群等，这些因素是华南至越南北部间新石器时代就已经确立的土著文化传统的延续。

属于瓯骆、西瓯、南越、闽越等百越诸王国社会文化交流与融合的因素包括：东山文化中器身装饰几何纹样的双肩和靴形铜斧（钺）见于两广②，人面纹铜短剑和人形柄铜短剑见于两广等地③，羊角形纽的铜钟见于滇、桂的周汉时期墓葬中④，满布几何纹的铜或陶的提桶、双腹圜底甗形器等特征性很强的土著器物也在两广到闽赣等华南百越文化中不同程度地出现（图二）。

更为重要的是，东山铜鼓与滇、黔、桂古代社会发达的铜鼓文化紧密联系在一起，东山铜鼓的不同形态分别与万家坝型、石寨山型、冷水冲型等铜鼓有很大的共性，是古代华南至东南亚地区跨越时间长、分布空间广的特殊文化现象，所以研究铜鼓谱系、东山鼓在铜鼓谱系中的地位是认识东山文化性质及其与周邻文化

① Jeremy H.C.S.Davidson. Recent Archaeology Activity in Viet-Nam. *Journal of the Hongkong Archaeology Society*, Vol.VI(1975): 80-99, Hongkong, 1976.

② 徐恒彬：《广东青铜器时代概论》，《广东出土先秦文物》，香港中文大学文物馆，1984年；蓝日勇：《广西先秦越族青铜兵器研究》，《铜鼓与青铜文化的新探索》，广西民族出版社，1993年；黄展岳：《论两广出土的先秦青铜器》，《考古学报》1986年第4期。

③ 邓聪：《人面弓形格铜剑刍议》，《文物》1993年第11期；《再论人面弓形格铜剑》，《东南亚考古论文集》，香港大学美术博物馆，1995年，231～239页；陈光祖：《“南方文明”的南方——越南东山文化人形柄青铜短剑初探》（打印稿）。

④ 蒋廷瑜：《羊角纽铜钟初论》，《文物》1984年第5期；广西壮族自治区文物工作队：《广西贵县罗泊湾一号墓发掘简报》及《广西西林普驮铜鼓墓葬》，《文物》1978年第9期；云南省博物馆：《云南晋宁石寨山古墓群发掘报告》，文物出版社，1959年；云南省博物馆：《云南省楚雄县万家坝古墓群发掘简报》，《文物》1978年第10期。

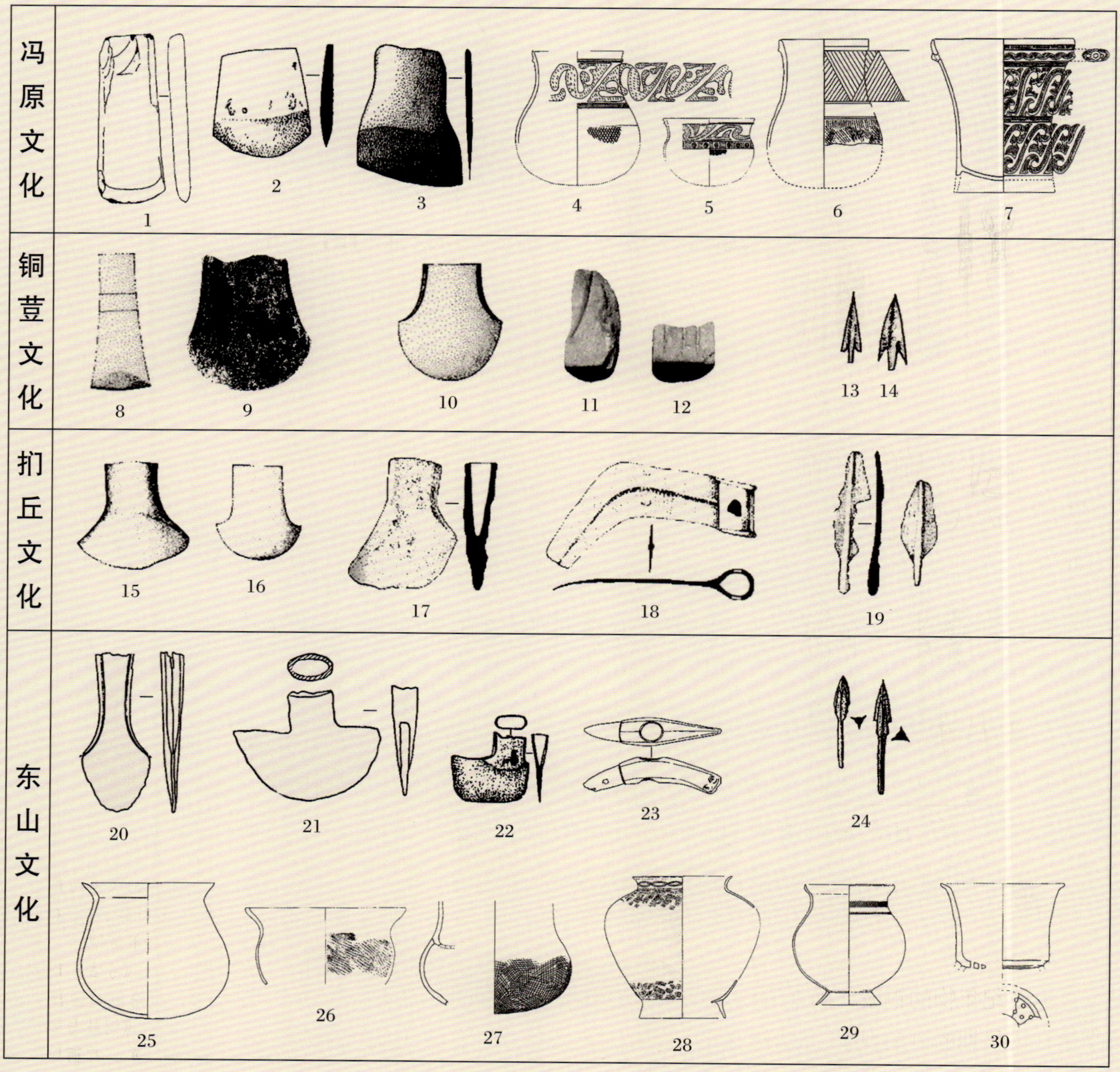

图一　东山文化与先东山诸文化的传承

1、4～7.山岭　8～14.铜荳　15～19.扪丘　20、23、25～30.老盔　21.岗河　22、24.古螺城

关系的关键。对东南亚铜鼓最早进行系统类型学研究的是奥地利考古学家黑格尔（F.Heger），早在1902年就在著名的《东南亚古代金属鼓》一书中，将欧洲和东南亚各大博物馆收藏的165面铜鼓分成自早到晚的Ⅰ、Ⅱ、Ⅲ、Ⅳ四型和Ⅰ－Ⅱ、Ⅱ－Ⅲ、Ⅲ－Ⅳ三个过渡型，东山铜鼓属于Ⅰ型鼓，代表了越南及华南、东南亚最古老的铜鼓形态①。近半个世纪以来，中国学者根据滇、黔、桂三省发现的有地层、

①〔奥〕弗兰茨·黑格尔著，石钟健、黎广秀、杨才秀译，中国古代铜鼓研究会编：《东南亚古代金属鼓》，上海古籍出版社，2004年。

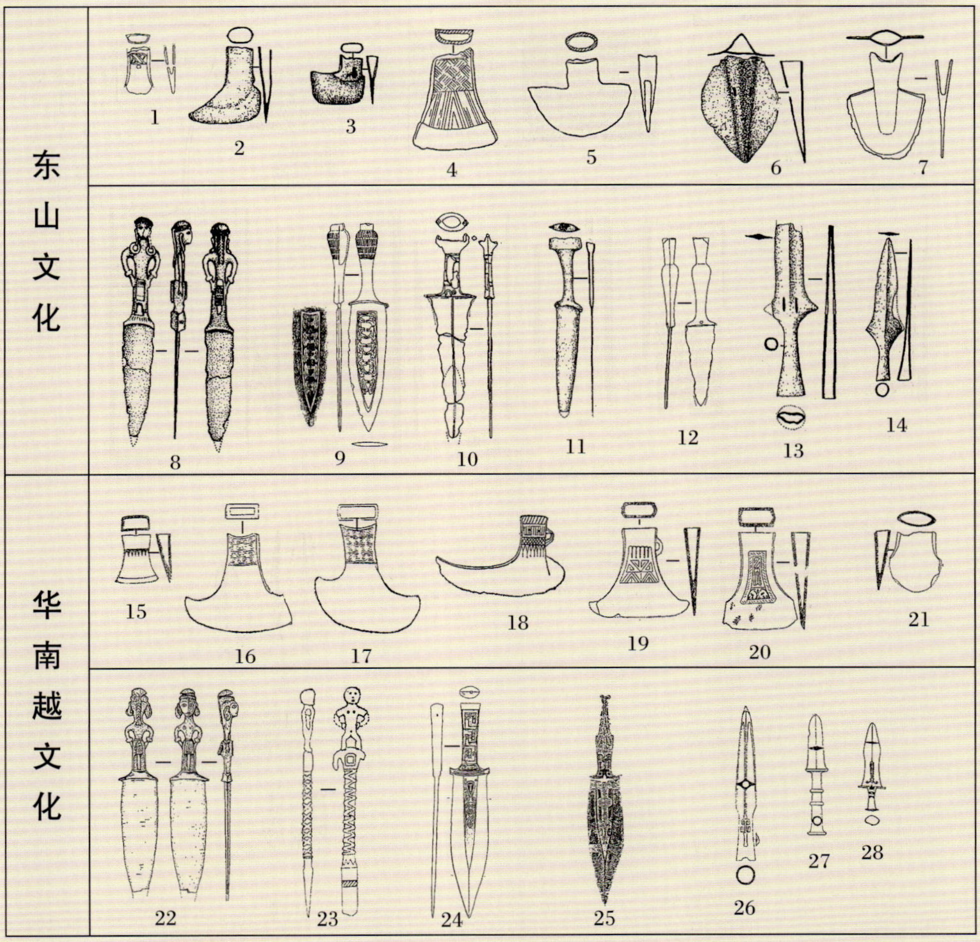

图二 东山文化与华南越文化共存青铜兵器、工具比较

1、7～10、12. 老盎 2、3、6、11、13、14. 古螺城 4、5. 岗河 15、18～21、26～28. 平乐银山岭 16、17. 恭城秧家 22. 长沙树木岭 23.清远 24.香港石壁 25. 广州暹岗①

共出关系或纪年物的铜鼓，确立了较黑格尔四型序列更为完整的铜鼓谱系，即春秋晚期至战国早期的万家坝型、战国至东汉初的石寨山型和北流型、西汉中期至隋唐间的冷水冲型和灵山型、唐代至宋代的遵义型和西盟型、南宋末至清末的麻江型。这一谱系一方面证明了黑格尔四型所代表的铜鼓发展、演变的逻辑关系是基本正确的，石寨山型和冷水冲型相当于黑格尔Ⅰ型、北流型和灵山型相当于Ⅱ型、西盟型相当于Ⅲ型、麻江型相当于最晚的Ⅳ型，另一方面又补充发展了黑格尔序列，尤其是确立比黑格尔Ⅰ型鼓更为古老的万家坝型铜鼓。根据这一谱系，东山铜鼓与石寨山型、冷水冲型鼓相当，处于铜鼓谱系中较早的阶段，但晚于万家坝型鼓，因此云贵高原是东亚南部铜鼓文化的发源地，东山文化的铜鼓是延续中国西南铜鼓文化发展来的②（图三）。

① 黄展岳:《论两广出土的先秦青铜器》，《考古学报》1986年第4期；《铜提桶考略》，《考古》1989年第9期；《论南越国出土的青铜器》，《铜鼓与青铜文化的新探索》，广西民族出版社，1993年；福建博物院等:《武夷山城村汉城遗址发掘报告》，福建人民出版社，2004年，图版145、146；刘茵:《印纹陶文化中的甗形器初探》，《东南考古研究》（第三辑），厦门大学出版社，2003年。

② 中国古代铜鼓研究会:《中国古代铜鼓》，文物出版社，1988年。

不过，最近的一些发现、研究表明，铜鼓问题没有那么简单。所谓比黑格尔Ⅰ型鼓原始的“万家坝型”鼓，在越南的红河流域的河东、永福、老街等省也有不断的发现。在越南学者的分类研究中，并不认为存在黑格尔四型序列之外的独立的“万家坝型”，东山鼓更不是来源于“万家坝型”。他们将东山鼓（黑格尔Ⅰ式鼓）A、B、C、D、E五组，其中A、B型相当于石寨山型，C、E相当于冷水冲型，

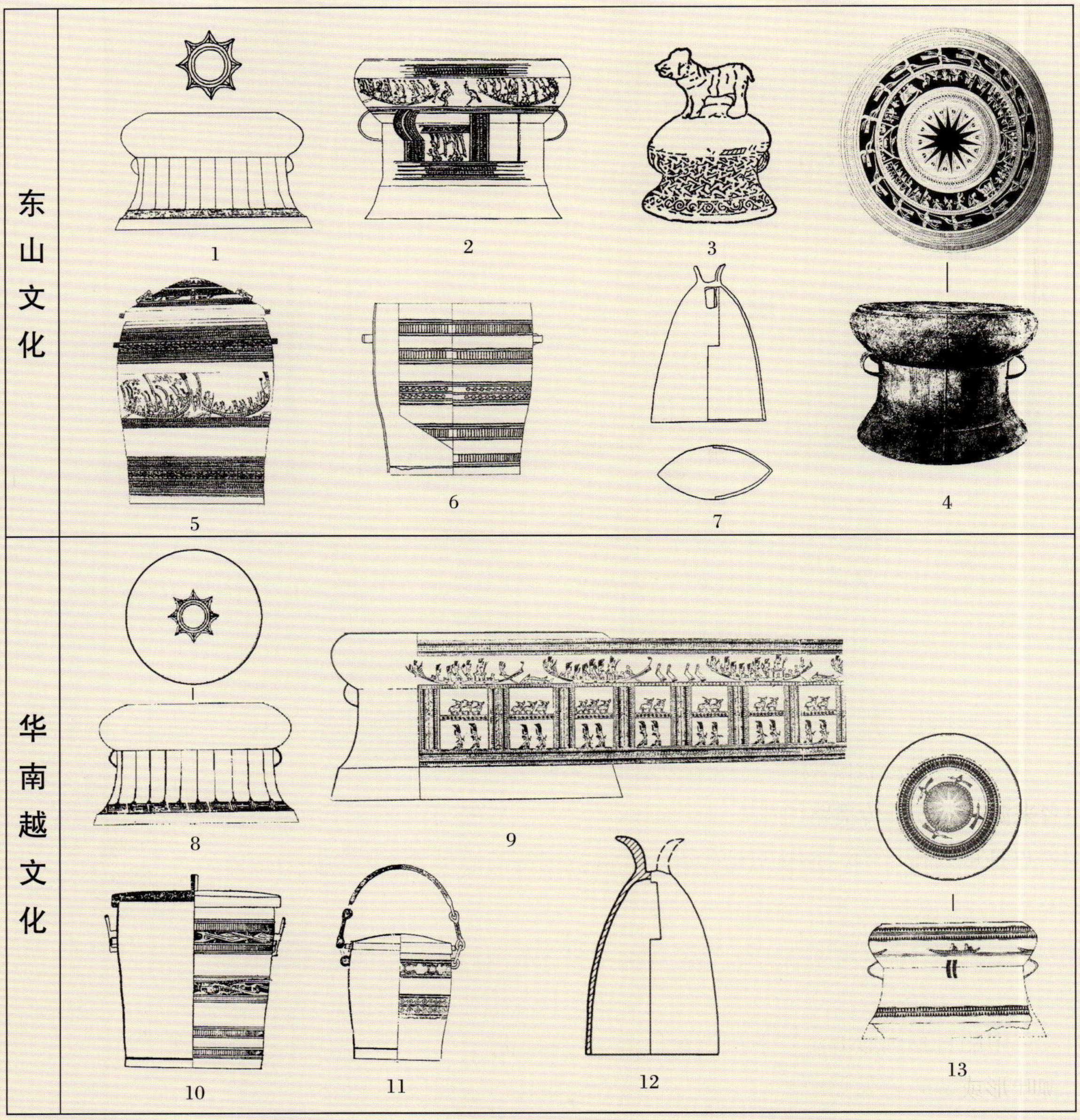

图三　东山文化与华南越文化共存青铜乐器、容器比较

1. 老街鼓　2. 玉镂鼓　3. 东山明器鼓　4. 古螺城鼓　5. 道清提桶　6. 老盔提桶　7. 越南羊角纽铜钟　8. 万家坝鼓　9. 西林鼓　10.罗泊湾提桶　11. 广州南越王墓　12. 恭城东寨羊角纽铜钟　13. 石寨山鼓

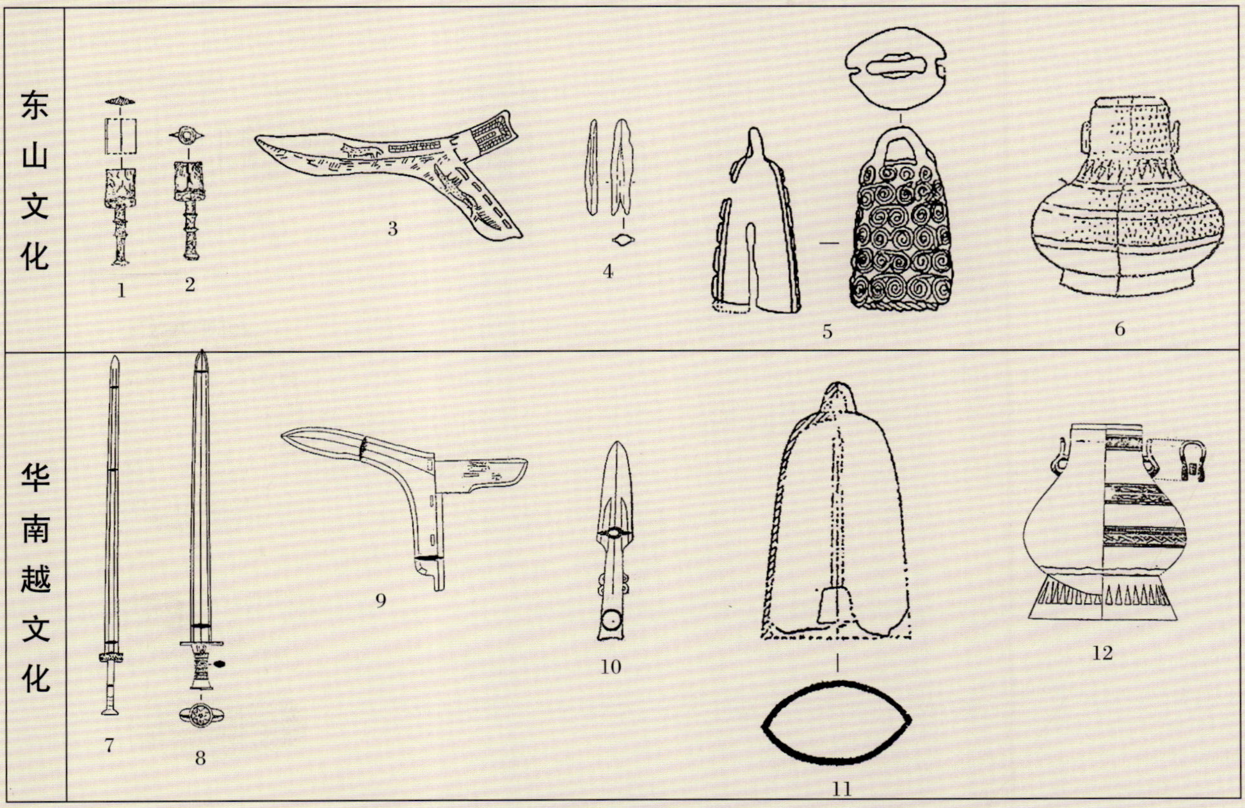

图四 东山与华南越族青铜文化中共存的“周汉”因素
1、2、6. 东山 3. 象山 4. 古螺城 5. 老蚕 7、8、12. 广州 9、10. 平乐银山岭 11. 武鸣

D型相当于“万家坝型”①。张增祺先生也曾通过万家坝型与石寨山型铜鼓的比较，认为万家坝型的年代是春秋晚期到西汉初中期，石寨山型的年代是春秋末期到西汉早期，两者来源、民族、传播路线均不同，是平行发展而不是前后继承的②。但无论如何，有一点是可以肯定的，东山文化及越南北方的铜鼓与华南早期铜鼓是一个文化体系，关系十分密切。

（三）中原华夏与汉文化透过岭南地区对东山文化的影响

东山文化中的直颈圆腹圈足铜壶与楚汉墓葬中的礼器壶一致，扁茎无格或圆茎宽格剑、柳叶形或两叶内弧形铜矛、长胡直内戈等也都与东周铜兵器没有大的差别（图四），这些共性反映了周汉时期中原华夏、汉民族文化圈与东亚南部的土著民族文化圈之间的互动关系，这是典型的“中心–边缘”、“中国–四方万国”形态的政治、经济与文化关系。正是这些外来文化因素的存在，发掘过东山遗址的瑞典

① 蒋廷瑜:《铜鼓是东盟古代文化的共同载体》，《广西民族学院学报》（哲学社会版）2005年第1期；〔越〕范明玄、阮文煊、郑生:《东山铜鼓》，越南社会科学出版社，1987年。

② 张增祺:《“万家坝型”铜鼓与“石寨山型”铜鼓的关系》，《铜鼓与青铜文化的新探索》，广西民族出版社，1993年。

考古学家简斯就认为，东山文化的戈、矛、剑等与中国许多地方发现的铜器十分相似，从而推定中国古代青铜文化对东山文化的影响，奥地利考古学家海因·戈尔登也曾提出东山文化铜器与中国周末铜器的相同之处。

（四）东山文化与东南亚半岛同期古文化的不同程度共性或交流

在越南中部沿海至湄公河三角洲，沙莹（Sa Huynh）文化从前600年延续发展至公元前后，共出东山文化铜鼓以及周汉式铜剑，沙莹文化典型的三或四凸纽形的玉石玦饰也发现于北越的扪丘、东山文化中。在湄公河中游的呵叻高原能诺他、班清、诺乌罗（Noen U-Loke）、能芒考（Non Muang Kao）以及湄南河平原的班多塔菲（Ban Don Ta Phet）等早期铁器时代地层中，也不同程度共出青铜双肩斧、矛、周汉式剑、铁箭铜矛、包铁铜镯、青铜人像、人头、动物雕像、钟、容器、铜鼓等金属器，相当部分因素与东山文化没有多大差别。北碧府的班多塔菲是湄南河平原早期铁器时代的最重要墓地，出土钵、杯、罐、桶形器、器盖、牌形饰、手镯、脚镯等铜器近300件，鱼叉、箭镞、矛、凿、锄形器、斧、钩形器等铁器300多件，数量不少的玉石和玻璃制装饰品，装饰绳纹、印纹、戳印纹的圜底釜、矮圈足罐、圜底钵等陶器也与东山文化有相当的可比性①。

二

从“雄王”之“文郎国”到安阳王之“瓯骆国”的考古推测

与华南的百越民族一样，上古时期的越南土著没有本民族的文献历史，加上宋代以前越南北方一直就在中国历代王朝的版图之内，它们的早期历史零星地记录在汉文史籍中。根据中国的史、汉正史及《交州外域记》、《广州记》等汉晋史籍以及越南的《岭南摭怪》、《大越史记全书》等汉文古史文献，大致可以复原起红河下游早期文明起源与发展的两个重要阶段，“雄王”所建“文郎国”时代和“安阳王”所建的“瓯骆国”时代，相当于考古学上的铜荳、扪丘文化和东山文化阶段。

（一）铜荳、扪丘文化——“雄王”之“文郎国”史迹

铜荳、扪丘文化距今3500～2500年间的前后两个阶段，是红河三角洲青铜文化初步发展期，也是东山（Dong Son）文化的重要基础②。铜荳、扪丘文化正值越南上古传说的“雒（骆）王”时代，也就是越南人民引以为民族精神支柱的所谓“雄

① Charles Higham. *The Archaeology of Mainland Southeast Asian*. Cambridge University Press, 1989: 99-113, 207-209,230-233. Charles Higham. *Early Cultures of Mainland Southeast Asia*. Chicago:Art Media Resources Ltd, 2002: 179-228. Peter Bellwood. *Prehistory of the Indo-Malaysian Archipelago*. Honolulu: University of Hawaii Press, 1997: 271-275. D.T.Bayard. Excavations at Non Nok Tha, Northeastern Thailand 1968: an interim report. *Asian Perspectives*, 1972(13). C. F. Gorman and Pisit Charoenwongsa. Ban Chiang: a Mosaic of Impressions from the Forst Two Yeas. *Expedition*, 1976(4). Jerome Feldman. Ban Chiang: Disciversity of a Lost Bronze Age, The Exhibition of in Hawaii in 1985. Jogce C.White. The Ban Chiang Chronology Revised, Southeast Asian Archaeology 1986: Proceeding of the First Conference of the Association of Southeast Asian Archaeologists in Western Europe, BAR International Series 561, 1990, England. Ian C. Glover, Ban Don Ta Phet: the 1984-1985 Excavation, Southeast Asian Archaeology 1986: Proceeding of the First Conference of the Association of Southeast Asian Archaeologists in Western Europe, BAR International Series 561, 1990, England.

② Charles Higham. *The Archaeology of Mainland Southeast Asian*. Cambridge University Press, 1989: 173-182. Charles Higham. *Early Cultures of Mainland Southeast Asia*. Chicago:Art Media Resources Ltd, 2002: 151-153. Peter Bellwood. *Prehistory of the Indo-Malaysian Archipelago*. Honolulu: University of Hawaii Press, 1997: 269-271, 277-284. Jeremy H.C.S.Davidson. Recent Archaeology Activity in Viet-Nam. *Journal of the Hongkong Archaeology Socitet*. Vol.VI(1975), Hongkong, 1976: 80-99.

王”创立“文郎国”时期[①]。

根据汉晋文献，先秦时期活跃在交趾一带的“骆（雒）越”是百越的一个支系，或曾割据称“王”。《汉书·地理志》注引臣瓒语：“自交趾至会稽七八千里，百粤杂处，各有种姓，不得尽云太康之后也。”《史记·南越列传》载：“佗因此以兵威边，财物赂遗闽越、西瓯、骆，役属焉，东西万余里。”“尉佗之王，本由任嚣。遭汉初定，列为诸侯。隆虑离湿疫，佗得以益骄。瓯、骆相攻，南越动摇。汉兵临境，婴齐入朝。”又引赵佗语：“南方卑湿，蛮夷中间，其东闽越千人众，号称王，其西瓯、骆、裸国亦称王。”《水经注》卷37“叶榆河”引成书于3、4世纪的《交州外域记》有“骆田”、“骆民”、“骆将”、“骆侯”、“骆王”的记载，所谓“交趾昔未有郡县之时，土地有骆田，其田随潮水上下。民垦食其田，因名为骆民，设骆王骆侯，主诸郡县。县多为骆将，骆将铜印青绶。后蜀王子将兵三万，来讨骆王骆将，蜀王子因称为安阳王。后南越王尉佗，举众攻安阳王”。据张一民先生考，左右江流域、红河三角洲的骆越与西江中游流域、桂江流域的西瓯是百越中两个不同的支系[②]。

所谓“雄王”的记载最早见于5世纪沈怀远《南越志》，该书已佚，辗转传抄见于宋代的《太平寰宇记》，与前引《交州外域记》中所记相似的历史却成为“人称其地为雄地（雄田），其民为雄民，旧有君长曰雄王，其佐曰雄侯，其地分封各雄将”。实际情况正如法国汉学家乔治·马斯佩罗（Georges Maspero）在《文郎国》（Le Royaume de Van-lang）一文中的考证，《南越志》的作者将汉字字型相近的“雒（骆）”混淆成“雄”，因而将交趾历史上的“骆（雒）王”误写作“雄王”了，而到了15世纪越南黎朝人吴士连编《大越史记全书》时因此抄出了错误的“雄王”时代历史，这一点越南历史学家陶维英也完全赞同，他还指出《大越史记全书》的一个注释家已经注意到这个错误，“貉将后讹为雄将”[③]。有趣的是，13世纪越南陈朝人陈世法撰《岭南摭怪》记载的并被《大越史记全书》收编的越南民族的起源传说“鸿庞氏”，却仍然保持原汁原味的“貉龙君”，即“按黄帝时，建万国，以交趾界于西南，远在百粤之表……鸿庞纪。泾阳王讳禄续，神龙氏之后也……封王为泾阳王，治南方，号赤土国。王娶洞庭君女曰神龙，生貉龙君”。“貉龙君”娶嫗姬为妻，生百男，“嫗姬与五十男居封州，自相惟服，立作君臣，以其雄长，尊立为主，号曰雄王，国号文郎……置其弟为相，相曰貉相，将曰貉将”[④]。

就是说，史籍和传说中的骆越王、骆王、骆侯、雄王、泾阳王、貉龙君、文郎国等，反映了先秦时期百越支系之一、活跃在越南北部的骆越、骆民聚族而居的历史。所谓“雄（雒）王”建“文郎国”，实际上都是“中国”早期边疆人文的“四方万国”状态的有机环节之一，与真正意义上的“国家文明”社会还有一段距离，与同一时期华南东瓯、闽越、南越、西瓯等大分散、小聚居的百越其他支系一样，是骆越部落社会生活状态的反映。从铜荳、扪丘文化的内涵看，这一时空的社会文

① 文新等:《雄王时代》，越南科学出版社，1976年（云南省历史研究所:《东南亚资料译丛》（第一种），1980年。

② 张一民:《西瓯骆越考》，《百越民族史论丛》，广西人民出版社，1985年。

③ 陶维英:《越南古代史》（上册），商务印书馆，1976年，181～183页。

④ 陶维英:《越南古代史》（上册），商务印书馆，1976年，33、34、179页。

化发展水平是有限的，石器生产工具仍是主流，虽然进入青铜时代，但主要是斧、刀、矛、镞、鱼钩等小型铜工具，缺乏大型青铜礼器和戈、剑等青铜兵器，更缺乏大规模中心聚落乃至城防设施等，不及方国社会应有的社会复杂化程度。

（二）东山文化——瓯骆国的史迹

西瓯、骆越的异同是百越民族史研究上争论已久的问题，一般认为左右江流域、红河三角洲的骆越与西江中游流域、桂江流域的西瓯是百越中两个不同的支系[①]。

东山文化是红河流域史前史上青铜文化的鼎盛和铁器时代的初始阶段，以河内古螺的都城聚落、越窠与曹村等墓地的大型贵族船棺墓葬、发达的青铜兵器、大型精美的东山铜鼓、铜鼓纹饰中的羽人竞渡、武士征战等场面，反映了东山文化已经不是一般的氏族部落社会。尤其是河内的古螺城遗址，据勘测及笔者的实地调查，该城现存地面上的三重夯土城圈，城圈外分别环绕城壕，三重城壕与城内外的水系连成一体。外城、内城大致椭圆形，宫城为方形，其中外城周长8公里，墙基宽达25米，残存高度4～5米。越南考古学者尚未对古螺城址做系统的勘探和发掘，唯内城的小规模发掘发现有东山文化陶器、完整的东山铜鼓、铜鼓内盛放的铜犁和铜镞，迄今城址地表仍可以采集到秦汉时代特征的绳纹筒瓦、板瓦等遗存。古螺城遗址是迄今东山文化时期保存最完好的、规模最大、规格最高的聚落单位，表明东山文化已经形成了围城自重、割据一方、武力强大的边疆王国或民族国家。

古螺城的三重夯土城圈、三重水城布局与苏南吴都淹城遗址的三重圆形土城、水城布局惊人相同[②]。在邻近的东南亚半岛上，泰国的班清、诺乌罗、班蒙河（Ban Mung Fang）等青铜时代遗址也发现了与红河下游古螺、华南吴国淹城相似的多重圆形土城建筑遗存[③]。这些早期城市形态与结构上的共性，可能反映了上古时期华南百越系统的早期城市建设与以黄河流域为中心的秦汉王朝都城形态的区别。

汉文史籍记载，约秦汉时代安阳王在红河下游的骆越故地上“灭文郎国，改曰瓯骆国”。前引《交州外域记》语“后蜀王子将兵三万，来讨骆王骆将，蜀王子因称为安阳王。后南越王尉佗，举众攻安阳王”。《史记索隐》引5世纪文献《广州记》类似的内容：“后蜀王子将兵讨骆侯，自称为安阳王，治封溪县。后南越王尉佗，攻破安阳王，令二使典主交趾、九真二郡，即瓯骆也。”13世纪的越史《岭南摭怪》有创始神话“金龟传”，很详细地记载了安阳王蜀泮建、南越王赵佗灭“瓯骆国”的过程：“瓯貉国安阳王，巴蜀人也，姓蜀名泮，因先祖求雄王之女媚娘为婚，不许，怨之，泮欲成前志，兴兵攻雄王，灭文郎国，改曰瓯骆国。筑城于越裳之地……其城延广千丈，盘旋如螺形，鼓曰螺城，又曰思龙城。”“王乃命臣皋鲁为弩，以爪为机，名曰灵光金龟爪神机。赵佗来侵，与王交战，王以神弩射之，佗军大溃，驻于邹山，与王对垒，不敢再战，遂和，王许之。未几，佗托求婚，王不

① 张一民：《西瓯骆越考》，《百越民族史论丛》，广西人民出版社，1985年；蒋廷瑜：《西瓯骆越青铜文化比较研究》，《百越研究》（第一辑），广西科技出版社，2007年。

② 陈颂华：《江南古国遗址——淹城》，《江苏省考古学会1983年考古论文选》，江苏省考古学会，1983年。

③ Charles Higham. *The Archaeology of Mainland Southeast Asian*. Cambridge University Press, 1989: 99-113, 207-209, 230-233. Charles Higham. *Early Cultures of Mainland Southeast Asia*. Chicago: Art Media Resources Ltd, 2002: 179-228. Peter Bellwood. *Prehistory of the Indo-Malaysian Archipelago*. Honolulu: University of Hawaii Press, 1997: 271-275.

意，以女媚珠嫁佗子仲始，仲始诱媚珠，观神机弩，潜作别机，代金龟爪……仲始挟机而归，佗得之大喜，发兵攻王，王不知机弩已失矣！众崩溃”。“王拔剑欲斩媚珠……王竟斩之……佗军追至，未见何物，仅见媚珠之尸，仲始抱其尸，装还螺城，封葬……竟投身井底死”。《大越史记全书》删除了“金龟传”的神话部分，保留安阳王蜀泮建瓯骆国、被赵佗灭并的故事，其建国部分说：“王既并文郎国……王既并其国，乃改国号曰瓯貉，都封溪。”看来，安阳王蜀泮建瓯骆国、赵佗灭瓯骆国并为南越国而后为汉武帝所有，中、越两国的汉文史籍与民间传说的记载是相符的，应是史实。骆越国都城所在地封溪后汉置封溪县，《后汉书·郡国志》“交趾郡（武帝置，即安阳王国，洛阳南万一千里）十二城”，“封溪建武十九年置”，越南学者考证封溪今地望山西、和平、永福、富寿交界地带[①]，河内西北的古螺城遗址地望与之吻合，笔者考察古螺城遗址时，也在古螺村找到了祭祀骆越国神弩的发明者皋鲁的神庙及安阳王祠，古螺城采集绳纹瓦片也是典型的秦汉时代特征以及城内的东山文化青铜器等，应可佐证骆越在这里筑城建国的历史。

在百越的先民文化体系中，约当商周时期的西瓯、骆越是分别活动于西江中游流域与左右江、红河三角洲的两个不同的氏族部落文化，文献历史的记载不同，考古文物有别，而秦汉前后安阳王所建的红河王国得名“瓯骆”，似乎又与历史不符。类似的情形也出现在百越王国的其他支系中，由于江浙吴、越文化的向南传播与融合，商周时期东南的土著诸蛮如“越沤”、“瓯”、“闽”、“粤”等逐步发展为于越、东瓯（越）、闽越、南越、干越、扬越等“百越”支系，秦汉时代的“闽越”就是商周“七闽”与南来的吴越融合生成的[②]。《史记·东越列传》语“闽越王无诸及越东海王摇者，其先皆越王句践之后”与《汉书·地理志》语“自交趾至会稽七八千里，百粤杂处，各有种姓”这两句，真实地反映了“百越”民族文化内在关系的两个方面。瓯骆建国的历史也是这种情形，前引“金龟传”载灭文郎国、建瓯骆国的安阳王蜀泮为巴蜀人。安阳王是否就是所谓的巴蜀人，这并不重要，但“巴蜀”是一个符号、一个象征，重要的是从蜀泮这个人物的移民事件我们看到了瓯骆国文化的土著（骆越的“文郎国”）与外来两种力量的整合作用。换句话说，瓯骆国的创始人不是土著的骆越人，瓯骆建国有来自北部势力、北方“移民”的介入。类似的情形在百越王国的建立过程中是很常见的，如周太伯与仲雍“奔荆蛮”建吴国（《史记·吴太伯世家》），越王句践之后无诸南下建立闽越国、摇南下东瓯国（《史记·东越列传》）、河北真定人赵佗建南越国（《史记·南越列传》）等。历史与考古资料显示，虽然这些边疆民族王国社会的一些上层贵族是外来的“移民”，但其社会文化基础却都是土著的延续和部分外来文化因素的融合。前述东山文化主体延续了铜荳、扪丘等土著青铜文化基础，也吸收融合西瓯、南越、滇越等百越其他支系及中原周汉文化因素的影响，证明了蜀泮建瓯骆国的历史也是遵循这样的规律，瓯骆国的东山文化正是在华南百越王国、中原周汉帝国间南征北伐、激流涌荡的社会文化背景下融合形成的。

① 陶维英：《越南古代史》（下册），商务印书馆，1976年，174页。

② 吴春明：《中国东南土著民族历史与文化的考古学观察》，厦门大学出版社，1999年。

后 记

Postscript

广西与东盟的交往不仅具有悠久的历史，而且在青铜文化上形成了独特的区域性文化，尤其是铜鼓文化的特色十分突出。为此，由广西壮族自治区文化厅主办，广西壮族自治区博物馆、广西文物考古研究所、广东省博物馆、云南省博物馆、海南省博物馆、贵州省博物馆5省6个文博单位联合承办的“广西与东盟青铜文化学术研讨会”，于2011年10月18～23日在南宁召开。来自国内11个省、市、自治区的25个单位以及越南、老挝、日本等60多名专家、学者提供了46篇论文，内容包括铜鼓文化研究、青铜文化研究、青铜科技保护等方面的文章，因有的文章已另处发表，不再编入本书。现将37篇文章汇编成《广西与东盟青铜文化学术研讨会论文集》一书，为研究中国与东盟青铜文化提供一部新的研究成果文集。这既是搭建文化交流的新平台，也是为构建区域文博事业新发展打牢基础，更是广西与东盟地区青铜文化研究新成果的首次展示。

全书由黄启善担任执行主编，蒋廷瑜、蓝日勇、郑超雄、陈小波等对部分论文进行了修改补充。

为使本次会议得以顺利举行，广西壮族自治区文化厅、广西壮族自治区文物局的领导十分重视会议的召开，多次听取筹备工作的汇报，广西壮族自治区博物馆吴伟峰馆长、广西文物考古研究所林强所长等领导多次召开会议部署工作，吴伟峰馆长还邀请承办单位的领导在南宁召开联席会，云南省博物馆马文斗馆长、李黎副馆长和4名工作人员、广东省博物馆莫鹏副馆长、海南省博物馆丘刚馆长等领导出席会议，共商研讨会召开事宜，各承办单位都建立了联络人员，广东省博物馆的黄青松，云南省博物馆范舟、樊海涛，广西壮族自治区博物馆的黄启善、陶少艺、黄念等人积极地做好会议的筹备工作，保证了会议的顺利召开。会议召开之际，云南省博物馆马文斗馆长、海南省博物馆丘刚馆长、广东省博物馆莫鹏副馆长、贵州省博物馆党总支张兰冰书记等领导出席了会议。

会议召开期间，周敏副书记亲自带领办公室、财务科等有关人员布置会场、接待国内外专家和嘉宾，为会议的顺利召开做了大量的后勤保障工作。黄巍、陈洪波、张利敏、黄念等人负责英文翻译和校对。科学出版社李茜不仅参加了会议，还为本书的编辑出版付出了辛勤的劳动。在此一并表示衷心的感谢！

广西与东盟青铜文化学术研讨会筹委会

2012年1月